D0667162

# STATISTICAL METHODS FOR TESTING, DEVELOPMENT, AND MANUFACTURING

# STATISTICAL METHODS FOR TESTING, DEVELOPMENT, AND MANUFACTURING

**FORREST W. BREYFOGLE III**
IBM Corporation
Austin, Texas

A Wiley-Interscience Publication
JOHN WILEY & SONS, INC.
New York • Chichester • Brisbane • Toronto • Singapore

*Library of Congress Cataloging in Publication Data:*
Breyfogle, Forrest W., 1946—
    Statistical methods for testing, development, and manufacturing /
Forrest W. Breyfogle III.
        p.     cm.
    Includes bibliographical references.
    1. Production management—Statistical methods.     2. Quality
control—Statistical methods.     3. Reliability (Engineering)—
Statistical methods.     4. Factorial experiment design.     I. Title.

TS155.B66   1991
658.5′62′015195—dc20                                               91-14539
                                                                  CIP

ISBN 0-471-54035-8

Printed in the United States of America

10   9   8   7   6   5   4   3

*To my wife, Becki*

# CONTENTS

**PREFACE**                                                        xix

**ACKNOWLEDGMENTS**                                               xxiii

**1   Getting Started**                                             1

**PART I   MANAGEMENT PHILOSOPHY AND BASIC
            STATISTICAL CONCEPTS**                                  5

**2   Introduction**                                               7

   2.1. Example 2-1: Automobile Test—Answering the Right
      Question, 9
   2.2. Do-It-Smarter Considerations, 11
   2.3. Computer Programs, 13
   2.4. Nomenclature, 14

**3   Managing Problem Solving, Decision Making, and Process
     Improvement**                                                15

   3.1.   Management Structure, 15
   3.2.   Deming's 14 Points for Management, 17
   3.3.   Chronic versus Sporadic Problems and Common
       Causes versus Special Causes, 22
   3.4.   Problem Solving and Decision Making, 23
   3.5.   Brainstorming, 24

3.6.  Cause-and-Effect Diagram, 25

3.7.  Example 3-1: Improving a Process with Subjective Information, 26

3.8.  Example 3-2: Reducing the Total Cycle Time of a Process, 29

3.9.  Example 3-3: Improving a Process That Has Defects, 33

3.10. Example 3-4: Automobile Test—Brainstorming for Test Considerations, 34


**4  Descriptive Statistics and Experimentation Traps**                    **37**

4.1.  Sampling Considerations, 37

4.2.  Simple Data Presentation, 39

4.3.  Example 4-1: Histogram Plot, 40

4.4.  Measurements from a Sample, 40

4.5.  Hypothesis Testing, 42

4.6.  Confidence Interval Statements, 45

4.7.  Central Limit Theorem, 46

4.8.  Experimental Error in Measurement Data, 46

4.9.  Example 4-2: Experimentation Errors, 48

4.10. Experimentation Traps, 49

4.11. Example 4-3: Experimentation Trap—Lack of Randomization, 49

4.12. Example 4-4: Experimentation Trap—Confused Effects, 50

4.13. Example 4-5: Experimentation Trap—Interaction of Factors, 51

4.14. Example 4-6: Experimentation Trap—Independently Designing and Conducting an Experiment, 52

4.15. Some Sampling Considerations, 54

4.16. Do-It-Smarter Considerations, 55


**5  Probability and Hazard Plotting**                                      **57**

5.1. Probability and Hazard Plotting Concepts, 57

5.2. Probability Plotting, 58

5.3. Example 5-1: PDF, CDF, and Then a Probability Plot, 58

5.4. Probability Plot Positions and the Interpretation of Plots, 60

5.5. Hazard Plots, 63

5.6. Example 5-2: Hazard Plotting, 64

5.7. Summarizing the Creation of Probability and Hazard Plots, 64

5.8. "Percent of Population" Statement Considerations, 65

**6  Distributions and Statistical Processes**    68

6.1.  An Overview of the Application of Distributions, 68
6.2.  Normal Distribution, 70
6.3.  Binomial/Hypergeometric Distributions, 72
6.4.  Poisson Distribution, 74
6.5.  Exponential Distribution, 74
6.6.  Weibull Distribution, 76
6.7.  Log-Normal Distribution, 78
6.8.  Tabulated Probability Distribution: Chi-Square Distribution, 80
6.9.  Tabulated Probability Distribution: $t$ Distribution, 81
6.10. Tabulated Probability Distribution: $F$ Distribution, 81
6.11. Hazard Rate, 82
6.12. Nonhomogeneous Poisson Process (NHPP), 83
6.13. Homogeneous Poisson Process (HPP), 84
6.14. Applications for Various Types of Distributions and Processes, 84

**PART II  SOLVING DEFINED PROBLEMS**    89

**7  Inferences: Continuous Response**    91

7.1.  Summarizing Sampled Data, 91
7.2.  Sample Size: Hypothesis Test of a Mean Criterion for Continuous Response Data, 92
7.3.  Example 7-1: Sample Size Determination for a Mean Criterion Test, 92
7.4.  Confidence Intervals on the Mean and Hypothesis Test Criteria Alternatives, 93
7.5.  Example 7-2: Confidence Intervals on the Mean, 95
7.6.  Standard Deviation Confidence Interval, 96
7.7.  Example 7-3: Standard Deviation Confidence Statement, 97
7.8.  Percentage of the Population Assessments, 97
7.9.  Example 7-4: Percentage of the Population Statements, 98
7.10. Tolerance Analyses, 100
7.11. Example 7-5: Combining Analytical Data with a Tolerance Analysis, 101
7.12. Do-It-Smarter Considerations, 103

**8  Inferences: Attribute Response**    105

8.1.  Attribute Response Situations, 106
8.2.  Sample Size: Hypothesis Test of an Attribute Criterion, 106

8.3. Example 8-1: Sample Size—A Hypothesis Test of an Attribute Criterion, 107
8.4. Confidence Intervals for Attribute Evaluations, 107
8.5. Reduced Sample Size Testing for Attribute Situations, 110
8.6. Example 8-2: Reduced Sample Size Testing—Attribute Response Situations, 110
8.7. Attribute Sample Plan Alternatives, 112
8.8. Do-It-Smarter Considerations, 112

**9  Comparison Tests**                                                    **114**

9.1.  Comparing Data, 114
9.2.  Sample Size: Comparing Two Means, 115
9.3.  Comparing Two Means, 115
9.4.  Example 9-1: Comparing the Means of Two Samples, 116
9.5.  Comparing the Variance of Two Samples, 117
9.6.  Example 9-2: Comparing the Variance of Two Samples, 118
9.7.  Comparing Populations Using a Probability Plot, 118
9.8.  Example 9-3: Comparing Samples Using a Probability Plot, 118
9.9.  Paired Comparison Testing, 119
9.10. Example 9-4: Paired Comparison Testing, 120
9.11. Comparing Two Proportions, 122
9.12. Example 9-5: Comparing Two Proportions, 122
9.13. Analysis of Means, 123
9.14. Example 9-6: Analysis of Means, 124
9.15. Do-It-Smarter Considerations, 126

**10  Reliability Testing: Overview**                                       **128**

10.1.  Product Life Cycle, 128
10.2.  Repairable versus Nonrepairable Testing, 130
10.3.  Nonrepairable Device Testing, 131
10.4.  Repairable System Testing, 132
10.5.  Accelerated Testing: Discussion, 133
10.6.  High-Temperature Acceleration, 134
10.7.  Example 10-1: High-Temperature Acceleration Testing, 136
10.8.  Eyring Model, 136
10.9.  Thermal Cycling: Coffin–Manson Relationship, 137
10.10. Model Selection: Accelerated Testing, 138
10.11. Do-It-Smarter Considerations, 139

**11  Reliability Testing: Repairable System**                    **141**

11.1.  Considerations When Designing a Test of a
       Repairable System Failure Criterion, 141
11.2.  Sequential Testing: Poisson Distribution, 144
11.3.  Example 11-1: Sequential Reliability Test, 145
11.4.  Total Test Time: Hypothesis Test of a Failure Rate
       Criterion, 146
11.5.  Confidence Interval for Failure Rate Evaluations, 147
11.6.  Example 11-2: Time-Terminated Reliability Testing
       Confidence Statement, 147
11.7.  Reduced Sample Size Testing: Poisson
       Distribution, 148
11.8.  Example 11-3: Reduced Sample Size Testing—
       Poisson Distribution, 149
11.9.  Reliability Test Design with Test Performance
       Considerations, 149
11.10. Example 11-4: Time-Terminated Reliability Test
       Design—with Test Performance Considerations, 151
11.11. Posttest Assessments, 152
11.12. Example 11-5: Postreliability Test Confidence
       Statements, 154
11.13. Repairable Systems with Changing Failure Rate, 155
11.14. Example 11-6: Repairable Systems with Changing
       Failure Rate, 156
11.15. Do-It-Smarter Considerations, 160

**12  Reliability Testing: Nonrepairable Devices**                **162**

12.1.  Reliability Test Considerations for a Nonrepairable
       Device, 162
12.2.  Weibull Probability Plotting and Hazard Plotting, 163
12.3.  Example 12-1: Weibull Probability Plot for Failure
       Data, 165
12.4.  Example 12-2: Weibull Hazard Plot with Censored
       Data, 167
12.5.  Nonlinear Data Plots, 169
12.6.  Reduced Sample Size Testing: Weibull
       Distribution, 170
12.7.  Example 12-3: A Zero Failure Weibull Test
       Strategy, 171
12.8.  Log-Normal Distribution, 172
12.9.  Example 12-4: Log-Normal Probability Plot
       Analysis, 173
12.10. Do-It-Smarter Considerations, 173

**13  Factorial Experiments and Variance Components Analysis:
Concepts/Designs**                                                           **176**

13.1.  The Need for Fractional Factorial Experiments, 176
13.2.  Initial Thoughts When Setting Up a Factorial
       Experiment, 177
13.3.  Experiment Design Considerations, 178
13.4.  Experiment Design Considerations: Factor
       Significance, 180
13.5.  Experiment Design Considerations: Factors and
       Responses, 180
13.6.  Experiment Design Considerations: Experiment
       Resolution, 182
13.7.  Conceptual Explanation: Two-Level Full Factorial
       Experiments and Two-Factor Interactions, 182
13.8.  Conceptual Explanation: Saturated Two-Level
       Fractional Factorial Experiments, 185
13.9.  Two-Level Fractional Factorial Design
       Alternatives, 186
13.10. Designing a Two-Level Fractional Factorial
       Experiment Using Tables M and N, 188
13.11. Blocking, 189
13.12. Curvature Check, 190
13.13. Experimental Error and Data Analyses, 190
13.14. Example 13-1: A Resolution V Fractional Factorial
       Experiment Design, 191
13.15. Example 13-2: A Resolution III Fractional Factorial
       Screening Experiment Design, 194
13.16. Example 13-3: Automobile Test—Fractional Factorial
       Experiment Design, 196
13.17. Factorial Designs That Have More Than Two
       Levels, 198
13.18. Sample Size: A Simple Strategy for Fractional
       Factorial Experiments That Have a Continuous
       Response Output, 199
13.19. Fractional Factorial Experiment: Attribute
       Response, 200
13.20. Fractional Factorial Experiment: Reliability
       Evaluations, 200
13.21. Modeling Equation Format for Two-Level Factorial
       Experiments, 201
13.22. Variance Components, 202
13.23. Example 13-4: Nested Variance Components, 202
13.24. Example 13-5: Variance Components, 203
13.25. Do-It-Smarter Considerations, 204

**14  Factorial Experiments: Basic Analyses**                                    **206**

14.1. Determining the Significant Effects and a Probability
      Plotting Procedure, 206
14.2. Example 14-1: Analysis of a Resolution III Fractional
      Factorial Screening Experiment, 208
14.3. A Significance Test Procedure for These Two-Level
      Experiments, 211
14.4. Example 14-2: Analysis of a Resolution V Fractional
      Factorial Experiment Design, 213
14.5. Example 14-3: Analysis of a Resolution III Experiment
      with Two-Factor Interaction Assessment, 217
14.6. Analysis of Means, 218
14.7. Do-It-Smarter Considerations, 218

**15  Factorial Experiments and Variance Components:
Computer Analyses**                                                              **219**

15.1. Considerations When Analyzing Fractional Factorial
      Data, 219
15.2. Example 15-1: Computer Analysis of a Resolution V
      Fractional Factorial Experiment Design, 220
15.3. Example 15-2: Computer Analysis of a Fractional
      Factorial Experiment Design with Missing Data, 233
15.4. Data Transformations, 237
15.5. Variance Components: Analysis, 238
15.6. Example 15-3: Nested Variance Components
      Analysis, 238
15.7. Example 15-4: Variance Components Analysis, 241
15.8. Do-It-Smarter Considerations, 243

**16  Factorial Experiments: Taguchi Contributions**                             **244**

16.1. Test Strategies, 244
16.2. Loss Function, 245
16.3. Example 16-1: Loss Function, 247
16.4. Standard Deviation as a Response, 248
16.5. Do-It-Smarter Considerations, 249

**17  Response Surface and Mixture Designs**                                      **250**

17.1. Modeling Equations, 250
17.2. Central Composite Design, 252
17.3. Example 17-1: Response Surface Design, 254
17.4. Box–Behnken Designs, 255
17.5. Mixture Designs, 257

17.6. Simplex Lattice Designs for Exploring the Whole Simplex Region, 258

17.7. Example 17-2: Simple-Lattice Designed Mixture Experiment, 260

17.8. Mixture Designs with Process Variables, 262

17.9. Example 17-3: Mixture Experiment with Process Variables, 262

17.10. Extreme Vertices Mixture Designs, 267

17.11. Example 17-4: Extreme Vertices Mixture Experiment, 267

17.12. Computer-Generated Mixture Designs/Analyses, 268

17.13. Example 17-5: Computer-Generated Mixture Design/ Analyses, 268

17.14. Additional Response Surface Design Considerations, 270

17.15. Do-It-Smarter Considerations, 271

**18 Pass/Fail Functional Testing**     **273**

18.1. The Concept of Pass/Fail Functional Testing, 273

18.2. Example 18-1: Automobile Test—Pass/Fail Functional Testing Considerations, 274

18.3. A Test Approach for Pass/Fail Functional Testing, 276

18.4. Example 18-2: A Pass/Fail System Functional Test, 278

18.5. Example 18-3: A Pass/Fail Hardware/Software System Functional Test, 280

18.6. General Considerations When Assigning Factors, 281

18.7. Factor Levels Greater Than 2, 281

18.8. Example 18-4: A Software Interface Pass/Fail Functional Test, 282

18.9. A Search Pattern Strategy to Determine the Source of Failure, 284

18.10. Example 18-5: A Search Pattern Strategy to Determine the Source of Failure, 284

18.11. Additional Applications, 288

18.12. Do-It-Smarter Considerations, 289

**19 Analyses of Processes**     **290**

19.1. Monitoring Processes, 290

19.2. Statistical Process Control Charts, 292

19.3. $\bar{x}$ and $R$ and $\bar{x}$ and $s$ Charts: Mean and Variability Measurements, 293

19.4. Example 19-1: $\bar{x}$ and $R$ Charts, 294

19.5.  $X$ Chart: Individual Measurements, 297

19.6.  Example 19-2: $X$ Chart, 298

19.7.  $p$ Chart: Fraction Nonconforming Measurements, 299

19.8.  Example 19-3: $p$ Chart, 300

19.9.  $np$ Chart: Number of Nonconforming Items, 302

19.10. $c$ Chart: Number of Nonconformities, 302

19.11. $u$ Chart: Nonconformities per Unit, 303

19.12. Interpretation of Control Chart Patterns, 303

19.13. CUSUM Chart: Cumulative Sum of Measurements, 305

19.14. Example 19-4: CUSUM Chart, 307

19.15. Process Capability Studies, 309

19.16. Example 19-5: Process Capability, 311

19.17. Pareto Diagrams, 313

19.18. Example 19-6: Pareto Diagram, 313

19.19. Implementation Considerations, 315

19.20. Do-It-Smarter Considerations, 315

**PART III  COMBINING VARIOUS STATISTICAL CONCEPTS AND OTHER IMPLEMENTATION TOOLS**                               **317**

**20  Determining the Needs of the Customer**                        **319**

20.1. Meeting the Needs of the Customer, 319

20.2. Quality Function Deployment (QFD), 320

20.3. Example 20-1: Creating a QFD Chart, 325

20.4. A Simple Methodology to Assess the Needs of Customers, 328

20.5. Do-It-Smarter Considerations, 330

**21  Development and Manufacturing Process Improvement "Tools"**                                                    **332**

21.1. Motorola's Six Sigma Program, 332

21.2. A Six Sigma Approach to Product Development, 338

21.3. A Process to Manage Product Development with Fractional Factorial Experiments, 343

21.4. Example 21-1: Managing Product Development Using Fractional Factorial Experiments, 344

21.5. Other Tools, 347

21.6. Do-It-Smarter Considerations, 348

**22  Examples with Do-It-Smarter Considerations**                    **349**

22.1. Example 22-1: A QFD Evaluation with Fractional Factorial Experimentation, 349

22.2. Example 22-2: A Reliability and Functional Test of an Assembly, 356

22.3. Example 22-3: A System Fractional Factorial Stress to Fail Test, 365

22.4. Example 22-4: Creating a Two-Level Fractional Factorial Experiment Strategy from a "Many-Level" Full Factorial Initial Proposal, 368

22.5. Example 22-5: Fractional Factorial Screening (Resolution III) Experiment with Interaction Consideration, 371

22.6. Example 22-6: A Development Strategy for a Chemical Product, 372

22.7. Example 22-7: A Process Capability Study, 374


**Appendix A. Equations for the Distributions**    **378**

A.1. Normal Distribution, 378
A.2. Binomial Distribution, 379
A.3. Hypergeometric Distribution, 379
A.4. Poisson Distribution, 380
A.5. Exponential Distribution, 380
A.6. Weibull Distribution, 380


**Appendix B. Histogram Creation, Probability Plotting, and Lack of Fit**    **383**

B.1. Creating Histograms Manually, 383
B.2. Example B-1: Histogram Plot, 384
B.3. Theoretical Concept of Probability Plotting, 385
B.4. Plotting Positions, 386
B.5. Manual Estimation of a Best-Fit Probability Plot Line, 387
B.6. Computer-Generated Plots and Lack of Fit, 390


**Appendix C. Fractional Factorial and Response Surface Analyses**    **391**

C.1. Computer Output Description: Analysis of Variance, 391
C.2. Computer Output Description: General Linear Model, 393
C.3. Computer Output Description: Response Surface Regression, 395
C.4. Sample Size: Fractional Factorial Experiment with a Continuous Response Output—Mathematical Considerations, 397
C.5. Derivation of Equation for Contrast Column SS, 398
C.6. Example 15-1: Computer Analysis Program Steps and Manual Calculations, 400

C.7.   Example 15-3: Computer Analysis Program Steps, 406
C.8.   Example 15-4: Computer Analysis Program Steps, 406
C.9.   Example 17-1: Computer Analysis Program Steps and
       Lack-of-Fit Assessments, 406
C.10.  Example 17-3: Computer Analysis Program Steps, 411
C.11.  Example 22-1: Computer Analysis Program Steps, 411

## Appendix D.  Reference Tables                                417

A.   Area under the Standardized Normal Curve, 418
B.   Probability Points of the Normal Distribution:
     Single Sided ($\sigma^2$ known), 420
C.   Probability Points of the Normal Distribution:
     Double Sided ($\sigma^2$ known), 420
D.   Probability Points of the $t$ Distribution: Single Sided, 421
E.   Probability Points of the $t$ Distribution: Double Sided, 422
F.   Probability Points of the Variance Ratio
     ($F$ Distribution), 424
G.   Cumulative Distribution of $\chi^2$, 428
H.   Gamma Function, 430
I.   Exact Critical Values for Use with the Analysis of
     Means, 431
J.   Factors for Constructing Variables Control Charts, 437
K.   Poisson Distribution Factors, 438
L.   Weibull Mean: Percentage Fail Value for Given
     Weibull Slope, 440
M1.  Two-level Full and Fractional Factorial Designs,
     4 Trials, 440
M2.  Two-level Full and Fractional Factorial Designs,
     8 Trials, 442
M3.  Two-level Full and Fractional Factorial Designs,
     16 Trials, 443
M4.  Two-level Full and Fractional Factorial Designs,
     32 Trials, 444
M5.  Two-level Full and Fractional Factorial Designs,
     64 Trials, 446
N1.  Two-factor Interaction Confounding in the Contrast
     Columns of the Tables M1–M5 Resolution V Fractional
     Factorial Designs, 450
N2.  Two-factor Interaction Confounding in the Contrast
     Columns of the Tables M1–M5 Resolution IV Fractional
     Factorial Designs, 451
N3.  Two-factor Interaction Confounding in the Contrast
     Columns of the Tables M1–M5 Resolution III Fractional
     Factorial Designs, 454
O.   Pass/fail Functional Test Matrix Coverage, 459

P.   Generic Percent Plot Positions ($F_i$) for Probability Papers, 460
Q1.  Normal Probability Paper, 462
Q2.  Log-normal Probability Paper, 463
Q3.  Weibull Probability Paper, 464
R1.  Normal Hazard Paper, 465
R2.  Log-normal Hazard Paper, 466
R3.  Weibull Hazard Paper, 467

**Appendix E.  List of Symbols**                              **468**

**Appendix F.  Glossary**                                     **472**

**References**                                                **487**

**Author Index**                                              **495**

**Subject Index**                                             **499**

# PREFACE

And . . . the competition in industry continues to get tougher. There is much pressure on both product development and manufacturing organizations to become more productive and efficient. Developers need to create innovative products in less time, even though the product may be very complex. Manufacturing organizations experience growing pressure to improve quality, while decreasing costs and increasing production volumes with fewer resources.

Companies are now making honest self-evaluations that yield the conclusion that they need to do things differently in order to survive. Management understands, for example, that variation is a fact of life (e.g., there can be good automobiles and "lemons" produced from a manufacturing process). Management realizes that more effort needs to be taken to reduce the magnitude of variability so that products can be produced better and more consistently (e.g., no "lemons" will be produced). Companies also note that often processes need to be better optimized in order to increase/decrease a performance characteristic of the product. Perhaps also shorter test durations are needed to determine whether products will perform all the intended functions in concert with other mating products or components. Management cannot solve these types of problems with simple slogans and/or charts. The techniques discussed in this text can help define the road map for change (perhaps revolutionary) that needs to be followed in order to meet these challenges.

Many business processes could be improved if wisely applied statistical concepts were a part of these processes. However, even after the discovery of this fact, how should one begin? The reading you are *now* doing can be the starting point to answer these tough questions. This book is not a classical statistical text. It is an easy-to-understand guide that can help solve complex industrial problems oftentimes with much less effort than with a "traditional approach." This guide illustrates how statistical techniques can be easily understood and applied with a sample size that is smaller than that typically envisioned.

I had three basic goals when developing this "guide." The first goal was to provide a tool such that a practitioner could read an applicable chapter to understand how to structure his or her experiment with both "traditional" and then with "do-it-smarter" considerations. The second goal was to make the topics practical to such an extent that this reference guide would become worn out through continual use. Finally, the third goal was for the text to "sell" employees and all levels of management on the power of wisely applied statistical concepts in their field. Perhaps after reading this guide some individuals will better understand the power of wisely applied statistical concepts to such an extent that they undertake additional research in an area they find most interesting.

Statistical texts normally identify techniques to use when solving classical problems of various types. A practitioner could use a text to determine, for example, the sample size that is needed to check a failure rate criterion. However, the practitioner may find that the execution of this "simple test plan" is impossible because the low failure rates of today can require a very large sample size and a very long test duration. Instead of blindly running this type of test, this text suggests that there may be other considerations that can make the test more manageable and meaningful. Effort needs to be expended upon a basic strategy and the definition of problems that focus on meeting the real needs of customers with less time, effort, and costs.

This text breaks from the traditional bounds maintained by many texts. In this guide emphasis is given to identifying techniques for restructuring, if necessary, the original (or defining the "right") question and then designing a more informative test plan/procedure that requires fewer samples and gives more information with often less test effort.

This guide will address how very complicated problems can be subdivided and solved with minimal test effort. Instruction in this guide is intended to be at such a level that a novice can quickly understand many of the concepts and in a short time begin doing his or her job smarter. To help the "typical practitioner," theoretical and detailed information that is pertinent but possibly disruptive to the flow of reading is relegated to the appendices.

To prove ease of use, consider opening this guide to any chapter and reading the discussion. The text should be easy to understand. The examples found in most chapters can be very beneficial to expedite an understanding of the concepts. The glossary can be consulted for a description of unfamiliar terms and symbols.

This guide can help developers and manufacturers of mechanical devices, electrical equipment, software, and chemical products. This guide is a practical solution manual for problems/dilemmas that often occur within the work disciplines of mechanical, electrical, aeronautical, and chemical engineers, as well as reliability, product test, and quality engineers. Chemists, physicists, programmers, technicians, statisticians, and managers will also find this book a valuable guide.

Managers are included in this list since they need to be aware of the concepts so that they can direct efforts toward doing "the job smarter." Similarly, statisticians who work in product development and manufacturing can also receive benefits from this text, even if they are familiar with all the basic concepts. Examples are included that can give many statisticians more insight into the challenge of optimizing experimental work to better meet the real needs of the business/customer.

This guide discusses brainstorming, reliability testing, factorial analyses, response surface analysis, statistical process controls (SPC), and quality function deployment (QFD) individually and as a collective entity to "do-it-smarter." Because of this diversification in content, I suggest first reading the "Getting Started" chapter. This chapter along with the Contents can then give a reader direction to locate the most effective point to enter this guide.

For example, perhaps a reader has a reliability test sample size question. The reader can note from Table 1.1 in Chapter 1 that Chapter 10 has an overview of reliability testing, while Chapter 11 discusses repairable systems. From the Contents, the reader may then choose to read Example 11-3 in Chapter 11 for a quick illustrative explanation. The reader then may consult other portions of this chapter and Chapter 10 for more information about the analysis technique and "testing smarter" alternatives.

A company may need to make revolutionary changes in order to become more competitive (or maintain competitiveness). The techniques described in this text are tools that can help both orchestrate this change and give direction to procedural changes that should be made in this transition.

FORREST W. BREYFOGLE III

# ACKNOWLEDGMENTS

I am grateful to Bill Diamond for introducing me to the power of design of experiments. If it weren't for him, I may still be doing "one-at-a-time" tests. Special thanks needs to go to Becki Breyfogle, Stan Wheeler, and my IBM management. My wife, Becki, has been very supportive of the effort and time required to write this book. She also has given some helpful comments. My friend Stan has given me much guidance over the years when applying statistical concepts to my real engineering problems. Stan helped answer many of the questions that arose when I wrote this text. I consider him a great practical statistician. My IBM management has been very supportive of me over the years. They have let me work on the application and development of statistical techniques to solve many types of problems, even though the work was often outside my immediate organization.

I appreciate the detailed critiques from Wes Breyfogle, Jim King, and the reviewers from John Wiley and Sons, Inc. Because of these critiques, I made significant changes that improved the accuracy and usability of this book. I appreciate the help that several have given me with creating some of the tables in the appendix: Lally Marwah with Table K, Forrest Steely with Tables N, and Angelo Aloia with Table O. Many others have helped with critiques, composition of examples, or administrative help. I wish to thank the following for their help in various capacities: John Albrecht, Bill Barton, Tony Bateman, Dan Breyfogle, Dave Brewster, Neal Brinson, Don Brown, Eliott Burrell, Anita Choate, George Clausen, Jack Coulters, Charles Fieselman, Herman Friedman, Jo Jo Freeman, Paolo Gazzaniga, Barney Hallman, Sue Hynes, Karen Kolar, Tien Le, Jerry Lorenzen, LaShawna McKoy, Bill Messina, Vivian Morabito, Dan Rand, Les Record, Wayne Rogers, John

Sabol, Marty Schatzoff, Jim Shelton, Marv Smoak, Paul Tobias, Larry Toups, Susan True, Lorraine Valenta, Peter Welch, Jim Werner, Don Whitley, and Elias Zachos.

I am grateful to the Literary Executor of the late Sir Ronald A. Fisher, F.R.S., to Dr. Frank Yates, F.R.S., and the Longman Group Ltd., London for permission to reprint Tables D and F from their book *Statistical Tables for Biological, Agricultural and Medical Research* (6th edition 1974).

Output from SAS procedures is printed with the permission of SAS Institute Inc., Cary, NC, USA. Copyright © 1990. Many of the computer-generated graphs were created using GRAFSTAT, an IBM statistical analysis software package (Heidelberg et al. 1983; Buckland et al. 1984; Lane and Welch 1987).

F.W.B.

# STATISTICAL METHODS FOR TESTING, DEVELOPMENT, AND MANUFACTURING

# 1

# GETTING STARTED

This text can help people solve a wide range of problems. To illustrate the diverse application of this text consider the following three scenarios.

1. A high-level manager can read parts of this text to get quick insight into the potential power of statistical concepts. From this reading the manager might begin asking subordinate managers to do tasks using "do-it-smarter" considerations (e.g., a factorial experiment is needed before this issue is resolved). The manager might also have a staff person use this text as a guide for a more in-depth reevaluation of the traditional objectives, definitions, and procedures of his or her organization.
2. An engineer or technician can, with minimal statistical training, easily determine how to answer the original question and perhaps determine a "smarter" approach that better addresses the "real" question.
3. Individuals can get a concise explanation of factorial experiments, response surface analysis, reliability testing, statistical process control (SPC), and quality function deployment (QFD) within one text, and how a total problem solution considers a blend of all these techniques.

To meet the needs of a diverse audience, the following things were done to illustrate the applicability of these techniques to a variety of situations. In addition, these items are intended to aid the reader in locating and understanding applicable sections without reading the entire book.

1. The Contents is useful to locate examples that can give guidance to help solve a particular problem.

2. Part I contains introductory material. Part II discusses the methodology used to solve a variety of defined problems along with do-it-smarter considerations. Part III discusses the use of multiple statistical concepts when solving a problem, along with illustrating other implementation tools.

3. Each chapter begins with an overview discussion that can help readers determine whether the concepts within the chapter are applicable to their situation.

4. The glossary is a useful reference point whenever a concise definition or an unfamiliar statistical term or symbol is encountered in a chapter that may be located "in the middle of the book."

5. Examples are included frequently. The examples normally follow a description of a technique and are intended to further clarify confusing information. Chapter 22 considers the combination of statistical concepts discussed in previous chapters toward a "total problem solution."

6. Cross references are made to previous chapters whenever a chapter uses an analysis technique previously described.

7. Detailed mathematics and computer program steps to create various outputs in this guide are collected in the appendices to prevent disruption of the flow of dialog in the chapters and to make it easier for the reader to find and use these tools.

8. References are cited so that other articles and books may be used to obtain more in-depth information about a particular subject.

Table 1.1 is useful to determine which sequence of chapters should be consulted first when using this text to solve a particular type of problem or receive instructional information.

To illustrate one use of Table 1.1, consider the situation where someone wishes to determine how to compare products received by two suppliers. He or she wishes to determine the sample size and statistical comparative procedures needed to compare the quality of picture produced on television cathode ray tubes supplied by the two vendors.

From Table 1.1 information about this type of problem is noted to be found in Chapter 9 (under "sample testing" and then "comparison tests"). The Contents can then be consulted to locate particular sections in this chapter that contain the methodology of interest and an illustrative example. There is also a section on do-it-smarter concepts in this chapter. After reading this section in Chapter 9, the tester might now consider that a factorial-type test (which evaluates several factors in one experiment) could be more suitable for the test evaluation. Table 1.1 can then be consulted for guidance on how to get training in factorial testing. It is noted from Table 1.1 that the sequence of chapters addressing factorial testing concepts is 13, 14, 15, and 16.

Previous chapters that are recommended for introductory reading are also noted at the beginning of each chapter.

**TABLE 1.1. How Can Someone Begin and Then Sequence Their Reading in This Text?[a]**

Chapter Numbers[b] — Part 1 = chapters 1–9, Part 2 = chapters 10–19, Part 3 = chapters 20–22. (For chapters 10 through 22, numerals are written vertically in the original.)

| Topics | 1 | 2 | 3 | 4 | 5 | 6 | 7 | 8 | 9 | 10 | 11 | 12 | 13 | 14 | 15 | 16 | 17 | 18 | 19 | 20 | 21 | 22 |
|---|---|---|---|---|---|---|---|---|---|---|---|---|---|---|---|---|---|---|---|---|---|---|
| Overview | 1 | 2 | 3 | | | | | | | | | | | | | | | | | 4 | | |
| Basic concepts | X | X | X | X | X | | | | | | | | | | | | | | | | | |
|   Hypothesis testing | X | | | | | | | | | | | | | | | | | | | | | |
|   Confidence statements | X | | | | | | | | | | | | | | | | | | | | | |
|   Experimentation traps | X | | | | | | | | | | | | | | | | | | | | | |
|   Probability/hazard plots | | X | | | | | | | | | | | | | | | | | | | | |
|   Distributions/processes | | | X | | | | | | | | | | | | | | | | | | | |
| Sample testing | | | | | | | | | | X | X | X | | | | | | | | | | |
|   Continuous response | | | | | | | | | | X | | | | | | | | | | | | |
|   Attribute response | | | | | | | | | | | X | | | | | | | | | | | |
|   Comparison tests | | | | | | | | | | | | X | | | | | | | | | | |
| Reliability testing | | | | | | | | | | | | | X | X | X | | | | | | | |
|   Overview of reliability testing | | | | | | | | | | | | | X | | | | | | | | | |
|   Accelerated testing | | | | | | | | | | | | | X | | | | | | | | | |
|   Repairable systems | | | | | | | | | | | | | | X | | | | | | | | |
|   Nonrepairable devices | | | | | | | | | | | | | | | X | | | | | | | |
| Factorial testing (DOE) | | | | | | | | | | | | | | | | X | X | X | X | | | |
|   Overview of factorials | | | | | | | | | | | | | | | | X | | | | | | |
|   Designing an experiment | | | | | | | | | | | | | | | | X | | | | | | |
|   Basic analysis | | | | | | | | | | | | | | | | | X | | | | | |
|   Computer analyses | | | | | | | | | | | | | | | | | | X | | | | |
|   Taguchi considerations | | | | | | | | | | | | | | | | | | | X | | | |
| Response surface analysis | | | | | | | | | | | | | | | | | | | | X | | |
| Pass/fail functional test | | | | | | | | | | | | | | | | | | | | | X | |
| Process control (SPC) | | | | | | | | | | | | | | | | | | | | | | X |
| Meeting needs of the customer | | | | | | | | | | | | | | | | | | | | X | X | |
| Project management | 1 | 2 | 3 | | | | | | | | | | | | | | | | | 4 | 5 | |
| Decision techniques | 1 | 2 | 3 | | | | | | | | | | | | | | | | | 4 | | |
| Basics and sampling | 1 | 2 | 3 | 4 | 5 | 6 | 7 | 8 | 9 | | | | | | | | | | | | | |
| Reliability testing | | | | | | | | | | | | | 1 | 2 | 3 | | | | | | | |
| Factorial testing | | | | | | | | | | | | | | | | 1 | 2 | 3 | 4 | | | |
| Response surface analysis | | | | | | | | | | | | | | | | 1 | 2 | 3 | 4 | 5 | | |
| Development of | X | X | X | | | | | | | | | | | X | X | X | X | X | X | X | X | X |
|   Hardware–Elect./Mech. | 1 | 2 | 3 | | | | | | | | | | | 4 | 5 | 6 | 7 | 8 | 9 | A | B | C |
|   Chemical mixture Exp. | 1 | 2 | 3 | | | | | | | | | | | 4 | | | 5 | | | 6 | 7 | 8 |
|   Software/logic | 1 | 2 | 3 | | | | | | | | | | | 4 | | | | 5 | | | 6 | 7 |
| Manufacturing/quality | 1 | 2 | 3 | | | | | | | | | | 4 | 5 | 6 | 7 | 8 | 9 | A | B | C | D |

[a]X indicates a chapter contains information on the subject; numbers and letters indicate a sequence of study.

[b]For chapters 10 through 22, numerals are written vertically; e.g., 1 = 10; 1 = 11. (with 0 and 1 beneath, respectively)

3

# PART I

# MANAGEMENT PHILOSOPHY AND BASIC STATISTICAL CONCEPTS

In Part I there is discussion on management philosophy and the advantage of using team concepts to get the right focus within an organization. Simple illustrative examples are included to illustrate the concepts.

There is also discussion on a variety of basic statistical concepts that are applied later in the text. Sampling measurements, confidence interval statements, hypothesis testing, and probability plotting are covered along with discussion on experimental error and statistical distributions.

# 2

# INTRODUCTION

Many (if not most) engineers believe that statistics is "only" applicable to baseball and is not helpful to their situation since "too many samples are always required." Bill Sangster, dean of the Engineering School and faculty athletic representative at Georgia Tech states that: "Statistics in the hands of an engineer are like a lamppost to a drunk. They're used more for support than illumination" (*The Sporting News* 1989).

It is unfortunate that in the college curriculum of many engineering disciplines there is only a small amount of time allocated to training in statistics. It is also unfortunate that within these classes and other "week-long short classes" the students often cannot relate to how the techniques can be helpful in solving problems in their discipline.

Both development and manufacturing engineers need concise training on how statistics is applicable to their profession with a "do it (my job) smarter" philosophy. Managers need concise training so that they can give direction to their employees in order to accomplish tasks in the most efficient manner and present information in a concise fashion. If all individuals within an organization would apply do-it-smarter statistical concepts, many meetings that are conducted for the purpose of problem discussion would either be avoided or yield increased benefits with more efficiency. Engineering management and general problem solvers need to have statistical concepts presented to them in an accessible format so they can understand how to use these tools for illumination. This guide addresses these needs.

What type of people should be trained and use the concepts discussed in this text? In some organizations there are already statisticians to aid engineers in setting up and analyzing experiments. The size of other organizations may prohibit having a statistical consultant, while a third type of organization may not in the past have appreciated the value of wisely applied statistical concepts.

Even when a statistical consultant is available, engineers need to know what questions to ask. If the engineer does not realize the power of statistics, he or she may not solicit help when statistical techniques are appropriate. If a statistical consultant is approached for assistance by an engineer who has no knowledge of statistics, the statistician should learn all the technical aspects of the dilemma in order to give the best possible assistance. Most statisticians have not the time, background, or desire to understand all engineering dilemmas within their corporate structure. Engineers need to have at a minimum some basic knowledge of the concepts in this text so that they can first identify an application of the concepts and then solicit help, if needed, in an effective manner.

In any case detailed knowledge transfer to statisticians can be very time consuming and in most cases will be incomplete. Engineers that have knowledge of basic statistical concepts can intelligently mix engineering concepts with statistical techniques to maximize test quality and productivity. Earlier problem detection and better quality can then be expected when testing is considered as an integral part of the design and manufacturing process development.

This guide does not suggest that engineers replace statisticians in the areas of product development and manufacturing, but it does suggest that more communication and understanding is required between these disciplines. An objective of this guide is for engineers to get an appreciation of the power of statistical concepts so that they can do efficient experimentation and can communicate better with statisticians when needing assistance. From this guide hopefully statisticians can better appreciate engineering dilemmas so that they can add more value to improving the product development and manufacturing processes.

Theoretical derivations and manual statistical analysis procedures can be very laborious and confusing to many practitioners. In this guide there is minimal discussion on these issues; these topics are presently covered sufficiently in other texts. This information was excluded for the purpose of making the text more readable by a diverse audience that does not have an interest in detailed theoretical or manual considerations. In lieu of theory, illustrations are sometimes included for the purpose of showing why the concepts "work." In lieu of illustrating manual analysis concepts, computer analysis techniques are discussed since most practitioners would implement the concepts using one of the many commercially available computer packages.

This guide also has a "keep-it-simple" (KIS) objective. To achieve maximum effectiveness for developing or manufacturing a product, many "quick tests" (in lieu of one "big" test) could be best for a given situation. Engineers do not have enough time to investigate statistical literature to determine, for example, the "best" theoretically possible fractional factorial design alternative (see Chapter 13) to use for a given situation. An engineer needs to spend his or her time choosing a good overall statistical strategy assessment that

EXAMPLE 2-1: AUTOMOBILE TEST—ANSWERING THE RIGHT QUESTION    **9**

minimizes the risk of customer dissatisfaction. These strategies often need a blend of statistical approaches with technical considerations.

Classical statistical texts and classes usually emphasize either factorial experimentation, statistical process controls, or reliability testing. This guide illustrates that the mixture of all these techniques with brainstorming yields a very powerful combination when developing and producing a high-quality product in a timely fashion. Engineers need to be equipped with all these skills in order to maximize the effectiveness of their job performance.

Classical statistical texts do not typically emphasize "defining the problem(s)." For example, a classical text may give a procedure to choose the sample size to verify a failure criterion. A more important consideration would be to determine how to implement a factorial test that considers how several factors could be changed to improve the quality of the product. This guide emphasizes defining the "best" problem to solve for a given situation; individuals should continually assess their work environment by asking: Are we trying to answer the right question, and are we using the best basic test, development, and manufacturing strategies?

In many industries problems are getting more difficult to solve using traditional techniques. Failure rates are getting lower and the product applications are getting more complex. A classic question in this type of industry is: "What sample size do I need to verify a failure criterion?" The answer to this type of question is that, in general, it will be "too large." In lieu of addressing a sample size issue, individuals should consider what will be done "for the customer" with information obtained from the test. To make this self-evaluation, consider that a test was designed such that the criterion was met if no failures occurred. What would be the reaction from management if several failures occurred during the test? Might the failures be "talked away" (i.e., the numbers game)? If the process is not changed so that the root cause is avoided in the future, there may not be much gained from the test effort. Another example is that it is generally ineffective to arbitrarily conduct a test for the purpose of observing and fixing failures that occur. This approach is in general inefficient for problem determination. When testing to find a problem, it is usually better to structurally change things and observe the response.

Many questions should perhaps take a general form: What can be done to obtain customer satisfaction? The following example illustrates how a rephrasing of the question leads to a different test strategy that requires less test time and a smaller sample size.

## 2.1. EXAMPLE 2-1: AUTOMOBILE TEST—ANSWERING THE RIGHT QUESTION

Consider the hypothetical situation in which the insurance industry and automotive industry want to work together to determine whether the average accident rate of an automobile that has an innovative steering and braking mechanism will occur no more frequently than with the previous design (one accident every 5 years). [For those readers who are familiar with reliability testing, this initial question form is similar to a mean time between failure (MTBF) criterion test of a product.]

To answer this specific question, one can use the techniques discussed later to determine the number of prototype vehicles to build and then the number of miles to test drive this "random sample." For these test vehicles the desired accident rate must be achieved with some level of belief that the criterion will not be exceeded by the customer after shipment begins. The test would surely require a rather large random sample of automobiles, "typical drivers," and test time. The experimenter would probably also require that the cause of accidents be investigated to note if there was a design problem that caused the accident. However, with the current definition, this "problem diagnosis" is not a formal requirement of the experiment.

When reassessing the problem definition, it seems that the "real question of concern" may not be addressed by the test. Perhaps the test should directly assess whether this new design is going to increase the chance of accidents under varying road and driver situations. For example, if the initial test were performed in a locality during dry months, design problems that can cause accidents on wet pavements may not be detected. Other concerns may also be expressed. For example, speed, driver's age, sex of driver, alcohol content in driver, traffic conditions, and road curvature are not formally considered individually or in combination. Care needs to be given to create driving scenarios that match the frequency of customer situations during such a "random" test strategy. Often it is not practical to consider a random sampling plan where all infrequent situations are covered during test; however, in such situations a very serious problem could be overlooked because it was considered a "rare event" and was not tested. When such a rare event occurs later to a customer, the situation might result in a very serious problem. In lieu of verifying an overall failure criterion, a test alternative is to structurally force various situations, to assess whether a problem exists with the design. A fractional factorial experiment design offers such a structure (see Chapter 13).

Next, alternative responses should be considered since the sole output of "accidents" is expensive and can be catastrophic. In this example two possible output alternatives to the experiment are operator and vehicle response time to a simulated adverse condition. These outputs can be assessed relative to each other for a simulated obstacle to determine if an accident would have occurred. If the accident was avoided, the "safety factor" time could also then be determined for each adverse condition.

Reflecting back to the original problem definition, it is noted that the failure rate criterion validation question was changed to a test that focused directly on meeting the needs of the customer. A test strategy that attempted to answer the original question would not focus on the different customer situations that might cause a basic problem (or very hazardous situation) for some users. The redefined question would also save monies in that the test could be conducted earlier in the development cycle with fewer test systems. This earlier test strategy would permit more expedient (and less costly) fixes to those problems that are identified during the test. Examples 3-4, 13-3, and 18-1 build further upon the details of designing this test.

## 2.2. DO-IT-SMARTER CONSIDERATIONS

Examples in this text are structured given the assumption that samples and trials are expensive. In this text focus is given to using a minimum number of samples or trials while striving for the maximum amount of useful information. To achieve this, some examples will illustrate the blending of engineering judgment with statistics as part of a decision process.

Examples also assume that time is money. "Analysis paralysis" (i.e., analyzing the data to "death") is discouraged. Also, emphasis is given not to lose the "big picture" by too close examination of phenomena that may be statistically interesting but of little value to meet the needs of the customer.

When choosing an effective test strategy, one hurdle that often needs to be overcome is an appreciation of the fact that a fractional factorial experiment (where several factors are considered in one experiment) is a tool that can often help solve problems quicker than a one-at-a-time approach. When developing a process or product or fixing a problem, the "let's try this next" (i.e., one-at-a-time) strategy often prevails when attempting to get a "quick" solution. This type of test strategy can yield erroneous conclusions and the problems may never really get "fixed" (see Example 4-5). Individuals should, in general, consider the more efficient alternative of evaluating several factors simultaneously using a factorial experiment strategy (see Chapter 13).

When setting up tests using a do-it-smarter strategy, some problems can be broken up into subgroupings for statistical assessment (see Example 21-1). However, for this strategy to be successful all areas of management in an organization must have an appreciation for the value of statistical concepts. If a do-it-smarter strategy is incorporated, less emergency testing and fixing (i.e., less "fire fighting") in both product development and the manufacturing process can be expected. One might say: Use statistics for fire prevention. Constant job pressure to fix individual problems "now" can be very stressful. With less fire fighting, there could be less employee stress, which could lead to healthier and happier employees.

A do-it-smarter philosophy means directing efforts toward objectives that have the most benefit. If this is not done, development and manufacturing work can have many misdirections. Efforts must be taken to avoid magnifying the small and missing the big. More emphasis also needs to be placed on having a product that is satisfactory to "all" customers as opposed to "certifying" an "average" criterion (see Example 2-1). Sometimes only very simple changes are needed to make a process much better (see Examples 3-1, 3-2, and 3-3).

In development, doing-it-smarter techniques can lead to earlier problem detection and fewer problem escapes, with reduced development time. In manufacturing, these techniques can lead to reduced problem escapes, fixing the problem the first time, and better process understanding. The economics associated with these results can be very significant.

When developing and maintaining processes, emphasis should be given to reducing manufacturing variability—preferably during initial design stages of the development effort. If there is less variability in the process, there will be fewer defects or out-of-compliance product—fewer "fires" will need to be fought. Simple experiments in critical process steps initially can be very beneficial to reducing variability.

Large objectives can be achieved using do-it-smarter considerations; however, there is a price to pay—test objectives may need to be redefined. Classical statistical problem definitions often assume no engineering knowledge (e.g., will this product meet the failure criterion?). Typically within any product or process development there are individuals who have engineering knowledge of where product risks exist. Combining all sources of knowledge structurally is important to problem redefinition and a do-it-smarter philosophy. If test efforts are directed toward these risk areas, favorable customer satisfaction and higher product quality can result with less test effort.

Consider the situation where a product failure rate criterion is to be certified before first customer shipment. Samples that are taken should not be assumed to represent a random sample of future machine builds. Random samples can only be presumed to represent the population from which they are taken. With an early production sample, the production volume may not be much larger than the sample used in the test. In addition, the lack of precision of acceleration test factors (see Section 10.5) that may be used in a test adds to the uncertainty about confidence statements relative to certifying that a failure criterion is not exceeded.

Instead of taking a "random sample" of the first production builds, a do-it-smarter strategy may be to make the sample represent future builds with configurations, part tolerances, and/or process tolerances that are typical of what is expected to be within a customer environment. Fractional factorial experiment designs are useful when implementing such a test strategy. Within this approach many manufacturing and design factors are structurally changed to assess whether the product will perform satisfactorily within the designed or manufactured "space." The input parameters to a fractional factorial experiment design can be set to their specification limits, and the output response is then evaluated to determine if it is "acceptable." This basic test approach can often require more initial planning and effort; however, this strategy typically leads to a much better understanding of the process which can lead to early improvements, resulting in a smaller number of future "fire fights." Overall this strategy can yield higher quality with reduced costs.

In addition to input differences with this philosophy, other output considerations beyond a defect rate can give more "statistical power" and insight to the process and design. In addition, in an established process, surprising conclusions may often result by looking at the data differently. Data analysis paralysis should be avoided. For example, an analysis may indicate that a factor affects the response—who cares if all response data are satisfactory by a large amount? Another example is confusion over confidence interval statements—best estimate indicators may be the best economical choice for a particular situation. In addition, graphical techniques can be very powerful not only in giving additional knowledge but can also be a form that is useful in presentations to management.

Many organizations have accepted the value of process control charts (see Chapter 19); however, initial process capability studies might not have been considered. The procedure to manufacture a subassembly by a subcontractor (i.e., a vendor process) may be initially approved for "start-up" by sample lot inspection, while a process capability study (see Chapter 19) may indicate that the current process will not produce quality product on an ongoing basis.

Another do-it-smarter consideration may be to assess the "design or manufacturing safety factor." With this technique stress factors are changed until failures occur. Probability plotting techniques (see Chapter 5) are then used to project failure rates back to nominal conditions. This technique can be either considered with random samples or structurally with fractional factorial experiment designs. True randomization of the current "build vintage" will be sacrificed when using factorial concepts with this approach; however, a more desirable output of earlier problem detection and resolution may be achievable by reconsidering the test objective. This, in combination with good data analyses, can yield a more useful test result.

For a given situation, defining the best problem to solve and convincing others that this is the best problem to solve can be much more difficult than the analytical portion of the problem. Hopefully the examples discussed in this text can be used as a model for *you* to help define and convince others of the *best* problem to solve for *your* specific situation.

## 2.3. COMPUTER PROGRAMS

Most laborious manual statistical calculations can now easily be relegated to a computer. *Quality Progress* (a magazine of the American Society for Quality Control, Milwaukee, WI) periodically has an article that describes the features of computer program packages that can aid the practitioner with many of these tasks.

Unfortunately, program packages do not currently give the practitioner the knowledge to "ask the right question." This text addresses this most important task along with giving the basic knowledge of how to use computer program packages most effectively.

## 2.4. NOMENCLATURE

I have tried to be consistent with other texts when assigning characters to parameters (e.g., $\mu$ represents mean or average). However, there is an overlap in nomenclatures commonly found in texts that address differing areas of statistics. Since this guide spans many areas of statistics, compromises had to be made. Appendix E summarizes the assignments that are used globally in this guide.

In this guide both continuous response and reliability analyses are discussed. The independent variable $x$ is used in models that typically describe continuous responses, while $t$ is used when time is considered the independent variable in reliability models.

References are cited to indicate from where the information was taken or where additional information can be found on the subject. The numbering of examples in the text follows a "chapter sequence" numbering convention. Tables with a letter designation are located in Appendix D.

# 3

# MANAGING PROBLEM SOLVING, DECISION MAKING, AND PROCESS IMPROVEMENT

Recommended introductory reading: Chapters 1 and 2.

A basic theme of this text is to always strive for improvement (i.e., do-it-smarter) and not "play games" with the numbers. It is hoped that the reader will note a consistency between the philosophies discussed in this text and the basic quality management styles of two authorities on the subject: W. Edwards Deming and J. M. Juran. This chapter discusses the steps to both Deming's 14 points of management philosophy and Juran's control sequence and breakthrough sequence.

Also included in this chapter are the steps for effective decision making and the management attitude needed to support this activity. Group input techniques such as brainstorming and cause-and-effect diagraming are also discussed. Examples show some simple applications of these techniques along with a general discussion of some future topics that are discussed in this text.

## 3.1. MANAGEMENT STRUCTURE

Management structure can discourage effective decision making (Scholtes 1988). American managers often conduct much of their business through an approach that is sometimes called management by results. This type of management tends to focus only on the end result—return on investment. Emphasis is placed on a chain of command with a hierarchy of standards, objectives, controls, and accountability. Objectives are translated into work standards or quotas that guide the performance of employees. Use of these

**15**

numerical goals can cause short-term thinking, misdirected focus, fear (e.g., of a poor job performance rating), fudging the numbers, internal conflict and blindness for customer concerns. This type of management is said to be like trying to keep a dog happy by forcibly wagging its tail.

Quality leadership is an alternative that emphasizes results by working on methods. In this type of management every work process is studied and constantly improved so that the final product or service not only meets but exceeds customer expectations. The principles of quality leadership are customer focus, obsession with quality, effective work structure, control—yet freedom (e.g., management in control of employees yet freedom given to employees), unity of purpose, process defect identification, teamwork, and education and training. These principles are more conducive to long-term thinking, correctly directed efforts, and a keen regard for the customer's interest.

Quality leadership does have an effect on the return on investment. In 1950 Deming described this chain reaction of getting a greater return on investment as: improve quality—decrease costs—improve productivity—decrease prices—increase market—stay in business—provide jobs—increase return on investment. Quality is not something that can be delegated to others. Management must lead the transformation process.

To give quality leadership, the conventional hierarchical management structure (Figure 3.1) needs to be changed to management teams that have a unity of purpose (Figure 3.2). A single person using these concepts can make a big difference in an organization. However, one person rarely has enough knowledge or experience to understand everything within a process. Major gains in both quality and productivity can often result when a team of people pool their skills, talents, and knowledge.

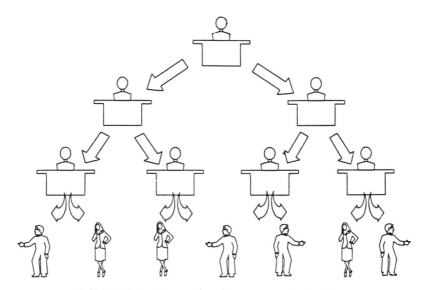

**FIGURE 3.1.** Conventional management structure.

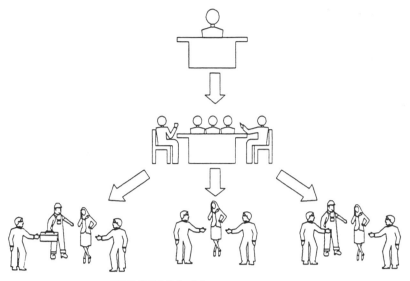

**FIGURE 3.2.** Management teams.

Teams need to have a systematic plan to improve the process that creates mistakes/defects, breakdowns/delays, inefficiencies, and variation. For a given work environment, management needs to create an atmosphere that supports team effort in all aspects of business. In some organizations management may need to create a process that describes hierarchical relationships between teams, the flow of directives, how directives are transformed into actions and improvements, and the degree of autonomy and responsibility of the teams. The change to quality leadership can be very difficult. It requires dedication and patience to transform an entire organization.

## 3.2. DEMING'S 14 POINTS FOR MANAGEMENT

Deming had a great influence on the rise of quality and productivity within Japan. The Japanese have embraced his concepts and have named their highest quality award after him.

Based on many years of industrial experience, I agree with Deming's basic philosophy and believe that many companies need to make the changes proposed by Deming in order to become more competitive. This text is a "how-to" guide toward the implementation of many of Deming's concepts.

The following discussion is a summary of Deming's 14 points for management[1]:

---

[1] The quoted material is reprinted from *Out of the Crisis* by W. Edwards Deming by permission of MIT and W. Edwards Deming; published in 1986 by MIT, Center for Advanced Engineering Study, Cambridge, MA 02139.

**1.** "Create constancy of purpose toward improvement of product and service, with the aim to become competitive and to stay in business and to provide jobs."

For the company that wants to stay in business, the two general types of problems that exist are the problems of today and the problems of tomorrow. It is easy to become wrapped up with the problems of today; however, the problems of the future command first and foremost constancy of purpose and dedication to keep the company alive. Obligations need to be made to cultivate innovation, fund research and education, and improve the product design and service, remembering the customer is the most important part of the production line.

**2.** "Adopt the new philosophy. We are in a new economic age. Western management must awaken to the challenge, must learn their responsibilities, and take on leadership for change."

Government regulations and antitrust activities need to be changed to support the well-being of people (not depress it). Commonly accepted levels of mistakes and defects can no longer be tolerated. People must receive effective training so that they understand their job and also understand that they should not be afraid to ask for assistance when help is needed. Supervision must be adequate and effective. Management must be rooted in the company and must not job hop between positions within a company.

**3.** "Cease dependence on inspection to achieve quality. Eliminate the need for inspection on a mass basis by building quality into the product in the first place."

Inspection is too late, ineffective, and costly to improve quality. It is too late to react to the quality of a product when the product leaves the door. Quality comes from improving the production process, not inspection. Corrective actions are not inspection, scrap, downgrading, and rework on the process.

**4.** "End the practice of awarding business on the basis of price tag. Instead, minimize total cost. Move toward a single supplier for any one item, on a long-term relationship of loyalty and trust."

Price and quality go hand in hand. Trying to drive down the price of anything purchased without regard to quality and service can drive good vendors and good service out of business. Single-source suppliers are desirable for many reasons. For example, a single-source supplier can become innovative and develop an economy in the production process that can only result from a long-term relationship with their purchaser. Another advantage is that often the lot-to-lot variability within the process of one vendor process is enough to disrupt the purchaser's process. Only additional variation can be expected with two suppliers. To qualify a vendor as a source for parts in a manufacturing process, perhaps it is better to first discard manuals that may have been used as guidelines by unqualified examiners when visiting suppliers to rate them. Instead suppliers could be asked to present evidence of active involvement of management that encourages the application of many of the do-it-smarter concepts discussed in this text. Special note should be given to the methodology used for continual process improvement.

**5.** "Improve constantly and forever the system of production and service, to improve quality and productivity, and thus constantly decrease costs."

There is a need for constant improvement in test methods and a better understanding of how the customer uses and misuses a product. In the past American companies have often worried about meeting specifications, while the Japanese have worried about uniformity (i.e., reducing variation about the nominal value). Continual process improvement can take many forms. For example, never ending improvement in the manufacturing process means that work must be done continually with vendors to improve their processes. It is important to note that putting out "fires" is not a process improvement.

**6.** "Institute training on the job."

Management needs training to learn about the company from incoming materials (with an appreciation of variation) to customer needs. Management must understand the problems the worker has in performing his or her tasks satisfactorily. A large obstacle exists in training and leadership when there are flexible standards to acceptable work. The standard may often be most dependent on whether a foreperson is having difficulty in meeting a daily production quota. It should be noted that money and time spent will be ineffective unless the inhibitors to good work are removed.

**7.** "Institute leadership. The aim of supervision should be to help people and machines and gadgets to do a better job. Supervision of management is in need of overhaul, as well as supervision of production workers."

Management is to lead, not supervise. Leaders must know the work that they supervise. They must be empowered and directed to communicate and act on conditions that need correction. They must learn to fix the process, not react to every fault as if it were a special cause, which can lead to a higher defect rate.

**8.** "Drive out fear, so that everyone may work effectively for the company."

No one can give their best performance without feeling secure. Employees should not be afraid to express their ideas or ask questions. Fear can take many forms, resulting in impaired performance and padded figures. Industries should embrace new knowledge since it can yield better job performance, not be fearful of this knowledge since it could disclose some of our failings.

**9.** "Break down barriers between departments. People in research, design, sales, and production must work as a team to foresee problems of production and in use that may be encountered with the product or service."

Teamwork is needed throughout the company. Everyone can be doing superb work (e.g., design, sales, manufacturing), and yet the company can be failing. Why? Functional areas are suboptimizing their own work and not working as a team for the company. Many types of problems can occur when communication is poor. For example, service personnel working with customers know a great deal about their products; however, it is unfortunate that there is often no routine procedure for disseminating this information.

**10.** "Eliminate slogans, exhortations, and targets for the work force asking for zero defects and new levels of productivity. Such exhortations only create adversary relationships, as the bulk of the causes of low quality and low productivity belong to the system and thus lie beyond the power of the work force."

Exhortations, posters, targets, and slogans are directed at the wrong people, causing general frustration and resentment. Posters and charts do not consider the fact that most trouble comes from the basic process. Management needs to learn that its main responsibility should be to improve the process and remove any special causes found by statistical methods. Goals need to be set by an individual for the individual, but numerical goals set for other people without a road map to reach the objective have an opposite effect in achieving the goal.

**11a.** "Eliminate work standards (quotas) on the factory floor. Substitute leadership."

It is incompatible to achieve never-ending improvement with a quota. Work standards, incentive pay, rates, and piece work are manifestations of management's lack of understanding, which leads to inappropriate supervision. Pride of workmanship needs to be encouraged, while the quota system needs to be eliminated. Whenever work standards are replaced with leadership, quality and productivity have increased substantially and people are happier on their jobs.

**11b.** "Eliminate management by objective. Eliminate management by numbers, numerical goals. Substitute leadership."

Goals such as "improve productivity by 4 percent next year" without a method are a burlesque. The data behind plots that track these targets are often questionable; however, a natural fluctuation in the right direction is often interpreted as success while small fluctuation in the opposite direction causes a scurry for explanations. If there is a stable process, a goal is not necessary since the output level will be what the process produces. A goal beyond the capability of the process will not be achieved. A manager must understand the work that is to be done in order to lead and manage the sources for improvement. New managers often short circuit this and instead focus on outcome (e.g., getting reports on quality, proportion defective, inventory, sales, and people).

**12a.** "Remove barriers that rob the hourly worker(s) of their right to pride of workmanship. The responsibility of supervisors must be changed from sheer numbers to quality."

In many organizations the hourly worker becomes a commodity. They may not even know whether they will be working next week. Management can face declining sales and increased costs of almost everything; however, it is helpless to face the problems of people. The establishment of employee involvement and participation plans have all been a smoke screen. Management needs to listen and correct problems with the process that are robbing the worker of pride of workmanship.

**12b.** "Remove barriers that rob people in management and in engineering of their right to pride of workmanship. This means, inter alia, abolishment of the annual or merit rating and of managing by objective."

Merit rating rewards people that are doing well in the system; however, it does not reward attempts to improve the system (i.e., don't rock the boat). The performance appraisal erroneously focuses on the end product, not leadership to help people. People that are measured by counting are deprived pride of workmanship. The indexes for these measurements can be ridiculous. For example, an individual is rated on the number of meetings he or she attends; hence in negotiating a contract, the worker extends the number of meetings needed to reach a compromise. One can get a good rating for "fire fighting" since the results are visible and quantifiable, while another person only satisfied requirements since he or she did the job right the first time (i.e., mess up your job and correct it later to become a hero). A common fallacy is the supposition that it is possible to rate people by putting them in rank order from last year's performance. There are too many combinations of forces (i.e., the worker, co-workers, noise, confusion, etc.). Apparent differences in people will arise almost entirely from these actions in the system. A leader needs to be a colleague and counselor that leads and learns with his or her people on a day-to-day basis, not be a judge. In absence of numerical data, a leader must make subjective judgment when discovering who, if any, of his or her people are outside the system (on the good or the bad side) or within the system.

**13.** "Institute a vigorous program of education and self-improvement."

An organization needs good people that are improving with education. Management should be encouraging everyone to get additional education and self-improvement.

**14.** "Put everybody in the company to work to accomplish the transformation. The transformation is everybody's job."

Management needs to take action to accomplish the transformation. To do this, first consider that every job and activity is part of a process. A flow diagram breaks a process into stages. Questions then need to be asked about what changes could be made to each stage to improve the effectiveness of other upstream or downstream stages. An organization structure is needed to guide continual improvement of quality. Statistical process control (SPC) charts are useful to quantify chronic problems and identify the sporadic problems. Everyone can be a part of the team effort to improve the input and output of the stages. Everyone on a team has a chance to contribute ideas and plans. A team has an aim and goal toward meeting the needs of the customer.

### 3.3. CHRONIC VERSUS SPORADIC PROBLEMS AND COMMON CAUSES VERSUS SPECIAL CAUSES

J. M. Juran (Juran and Gryna 1980) considers the corrective action strategy for sporadic and chronic problems, while W. Edwards Deming addresses this basic issue using a nomenclature of special causes and common causes (Deming 1986). Process control charts are tools that can be used to distinguish these two types of situations (see Section 19.1).

Sporadic problems are defined to be an unexpected change in the normal operating level of a process, while chronic problems exist when the process is at a long-term unacceptable operating level. With sporadic problems the corrective action is to bring the process back to the normal operating level, while the solution to chronic problems is a change in the normal operating level of the process. Solving these two types of problems involves different basic approaches.

The Juran's control sequence (Juran and Gryna 1980) is basically a feedback loop that involves the following steps:

1. Choose the control subject (i.e. what we intend to regulate).
2. Choose a unit of measure.
3. Set a standard or goal for the control subject.
4. Choose a sensing device that can measure the control subject in terms of unit of measure.
5. Measure actual performance.
6. Interpret the difference between the actual and standard.
7. Take action (if any needed) on the difference.

The process control charting techniques discussed in Chapter 19 are useful tools to monitor the process stability and identify the existence of both chronic and sporadic problems in the process.

Chronic problems often involve extensive investigation time and resources. Juran describes the following breakthrough sequence for solving this type of problem:

1. Convince others that a breakthrough is needed—convince those responsible that a change in quality level is desirable and feasible.
2. Identify the vital few projects—determine which quality problem areas are most important.
3. Organize for breakthrough in knowledge—define the organization mechanisms for obtaining missing knowledge.
4. Conduct the analysis—collect and analyze the facts that are required and recommend the action needed.

5. Determine the effect of proposed changes on the people involved and find ways to overcome the resistance to change.
6. Take action to institute the changes.
7. Institute controls to hold the new level.

The Pareto chart, discussed in more detail in Section 19.17, is a tool that is used to identify the most likely candidates or areas for improvement. Within a given area of improvement, fractional factorial experiment techniques (see Chapter 13) can often be used to efficiently determine which of the considered changes are the most important alterations that should be made to the process.

It is important to note that sporadic problems usually receive more attention because of high visibility. However, more gains can often be made by constant effort of continually working on chronic problems.

## 3.4. PROBLEM SOLVING AND DECISION MAKING

The following are steps to effective decision making:

Become aware of a problem or needed action.
Define the problem or needed action.
Consider alternatives and their consequences.
Select an approach.
Implement the approach.
Provide feedback.

Everyone follows this basic flow automatically to solve a problem—don't they? Not necessarily. For example, someone may determine a "quick fix" to a "crisis" in the manufacturing line. The person may have created other problems with the quick fix since he or she did not discuss the alternatives with other individuals. In addition, there may be no feedback to determine if the problem fix was effective for future production.

An additional concern arises in that the "wrong" basic problem is often solved (often called a type III error—type I and type II errors are discussed in Chapter 4). To address this issue, consider a manufacturing facility that produces printed circuit boards. This company may need to reduce their total defect rate at final test. Without proper understanding and investigation, the problem initially may be defined as: How should we get the assembly line employees to work more carefully so that they will reduce variability at their stations? However, perhaps a better starting point would be to state the problem as being too high of a defective rate at the end of the manufacturing process. From this more general definition, Pareto diagrams (see Section

19.17) can be used to direct efforts toward the sources that are causing most of the failures.

A cause-and-effect diagram (see Section 3.6) can then be used to consider alternatives and possible experiments for data collection as part of the decision-making process. Kepner and Tregoe (1981) discuss other structured problem solving approaches.

## 3.5. BRAINSTORMING

To begin this process of gathering information by brainstorming (Moody 1983; Dewar 1980), a group of people is assembled in a room where it is preferable that tables are positioned in a manner to encourage discussion (e.g., the tables are positioned in the shape of a U). The people who are assembled should have different perspectives on the topic that is to be addressed. The problem or question is written down so that everyone can see it (e.g., on a chalkboard), and the following basic rules of the exercise are followed by the leader (and explained to the members). It is preferable that the meeting leader (i.e., facilitator) has experience in conducting a brainstorming session. At a minimum a facilitator should have been a member of a previous brainstorming session.

1. Ask each member in rotation for one idea. This continues until all ideas are exhausted. It is acceptable for a member to pass a round.
2. Rule out all judgments. No idea is evaluated or criticized before considering all thoughts relevant to the problem.
3. Encourage wild ideas. It may be difficult to generate them; hence, wild ideas should not be discouraged since they encourage other wild ideas. They can always later be tamed down.
4. Encourage good natured laughter and informality.
5. Target for quantity, not quality. When there are many ideas, there is more chance of a good one being within the group.
6. Look for improvements and combinations of ideas. Participants should feel free to modify or add to the suggestions of others.

For the most effective meeting the leader should consider the following guidelines:

1. The problem needs to be simply stated.
2. Two or more people should document the ideas in plain sight so that the participants can see the proposed ideas and build on the concepts.
3. The person's name should be placed next to the idea so that the flow of ideas is not disrupted.

4. Ideas typically start slowly and build speed. Change in speed often occurs after someone proposes an off-beat idea. This change typically encourages others to try to surpass it.

5. A single session can produce over 100 ideas, but many will not be practical.

6. Many innovative ideas can occur after "sleeping on it."

A follow-up session can be used (or perhaps a survey of the participants can be conducted; see Section 20.4) to sort the ideas into categories and rank the ideas. When ranking ideas, members vote on each idea that they think has value. For some idea considerations it is beneficial to have a discussion of the pros and cons about the idea before the vote. A circle is drawn around the ideas that receive the most votes. Through sorting and ranking many ideas can be combined while others are eliminated.

Brainstorming can be a useful tool for a range of questions, from defining the right question to ask to determining the factors to consider within a fractional factorial experiment. This technique can be used to determine, for example, a more effective general test strategy that considers a blend of reliability testing, SPC, and factorial experiments. The cause-and-effect diagraming tool, as discussed in the next section, can be used to assemble thoughts from the sessions.

It should be noted that computers are sometimes now used with specialized software in a network to aid with administering brainstorming sessions. This tool can be a very effective means to gather honest opinions since inputs are often anonymous.

## 3.6. CAUSE-AND-EFFECT DIAGRAM

An effective tool as part of a problem-solving process is the cause-and-effect diagram (Crocker, Cuiu, and Charney 1984), also known as an Ishikawa diagram (after its originator Karoru Ishikawa) or fishbone diagram. This technique (Ball and Barney 1982) is useful in group brainstorming sessions where individuals list the perceived sources (causes) of a problem (effect). The technique can be useful to determine the factors to consider within a factorial experiment.

When constructing a cause-and-effect diagram, it is convenient to think in terms of four areas (causes) that contribute to a characteristic used to monitor quality (effect): materials, equipment, methods, and personnel. Each one of these characteristics is then investigated for subcauses. Subcauses are specific items or difficulties that are identified as a factual or potential cause to the problem (effect).

Figure 3.3 exemplifies a cause-and-effect diagram. In this figure the most likely causes, which are circled, could be used as initial factor considerations within a fractional factorial experiment design.

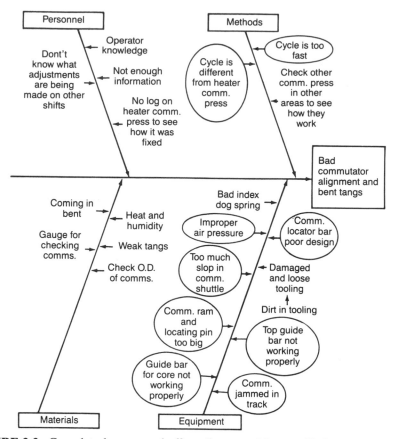

**FIGURE 3.3.** Completed cause-and-effect diagram with most likely causes circled. "Comm." = commutator. [Reproduced with permission: R. A. Ball and S. P. Barney, *Quality Circle Project Manual*, Dearborn, MI, p. 23.]

## 3.7. EXAMPLE 3-1: IMPROVING A PROCESS WITH SUBJECTIVE INFORMATION

Measurements may be nonexistent in a service organization because of the difficulty of determining a meaningful number. Measurements within the typing center, for example, could conceivably be the number of pages produced; however, this form of measurement could lead to a detrimental quota system (see Section 3.2, point 11a of Deming's 14 points to management). Monitoring of this measurement, or even monitoring the number of returns because of errors can also result in lost vision of what should be done to change the basic process in order to better meet the needs of customers.

Consider that an opportunity for improvement (see Step 1 in Figure 21.4) was identified in the typing center. A team was organized and the basic process in this area was identified to be as shown in Table 3.1.

**TABLE 3.1. Example 3-1: The Current Process in the Typing Center**

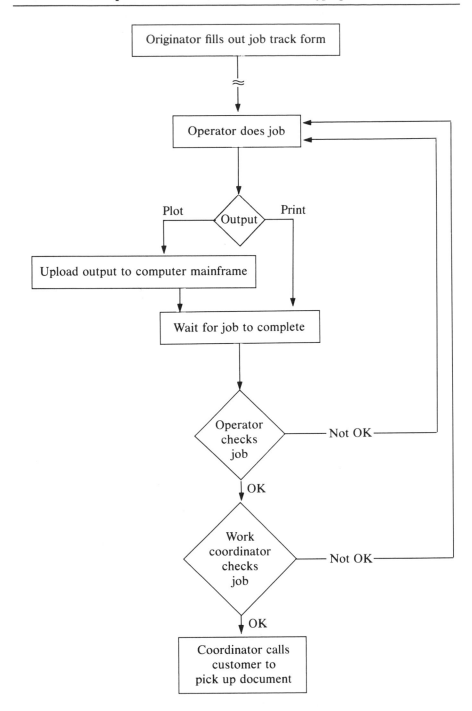

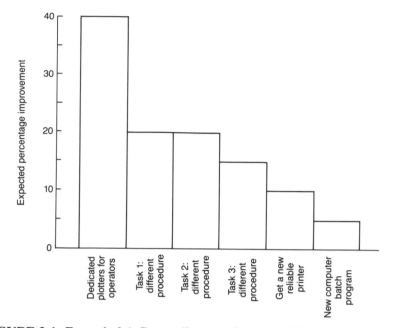

**FIGURE 3.4.** Example 3-1: Pareto diagram of opportunities for improvement.

A brainstorming session was conducted by the team to determine changes that could be made to improve work efficiency. During this session, the estimated percentage improvement in efficiency was noted for each change proposal. A Pareto diagram (see Section 19.17) of the items was created (Figure 3.4) to illustrate the relative magnitude of these items. Note tasks 1, 2, and 3 in the Pareto chart affected other areas of the business; hence, they were not included in the previous process flowchart. The meaning of the issue, "dedicated plotters for operators," needs next to be addressed since this is perceived as the most important change to make.

To address this issue it was noted that if two plotters were purchased, each operator could have a dedicated plotter, which would be much more efficient than the current queuing of jobs on the shared plotters. The cost would be

Cost for two plotters = (2 plotters)($4000/plotter) = $8000

Given a 40% efficiency and the additional factors of a 160-hr work month for five employees at a company burden rate of $100/hr, the estimated annual cost savings after purchasing the equipment would be

0.40(160 hr/month)(12 month/yr)($100/hr)(5 people) = $384,000

EXAMPLE 3-2: REDUCING THE TOTAL CYCLE TIME OF A PROCESS    **29**

The percentile estimates made by the operators could have considerable error and yet the purchase of these plotters would still be cost effective. It is also expected that there will be fewer operator errors after the purchase of the plotters since the removal of job queuing will eliminate one major source of frustration in the typing center.

A similar analysis might also be done of the lesser "leverage" items that were mentioned in the brainstorming session.

## 3.8. EXAMPLE 3-2: REDUCING THE TOTAL CYCLE TIME OF A PROCESS

Sometimes individuals are great at fixing the small problems; however, they sometimes miss the "big picture." This example addresses a big-picture issue.

Consider the development cycle time of a complex product that needs shortening so that the needs of the customer can more expediently be met. The total development process is described in Table 3.2.

**TABLE 3.2. Example 3-2: Total Overall Process**

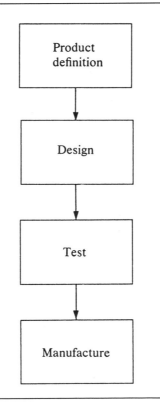

The total development cycle time of a product is typically between 2 and 3 years. Since absolute numbers were not available from previous development cycles, brainstorming sessions were conducted to identify possible sources of improvement. Several sessions were conducted to identify areas that could be targeted for improvement (i.e., processes). Consider that after all the group sessions were completed, the total list was presented back to each group for quantification in the form of a survey. Such a survey might ask for the amount of perceived improvement for each of the items, resulting in a Pareto diagram (similar to Figure 3.4). Another alternative question approach in the survey would be to format the questions such that a perceptual map results (see Section 20.4).

Management might be surprised to learn that an item such as the procurement of standard equipment and components was the biggest deterrent to a shortened development cycle time. Management might have expected to hear something more complex such as availability of new technology.

A team was then formed for the purpose of improving the procurement cycle. The current procurement process was defined by the team, as in Table 3.3a.

To better understand the existing process, the team considered a sample situation where a new piece of computer equipment is needed by an employee in her office. The equipment costs $1000. There should be much improvement in work efficiency after the equipment item is installed. An overhead rate of $100/hr exists (i.e., it costs the company $100 for the employee's salary, benefits, space allotment, etc.) and an improvement in efficiency of $\frac{1}{8}$ is expected when the equipment is available for use (i.e., 5 hr for every 40-hr week). The estimated cost to procure the item is noted in the following breakdown. Since the cost is over $500, the approval process is lengthy. The itemized costs include lost efficiency because of the time it takes to receive the item (e.g., consider that the company might not have to spend so much money subcontracting out work if the employee could get more done in less time).

Because of this, time expenditures and lost revenue increased the purchase price by a factor larger than 20 (i.e., $22,100 compared to $1000; see Table 3.3b). This process flow encourages the purchase of antiquated equipment. To illustrate this point, consider that during the 36 weeks of justification and budgeting a new more expensive piece of equipment is marketed. This equipment offers the opportunity of having much more productivity, which would be cost effective. But, if the purchase of this equipment would require additional delays, the employee would probably opt to purchase the "obsolete" piece of equipment in lieu of going through another justification and budget cycle. This action could cause a decrease in product quality and/or an increase in product development time.

In addition, the team also noted that with this process, it becomes only natural to play games. A department may often "justify" equipment with the anticipation that in 36 weeks it can replace this "justified" equipment with

**TABLE 3.3a. Example 3-2: The Procurement Process**

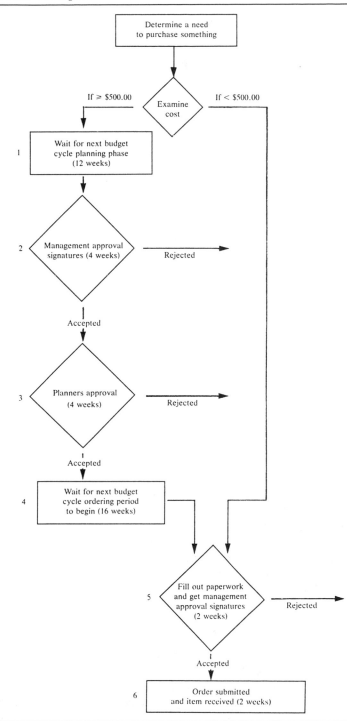

**TABLE 3.3b. Example 3-2: Lost Time and Revenue in Equipment Procurement**

| Step Number | Item | Cost |
|:---:|---|---:|
| 1 | Lost efficiency while waiting for next budget cycle time to begin: <br> (12 weeks) (5 hr/week) ($100/hr) = | $6,000 |
| 2 | Time writing justification and time for approval signatures: <br> (4 hr × $100/hr) = | $400 |
| 2 | Lost efficiency while waiting for equipment approval: <br> (4 weeks) (5 hr/week) ($100/hr) = | $2,000 |
| 3 | Planners' time for approving item: <br> (2 hr × $100/hr) = | $200 |
| 3 | Lost efficiency during planners' approval step: <br> (4 weeks) (5 hr/week) ($100/hr) = | $2,000 |
| 4 | Lost efficiency while waiting for next budget ordering cycle time to begin:   (16 weeks) (5 hr/week) ($100/hr) = | $8,000 |
| 5 | Time writing purchase order and time for approval signatures: <br> (4 hr × $100/hr) = | $400 |
| 5 | Lost efficiency while waiting for purchase order approval: <br> (2 weeks) (5 hr/week) ($100/hr) = | $1,000 |
| 6 | Time people spend in delivery of the item to correct internal location:   (1 hr × $100/hr) = | $100 |
| 6 | Lost efficiency while waiting for delivery of item: <br> (2 weeks) (5 hr/week) ($100/hr) = | $1,000 |
| | Total "process expense" | $21,100 |
| | Item expense | 1,000 |
| | | $22,100 |

some other piece of equipment that it really needs. However, what is done if there is allotted money and they find that they really don't need the justified equipment or any substitute equipment? The team discovered that departments typically buy some equipment anyway since they may lose their typical allotted monies in the next budget cycle.

The team next had a brainstorming session with people who often procure this type of equipment along with key people from the purchasing department (including managers). One outcome from this session might be that some capital equipment monies would be budgeted in the future more like existing expense monies. Each department would then be allotted a certain amount of money for engineers, secretaries, technicians, and so forth for improvements to their office equipment and other expenditures. Department managers would have the sole responsibility to authorize expenditures from these resources wisely. The team also noted that the future budget allotment for a department should not be reduced if they did not spend all their budget monies. Also, very large expenditures would be addressed in a different process flow.

EXAMPLE 3-3: IMPROVING A PROCESS THAT HAS DEFECTS    33

## 3.9. EXAMPLE 3-3: IMPROVING A PROCESS THAT HAS DEFECTS

As noted earlier, process control charts (see Chapter 19) are useful to monitor the process stability and identify when special cause situations occur. A process is generally considered to be "in control" whenever the process is sampled periodically in time and the measurements from the samples are within the upper control limit (UCL) and lower control limit (LCL), which are positioned around a center line (CL) (see Sections 19.2 and 19.12). Note that these control limits are independent of any specification limits.

Consider the final test of a printed circuit board assembly in a manufacturing facility that had a hypothetical process control $p$ chart (i.e., fraction nonconforming control chart) shown in Figure 3.5. In this chart it is noted that sample number 1 had a defect rate approximately equal to 0.18, while the overall average defect rate was 0.244.

This process is in control (i.e., no special causes noted); however, the defect rate needs to be reduced so that there will be less rework and scrap (i.e., reduce the magnitude of common causes).

After a team was selected and the process was described, a Pareto diagram was made to describe the type of defects. This Pareto diagram, shown in Figure 3.6, indicates that insufficient solder is the largest source of defects.

A brainstorming session with experts (i.e., engineers, technicians, manufacturing workers, chemists, management, etc.) in the field could then be conducted to create a cause-and-effect diagram for the purpose of identifying the most likely sources of the defects. A fractional factorial or response surface experiment is then often appropriate (see Chapters 13 and 17) to determine which of the factors are the most important.

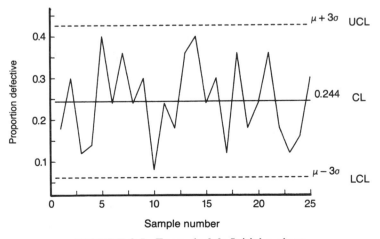

**FIGURE 3.5.** Example 3-3: Initial $p$ chart.

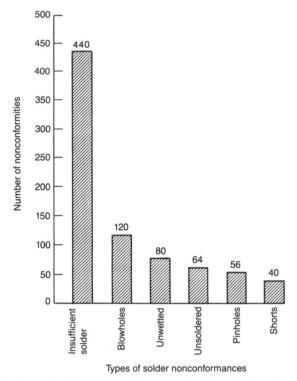

**FIGURE 3.6.** Example 3-3: Pareto diagram of solder defects [Reproduced with permission: William S. Messina, *Statistical Quality Control for Manufacturing Managers*, John Wiley and Sons, New York, 1987.]

Changes should then be made to the manufacturing process after a confirmation experiment verifies the changes suggested by the experiments. The data pattern of the *p* chart shown in Figure 3.5 should now shift downward in time because of these changes, to another region of stability. As part of a continuing process improvement program, the preceding steps can be repeated to identify other areas to improve.

### 3.10. EXAMPLE 3-4: AUTOMOBILE TEST—BRAINSTORMING FOR TEST CONSIDERATIONS

The automobile test described in Example 1-1 contained the logic that was used to change test considerations from a failure rate criterion test to a fractional factorial experiment approach (i.e., to answer the right question). This next example illustrates for this fractional factorial experiment how brainstorming and cause-and-effect techniques can aid with the selection of factors and their levels.

EXAMPLE 3-4: BRAINSTORMING FOR TEST CONSIDERATIONS     **35**

Consider that a group of people initially chose the factors and factor levels along with the test assumptions as noted in Table 3.4 for the fractional factorial experiment, where the factor levels are indicated by a + or − designation in this table. Next, a meeting of peers from all affected areas was conducted to consider expansion/deletion of selected factors, outputs, and limiting assumptions for the experiment.

In the meeting, inputs to the basic test design will depend on the experience and perspective of each individual. Probably everyone would not agree to the initial proposal. The following scenario could typify such a meeting.

Someone indicates that historically there has been no difference in driving capabilities between men and women; he suggests using men for the test since there was a shortage of women workers in the area. The group agreed to this change along with other suggestions that both automobile performance on curves and operator age should be included. The group thought that operator age should be considered since they did not want to jeopardize the safety of elderly people who might have trouble adapting to the new design. Also, the excellent suggestion was made that a comparison be made between the new design and the existing vehicle design within the same experiment to determine whether the new vehicle caused a difference in response under similar conditions. Also, it was agreed that operators should have one hour to get experience operating the new vehicle design before experiencing any simulated hazards. The

**TABLE 3.4. Example 3-4: Initial Proposal**

Objective
    Test operators under simulated road hazards to assess their reaction time along with automobile performance to determine if the new design will perform satisfactorily in various customer driving situations.
Limiting Assumptions
    No passing
    Flat terrain
    No traffic
Outputs
    Operator response time to adverse condition
    Automobile response characteristics to operator input
    Pass/fail expectation

| Factor | Factor Level Conditions | |
| Consideration | (−) | (+) |
| --- | --- | --- |
| Weather | Wet | Dry |
| Alcohol | None | Legal limit |
| Speed | 40 mph | 70 mph |
| Sex | Male | Female |

**TABLE 3.5. Example 3-4: Revised Proposal**

Objective
  Test operators under simulated road hazards to assess their reaction time along
  with automobile performance to determine if the new design will perform
  satisfactorily within customer driving situations.
Limiting assumptions
  No passing
  Flat terrain
  No traffic
  Operators will have one hour to get accustomed to the car before experiencing
  any hazards
  Only male drivers will be used since previous testing indicates that there is no
  difference between male and female drivers.
Outputs
  Operator response time to adverse condition
  Automobile response characteristics to operator input
  Pass/fail expectation

| Factor | Factor Level Conditions | |
| Consideration | (−) | (+) |
|---|---|---|
| Weather | Wet | Dry |
| Alcohol | None | Legal limit |
| Speed | 40 mph | 70 mph |
| Age of driver | 20–30 | 70–80 |
| Car design | Current | New |
| Road curvature | None | Curved |

revised test design shown in Table 3.5 was created, where each factor
will be tested at either a − or + factor level condition in an experiment
discussed in Example 13-1.

Note that this example is a conceptual example to illustrate the power of
using factorial tests versus a "random" test strategy. In reality for this particular
situation there would be other statistical concerns for the factor levels. For
example, it would be unreasonable to assume that one elderly driver could
accurately represent the complete population of elderly drivers. Several
drivers, for example, may be needed for each trial to determine whether
they all would respond favorably to the test situation.

# 4

# DESCRIPTIVE STATISTICS AND EXPERIMENTATION TRAPS

Recommended introductory reading: Chapters 1, 2, and 3.

A sample is a portion of a larger aggregate (population) from which information is desired. The sample is observed and examined, but information is desired about the population from which the sample is taken. From the sample (which is randomly obtained) a confidence interval can be determined that gives an expected range of values that contain a true population characteristic (e.g., an average output value).

A test may be used to evaluate a characteristic of a population to determine whether it meets or does not meet a criterion. Such a test is called a hypothesis test. Since the measurements from a sample do not usually yield a value that is exactly equal to a characteristic of the population, some decision needs to be made relative to the details of the test. Even with these plans there is always some risk of making a decision in error. Hypothesis tests address these details such that decisions risks are quantifiable and at acceptable levels.

This chapter gives an overview of some basic descriptive statistics used when sampling from a population. Some of the methodologies discussed are test hypotheses, confidence interval statements, and some plotting techniques. To get a valid answer, care must be exercised when performing a test. This chapter also includes four examples of experiment traps that need to be consciously avoided when conducting an experiment.

## 4.1. SAMPLING CONSIDERATIONS

Variability is everywhere. Consider a person who parks his car inside his garage. The final position of the car is not the same exact place day after day. The driver has variability when parking the car. If his variability when parking is too large from the center parking position in the garage, he might sometimes hit the garage door frame.

For the purpose of illustration, consider a person who wants to determine her average parking position and the consistency she has in parking her car inside the garage. It is not reasonable to expect that she would need to make measurements every time that she parks the car. During some period of time (e.g., one month), she could periodically take measurements of the parked position of the car. These measurements would then be used to estimate, for example, her average parking position for that period of time.

Similarly, all automobiles from a manufacturing line will not be manufactured exactly the same. Automobiles will exhibit variability in many different ways. Manufacturers have many criteria (or specifications) that must consistently be achieved. These criteria can range from dimensions on parts in the automobile to various performance specifications. For example, one criterion could be the stopping distance of the automobile at a certain speed. To test this criterion, the automobile manufacturer obviously cannot test every vehicle under actual operating conditions to determine whether it meets this criterion. In lieu of this, the manufacturer could test against this criterion using a sample from the population of automobiles manufactured.

A sample can yield information that can be used to predict characteristics of a population; however, beginning experimenters often have a misconception about the details of performing such a test. They may suggest taking a sample of five from today's production, making a measurement, averaging the results, and then reporting this value to management (for the purpose of making a decision).

Arbitrary sampling plans such as this can yield erroneous conclusions since the test sample may not accurately represent the population of interest. A sample that is not randomly selected from a population can give experimental bias, yielding a statement that is not representative of the population that is of interest. A sample of automobiles to address some criterion characteristic, for example, should be taken over some period of time with the consideration of such parameters as production shifts, workers, and differing manufacturing lines (i.e., a random sample without bias). A response $(x)$ from samples taken randomly from a population is then said to be a random variable.

Another consideration when sampling is that if there is much variability within a population, then there may not be much confidence in the precision of the point that is estimated (e.g., average or mean response). A confidence interval statement quantifies the uncertainty in the estimate since the width of the interval is a function of both sample size and sample variability. When a population characteristic such as the mean is noted to be within a confidence interval, the risk of the true value being outside this range is a quantifiable value.

Still another point not to overlook when evaluating data is that there may be another estimate besides the mean that better expresses the most important characteristic of a population. One of these considerations is the standard deviation (see Section 4.3) of a population, which quantifies the variability of a population. Another consideration is a population percentage value statement (see Section 5.3).

## 4.2. SIMPLE DATA PRESENTATION

It can be meaningful to present data in a form that illustrates the frequency of occurrence of values. A histogram is one form of plot to make such illustrations. To create a histogram when the response only "takes on" certain discrete values, a tally is simply made each time a discrete value occurs. After a number of responses are taken, the tally for the grouping of occurrences can then be plotted in histogram form. For example, Figure 4.1 shows a histogram of 200 rolls of two dice, where, for example, the sum of the dice was two for eight of these rolls.

However, when making a histogram of response data that are continuous, the data need to be placed into groups (i.e., cells). For example, in a set of data there might be six measurements that fall between the numbers of 0.501 and 1.500; these measurements can be grouped into a cell that has a center value of 1. Many computer programs internally handle this grouping. Section B.1 in Appendix B discusses a manual approach.

It should be noted that even though histograms are commonly used to illustrate data, the probability plotting techniques discussed in Chapter 5 often can give a more informative illustration about the population from which the data is sampled.

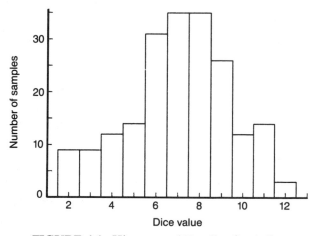

**FIGURE 4.1.** Histogram: 200 rolls of two dice.

## 4.3. EXAMPLE 4-1: HISTOGRAM PLOT

A sample yields the following 24 ranked (low to high value) data points:

> 2.2 2.6 3.0 4.3 4.7 5.2 5.2 5.3 5.4 5.7 5.8 5.8 5.9 6.3 6.7
> 7.1 7.3 7.6 7.6 7.8 7.9 9.3 10.0 10.1

Example B-1 in Appendix B illustrates the grouping of this data to yield the histogram shown in Figure 4.2.

## 4.4. MEASUREMENTS FROM A SAMPLE

A well-known statistic for a sample is the mean ($\bar{x}$). The mean is the arithmetic average of the data values ($x_1$, $x_2$, $x_3$, . . ., $x_i$), which is mathematically expressed in equation (4.1) using a summation sign ($\Sigma$) for sample size ($n$) as

$$\bar{x} = \frac{\sum\limits_{i=1}^{n} x_i}{n} \tag{4.1}$$

A sample yields an estimate ($\bar{x}$) for the true mean of a population ($\mu$) from which the sample is randomly drawn. Consider, for example, that the number of earned runs given by a baseball pitcher during six randomly chosen games

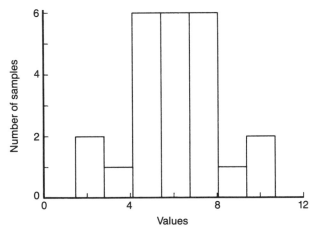

**FIGURE 4.2.** Example 4-2: Histogram of the data.

of his career were 6, 2, 3, 3, 4, and 5. Using Equation (4.1), an estimate for his actual "earned run average" (for all the games that were pitched) is

$$\bar{x} = \frac{6 + 2 + 3 + 3 + 4 + 5}{6} = 3.83$$

As noted earlier, standard deviation is a statistic that quantifies data variability. A baseball manager, for example, might not only be interested in the average runs given by a pitcher but also his consistency between games. One equation form for the standard deviation ($s$) of a sample is

$$s = \left[ \frac{\sum\limits_{i=1}^{n} (x_i - \bar{x})^2}{n - 1} \right]^{1/2} \tag{4.2}$$

A sample yields an estimate ($s$) for the true population standard deviation ($\sigma$). Figure 6.3 later illustrates that in some types of situations *approximately* 68.26% of the data is expected to be within a plus or minus one standard deviation range around the mean. For this example, the standard deviation of the runs given by the baseball pitcher would be

$$s = \left[ \frac{(6 - 3.83)^2 + \cdots}{6 - 1} \right]^{1/2} = 1.472$$

The $n$-1 term in the denominator is commonly called "degrees of freedom." This term will be used throughout this text and is assigned the Greek letter $\nu$ (pronounced *nu*, as noted in Appendix E). The number of degrees of freedom is a function of the sample size and is a tabular input value often needed to make various statistical calculations.

Variance is the square of the standard deviation. Variance is equivalent to moment of inertia, a term encountered in engineering. For this illustration, the sample variance $s^2$ is

$$s^2 = 1.472^2 = 2.167$$

The curves shown in Figure 4.3 have a frequency distribution shape that is often encountered when "smoothing" histogram data. The mathematic model corresponding to the frequency distribution is the probability density function (PDF). Each of these density function curves are bell-shaped and are called a normal probability density function.

For a given sample size, a smaller standard deviation will yield more confidence in the test results. This is pictorially illustrated in Figure 4.3 where case 2 has

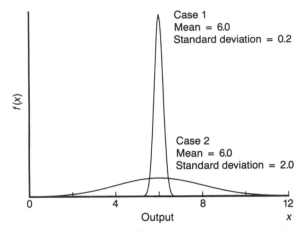

**FIGURE 4.3.** PDF: Effects of population variability.

more variability than case 1, which will cause more uncertainty in any estimated population parameter (e.g., true population mean). Chapter 7 discusses the calculation of the confidence interval that quantifies this uncertainty.

The sample median is the number in the middle of all the data. It can be represented as $x_{50}$. The 50 denotes that 50% of the measurements are lower than the $x$ value (similarly, e.g., $x_{30}$ indicates the 30th percentile). To determine the median of data, the data first need to be ranked. For the preceding set of data, the median is

$$2\ 3\ 3\ 4\ 5\ 6:\ \text{median} = \frac{3 + 4}{2} = 3.5$$

or the mean of the two middle values, because there is an even number of data points.

Note, however, that if the data were 1 2 4 5 6, the sample median would be 4, the middle of an odd number of data points.

## 4.5. HYPOTHESIS TESTING

Tests that require a yes or no answer as to whether the population meets or does not meet a criterion (or equality condition) are defined as hypothesis tests. At the conclusion of a hypothesis test, either the null hypothesis or the alternative hypothesis is accepted. The null hypothesis is accepted whenever the test results indicate that the criterion is met, while the alternative hypothesis is accepted (i.e., null hypothesis is rejected) whenever the results indicate that the criterion is not met.

Assume that there were a criterion that the mean for a population should be 6 and the ACTUAL mean value ($\mu$) of this population was exactly 6 (but the experimenter does not know this). When sampling from this population, the mean value of 6 would not always occur as the sample mean. If 10 different samples each of $n = 16$ are taken, the outputs could be as shown in Table 4.1, with the calculated mean and standard deviation values. (Note: These sample results were randomly generated from a normal PDF with mean 6 and standard deviation 2.)

In hypothesis tests the question of concern should be: Given any one of the preceding samples, should a criterion be accepted (accept null hypothesis, $H_0$) or rejected (accept alternative hypothesis, $H_a$)?

Since the data were in fact randomly generated from a distribution that had a mean of exactly 6, it is obvious that we would like to have a basic test strategy that would accept for all the samplings that the null hypothesis is met. However, none of the samples had an $\bar{x}$ value exactly equal to 6.

In most industrial situations a criterion value does not have to be exactly met. In other words an experimenter is typically willing to accept, from a process/design point of view, some amount of plus or minus shift from the value of 6.000000. A decision next needs to be made to determine the amount of shift that is acceptable. This amount of shift is defined as $\delta$ (Greek letter delta, as noted in Appendix E) and is an integral part of the preceding null hypothesis statement.

When sampling, we do not know the actual population mean; hence, the true mean value could be lower or higher than the sample mean value. At the end of a hypothesis test the tester will either accept or reject that the criterion is met for the population. Before starting the test, a person should decide upon the levels of risk (of being in error) that they are willing to take when making the final decision at the conclusion of the test. By convention, $\alpha$ risk relates to the risk of making the wrong decision when the alternative hypothesis ($H_a$) is accepted (i.e., the null hypothesis is rejected), while $\beta$ describes the risk of making the wrong decision when accepting the null hypothesis ($H_0$).

The previous illustration of testing for the criterion of 6 was a "double-sided" problem (i.e., two-sided problem). That is, the alternative hypothesis could be accepted because the conclusion from the sample would be that the population mean was either too large OR too small. Two-sided situations relate also to tests to determine whether two samples have equivalent means (e.g., population mean $\mu_1$ is either larger OR smaller than population mean $\mu_2$).

In addition to these double-sided tests, there are also single-sided tests where only one side of a statement is of interest. Table 4.2 illustrates both single-sided and double-sided hypothesis test scenarios as relates to tests of the mean. A similar table could be made for standard deviation.

Again, the $\beta$ risk corresponds to incorrect acceptance of the null hypothesis. This can be equated to the terms: type II error, "pass test" risk, test department

**TABLE 4.1. Example Data: 10 Random Samplings from a Normal PDF Where $\mu = 6$ and $\sigma = 2$**

| Within-Group Sample Number | Sampling Group Numbers | | | | | | | | | |
|---|---|---|---|---|---|---|---|---|---|---|
| | 1 | 2 | 3 | 4 | 5 | 6 | 7 | 8 | 9 | 10 |
| 1 | 2.99 | 7.88 | 9.80 | 6.86 | 4.55 | 4.87 | 5.31 | 7.17 | 8.95 | 3.40 |
| 2 | 6.29 | 6.72 | 4.04 | 4.76 | 5.19 | 8.03 | 7.73 | 5.04 | 4.58 | 8.57 |
| 3 | 2.65 | 5.88 | 4.82 | 6.14 | 8.75 | 9.14 | 8.90 | 4.64 | 5.77 | 2.42 |
| 4 | 10.11 | 7.65 | 5.07 | 3.24 | 4.52 | 5.71 | 6.90 | 2.42 | 6.77 | 5.59 |
| 5 | 5.31 | 7.76 | 2.18 | 8.55 | 3.18 | 6.80 | 4.64 | 10.36 | 6.15 | 9.92 |
| 6 | 5.84 | 7.61 | 6.91 | 3.35 | 2.45 | 5.03 | 6.65 | 4.17 | 6.11 | 4.63 |
| 7 | 2.17 | 7.07 | 4.18 | 4.08 | 7.95 | 7.52 | 2.86 | 6.87 | 5.74 | 7.48 |
| 8 | 4.13 | 5.67 | 8.96 | 7.48 | 7.28 | 9.29 | 8.15 | 8.28 | 4.91 | 8.55 |
| 9 | 7.29 | 8.93 | 8.89 | 5.32 | 3.42 | 7.91 | 8.26 | 6.60 | 6.36 | 6.10 |
| 10 | 5.20 | 4.94 | 7.09 | 3.82 | 7.43 | 5.96 | 6.31 | 4.46 | 5.27 | 6.42 |
| 11 | 5.80 | 7.17 | 7.09 | 5.79 | 5.80 | 6.98 | 8.64 | 7.08 | 5.26 | 4.46 |
| 12 | 5.39 | 2.33 | 3.90 | 4.45 | 6.45 | 6.94 | 1.67 | 6.97 | 5.37 | 7.02 |
| 13 | 10.00 | 3.62 | 5.68 | 5.19 | 7.72 | 7.77 | 7.49 | 4.06 | 2.54 | 5.86 |
| 14 | 9.29 | 7.16 | 7.18 | 5.57 | 3.53 | 7.12 | 6.14 | 10.01 | 6.69 | 4.80 |
| 15 | 4.74 | 9.39 | 7.14 | 4.42 | 7.69 | 3.71 | 2.98 | 2.20 | 7.89 | 9.60 |
| 16 | 5.19 | 7.98 | 2.36 | 7.74 | 5.98 | 9.91 | 7.11 | 5.18 | 5.67 | 5.92 |
| $\bar{x}$ | 5.77 | 6.74 | 5.96 | 5.42 | 5.74 | 7.04 | 6.23 | 5.97 | 5.88 | 6.30 |
| $s$ | 2.41 | 1.86 | 2.30 | 1.59 | 1.97 | 1.69 | 2.19 | 2.38 | 1.42 | 2.14 |

**TABLE 4.2. Hypothesis Testing: Single- and Double-Sided Tests on Population Mean**

| Single sided | | |
|---|---|---|
| $H_0$: $\mu \leq$ criterion value | or | $\mu \geq$ criterion value |
| $H_a$: $\mu >$ criterion value | | $\mu <$ criterion value |
| Double sided | | |
| $H_0$: $\mu =$ criterion value | or | $\mu_1 = \mu_2$ |
| $H_a$: $\mu \neq$ criterion value | | $\mu_1 \neq \mu_2$ |

risk, or consumer's risk. The $\alpha$ risk corresponds to incorrectly rejecting the null hypothesis. This can be equated to the terms: type I error, "fail test" risk, development risk, or producer's risk.

If there is a large difference between a population mean and its criterion, this difference can be detected with a small sample size. However, if there is not much difference, the sample size requirements may be very large. The sample size requirements (see, for example, Equation 7.1) can yield a very large number of samples whenever the $\alpha$, $\beta$ and $\delta$ input requirements are small.

Statistical statements about the mean of a population are robust to the data not being normally distributed in a bell-shaped curve like that shown in Figure 4.3 (see Section 4.7), while statistical evaluations about population standard deviations are not robust to a lack of normality.

It should also be noted that it is often good practice to "look at the data" in conjunction with making a formal statistical statement that addresses perhaps only a mean criterion. Probability plotting (see Chapter 5) is a good tool to use when making such observation. After "looking at the data" it might be determined that the wrong question was initially asked (e.g., a percentage of population statement would be more meaningful than a statement about the mean of a population).

## 4.6. CONFIDENCE INTERVAL STATEMENTS

As noted earlier, the mean of a sample does not normally equate exactly to the mean of the population from which the sample is taken. An experimenter has more "confidence" that a sample mean, for example, is close to the population mean whenever the sample size is large, as opposed to whenever a sample size is small.

There are statistical procedures discussed later in this text that quantify the uncertainty of a sample via a confidence interval statement. A confidence interval can be single sided or double sided. Plus, a confidence interval statement can relate to other characteristics besides mean values (e.g., population variance).

The following exemplify confidence interval statements on the mean:

$$\mu \leq 8.0 \text{ with } 95\% \text{ confidence}$$
$$2.0 \leq \mu \leq 8.0 \text{ with } 90\% \text{ confidence}$$

Similar statements can be made about standard deviation. The statements relative to robustness and answering the right question noted in Section 4.5 are similarly applicable to confidence interval statements. L. S. Nelson (1990) has more discussion on significance tests and confidence interval statements.

## 4.7. CENTRAL LIMIT THEOREM

The Central Limit Theorem states that a plot of *sampled mean values* from a population tend to be normally distributed (i.e., have a bell-shaped curve; see Section 6.2). Figure 4.4 indicates that a plot of the 10 sample mean values from Table 4.1 has the shape of a normal distribution. The distribution shape of mean values taken from a population will tend to be normally distributed even though the underlying distribution is not normal. The Central Limit Theorem is an important phenomenon that is a part of the theoretical basis to many procedures used in statistics (e.g., calculation of the confidence interval of a sample mean).

## 4.8. EXPERIMENTAL ERROR IN MEASUREMENT DATA

Experimental error can cause ambiguities during data analysis. The basic sources for error need to be understood so that a conscious effort can be

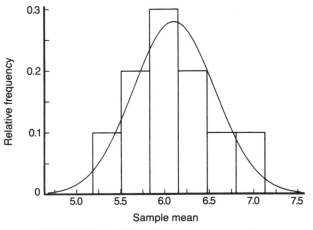

**FIGURE 4.4.** Plot of sample mean values.

taken to manage and reduce their magnitude so that clear and valid conclusions result.

The following definitions are useful to the discussion of experimental errors (Davies 1967). These errors are discussed further in Example 4-2.

*Accuracy*: It is usually impossible to ascertain the true value. Accuracy is a description of the closeness of agreement between the experimental value and the truth.

*Reproducibility*: When a method is highly reproducible, it is capable of yielding very similar results in replicated analyses. A result can be reproducible and not accurate since results can show a small amount of variations among themselves but do not necessarily vary about the true value.

*Error*: A difference from the truth that arises from causes that are inherent to the analytical methodology. For example, there is more error when measuring the width of a part using a ruler than with a micrometer.

*Mistake*: A difference from the truth arising from an unintentional departure from the usual procedure. For example, a reading was copied wrong from the data log.

*Random error*: An error that has an average that tends to be zero in the long run; however, it is unpredictable in an individual measurement.

*Bias or systematic error*: An error that persists during a series of similar measurements or analytical determinations. A total measurement error can consist of both bias and random error. Unlike the random component, averaging several measurements will not reduce the bias component.

Consider, for example, a test where measurements are taken on a piece equipment over time. Error can be caused by the following:

The variations in repeated tests performed under equivalent conditions at the same time. The results from such a test will vary around a mean value with a variance ($\sigma_1^2$).

The variations caused by operator bias. The means for a number of analyses will vary around some overall mean (i.e., bias) with a variance ($\sigma_2^2$).

The variations between analyses made at different times. The means for a number of analyses will vary around some overall mean with a variance ($\sigma_3^2$).

The total error variance ($\sigma_e^2$) is the sum of the error variance contributors; hence

$$\sigma_e^2 = \sigma_1^2 + \sigma_2^2 + \sigma_3^2 \cdots \tag{4.3}$$

It is often assumed that measurement tools and techniques do not contribute much to the measured variability of a process. However, measurement tool variability can be a large term in Equation (4.3) that can lead to erroneous conclusions about what should be done to reduce process variability (if not considered as an integral part of the analyses). The capability (see Section 19.15) of measurement tools should not be overlooked relative to needed measurement precision under various operating conditions. Example 15-3 illustrates a situation where the main source for error was found to be from operators using an invalid measurement procedure.

### 4.9.  EXAMPLE 4-2: EXPERIMENTATION ERRORS

Consider that the data in Table 4-1 are the readings [in 0.001 of a centimeter (cm)] of a functional "gap" measured between two mechanical parts. The design specifications for this gap was $0.008 \pm 0.001$ cm. The sample was taken from a population where the mean was 0.006 and the standard deviation was 0.002; hence, the part measurements will not be consistently within specification (which is unknown to the experimenter).

This type of data could be expected from the measurements in a manufacturing line, where the 16 random samples were taken over 10 days. A process control chart could be used to monitor the process average and variability over time (see Section 19.3), while a process capability study could be performed to determine whether the process will consistently produce product to specification (see Section 19.15).

However, for the purpose of making a decision, these measurement tools assume that the measurement technique is accurate. An experimenter typically desires that measurement precision be at least 10 times better than the range of the response that is of interest.

For this example the measurement variability could include the variabilities from part to part ($\sigma_1^2$), reproducibility ($\sigma_2^2$), operator to operator ($\sigma_3^2$), measurement tool to tool ($\sigma_4^2$), and day to day ($\sigma_5^2$). The total variability ($\sigma_e^2$) would be equal to the sum of the variance components; hence,

$$\sigma_e^2 = \sigma_1^2 + \sigma_2^2 + \sigma_3^2 + \sigma_4^2 + \sigma_5^2 \qquad (4.4)$$

The precision of the measurements is dependent on $\sigma_e^2$ and any bias that occurs during the measurements.

A manufacturing environment could be confronted with the question whether to reject initial product parts, given the information in Table 4.1. With no knowledge of the precision of the measurements, it might be concluded that the parts are bad, using the techniques described later in this text. However, if there were a large reproducibility term ($\sigma_2^2$), for example, in Equation (4.4), good parts could appear much worse than they actually are.

Each of these error terms could be estimated individually. For example, one part could be remeasured several times during the day by an operator using the same equipment (without the knowledge of the operator that it

EXAMPLE 4-3: EXPERIMENTATION TRAP—LACK OF RANDOMIZATION    **49**

was the same part). The variance of these measurements would be an estimate for reproducibility for that operator on that day.

It is obvious that the effort would get quite large if all the other factors are considered independently. Also, one can speculate that the reproducibility of an operator would probably be somewhat different overall than what could be projected by monitoring the activity of one day. A more structured approach to answering this question is to conduct a variance components experiment (see Section 13.22) for the purpose of estimating the magnitude of each of these sources for error.

## 4.10. EXPERIMENTATION TRAPS

Randomization is used in experiments when attempting to avoid experimental bias. However, there are other traps that can similarly yield erroneous conclusions. For example, erroneous statements can result from poor experiment design strategy, erroneous assumptions, and/or data analysis errors.

Invalid conclusions can easily result when good statistical experimentation techniques are not followed. Perhaps more erroneous conclusions occur because of this than from inherent risks associated with the probability of getting a sample that is atypical. The next four sections illustrate examples associated with poor experiment methodology. These problems emphasize the risks associated with lack of randomization, confused effects, factor interactions, and not tracking the details of the implementation of an experiment design.

## 4.11. EXAMPLE 4-3: EXPERIMENTATION TRAP—LACK OF RANDOMIZATION

The following measurements were made to assess the effect of pressure duration on product strength:

| Test Number | Duration of Pressure (sec) | Strength (lb) |
|:---:|:---:|:---:|
| 1 | 10 | 100 |
| 2 | 20 | 148 |
| 3 | 30 | 192 |
| 4 | 40 | 204 |
| 5 | 50 | 212 |
| 6 | 60 | 208 |

From the data plot of Figure 4.5, the strength appears to have increased with duration, however, from the preceding table it is noted that the magnitude of pressure duration was not randomized relative to the test number.

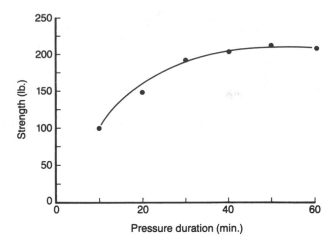

**FIGURE 4.5.** Example 4-3: Plot of the first set of data.

The collection of data was repeated in a random fashion to yield the following:

| Test Number | Duration of Pressure (sec) | Strength (lb) |
|---|---|---|
| 1 | 30 | 96 |
| 2 | 50 | 151 |
| 3 | 10 | 190 |
| 4 | 60 | 200 |
| 5 | 40 | 210 |
| 6 | 20 | 212 |

From the data plot in Figure 4.6, strength does not now appear to increase with duration. For an unknown reason the initial data indicates that strength increases with the test number. Often such unknown phenomena can cloud test results. Perhaps the first two samples of the initial experiment were taken when the machine was cold, and this was the real reason that the strength was lower. Randomization reduces the risk of an unknown phenomenon affecting a response, which can lead to an erroneous conclusion.

## 4.12. EXAMPLE 4-4: EXPERIMENTATION TRAP— CONFUSED EFFECTS

The following strategy was used to determine if resistance readings on wafers are different when taken with two types of probes and/or between automatic

EXAMPLE 4-5: EXPERIMENTATION TRAP—INTERACTION OF FACTORS    **51**

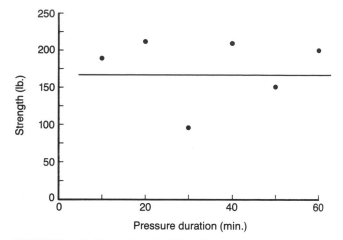

**FIGURE 4.6.** Example 4-3: Plot of the second set of data.

and manual readings. Wafers were selected from 12 separate part numbers $G_1$ through $G_{12}$, as shown in Table 4.3.

However, with the experiment design proposed by Table 4.3, the differences between probes are confused with the differences between part numbers. For example, wafer $G_1$ is never tested with probe type 2; hence, this part number could affect our decision whether probe type significantly affects the resistance readings. Table 4.4 indicates a full factorial design that removes this confusing effect. Note that future chapters will illustrate other test alternatives to full factorial experiment designs that can reduce experiment time dramatically.

## 4.13. EXAMPLE 4-5: EXPERIMENTATION TRAP— INTERACTION OF FACTORS

A one-at-a-time experiment was conducted when there was interest in reducing the photoconductor speed of a process. Bake temperature and percent additive were the factors under consideration.

The experimenter first chose to set bake temperature and percent additive to their lowest level setting (see Table 4.5) because this was the cheapest manufacturing alternative. The percent additive was then increased while the bake temperature remained constant. Because the photoconductor speed

**TABLE 4.3. Example 4-4: Initial Experiment Strategy**

|  | Automatic | Manual |
|---|---|---|
| Probe type 1 | $G_1, G_2, G_3, G_4$ | $G_1, G_2, G_3, G_4$ |
| Probe type 2 | $G_5, G_6, G_7, G_8, G_9, G_{10}, G_{11}, G_{12}$ | $G_5, G_6, G_7, G_8, G_9, G_{10}, G_{11}, G_{12}$ |

**TABLE 4.4. Example 4-4: Revised Experiment Strategy**

|          | Auto |  | Manual |  |
|----------|---------|---------|---------|---------|
|          | Probe 1 | Probe 2 | Probe 1 | Probe 2 |
| $G_1$    | —[a]    | —       | —       | —       |
| $G_2$    | —       | —       | —       | —       |
| .        | .       | .       | .       | .       |
| .        | .       | .       | .       | .       |
| .        | .       | .       | .       | .       |
| $G_{11}$ | —       | —       | —       | —       |
| $G_{12}$ | —       | —       | —       | —       |

[a] The — sign indicates the tabular position of a datum point.

degraded (i.e., a higher number resulted), the bake temperature was next increased while the percent additive was set to its original level. This combination yielded the lowest results; hence, the experimenter suggested this combination to management as the "optimum combination."

From the summary of results shown in Table 4.5, it is obvious that one combination of bake temperature with additive percentage was not evaluated. Consider now that another trial was added to address this combination of parameters and the resulting photoconductor speed was measured as 0.6. The two factors, bake temperature and percent additive, "interact" together to affect the output level. Figure 4.7 indicates an interaction plot of this data where the lowest (best) speed of conductor is obtained by adjusting both parameters concurrently.

Note that the straight line interconnecting the points assumes a linear relationship between the test point combinations, which may not be precise. However, this is surely a better initial test evaluation than using the original one-at-a-time approach.

## 4.14. EXAMPLE 4-6: EXPERIMENTATION TRAP— INDEPENDENTLY DESIGNING AND CONDUCTING AN EXPERIMENT

A system under development had three different functional areas. In each of these areas there were two different designs that could be used in production.

**TABLE 4.5. Example 4-5: Test Results as a Function of Factor Levels**

| Sequence Number | Bake Temperature (°C) | Percent Additive (%) | Speed of Photoconductor |
|-----------------|-----------------------|----------------------|-------------------------|
| 1               | 45                    | 1                    | 1.1                     |
| 2               | 45                    | 3                    | 1.2                     |
| 3               | 55                    | 1                    | 1.0                     |

EXAMPLE 4-6: EXPERIMENTATION TRAP—DESIGNING AND CONDUCTING     **53**

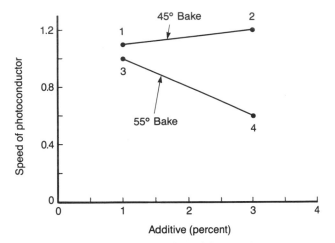

**FIGURE 4.7.** Example 4-5: Interaction of factors (test sequence noted).

To evaluate the designs, an engineer built eight special systems, which contained all combinations of the design considerations (i.e., a full factorial; see Chapter 13). The systems were built according to the following matrix, where the functional areas are designated as $A$, $B$, and $C$ and the design considerations within these areas are designated either as plus $(+)$ or minus $(-)$.

| System Number | Functional Area | | |
|:---:|:---:|:---:|:---:|
| | *A* | *B* | *C* |
| 1 | + | + | + |
| 2 | + | + | − |
| 3 | + | − | + |
| 4 | + | − | − |
| 5 | − | + | + |
| 6 | − | + | − |
| 7 | − | − | + |
| 8 | − | − | − |

The engineer than gave the eight systems to a technician to perform an accelerated reliability test. The engineer told the technician to note the time when each system failed and call her after all the systems had failed. The engineer did not tell him that there were major differences between each of the test systems. The technician did not note any difference since the external appearance of the systems were similar.

After running the systems for one day, the technician accidentally knocked one of the systems off the table. There was no visible damage; however, the system now made a different sound when operating. The technician chose not to mention this incident because of the fear that the incident might affect his work performance rating. At the end of the test, the technician called the engineer to give the failure times for the eight systems.

During the analysis, the engineer did not note that one of the systems had an early failure time with an unexpected mode of failure. Because of schedule pressures from management, the engineer's decision was based only on "quick and dirty" statistical analysis of the mean effects of the factors without residual analysis (i.e., all the failure times were used in the analysis—see Example 15-1). Unknown to the engineer, the analytical results from this experiment led to an erroneous decision that was very costly.

This type of experiment trap can occur in industry in many forms. It is important for the person who designs a test to have some involvement in the details of the test activity. When breaking down the communication barrier that exists in this example, the test designer may also find some other unknown characteristic of the design/process that is important. This knowledge along with some interdepartmental brainstorming can yield a better overall basic test strategy.

## 4.15. SOME SAMPLING CONSIDERATIONS

Readers often state that it is hard to believe that they could ever fall into one or more of the preceding example traps. However, within an individual experiment these traps can be masked; they may not be readily identifiable to individuals who are not aware of the potential pitfalls.

The reader may conclude from Examples 4-4, 4-5, and 4-6 that this text will suggest that all combinations of the parameters (factors) need direct experimental assessment during test. This is not usually true; experimental design techniques are suggested that are manageable within the constraints of industry. This objective is achieved by using design matrices that yield much information for each test trial.

Random sampling plans are based on the assumption that errors are independent and normally distributed. In real data this independence assumption is often invalid, which can yield serious inaccuracies. If appropriate, randomization is introduced when conducting an experiment, as an approximation alternative. The adoption of the randomization approach has the advantage that it does not require information about the nature of dependence. However, there are situations where randomization is not appropriate. To illustrate this, consider stock market prices. The magnitude of the closing price on a given day is dependent on its closing price the previous day.

One approach to this data dependence issue is to use a specific model for dependence. If such a model is valid, it is possible to develop procedures that are more sensitive than those that depend only on randomization. Box et al. (1978) illustrates with elementary examples that the ability to model dependence using time series can lead to problem solutions in the areas of forecasting, feedback control, and intervention analysis.

The sampling plans discussed later in this text assume that the process is stable (see Chapter 19). If the measurements are not from a stable process, the test methodology and confidence statements can be questionable. Even if an experiment strategy is good, the lack of stability can result in conclusions that can be erroneous.

This chapter has only given a brief overview of basic statistical concepts that are used later in this text. The bibliography section at the end of the book lists some other sources that give more detailed information on these basic concepts.

## 4.16. DO-IT-SMARTER CONSIDERATIONS

An experimenter could collect random data such as that shown in sample group 1 from Table 4.1. The experimenter might then want to make a statement about the data. The following statements could be made about the population from which the sample is taken when there is a continuous response (reference chapters are noted):

- Confidence interval on the mean and standard deviation (Chapter 7).
- Hypothesis statement relative to an average criterion (Chapter 7).
- Percent of population statements (Chapter 7).
- Process capability statement of frequency of meeting a criterion (Chapter 19).
- Comparing mean and standard deviation of one set of data to another set of data (Chapter 9).

Data is often generated for the purpose of discussing one or more of these considerations. However, there are often other questions that can be more important to consider. Would it be better for the experimenter to first attempt to understand the source of variability in the measurements (see Example 4-2)? A random effects model (see Section 15.5) could be used in an experiment design having such considerations. Or, perhaps there should be an emphasis to understand what factors affect the average response output of an experiment. This fixed effect model alternative differs from the random effects model discussed in Example 4-2 in that with this approach there could be an attempt to determine, for example, if there were an average difference in response output between two operators, along with other considerations such as tool adjustments (see Chapter 13).

Another possibility for experimental data collection is the proportion of product that either passes or fails a test. An experimenter may want to make a confidence statement about the population from this information. Chapter 8 discusses procedures to answer this attribute question, while Chapter 9 discusses the comparison of two different populations. The do-it-smarter consideration section (Section 8.8) of Chapter 8 discusses test considerations to this type of basic test strategy.

Reliability tests are another source for data. Chapters 10, 11, and 12 are useful to make statements with this type of information. Again, the do-it-smarter sections of these chapters discuss test alternatives to this type of testing.

# 5

# PROBABILITY AND HAZARD PLOTTING

Recommended introductory reading: Chapters 2, 3, and 4.

This chapter illustrates the concepts of probability density function (PDF), cumulative distribution function (CDF), probability plotting, and hazard plotting, while Chapter 6 discusses various types of PDFs and their associated CDFs.

Probability plotting, in particular, is a very powerful tool that is used in many different situations throughout this text. When sampling from a population, a probability plot of the data can often yield a better understanding of the population than traditional statements made only about the mean and standard deviation.

## 5.1. PROBABILITY AND HAZARD PLOTTING CONCEPTS

Percent characteristics of a population can be determined from the cumulative distribution function (CDF), which is the integration of the probability density function (PDF, e.g., the bell-shaped normal distribution curve shown in Figure 4.3). Probability and hazard plots are useful to estimate from data the unknown parameters of a PDF/CDF (see Appendix A) and the percent less than (or greater than) characteristics of a population.

A basic concept behind probability plotting is that if data plotted on a probability distribution scale (e.g., normal probability paper, see Table Q1) follow a straight line, then the population from which the samples are drawn can be represented by that distribution. When the distribution of data is noted, statements can be made about percentage values of the population, which can often be more enlightening than the mean and standard deviation statistics.

There are many different types of probability papers (i.e., coordinate systems) to address data from differing distributions [e.g., normal PDF (Figure 6.1) or Weibull PDF (Figure 6.10)]. Some computer programs can generate probability plots conveniently and yield precise parameter estimations. However, manual plots can also be generated using probability paper, which can be obtained from sources such as TEAM (see bibliography section). Some blank probability papers are included near the end of this text so that the reader has the opportunity to immediately apply this powerful tool to a variety of problems. (Figure 5.3 shows a probability plot.)

Probability and hazard plots of the same data are interchangeable for practical purposes (W. Nelson 1982). For ease of manual calculations, this text will use probability plotting when the data are not censored (e.g., all component failure times are available from a reliability test), while hazard plotting will be used when there are censored data (e.g., all the components did not fail during a reliability test).

## 5.2. PROBABILITY PLOTTING

As noted in Chapter 4, a plot of data that are grouped in intervals is called a histogram. A PDF can describe the shape of a histogram, where the area under the PDF is equal to 100% of the population. The median of the variable described by a PDF, for example, is the value where the area under the curve is split 50/50 [i.e., 50% of the population is less than (or greater than) the median value]. Other percentiles of population values can similarly be determined; however, since this percentage value is the area under a curve, it is difficult to get an accurate value for any given value of the variable on the abscissa of a PDF.

As noted earlier, the PDF is integrated to yield the CDF, which graphically yields population percentile (less than or greater than) values on one axis of the plot. However, drawing a line through test data to determine population characteristics is not accurate since the data do not typically follow a straight line on commonly used graph papers.

To address this nonlinear plotting situation, probability paper can be used since the axes are transformed such that a particular CDF shape will appear as a straight line if the data are from that distribution. The mathematics behind this transformation is illustrated for the Weibull PDF (see Section 6.6 and Section A.6 of Appendix A). The following example illustrates this transformation from a conceptual point of view.

## 5.3. EXAMPLE 5-1: PDF, CDF, AND THEN A PROBABILITY PLOT

Consider the following 25 ranked (low to high) measurements:

3.8 4.6 4.6 4.9 5.2 5.3 5.3 5.4 5.6 5.6 5.7 5.8 5.9
6.0 6.1 6.1 6.3 6.3 6.4 6.5 6.6 6.8 7.0 7.4 7.6

EXAMPLE 5-1: PDF, CDF, AND THEN A PROBABILITY PLOT    **59**

**TABLE 5.1. Example 5-1: Data Groupings**

| Response | Test Data[a] (number of items) | Test Data[b] Integration (number of items less then or equal to a value) |
|---|---|---|
| 3.6–4.5 | 1 | 1 |
| 4.6–5.5 | 7 | 8 |
| 5.6–6.5 | 12 | 20 |
| 6.6–7.5 | 4 | 24 |
| 7.6–8.5 | 1 | 25 |

[a] For Figure 5.1.
[b] For Figure 5.2.

In this data there is, for example, one output response between 3.6 and 4.5, while there are seven between 4.6 and 5.5. These ranked values can be grouped into cells (see Table 5.1) and then be plotted to create the histogram shown in Figure 5.1. These measurements form a bell-shaped PDF that is characteristic of a normal distribution. Figure 5.2 illustrates an integration plot of the data from Figure 5.1, yielding the characteristic S-shaped curve of the normal CDF (see Section 6.2).

Figure 5.3 next illustrates a transformation of the raw data via a normal probability plot. To make this plot, the following probability plot coordinate positions were used in conjunction with the original data set. The origin of these positions will be discussed in the next section of this chapter.

Data point:   3.8 4.6  4.6  4.9  5.2  5.3  5.3  5.4  5.6  5.6
Plot position:   2.0 6.0 10.0 14.0 18.0 22.0 26.0 30.0 34.0 38.0

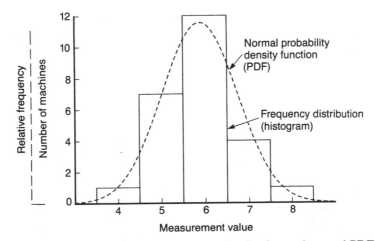

**FIGURE 5.1.** Example 5-1: Frequency distribution and normal PDF.

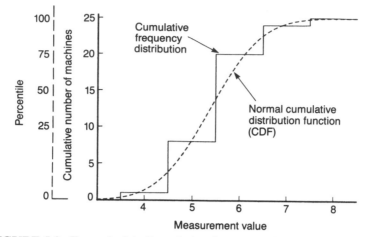

**FIGURE 5.2.** Example 5-1: Cumulative frequency distribution and CDF.

| Data point: | 5.7 | 5.8 | 5.9 | 6.0 | 6.1 | 6.1 | 6.3 | 6.3 | 6.4 | 6.5 |
|---|---|---|---|---|---|---|---|---|---|---|
| Plot position: | 42.0 | 46.0 | 50.0 | 54.0 | 58.0 | 62.0 | 66.0 | 70.0 | 74.0 | 78.0 |

| Data point: | 6.6 | 6.8 | 7.0 | 7.4 | 7.6 |
|---|---|---|---|---|---|
| Plot position: | 82.0 | 86.0 | 90.0 | 94.0 | 98.0 |

## 5.4. PROBABILITY PLOT POSITIONS AND THE INTERPRETATION OF PLOTS

As illustrated in Example 5-1, probability paper has one axis that describes percentage of the population, while the other axis describes the variable of concern. For example, a straight line on probability paper intersecting a point having the coordinates 30% (less than) and 2.2 can be read as 30% of the population is estimated to have values equal to or less than 2.2. Note that this could mean that 30% of the devices exhibit failure before a usage of 2.2 or that a measurement is expected to be less than 2.2 for 30% of the time. The precise statement wording depends on the type of data under consideration.

Consider an evaluation in which components were to be tested to failure, however, some of the samples had not yet experienced a failure at the test termination time. Only measured data (e.g., failure times) can be plotted on probability paper; individual censored datum points (e.g., times when components were removed from test without failure) cannot be plotted. When there are censored data, these data affect the percentage value plot considerations of the uncensored data. Since the adjustment of these plot positions utilizes a cumbersome and difficult algorithm, this text will use hazard plots, as discussed later in this chapter, to address the manual analysis of data that contains some censored datum points.

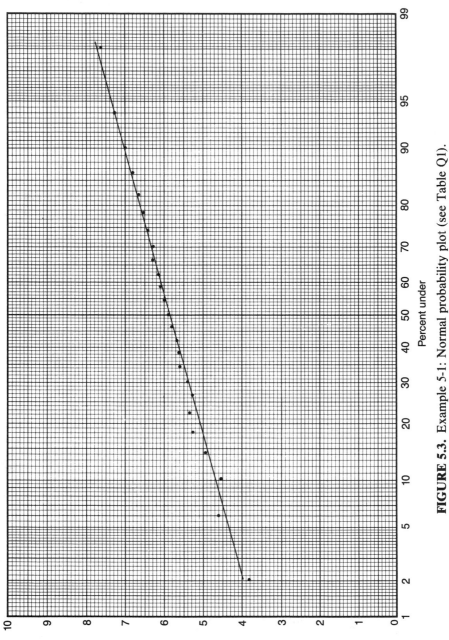

**FIGURE 5.3.** Example 5-1: Normal probability plot (see Table Q1).

With uncensored data, the coordinate position of each plot point relates to the measured value and a percentage value. For a sample of uncensored data, a simple generic form commonly used to determine the percentage value for ranked data ($F_i$) (W. Nelson 1982) is

$$F_i = \frac{100(i - 0.5)}{n} \qquad i = 1, 2, \ldots n \qquad (5.1)$$

where $n$ is the sample size and $i$ is the ranking number of the data points. For convenience, values from this equation are tabulated within Table P for sample sizes up to 26. Section B.4 in Appendix B discusses some other probability plot position equations that may, in general, yield a more precise plot position for a given set of data.

There are many types of probability paper. Within this text, normal, log-normal, and Weibull are discussed. Data from a distribution follow a straight line when plotted on a probability paper created from that distribution. Hence, if a distribution is not known, data can be plotted on different papers in an attempt to find the probability paper distribution that best fits the data. In lieu of a manual plot, a computer program (Section 2.3) could be used to generate a probability plot and make a lack of fit assessment of how the data fit the model.

Probability plots have many applications. These plots are an excellent tool to gain better insight to what may be happening physically in an experiment. A probability plot tells a story. For example, a straight line indicates that a particular distribution may adequately represent a population, while a "knee" can indicate that the data are from two (or more) distributions. One data point that deviates significantly from an otherwise straight line on probability plot could be an outlier that is caused, for example, by an erroneous reading.

In this text, Chapter 7 discusses the application of probability plotting relative to measured data, Chapter 12 utilizes the technique to determine the reliability of a device, and Chapter 15 discusses applications relative to fractional factorial test analyses. The following detailed examples are used to illustrate the application of these concepts:

Normal probability plotting, Example 7-4.

Comparing samples using a probability plot, Example 9-3.

Weibull probability plotting of failure data, Example 12-1.

Log-normal probability plotting, Example 12-4.

Normal probability plotting in factorial experiment analyses, Example 14-1.

Residual plot in a factorial experiment analysis, Example 15-1.

Quality function deployment with factorial experiment, Example 22-1.

Reliability and functional testing an assembly, Example 22-2.

Other texts discuss the mathematics that is used to perform the various formal lack of fit tests discussed in Section B.6 (Appendix B). A manual lack-of-fit check procedure is discussed in Section B.5. However, in many situations a simple visual examination can be adequate if care is taken not to overreact and conclude that a distribution assumption is not valid because the data do not visually fit a straight line "well enough." For example, Figure 7.1 has enough dispersion that one could question the validity of the normal distribution to describe the data. This figure is a probability plot of 16 random numbers that were taken from a normal distribution. Visually assessing data fit is further illustrated by Daniel and Wood (1980) where 40 normal probability plots of 16 independent standard normal deviates ($\mu = 0$ and $\sigma = 1$) contain more dispersion than may intuitively be expected.

## 5.5. HAZARD PLOTS

Most nonlife data are complete (i.e., not censored). Reliability test of life data may also be complete when the time to failure of each sample is noted. However, reliability tests of this type commonly contain failure times for some samples and cumulative usages for other test samples that have not experienced failure. There are several types of censoring possible (W. Nelson 1982); however, this text considers only multiple time censoring where failure times are noted and test samples may be removed from test at any time (in general, some can be removed earlier than others). Graphically this is shown in Figure 5.4.

As noted earlier, this problem is addressed manually in this text using hazard plots. The following procedure can be used to plot data on hazard paper (see Tables R1 to R3 for blank normal, lognormal and Weibull hazard papers).

1. Ranked data are assigned a reverse rank number ($j$), which is independent of whether the data points were from censoring or failure. A "+" sign indicates that the device has not yet failed at the noted time.

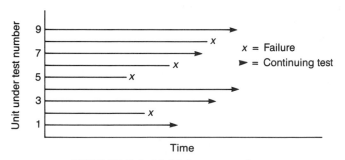

**FIGURE 5.4.** Multiply censored test.

2. A hazard value (100/$j$) for each *failure* point is determined, where $j$ is the reverse ranking.
3. Cumulative hazard values are determined for these failure points. This value is the sum of the current hazard value and the previous failed cumulative hazard value. These hazard values may exceed 100%.
4. The cumulative hazards are plotted with the failure times on hazard plotting paper.

If the data follow a straight line on the hazard plot, the data are from the distribution described by that paper. Example 5-2 illustrates the creation of a hazard plot.

## 5.6. EXAMPLE 5-2: HAZARD PLOTTING

Consider that the ranked data from the previous example were from an accelerated reliability test that had some censoring. In Table 5.2 the data (censored data are noted by a + sign) are shown along with the results from applying the steps noted in Section 5.5.

From the hazard plot of this data in Figure 5.5, it is noted that the data can be fitted by a Weibull distribution (see section 6.6) since the data follow a straight line on Weibull hazard paper. Percentage values for a failure time are then estimated by using the upper probability scale. For example, in Figure 5.5 90% of the population is expected to have a value less than 7.0. An example of a reliability statement given these numbers from a test would be: a "best estimate" is that 90% of the devices will fail in the customer's office before a usage of 7.0 years.

There is more discussion about the application of hazard plots to reliability data in Example 12-2.

## 5.7. SUMMARIZING THE CREATION OF PROBABILITY AND HAZARD PLOTS

A histogram is a graphical representation of a frequency distribution determined from sample data. The empirical cumulative frequency distribution is then the accumulation of the number of observations less than or equal to a given value.

Both the frequency distribution and cumulative frequency distribution are determined from sample data and are estimates of the actual population distribution. Mathematically, the PDF and CDF are used to model the probability distribution of the observations. The PDF is a mathematical function that models the probability density reflected in the histogram. The CDF evaluated at a value $x$ is the probability that an observation takes a value less than or equal to $x$. The CDF is calculated as the integral of the PDF from minus infinity to $x$. The procedure often used to determine a PDF for

**TABLE 5.2. Example 5-2: Hazard Plot Data/Calculations**

| Time of Failure or Censoring Time (yr) | Reverse Rank ($j$) | Hazard ($100/j$) | Cumulative Hazard |
|---|---|---|---|
| 3.8 | 25 | 4.0 | 4.0 |
| 4.5 | 24 | 4.2 | 8.2 |
| 4.6 | 23 | 4.3 | 12.5[b] |
| 4.9 | 22 | 4.5 | 17.0 |
| 5.2+[a] | 21 | | |
| 5.3 | 20 | 5.0 | 22.0 |
| 5.3 | 19 | 5.3 | 27.3 |
| 5.4+ | 18 | | |
| 5.6 | 17 | 5.9 | 33.2 |
| 5.6 | 16 | 6.3 | 39.5 |
| 5.7 | 15 | 6.7 | 46.2 |
| 5.8+ | 14 | | |
| 5.9 | 13 | 7.7 | 53.9 |
| 6.0 | 12 | 8.3 | 62.2 |
| 6.1 | 11 | 9.1 | 71.3 |
| 6.1 | 10 | 10.0 | 81.3 |
| 6.3+ | 09 | | |
| 6.3 | 08 | 12.5 | 93.8 |
| 6.4 | 07 | 14.3 | 108.1 |
| 6.5 | 06 | 16.7 | 124.8 |
| 6.6 | 05 | 20.0 | 144.8 |
| 6.8+ | 04 | | |
| 7.0 | 03 | 33.3 | 178.1 |
| 7.4 | 02 | 50.0 | 228.1 |
| 7.6+ | 01 | | |

[a] Censoring times are identified by a + sign
[b] For example, $12.5 = 8.2 + 4.3$

a given set of data is to first assume that the data follow a particular type of distribution and then observe whether the data can be adequately modeled by the selected distribution shape. This observation of data fit to a distribution can be evaluated using a probability plot or hazard plot.

Chapter 6 gives an overview of the common PDFs that describe some typical frequency distribution shapes, while Table 6.1 summarizes the application of distributions and processes to solve a variety of problems found in this text.

## 5.8. "PERCENT OF POPULATION" STATEMENT CONSIDERATIONS

Appendix B discusses other things to consider to make when generating either manual or computer probability plots. This appendix discusses techniques

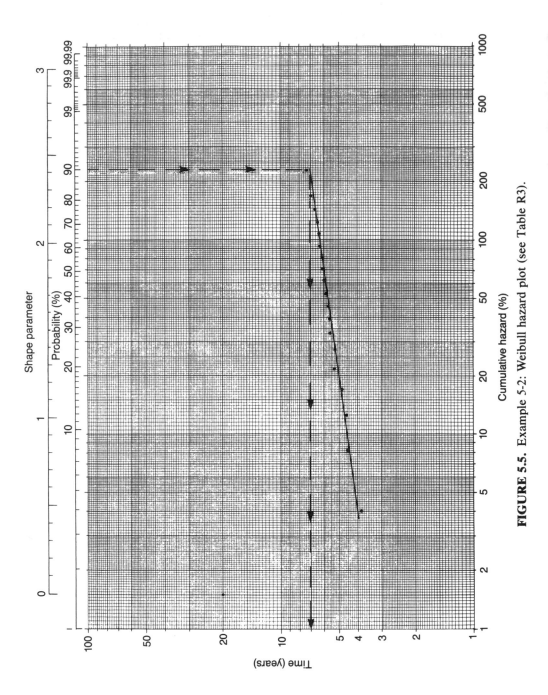

**FIGURE 5.5.** Example 5-2: Weibull hazard plot (see Table R3).

for determining the best-fit line on a probability plot and whether this line (i.e., the PDF) adequately describes the data.

Confidence interval statements relative to a percent of population plot can take one of two general forms. For example, in Figure 5.3 the following two questions could be asked:

1. The population percentile estimate below 7.0 is 90%. What are the 95% confidence bounds for this percentile estimate?
2. The 90% population percentile is estimated to have a value of 7.0. What are the 95% confidence bounds around this estimate?

This text does not address the confidence interval calculations for percentiles. Nelson (1982) includes an approximation for these limits, while King (1980b) addresses this issue by using graphical techniques with tabular plot positions.

This text focuses on the normal, Weibull, and log-normal distributions (see Chapter 6) to solve common, industrial problems. W. Nelson (1982) and King (1980b, 1981) discuss other distributions that may be more appropriate for a given set of data.

# 6

# DISTRIBUTIONS AND STATISTICAL PROCESSES

Recommended introductory reading: Chapters 2, 3, 4, and 5.

A practitioner does not need an in-depth understanding of all the detailed information that is presented in this chapter to solve most types of problems. A reader may choose to initially scan this chapter and then refer to this information again as needed in conjunction with the reading of other chapters in this text.

This chapter gives an overview of some statistical distributions (e.g., normal PDF) that are applicable to various engineering situations. In some situations a general knowledge of distributions can be helpful when choosing a good test/analysis strategy to answer a specific question. Detailed analysis techniques using these distributions are discussed in later chapters. Mathematics associated with these distributions is in Appendix A.

Hazard rate, the homogeneous Poisson process (HPP), and the nonhomogeneous Poisson process (NHPP) with Weibull intensity are also discussed in this chapter. The hazard rate is the instantaneous failure rate of a device as a function of time. The HPP and NHPP are used later in this text to model the failure rate for repairable systems. The HPP can be used to model situations where a failure rate is constant with respect to time. The NHPP can be used to model situations in which the failure rate increases or decreases with time.

## 6.1. AN OVERVIEW OF THE APPLICATION OF DISTRIBUTIONS

As noted in Section 4.7, the shape of a distribution is not usually considered when making statements about the mean because of the Central Limit Theorem;

however, often more useful knowledge relative to the needs of the customer is obtained by better understanding percentiles of the population. To be able to get this information, knowledge is needed about the shape of the distribution. Instead of representing continuous response data using a normal distribution, the three-parameter Weibull distribution or log-normal distribution may, for example, better explain the general probability characteristics of the population.

The normal distribution is often encountered within statistics. This distribution is characterized by the bell-shaped, Gaussian curve, as was illustrated in Figure 5.1. The normal PDF is applicable to many sampling statistical methodologies when the response is continuous.

The binomial distribution is another common distribution. In this distribution a pass/fail condition is the response that is analogous to a flip of the coin (one chance in two of passing) or a roll of a die (one chance in six of getting a particular number, which could equate to either a passing or failing probability). An application for the hypergeometric distribution is similar to the binomial distribution except this distribution addresses the situation where the sample size is large relative to the population. These distributions are compared further in the binomial/hypergeometric distribution section (i.e., Section 6.3) of this chapter.

In addition to a continuous output or a pass/fail response, another output possibility is that multiple defects or failures can occur on a sample. The Poisson distribution is useful to design tests when the output takes this form.

Reliability tests are somewhat different than the previously noted sampling plans. For a reliability test, the question of concern is how long the sample will perform before failure. Initial start-up tests can be binomial (i.e., samples either pass or fail start-up). If the sample is not DOA (dead on arrival), then a reliability test model can be used to analyze the failure times from the samples.

If reliability test samples are not repairable (e.g., spark plugs in an automobile), the response of interest is percentage failure as a function of usage. The Weibull and log-normal distributions (which are discussed later in this chapter) typically can model this scenario.

If the reliability test samples are repairable (e.g., an automobile), the natural response of interest is a failure rate model (i.e., intensity function). In this type of test, systems are repaired and placed back on test after failures have occurred. The HPP is used to describe system failure rate when it has a constant (i.e., a constant intensity function) value that is independent of usage that the system has previous experienced. The NHPP can be used to model system failure rate when the instantaneous failure rate (i.e., intensity function) either increases or decreases as a function of system usage. Both of these models use the Poisson distribution (see Chapter 11) to calculate the probability of seeking a certain number of failures during a fixed interval of time.

The following discussion in this chapter expands on the preceding overview. The mathematics associated with these distributions is found in Appendix A, while Mann et al. (1974) gives a more theoretical discussion. In this chapter there is also discussion on the application of other frequently encountered distributions that have tabular probability values, which are found in the back of this text. These distributions are referenced as sampling distributions. Sampling distributions are derived from the parent distribution by random sampling. Later chapters in this text expand upon the practical implementation of these distributions/processes. Lentner (1982) contains additional reference tables.

## 6.2. NORMAL DISTRIBUTION

The following two scenarios exemplify data that follow a normal distribution.

A dimension on a part is critical. This critical dimension is measured daily on a random sample of parts from a large production process. The measurements on any given day are noted to follow a normal distribution.

The mean value of the averages for the daily readings of the part in the previous illustration follows a normal distribution.

Note, because of the Central Limit Theorem, that the second scenario would tend to be true even if the first scenario did not follow a normal distribution.

Figure 6.1 illustrates the characteristic bell shape of the normal PDF, while Figure 6.2 shows the corresponding S shape of the normal CDF. These curves were generated for $\mu = 0$ and $\sigma = 1$. The area shown under the PDF (with the corresponding ordinate value of the CDF) will be referenced later in this section.

A commonly applied characteristic of the normal distribution is the relationship of percent of population to the standard deviation. To pictorially illustrate this relationship, note from the normal PDF equation (A.2)* that the CDF is dependent only on the mean $\mu$ and standard deviation $\sigma$ [see Equations (4.1) and (4.2)]. Figure 6.3 pictorially quantifies the percent of population as a function of its standard deviation.

Percentage values for the normal distribution are noted in Reference Tables A, B, and C (Appendix D). To conceptually illustrate the origin of these tables, the reader can note from Table B that $U_\alpha = U_{0.05} = 1.645$, which is the area marked in Figure 6.1. Also the quantity for $U_\alpha$ is noted to equal the double-sided value in Table C when $\alpha = 0.10$ (i.e., the single-sided probability is multiplied by 2). In addition, the single-sided value equates to

---

* Equations in Appendix A are numbered A.1, A.2, etc. in Appendix B, B.1, B.2, etc.

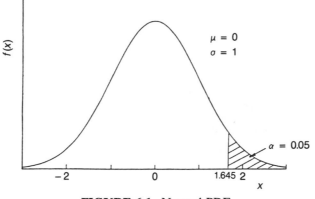

**FIGURE 6.1.** Normal PDF.

the value that can be determined from Table A for $Z_\alpha = Z_{0.05}$ (i.e., a more typical table format).

As an additional point to illustrate the preceding concept, the reader can also note that the $2\sigma$ value of 95.46% from Figure 6.3 equates to a double-tail ($\alpha$) area of approximately 0.05 [i.e., $(100 - 95.46)/100 \simeq 0.05$]. For an $\alpha = 0.05$, Table C yields a value of 1.960, which approximately equates to the $\sigma$ value of 2.0 shown in Figure 6.3 (i.e., $\pm 2\sigma$ contains approximately 95% of the population).

As a side note, most texts consider only one type of table for each distribution. The other table forms were included in this text so that the practitioner can more easily determine the correct tabular value to use when solving the types of problems addressed in this text.

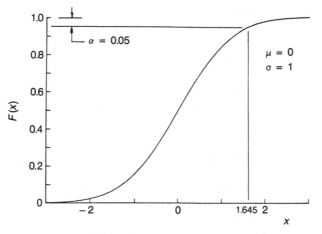

**FIGURE 6.2.** Normal CDF.

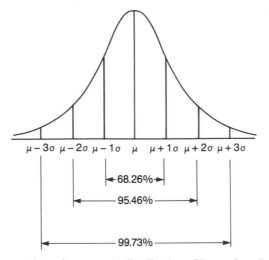

**FIGURE 6.3.** Properties of a normal distribution. [Reproduced with permission: William S. Messina, *Statistical Quality Control for Manufacturing Managers*, John Wiley and Sons, New York, 1987.]

## 6.3. BINOMIAL/HYPERGEOMETRIC DISTRIBUTIONS

Altering the first scenario discussed under the normal distribution section (Section 6.2) to a binomial distribution scenario yields:

A dimension on a part is critical. This critical dimension is measured daily on a random sample of parts from a large production process. To expedite the inspection process a tool is designed to either pass or fail a part that is tested. The output now is no longer continuous. The output is now binary (pass or fail for each part); hence, the binomial distribution can be used to develop an attribute sampling plan.

In Equation (A.3) it is shown that the shape of a binomial distribution is dependent on the sample size ($n$) and proportion of the population having a characteristic ($p$) (e.g., proportion of the population that is not in compliance). For an $n$ of 8 and various $p$ values (i.e., 0.1, 0.5, 0.7, and 0.9), Figure 6.4 illustrates these four binomial distributions (for the probability of an occurrence Pr), while Figure 6.5 shows the corresponding cumulative distributions.

When there is an alternative, attribute sampling inspection plans are not, in general, as desirable as a continuous sampling plan, which monitors the measurement values. For the parts in the above sampling plan, no knowledge is gained as to the level of goodness or badness of the dimension relative to the criterion. Attribute test plans can often require a much larger sample size than sampling plans that evaluate measurement values.

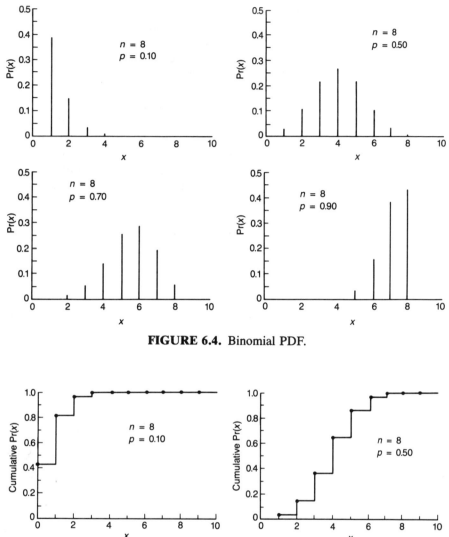

**FIGURE 6.4.** Binomial PDF.

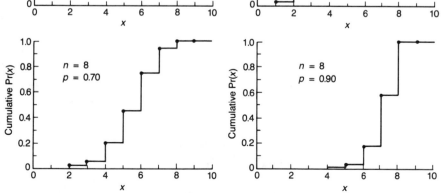

**FIGURE 6.5.** Binomial CDF.

Use of the hypergeometric distribution in sampling is similar to that of the binomial distribution except that the sample size is "large" relative to the population size. To illustrate this difference, consider that the first 100 parts of a new manufacturing process were given a pass/fail test where one part failed. Section 8.4 shows how a confidence interval for the proportion defective of a process can be determined given the one failure in a sample of 100. However, in reality the complete population was tested; hence, there is no confidence interval. The experimenter is 100% confident that the failure rate for the population that was sampled (i.e., the 100 parts) is 0.01 (i.e., 1/100). This illustration considers the extreme situation where the sample size equals the population size. The hypergeometric distribution should be considered whenever the sample size is larger than approximately 10% of the population (Miller and Freund 1965). Equation (A.8) shows the mathematics of this distribution. McWilliams (1990) gives a FORTRAN program for acceptance sampling plans based on the hypergeometric distribution.

## 6.4. POISSON DISTRIBUTION

The following two scenarios exemplify data that can follow a Poisson distribution.

> There are a large number of dimensions on a part that are critical. Dimensions are measured on a random sample of parts from a large production process. The number of "out-of-specification conditions" are noted on each sample. This collective "number-of-failures" information from the samples can often be modeled using a Poisson distribution.

> A repairable system is known to have a constant failure rate as a function of usage (i.e., follows a HPP). In a test a number of test systems are exercised and the number of failures are noted for the systems. The Poisson distribution can be used to design/analyze this test.

In this text the repairable system scenario gets the most focus of these two situations.

In Equations (A.10) and (A.11) it is noted that the Poisson distribution is dependent only on one parameter, the mean ($\mu$) of the distribution. Figure 6.6 shows the Poisson distributions (for the probability of an occurrence Pr) for the mean values of 1, 5, 8, and 10, while Figure 6.7 shows the corresponding cumulative distributions.

## 6.5. EXPONENTIAL DISTRIBUTION

The following scenario exemplifies a situation that follows an exponential distribution.

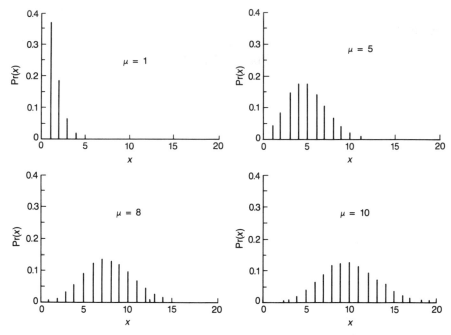

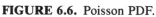

**FIGURE 6.6.**  Poisson PDF.

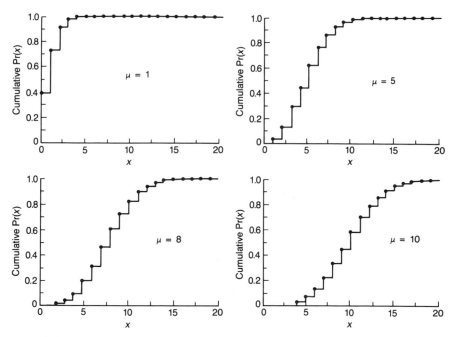

**FIGURE 6.7.**  Poisson CDF.

A repairable system is known to have a constant failure rate as a function of usage. The time between failures will be distributed exponentially. The failures will have a rate of occurrence that is described by a HPP. The Poisson distribution can be used to design a test where sampled systems are tested for the purpose of determining a confidence interval for the failure rate of the system.

The PDF for the exponential distribution is simply

$$f(x) = (1/\theta)e^{-x/\theta} \tag{6.1}$$

Integration of this equation yields the CDF for the exponential distribution

$$F(x) = 1 - e^{-x/\theta} \tag{6.2}$$

The exponential distribution is only dependent on one parameter ($\theta$), which is the mean of the distribution (i.e., mean time between failures). Equation (A.17) shows that the instantaneous failure rate (i.e., hazard rate; see Section 6.11) of an exponential distribution is constant and equals $1/\theta$. Figure 6.8 illustrates the characteristic shape of the PDF, while Figure 6.9 shows the corresponding shape for the CDF. The curves were generated for a $\theta$ value of 1000.

## 6.6. WEIBULL DISTRIBUTION

The following scenario exemplifies a situation that can follow a two-parameter Weibull distribution.

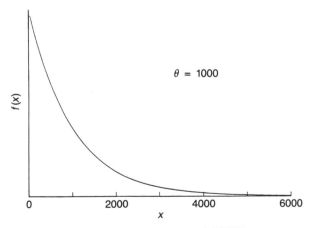

**FIGURE 6.8.** Exponential PDF.

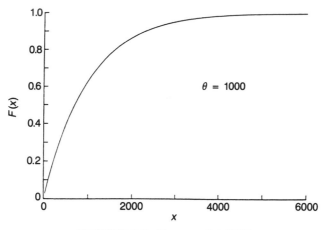

**FIGURE 6.9.** Exponential CDF.

A nonrepairable device experiences failures through either early-life, intrinsic, or wear-out phenomena. Failure data of this type often follow the Weibull distribution.

The following scenario exemplifies a situation where a three-parameter Weibull distribution is applicable.

A dimension on a part is critical. This critical dimension is measured daily on a random sample of parts from a large production process. Information is desired about the "tails" of the distribution. A plot of the measurements indicate that they follow a three-parameter Weibull distribution better than a normal distribution.

As illustrated in Figures 6.10 and 6.11, the Weibull distribution has shape flexibility; hence, this distribution can be used to describe many types of data. The shape parameter ($b$) in the Weibull equation (see Appendix A) defines the PDF shape. Another parameter is $k$ (scale parameter or characteristic life), which describes conceptually the magnitude of the $x$-axis scale. The other parameter contained within the three-parameter model is the location parameter ($x_0$), which is the $x$-axis intercept equating to the value where there is zero probability of lesser values.

For reliability models, $x_0$ usually equals zero. From Equation (A.19) the proportion of failures $F(x)$ at a certain time reduces to simply

$$F(x) = 1 - \exp\left[ -\left(\frac{x}{k}\right)^b \right]$$

(6.3)

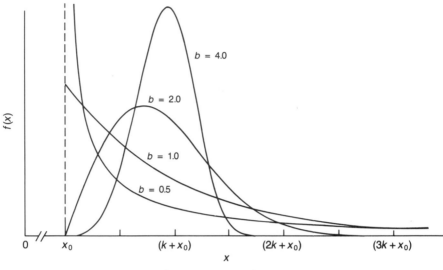

**FIGURE 6.10.** Weibull PDF.

Section A.6 in Appendix A has more detailed information on the mathematical properties of the Weibull distribution.

## 6.7. LOG-NORMAL DISTRIBUTION

The following scenario exemplifies a situation that can follow a log-normal distribution.

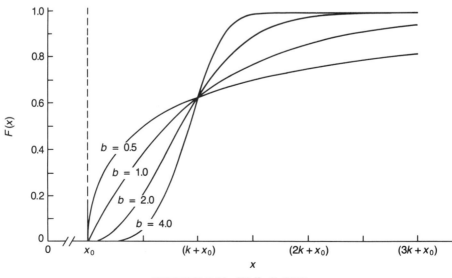

**FIGURE 6.11.** Weibull CDF.

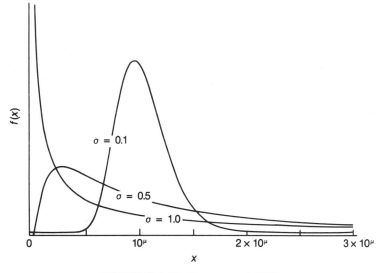

**FIGURE 6.12.** Log-normal PDF.

A nonrepairable device experiences failures through metal fatigue. Time-of-failure data from this source often follows the log-normal distribution.

Like the Weibull distribution, the log-normal distribution exhibits many PDF shapes, as illustrated in Figures 6.12 and 6.13. This distribution is often useful in the analysis of economic, biological, life data (e.g., metal fatigue and electrical insulation life), and the repair times of equipment. The distribution can often be used to fit data that has a large range of values.

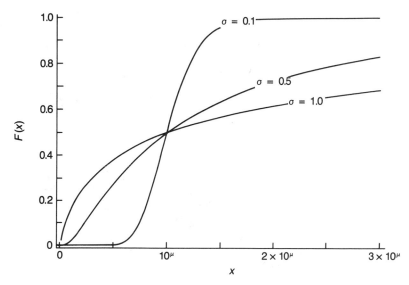

**FIGURE 6.13.** Log-normal CDF.

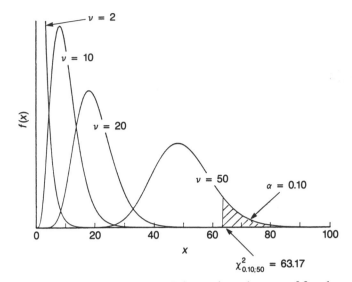

**FIGURE 6.14.** Chi-square PDF for various degrees of freedom.

The logarithm of data from this distribution is normally distributed; hence, with this transformation, data can be analyzed as if they came from a normal distribution. Note in Figures 6.12 and 6.13 that $\mu$ and $\sigma$ are determined from the transformed data.

## 6.8. TABULATED PROBABILITY DISTRIBUTION: CHI-SQUARE DISTRIBUTION

The chi-square distribution is an important sampling distribution. One application of this distribution is illustrated in Equation (7.3) where the chi-square distribution (Table G)* is used to determine the confidence interval for the standard deviation of a population.

If $x_i$, where $i = 1, 2, \ldots, \nu$, are normally and independently distributed with means $\mu_i$ and variances $\sigma_i^2$, the chi-square variable can be defined as

$$\chi^2(\nu) = \sum_{i=1}^{\nu} \left[ \frac{x_i - \mu_i}{\sigma_i} \right]^2 \qquad (6.4)$$

In Figure 6.14 the chi-square distribution is shown to be a family of distributions that is indexed by the number of degrees of freedom ($\nu$). The chi-square distribution has the characteristics $\mu = \nu$ and $\sigma^2 = 2\nu$.

Table G gives percentage points of the chi-square distribution. From this table, for example, $\chi_{\alpha;\nu}^2 = \chi_{0.10;50}^2 = 63.17$, which is illustrated pictorially in Figure 6.14.

* Tables A through R3 are located in Appendix D of this book.

## 6.9. TABULATED PROBABILITY DISTRIBUTION: *t* DISTRIBUTION

Another useful sampling distribution is the *t* distribution. Applications of the *t* distribution are shown in Tables 7.1 and 9.1. In these equations probability values from the *t* distribution (see Tables D and E) are used to determine confidence intervals and comparison statements about the population mean(s).

In Figure 6.15 the *t* distribution is shown to be a family of distributions that is indexed by the number of degrees of freedom ($v$). The distribution is symmetrical; hence, $t_{1-\alpha;v} = -t_{\alpha;v}$. Tables D and E give percentage points from the *t* distribution. Table D considers the single-sided probability of the distribution tail, while Table E contains the probability of both tails (i.e., double sided). From Table D, for example, $t_{\alpha;v} = t_{0.10;1} = 3.078$, which is illustrated pictorially in Figure 6.15. A double-sided value equates to the single-sided value when the single-sided probability is multiplied by 2. For example, the double-sided 0.20 level equates to the 0.10 single-sided value (i.e., from Table E [$t_{\alpha;v}$ (double-sided) = $t_{0.20;1} = 3.078$] equates to the preceding value).

As the number of degrees of freedom approaches infinity, the distribution approaches a normal distribution. To illustrate this note that from Table D, $t_{0.10;\infty} = 1.282$, which equates to the value $U_{0.10}$ in Table B and $Z_{0.10}$ in Table A.

## 6.10. TABULATED PROBABILITY DISTRIBUTION: *F* DISTRIBUTION

The *F* distribution is another useful sampling distribution. An application of the *F* distribution (see Table F) is within Equation (9.1). In this equation the

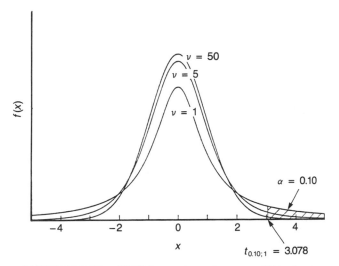

**FIGURE 6.15.** *t* PDF for various degrees of freedom.

$F$ distribution is used to determine if two population variances are statistically different in magnitude.

The $F$ distribution is a family of distributions defined by two parameters, $v_1$ and $v_2$. Figure 6.16 shows example shapes for this distribution. Table F gives percentage points of the $F$ distribution. From this table, for example, $F_{\alpha;v1;v2} = F_{0.10;40;40} = 1.51$, which is illustrated pictorially in Figure 6.16.

## 6.11. HAZARD RATE

Hazard rate is the probability that a device on test will fail between $(t)$ and an additional infinitesimally small increment unit of time (i.e., $t + dt$), if the device has already survived up to time $(t)$. The general expression for the hazard rate $(\lambda)$ is

$$\lambda = \frac{f(t)}{1 - F(t)} \tag{6.5}$$

where $f(t)$ is the PDF of failures and $F(t)$ is the CDF of failures at time $t$. The $[1 - F(t)]$ quantity is often described as the reliability of a device at time $t$ (i.e., survival proportion).

The hazard rate (failure rate) can often be described by the classical reliability bathtub curve shown in Figure 6.17. For a nonrepairable system, the Weibull distribution can be used to model portions of this curve. In the Weibull equation a value of $b < 1$ is characteristic of early-life manufacturing failures, a value of $b > 1$ is characteristic of a wear-out mechanism, and a

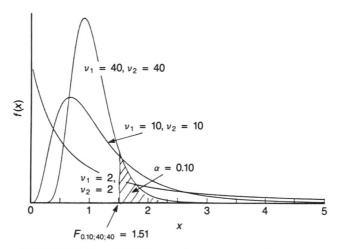

**FIGURE 6.16.** $F$ PDF for various degrees of freedom.

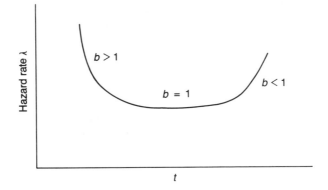

**FIGURE 6.17.** Bathtub curve with Weibull shape parameters.

value of $b = 1$ is characteristic of a constant failure rate mode (also known as intrinsic failure period).

The hazard rate equations for the exponential and Weibull distributions are shown in Appendix A as equation numbers (A.17) and (A.23), respectively.

## 6.12. NONHOMOGENEOUS POISSON PROCESS (NHPP)

The Weibull distribution can be used to estimate the percent of the population that is expected to fail by a given time. However, if the unit under test is repaired, then this percentage value does not have much meaning. A more desirable unit of measure would be to monitor the system failure rate as a function of usage. For a repairable system, this failure rate model is called the intensity function. The NHPP with Weibull intensity is a model that can consider system repairable failure rates that change with time. The following scenario exemplifies the application of this NHPP.

A repairable system failure rate is not constant as a function of usage. The NHPP with Weibull intensity process can often be used to model this situation when considering the general possibilities of early-life, intrinsic, or wear-out characteristics.

The NHPP with Weibull intensity function can be expressed mathematically as

$$r(t) = \lambda b t^{b-1} \tag{6.6}$$

where $r(t)$ is instantaneous failure rate at time $t$ and $\lambda$ is the intensity of the Poisson process.

## 6.13. HOMOGENEOUS POISSON PROCESS (HPP)

This model considers that the failure rate does not change with time (i.e., a constant intensity function). The following scenario exemplifies the application of the HPP.

> A repairable system failure rate is constant with time. The failure rate is said to follow an HPP process. The Poisson distribution is often useful when designing a test of a criterion that has an HPP.

The HPP is a model that is a special case of the NHPP with Weibull intensity, where $b$ in Equation (6.6) equals 1. With this substitution the HPP model is shown in Equation (6.7) to have a constant failure rate. It can be noted that the intensity of the HPP equates to the hazard rate of the exponential distribution (i.e., they both have a constant failure rate).

$$r(t) = \lambda \tag{6.7}$$

## 6.14. APPLICATIONS FOR VARIOUS TYPES OF DISTRIBUTIONS AND PROCESSES

Table 6.1 summarizes the application of distributions and processes to solve a variety of problems found in this text.

For engineering applications the previous sections of this chapter have shown common density functions for continuous responses and the discrete distribution function for a binary response. In addition, this discussion has shown some models to describe the instantaneous failure rate of a process.

The equation forms for the discrete distributions noted in Appendix A are rather simple to solve even though they initially look complex. By knowing the sample size and the percentage of good parts, the mechanics of determining

**TABLE 6.1. Distribution/Process Application Overview**

| Distribution or Process | Applications | Examples |
|---|---|---|
| Normal distribution | Can be used to describe various physical, mechanical, electrical, and chemical properties. | Part dimensions Voltage outputs Chemical composition level |
| Binomial distribution | Can be used to describe the situation where an observation can either pass or fail. | Part sampling plan where the part meets or fails to meet a specification criterion |

**TABLE 6.1.** (*Continued*)

| Distribution or Process | Applications | Examples |
| --- | --- | --- |
| Hypergeometric distribution | Similar to the binomial distribution; however, the sample size is large relative to the population size. | Binomial sampling where a sample of 50 is randomly chosen from a population of size 100 |
| Log-normal distribution | Shape flexibility of density function yields an adequate fit to many types of data. Normal distribution equations can be used in the analysis. | Life of mechanical components that fail by metal fatigue<br>Describes repair times of equipment |
| Weibull distribution (2-parameter) | Shape flexibility of density function conveniently describes increasing, constant and decreasing failure rates as a function of usage (age). | Life of mechanical and electrical components |
| Weibull distribution (3-parameter) | Shape flexibility of two-parameter distribution with the added flexibility that the zero probability point can take on values that are greater than zero. | Mechanical part tensile strength<br>Electrical resistance |
| Exponential distribution | Shape can be used to describe device system failure rates that are constant as a function of usage. | MTBF or constant failure rate of a system |
| Poisson distribution | Convenient distribution to use when designing tests that assumes that the underlying distribution is exponential. | Test distribution to determine whether a MTBF failure criterion is met |
| HPP | Model that describes occurrences that happen randomly in time. | Modeling of constant system failure rate |
| NHPP | Model that describes occurrences that either decrease or increase in frequency with time. | System failure rate modeling when the rate increases or decreases with time |

the probability (chance) of getting a "bad" or "good" individual sample involves only simple algebraic substitution. Unfortunately in reality the percent of good parts is the unknown quantity, which cannot be determined from these equations without using an iterative solution approach.

An alternative approach to this binomial criterion validation dilemma is to use another distribution that closely approximates the shape of the binomial distribution. As mentioned earlier, the Poisson distribution is applicable to address exponential distribution problems. The Poisson distribution can also be used for some binomial problems. This can be better understood by noting how the binomial distribution shape in Figure 6.4 skews toward the shape of the exponential distribution in Figure 6.9 when the proportion defective ($p$) is a low number. However, when the proportions of good parts approach 0.5, the normal distribution can be utilized. This can again be conceptually understood by comparing the distribution shapes between Figure 6.4 (when $p$ is near 0.5) and Figure 6.1.

Table 6.2 gives some rules of thumb to determine when the preceding approximations can be used, along with determining whether the binomial distribution is applicable in lieu of the hypergeometric distribution. Chapters 8 and 11, respectively, discuss the application of the binomial and Poisson distribution further.

The distributions previously discussed are a few of the many possible alternatives. However, these distributions are, in general, sufficient to solve most industrial engineering problems.

An exception to this statement is the multinomial distribution, where the population can best be described with more than one distribution (e.g., bimodal distribution). This type of distribution can occur, for example, when a supplier sorts and distributes parts that have a small plus or minus tolerance at an elevated piece price. The population of parts that are distributed to the larger plus or minus tolerance will probably have a bimodal distribution.

**TABLE 6.2. Distribution Approximations**

| Distribution | Approximate Distribution | Situation |
|---|---|---|
| Hypergeometric | Binomial | $10n \leq$ population size (Miller and Freund 1965) |
| Binomial | Poisson | $n \geq 20$ and $p \leq 0.05$. If $n \geq 100$, the approximation is excellent as long as $np \leq 10$ (Miller and Freund 1965) |
| Binomial | Normal | $np$ and $n(1 - p)$ are at least 5 (Dixon and Massey 1969) |
| | $n$ = sample size; $p$ proportion (e.g., rate of defective parts) | |

A specific example of this situation is the distribution of resistance values for resistors that have a ±10% tolerance. A manufacturer may sort and remove the ±1% parts that are manufactured; hence, creating a bimodal situation for the parts that have the larger tolerance.

# PART II

# SOLVING DEFINED PROBLEMS

In this part of the text there is a discussion of the solution methodologies to a wide variety of problems. At the end of each chapter, there is also a section that addresses do-it-smarter considerations. This section, among other things, encourages the reader to consider the possibility that the original problem definition is directed toward "answering the wrong question." Possibly by rephrasing the question, a better approach can then be taken toward meeting the needs of the customer.

The analysis of random sampled data is discussed for both continuous and attribute situations. The chapters on reliability testing are directed toward tests that involve either repairable systems or nonrepairable devices. The chapters covering factorial experiments include tabular experiment designs along with both some basic and computer analysis approaches. A unique approach to pass/fail functional testing is also suggested. With this test approach, a value for *test coverage* can simply be determined from a table. The discussion on statistical process control involves techniques that are used to assess both the stability of processes and whether or not the process will consistently yield a response that meets specifications.

# 7

# INFERENCES: CONTINUOUS RESPONSE

Recommended introductory reading: Chapters 2, 3, 4, and 5.

This chapter covers random sampling evaluations from a population that has a continuous response. An example of a continuous response is the amount of tire tread that exists after 40,000 kilometers (km) of automobile usage. One tire might, for example, have 6.0 millimeters (mm) remaining tread, while another tire might measure 5.5 mm.

In this chapter the estimation of population mean and standard deviation from sampled data is discussed in conjunction with probability plotting.

## 7.1. SUMMARIZING SAMPLED DATA

Classically the analysis of sampled data taken from a continuous response population has focused on determining a sample mean ($\bar{x}$) and standard deviation ($s$), along with perhaps confidence interval statements that can relate both these sampled characteristics to the actual population values ($\mu$ and $\sigma$, respectively). Experimental considerations of this type answer some basic questions about the sample and population. However, often a person responsible for either generating a criterion specification or making a pass/ fail decision does not consider the other information that data analyses can convey. For example, an experiment might be able to indicate that 90% of the automobiles using a certain type of tire will have at least 4.9 mm tire tread after 40,000 km. This type of statement can be more informative than a statement that only relates to the mean tire tread after 40,000 km.

## 7.2. SAMPLE SIZE: HYPOTHESIS TEST OF A MEAN CRITERION FOR CONTINUOUS RESPONSE DATA

One of the most traditional questions asked of a statistical consultant is: "What sample size do I need (to verify this mean criterion)?" Equation (7.1) (Diamond 1989) can be used to determine the sample size ($n$) to evaluate a hypothesis test criterion (see Table 4.2) at given values for $\alpha$, $\beta$, and $\delta$ (i.e., producer's risk, consumer's risk, and an acceptable amount of uncertainty, respectively; see Section 4.5). Sometimes the population standard deviation ($\sigma$) is know from previous test activity; however, this is not generally true. For this second situation $\delta$ can be conveniently expressed in terms of $\sigma$, when using Equation (7.1).

$$ n = (U_\alpha + U_\beta)^2 \frac{\sigma^2}{\delta^2} \tag{7.1} $$

In this equation $U_\beta$ is determined from the single-sided Table B in Appendix D*. If the alternate hypothesis (see Section 4.5) is single sided (e.g., $\mu <$ criterion), $U_\alpha$ is also determined from Table B (see Section 6.2); however if the alternate hypothesis is double sided (e.g., $\mu <$ or $>$ criterion), $U_\alpha$ is determined from Table C.

If the standard deviation is not known, the sample size should be adjusted using Equation (7.2) (Diamond 1989)

$$ n = (t_\alpha + t_\beta)^2 \frac{s^2}{\delta^2} \tag{7.2} $$

In this equation $t_\beta$ is determined from the single-sided Table D (see Section 6.9). If the alternate hypothesis is single sided (e.g., $\mu <$ criterion), $t_\alpha$ is also determined from Table D; however, if the alternate hypothesis is double sided (e.g., $\mu <$ or $>$ criterion), $t_\alpha$ is determined from Table E.

There is discussion on sample size selection in Natrella (1966), Brush (1988), and Cochran (1977).

## 7.3. EXAMPLE 7-1: SAMPLE SIZE DETERMINATION FOR A MEAN CRITERION TEST

A stereo amplifier output power level is to be on the average at least 100 watts (W) per channel. Determine the sample size that is needed to verify this criterion given the following:

$\alpha = 0.1$, which from Table B yields $U_\alpha = 1.282$.
$\beta = 0.05$, which from Table B yields $U_\beta = 1.645$.
$\delta = 0.5\sigma$.

* Tables A through R3 are located in Appendix D of this book.

Substitution into Equation (7.1) yields

$$n = (1.282 + 1.645)^2 \frac{\sigma^2}{(0.5\sigma)^2} = 34.26$$

Rounding upward to a whole number yields a sample size of 35.

If the standard deviation is not known, this sample size needs to be adjusted using Equation (7.2), where the number of degrees of freedom for the $t$ table value equals 34 (i.e., 35 − 1). Interpolation in Table D yields $t_{0.1; 34} = 1.307$ and $t_{0.05; 34} = 1.692$ hence

$$n = (1.692 + 1.307)^2 \frac{s^2}{(0.5s)^2} = 35.95$$

Rounding upward to a whole number yields a sample of 36. Equation (7.2) could be iterated again with this new sample size; however, this is not normally necessary.

Because individuals want to make sure that they are making the correct decision, they often specify very low $\alpha$ and $\beta$ values, along with a low $\delta$ value. This can lead to a sample size that is unrealistically large with normal test time and resource constraints. When this happens, the experimenter may need to accept more risk than he or she was originally willing to tolerate. The sample size can then be recalculated permitting the larger risks (i.e., a higher $\alpha$ and/or $\beta$ value) and/or an increase in uncertainty (i.e., a higher $\delta$ value).

## 7.4. CONFIDENCE INTERVALS ON THE MEAN AND HYPOTHESIS TEST CRITERIA ALTERNATIVES

The sample mean ($\bar{x}$) and standard deviation ($s$) are determined from the data using Equations (4.1) and (4.2). Table 7.1 gives a summary of the equations used to determine from these population estimates the intervals that contains the true mean ($\mu$) at a confidence level of [$(1 - \alpha)100$]. The equations in Table 7.1 utilize the $t$ tables (as opposed to the $U$ tables) whenever the population standard deviation is not known. Because of the Central Limit Theorem, the equations noted in this table are robust to the data not being from a normal distribution (see Section 4.7).

If either Equation (7.1) or (7.2) was used to determine the sample size, the null hypothesis is accepted if the criterion is contained within the appropriate confidence interval for $\mu$ (see Table 7.1). This decision is made with the $\beta$ risk of error that was used in calculating the sample size (given the underlying $\delta$ input level of uncertainty). However, if the criterion is not contained within the interval, then the alternative hypothesis is accepted. This decision is made with $\alpha$ risk of error.

**TABLE 7.1. Mean Confidence Interval Equations**

|  | Single Sided | Double Sided |
|---|---|---|
| $\sigma$ Known | $\mu \leq \bar{x} + \dfrac{U_\alpha \sigma}{\sqrt{n}}$<br><br>or<br><br>$\mu \geq \bar{x} - \dfrac{U_\alpha \sigma}{\sqrt{n}}$ | $\bar{x} - \dfrac{U_\alpha \sigma}{\sqrt{n}} \leq \mu \leq \bar{x} + \dfrac{U_\alpha \sigma}{\sqrt{n}}$ |
| $\sigma$ Unknown | $\mu \leq \bar{x} + \dfrac{t_\alpha s}{\sqrt{n}}$<br><br>or<br><br>$\mu \geq \bar{x} - \dfrac{t_\alpha s}{\sqrt{n}}$ | $\bar{x} - \dfrac{t_\alpha s}{\sqrt{n}} \leq \mu \leq \bar{x} + \dfrac{t_\alpha s}{\sqrt{n}}$ |
| Using reference tables | $U_\alpha$: Table B<br>$t_\alpha$: Table D[a] | $U_\alpha$: Table C<br>$t_\alpha$: Table E[a] |

[a] $\nu = n - 1$ (i.e., the number of degrees of freedom used in the $t$ table is equal one less than the sample size).

Other methods can be used when setting up a hypothesis test criterion. Consider, for example, the alternative hypothesis ($H_a$) of $\mu > \mu_a$, where $\mu_a$ is a product specification criterion. It can be determined from Table 7.1 that

$$\bar{x}_{\text{criterion}} = \mu_a + \frac{t_\alpha s}{\sqrt{n}}$$

When $\bar{x}$ is equal to or greater than the test $\bar{x}_{\text{criterion}}$, the alternative hypothesis is accepted. When $\bar{x}$ is less than $\bar{x}_{\text{criterion}}$, the null hypothesis is accepted. An alternative approach for this problem is to use the equation form

$$t_0 = \frac{(\bar{x} - \mu_a)\sqrt{n}}{s}$$

where the alternative hypothesis is accepted if $t_0 > t_\alpha$.

The above equations apply to planned statistical hypothesis testing where a decision was made prior to test start about $\alpha$, $\beta$, and $\delta$. However, in reality, data is often taken without making these pretest decisions. The equations

EXAMPLE 7-2: CONFIDENCE INTERVALS ON THE MEAN    **95**

in Table 7.1 are still useful to make an assessment of the population, as noted in Example 7-2.

## 7.5. EXAMPLE 7-2: CONFIDENCE INTERVALS ON THE MEAN

Consider the 16 data points from sample 1 of Table 4.1, which had a sample mean of 5.77 and a sample standard deviation of 2.41. Determine the various 90% confidence statements that can be made relative to the true population mean given that the standard deviation is known to equal 2.0 and then as an unknown parameter.

Given $\sigma$ is known to equal 2.0 and the $U_\alpha$ values from the tables noted in Table 7.1, the single-sided and double-sided 90% confidence (i.e., $\alpha = 0.1$) interval equations are as shown below. The $U_\alpha$ value of 1.282 is from the single-sided Table B given $\alpha = 0.1$. The $U_\alpha$ value of 1.645 is from the double-sided Table C given $\alpha = 0.1$.

Single-sided scenarios:

$$\mu \leq \bar{x} + \frac{U_\alpha \sigma}{\sqrt{n}} \qquad\qquad \mu \geq \bar{x} - \frac{U_\alpha \sigma}{\sqrt{n}}$$

$$\mu \leq 5.77 + \frac{1.282(2.0)}{\sqrt{16}} \qquad\qquad \mu \geq 5.77 - \frac{1.282(2.0)}{\sqrt{16}}$$

$$\mu \leq 5.77 + 0.64 \qquad\qquad \mu \geq 5.77 - 0.64$$

$$\mu \leq 6.41 \qquad\qquad \mu \geq 5.13$$

Double-sided scenario:

$$\bar{x} - \frac{U_\alpha \sigma}{\sqrt{n}} \leq \mu \leq \bar{x} + \frac{U_\alpha \sigma}{\sqrt{n}}$$

$$5.77 - \frac{1.645(2.0)}{\sqrt{16}} \leq \mu \leq 5.77 + \frac{1.645(2.0)}{\sqrt{16}}$$

$$5.77 - 0.82 \leq \mu \leq 5.77 + 0.82$$

$$4.95 \leq \mu \leq 6.59$$

If we consider that we do not know the standard deviation, then the equations and referenced tables of Table 7.1 yield the following single- and double-sided 90% confidence intervals. The $t_\alpha$ value of 1.341 is from the single-sided Table D given $\alpha = 0.1$ and $\nu = 16 - 1 = 15$. The $t_\alpha$ value of 1.753 is from the double-sided Table E given $\alpha = 0.1$ and $\nu = 16 - 1 = 15$.

Single-sided scenarios:

$$\mu \leq \bar{x} + \frac{t_\alpha s}{\sqrt{n}} \qquad\qquad \mu \geq \bar{x} - \frac{t_\alpha s}{\sqrt{n}}$$

$$\mu \leq 5.77 + \frac{(1.341)(2.41)}{\sqrt{16}} \qquad \mu \geq 5.77 - \frac{(1.341)(2.41)}{\sqrt{16}}$$

$$\mu \leq 5.77 + 0.81 \qquad\qquad \mu \geq 5.77 - 0.81$$

$$\mu \leq 6.58 \qquad\qquad\qquad \mu \geq 4.96$$

Double-sided scenario:

$$\bar{x} - \frac{t_\alpha s}{\sqrt{n}} \leq \mu \leq \bar{x} + \frac{t_\alpha s}{\sqrt{n}}$$

$$5.77 - \frac{1.753(2.41)}{\sqrt{16}} \leq \mu \leq 5.77 + \frac{1.753(2.41)}{\sqrt{16}}$$

$$5.77 - 1.06 \leq \mu \leq 5.77 + 1.06$$

$$4.71 \leq \mu \leq 6.83$$

The mean and standard deviation used in the preceding calculations were taken from Table 4.1, which was randomly created from a normal distribution where $\mu = 6.0$. Note that this true mean value is contained in these confidence intervals.

## 7.6. STANDARD DEVIATION CONFIDENCE INTERVAL

When a sample of size $n$ is taken from a population that is normally distributed, the double-sided confidence interval equation for the population's standard deviation ($\sigma$) is

$$\left[ \frac{(n-1)s^2}{\chi^2_{\alpha/2;\nu}} \right]^{1/2} \leq \sigma \leq \left[ \frac{(n-1)s^2}{\chi^2_{(1-\alpha/2;\nu)}} \right]^{1/2} \tag{7.3}$$

where $s$ is the standard deviation of the sample and the $\chi^2$ values are taken from Table G with $\alpha/2$ risk and $\nu$ degrees of freedom equal to the sample size minus 1.

It should be noted that Equation (7.3) is not robust to data not being from a normal distribution (see Section 4.5).

## 7.7. EXAMPLE 7-3: STANDARD DEVIATION CONFIDENCE STATEMENT

Consider again the 16 data points from sample 1 of Table 4.1, which had a mean of 5.77 and a standard deviation of 2.41. Given that the standard deviation was not known, from Equation (7.3) the 90% confidence interval for the standard deviation of the population would then be

$$
\left[ \frac{(16 - 1)(2.41)^2}{\chi^2_{(0.1/2;[16-1])}} \right]^{1/2} \leq \sigma \leq \left[ \frac{(16 - 1)(2.41)^2}{\chi^2_{(1-[0.1/2];[16-1])}} \right]^{1/2}
$$

$$
\left[ \frac{87.12}{25.00} \right]^{1/2} \leq \sigma \leq \left[ \frac{87.12}{7.26} \right]^{1/2}
$$

$$
1.87 \leq \sigma \leq 3.46
$$

The standard deviation used in this calculation was from a random sample taken from a normal distribution where $\sigma = 2.0$. Note that this true standard deviation value is contained in this confidence interval.

## 7.8. PERCENTAGE OF THE POPULATION ASSESSMENTS

Criteria are often assumed to apply to the mean response of the product's population, with no regard to the variability of the product response. Often what is really needed is that all of the product should have a response that is less than or greater than a criterion.

For example, a specification may exist that a product should be able to withstand an electrostatic discharge (ESD) level of 700 volts (V). Is the intent of this specification that the mean of the population (if tested to failure) should be above 700 V? Or, perhaps all products built should be able to resist a voltage level of 700 V.

It is impossible to be 100% certain that every product will meet such a criterion without testing every product that is manufactured. For criteria that require much certainty and a 100% population requirement, 100% testing to a level that anticipates field performance degradation may be required. However, a reduced confidence level may be acceptable with a lower percent confidence requirement (e.g., 95% of the population). Depending on the situation, the initial criterion may need adjustment to reflect the basic test strategy.

There are approaches such as *K* factors (Natrella 1966) noted within other texts that address this situation using tables and equations that consider both the mean and standard deviation of the sample. However, with this approach, the assumption of normality is very important and the sample size requirements may often be too large.

A "best estimate" probability plot is another approach consideration, which can give visual indications to population characteristics that may not otherwise be apparent. A probability plot may indicate, for example, that data outliers are present or that a normal distribution assumption is not appropriate.

## 7.9. EXAMPLE 7-4: PERCENTAGE OF THE POPULATION STATEMENTS

Consider again the first sample from Table 4.1 that yielded a mean value of 5.77 and a standard deviation of 2.41. Using the techniques illustrated within Chapter 5 and Table P, the ranked sample values are noted with the percentage plot values for a sample size of 16 to be that shown in Table 7.2. These coordinates can then be manually plotted on normal probability paper (see Table Q1). Figure 7.1 is a computer generated normal probability plot of the data.

From this plot it is first noted that only evaluating the mean value for this sample may yield deceiving conclusions since the standard deviation is rather

**TABLE 7.2. Example 7-4: Ranked Data and Plot Positions**

| Original Sample Number | Ranked Sample Value | Percentage Plot Position |
|---|---|---|
| 7 | 2.17 | 3.1 |
| 3 | 2.65 | 9.4 |
| 1 | 2.99 | 15.6 |
| 8 | 4.13 | 21.9 |
| 15 | 4.74 | 28.1 |
| 16 | 5.19 | 34.4 |
| 10 | 5.20 | 40.6 |
| 5 | 5.31 | 46.9 |
| 12 | 5.39 | 53.1 |
| 11 | 5.80 | 59.4 |
| 6 | 5.84 | 65.6 |
| 2 | 6.29 | 71.9 |
| 9 | 7.29 | 78.1 |
| 14 | 9.29 | 84.4 |
| 13 | 10.00 | 90.6 |
| 4 | 10.11 | 96.9 |

EXAMPLE 7-4: PERCENTAGE OF THE POPULATION STATEMENTS      **99**

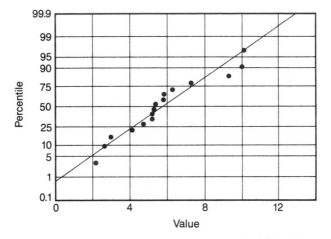

**FIGURE 7.1.** Example 7-4: Normal probability plot.

large compared to the reading values. It is also noted that the normal distribution can be used to represent the population, since the data tends to follow a straight line. If a criterion of 20 was specified for 95% of the population (given that a low number indicates goodness), an individual would probably feel comfortable that the specification was met since the "best estimate" plot estimates that 95% of the population is less than 9.5. However, if the criterion were 10 for this percentage of the population, we would probably conclude that too many of the machines might be beyond specification. To better meet this criterion of 10, perhaps the manufacturing process needs to be examined for ways that it could be improved. A fractional factorial experiment (see Chapter 13) might be appropriate to assess which of those parameters considered (from perhaps a brainstorming session; see Section 3.5) are significant in reducing the mean and/or standard deviation of the process.

Probability plots of data can often be enlightening. From these plots one may find, for example, that the data are not normally distributed. If there is a knee in the curve, this may indicate that there are two distributions within the process (i.e., a bimodal distribution). In this case it might be beneficial to try to determine why one sample is from one distribution while another sample is from another distribution. This phenomenon may happen, for example, because there are two vendors where one vendor produces a better part than the other vendor. Or, another possibility is that the normal probability plot may have curvature and be better fitted to some other distribution (e.g., a three-parameter Weibull distribution).

As a *minimum* when choosing a sample size for making a decision about the percentage of population, extrapolation should be avoided to reach the desired percentage value. In this example it is noted from Table 7.2 that the percentage plot position extremes are 3.1 and 96.9. This means that a probability plot of the 16 data points has no extrapolation when single-sided (high value) statements are made about 95% of the population. The percentage plot positions in Table P indicate that 26 data points are needed to yield nonextrapolated single-sided statements about 98% of the population.

Another valid concern can emerge from this type of experiment. If the sample is drawn from a process over a short period of time, this sample does not necessarily represent what the process will do in the future. Fractional factorial experiment design matrices again can be used as a guide to adjust parameters used to manufacture the parts. The procedure within Example 7-4 could then still be applied to get a "big picture spatial representation" (i.e., the data are from the factorial trials and are not a true random sample of a population) of what could be expected of the process in the future (see Example 22-2). In addition, any significant parameters could then be focused upon, to perhaps improve the process mean and/or reduce the process variability. The process then could be continually monitored via control charts (discussed later in this text) for drifts of the process mean and standard deviation.

## 7.10. TOLERANCE ANALYSES

When designing a product, the quality of the output (or whether the assembly will work or fail) can depend on the tolerances of the component parts used in the assembly process. A pencil-and-paper worst-case tolerance analysis is sometimes appropriate to make sure that tolerances do not "stack," causing an overall out-of-specification condition. However, if there are many components within the assembly process, it may be impossible to ensure that the completed product will perform in a satisfactorily way if all the component tolerances were at worst-case conditions.

The overall effect of a component can sometimes be considered to follow a normal distribution with $\pm 3\sigma$ bounds equivalent to the tolerance limits (or some other tighter limits) of the component, and where the mean ($\mu$) of the distribution is the midpoint between the tolerance limits.

Consider that measurements for $n$ components that are each centered at mean ($\mu_i$) of a normal distribution with plus or minus tolerances ($T_i$) around this mean value. The worst-case overall tolerance ($T_w$) for this situation is simply the addition of these tolerances.

$$T_w = \pm \sum_{i=1}^{n} T_i = \pm(T_1 + T_2 + \cdots + T_n) \qquad (7.4)$$

The serial $3\sigma$ combination of the component tolerances (see Figure 22.12) yields an overall product $3\sigma$ tolerance ($T_{3\sigma}$) (Mauritzson 1971) of

$$T_{3\sigma} = \pm \left[ \sum_{i=1}^{n} T_i^2 \right]^{1/2} = \pm(T_1^2 + T_2^2 + \cdots + T_n^2)^{1/2} \qquad (7.5)$$

EXAMPLE 7-5: ANALYTICAL DATA/TOLERANCE ANALYSIS    **101**

Care must be exercised when using Equation (7.5). The accuracy of the assumption that each component follows a normal distribution is very important. There are situations where this assumption will not be valid. For example, a ± 10% tolerance resistor may follow a bimodal distribution since the best parts can be sorted out and sold at a higher price with a ± 1% or ± 5% tolerance. Another situation where the normality assumption may be invalid is in the case where a manufacturer initially produces a part at one tolerance extreme, anticipating tool wear within the manufacturing process.

An alternative approach to Equation (7.5) is to estimate a distribution shape for each component. Then, via a computer, randomly choose a component characteristic from each distribution; then combine these values to yield an overall expected output. A computer can easily simulate thousands of assemblies to yield the expected overall distribution of the combined tolerances.

## 7.11. EXAMPLE 7-5: COMBINING ANALYTICAL DATA WITH A TOLERANCE ANALYSIS

An automatic sheet feed device is to load a sheet of paper into a printer such that the first character printed on the paper will be 1.26 ± 1.26 mm from the edge of the paper (Figure 7.2).

There are two variabilities that need consideration within this problem. First, the variability within machines and then the variability between machines. For some problem types only variability between machines will be needed when there is only one output for the device. However, with this situation each machine will have multiple outputs since each printed page is basically an output.

Within industry this type of question may need to be addressed early within a development cycle when there are only a few models available to test. The following will consider three alternatives given this physical test constraint. The first approach will be that all tolerances including some measurement data will be combined via Equation (7.4) to yield a worst-case analysis. The second approach will consider the population to be all sheets of paper produced on all printers manufactured. The third consideration will be that the real intent of the question is to determine whether 99.7% ($\approx 3\sigma$)

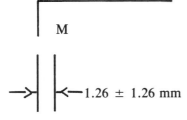

—←1.26 ± 1.26 mm    **FIGURE 7.2.** Example 7-5: Diagram showing specification limits.

of the sheets printed on 99.7% of the printers will be within the tolerance limits.

The design group determined that there were 14 tolerances involved with either the placement of the page within the printer or the printing of the character on the page. The tolerance analyses also indicated a nominal character position of 1.26 mm. All the tolerances were plus or minus values; hence, the tolerances can be algebraically combined as later shown. The plus or minus tolerances $(T_i)$ $(i = 1$ to 14) are

$$0.1, 0.2, 0.2, 0.03, 0.34, 0.15, 0.05, 0.08, 0.1, 0.1, 0.1, 0.1, 0.06, 0.1$$

When a machine is assembled it takes on one of these values. However, for various reasons, the first print character will not always be positioned in the same position. Things that could affect this positioning are paper type, platen imperfections, initial loading of the paper tray, and so forth. The assessment of all these considerations suggests a fractional factorial experiment design (see Chapter 13). Assume that this experiment was performed and it was concluded from the test that a machine repeatability $(\sigma_r)$ estimate of 0.103 mm would be used for any further calculations.

**1.** Considering a worst-case analysis approach, the worst-case machine tolerances $(T_A)$ are then combined with the $3\sigma_r$ limits of machine repeatability to yield

$$T_A = \pm \sum_{i=1}^{n} T_i \pm 3\sigma_r$$

$$= \pm(0.1 + 0.2 \cdots 0.1) \pm 3(0.103)$$

$$= \pm 1.71 \pm 0.31 = \pm 2.02$$

Since $\pm 2.02$ is greater than the specification $\pm 1.26$ tolerance, the assembly is not expected to perform satisfactorily with this worst-case scenario.

**2.** Considering the specification as addressing 99.7% of all pages produced on the printers, Equation (7.5) yields

$$T_B = \pm \left\{ \left[ \sum_{i=1}^{n} T_i^2 \right] + (3\sigma)^2 \right\}^{0.5}$$

$$= \pm \{(0.1^2 + 0.2^2 \cdots 0.1^2) + [3(0.103)]^2\}^{0.5}$$

$$= \pm 0.622$$

This combination yields a favorable result since $\pm 0.622$ is less than the specification tolerance of $\pm 1.26$. However, consider the person that has a printer with manufacturing tolerances at a $3\sigma$ limit. This individual will still experience the full effects of variations when loading the paper in addition to the adverse printer tolerance considerations. Hence, this approach may yield a conclusion that is too optimistic from a user perspective.

**3.** Considering that the specification should be met on 99.7% of the sheets produced on a "statistical worst-case" machine (i.e., $3\sigma$ combination), this yields

$$T_C = \pm \left[ \sum_{i=1}^{n} T_i^2 \right]^{0.5} \pm (3\sigma)$$

$$= \pm (0.1^2 + 0.2^2 \cdots 0.1^2)^{0.5} \pm [3(.103)]$$

$$= \pm 0.85$$

This approach yields a favorable result since $\pm 0.85$ is less than the specification tolerance of $\pm 1.26$.

This example illustrates an approach to combine experimental results with a tolerance analysis. Also, it was illustrated how the basic analysis strategy can change depending on the intent of the problem definition. Chapter 16 on Taguchi contributions will take this a step further. This chapter will challenge the historical logic of assuming that an assembly that just meets a criterion is good, while an assembly that just misses the criterion is bad (i.e., for this example, a $\pm 1.25$ value around the criterion would be considered "good," while a $\pm 1.27$ value around the criterion would be judged "bad").

Example 22-5 combines the use of process capability indices (see Section 19.15) with statistical tolerancing techniques.

## 7.12. DO-IT-SMARTER CONSIDERATIONS

Within industry, a generic random test strategy is often suggested during initial problem definition. This chapter illustrates approaches to answer this question. However, is this the do-it-smarter approach that should be taken?

Questions to consider:

1. Is the sample really taken from the population of interest? If, for example, a sample is taken from the start-up of a manufacturing process, the sample output will not necessarily represent future machine builds. Hence, a machine failure rate test during this early phase of production may not yield a failure rate that is similar to that which the customer will later be experiencing.

2. Is the process that is being sampled stable? If it is not, then the test methods and confidence statements cannot be interpreted with much precision. Process control charting techniques (see Chapter 19) can be used to determine the stability of a process.

3. What is going to be done if the process does not meet a test criterion? Are the parts going to be shipped anyway, as long as the output is "reasonable"?

4. Would a fractional factorial test strategy (see Chapter 13) be more beneficial than a "random sample" taken at some point in time? A fractional factorial test strategy can yield information as to where the process/design may be improved.

Let's not play games with the numbers. Future chapters will illustrate approaches that can be more beneficial in answering the real questions: How can we design, build, or test this product smarter to give the customer the best possible product at the lowest possible price?

# 8

# INFERENCES: ATTRIBUTE RESPONSE

Recommended introductory reading: Chapters 2, 3, and 4.

This chapter discusses the evaluation of attribute data (e.g., go/no-go type information). An example of an attribute (pass/fail) response situation would be that of a copier that fed or failed to feed individual sheets of paper satisfactorily (i.e., a copier may feed 999 sheets out of 1000 sheets of paper on the average without a jam). The purpose of these experiments may be to assess an attribute criterion or evaluate the proportion of parts beyond a continuous criterion value (e.g., 20% of the electrical measurements are less than 100,000 ohms).

Samples are evaluated to determine whether they will either pass or fail a requirement (a binary response). Experiments of this type can assess the proportion of a population that is "defective" through either a confidence interval statement or a hypothesis test of a criterion.

It will be illustrated later that tests of attribute information can require a much larger sample size than tests of a continuous response. Because of this fact, this chapter also includes suggestions on how an original attribute test approach could be changed to a continuous response test alternative. With this change more relevant information can often be obtained with a large reduction in sample size requirements.

The binomial distribution is used for this type of analyses given that the sample size is small relative to the size of the population (e.g., less than 10% of the population size; see Table 6.2). A hypergeometric distribution (see Section A.3 of Appendix A*) can be used when this assumption is not valid.

* Sections and equations preceded by letter A [e.g., Section A.3, Equation (A.3)] are located in Appendix A of the book. Tables with letters A–R3 are located in Appendix D.

## 8.1. ATTRIBUTE RESPONSE SITUATIONS

The equation forms for the discrete distributions shown in Sections A.2 and A.3 initially look complex; however, they are rather mathematically simple to apply. By simply knowing the sample size and the percentage of "good" parts, it is easy to determine the probability (chance) of getting a "bad" or "good" sample part.

However, a typical desired response is to determine whether a criterion is met with a manageable risk of making the wrong decision. For example, the experimenter may desire to state that at least 99% of the parts are satisfactory with only a risk of 0.10 of making the wrong decision. Or, an experimenter may desire the 90% confidence interval for the defective proportion of the population.

The binomial equation [see Equation (A.3)] can be used to assess this situation using an iterative computer routine; however, care must be taken when writing the program to avoid computer number size limitation problems. The Poisson or the normal distribution can be used to approximate the binomial distribution under the situations noted within Table 6.2. Because failure rates typically found within industry are low, the Poisson distribution often is a viable alternative distribution to use for these attribute tests.

## 8.2. SAMPLE SIZE: HYPOTHESIS TEST OF AN ATTRIBUTE CRITERION

Equation (8.1) is a simple approximation for the sample size needed to make a hypothesis test using the binomial distribution with $\alpha$ and $\beta$ risks (Section 4.5) (Diamond 1989), where the failure rate at which $\alpha$ applies is $\rho_\alpha$, while the failure rate at which $\beta$ applies is $\rho_\beta$.

$$n = \left( \frac{(U_\alpha)[(\rho_\alpha)(1 - \rho_\alpha)]^{1/2} + (U_\beta)[(\rho_\beta)(1 - \rho_\beta)]^{1/2}}{\rho_\beta - \rho_\alpha} \right)^2 \tag{8.1}$$

$U_\alpha$ is the value from Table B or C (depending on whether $H_a$ is single or double sided) and $U_\beta$ is from the single-sided Table B. After the test, if the failure rate is not shown to be outside the confidence bounds (see Section 8.4), the null hypothesis is then accepted with $\beta$ risk. (Section 7.4 discusses other approaches to create a hypothesis test criterion.)

For those readers who are interested, this sample size equation assumes that a normality approximation to the binomial equation is appropriate. In general, this is a valid approximation (see Table 6.2) since the sample size required for typical $\alpha$ and $\beta$ risk levels is high enough to approximate normality, even though the failure criterion is low. Example 8-1 exemplifies this point.

Natrella (1966), Brush (1988) and Cochran (1977) have more discussion on choosing a sample size.

## 8.3. EXAMPLE 8-1: SAMPLE SIZE—A HYPOTHESIS TEST OF AN ATTRIBUTE CRITERION

A vendor is to supply a component that is not to have more than 1 defect every 1000 parts (i.e., a 0.001 failure rate criterion). How many parts need to be tested?

The failure rate that is desired is 1/1000 (i.e., 0.001); however Equation (8.1) requires two failure rates (i.e., $\rho_\beta$ and $\rho_\alpha$). To determine values for $\rho_\beta$ and $\rho_\alpha$, assume that a shift of 200 was thought to be a minimal "important increment" from the above 1000-part criterion, along with $\alpha = \beta = 0.05$. The value for $\rho_\beta$ would then be 0.00125 [i.e., $1/(1000 - 200)$], while the value for $\rho_\alpha$ would be 0.000833 [i.e., $1/(1000 + 200)$]. For this single-sided problem the values are determined from Table B. Substitution into Equation (8.1) yields

$$n = \left( \frac{(1.645)[(0.000833)(1 - 0.000833)]^{1/2} + (1.645)[(0.00125)(1 - 0.00125)]^{1/2}}{0.00125 - 0.000833} \right)^2$$

$$n = 64{,}106$$

Ready to suggest this to your management? There goes your next raise! This is not an atypical type of sample size problem that is encountered when developing an attribute sampling plan. These calculations could be repeated for relaxed test considerations for $\alpha$, $\beta$, $\rho_\beta$, and/or $\rho_\alpha$. Section 8.5 discusses another test design alternative approach while Section 8.8 discusses do-it-smarter alternatives.

In Section 8.2 it was stated that the origin of Equation (8.1) involved a normal distribution approximation. To illustrate why this approximation is reasonable for this test situation, first note from Table 6.2 that normality is often assumed if $np > 5$ and $n(1 - p) > 5$. In the example $p = 0.001$ and $N = 64{,}106$, which yields an $np$ value of 64.106 [i.e., $64{,}106 \times 0.001$], which is greater than 5, and $n(1-p)$ value of 64,042 [i.e., $64{,}106 \times 0.999$], which is also greater than 5.

## 8.4. CONFIDENCE INTERVALS FOR ATTRIBUTE EVALUATIONS

If there are $r$ failures from a sample size of $n$, the simplest way to make a double-sided confidence interval statement for this pass/fail test situation is to use Clopper and Pearson (1934) charts (Figures 8.1 through 8.4). To use these charts, a sample failure rate is first determined ($r/n$). The confidence intervals are then read from the ordinate of the curve at the values of the intersection of the abscissa value and the sample size $n$.

For example, if we find 30 defects out of a sample of 100, the sample failure rate would be 0.3 (i.e., 30/100). The intersection of this abscissa value

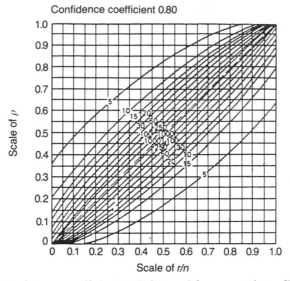

**FIGURE 8.1.** Confidence coefficient (0.8) interval for proportions. [Reproduced by permission of Biometrics Trustees from C. J. Clopper and E. S. Pearson, *Biometrika*, **26**: 404 (1934).] The axis labels $r/n$ and $\rho$ reflect the nomenclature used in this text.

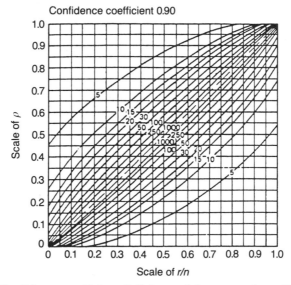

**FIGURE 8.2.** Confidence coefficient (0.9) interval for proportions. [Reproduced by permission of Biometrics Trustees from C. J. Clopper and E. S. Pearson, *Biometrika*, **26**: 404 (1934).]

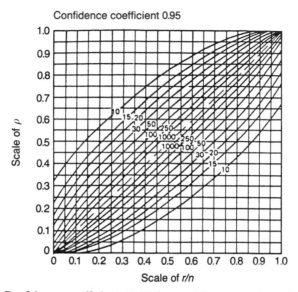

**FIGURE 8.3.** Confidence coefficient (0.95) interval for proportions. [Reproduced by permission of Biometrics Trustees from C. J. Clopper and E. S. Pearson, *Biometrika*, **26**: 404 (1934).]

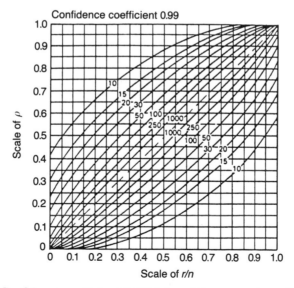

**FIGURE 8.4.** Confidence coefficient (0.99) interval for proportions. [Reproduced by permission of Biometrics Trustees from C. J. Clopper and E. S. Pearson, *Biometrika*, **26**: 404 (1934).]

with the sample size of 100 yields from the ordinate an 80% confidence interval of 0.24—0.37.

However, these tables are difficult to read for low test failure rates, which often typify the tests of today's products. In lieu of using a computer algorithm to determine the confidence interval, the Poisson distribution can often be used to yield a satisfactory approximation (see Table 6.2 and Section 11.5). Given this assumption with a small number of failures, Table K can be used for a simplified approach (See Example 11-2) to calculate a confidence interval for the population failure rate.

## 8.5. REDUCED SAMPLE SIZE TESTING FOR ATTRIBUTE SITUATIONS

The sample size procedure illustrated in Section 8.2 protects both the customer (with $\beta$ risk) and the producer (with $\alpha$ risk). A reduced sample size test is achievable for a criterion verification test when the test sample size is chosen such that the criterion is set to a bound of the confidence interval with a given number of allowed failures (i.e., the failure rate criterion will be equal to or less than the bound at the desired confidence level).

Example 8-2 illustrates the simple procedure to use when designing such a test; this example also shows that in order to pass a test of this type the sample may be required to perform at a failure rate that is much better than the population criterion. Chapter 11 has additional discussion on this topic when referencing the certification of a repairable system failure rate.

If the Poisson distribution is an appropriate approximation for this binomial test situation (see Table 6.2), sample size requirements can be determined from Table K. A tabular value ($B$) can be determined for the chosen number of permissible failures ($r$) and desired confidence value ($c$). This value is then substituted with the failure rate criterion ($\rho_a$) into Equation (8.2) to yield a value for $T$, the necessary test sample size.

$$T = B_{r;\,c}/\rho_a \qquad (8.2)$$

## 8.6. EXAMPLE 8-2: REDUCED SAMPLE SIZE TESTING— ATTRIBUTE RESPONSE SITUATIONS

Given the failure rate criterion ($\rho_a$) of 0.001 (i.e., 1/1000) from Example 8-1, determine a zero failure test sample size such that a 95% confidence interval bound will be

$$\rho \leq 0.001$$

From Table 6.2 it is noted that the Poisson approximation seems to be a reasonable simplification since the failure rate criterion of 0.001 is much less than 0.05 and will surely require a sample size larger than 20.

EXAMPLE 8-2: REDUCED SAMPLE SIZE TESTING    **111**

From Table K, $B_{0;0.95}$ equals 2.996. The sample size from Equation (8.2) is

$$T = B_{0;\,0.95}/\rho_a = 2.996/0.001 = 2996$$

The sample size for this example is much less than that calculated in Example 8-1 (i.e., 64,106); however, this example does not consider both $\alpha$ and $\beta$ risks. With a zero failure test strategy, there is a good chance that the samples will not perform well enough to pass the test objectives, unless the actual failure rate (which is unknown to the experimenter) is much better than the criterion.

To illustrate this, consider, for example, that only one failure occurred while testing the sample of 2996. For this sample the failure rate is lower than the 0.001 criterion (i.e., $1/2996 = 0.00033$). However, from Table K, $B_{1;0.95}$ equals 4.744 for one failure and a level equal to 0.95. The single-sided 95% confidence interval for the failure rate given information from this test using the form of Equation (8.2) shown at the bottom of Table K is

$$\rho \leqslant B_{1;\,0.95}/T = 4.744/2996 = 0.00158 \quad (\text{i.e., } \rho \leqslant 0.00158)$$

The 0.001 failure rate criterion value is contained in the above 95% confidence bounds. The original test objectives were not met (i.e., there was a failure that occurred during test); hence, from a technical point of view the "product did not pass test." However, from a practical point of view, the experimenter may want to determine (for reference only) a lesser confidence interval (e.g., 80% confidence) that would have allowed the test to pass if this value were chosen initially.

From Table K the single-sided 80% confidence for the failure rate is

$$\rho \leqslant B_{1;\,0.80}/T = 2.994/2996 = 0.0009993 \quad (\text{i.e., } \rho \leqslant 0.0009993)$$

The 0.001 criterion is now outside the single-sided 80% confidence interval. A major business decision may rest upon the outcome of this test. From a practical point of view, it seems wise for the experimenter to report this lower confidence interval information to management along with the cause of the failure and a corrective action strategy (i.e., don't we really want to have zero failures experienced by the customer?). The experimenter might also state to management that a fractional factorial experiment (see Chapter 13) is being planned to determine the changes that should be made to improve the manufacturing process so that there is less chance that this type of failure will occur again. From this information management may decide that a limited shipment plan is appropriate for the current product. Note that the same general methodology could be used if more than one failure occurred during the test. Other confidence statements that might similarly be appropriate under certain situations are a double-sided confidence interval statement or a single-sided statement where ($\rho \geqslant$ a value) may be appropriate.

In the above situation the experimenter may have been surprised to find that one failure technically means the test was not passed, even though the sample failure rate was much better than the criterion. To avoid this (perhaps) surprise when using this test strategy, Section 11.9 illustrates how a test performance ratio can be used to create pretest graphical information that can be an aid when choosing the number of permissible failures and test confidence interval level (a lower level than initially desired may be needed in order to create a reasonable test).

## 8.7. ATTRIBUTE SAMPLE PLAN ALTERNATIVES

The preceding discussion assumes that the sample size is small relative to the population size. If the sample size is greater than $1/10$ of the population size, the hypergeometric distribution should be considered.

In addition, it is also important to reemphasize that the sample needs to be randomly taken from the population and that the outcome of the experiment only characterizes the population from which the sample is taken. For example, a sample taken from an initial production process may be very different from the characteristics of production parts manufactured in the future and sent to the customer.

Military standards could be used as an alternative approach to choosing an attribute sampling plan. Messina (1987) discusses traditional application of the following military standards:

MIL-STD-105D: Sampling for attributes (US Department of Defense 1963)

MIL-STD-414: Sampling by variables for percent defective (US Department of Defense 1957)

MIL-STD-1235B: Single- and multi-level continuous sampling procedures for attributes (US Department of Defense 1981b)

Still another approach is to consider sequential binomial test plans, which are similar in form to that shown in Section 11.3 for the Poisson distribution. Ireson (1966) discusses the equations necessary for the application of this approach, which was originally developed by Wald (1947). However, with the low failure rate criteria of today, I believe that this sequential test approach is not usually a realistic test alternative.

## 8.8. DO-IT-SMARTER CONSIDERATIONS

When determining a test strategy, the question of process stability needs to be addressed. If a process is not stable, the test methods and confidence statements cannot be interpreted with much precision. Process control charting techniques (see Chapter 19) can be used to determine the stability of a process.

Consider also what actions will be taken when a failure occurs in a particular attribute sampling plan. Will the failure be "talked away"? Often no knowledge is obtained about the "good" parts. Are these "good parts" close to "failure"? What direction can be given to fixing the source of failure so that the failure will not occur with a customer environment? One should not "play games with numbers"! Tests need to be considered such that they can give useful information to continually improve the manufacturing process.

The examples in this chapter illustrate that a test sample size can become very large when verifying a low failure criterion. To make matters worse, large sample size requirements may actually be needed for each lot that is produced.

It is fortunate, however, that many problems that are initially defined as an attribute test can be redefined to a continuous response output. For example, a tester may reject an electronic panel if the electrical resistance of any circuit is below a certain resistance value. In this example more benefits could be obtained from the test if actual resistance values are evaluated. With this information, percent of population projections for failure at the resistance threshold could then be made using probability plotting techniques (see Example 7-4). After an acceptable level of resistance is established within the process, resistance could then be monitored using control chart techniques for variables. These charts can then indicate when the resistance mean and standard deviation is decreasing/increasing, respectively, with time, which would be an expected indicator of an increase in the percentage builds that are beyond the threshold requirement.

Another test consideration is that fractional factorial techniques (discussed later in this text) could be used as a guide to manufacture the test samples such that they represent the limits of the process. This test could then perhaps yield parts that are more representative of future builds and future process variabilities. These samples will not be "random" from the process; however, this technique can potentially identify future process problems that a random sample from an initial "batch" lot would miss.

# 9

# COMPARISON TESTS

Recommended introductory reading: Chapters 2, 3, 4, and 5.

This chapter discusses statistical tests that can be used to compare the equality of populations (e.g., do two machines manufacture on the average the diameter of a shaft to the same dimension). Distributions that will be considered are the normal and binomial. Analysis of means (ANOM) graphical techniques will be used for the comparisons of means when more than two samples are considered.*

## 9.1. COMPARING DATA

The methods discussed in this chapter can be used, for example, to compare two production machines or vendors. Both mean and standard deviation output can be compared between the samples to determine if a difference is large enough to be statistically significant. The comparison test of means is robust to the shape of the underlying distribution not being normal; however, this is not true when comparing standard deviation.

In the situation where two means are compared, a basic equation in this chapter (see Table 9.1) applies also to the analysis of two-level fractional factorial experiment data [see Equation (14.5)].

---

* Tables A through R3 are located in Appendix D of the book.

**TABLE 9.1. Significance Tests for the Difference between the Means of Two Samples**

| $\sigma_1^2 = \sigma_2^2$ | $\sigma_1^2 \neq \sigma_2^2$ |
|---|---|

*$\sigma$ Known*

$$U_0 = \frac{|\bar{x}_1 - \bar{x}_2|}{\sigma\sqrt{\dfrac{1}{n_1} + \dfrac{1}{n_2}}} \qquad\qquad U_0 = \frac{|\bar{x}_1 - \bar{x}_2|}{\sqrt{\dfrac{\sigma_1^2}{n_1} + \dfrac{\sigma_2^2}{n_2}}}$$

Accept $H_a$ if $U_0 > U_\alpha$ $\qquad\qquad$ Accept $H_a$ if $U_0 > U_\alpha$

*$\sigma$ Unknown*

$$t_0 = \frac{|\bar{x}_1 - \bar{x}_2|}{s\sqrt{\dfrac{1}{n_1} + \dfrac{1}{n_2}}} \qquad\qquad t_0 = \frac{|\bar{x}_1 - \bar{x}_2|}{\sqrt{\dfrac{s_1^2}{n_1} + \dfrac{s_2^2}{n_2}}}$$

$$s = \sqrt{\frac{(n_1 - 1)s_1^2 + (n_2 - 1)s_2^2}{n_1 + n_2 - 2}}$$

Accept $H_a$ if $t_0 > t_\alpha$ where

Accept $H_a$ if $t_0 > t_\alpha$ where

$$\nu = \frac{[(s_1^2/n_1) + (s_2^2/n_2)]^2}{\dfrac{(s_1^2/n_1)^2}{n_1 + 1} + \dfrac{(s_2^2/n_2)^2}{n_2 + 1}} - 2$$

$$\nu = n_1 + n_2 - 2$$

*Reference Tables*

| $H_a$ | $U_\alpha$ | $t_\alpha$ |
|---|---|---|
| $\mu_1 \neq \mu_2$ | Table C | Table E |
| $\mu_1 > \mu_2$ (if $\bar{x}_1 > \bar{x}_2$) | | |
| or | Table B | Table D |
| $\mu_1 < \mu_2$ (if $\bar{x}_1 < \bar{x}_2$) | | |

## 9.2. SAMPLE SIZE: COMPARING TWO MEANS

Natrella (1966) gives tables for sample size selection when comparing the attribute response characteristics of two populations. Brush (1988) gives graphs that can be used to aid with selection of sample sizes. Diamond (1989) multiplies the appropriate single sampled population equation [i.e., Equation (7.1), (7.2), or (8.2)] by 2 to determine a sample size for each of the two populations.

## 9.3. COMPARING TWO MEANS

When comparing the means between two samples, the null hypothesis is that there is no difference between the population means, while the alternative hypothesis is that there is a difference between the population means. A difference between two means could be single sided (i.e., $\mu_1 > \mu_2$ or $\mu_1 < \mu_2$) or double sided (i.e., $\mu_1 \neq \mu_2$). Table 9.1 summarizes the equations and tables to use when making these comparisons to determine if there is a significant difference at the desired level of risk (Natrella 1966; Diamond 1989). The alternate hypothesis acceptance criterion is noted for each of the tabulated scenarios. See Section 7.4 for more discussion on hypothesis test criteria.

## 9.4. EXAMPLE 9-1: COMPARING THE MEANS OF TWO SAMPLES

A fractional factorial experiment (see Chapter 13) was designed to improve the voice quality of a portable recording machine. The experiment results indicated that three design changes should improve this quality. A comparison experiment was done to confirm this conclusion. The results from the test were as follows, where a lower number indicates that a machine has better voice quality:

| Sample Number | Current Design (voice quality measurement) | New Design (voice quality measurement) |
|:---:|:---:|:---:|
| 1 | 1.034 | 0.556 |
| 2 | 0.913 | 0.874 |
| 3 | 0.881 | 0.673 |
| 4 | 1.185 | 0.632 |
| 5 | 0.930 | 0.543 |
| 6 | 0.880 | 0.748 |
| 7 | 1.132 | 0.532 |
| 8 | 0.745 | 0.530 |
| 9 | 0.737 | 0.678 |
| 10 | 1.233 | 0.676 |
| 11 | 0.778 | 0.558 |
| 12 | 1.325 | 0.600 |
| 13 | 0.746 | 0.713 |
| 14 | 0.852 | 0.525 |

Using Equations (4.1) and (4.2), the mean $(\bar{x})$ and standard deviation (s) of the 14 samples are

| Current Design | New Design |
|:---|:---|
| $\bar{x}_1 = 0.955$ | $\bar{x}_2 = 0.631$ |
| $s_1 = 0.188$ | $s_2 = 0.099$ |

From the sample data the mean level from the new design is better than the current design; however, the question of concern is whether the difference is large enough to be considered significant. The following equation is used from Table 9.1 since the standard deviations are unknown and are thought to be different (see Example 9-2):

$$t_0 = \frac{|\bar{x}_1 - \bar{x}_2|}{\sqrt{\dfrac{s_1^2}{n_1} + \dfrac{s_2^2}{n_2}}} = \frac{|0.955 - 0.631|}{\sqrt{\dfrac{(0.188)^2}{14} + \dfrac{(0.099)^2}{14}}} = 5.71$$

Accept $H_a$ if $t_0 > t_\alpha$, where the degrees of freedom for $t_\alpha$ is determined to be

$$\nu = \frac{[(s_1^2/n_1) + (s_2^2/n_2)]^2}{\dfrac{(s_1^2/n_1)^2}{n_1 + 1} + \dfrac{(s_2^2/n_2)^2}{n_2 + 1}} - 2 = \frac{[(0.188^2/14) + (0.099^2/14)]^2}{\dfrac{(0.188^2/14)^2}{14 + 1} + \dfrac{(0.099^2/14)^2}{14 + 1}} - 2 = 20.7$$

Assume that there is agreement to make the changes if this confirmation experiment shows significance at a level of 0.05. For 20 degrees of freedom, Table D yields a $t_{0.05}$ value of 1.725.

The test question is single sided (i.e., is the new design better than the old design?). It does not make sense for this situation to address whether the samples are equal (double-sided scenario). Money should only be spent to make the change if the design changes show an improvement in voice quality.

Since $5.71 > 1.725$ (i.e., $t_0 > t_\alpha$), the design changes should be made.

## 9.5. COMPARING THE VARIANCE OF TWO SAMPLES

Hypothesis tests (see Section 4.5) can be conducted focusing on variance (i.e., the square of standard deviation) as the primary response of an experiment (Diamond 1989; Messina 1987; and Montgomery 1984). Unlike the test for differing means, this test is sensitive to the data being from a normal distribution. Care must be exercised when doing the following test because, for example, a "significant difference" may in reality be a violation of this underlying assumption. A probability plot of the data, as discussed in Section 9.7, can yield information that can be used to make this assessment.

A methodology to determine if two sample variances are significantly different is to first determine

$$F_0 = \frac{s_1^2}{s_2^2} \qquad s_1^2 > s_2^2 \tag{9.1}$$

For the two variances to be significantly different, this ratio needs to be larger than the appropriate tabular value of the $F$ distribution noted in Table

F. From this table is taken $F_{\alpha;\nu1;\nu2}$ where $\nu_1$ is the number of degrees of freedom (sample size minus one) of the sample with the largest variance, while $\nu_2$ is the number of degrees of freedom of the smallest variance. A variance ratio that is larger than the tabular value for $\alpha$ indicates that there is a significant difference between the variances at the level of $\alpha$.

### 9.6. EXAMPLE 9-2: COMPARING THE VARIANCE OF TWO SAMPLES

The two standard deviations of the 14 samples from Example 9-1 were 0.188 for the current design and 0.099 for the new design. The question of concern is whether there is reason to believe (at the 0.05 significance level) that there is a difference in variance between the machine designs. From Equation (9-1)

$$F_0 = \frac{s_1^2}{s_2^2} = \frac{0.188^2}{0.099^2} = 3.606$$

The number of degrees of freedom are

$$\nu_1 = 14 - 1 = 13 \qquad \nu_2 = 14 - 1 = 13$$

With these degrees of freedom, interpolation in Table F yields

$$F_{\alpha;\,\nu1;\,\nu2} = F_{0.05;\,13;\,13} = 2.58$$

Since $3.606 > 2.58$ (i.e., $F_0 > F_{\alpha;\nu1;\nu2}$), it is concluded that there is a difference in the variances between the two populations at a significance level of 0.05.

### 9.7. COMPARING POPULATIONS USING A PROBABILITY PLOT

Probability plots of experimental data can supplement the traditional comparison tests. These plots can show information that may yield a better basic understanding of the differences between the samples. Two probability plots on one set of axes can indicate graphically the differences in means, variances, and possible outliers (i.e., data points that are "different" from the other values; e.g., there may have been an error when recording some of the data). This type of understanding can often be used to help improve the manufacturing processes.

### 9.8. EXAMPLE 9-3: COMPARING SAMPLES USING A PROBABILITY PLOT

Consider the data presented in Example 9-1. The normal probability plots for the data (see Chapter 5) in Figure 9.1 shows graphically the improvement

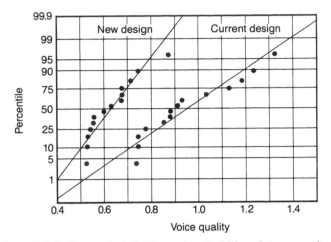

**FIGURE 9.1.** Example 9-3: Normal probability plot comparison.

in mean and standard deviation (i.e., increased slope with new design). The data tends to follow a straight line on the normal probability paper; however, the experimenter in general should investigate any outlier points or slope changes (e.g., the highest "new design" value should probably be investigated).

Additional information can be obtained from the normal probability plot. If, for example, a final test criterion of 1.0 exists, the current design would experience a rejection rate of approximately 40%, while the new design would be close to zero.

The probability plot is a powerful tool; however, management may not be familiar with the interpretation of the graph. Since the data do seem to follow a normal distribution, perhaps a better understood final presentation format would be to use the sample means and standard deviations to draw the estimated PDFs. These graphs can then be illustrated together as shown in Figure 9.2 for comparative purposes.

## 9.9. PAIRED COMPARISON TESTING

When possible it is usually advantageous to pair samples during a comparison test. In a paired comparison test, a reduction in experimental variability can permit the detection of smaller data shifts; even though, the total number of degrees of freedom is reduced since the sample size becomes now the number of comparisons.

An example of this type of test is the evaluation of two pieces of inspection equipment to determine if any significant difference exists between the equipment. With this technique products could be inspected on each piece of equipment. The differences between the paired trials are statistically tested against a value of zero using the equations noted in Table 7.1. Note that the sample size now becomes the number of comparisons, and the degrees of freedom is one minus the number of comparisons.

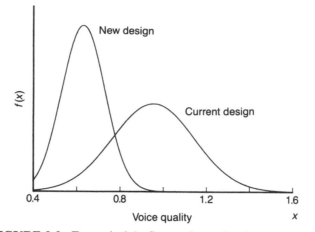

**FIGURE 9.2.** Example 9-3: Comparison of estimated PDFs.

## 9.10. EXAMPLE 9-4: PAIRED COMPARISON TESTING

The data in Example 9-1 was previously considered as two separate experiments. However, the data was really collected in a paired comparison fashion. Fourteen existing drive mechanisms were labeled 1 through 14. The voice quality was measured in a machine using each of these drives. The drives were then rebuilt with the new design changes. The voice quality was noted again for each drive, as shown:

| Sample Number | Current Design | New Design | Change (current − new) |
|---|---|---|---|
| 1 | 1.034 | 0.556 | 0.478 |
| 2 | 0.913 | 0.874 | 0.039 |
| 3 | 0.881 | 0.673 | 0.208 |
| 4 | 1.185 | 0.632 | 0.553 |
| 5 | 0.930 | 0.543 | 0.387 |
| 6 | 0.880 | 0.748 | 0.132 |
| 7 | 1.132 | 0.532 | 0.600 |
| 8 | 0.745 | 0.530 | 0.215 |
| 9 | 0.737 | 0.678 | 0.059 |
| 10 | 1.233 | 0.676 | 0.557 |
| 11 | 0.778 | 0.558 | 0.220 |
| 12 | 1.325 | 0.600 | 0.725 |
| 13 | 0.746 | 0.713 | 0.033 |
| 14 | 0.852 | 0.525 | 0.327 |
| | | | $\bar{x} = 0.324$ |
| | | | $s = 0.220$ |

EXAMPLE 9-4: PAIRED COMPARISON TESTING    **121**

Noting that $t_{0.05} = 1.771$ in the single-sided Table D for $v = 13$ (i.e., $n - 1$) degrees of freedom, the change in voice quality for each drive sample can now be analyzed using the equation shown in Table 7.1. These calculations for the single-sided 95% confidence interval are

$$\mu \leqslant \bar{x} - \frac{t_\alpha s}{\sqrt{n}}$$

$$\mu \leqslant 0.324 - \frac{1.771(0.220)}{\sqrt{14}} = 0.220$$

The lower side of the single-sided 95% confidence interval is greater than zero, which indicates that the new design is better than the current design. Another way to determine if there is a significant difference is to consider

$$\text{Test criterion} = \frac{t_\alpha s}{\sqrt{n}} = \frac{1.771(0.220)}{\sqrt{14}} = 0.104$$

Since $0.324 > 0.104$, there is a significant difference in the population means (i.e., the new design is better than the old design) at the 0.05 level. The normal probability plot of the change data, as shown in Figure 9.3, can be helpful to better understand the magnitude of improvement as it relates to percent of population. In addition, a best estimate of the PDF describing the expected change, as shown in Figure 9.4, can be a beneficial pictorial presentation to management. This PDF was created using the $\bar{x}$ and $s$ estimates for change since the normal probability plot followed a straight line.

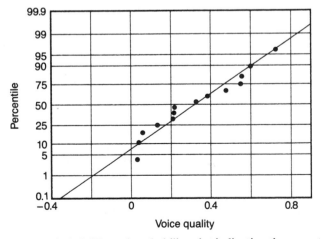

**FIGURE 9.3.** Example 9-4: Normal probability plot indicating the expected difference between the new and old design.

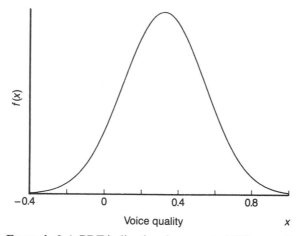

Voice quality

**FIGURE 9.4.** Example 9-4: PDF indicating the expected difference between the new and old design.

## 9.11. COMPARING TWO PROPORTIONS

Consider that samples are taken from two different populations (Natrella 1966) and the response is a proportion of pass/fail (i.e., an attribute test). For small sample sizes tables (Natrella 1966) can be used to determine whether there is a significant difference in the number of failures found for the two samples. However, the following chi-square test statistic can be used with large sample sizes (Natrella 1966). For this situation there is a significant difference between the proportions at an $\alpha$ level of significance if the chi-square value calculated in the following equation is greater than the $\chi^2_{\alpha;\nu}$ value for one degree of freedom ($\nu = 1$) in Table G.

$$\chi^2_0 = \frac{(n_1 + n_2)\left[|x_1 y_2 - x_2 y_1| - \dfrac{(n_1 + n_2)}{2}\right]^2}{n_1(x_1 + x_2)n_2(y_1 + y_2)} \qquad (9.2)$$

where $n_1$ and $n_2$ are the sample sizes, $x_1$ and $x_2$ are the number of no fails, and $y_1$ and $y_2$ are the number of fails. Note that if the question is whether one proportion is larger than another proportion at a level of $\alpha$, $\chi^2_{2\alpha;\nu}$ is the tabular value that should then be used for the test of significance.

## 9.12. EXAMPLE 9-5: COMPARING TWO PROPORTIONS

A forming machine makes frozen orange juice concentrate containers. Some of the packages that it makes are defective since they would leak if they were filled with orange juice. The containers (Montgomery 1985) were monitored on a continuing basis using a process control $p$ chart (see Example 19-3). Consider that after some later point in time, it was noted that a shift in the mean occurred in the process control chart after some machine adjustments. The single-sided question of concern is whether the change that was noted was large enough to be considered significant at a level of 0.05. In the following table the before adjustment parameters contain the subscript 1, while the after adjustment parameters contain the subscript 2.

| Not Failed | Failures | Total |
|---|---|---|
| $x_1 = 1099$ | $y_1 = 301$ | $n_1 = 1400$ |
| $x_2 = \underline{1067}$ | $y_2 = \underline{133}$ | $n_2 = \underline{1200}$ |
| $x_1 + x_2 = 2166$ | $y_1 + y_2 = 434$ | $n_1 + n_2 = 2600$ |

Substitution into Equation (9.2) yields

$$\chi_0^2 = \frac{(2600)\left(|(1099)(133) - (1067)(301)| - \dfrac{(2600)}{2}\right)^2}{(1400)(2166)(1200)(434)} = 51.17$$

Using Table G, it is noted that $\chi_0^2 > \chi_{[(0.05 \times 2);1]}^2$ (i.e., $51.17 > 2.71$); hence, the difference is significant at the 0.05 level. We then conclude that there is a significant reduction in the defect rate and will want to adjust our control chart limits accordingly using the most recent data.

## 9.13.  ANALYSIS OF MEANS

Analysis of means (ANOM) (Ott 1983 and Ramig 1983) is a graphical approach that can be used to compare $k$ groups of size $n$. Consider the following $x_{ij}$ data format where there are $n$ observations within $k$ groups.

| | Groups | | | |
|---|---|---|---|---|
| 1 | 2 | 3 | $\cdots$ | $k$ |
| | | Observations | | |
| $x_{11}$ | $x_{21}$ | $x_{31}$ | $\cdots$ | $x_{k1}$ |
| $x_{12}$ | $x_{22}$ | $x_{32}$ | $\cdots$ | $x_{k2}$ |
| $x_{13}$ | $x_{23}$ | $x_{33}$ | $\cdots$ | $x_{k3}$ |
| $\vdots$ | $\vdots$ | $\vdots$ | | $\vdots$ |
| $x_{1j}$ | $x_{2j}$ | $x_{3j}$ | $\cdots$ | $x_{kj}$ |
| $\bar{x}_1$ | $\bar{x}_2$ | $\bar{x}_3$ | $\cdots$ | $\bar{x}_i$ |
| $s_1$ | $s_2$ | $s_3$ | $\cdots$ | $s_i$ |

The grand mean $\bar{\bar{x}}$ of the group means $(\bar{x}_i)$ [see Equation (4.1)] is simply the average of these mean values, which is written

$$\bar{\bar{x}} = \frac{\sum\limits_{i=1}^{k} \bar{x}_i}{k} \tag{9.3}$$

The pooled estimate for the standard deviation is the square root of the average of $s_i^2$ for the individual observations [see Equation (4.2)].

$$s = \sqrt{\frac{\sum\limits_{i=1}^{k} s_i^2}{k}} \tag{9.4}$$

The lower and upper decision lines (LDL and UDL) are

$$\text{LDL} = \bar{\bar{x}} - h_\alpha s \sqrt{\frac{k-1}{kn}} \qquad \text{UDL} = \bar{\bar{x}} + h_\alpha s \sqrt{\frac{k-1}{kn}} \tag{9.5}$$

where $h_\alpha$ is from Table I (Appendix D) for risk level $\alpha$, number of means $k$, and degrees of freedom $[(n-1)k]$. The means are then plotted against the decision lines. If any mean falls outside the decision lines, there is a statistically significant difference among the means.

If normality can be assumed, analysis of means is also directly applicable to attribute data. As noted in Table 6.2, it is reasonable to consider a normality approximation if both $np$ and $n(1-p)$ are at least 5. For a probability level $p$ of 0.01, this would require a sample size of 500 [i.e., 500(0.01) = 5]. Nelson (1983b) describes transformations that can be used to reduce this sample size requirement, for example, to 100 for both attribute data (binomial distribution) and count data (Poisson distribution).

Ramig (1983) discusses also the application of ANOM to attribute data, count data, and cross classifications (e.g., 3 × 5 factorial).

## 9.14. EXAMPLE 9-6: ANALYSIS OF MEANS

The bursting strengths of diaphragms were determined in an experiment. In this experiment there were seven different types of rubber ($k = 7$) each having four observations ($n = 4$). A data summary of the mean and variance for each rubber type is

EXAMPLE 9-6: ANALYSIS OF MEANS    **125**

|  | ith Sample Number | | | | | | |
|---|---|---|---|---|---|---|---|
|  | 1 | 2 | 3 | 4 | 5 | 6 | 7 |
| $\bar{x}_i$ | 63.0 | 62.0 | 67.0 | 65.0 | 65.0 | 70.0 | 60.0 |
| $s_i^2$ | 9.2 | 8.7 | 8.8 | 9.8 | 10.2 | 8.3 | 8.0 |

From Equation (9.3) the overall mean is

$$\bar{\bar{x}} = \frac{\sum_{i=1}^{k} \bar{x}_i}{k} = \frac{63 + 62 + 67 + 65 + 65 + 70 + 60}{7} = 64.57$$

From Equation (9.4) the pooled estimate for the standard deviation is

$$s = \sqrt{\frac{\sum_{i=1}^{k} s_i^2}{k}}$$

$$= \left(\frac{9.2 + 8.7 + 8.8 + 9.8 + 10.2 + 8.3 + 8.0}{7}\right)^{1/2}$$

$$= 3.0$$

The number of degrees of freedom is $(n - 1)k = (4 - 1)(7) = 21$. For a significance level of 0.05 with 7 means and 21 degrees of freedom, it is determined by interpolation from Table I that $h_{0.05} = 2.94$. From Equation (9.5) the upper and lower decision lines are then

$$\text{UDL} = \bar{\bar{x}} + h_\alpha s \sqrt{\frac{k-1}{kn}} = 64.57 + (2.94)(3.0) \sqrt{\frac{7-1}{7(4)}} = 68.65$$

$$\text{LDL} = \bar{\bar{x}} - h_\alpha s \sqrt{\frac{k-1}{kn}} = 64.57 - (2.94)(3.0) \sqrt{\frac{7-1}{7(4)}} = 60.49$$

An ANOM chart with the limits and measurements is shown in Figure 9.5. This plot illustrates graphically that $\bar{x}_6$ and $\bar{x}_7$ are significantly different from the other measurements.

Other mathematical techniques could also be used to compare the means of more than two samples (see Duncan method in Table 15.3). A probability plot can again be beneficial where the data are plotted for individual groups on one graph. This graph can pictorially show possible outliers, standard

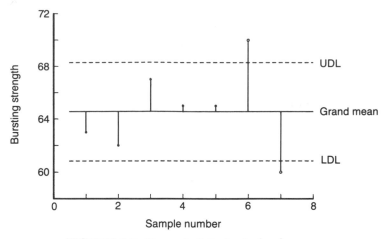

**FIGURE 9.5.** Example 9-6: Analysis of means.

deviation differences, and percent of population statements that may not be obvious when evaluating overall differences between means.

## 9.15. DO-IT-SMARTER CONSIDERATIONS

As noted earlier, the methods included within this chapter are traditionally used to compare vendors, machines, and so forth by taking samples from the populations. In general, when designing a test, attempts should be made to use a continuous response output, as opposed to an attribute response, whenever possible. For example, a particular part may be considered a failure when it tests beyond a certain level. Instead of analyzing what proportion of parts are beyond this level, fewer samples are required if the actual measurement data is analyzed. Also, fewer samples, in general, are required if the test objective can be met using paired comparison techniques, as opposed to comparison tests between samples. In addition, probability plotting techniques can be very useful to better understand the data; a probability plot of the data may indicate that there is something worth investigating, which was not obvious when comparing mean or standard deviation values.

There are problems that can occur when making comparisons. For example, the quality of a part that is to be supplied by a vendor is compared from two sources. A problem with this type of test is that the samples that are drawn do not necessarily represent the type of parts manufactured in the future. Also, the samples need to be taken from processes that are stable. If the processes are not stable, a conclusion may not have much precision.

For this situation a do-it-smarter consideration might be to have the vendors manufacture (and label) specially made parts that reflect normal boundaries experienced within their processes. A fractional factorial experiment design structure (see Chapter 13) can be used to describe how these specially built parts are to be manufactured, where one of the factors under consideration might be vendor A versus vendor B. Other factors to consider are new versus experienced operator, first shift versus second shift, raw material supply source A versus B, high versus low machine tolerance limits, manufacturing line A versus B, tester A versus B, and so forth. This comparison test build strategy can also give indications on what factors are causing a degraded response (so that these problems can get "fixed").

For some added insight to the range of variability that might be expected from the current process, a probability plot could be made of all the fractional factorial trial data (see Example 22-2; note that care should be made intrepreting this type of plot since the data are not random).

After a vendor is "qualified" using the preceding procedure, process control charts (see Chapter 19) should be implemented for the purpose of tracking and stopping the process if degradation should later occur. A fractional factorial experiment strategy may again be needed in the future to better understand the source of any degradation.

# 10

# RELIABILITY TESTING: OVERVIEW

Recommended introductory reading: Chapters 2, 3, 4, 5, and 6.

This chapter is an introduction to Chapters 12 and 13, which discuss the reliability testing of repairable systems and nonrepairable devices, respectively. In this text the Weibull and log-normal distributions are used for nonrepairable device analyses, while the Poisson distribution and NHPP are used for repairable system analyses.

A test that evaluates the frequency of failure for systems (or the time of failure for devices) can take a long time to complete when the failure rate criterion is low (or the average life is high). To complete a test in a reasonable period of time, considerations may need to be made to have the sample tested in an environment that accelerates usage. Alternatives to achieve this acceleration within the electronic industries include tests at high temperature, high humidity, thermal cycling, vibration, corrosive environments, and increased duty cycle. This chapter covers some accelerated testing models and a general accelerated reliability test strategy.

## 10.1. PRODUCT LIFE CYCLE

The "bathtub" curve shown Figure 10.1 describes the general life cycle of a product. The downward sloping portion of the curve is considered the "early-life" portion where the chance of a given product failing during a unit of time decreases with usage. The flat portion is the portion of the cycle where the failure rate does not change with additional usage. Finally, the

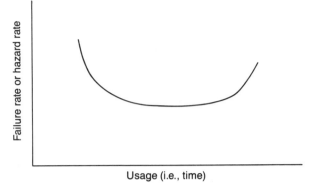

**FIGURE 10.1.** Bathtub curve.

increasing slope portion is the "wear-out" region where the chance of failure in a unit of time increases as the product's usage increases.

An automobile is a repairable system that can experience a bathtub life cycle. New car owners may have to return the vehicle several times to the dealer to remove the "bugs." Failures during this time are typically due to manufacturing workmanship problems; a customer may experience problems with a wheel alignment adjustment, a door not closing properly, or a rattle in the dashboard. During this early-life period, the frequency of returning the vehicle decreases with vehicle age. After these initial bugs are removed, usually the car will start to approach a relative constant failure rate. When the constant failure rate portion of life is reached, the vehicle may experience, for example, a mean time between failure (MTBF) rate of 6 months or 10,000 miles. Failures during this period will normally differ from early-life failures for an automobile; problems may occur with the water pump bearings, wheel bearings, brake linings, and exhaust systems. Note that at the device level the parts may be wearing out; however, at the system level the overall failure rate may be constant as a function of usage of the vehicle. However, with usage an automobile then may start to experience an overall increasing failure rate. During this period, the frequency of component wear-out and required adjustments increases with time. This period of time may contain many of the same failures as the constant failure rate period; however, now the frequency of repair will be increasing with the addition of wear-out from other components. Wear-out might now involve such components as the steering linkage, differential, suspension, and valve lifters.

As discussed earlier, there are repairable systems and nonrepairable devices. The automobile is obviously a repairable system since we don't throw the vehicle away after its first failure. Other items are not so obvious. For example, a water pump may be repairable or nonrepairable. The most frequent failure mode for a water pump may be its bearings. If a water pump is repaired (rebuilt) because of a bearing failure, then that water pump could be considered a repairable system. If a water pump that has never been rebuilt is discarded after a failure, then this device would be considered a nonrepairable device.

There are other devices that are easier to classify as a nonrepairable device. These devices include brake pads, headlights, wheel bearings, exhaust pipe, muffler, and the bearings of the water pump. These devices are discarded after failure.

## 10.2. REPAIRABLE VERSUS NONREPAIRABLE TESTING

Consider first a nonrepairable device. Assume that 10 tires were randomly selected from a warehouse and were tested to wear-out or failure. With this situation input to an analysis may simply be 10 customer equivalent mileage numbers reflecting when the tire treads decreased to 2.0 mm. From this information an "average life" (e.g., 60,000 km) and other characteristics could be determined (e.g., 90% of the tires are not expected to fail by 40,000 km; see Chapter 5). Chapter 12 addresses this problem type (reliability of nonrepairable devices) using Weibull or log-normal analysis techniques.

Consider now a repairable system such as an overall automobile failure rate. The data from this test analysis might be in the following form:

2000 km: repaired electronic ignition, idling problems
8000 km: pollution device replacement, acceleration problems
18,000 km: dashboard brake light repair
30,000 km: water pump bearing failure
40,000 km: test terminated

This above information may apply to one of 10 cars that were monitored that had similar information. Since multiple failures can occur on each test device, a Weibull probability plot, for example, is not an appropriate direct analysis tool. For this situation we are not interested in the percentage of population that fails at a given test time or an average life number; we are interested in the failure rate of the car (or the time between failures).

Extending this conceptual automobile failure example further, the following is then considered. If the failure rate is believed not to be dependent on the age of the automobile, then in the above example we may estimate that the failure rate for the vehicle during a 20,000-km test would be on the average 0.0001 failures/km (4 failures/40,000 km = 0.0001) or 10,000 km MTBF (40,000 km/4 failures = 10,000) [note, this is a biased estimate for MTBF]. However, the logic behind the "constant failure rate" assumption seems questionable since the time between each succeeding failure seems to be increasing. Chapter 11 address this type of problem (reliability of repairable systems with constant and decreasing/increasing failure rates) using the Poisson distribution or the nonhomogenous Poisson process (NHPP) with Weibull intensity.

## 10.3. NONREPAIRABLE DEVICE TESTING

The two-parameter Weibull distribution is often used for the analysis of nonrepairable device failure times since it can model any one of the three situations commonly encountered as a function of device age: reducing chance of failure, constant chance of failure, and increasing chance of failure for a time increment.

As noted in Equation (6.3), the Weibull cumulative distribution function takes the form (where $t$ is used to represent time)

$$F(t) = 1 - \exp\left[-(t/k)^b\right] \tag{10.1}$$

where the $b$ is the shape parameter and $k$ is the scale parameter (or characteristic life). If both $k$ and $b$ are known, a cumulative failure value [$F(t)$] can be determined for any value of time ($t$). For example, $F(100,000 \text{ hr}) = 0.9$ indicates that 90% of the population is expected to fail before a usage of 100,000 hr. The purpose of a test and corresponding data analyses then becomes a means to estimate the unknown parameters of Equation (10.1).

Much can be understood about a device failure mode if the shape parameter $b$ is known. The PDF for differing shape parameters is shown in Figure 10.2. Numerically, this shape parameter $b$ indicates the following relative to Figure 10.1:

$b < 1$: early life, decreasing failure rate with usage
$b = 1$: random or intrinsic failures, constant failure rate with usage
$b > 1$: wear-out mode, increasing failure rate with usage

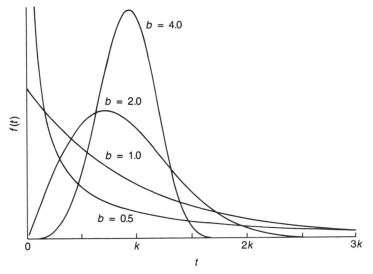

**FIGURE 10.2.** Weibull PDF.

The log-normal distribution is another alternative often found suitable to describe the underlying failure distribution of electrical/mechanical components (e.g., resistors and journal bearings). This distribution is applicable when the logarithms of the failure time data are normally distributed. With this distribution the model parameters take the form of a mean and standard deviation; hence, the mathematical tools of the normal distribution are applicable to the log-normal distribution. Figures 6.12 and 6.13 show PDFs and CDFs for this distribution.

## 10.4. REPAIRABLE SYSTEM TESTING

The Poisson distribution is commonly used when determining the details of a repairable system test. The underlying assumption when using this distribution is that the system failure rate will be constant as a function of usage (i.e., follows an exponential distribution). Conceptually this means that systems will have the same mean time between failure during their first year of service as they will have in their tenth year of service. In reality this may not often be true. However, the ease of using this type of test strategy makes it very popular, and it can be satisfactory for many situations, if care is taken when designing and implementing the test (even though the test is not technically robust relative to the validity of this underlying assumption).

A reasonable basic overall reliability test strategy for repairable systems can be to first select a satisfactory sample size and test interval using the Poisson distribution (see Chapter 11). Then, if enough failures occur during test, analyze the data to determine if a better fit could be made using the NHPP model, which can consider failure rate change as a function of usage.

When designing a test to certify a criterion (failures/unit time or MTBF) using the Poisson distribution, the design consideration to determine is the total test time. For example, a test criterion for an automobile might be 7000 km MTBF or 1/7000 failures/km. From Table K (using the concepts illustrated in Section 11.7), a proposed test to verify that the 90% confidence interval (i.e., for $\rho \leq 1/7000$ failures/km), while permitting 8 failures would require a total test time of about 90,965 km.

Since the underlying assumption is that the failure rate does not change as a function of usage on the system, two extremes for the physical test are to either test one automobile for 90,965 km or to test 90,965 automobiles for 1 km. The first test alternative is perhaps physically achievable; however, by the time the test is completed, knowledge gained from the test relative to its criterion may be too late to impact the design. These test results may then be used for information only. The 90,963 sample size alternative extreme is not realistic since this sample size is typically too large for a complex system test. It should be noted that both these test extremes would be very sensitive to the accuracy of the underlying assumption of there being a constant failure rate.

Chapter 11 discusses realistic compromises that can be made between the sample size and the test duration for individual systems. This chapter also discusses analyzing the results to consider the failure rate changing as a function of usage.

Another test consideration that might be applicable and advantageous to consider is the modeling of the positive improvement displayed during reliability tests over a period of time due to changes in product design or the manufacturing process. US Department of Defense (1980 and 1981a), Crow (1975), and Dwaine (1964) discuss the modeling of "reliability growth."

## 10.5. ACCELERATED TESTING: DISCUSSION

Reliability certification of electronic assemblies can be difficult since often the failure rate criterion is low and there are usually aggressive time and resource constraints. Accelerated testing techniques are often essential to complete certification within a reasonable period of time and with reasonable resources.

However, care must be exercised when choosing an accelerated test strategy. A model that does not closely follow the characteristics of a device can result in an invalid conclusion. The following sections give a general overview of some accelerated test models. In later sections of this chapter, literature is referenced for additional information about the applicability of models; traditional statistical lack of fit analysis techniques (Tobias and Trindade 1986) for the models is sometimes discussed in this literature (see Section B.6, Appendix B).

Product technology, design, application, and performance objectives need to be considered when choosing stress tests for a product. After the stress tests are chosen, stress levels must not change the normal product failure modes. Without extensive model validation within the proposed experiment, an acceleration model should technically be known and implemented to contain both sample size and test duration limitations. Unfortunately, because of test constraints, model applicability may only be speculative. In addition, the results from a lack of fit analysis might not very decisive because of test sample size constraints.

Often a simple form of acceleration is implemented without any awareness that the test is being accelerated. For example, a device under test may be subjected to a reliability test 24 hr per day, 7 days a week (i.e., 168 hr per week). If we believe that a customer will only use the device 8 hr a day, 5 days a week (i.e., 40 hr per week), we could consider that our test has a customer usage time acceleration of 4.2 (i.e., 168/40). Even with this simple form of acceleration, traps can be encountered. With this test the assumption is made that the sample is tested exactly as a customer uses the product. This assumption may not be valid; for example, on/off cycling may be ignored during the test. This cycling might contribute to thermal or electrical changes that may result in a big contribution to failures within the customer environment. Or, perhaps even no run time within the customer's facility causes a significant number of failures due to large corrosive or high-humidity conditions. Again, care must be exercised to protect against performing an accelerated test that either ignores an underlying phenomenon that can cause a significant number of failures or has an erroneous acceleration factor. Perhaps too much emphasis is often given to the question of the confidence level that the product will be equal to or better than the criterion, as opposed to the basic assumptions that are made in the test design.

Accelerated tests can use one or more of many stress test environments (e.g., high temperature, thermal cycling, power cycling, voltage, high current, vibration, high humidity, and mechanical stress). The following discussion includes model considerations for elevated temperature and thermal cycling tests.

## 10.6.  HIGH-TEMPERATURE ACCELERATION

A common acceleration model used in the electronics industry is the Arrhenius equation. This model suggests that degradation leading to component failure is governed by a chemical and physical process reaction rate. This high-temperature model yields a temperature acceleration factor ($A_t$) of

$$A_t = \exp\left[(E_a/k)(1/T_u - 1/T_s)\right] \tag{10.2}$$

where $E_a$ = activation energy (eV),
    function of device type/technology/mechanism
    $k$ = Boltzmann's constant, $8.617 \times 10^{-5}$ (eV/K)
    $T_u$ = unstress temperature (K)
    $T_s$ = stress temperature (K)
    K = $273.16 + \,°C$

Equation (10.2) was originally generated to predict the rate of chemical reactions. It is applied often to electronic component testing since many failure mechanisms are dependent on such reactions. A key parameter within this equation is the activation energy, which commonly ranges from 0.3 to 0.7 eV, depending on the device. Jensen and Petersen (1982) summarize activation energies that have been found applicable for certain device types, while Figure 10.3 illustrates the sensitivity of the equation to any activation energy constant assumption.

Multiple temperature stress cells can be used to determine the activation energy. Equation (10.2) can be rearranged in the form of Equation (10.3), which is in a form conducive to a simple analysis of a two-cell temperature test $T_1$ and $T_2$. To use this equation, first determine the 50% failure point

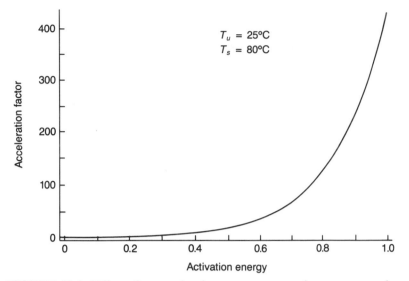

**FIGURE 10.3.** Effects from activation energy assumptions: an example.

for each cell ($T_{50_1}$ and $T_{50_2}$) using Weibull or other analysis techniques discussed in this text (note that it is not required that 50% of the sample fail to make a $T_{50}$ estimate). The ratio of $T_{50_1}/T_{50_2}$ is the best estimate for the acceleration factor ($A_t$). The activation energy ($E_a$) can then be determined using the equation (Tobias and Trindad 1986)

$$ E_a = k \left[ \ln \left( \frac{T_{50_1}}{T_{50_2}} \right) \right] \left( \frac{1}{T_1} - \frac{1}{T_2} \right)^{-1} \quad (T_2 > T_1) \qquad (10.3) $$

Assembly testing offers the additional challenge of having multiple component types that have various activation energies. One approach when addressing this issue for a test is to determine an overall activation energy for the assembly. Jensen and Petersen suggest that "at the present time, and lacking further information, we would, for integrated circuits, be inclined to follow Peck and Trapp (1978) and suggest a value of 0.4 eV for an otherwise unspecified freak population failure," where a freak population is produced by random occurrences in the manufacturing process as it describes a population of substandard products. To add more uncertainty to the number, Jensen & Petersen state that activation is not necessarily constant as a function of test temperature.

In addition to an activation energy constant, the Arrhenius equation needs temperature inputs. In component tests these inputs should be measured on the component in degrees Kelvin where the failure process is taking place. Within an assembly, temperature varies as a function of component position, type, and usage; hence, for practical considerations, some test designers use the module ambient temperature.

Additional discussion on the application of the Arrhenius equation is found in Nelson (1990), Tobias and Trindade (1986), Jensen and Petersen (1982), and Sutterland and Videlo (1985).

## 10.7. EXAMPLE 10-1: HIGH-TEMPERATURE ACCELERATION TESTING

The life criterion of an electronic component needs verification using a high-temperature test. Given an ambient operating temperature of 35°C, a stress temperature of 85°C, and an activation energy of 0.6, determine the test acceleration $(A_t)$.

Converting the centigrade temperatures to units of Kelvin yields

$$T_o = 35 + 273 = 308$$

$$T_s = 85 + 273 = 358$$

Substituting the quantities into Equation (10.2) yields

$$A_t = \exp [(E_a/k)(1/T_u - 1/T_s)]$$

$$= \exp [(0.6/8.617 \times 10^{-5})(1/308 - 1/358)]$$

$$= \exp [(6963)(1/308 - 1/358)] = 23.5$$

## 10.8. EYRING MODEL

Most of the well-known acceleration functions can be considered to be a special case of the general Eyring acceleration function (Tobias and Trindade 1986). This model also offers a general solution to the problem of combining additional stresses.

The Arrhenius model is an empirical equation that justifies its use by the fact that it "works" in many situations. The Eyring model has the added strength of having a theoretical derivation based on chemical reaction rate theory and quantum mechanics. For the time to fail of 50% of the population $(T_{50})$, the generalized form of the Eyring model equation is

$$T_{50} = AT^Z[\exp (E_a/kT)]\{\exp [B + (C/T)]S_1\} \qquad (10.4)$$

where temperature $(T)$ is one stress and $S_1$ is a second stress; $A$, $B$, $C$, and $Z$ are constants. Several notes should be made about this equation:

1. The Eyring model equation describes failures at one condition. A test acceleration factor can be calculated by taking the ratio of two of these equations with differing input conditions. When this mathematical operation is performed, the $A$ constant will cancel.

2. Many expressions may not initially appear to originate from an Eyring model, but in fact have this origination there. For example, the temperature/voltage stress model in Equation (10.5) may be thought to be applicable under a certain situation.

$$T_{50} = A[\exp (E_a/kT)](V^B) \qquad (10.5)$$

The generalized two-stress Eyring equation reduces to this form by substituting $Z = 0$, $C = 0$, and $S_1 = \ln V$ (where $V$ is in volts).

3. $T_{50}$ describes the time when 50% of the test units will fail. However, other percentiles can likewise be determined.

4. The term $T^Z[\exp (E_a/kT)]$ models the effect of temperature and compares with the Arrhenius model if $Z$ is close to 0.

5. Additional stresses (e.g., $S_2$) can be added as factors in the following form:

$$T_{50} = AT^Z[\exp (E_a/kT)]\{\exp [B + (C/T)]S_1\}\{\exp [D + (E/T)]S_2\} \qquad (10.6)$$

Each additional set of factors adds two more unknown constants (e.g., $D$ and $E$), making the model more difficult to work with in a general state. Considering all the constants as unknowns requires at least as many separate experimental stress cells as there are unknown constants in the model.

6. Choosing the units to use in a model equation can be a problem. Temperature is in degrees Kelvin. But, for example, how should voltage or humidity be input? The theoretical model derivation does not specify; hence, the experimenter must either work it out by trial and error, or derive an applicable model using arguments from physics and statistics.

## 10.9. THERMAL CYCLING: COFFIN–MANSON RELATIONSHIP

The inverse power law is used to model fatigue failure of metals that are subjected to thermal cycling. For the purpose of accelerated testing, this model relationship is called the Coffin–Manson relationship (Coffin 1954, 1974; Manson 1953, 1966) and can be expressed in the form

$$A_t = (\Delta T_s/\Delta T_u)^B \qquad (10.7)$$

where $A_t$ is the acceleration factor and $B$ is a constant characteristic of the metal and test method and cycle. $\Delta T_u$ is the temperature change under normal operation, while $\Delta T_s$ is the temperature change under stress operation. The constant $B$ is near 2 for metals, while Nelson (1990) states that for plastic encapsulates for microelectronics $B$ is near 5.

An application of Equation (10.7) is in the electronic industry. Heating/cooling conditions can often occur within the covers of a product because of simple on/off cycling. Thermal changes cause expansion/contraction processes to occur within a product. If solder joints are weak and the thermal change is sufficiently large, stresses can then occur within solder joints thus causing fractures, which can lead to product failure.

In the electronics industry modifications are sometimes needed to Equation (10.7). For example, Norris and Landzberg (1969) noted that for tin–lead solders used in C-4 (Controlled Collapse Chip Connections), joints at room temperature are at about 50% of their absolute melting temperature. They state: "the Coffin–Manson equation was found to be inadequate for projecting the thermal failure of solder interconnections; in laboratory experiments it was found to yield very pessimistic estimates of fatigue lifetimes." They added a frequency dependent term and an Arrhenius temperature dependent term to form a "modified Coffin–Manson" equation.

Tummala and Rymaszewski (1989) shows a modified Coffin–Manson relationship of

$$A_t = \exp\left[(0.123/k)(1/T_u - 1/T_s)\right]\left(\frac{f_u}{f_s}\right)^{0.3}\left(\frac{\Delta T_s}{\Delta T_u}\right)^{1.9} \tag{10.8}$$

where the added terms $f_u$ and $f_s$ reflect the frequency of cyclic changes in use and stress conditions, respectively. $T_u$ and $T_s$ represent the maximum use and stress temperature in the cycles in degrees Kelvin; $k$ is the Boltzmann constant noted in Equation (10.2).

Other sources for information about the Coffin–Manson relationship are Engelmaier (1985), Goldmann (1969), Tobias and Trindade (1986), Nachlas (1986), and Nishimura et al. (1987). Saari et al. (1982) has an additional discussion on thermal cycle screening strengths in a manufacturing environment.

## 10.10. MODEL SELECTION: ACCELERATED TESTING

Previous sections within this chapter included only a few of the test alternatives suggested within the literature to accelerate certain types of failure modes. In addition, there are other stress alternatives such as humidity, voltage, current, corrosive gas, and vibration that are sometimes used in industry for accelerated tests.

Whenever one must choose an accelerated test strategy to address reliability certification, it becomes immediately obvious that model selection and test strategy can dramatically affect a product pass versus fail test position. For the model to be valid, the accelerated test methodology must not change the failure mode of the component. Care must be exercised when making a confidence interval assessment after using an accelerated test model since, in reality, much unknown error can exist within the "acceleration factor number."

Each model is most appropriate for a specific component failure mechanism. Assemblies can contain many components with different failure mechanisms, which make the selection of test models even more difficult. There is additional discussion on the application of acceleration models in Nelson (1990) and Tobias and Trindade (1986). These references also discuss step stress testing where, for example, the temperature stress on a set of test components is increased periodically and the times to failure are noted at each temperature level.

## 10.11. DO-IT-SMARTER CONSIDERATIONS

When choosing a basic test strategy for a given situation, one should consider the following:

1. Determine whether the units under test are repairable or nonrepairable.
2. Determine through consultation and literature searching the most accurate accelerated test modeling strategy that will suffice for the test constraints yet capture the failure modes that the customer might experience. Note, for example, that a test that constantly exercises a component only at an accelerated high-temperature environment is not evaluating possible failure modes caused by thermal cycling.
3. Determine a sample size, test duration (per unit), and number of permissible failures using detailed test strategies discussed within one of the two following chapters.
4. List all the test assumptions.

Reliability tests are often performed to "ensure" that the frequency of failures of a component or assembly is below a criterion. Often this test is performed during initial model builds or initial production.

One of the major assumptions that is often compromised in a typical reliability test is that the sample is randomly taken from the population of interest. Often with qualification tests the population of interest is really future product production. For this situation a perhaps better strategy is to test a product that has been specially manufactured to represent the variability "space" of a production process. Special test samples could be manufactured according to fractional factorial design considerations (discussed in Chapter 13). With this strategy there is the added advantage that a major process problem could be detected before mass production is begun (e.g., when a manufacturing factor is at its low tolerance setting, the product failure rate is significantly increased). This advantage can outweigh the sacrifice in a loss of randomization when it is considered that a "random" sample from an early manufacturing process may be far from representing product that the customer will actually receive.

Fractional factorial experiments can also have reliability test output considerations for each trial (see Section 13.20). For example, consider that the failure rate of a system needs to be reduced in order to increase customer satisfaction. A fractional factorial experiment could be used to evaluate proposed design changes, where special systems would be built according to the trial factor considerations. If all test units were operated to failure, the time of failure or a failure rate for the test units could be analyzed as a response for each trial. (Note that a data transformation may be required, Table 15.11.) However, it may be difficult to test long enough for all test units to fail. Because of this, it would be advantageous to monitor periodically during test some response that typically degrades in unison with the life characteristics of the device. The factors that appear significant for this response would then be presumed to significantly affect the system failure rate. The factor levels that are found best from this experiment should then be considered important when making changes to the design if appropriate.

In some system situations it might erroneously be assumed that the major source of customer problems is component failures. Example 22-2 illustrates a situation where the customer would have experienced a problem that was dependent on how he or she used the product. When the inherent failure rate of components is very low, it is very difficult to quantify a reliability failure rate. Because of this, perhaps more effort should be given toward ensuring that the product meets the real needs of the customer, in lieu of a simple "build them and test them" strategy.

# 11

# RELIABILITY TESTING: REPAIRABLE SYSTEM

Recommended introductory reading: Chapters 2, 3, 4, 5, 6, and 10.

This chapter explores the problem of "certifying" the failure rate criterion (failures per unit of time, $\rho_a$) or mean time between failures (MTBF) criterion of a system, where a system is defined as a collection of components, and components are replaced or repaired whenever a failure occurs.

Both constant and changing failure rate situations are considered. The Poisson distribution can be used when the system failure rate is constant as a function of the age of a system. The NHPP (nonhomogeneous Poisson process) with Weibull intensity can often be used when the failure rate is considered to change as a function of system usage.


## 11.1. CONSIDERATIONS WHEN DESIGNING A TEST OF A REPAIRABLE SYSTEM FAILURE CRITERION

One of several test design alternatives could be chosen when "certifying" a repairable system failure rate criterion. In this chapter classical test design alternatives are discussed along with some extensions and do-it-smarter considerations.

The techniques discussed within this chapter address the rate at which systems experience failures as a function of time. Criteria that are expressed in units of MTBF will need to be transformed by a simple reciprocal conversion. For example, a MTBF rate of 10,000 hr can be converted to a failure rate criterion of 0.0001 failures/hour (i.e., 1/10,000 = 0.0001).

Reliability tests can be either sequential or fixed length. With the sequential approach test termination is generally after either the product has exhibited few enough failures at some point in time during test for a "pass" decision (with β risk) or enough failures have occurred to make a "fail" decision (with α risk). The other alternative is either fixed length or fixed failure tests. Since fixed failure tests are not terminated until a predetermined number of failures have occurred and most test situations have schedule/time constraints, time-terminated tests are the normal choice for fixed length test strategies. Because of this application preference, only time-terminated tests will be discussed in this text; MIL-HDBK 781 (US Department of Defense 1987) addresses failure terminated tests.

System failure rate test designs often initially assume that the failure rate is constant as a function of system age. This limiting assumption can lead to the selection of the Poisson distribution for these test designs and analyses. With the Poisson distribution total usage on all systems is the parameter of concern; it theoretically does not matter how many units are on test to achieve this total test usage value. For example, with a 15,000-hr fixed length test, it does not technically matter if one unit is exercised for 15,000 hr or 15,000 units are exercised for 1 hr.

Theoretically, these scenarios may be the same; however, in reality the two test extremes may yield quite different results. If one of these two extremes were chosen, dramatic differences can be expected if the "constant failure rate" assumption is invalid. That is, this type of test evaluation is not robust to the underlying assumption not being valid. The following discussion considers test strategies that can be used to reduce the risk of getting an answer that has minimal value.

Technically, before using the Poisson distribution for test design, the failure rate of the system should be a known constant (flat part of a bathtub curve; see Figure 10.1) for the time of concern (e.g., product warranty or product useful life). However, process problems can cause more early-life failures, while wear-out phenomena can cause the instantaneous system failure rate to increase as a function of usage on the product. In reality, the experimenter does not know for sure that this response will be constant. However, if care is exercised when making initial decisions relative to sample size versus individual sample usage, error due to unknown information about the shape of this intensity function can be minimized.

When a test is being designed, consideration must be given to the real objective or concern. If concerns are about capturing wear-out problems, a small number of systems need to be tested for a long period of time. If concern is whether manufacturing or early-life problems exist, a larger number of samples should be tested for a shorter period of time. If there are concerns about early life and wear out, it may be the best economics to exercise a large sample for a "short" period and then continue the test for a subset of machines to "product life" usage to assess system wear-out exposures.

If a warranty or maintenance criterion needs to be assessed to ensure that failures will not exceed targets, then it may be best that the test duration per unit equals the warranty or maintenance agreement period. If a sufficient number of failures occurs during this test, then the NHPP can be used to determine if (and how) failure rates are changing as a function of usage on individual systems.

Failure rate tests during product development are sometimes expected to give an accurate confidence interval assessment of what the failure rate will be when the product is built within production. If there is concern about design and manufacturing problems, does it make sense to take a "random" sample of the first parts that are produced to certify a criterion? A "random" sample of future products is needed to test for design and manufacturing problems. Assemblies produced within a short time period tend to be similar; these samples do not necessarily represent the product "space" (i.e., boundary limits) of design tolerances and manufacturing variability.

In lieu of classical reliability testing, there are other economical alternatives that may capture these problems that can haunt a manufacturer later during production. Initial lot sampling may not expose design and process problems that in fact exist, since the sample is representative of only the current lot sample. Example 22-2 discusses alternatives that may be appropriate to replace or supplement this classical test approach in capturing these elusive problems earlier within the development of the product design and manufacturing processes.

Again, fixed length and sequential test plans (U.S. Department of Defense 1986, 1987) are the two general types of test strategies applicable to system failure rate "certification." Fixed length test plans are perhaps more commonly used; however, sequential test plan alternatives are also discussed in Section 11.2. The results from these tests could also be used to give a confidence interval for the failure rate of the product population from which the sample is drawn. It is assumed with this test that the manufacturing process is stable and that there will be no design changes to the product during test. In addition, it is also assumed for the described tests that the sample size is small relative to the population size. For this last assumption to be true, it is best that the ratio of sample size to population size does not exceed 10%.

A sequential test plan is considered the best test alternative when it is a requirement to either accept or reject predetermined failure rate values ($\rho_0$ and $\rho_1$) with predetermined risks of error ($\alpha$ and $\beta$) (see Section 4.5). With sequential testing, uncertainty must be expected in regards to total test time.

A fixed length test plan is appropriate when the total test time must be known in advance. In this chapter two test alternatives for this type of test are discussed. In Section 11.4 the sample size for a hypothesis test is discussed where both $\alpha$ and $\beta$ risks are considered. In Section 11.7 a reduced sample size testing strategy is addressed. This second test approach can be used to "certify" system criteria, with the understanding that the real test purpose is to obtain a confidence interval for the true failure rate and then compare the single-sided bound to the criterion.

## 11.2. SEQUENTIAL TESTING: POISSON DISTRIBUTION

For sequential plans, in addition to both $\alpha$ and $\beta$ risks, two failure rates ($\rho_0$ and $\rho_1$) are needed as input to this model. If a system has only one criterion ($\rho_a$) and this criterion is be "certified" with a consumer risk $\beta$, the highest failure rate $\rho_1$ should probably be set equal to the criterion. Perhaps then the easiest way to select a $\rho_0$, which relates to $\alpha$ risk, is to select first a discrimination ratio ($d$), which relates the two failure rate test extremes (U.S. Department of Defense 1987). This ratio can be defined as the ratio of a higher failure rate ($\rho_1$) to a lower failure rate ($\rho_0$):

$$d = \frac{\rho_1}{\rho_0} \qquad \rho_1 > \rho_0 \qquad (11.1)$$

The discrimination ratio input is a key parameter, along with $\alpha$ and $\beta$, when determining the specifics of the test. Before test, all concerned groups need to agree to all parameter inputs.

A sequential probability ratio plan for repairable systems can then be expressed as two straight lines with coordinates of failures ($r$) and total test time ($T$):

$$\frac{\ln[\beta/(1 - \alpha)]}{\ln(\rho_1/\rho_0)} + \frac{(\rho_1 - \rho_0)}{\ln(\rho_1/\rho_0)} T < r < \frac{\ln[C(1 - \beta)/\alpha]}{\ln(\rho_1/\rho_0)} + \frac{(\rho_1 - \rho_0)}{\ln(\rho_1/\rho_0)} T$$
$$(11.2)$$

where $C = 1$ when there is no test truncation time. The actual test failures are then plotted versus test time. The test is terminated whenever this plot intersects either the pass or fail line determined from Equation (11.2).

The factor $C$ in equation 11.2 takes on the value of ($[1 + d]/2d$) when the following test truncation procedure is used (U.S. Department of Defense 1987 and Epstein and Sobel 1955). In this procedure, the parallel lines from equation 11.2 have truncation lines added at $T_0$ and $r_0$. To determine $r_0$, an appropriate value of $r$ is first determined to be the smallest integer such that

$$\frac{\chi^2_{(1-\alpha);2r}}{\chi^2_{\beta;2r}} \geq \frac{\rho_0}{\rho_1}$$

In this equation, values are then determined for the numerator and denominator by simultaneously searching the Chi-square tables (see table G, Appendix D*) until the ratio of the variables is equal to, or greater than $\rho_0$/

---

* Tables A through R3 are located in Appendix D of this book.

EXAMPLE 11-1: SEQUENTIAL RELIABILITY TEST    **145**

$\rho_1$. The number of degrees of freedom $r_0$ will be half of this value that is determined; values for $r_0$ are rounded to the next higher integer. The test truncation time $T_0$ is then determined to be

$$T_0 = \frac{\chi^2_{(1-\alpha);2r_0}}{2\rho_0}$$

## 11.3. EXAMPLE 11-1: SEQUENTIAL RELIABILITY TEST

1. A sequential test is to assess whether a criterion of 1000 hr MTBF (i.e., 0.001 failures/hr) is met on a system given the following:
   a. $\beta = 0.1$ for $\rho_1 = $ criterion $= 0.001$
   b. Discrimination ratio $= d = 1.6$
   c. $\alpha = 0.05$
   hence, $\rho_0 = \rho_1/d = 0.001/1.6 = 0.000625$
   $C = (1 + 1.6)/(2[1.6]) = 0.8125$
2. The test was then conducted. The accumulated usages on the systems when there was a system failure was 2006, 3020, 6008, 8030, and 9010. With a given total test time of 12,268 hours it was necessary to determine what action should be taken (i.e., continue test, pass test, or fail test).

Substitution into equation 11.2 yields the following sequential decision lines.

$$\frac{\ln[0.1/(1 - 0.05)]}{\ln(0.001/0.000625)} + \frac{(0.001 - 0.000625)}{\ln(0.001/0.000625)}\ T < r$$

$$-4.790 + 0.000798\ T < r$$

$$r < \frac{\ln[0.8125(1 - 0.1)/0.05]}{\ln(0.001/0.000625)} + \frac{(0.001 - 0.000625)}{\ln(0.001/0.000625)}\ T$$

$$r < 5.708 + 0.000798\ T$$

To determine a termination time using the procedure described in Section 11.2, table G yields the following since $\rho_0/\rho_1 = 0.000625/0.001 = 0.625$.

$$\frac{\chi^2_{[(1 - 0.05);80]}}{\chi^2_{[0.1;80]}} = \frac{60.39}{96.58} = 0.6253 \geqslant 0.625$$

It then follows that $r_0 = 40$ failures (i.e., 80/2) and

$$T_0 = \frac{\chi^2_{(1-\alpha);2r_0}}{2\rho_0} = \frac{\chi^2_{(1-0.05);80}}{2(0.000625)} = \frac{60.39}{0.00125} = 48,312$$

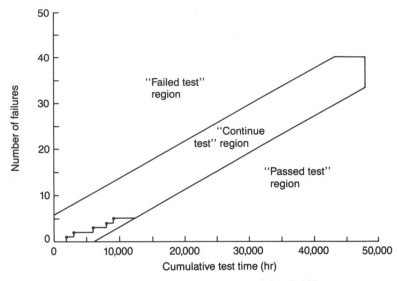

**FIGURE 11.1.** Example 11-1: Sequential reliability test.

Figure 11.1 illustrates the plotting of these sequential test boundary conditions with the failure data to determine that the test indicates that the systems in test "passed" at the test usage of 12,268 hr., i.e. from the first equation above: $T = [(5 + 4.79)/0.000798] = 12,268$.

At the "passed test" time of 12,268 hr for this example, the product sample was performing at a failure rate of 0.00041 (i.e., $5/12,268 = 0.00041$), which is 41% of the 0.001 criterion. If the test system actually performed close to the specification limit, the test duration time could be much larger.

In general, a sequential test strategy will yield a shorter test duration than a fixed test strategy that verifies both $\alpha$ and $\beta$. However, planning termination times before the "truncation time" can make accurate scheduling difficult.

## 11.4. TOTAL TEST TIME: HYPOTHESIS TEST OF A FAILURE RATE CRITERION

When the underlying distribution is Poisson, the total run time (in the case of a reliability test) for a hypothesis test about one population (see Table 4.2 and Section 7.4) can be determined from Equation (11.3):

$$T = \left[ \frac{(U_\alpha)(\rho_\alpha)^{1/2} + (U_\beta)(\rho_\beta)^{1/2}}{\rho_\beta - \rho_\alpha} \right]^2 \qquad (11.3)$$

where $T$ is the total test time given the failure rates $\rho_\beta$ and $\rho_\alpha$ that relate to the null ($H_0$) and alternate ($H_a$) hypotheses, respectively. $U_\alpha$ is the value

EXAMPLE 11-2: TIME-TERMINATED RELIABILITY TESTING     **147**

from Table B or C, depending on whether $H_a$ is single or double-sided, and $U_\beta$ is from Table B (Diamond 1989). Note, $T$ represents the sample size in the situation where the Poisson distribution is used as an approximation for the binomial distribution in an attribute hypothesis test. To illustrate this point, consider the units of these two types of failure rates. A reliability failure rate criterion could be 0.0001 failures/hour, while an attribute criterion could be 0.0001 jams/sheet of paper loaded. In the second example the experimenter is interested in determining the total number of sheets of paper to load into devices.

## 11.5. CONFIDENCE INTERVAL FOR FAILURE RATE EVALUATIONS

$$\frac{\chi^2_{2r;(1+c)/2}}{2T} \leq \rho \leq \frac{\chi^2_{2r+2;(1-c)/2}}{2T} \tag{11.4}$$

where $T$ = total cumulative usage
$\quad\quad r$ = number of failures
$\quad\quad \chi^2$ = chi-square value from Table G for $2r + 2$ or $2r$ degrees of freedom
$\quad\quad c$ = level of confidence selected expressed in decimal form.

An alternative approach is to use Table K with the equation

$$\frac{A_{r;(1+c)/2}}{T} \leq \rho \leq \frac{B_{r;\ (1+c)/2}}{T} \tag{11.5}$$

where $B$ = factor from Table K with $r$ failures and $[(1 + c)/2]$ decimal confidence value
$\quad\quad A$ = factor from Table K with $r$ failures and $[(1 + c)/2]$ decimal confidence value.

The single-sided confidence statement takes a similar form using the decimal confidence value directly.

## 11.6. EXAMPLE 11-2: TIME-TERMINATED RELIABILITY TESTING CONFIDENCE STATEMENT

Ten systems are tested for 1000 equivalent customer usage hours each. When a failure occurs, the system is repaired and placed back on test. Ten failures occurred during the time terminated test. The 90% confidence interval for the failure rate can be determined using either of the following two procedures.

Using Equation (11.4)

$$\frac{\chi^2_{[(2)(10)];[(1+0.9)/2]}}{2[(10)(1000)]} \leqslant \rho \leqslant \frac{\chi^2_{[(2)(10)+2];[(1-0.9)/2]}}{2[(10)(1000)]}$$

from the chi-square distribution (Table G)

$$\chi^2_{20;0.95} = 10.85 \qquad \chi^2_{22;0.05} = 33.92$$

substitution yields

$$0.0005425 \leqslant \rho \leqslant 0.001696$$

Similarly Table K could be used to get the same answer:

$$\frac{A_{10;(1+0.9)/2}}{(10)(1000)} \leqslant \rho \leqslant \frac{B_{10;(1+0.9)/2}}{(10)(1000)}$$

$$\frac{5.425}{10,000} \leqslant \rho \leqslant \frac{16.962}{10,000}$$

$$0.0005425 \leqslant \rho \leqslant 0.0016962$$

Since concerns are usually about ensuring the upper limits of the failure rate, the preceding double-sided 90% confidence interval could be expressed as a single-sided 95% confidence level of

$$\rho \leqslant 0.001696$$

## 11.7. REDUCED SAMPLE SIZE TESTING: POISSON DISTRIBUTION

The sample size procedure illustrated in Section 11.4 protects both the customer (with $\beta$ risk) and the producer (with $\alpha$ risk). The test objective of the plan described in this section is to only "certify" that the product does not exceed a criterion $\rho_a$. This single-sided test strategy will yield a similar test plan to those proposed by commercially available "reliability slide rules." In this strategy fewer than $r$ failures must occur within a total test time $T$ for "certification".

This reduced sample size testing strategy is applicable to a criterion certification test when the total test time is chosen such that the criterion is set to a bound of the confidence interval with a given number of allowed failures (i.e., the failure rate of the population is equal to or less than the criterion failure rate at the desired confidence level).

To get the total test duration that is required for such an evaluation, $B_{r;c}$ can be determined using Table K for the chosen number of permissible failures and desired confidence interval value. $B_{r;c}$ is then substituted with the failure rate criteron ($\rho_a$) into Equation (11.6) to yield a value for $T$, the total test time.

$$T = \frac{B_{r;c}}{\rho_a} \qquad (11.6)$$

Example 11-3 illustrates the simple procedure to use when designing such a test. In order to pass a test of this type, the sample may be required to perform at a failure rate that is much better than the population criterion.

## 11.8. EXAMPLE 11-3: REDUCED SAMPLE SIZE TESTING—POISSON DISTRIBUTION

Product planning states that a computer system is to have a failure rate (i.e., a failure rate criterion) that is not to exceed 0.001 failures/hour (i.e., $\rho_a = 0.001$). The projected annual customer usage of the system is 1330 hr. A test duration is desired such that two failures are acceptable and a 90% confidence interval bound on the failure rate will be

$$\rho \leqslant 0.001$$

Table K is used to determine that $B_{2;0.90} = 5.322$. Equation (11.6) then yields

$$T = \frac{B_{r;c}}{\rho_a} = \frac{B_{2;0.90}}{0.001} = \frac{5.322}{0.001} = 5322 \text{ hr}$$

As previously noted for this type of test, one system could be tested for 5322 hr or 5322 systems for 1 hr. A reasonable approach might be to test 4 units 1330 hr each [i.e. (4)(1330) $\approx$ 5322 total hr]. With this scenario each unit would experience usage equal to the annual warranty usage of 1330 hr. If a total of two or less failures occur on the test machines, the test is "passed."

## 11.9. RELIABILITY TEST DESIGN WITH TEST PERFORMANCE CONSIDERATIONS

The test strategy discussed in the previous section does not consider how difficult it might be for a product to pass a given test design. To illustrate this consider what position should be taken if a zero failure, 99% confidence bound test plan had 1 failure? 2 failures? 10 failures? Technically in all these cases the test was failed since the zero failure objective was not met. However, care needs to be exercised with this "failed test" position. It seems unreasonable to take an equal failed test position with the three posttest scenarios. With a 99% confidence bound test plan and one or two failures at test completion, the sample failure rate (i.e., number of failures divided by total test time) would be found to be better than criterion. However, if 10 failures occurred during test, the sample failure rate would be much worse than the criterion. The following discussion proposes a methodology to guide the experimenter in making better test input decisions.

Within corporations test groups could have an adversary relationship with the manufacturing and development communities. Testers want certainty that criteria objectives are met, while other groups may have the primary emphasis of meeting schedule and production volume requirements. Posttest confrontation between testers and others can be expected when certifying aggressive failure criteria with a fixed length test design that permits only a small number of failures and a high amount of confidence that the criterion will be met. If the product had one too many failures, the development or manufacturing organizations may take the position that the product should be considered satisfactory since the test failure rate was better than specification. There is some merit to this position, since with this type of test strategy the development/manufacturing organizations are taking the full impact of test uncertainty resulting from the test requirements of a high "pass test" confidence level and a small number of permissible failures.

One alternative to this uncertainty dilemma is to design a test that will address both $\alpha$ and $\beta$ risks collectively. The disadvantage to this strategy is that the test sample size [see Equation (11.3)] and test duration are normally "too large."

A compromise to this approach is to address what-if scenarios "up front" with possible outcomes before the test is begun. To aid this pretest scenario process, I suggest considering the "test performance ratio" ($P$) factor of various test alternatives before test start.

To explain this factor, consider a test alternative that permits $r$ failures with $T$ total test time. The sample failure $\rho_t$ rate for this test design would then be

$$\rho_t = \frac{r}{T} \qquad (11.7)$$

This test design failure rate ($\rho_t$) is then a function of both the number of allowable failures and desired percent confidence interval consideration for the chosen scenario. The test performance ratio ($P$) is then used to compare this test design failure rate ($\rho_t$) to the criterion ($\rho_a$) by the relationship

$$P = \frac{\rho_t}{\rho_a} \qquad (11.8)$$

EXAMPLE 11-4: TIME-TERMINATED RELIABILITY TEST DESIGN    **151**

Note that low values for $P$ indicate that the product will need to perform at a failure rate much better than the criterion to achieve a "pass test" position. For example, if $P$ were equal to 0.25, this means that for a pass test position to occur the product will need to perform four times better than specification during the test. If this ratio is assessed before the test, perhaps tests that are doomed to failure can be avoided. In this example the development organization may state that this proposed test is not feasible since it is highly unlikely the product sample will perform four times better than the criterion.

The following example illustrates the application of the test performance ratio to help achieve test design inputs that are agreeable to all concerned organizations before test initiation.

## 11.10. EXAMPLE 11-4: TIME-TERMINATED RELIABILITY TEST DESIGN—WITH TEST PERFORMANCE CONSIDERATIONS

A test performance ratio graph is desired to aid in the selection of the number of permissible test failures to allow when verifying the criterion noted in Example 11-3. The failure criterion in this example was 0.001 failures/hour with a test 90% confidence interval bound.

From Table K the following $B$ values for 90% confidence given the 0, 1, 2, and 3 failure(s) scenarios are

| $r$ | 0 | 1 | 2 | 3 |
|-----|------|------|------|------|
| $B$ | 2.303 | 3.890 | 5.322 | 6.681 |

Using Equation (11.6) (e.g., 5.322/0.001 = 5322), these tabular values yield a total test time ($T$) for the differing failure scenarios of

| $r$ | 0 | 1 | 2 | 3 |
|-----|------|------|------|------|
| $T$ | 2303 | 3890 | 5322 | 6681 |

For these scenarios $\rho_t$ is determined from Equation (11.7) by dividing the number of failures by the total test time (e.g., 2/5322 = 0.0003758) to achieve

| $r$ | 0 | 1 | 2 | 3 |
|-----|---|-----------|-----------|-----------|
| $\rho_t$ | 0 | 0.0002571 | 0.0003758 | 0.0004490 |

Using Equation (11.8) with the failure criterion of 0.001, the test performance ratio ($P$) for each test possibility becomes (e.g., 0.0002571/0.001 = 0.2571)

| $r$ | 0 | 1 | 2 | 3 |
|-----|---|--------|--------|--------|
| $P$ | 0 | 0.2571 | 0.3758 | 0.4490 |

This table gives an indication how much better than criterion the sample needs to perform for the 90% confidence interval bounded tests. For example, one-failure test requires that the sample failure rate be at least 3.89 times (i.e., $1/0.2571 = 3.89$) better than criterion for passage, while a three-failure test needs to be a multiple of 2.23 ($1/0.4490 = 2.23$). Obviously a product will have a better chance of passing a three-failure test; however, the price to pay is additional testing. To get a better idea of the test alternatives, test performance ratio ($P$) can be plotted versus the corresponding test times for each failure, as shown in Figure 11.2.

Each of these points on the graph represent a test plan alternative. This plot is not "half" of a sequential test plot. It is noted that a zero-failure test requires usage of 2303, while the previous sequential test plan in the example requires 6003 (see Figure 11.1). This difference exists because with a fixed length test a decision is to be made after test time ($T$), while normally a sequential test plan will be continued for a much longer test time until a decision can be made with either $\alpha$ or $\beta$ risk.

Figure 11.2 addresses a test performance ratio that relates a "pass test" failure rate to a criterion. The plot shown in Figure 11.3 indicates in addition to the preceding curve, a test performance ratio curve that is appropriate if each possible test failure objective is exceeded by one, which is the minimal number of failures that is considered for a "failed test" decision.

The plot form shown in Figure 11.4 is useful to assess the effects of various input confidence level alternatives on the test performance ratio ($P$). With this information a more realistic pass/fail test can often be chosen that better considers the general economics of the test situation.


## 11.11.  POSTTEST ASSESSMENTS

More failures than originally permitted may occur within a reliability test. However, management may not be willing to stop the production build process purely on the test position that the targeted failure rate cannot be "passed" with the desired confidence level. Management may want to better understand what future failure rate can be expected with minimal process changes. Management may even be willing to accept the risk of a higher customer failure rate exposure for some period of time until long-term "fixes" can be incorporated within the design or manufacturing process. The question of concern to make this decision becomes: What customer failure rate can be expected with the given test data, given minor product alterations?

To address this question, each failure within the test should be evaluated to determine whether a fix was made to eliminate future occurrences of this failure. Many of the problems experienced may be "talked away" by either future design change proposals or process changes. Care must be exercised with this strategy since a "retest" may experience additional process or design problems that did not happen to occur with the initial test sample

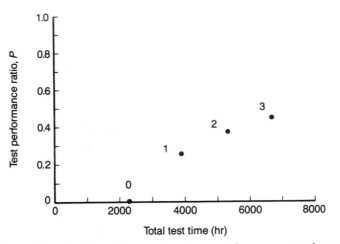

**FIGURE 11.2.** Example 11-4: Test performance ratio versus total test time for various test scenarios.

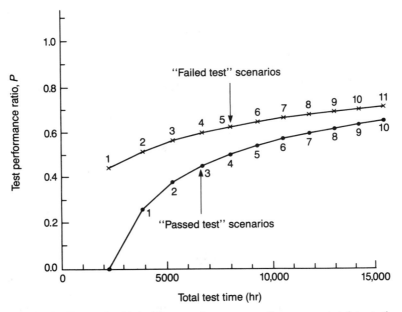

**FIGURE 11.3.** Example 11-4: Test performance ratio versus total test time for various test scenarios.

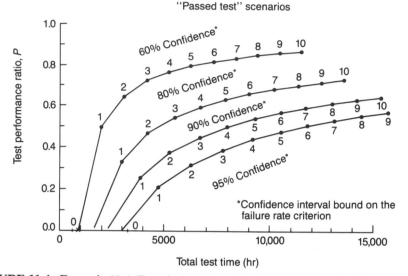

**FIGURE 11.4.** Example 11-4: Test design alternatives (60, 80, 90, and 95% confidence criterion bounded interval).

resulting in an overall failure rate that did not decrease to the extent that was expected.

However, a confidence interval could be calculated to illustrate the probabilistic range of failure rate for the population with a given test failure scenario. However, often two problems can exist with this strategy. First, differing organizations within a corporation do not often agree on the number of failures that "should be counted" from the test data. Also, the confidence level to be reported may not be in general agreement.

## 11.12. EXAMPLE 11-5: POSTRELIABILITY TEST CONFIDENCE STATEMENTS

From Example 11-4 the three-failure test of the 0.001 failures/hr criterion was chosen. A total test time of 6681 was planned to verify the criterion; however, the test did not actually stop until a total customer equivalent usage time of 7000 hr was achieved. This time-terminated test experienced a total of eight failures.

The eight failures were analyzed to determine what would be necessary to prevent future occurrences of each failure type. Representatives from all concerned organizations agreed that three of the failure types could happen again since the cost to alter the manufacturing process to eliminate these differing failure types would currently be cost prohibitive. These representatives also agreed that two of the failures would be transparent to a customer and should not be considered a failure. The manufacturing and development organizations believed that the other three would be fixed by either an engineering change to the process or the design; they believed that if this test were performed again with these changes, there would "probably be" three failures. The test organization was not so optimistic about these fixes, and they believed that some other type of failures might surface if the test were repeated. They wanted to consider six failures until proven otherwise.

To better assess the business risk relative to the 0.001 criterion, the following failure rate table was created for various confidence levels using Equation (11.5) and Table K.

|  | 3 Failures | 6 Failures |
|---|---|---|
| Sample failure rate | 3/7000 = 0.00043 | 6/7000 = 0.00086 |
| 70% upper limit | 4.762/7000 = 0.00068 | 8.111/7000 = 0.00116 |
| 90% upper limit | 6.681/7000 = 0.00095 | 10.532/7000 = 0.0015 |

Cost factors can be an appropriate extension to this table to aid with the business decision process.

The preceding discussion was relative to the goal of meeting a criterion. However, neither testers nor management should "play games with the numbers." A customer wants no failures to occur. Emphasis should be given to continually improve the process by eliminating first the source for the large problems and then smaller problems, with the target in mind of eventually improving the process so that no failures will occur. Chapters 3 and 21 discusses how brainstorming, Pareto diagrams, and fractional factorial experiments can be very beneficial tools to help improve processes.

## 11.13. REPAIRABLE SYSTEMS WITH CHANGING FAILURE RATE

The Weibull probability plot discussed in Chapter 5 yields an estimate for the percent of population failed as a function of device usage. For a system a question of concern is whether the "instantaneous" failure rate (e.g., failures/hr) changes as a function of usage, not percentage of population failures as a function of usage. The NHPP model is often applicable to this situation. In Equation (6.6) this model was noted to take the form

$$r(t) = \lambda b(t)^{b-1} \tag{11.9}$$

If $\lambda$ and $b$ in this equation were known, then the system failure rate, $r(t)$, is described as a function of time.

Consider that time of failure data was available either from a test or from a data base containing information about system failures in a customer's office. If we consider that these systems had multiple start times, iterative solutions are needed to determine the estimators to this model. However, the equations are closed form in the special case when the systems are considered to have the same start time (see Crow 1974); hence, this scenario does not require an iterative solution.

For a time-truncated scenario the conditional maximum-likelihood estimates $\hat{b}$ and $\hat{\lambda}$ when all the systems start at the same time are given by Equations (11.10) and (11.11). These equations can be used to estimate the unknown quantities $b$ and $\lambda$ in Equation (11.9).

$$\hat{b} = \frac{\sum\limits_{q=1}^{K} N_q}{\sum\limits_{q=1}^{K} \sum\limits_{i=1}^{Nq} \ln \dfrac{T_q}{X_{iq}}} \tag{11.10}$$

$$\hat{\lambda} = \frac{\sum\limits_{q=1}^{K} N_q}{\sum\limits_{q=1}^{K} T_q^{\hat{b}}} \tag{11.11}$$

where $K$ = total number of systems on test
$q$ = system number $(1, 2, \ldots, K)$
$N_q$ = the number of failures exhibited by $q$th system
$T_q$ = the termination time for $q$th system
$X_{iq}$ = age of the $q$ system for the $i$th occurrence of failure.

Example 11-6 illustrates how the NHPP can be used to assess a system failure rate as a function of usage on the system. The type of data in this example could have been collected either from a failure criterion test, from field tracking information, or an "in-house" stress screen test, if we assume the systems have the same "start time".

## 11.14. EXAMPLE 11-6: REPAIRABLE SYSTEMS WITH CHANGING FAILURE RATE

A manufacturing process is to produce systems that are to be tested before shipment within an accelerated test environment. This screen is to be long enough to capture most quality problems. Twenty systems were tested to a duration that was longer than the "planned" normal stress screen duration. This test yielded the results shown in Table 11.1, where the accelerated test

EXAMPLE 11-6: REPAIRABLE SYSTEMS WITH CHANGING FAILURE RATE    **157**

**TABLE 11.1. Example 11-6: System Failure Times**

| System Number | Failure Times ("Customer Days") | Termination Time ("Customer Days") |
|---|---|---|
| 1 | 0.3 | 58 |
| 2 | 14, 42 | 61 |
| 3 | 20 | 27 |
| 4 | 1, 7, 15 | 54 |
| 5 | 12, 25 | 27 |
| 6 | 0.3, 6, 30 | 35 |
| 7 | 6 | 40 |
| 8 | 24 | 31 |
| 9 | 1 | 42 |
| 10 | 26 | 54 |
| 11 | 0.3, 12, 31 | 46 |
| 12 | 10 | 25 |
| 13 | 3 | 35 |
| 14 | 5 | 25 |
| 15 | None | 67 |
| 16 | None | 40 |
| 17 | None | 43 |
| 18 | None | 55 |
| 19 | None | 46 |
| 20 | None | 31 |

usage was converted to expected "customer usage" values. Figure 11.5 pictorially illustrates these failures on the individual systems. Note, the following discussion assumes that multiple failures occur on a system by chance. In general, an experimenter should try to determine if (and then try to understand why) some systems perform significantly better/worse than the other systems.

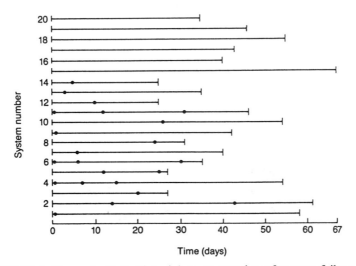

**FIGURE 11.5.** Example 11-6: Pictorial representation of system failure times.

Substituting into Equations (11.10) and (11.11) yields

$$\hat{b} = \frac{\sum\limits_{q=1}^{K} N_q}{\sum\limits_{q=1}^{K} \sum\limits_{i=1}^{N_q} \ln \dfrac{T_q}{X_{iq}}} = \frac{1 + 2 + 1 + 3 + \ldots}{\ln \dfrac{58}{0.3} + \ln \dfrac{61}{14} + \ln \dfrac{61}{42} + \ln \dfrac{27}{20} + \ldots} = 0.54$$

$$\hat{\lambda} = \frac{\sum\limits_{q=1}^{K} N_q}{\sum\limits_{q=1}^{K} T_q^{\hat{b}}} = \frac{1 + 2 + 1 + 3 + \ldots}{58^{0.54} + 61^{0.54} + 27^{0.54} + 54^{0.54} + \ldots} = 0.15$$

From Equation (11.9), the expected individual system failure rate is then

$$r(t) = \lambda b(t)^{b-1} = (0.15)(0.54)t^{0.54-1} = 0.081t^{-0.46}$$

Pictorially this intensity function is illustrated in Figure 11.6, where, for example, the failure rate at 10 days was determined to be:

$$r(10) = 0.081 \, (10)^{-0.46} = .028 \text{ failures/day.}$$

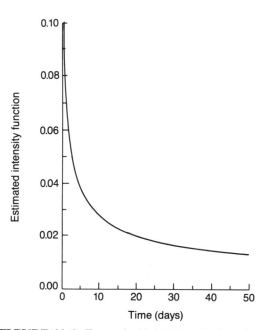

**FIGURE 11.6.** Example 11-6: Intensity function.

EXAMPLE 11-6: REPAIRABLE SYSTEMS WITH CHANGING FAILURE RATE     **159**

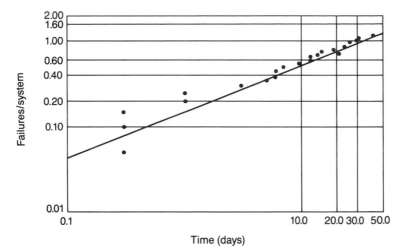

**FIGURE 11.7.** Example 11-6: Average failures per system.

One visual representation of the model fit to the data is to determine and then plot for each of the 22 failures the average system cumulative failure rate as a function of usage. Figure 11.7 shows the fitted equation along with these data points.

To determine the raw data plot positions in this figure, consider, for example, the plot position for the eighth ascending ranked data point. From the original data set, the failure time for both the eight and ninth data point was 6 days, which would be the abscissa value for both these points. The ordinate value for the eighth data point would be the average failure rate of the systems under test at this point in time. For the eighth data point the ordinate value is

$$\frac{8 \text{ total failures}}{20 \text{ systems in test}} = 0.4 \text{ failures/system}$$

From Figure 11.6 the rapidly decreasing intensity function curve indicates a decreasing failure rate and that the test is detecting early-life problems, which are often production quality issues. There does not appear to be a knee in the curve in Figure 11.7, which leads us to believe that our test duration is not getting past any initial early-life problem mode that could exist with the population (see Figure 12.3).

From Figure 11.6 it appears that a 10-day "customer usage test" screen reduces the initial failure rate from approximately 0.10 failures/day to 0.02 failures/day. Additional test time does not have as much benefit as this initial test period; hence, a 10-day customer equivalent usage test may initially seem to be a reasonable starting point for a production screen. Other economic factors could be added to this decision process; however, it should be noted that a "10-day screen"would not have captured all the failures noted in Figure 11.5. Hence, it might be appropriate to critique the screening procedure to determine if a better scheme can be found to get failures to occur sooner. Perhaps a vibration screen should be considered for use in conjunction with a thermal cycling screen.

After the specifics and duration of a screen test are established, a process control chart (see Chapter 19) could then be used to monitor this manufacturing process step for future changes in failure rate characteristics. An increase in the failure rate detected by the screen might be an indicator that the process has degraded (i.e., a sporadic problem; see Section 3.3) and that customers might also be expected to begin experiencing an increase in the failure rate. Because of early problem identification using a control chart, action can be taken to "fix" this degradation before it impacts the customer appreciably.

However, in reality it seems that for most products the noted failure rate would be too high to tolerate on a continuing basis (i.e., a chronic problem). A problem determination program should be used to find the cause of the failures (see Section 19.17). If the process is changed to minimize the number of problems that occur in this test, there is less risk of these problems occurring in a customer's office.

Pareto diagrams along with fractional factorial experiment techniques can be a valuable combination of tools to understand and give direction in reducing the number of problems. The control charts noted earlier could be used as a tool to determine when the process is creating fewer failures, which would be an indicator that the fixes are beneficial.

A significant reduction (or increase) in the process control chart mean value might also be considered as a trigger to repeat the above test to "reoptimize" the screening procedure. It may be later determined, for example, that our stress screen duration can be reduced appreciably, thus reducing costs.

## 11.15. DO-IT SMARTER CONSIDERATIONS

The reliability tests discussed in this chapter can be a useful portion of the process to get a quality product to the customer. However, these test should only be a portion of this total process to develop/manufacture a quality product. A false sense of security can result from a favorable reliability test at the beginning of production. Future production units may be quite different, and the customer may use the system much differently than simulated by the test driver, which could cause a higher field failure rate than anticipated. In addition, results from this test are typically late in the process; hence, problems that are discovered because of this test can be very difficult and expensive to fix. Reliability tests often can only be used as a sanity check, not as a means to "inspect in quality" (see Deming's point 3 in Section 3.2).

Fractional factorial experiments (see Chapter 13) early within the development and manufacturing process are usually a more effective means of creating an atmosphere in which quality can be designed within the product and its manufacturing process. Statistical process control charts are then an effective tool to monitor the manufacturing process for sporadic problems that could degrade product quality.

Determining the changing failure rate of a repairable system within tests in a manufacturing facility can be difficult since there may not be enough failures in the amount of test time to fit a model. However, the NHPP can be a useful tool to track a product within the customer environment if there is an accurate method of determining time to failure. With this information perhaps, for example, a better screen could be determined to use within the process to capture similar problems before units leave the manufacturing facility.

The logic used in Example 11-6 to optimize a manufacturing screening process could be also applied to nonrepairable situations using Weibull analysis techniques. Additional do-it-smarter considerations for reliability testing are noted at the end of Chapter 10 and in Example 22-2.

# 12

# RELIABILITY TESTING: NONREPAIRABLE DEVICES

Recommended introductory reading: Chapters 2, 3, 4, 5, 6, and 10.

This chapter is an extension of the concepts described in Chapter 10 relative to reliability tests that are performed on nonrepairable devices. The techniques discussed within this chapter are directed toward the situation where a random sample of a product is monitored for failure times during a reliability test assessment, given that samples that fail are *not* placed back on test after failure (i.e., a nonrepairable test plan). These techniques are applicable to the reliability testing of such devices as electronic modules, television displays, and automobile tires.

This chapter addresses the test situations where there are no accelerated stress conditions on the devices under test or there is a known acceleration factor (see Section 10.5). Section 10.10 discusses other test alternatives that can be more appropriate for a given reliability test consideration.

## 12.1. RELIABILITY TEST CONSIDERATIONS FOR A NONREPAIRABLE DEVICE

In this chapter the Weibull distribution is most often used when assessing the reliability of nonrepairable devices; however, many of the concepts apply similarly to the log-normal distribution, which is also discussed. As noted in Section 10.3, the Weibull distribution is appropriate to analyze this type of problem since this distribution can model the three usage-sensitive characteristics commonly encountered for a nonrepairable device: improving failure rate, constant failure rate, and degrading failure rate. As also noted, the log-normal distribution is an alternative approach to modeling these characteristics.

The unit of time considered in the data analysis can be chosen after acceleration factor adjustments are made to the test times on the devices. For example, a 1-hr test with an acceleration factor (see Section 10.5) of 20 can yield a test time input to the Weibull model of 20 hr.

In Chapter 11 the Poisson distribution was used to design tests for repairable systems that were assumed to experience a constant failure rate. For a given set of test requirements, Table K was used to determine the total test time, which would be spread between several test machines. However, for a non-repairable device following the Weibull distribution, the constant failure rate assumption often is not be appropriate; hence, the test time cannot be spread "arbitrarily" between the devices under test. The test time for each unit needs to be considered in conjunction with the sample size. To illustrate this point, consider that a wear-out problem would occur at 10,000 hr. Ten units tested to 1000 hr would not detect this problem; however, one unit tested to 10,000 hr would experience the problem.

From an analysis point of view, it is best to test long enough to have a failure time for each device under test. When this is done, the data can be analyzed using probability plotting techniques. However, often in this type of test all devices do not experience a failure before test termination. Data from this type of test can be analyzed manually using hazard plotting techniques (if no computer program is available to analyze this type of data using probability plotting techniques).

However, both of these test alternatives can involve a lot of test time. Section 12.6 considers another test alternative that can be used when the shape of the underlying Weibull distribution [$b$ in Equation (12.1)] is known (or can be assumed). With this approach probability plots are not anticipated since the test often would be planned to permit no failures. This section also illustrates how trade-offs can be made between the sample size and test duration for the individual samples.

## 12.2. WEIBULL PROBABILITY PLOTTING AND HAZARD PLOTTING

When planning a reliability test for a nonrepairable device, a sample size and test duration need to be considered along with a methodology that will be used to determine the time of failures during test. An accelerated test environment (see Section 10.5) may be needed so that the test can be completed in a reasonable period of time. The failure time data from such a test can be plotted on Weibull probability paper (see Table Q3*) or Weibull hazard paper (see Table R3) for the data analysis (see Sections 5.4 and 5.5).

When making trade-offs between sample size and test duration, the real test objective should be considered. If wear-out is of concern, perhaps a "smaller" number of units will then suffice; however, the test time for these devices could be very lengthy (e.g., the expected average life of the device or expected life usage in a customer's office). However, if early-life failures are of concern, more production parts need to be tested for a shorter period of time (e.g., 1 to 6 months equivalent "customer's usage").

Again, it is desirable from an analysis point of view to have a long enough test such that all test samples fail. Section 5.4 illustrates the mechanics of this analysis, while Example 12-1 exemplifies the probability plot procedure for a reliability test. However, this type of test is often not realistic, test analyses may often need to be done on data that has a mixture of failure and no failure (censored data) times.

If all the test samples have not failed, it is best that they have a consistent test termination time beyond the last failure point; however, other censoring times can be accommodated. Section 5.5 illustrates the mechanics of this manual hazard plot analysis, while Example 12-2 exemplifies this procedure.

A probability plot of the data from a Weibull distribution yields a slope equating to the shape parameter ($b$) and the 63.2% cumulative failure point equating to the characteristic life ($k$) (see Section A.6 in Appendix A). Note that $t$ is used in Equation (12.1) to designate time. In this equation $t$ replaces the $x$ parameter that was used in Equation (6.3).

$$F(t) = 1 - \exp\left[-(t/k)^b\right] \tag{12.1}$$

Examples 12-1 and 12-2 illustrate how the two unknown parameters of the Weibull distribution equation [see Equation (12.1)] can be estimated using a probability plot or hazard plot approach. Manual analysis techniques were used in these examples; however, computer programs are available that can give more accuracy to both the graphical illustration and parameter computations (see Section 2.3).

For a manual plot of the data, Section B.5 in Appendix B discusses an approach that can be used to determine a best-fit line. Computer-generated probability plots are an alternative that can have additional accuracy since the estimates are determined mathematically (e.g., maximum-likelihood estimators).

Again, Example 12-1 considers a test where all the samples are tested until failure. In this case all the data can be plotted using the percent plot position Table P (see also Section 5.4). Example 12-2 considers the test

---

* Tables A through R3 are located in Appendix D.

EXAMPLE 12-1: WEIBULL PROBABILITY PLOT FOR FAILURE DATA    **165**

where some of the units are removed from test before failure occurs. Example 12-4 analyzes the data from Example 12-1 using log-normal considerations.

## 12.3. EXAMPLE 12-1: WEIBULL PROBABILITY PLOT FOR FAILURE DATA

Seven printwheel components were tested and failed with the following number of months of usage: 8.5, 12.54, 13.75, 19.75, 21.46, 26.34, and 28.45.

The ranked data along with the Table P percentage plot positions for a sample size of seven yields the following:

| Ranked Life Data | Percentage Plot Position |
|:---:|:---:|
| 8.5 | 7.1 |
| 12.54 | 21.4 |
| 13.75 | 35.7 |
| 19.75 | 50.0 |
| 21.46 | 64.3 |
| 26.34 | 78.6 |
| 28.45 | 92.9 |

(See Section 5.4 for more information about probability plotting concepts.)

The ranked life data values are then plotted with the corresponding percentage plot position values on Weibull probability paper to create a best-fit line as noted by the solid line shown in Figure 12.1

The shape parameter ($b$) is determined from the slope of the curve to be 3.1 by drawing a line parallel to the best-fit line to a key that is found on the Weibull probability paper. The characteristic life ($k$) is determined by noting the usage value corresponding to a 63.2% percentage point, which yields an approximate value of 21.0. These values for $b$ and $k$ are considered the best estimates for the unknown parameter within Equation (12.1). Figure 12.1 illustrates these procedures to determine $b$ and $k$; King (1981) discusses the procedures in more depth.

Other information that can be noted from the graph is, for example, that the best estimate for $B_{25}$ is approximately 14.0 (i.e., 75% of the components are expected to survive a usage of 14.0 without failure) and the best estimate for the median life $B_{50}$ is approximately 18.6.

Since the output Weibull distribution is not generally symmetrical, the average life of a Weibull plot is not normally the 50% failure point. Table L is useful to determine the percentage value that relates to the average life as a function of Weibull shape parameters (Lipson and Sheth 1973). This table yields a value of 50.7%, which is only slightly larger than the median value for this particular shape parameter. Note that when all the data fails, an average (mean) life and confidence interval could be determined using the techniques discussed in Chapter 7; however, this approach is not appro-

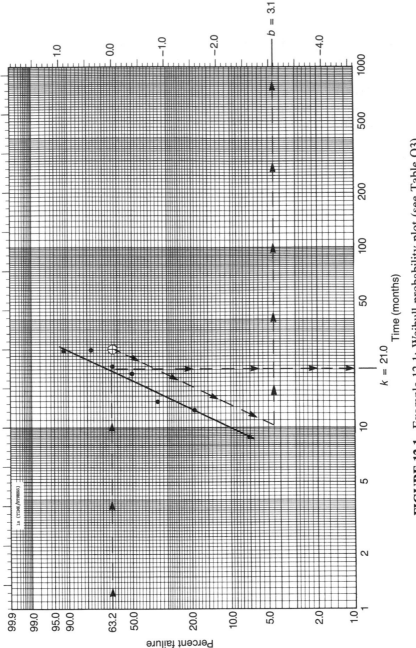

**FIGURE 12.1.** Example 12-1: Weibull probability plot (see Table Q3).

EXAMPLE 12-2: WEIBULL HAZARD PLOT WITH CENSORED DATA    **167**

priate with censored data and it cannot give information about the tails of the distribution.

## 12.4.  EXAMPLE 12-2: WEIBULL HAZARD PLOT WITH CENSORED DATA

Assume that the printwheel life failure times from Example 12-1 also contained four censored times of 13.00, 20.00, 29.00, and 29.00 (i.e., they were taken off test at these times). These times are noted in the following table by a plus sign.

As noted in Chapter 5, for ease of manual calculations, this text uses hazard plot techniques. The procedure described in Section 5.5 yields a cumulative hazard plot percentage shown in the following table.

| Time of Failure | Reverse Rank ($j$) | Hazard ($100/j$) | Cumulative Hazard |
|---|---|---|---|
| 8.50   | 11 | 9.1  | 9.1   |
| 12.54  | 10 | 10.0 | 19.1  |
| 13.00 + | 9 |      |       |
| 13.75  | 8  | 12.5 | 31.6  |
| 19.75  | 7  | 14.3 | 45.9  |
| 20.00 + | 6 |      |       |
| 21.46  | 5  | 20.0 | 65.9  |
| 26.34  | 4  | 25.0 | 90.9  |
| 28.45  | 3  | 33.3 | 124.2 |
| 29.00 + | 2 |      |       |
| 29.00 + | 1 |      |       |

The time to failure values are then plotted with the corresponding cumulative hazard values on Weibull hazard paper to create the plot shown in Figure 12.2. The percent probability value readings can then be noted and interpreted similar to Examples 5-2 and 12-1.

A comparison of the results from the manual analyses for Example 12-1 and 12-2 yields

| Data | $b$ | $k$ | $B_{50}$ | $B_{25}$ |
|---|---|---|---|---|
| 7 failures + 4 censored points | 2.3 | 26.0 | 22.0 | 15.0 |
| 7 failures | 3.1 | 21.0 | 18.6 | 14.0 |

The characteristic life ($k$) is noted to be obviously larger (as it should be) with the censored data set (which is also reflected in the values for $B_{50}$ and $B_{25}$).

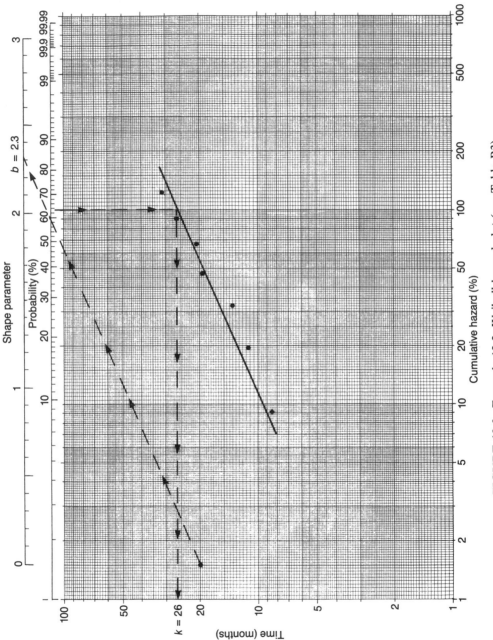

**FIGURE 12.2.** Example 12-2: Weibull hazard plot (see Table R3).

## 12.5. NONLINEAR DATA PLOTS

When the data do not follow a "straight line" on a Weibull probability or
hazard plot, the data are not from a Weibull distribution. In this case the
probability or hazard plot may be telling us a story; the appearance of data
plotted on probability or hazard paper can give insight to better understanding
the device failure modes. For example, when the data plot has a knee in the
curve, this could be indicating that the data are from two different distributions.
A knee may be prevalent in a plot when, for example, a device experiences
a definite transition between early-life failures to a constant failure rate.

To better describe the overall frequency of cumulative failures as a function
of usage when multiple distributions are present, the data can be split into
groups of data from the differing distributions. The data are then analyzed
in these groups and combined mathematically using the equation.

$$F(t) = 1 - \{[1 - F_1(t)] \times [1 - F_2(t)] \times \cdots \times [1 - F_n(t)]\} \quad (12.2)$$

Note that this equation does not require $F_1(t)$, $F_2(t)$, and so on to all be
from a Weibull distribution. Data should be split into groups of various
distributions that make physical sense; however, in reality it is often difficult
to have a large enough test effort to be able to get to this level of detail in
the analysis.

The above described "knee characteristic" of a Weibull plot from two
different distributions can be used in a basic test strategy. For example, a
test can be designed to optimize the duration of a screen that is going to be
installed in a manufacturing process (Navy 1979). It is desirable that the
screen duration is at a point where a knee occurs in the curve such that the
early-life problems are detected and fixed in the manufacturing plant, as
opposed to the customer's office. This situation can take the form described
by Jensen and Petersen (1982) and illustrated by the situation where a small
number of poor parts could be considered to be from a freak distribution,
while a larger portion of parts is from the main distribution (see Figure 12.3).
It should be noted that the parts in the freak distribution could have a Weibull
slope that indicates wear-out tendencies.

Another situation where one overall Weibull distribution may not be applicable is when analysis of test data indicates that a mechanism experienced
several distinctly different failure modes. In this situation the data might
again be split up, analyzed separately, and then combined via Equation
(12.2).

Still another common occurrence is for the data to have a convex shape.
Often with this scenario the data can be fitted by transforming the data into
a three-parameter Weibull model [see Equation (A.19)].* This can be done
by subtracting from all the data points a constant (i.e., location parameter,

* Equations beginning with letter A can be found in Appendix A.

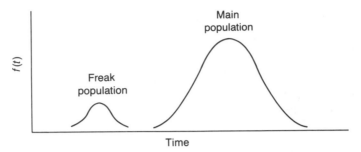

**FIGURE 12.3.** Freak and main distribution.

$x_0$) of such a magnitude that a two-parameter Weibull plot of the adjusted data follow a straight line.

Data transformation to a three-parameter Weibull distribution can make sense if the data are to describe a physical phenomena where the probability of failing at any value from zero up to the shift value is zero. This is not usually a reasonable physical restriction to make in the case of a reliability test since the device always has a chance of failing the instant after it has begun to perform its intended function (without considering dead on arrival devices).

However, there are situations where a three-parameter Weibull distribution may be applicable; for example, when considering the tensile strength of a material, it is a reasonable to assume that there is zero chance for a steel bar to break until some axial force much larger than zero is applied. This physical value of shift for the expected zero probability point is the location parameter (i.e., $x_0$) within the three-parameter Weibull distribution.

## 12.6. REDUCED SAMPLE SIZE TESTING: WEIBULL DISTRIBUTION

It is best to have a test where many components are tested long enough such that there are many failure points to plot using Weibull analysis considerations. However, because of economic constraints, it is not often possible to have a large number of devices under test for a long period of time.

This section describes a test strategy that can be used to assess the feasibility of a mean life criterion if the failure distribution is Weibull and the practitioner is able (and willing) to assume a value for the shape parameter ($b$).

For data $t_i$ the transformed values $U_i = t_i^b$ come from the exponential distribution with mean $\theta = k^b$ (Nelson 1982), where $k$ is the characteristic life constant. From these relationships the methodologies for exponential data can be used to obtain estimates, confidence limits, and predictions, noting that the precision of this approach is dependent on the accuracy of $b$.

To use this relationship, consider a test that is to have no failures and the resultant mean life $T_d$ confidence interval is to have the form $T_d \geqslant$

EXAMPLE 12-3: A ZERO FAILURE WEIBULL TEST STRATEGY    **171**

criterion. $T_d$ can then be translated to a characteristic life criterion by using equation A.22.

From the the exponential distribution that has a mean ($\theta$) of

$$\theta = k^b \tag{12.3}$$

the individual transformed test times are

$$t_i = U_i^{1/b} \tag{12.4}$$

From Table K it is noted that the total test time ($T$) to obtain a confidence interval for $\theta$ (i.e., $1/\rho$ in Table K) is

$$T = (B_{r;c})\theta \tag{12.5}$$

It then follows for a zero failure test strategy that when $n$ units are on test for an equal time period, $U_i$ would be

$$U_i = [(B_{r;c})(\theta)]/n \tag{12.6}$$

Substitution of Equations (12.3) and (12.6) into (12.4) yields

$$t_i = \{[(B_{r;c})(k^b)]/n\}^{1/b}$$

Reducing this equation results in Equation (12.7), which can be used to determine the amount of individual test time ($t_i$) that ($n$) devices need to experience during a "zero failure permissible" test:

$$t_i = k[(B_{r;c})/n]^{1/b} \tag{12.7}$$

## 12.7. EXAMPLE 12-3: A ZERO FAILURE WEIBULL TEST STRATEGY

A previous reliability test indicated that the Weibull shape parameter was 2.18 for an automobile clutch. How long should a test consisting of 1, 2, 3, or 10 samples be tested to yield an 80% confidence bound that the mean life ($T_d$) is greater than or equal to 100,000 km of automobile usage, given that no failures occur?

From Equation (A.22) and use of the $\Gamma$ function in Table H, the 100,000-km mean life criterion equates to a characteristic life criterion of

$$k = \frac{T_d}{\Gamma(1 + 1/b)} = \frac{100,000}{\Gamma(1 + 1/2.18)} = \frac{100,000}{\Gamma(1.459)} = \frac{100,000}{0.8856} = 112,918$$

For an 80% confidence interval with no permissible failures, Table K yields $B_{0;0.8} = 1.609$. If there were only one device on test, Equation (12.7) yields

$$t_i = 112{,}918 \left[ \frac{(1.609)}{1} \right]^{1/2.18} = 140{,}447$$

A summary of the individual test time requirements with no device failures for 1, 2, 3, and 10 sample size alternatives is

| Sample Size | Individual Device Test Time |
|:-----------:|:---------------------------:|
| 1 | 140,447 |
| 2 | 102,194 |
| 3 | 84,850 |
| 10 | 48,843 |

In general, the shape parameter estimate needs to be accurate so that the unit test times will be accurate. However, this accuracy requirement decreases as the test time for each unit approaches the average life criterion. Hence, when assessing wear-out concerns, it is normally better to test a smaller number of units to the approximate mean life usage than testing a large number to only a portion of this usage. When there is uncertainty about the accuracy of the shape parameter estimate, the sample size can be calculated for several differing shape parameters. This information can yield better understanding of the sensitivity of this underlying assumption when choosing a sample size.

The objective of this test approach is that no failures occur; however, at the completion of a test, many more failures may occur than originally anticipated. Times of failure data from a test could then be analyzed using probability or hazard plotting techniques to determine an experimental value for the shape parameter, and so forth.

## 12.8. LOG-NORMAL DISTRIBUTION

The log-normal distribution (see Section 6.7) is an analysis alternative to the Weibull distribution. If this distribution is applicable, the equations for the normal distribution are appropriate through a log transformation. Data can also be plotted on log-normal probability paper (see Table Q2) or hazard paper (see Table R2) using the plot positions noted in Table P.

## 12.9. EXAMPLE 12-4: LOG-NORMAL PROBABILITY PLOT ANALYSIS

Given the printwheel failure times of Example 12-1, analyze the data using log-normal probability plotting techniques.

Table P is used to yield the same percentage plot position values illustrated in Example 12-1; however, this time the data are plotted on log-normal probability paper to create Figure 12.4. It may be difficult from a manual plot to determine whether the Weibull or log-normal distribution fits the data better. With computer programs lack of fit output parameters (see Section B.6) could be compared to choose the best distribution. A comparison of conclusions from the two manual plots (i.e., Figures 12.2 and 12.4) yields:

| Analysis | Figure Number | $B_{50}$ | $B_{25}$ |
|---|---|---|---|
| Log-normal | 12.4 | 17.0 | 13.0 |
| Weibull | 12.2 | 18.6 | 14.0 |

## 12.10. DO-IT-SMARTER CONSIDERATIONS

When planning a reliability test for a device, the practitioner needs to remember that in order to plot a point on Weibull or log normal probability paper a failure must occur. With the reliability of components improving with technology, the task of quantifying the reliability of these components during test is becoming increasingly difficult. To address this issue, Chapter 10 described acceleration models that can be used to accelerate failure modes. As noted also in this chapter, step stress testing (Nelson 1990; Tobias and Trindade 1986) is another test alternative that can be considered.

However, even with accelerated testing methods, test durations can be very long. Another approach to address this problem is to consider monitoring another response in conjunction with noting when the device fails completely. From experience it might be "known" for a type of device that whenever a particular output signal degrades 10%, the device has reached 20% of its life expectancy. To project the expected device failure usage, the practitioner could then multiply five by the amount of usage that the device had experienced whenever the signal degraded 10%.

If there are wear-out exposures, testing a small number of samples for a long period of time is more effective than testing a large number of samples for a short period. The test duration for the components should be at least to the usage of concern (e.g., life of the assembly that will contain the device). If early-life problems are anticipated, a large number of parts from a manufacturing process should be tested for a relatively "short" period of time

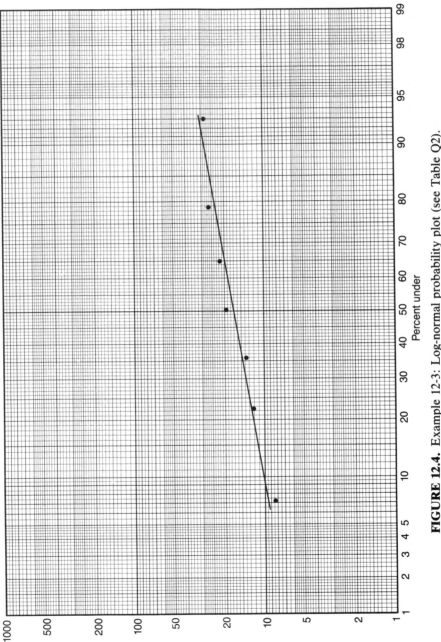

**FIGURE 12.4.** Example 12-3: Log-normal probability plot (see Table Q2).

to capture these failures. In some situations it may be best to conduct both types of tests (possibly concurrently) to evaluate the characteristics of both failure modes.

Time-to-failure data from a screen test of components on the manufacturing line could be tracked using control charting techniques (see Chapter 19). Information from a Weibull analysis of the failure data (from a stable screen test) can be used to optimize the duration of a manufacturer's in-house burn-in test that is used to capture early life failures before customer shipment (see Section 12.5). It should be noted, however, that a burn-in of all manufactured components does not preclude effort that should be taken to improve the manufacturing process so that the number of defects found during the screen test is lower in the future (see Example 3-3).

Additional do-it-smarter consideration thoughts for reliability testing are contained at the end of Chapter 10.

# 13

# FACTORIAL EXPERIMENTS AND VARIANCE COMPONENTS ANALYSIS: CONCEPTS/DESIGNS

Recommended introductory reading: Chapters 2, 3, 4, and 5.

Factorial experiments (i.e., design of experiments, or DOE) can be created such that they are an efficient basic strategy that has a wide range of applications. In fractional experiments the effects of several independent factors (variables) are considered simultaneously in one experiment without evaluating all possible combinations of the factor levels.

This chapter illustrates various experiment design alternatives and considerations with emphasis on two-level fractional factorial designs (as opposed to full factorial designs that consider all possible combinations of factor levels). In this chapter there is also a simple illustration on why two-level fractional factorial experiments work. Chapters 14 and 15 then cover how data can be analyzed using the structure of these designs. Chapter 17 discusses the extension of the concepts to response surface designs. The discussion in this chapter will focus primarily on continuous response designs; however, attribute factorial data is also discussed. Also, the primary discussion in this chapter is on fixed effect models; however, random effect models are discussed in Section 13.22 (see Section 4.8).

## 13.1. THE NEED FOR FRACTIONAL FACTORIAL EXPERIMENTS

To be competitive in today's markets, companies need to design and manufacture quality products within aggressive cost and schedule constraints. Organizations should use those experimentation techniques that are efficient and provide useful information. Fractional factorial experiment techniques are tools that can help satisfy these needs (see Example 2-1).

Because of time constraints, it is natural to focus experiment evaluations around nominal operating conditions. However, customers rarely either receive a "nominally" built machine or use a product under "nominal operating conditions." Similarly a manufacturing process rarely produces products under nominal toleranced conditions. Fractional factorial experiment techniques can aid in the development of quality products that meet the needs of customers even though they might have a variety of different applications. Fractional factorial experiment techniques can also help manufacturing with their process parameters and other considerations so that they create quality products on a continuing basis.

Factors to consider in an experiment (see Example 2-1) to determine whether a product will perform satisfactorily in a customer environment include such considerations as environmental conditions, external loads, product tolerances, and general human factor considerations. Factors for experimental consideration in the manufacturing process are part tolerances, process parameter tolerances, vendor sources, and manufacturing personnel.

If factors (e.g., part tolerances and environmental conditions) are assessed, it is natural for a novice in experimentation techniques to want to monitor changes in an output as a function of factors when they are changed individually (while holding all other factors constant). However, experiments performed at nominal conditions and then at other conditions using a basic one-at-a-time assessment for factor levels are not only inefficient but can also lead to erroneous conclusions (see Example 4-5). It is important to understand the effect factors have collectively on a product so that appropriate changes can be made to reduce variability and deliver a product that is price competitive.

In product development a test strategy needs to give early problem detection and isolation while promoting a reduced product development cycle time along with a low-cost basic design. In manufacturing, quick problem detection and resolution is most important. In addition, efficient techniques are needed to help maintain and continuously improve the manufacturing process. Fractional factorial experiment design techniques can give major benefits to both the development and manufacturing processes.

## 13.2. INITIAL THOUGHTS WHEN SETTING UP A FACTORIAL EXPERIMENT

One major obstacle in implementing an efficient fractional factorial design test strategy is that the initial problem definition may not imply that fractional factorial design concepts are appropriate, when in fact they are the best alternative (see Example 2-1).

A most effective blend is the combination of fractional factorial statistical methods with the skills of experts in a field of concern. Because of their structure, fractional factorial techniques are conducive to evaluating in one experiment a collection of agreed-upon conditions determined by team brainstorming sessions (see Section 3.5). This "team management strategy tool" can be dramatically more efficient than many individuals independently making one-at-a-time experiments.

When designing an experiment, it is most important to first agree upon a clear set of objectives and criteria for the experiment. A consultant or investigator needs to consider any history information and also ask many detailed questions before deciding upon the details of an experiment. Brainstorming and cause-and-effect diagram techniques (see Sections 3.5 and 3.6) can help with collecting this information.

The investigator or consultant should strive to identify all relevant sources of information about factors, their levels, and ranges. Factors that are believed important need to be included in an experiment design such that there will be meaningful results. Factor effects that are not of primary interest for consideration in an experiment should be held constant or blocked (see Section 13.11). In addition, the sequence of experiment trials should be randomized in order to reduce the risk of an unknown/unexpected occurrence jeopardizing accurate conclusions. Care needs to also be exercised such that there is minimal error in the measurements for each trial.

After a proposed experiment is determined, the structure of the experiment is conducive to an individual or team presentation to management and other organizations. The proposed factors, levels of factors, and outputs in the experiment can be presented in a fashion such that individuals can quickly understand the test strategy. Perhaps from this presentation there will be a constructive critique that results in a better implementation strategy.

## 13.3. EXPERIMENT DESIGN CONSIDERATIONS

Examples in this text propose using unreplicated two-level fractional factorial design matrices in Tables M1 to M5.* However, experiment design matrices are available in tabular form in other texts, journals, or computer programs (e.g., Bisgaard 1988; Morris and Mitchell 1988; Taguchi 1987; NBS 1961, 1959, 1957). The basic experiment design strategy suggested in this text is also applicable to many of these design matrix alternatives.

For most people it seems appropriate to have factors with many levels, which can make an experiment become very cumbersome and "impossible" (or unreasonable) to conduct. Reducing the number of factor levels and listing associated assumptions can change the experiment feasibility dramatically (see Example 22-4).

---

* Tables A through R3 are located in Appendix D.

The next question of concern is to determine what resolution (see Section 13.6) should be considered. I believe that many experimental design considerations fall into two general classifications. The first type needs to optimize a process (or help give direction toward a basic problem's resolution), while the second type needs to consider how a product will perform under various situations relative to meeting a specification.

For the first type of classification, factor interaction consideration (see Section 13.7) may be more important than with the second type. In this second type a continuous response may have many factors that are significant; however, if the product is well within criterion, additional analysis may not be necessary. If the significant factor information will not lead to a cost reduction or a reduction in manufacturing variability, the experimenter should avoid analysis paralysis and move on to the next problem/investigation.

There may be a higher probability of having problems in a fractional factorial experiment from either unconscious experimental bias or data collection techniques that introduce large amounts of error, as opposed to an experiment that has "too small a sample size." Good techniques can reduce this exposure to experimental problems. First, the sequence in which the experimental trials are performed should be random to avoid the type of problem illustrated in Example 4-3. Second, external experimentation factors should be blocked to avoid confusion between these external factors and experimental factor effects (see Section 13.11).

Note that for some factors, randomization may be a very difficult requirement to implement. Whenever the experiment is not randomized, care must be taken to consider that a bias (e.g., that may have been introduced in an experiment for convenience) could be the real reason that a factor is significant.

At the end of a fractional factorial experiment, a confirmation experiment should be performed to better quantify and confirm the magnitude of significant effects. A comparison test (see Example 9-1) may, for example, be appropriate to compare an old design with new design considerations that were found significant within the experiment.

The following is a checklist of items to consider when designing a two-level fractional factorial experiment. Note that both a team brainstorming session and historical information should be considered when addressing these issues.

List the objectives of the experiment.

List the assumptions.

List factors that might be considered in the experiment.

Choose factors and their levels to consider in the experiment.

List what "other factors" will not be evaluated in the experiment and will be held "constant."

Reduce "many-level" factors to "two-level" factors (see Section 13.5 and Example 22-4).

Choose the number of trials and resolution of the experiment (see Sections 13.6 and 13.9).

Determine if any of the factors will need to be blocked (see Section 13.11).

Change, if possible, from an attribute response consideration to a continuous response consideration (see Sections 13.5 and 13.19).

Determine if any design center points will be used to check for curvature (see Section 13.12).

Choose a fractional factorial design (see Section 13.10).

Determine whether the sample size is reasonable (see Section 13.18).

Determine a random order trial sequence to use.

Determine what can be done to minimize the amount of experimental error.

Determine what approach will be used to address experimental error.

Determine a follow-up experiment strategy (e.g., a higher resolution follow-up experiment or confirmation experiment).

Plan the approach to be used for the analysis (see Section 13.4).


## 13.4. EXPERIMENT DESIGN CONSIDERATIONS: FACTOR SIGNIFICANCE

Chapters 14 and 15 illustrate approaches to test for factor significance given an estimate for error. If a factor is "significant," the statement is made with an $\alpha$ risk of being wrong (i.e., the null hypothesis is rejected). However, the inverse is not true about factors not found to be significant. In other words there is *not* an $\alpha$ risk of being wrong when these factors are *not* significant. The reason for this is that the second statement relates to a $\beta$ risk (i.e., acceptance of the null hypothesis, which is a function of the sample size and $\delta$) (see Section 4.5). Section C.4 in Appendix C discusses an approach where the sample size of a factorial experiment is made large enough to address the statement of nonsignificance with $\beta$ risk.

Section 13.13 discusses alternatives that can be used to assess experimental error. Probability plotting of the factor effects (see Chapters 14 and 15) is an another approach that is used to visually assess the "significance" of effects.


## 13.5. EXPERIMENT DESIGN CONSIDERATIONS: FACTORS AND RESPONSES

Continuous outputs (as opposed to attribute outputs) are normally desired for fractional factorial designed experiments. A typical fractional factorial conclusion could be "voltage is significant at a level of 0.05." If voltage were a two-level factor consideration in the experiment, this statement means that a response is affected by changing the voltage from one level to another, and there is only an $\alpha$ risk of 0.05 of this statement not being true (see Section 4.5). Statements can also be made about the amount of change in output that is expected between the levels of factors. For example, a "best estimate" for a significant factor might be: a shift from the high tolerance level of the voltage factor to its low tolerance level will cause an output timing change of 4 milliseconds (msec).

Factor levels also can take different forms. Levels can be quantitative or qualitative. A quantitative level is when the factor can take on one of many different values (e.g., the temperature input in a manufacturing process step), while qualitative levels take on discrete values (e.g., material $x$ versus material $y$). The results obtained from the two-level manual fractional factorial analysis techniques discussed in this text are the same. However, the effect from two levels of a quantitative factor can be used to interpolate an output response for other magnitudes of the factor (assuming that a linear relationship exists between the two-level factors).

Choosing factors with appropriate levels is an important step when designing an experiment. It is "natural" to initially think that factors might need three, four, or more level state considerations when setting up an experiment. However, if, in general, all factors within an experiment can be creatively changed to two levels, greater benefits can be achieved from the experiment design (see Example 22-4).

In some situations this transition down from "many-level" to two-level considerations can take much thought. For example, instead of considering how a process operates at three temperatures, an experiment perhaps could first only be investigated at the tolerance extremes of temperature. If there were concern that the end condition levels of the factor have similar effects and the midpoint was significantly different, one tolerance extreme versus a nominal condition could be used in an initial experiment. If this factor is still considered important after the first experiment, the second tolerance extreme can be addressed in another experiment in conjunction with the nominal condition or another factor level setting. When the number of factors is not large, a response surface design may be an appropriate alternative (see Chapter 17).

If a factor has many levels (e.g., four vendor sources), perhaps previous knowledge can be used to choose the two extreme scenarios within the initial experiment considerations (realizing that there is a trade-off between the risk of making a wrong decision relative to the selection of vendors and the implications of a larger sample size). If there appears to be a difference between these two levels, then additional investigation of the other levels may naturally be appropriate. Example 22-4 has more discussion on the reduction of a many-level experiment down to a two-level experiment.

## 13.6. EXPERIMENT DESIGN CONSIDERATIONS: EXPERIMENT RESOLUTION

Full factorial designs are used to assess all possible combination of the factor levels under consideration. Within these designs, information is contained about all possible interactions of the factor levels. For example, a full factorial experiment consisting of 7 two-level factors will require 128 trials ($2^7 = 128$). There will be information in this experiment about all possible interactions, including whether all 7 factors work in conjunction to affect the output (defined as a seven-factor interaction). Also, information is contained about lower factor interactions—that is, any combination of 6, 5, 4, 3, and 2 factors.

In many situations three-factor and higher interaction effects can be considered small relative to the main effects and two-factor interaction effects. Because of this, interactions higher than two in many situations can be ignored. When this can be done, a smaller number of trials are needed to assess the same number of factors. A fractional factorial design can assess the factors with various "resolutions" (see instruction on Table M1). A resolution V design evaluates the main effects and two-factor interactions independently. A resolution IV design evaluates the main effects and confounded (i.e., mixed up) two-factor interactions (i.e., there is aliasing of the two-factor interactions). A resolution III design evaluates the main effects, which are confounded with the two-factor interactions. Tables M1 to M5 will later be used to give test alternatives for each of these resolutions. Plackett and Burman (1946) have other resolution III design alternatives; however, the fashion in which two factor interactions are confounded with main effects is often complicated.

## 13.7. CONCEPTUAL EXPLANATION: TWO-LEVEL FULL FACTORIAL EXPERIMENTS AND TWO-FACTOR INTERACTIONS

This section discusses the basics of two-level full factorial experiment designs. The next section illustrates why fractional factorial design matrices "work."

When executing a full factorial experiment, a response is achieved for all combinations of the factor levels. The three-factor experiment design in Table 13.1 is a two-level full factorial experiment. For analyzing three factors, eight trials are needed (i.e., $2^3 = 8$) to address all assigned combinations of the factor levels. The plus/minus notation illustrates the high/low level of the factors. When a trial is performed, the factors are set to the noted plus/minus limits (levels) and a response value(s) is then noted for the trial.

Within this experiment design each factor is executed at its high and low level an equal number of times. It can be noted that there are an equal number of plus and minus signs in each column. The best estimate factor effects can be assessed by noting the difference in the average outputs of

**TABLE 13.1. Two-Level Full Factorial Experiment Design**

| Number of Trial | Factor Designation | | | Experiment Response |
|---|---|---|---|---|
| | $A$ | $B$ | $C$ | |
| 1 | + | + | + | $x_1$ |
| 2 | + | + | − | $x_2$ |
| 3 | + | − | + | $x_3$ |
| 4 | + | − | − | $x_4$ |
| 5 | − | + | + | $x_5$ |
| 6 | − | + | − | $x_6$ |
| 7 | − | − | + | $x_7$ |
| 8 | − | − | − | $x_8$ |

the trials. Equation (13.1) shows the calculation of this relationship for the factor $A$ effect.

$$[(\overline{x}_{[A+]}) - (\overline{x}_{[A-]})] = \frac{x_1 + x_2 + x_3 + x_4}{4} - \frac{x_5 + x_6 + x_7 + x_8}{4} \quad (13.1)$$

The difference determined by the equation is an estimate of the average response change from the high to the low level of $A$. The other factor effects can similarly be calculated.

Interaction effects are a measurement of factor levels "working together" to affect a response (e.g., the product's performance degrades whenever temperature is high in conjunction with humidity being low). In addition to being able to calculate the main effects, all interaction effects can be assessed given these eight trials with three factors, as shown in Table 13.2. "Interaction columns" can be generated in the matrix by multiplying the appropriate

**TABLE 13.2. Full Factorial Experiment Design with Interaction Considerations**

| Number of Trial | Factors and Interactions | | | | | | | Experiment Response |
|---|---|---|---|---|---|---|---|---|
| | $A$ | $B$ | $C$ | $AB$ | $BC$ | $AC$ | $ABC$ | |
| 1 | + | + | + | + | + | + | + | $x_1$ |
| 2 | + | + | − | + | − | − | − | $x_2$ |
| 3 | + | − | + | − | − | + | − | $x_3$ |
| 4 | + | − | − | − | + | − | + | $x_4$ |
| 5 | − | + | + | − | + | − | − | $x_5$ |
| 6 | − | + | − | − | − | + | + | $x_6$ |
| 7 | − | − | + | + | − | − | + | $x_7$ |
| 8 | − | − | − | + | + | + | − | $x_8$ |

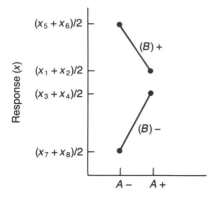

**FIGURE 13.1.** A two-factor interaction plot.

columns together and noting the resultant sign using conventional algebraic rules (as illustrated in Table 13.2). In this table the third trial sign, in the $AB$ column, for example, is determined by multiplying the $A$ sign $(+)$ by the $B$ sign $(-)$ to achieve an $AB$ sign $(-)$.

Two-factor interaction effects are similarly noted. For the $AB$ interaction, the best estimate of the effect can be determined from Table 13.2 by using Equation (13.2):

$$\bar{x}_{[AB^+]} - \bar{x}_{[AB^-]} = \frac{x_1 + x_2 + x_7 + x_8}{4} - \frac{x_3 + x_4 + x_5 + x_6}{4} \quad (13.2)$$

A question of concern in a factorial experiment is whether the calculated effects are large enough to be considered "significant." In other words is the resultant from Equation (13.1) [or (13.2)], for example, a large number relative to differences caused by experimental error (see Section 13.13)?

If a two-factor interaction is determined significant, more information is determined about the interaction through a plot such as that shown in Figure 13.1. From this plot it is noted that there are four combinations of the levels of the $AB$ factors ($AB$ levels: $++$, $+-$, $-+$, and $--$). To make the interaction plot, the average value for each of these combinations is first calculated [e.g., $AB = ++$ effect is $(x_1 + x_2)/2$]. The averages are then plotted as shown in Figure 13.1. In this plot a $A^-B^+$ yields a high output response, while $A^-B^-$ yields a low output; the levels of these factors interact to affect the output level.

If there is no interaction between factors, the lines on an interaction plot will be parallel. The overall effect initially determined for the interaction (i.e., $\bar{x}_{[AB^+]} - \bar{x}_{[AB^-]}$) was a measure for the lack of parallelism of the lines.

## 13.8. CONCEPTUAL EXPLANATION: SATURATED TWO-LEVEL FRACTIONAL FACTORIAL EXPERIMENTS

When many factors are considered, full factorials can yield a very large test sample size, whereas a saturated fractional factorial can require a much reduced sample size. For example, an 8-trial saturated fractional factorial experiment can assess the 7 two-level factors, while it would take 128 trials as a full factorial.

The basic concept of creating a saturated fractional factorial experiment design is illustrated in Table 13.3. In this table, the calculated interaction columns from Table 13.2 are used to describe the levels of 4 additional factors, which now makes the total number of two-level factor considerations 7 in 8 trials (i.e., a saturated fractional factorial design).

The disadvantage of this saturated fractional factorial experiment is the confounding of the two-factor interaction effects and the main effects. There is confounding of the $AB$ interaction and the main effect $D$; however, there is also confounding of factor $D$ and other two-factor interactions, because of the introduction of the additional factors $D$, $E$, $F$, and $G$.

Since each column can now have more than one meaning, each column is assigned a number, which in this text is referred to as a contrast column number (see Tables M1 to M5 and N1 to N3).

It may be hard for a reader to believe that all main effect information of seven two-level factors can be obtained in only eight trials. There may be a concern that the significance of one factor could affect the decision about another factor. To address this concern, assume $E$ is the only significant factor and there are no interactions. The question of concern, for example, is whether factor $E$ can affect the decision whether factor $A$ is significant.

**TABLE 13.3. Saturated Fractional Factorial Experiment: Eight Trials, Seven Factors**

| Number of Trial | \multicolumn{7}{c}{Factors and Interactions} | Experiment Response |
|---|---|---|---|---|---|---|---|---|
| | $A$ | $B$ | $C$ | $D$ $AB$ | $E$ $BC$ | $F$ $AC$ | $G$ $ABC$ | |
| 1 | + | + | + | + | + | + | + | $x_1$ |
| 2 | + | + | − | + | − | − | − | $x_2$ |
| 3 | + | − | + | − | − | + | − | $x_3$ |
| 4 | + | − | − | − | + | − | + | $x_4$ |
| 5 | − | + | + | − | + | − | − | $x_5$ |
| 6 | − | + | − | − | − | + | + | $x_6$ |
| 7 | − | − | + | + | − | − | + | $x_7$ |
| 8 | − | − | − | + | + | + | − | $x_8$ |

**TABLE 13.4. Example Output from Table 13.3 Design**

| Number of Trial | A | E | Experiment Response |
|:---:|:---:|:---:|:---:|
| 1 | + | + | 500 |
| 2 | + | − | 0 |
| 3 | + | − | 0 |
| 4 | + | + | 500 |
| 5 | − | + | 500 |
| 6 | − | − | 0 |
| 7 | − | − | 0 |
| 8 | − | + | 500 |

A subset of the matrix from Table 13.3 is shown in Table 13.4 with output that was designed to make factor $E$ very significant.

The $A$ and $E$ factor mean effects are

$$\bar{x}_{[E^+]} - \bar{x}_{[E^-]} = \frac{x_1 + x_4 + x_5 + x_8}{4} - \frac{x_2 + x_3 + x_6 + x_7}{4}$$

$$= \frac{500 + 500 + 500 + 500}{4} - \frac{0 + 0 + 0 + 0}{4} = 500$$

$$\bar{x}_{[A^+]} - \bar{x}_{[A^-]} = \frac{x_1 + x_2 + x_3 + x_4}{4} - \frac{x_5 + x_6 + x_7 + x_8}{4}$$

$$= \frac{500 + 0 + 0 + 500}{4} - \frac{500 + 0 + 0 + 500}{4} = 0$$

This example illustrates that even though factor $E$ was "very significant," this significance did not affect our decision about the nonsignificance of factor $A$. Like factor $A$, factors $B$, $C$, $D$, $F$, and $G$, can similarly be shown to be "not significant."

The purpose of this example is to illustrate that a main effect will not be confounded with another main effect in this seven-factor, eight-trial experiment design. However, the experimenter must be aware that it is possible that there is an interaction (e.g., $BC$) that could be making factor $E$ appear significant even though factors $B$ and $C$ individually were not determined significant.

## 13.9. TWO-LEVEL FRACTIONAL FACTORIAL DESIGN ALTERNATIVES

Section 13.8 describes the creation of a saturated fractional factorial experiment design from a full factorial design. However, there are other two-level fractional factorial design alternatives between full and saturated fractional factorial designs, which can give differing "resolutions" to the experiment design. If the procedure used in section 13.8 were used to create these test matrices, the question of concern is how to make the matches of the factors to the interaction columns such that there is minimal confounding (e.g., of main effects and two-factor interactions). Tables M1 to M5 (see Section 13.10) manage this issue by making the column selections for the practitioner, while Tables N1 to N3 show the aliasing structure of the design matrices.

Table 13.5 (and Table M1) indicates test possibilities for 4, 8, 16, 32, and 64 two-level factor designs with resolution V+, V, IV, and III, as defined in Table 13.5. To illustrate the use of Table 13.5, consider the eight-trial test alternatives that are shown. In the experiment design shown in Table 13.1, there were three two-level factors in eight trials; hence, it is a full factorial. This test alternative is shown in Table 13.5 as a 3 (number of factors) at the intersection of V+ column (full factorial) and the row designation 8 (number of trials).

Consider now the test design in Table 13.3. For this test design there are seven factors in eight trials. From Table 13.5 it is noted to be a resolution III design, which by definition describes designs that have the confounding of two-factor interactions and main effects. As noted earlier, there is confounding of the main effect $D$ in this design and the $AB$ interaction effect (and some other two-factor and higher order interactions); hence, the significance of this contrast could technically be caused by either the effect $D$ or $AB$ (or other interactions). In a resolution III (i.e., screening design), the experimenter normally initially assumes that the $D$ level is significant and

**TABLE 13.5. Number of Two-Level Factor Considerations Possible for the Various Full and Fractional Factorial Design Alternatives in Table M**

| Number of Trials | Experiment Resolution | | | |
|---|---|---|---|---|
| | V+ | V | IV | III |
| 4 | 2 | 3 | | |
| 8 | 3 | | 4 | 5–7 |
| 16 | 4 | 5 | 6–8 | 9–15 |
| 32 | 5 | 6 | 7–16 | 17–31 |
| 64 | 6 | 7–8 | 9–32 | 33–63 |

where resolution is defined as

V+: Full two-level factorial.
  V: All main effects and two-factor interactions are unconfounded with either main effects or two-factor interactions.
IV: All main effects are unconfounded by two-factor interactions. Two-factor interactions are confounded with each other.
III: Main effects confounded with two-factor interactions.

then confirm/rejects this theory via a confirmation experiment. It is noted from Table 13.5 that for these designs five, six, or seven factors in eight trials gives a resolution III design.

It is also noted from Table 13.5 that a resolution IV (see Example 22-1) is possible where four two-level factors can be assessed in eight trials such that there is no confounding of the main effects and two-factor interaction effects, however, two-factor interaction effects are confounded with each other. Table 13.5 also shows resolution V experiment alternatives where there is no confounding of the main effects and two-factor interaction effects, plus the two-factor interaction effects are not confounded with each other (e.g., 5 factors in 16 trials) (Diamond 1989).

It should be noted that a process called fold over can be used to create a resolution IV design from a resolution III design. To create a fold-over design simply include with the original resolution III design a second fractional factorial design with all the signs reversed (Box et al. 1978; Montgomery 1984). This fold-over process can be useful in the situation where the experimenter has performed a resolution III design initially and now wishes to remove the confounding of the main effects and the two-factor interaction effects.

The next section of this chapter will show how the experiment trials noted in Table 13.5 can be obtained from Table M.

## 13.10. DESIGNING A TWO-LEVEL FRACTIONAL FACTORIAL EXPERIMENT USING TABLES M AND N

In this text there are some useful two-level full and fractional factorial design alternatives (Diamond 1989) that are summarized (in an easy-to-use format) in Tables M1 to M5 of this text. The confounding structure of these designs are shown in Tables N1 to N3. These designs may look different from the two-level design matrices suggested by other texts; however, they are very similar (if not exactly the same) to other two-level design matrices.

A practitioner could use Table M to determine the experiment trials. Data analysis could then be done by probability plotting the effects as described in Chapter 14 or, using a computer program that permits the entry of the factor level considerations for each trial, as described in Chapter 15. It should be noted that a commercially available computer program might only permit the analysis of data taken from an experiment design structure in the format that it creates. If the practitioner chooses to use such a computer program, the experiment design trials should be created using the computer software that will be used for the data analysis.

In Tables M1 to M5 the rows of the matrix define the trial configurations; hence, if 16 rows are defined, there will be 16 trials. The columns are used to define the two-level states of the factors for each trial, where the level designations are + or −. A step-by-step description of how to create an experiment design using these tables is found in Table M1. Example 13-1 illustrates the use of Tables M1 to M5 along with Tables N1 to N3.

After the number of factors, resolution, and number of trials is chosen, a design can then be determined from the tables where columns are chosen from left to right using those identified by an asterisk (*) and the numbers sequentially in the header, until the number of columns equals the number of factors in the experiment. The contrast column numbers are then assigned sequential alphabetic characters from left to right. These numbers from the original matrix are noted and cross referenced to Tables N1 to N3, if information is desired about two-factor interactions and two-factor interaction confounding. Examples 13.1, 13.2, and 13.3 illustrate the use of these tables.

The next two sections of this chapter discuss blocking and center point considerations that may be needed when setting up a factorial experiment. There then follows a section that discusses experimental error.

## 13.11. BLOCKING

Many experiments can inadvertently give results that are biased. For example, error can occur in the analysis of experimental data if no consideration is given during the execution of an experiment toward the usage of more than one piece of equipment, operator, and/or test days. Blocking is a means to handle nuisance factors so that they do not distort the analysis of the factors that are of interest.

Consider, for example, that the experiment design in Table 13.3 as conducted sequentially in the numeric sequence shown over a two-day period (trials 1–4 on day 1 and trials 5–8 on day 2). Consider (unknown to the test designer) that humidity conditions affect the process results dramatically. As luck would have it, the weather conditions changed and it started raining very heavily on the second day. Results from the experiment would lead the experimenter to believe that factor $A$ was very significant since this factor was + on the first day and − on the second day, when, in fact, the humidity conditions caused by the rain was the real source of significance.

To avoid this unplanned confounding, experiments are blocked on such considerations. For example, in Table 13.3, "day" could have been blocked using the $ABC$ interaction column. The trial numbers 1, 4, 6, and 7 could then be exercised in random sequence the first day, while the other four trials could be exercised in random sequence on the second day. If the block on "day" was shown to be significant, then the conclusion would be that something changed from day 1 to 2; however, the specific cause of the difference may not be understood to the experimenter from a basic data analysis. More importantly this confounding would not affect decisions made about the other factors of interest.

High-factor interaction contrast columns can be used for the assignment of blocks when there are only two-level blocks to consider, as noted earlier.

However, care must be exercised when there are more than two levels in a block. Consider that four ovens were to be used in an experiment. Undesirable confounding can result if two high-factor interaction contrast columns are arbitrarily chosen to describe the trials that will use each of the ovens (i.e., $--$ = oven 1, $-+$ = oven 2, $+-$ = oven 3, and $++$ = oven 4). There is more discussion on this topic in other texts (Box et al. 1978; Montgomery 1984). Bisgaard (1988) has a booklet of experiment designs that considers blocking. Another alternative to creating a design matrix is to use a commercially available computer package that can create such designs (see Section 2.3).

## 13.12. CURVATURE CHECK

In a two-level experiment design, linearity is assumed between the factor level extremes (see Figure 13.1). When factors are from a continuous scale [i.e., a quantitative factor] (e.g., factor $A$ is an adjustment value that can take on any value from 1 to 10, as opposed to discrete levels [i.e., a qualitative factor] such as vendor 1 versus vendor 2), a curvature check can be made to evaluate the validity of this assumption by adding center points to the design matrix. To illustrate this procedure, the average of the four response trials for a $2^2$ full factorial (i.e., $--$, $+-$, $-+$, and $++$) can be compared to the average of the trials that were taken separately at the average of levels of each of the factor extremes. The difference between these two numbers can then be compared to see if there is a significant difference in their magnitude (i.e., curvature exists) (Box et al. 1978). In lieu of a manual approach when making this test, some computer programs can peform a statistical check for curvature. The examples discussed in this chapter do not have trials set up to make a curvature check; however, there is more discussion on this topic in the Chapter 17 on response surface methodology.

## 13.13. EXPERIMENTAL ERROR AND DATA ANALYSES

Given a set of continuous trial outputs, statistics is used to determine whether the differences between the levels of the factors on the response (i.e., factor effect) is large enough to be significant (e.g., was the difference between the mean response of factor $A$ at the plus level and the minus level large enough to be significant). To make this determination, an estimate of the error is needed.

Sometimes trials are replicated to give an estimate for this error. Unfortunately, this is often not a practical approach since the total number of experimental trials would double for one replication. Another alternative is to design the experiment with a resolution such that there are extra contrast columns that contain interactions higher than those the design is to capture.

EXAMPLE 13-1: RESOLUTION V FACTORIAL DESIGN     **191**

The information contained in these contrast columns can then be used to estimate the amount of experimental error. Still another alternative is to repeat one or more trials several times within the sequence of random trial selection. These approaches to experimental error can be handled directly via the data input by some computer programs.

An alternative is to use historical information. Equation (19.28) can be used to combine error estimates that originate from different sources. Equation (14.5) can then be used to determine a "significance test" criterion (Diamond 1989). Another approach to analyzing the results from a two-level fractional factorial experiment is to use a probability plot of the effects (see Examples 14-1 and 15-1).

In this text (Chapters 14 and 15) the preceding contrast column combination procedure is used to estimate the experimental error when making significance tests. In addition, probability plots of the effects (see Examples 14-1 and 15-1) is also used to give a visual assessment of the relative magnitude of contrast column effects.

## 13.14. EXAMPLE 13-1: A RESOLUTION V FRACTIONAL FACTORIAL EXPERIMENT DESIGN

The settle-out time of a stepper motor was a critical item within the design of a document printer. The product development organization proposed a change to the stepping sequence algorithm that they believed would improve the settle-out characteristics of the motor. Note that the wording of this problem is very typical within industry. Both specification vagueness and engineering change evaluation exist.

One approach to this problem would be to manufacture several motors and monitor their settle-out time. If we assume that these motors are a random sample (of future production parts?), a confidence interval on the average settle-out characteristics of the motor could then be determined (see Section 7.4). Another approach could also be to determine the percentage of population characters by using probability plotting techniques (see Section 7.8).

However, within the original problem description there was no mention of any specification. What the development organization really was proposing was an improved design. This problem redirection could lead one to perform a comparison test between the old design and new design (see Section 9.3).

Since there are several adjustments and environmental conditions that could effect this comparison, the next question is to determine test conditions for making this comparison. To address this question and perhaps get more information than just "between algorithm effects," a fractional factorial experiment design is useful.

Team brainstorming techniques (see Section 3.5) were used to determine what would be considered in the experiment when one evaluates the response (i.e., motor settle-out time). The resulting factor assignments and associated levels were

| | | Levels | |
|---|---|---|---|
| Factors and Their Designations | | (−) | (+) |
| A: Motor temperature | (mot_temp) | Cold | Hot |
| B: Algorithm | (algor) | Current design | Proposed redesign |
| C: Motor adjustment | (mot_adj) | Low tolerance | High tolerance |
| D: External adjustment | (ext_adj) | Low tolerance | High tolerance |
| E: Supply voltage | (sup_volt) | Low tolerance | High tolerance |

The development and test group team agreed to evaluate the 5 two-level factors in a resolution V design. Table 13.5 (or instructions on Table M1) shows that 16 test trials are needed to get this resolution with the 5 two-level factors. Table 13.6 illustrates the procedure to extract the design matrix trials from Table M3. Table 13.7 shows the resulting resolution V design matrix. From Table N1 it is noted for this design (and shown below) that all the contrast columns contain either a main or two-factor interaction effect; hence, there are no contrast columns that contain only three-factor and higher interactions, which could have been used to estimate experimental error.

From Table 13.7 it is noted that trial 5, for example, would be exercised with

$$
\begin{aligned}
\text{mot\_\_\_temp} \quad (−) &= \text{cold temperature} \\
\text{algor} \quad (+) &= \text{proposed redesign} \\
\text{mot\_\_\_adj} \quad (+) &= \text{high tolerance} \\
\text{ext\_\_\_adj} \quad (+) &= \text{high tolerance} \\
\text{sup\_\_\_volt} \quad (+) &= \text{high tolerance}
\end{aligned}
$$

The interaction assignment that is associated with each contrast column number noted in Table 13.6 from Table N1 is

| 1 | 2 | 3 | 4 | 5 | 6 | 7 | 8 | 9 | 10 | 11 | 12 | 13 | 14 | 15 |
|---|---|---|---|---|---|---|---|---|---|---|---|---|---|---|
| *A | *B | *C | *D | AB | BC | CD | ABD | AC | BD | ABC | BCD | ABCD | ACD | AD |
| | | | | | | | CE | | | DE | AE | *E | BE | |

The results from this experiment design will be analyzed in Examples 14-2 and 15-1. Again we note that all the contrast columns either have a two-factor interaction or main effect consideration. It should also be noted that the factors are highlighted with an asterisk (*) and that the higher order terms which were used to generate the design are also shown.

EXAMPLE 13-1: RESOLUTION V FACTORIAL DESIGN    **193**

**TABLE 13.6.  Example 13-1: Fractional Factorial Experiment Design Creation**

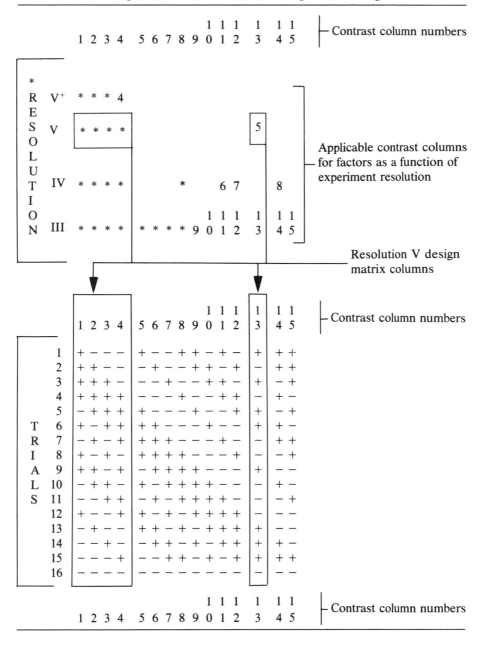

**TABLE 13.7. Example 13-1: Test Design**

| Number of Trial | Factors | | | | |
|---|---|---|---|---|---|
| | A mot__temp | B algor | C mot__adj | D ext__adj | E sup__volt |
| 1 | + | − | − | − | + |
| 2 | + | + | − | − | − |
| 3 | + | + | + | − | + |
| 4 | + | + | + | + | − |
| 5 | − | + | + | + | + |
| 6 | + | − | + | + | + |
| 7 | − | + | − | + | − |
| 8 | + | − | + | − | − |
| 9 | + | + | − | + | + |
| 10 | − | + | + | − | − |
| 11 | − | − | + | + | − |
| 12 | + | − | − | + | − |
| 13 | − | + | − | − | + |
| 14 | − | − | + | − | + |
| 15 | − | − | − | + | + |
| 16 | − | − | − | − | − |
| | 1 | 2 | 3 | 4 | 13 |

Contrast column numbers

## 13.15. EXAMPLE 13-2: A RESOLUTION III FRACTIONAL FACTORIAL SCREENING EXPERIMENT DESIGN

Consider a screening experiment where 15 two-level factors need assessment. Table M3 shows a 16-trial experiment design that can assess 15 factors with resolution III. This test design with factor designations $A-O$ is shown in Table 13.8.

Example 14-1 discusses the data analysis of results from this experiment design. Table N3 shows for this screening experiment, the large amount of aliasing in each contrast column (e.g., factor $A$ is confounded with $BE$, $CI$, $HJ$, $FK$, $LM$, $GN$, $DO$). Unknown two-factor interactions could lead the experimenter to an erroneous conclusion of significance for a main effect.

An experiment with enough trials to address all interaction concerns is desirable; however, the economics to perform such a test may be prohibitive. Instead, experimenters may consider fewer factors. This would lead to less confounding of interactions, but yields no information about the factors not considered within the experiment.

The concerns and issues of missing significant factors during an initial experiment of reasonable size are addressed when using a basic multiexperiment

EXAMPLE 13-2: RESOLUTION III FACTORIAL DESIGN    **195**

test strategy. A screening experiment (perhaps 25% of the resource allottment for the total experimental effort) should "weed out" small effects so that more detailed information can be obtained about the large effects and their interactions via a higher resolution experiment. A resolution III or IV design can be used for a screening experiment. [Daniel (1976) discusses problems associated with resolution III designs.]

There are situations where an experimenter would like a resolution III or IV design but yet manage a "few" two-factor interactions. This is achievable by using Tables M1 to M5 and N1 to N3 collectively when designing an experiment. When using Tables M1 to M5, if there are columns remaining above the number of main effect assignments, these columns can be used for interaction assignments. This is done by using Tables N1 to N3 to assign the factor designations such that these interactions appear within these columns. Example 22-5 exemplifies this procedure. It should be noted that in Tables N1 to N3 the lower tabular interaction considerations are dropped if they are not possible in the experiment (e.g., an $AO$ interaction should be dropped from the list of confounded items if there is no $O$ main effect in the design). This type of test philosophy is suggested sometimes by Taguchi (Taguchi and Konishi 1987).

**TABLE 13.8. Example 13-2: Example 13-2: Sixteen-Trial Experiment Design**

| | A | B | C | D | E | F | G | H | I | J | K | L | M | N | O | |
|---|---|---|---|---|---|---|---|---|---|---|---|---|---|---|---|---|
| | | | | | | | | | | 1 | 1 | 1 | 1 | 1 | 1 | Factor designations |
| | 1 | 2 | 3 | 4 | 5 | 6 | 7 | 8 | 9 | 0 | 1 | 2 | 3 | 4 | 5 | Column contrast designations |
| 1 | + | − | − | − | + | − | − | + | + | − | + | − | + | + | + | |
| 2 | + | + | − | − | − | + | − | − | + | + | − | + | − | + | + | |
| 3 | + | + | + | − | − | − | + | − | − | + | + | − | + | − | + | |
| 4 | + | + | + | + | − | − | − | + | − | − | + | + | − | + | − | |
| 5 | − | + | + | + | + | − | − | − | + | − | − | + | + | − | + | |
| 6 | + | − | + | + | + | + | − | − | − | + | − | − | + | + | − | |
| 7 | − | + | − | + | + | + | + | − | − | − | + | − | − | + | + | |
| 8 | + | − | + | − | + | + | + | + | − | − | − | + | − | − | + | |
| 9 | + | + | − | + | − | + | + | + | + | − | − | − | + | − | − | |
| 10 | − | + | + | − | + | − | + | + | + | + | − | − | − | + | − | |
| 11 | − | − | + | + | − | + | − | + | + | + | + | − | − | − | + | |
| 12 | + | − | − | + | + | − | + | − | + | + | + | + | − | − | − | |
| 13 | − | + | − | − | + | + | − | + | − | + | + | + | + | − | − | |
| 14 | − | − | + | − | − | + | + | − | + | − | + | + | + | + | − | |
| 15 | − | − | − | + | − | − | + | + | − | + | − | + | + | + | + | |
| 16 | − | − | − | − | − | − | − | − | − | − | − | − | − | − | − | |

Number of Trial

Much care needs to be exercised when using this pretest interaction assignment approach because erroneous conclusions can result, if there was, in fact, a significant interaction that was overlooked when setting up the experiment (especially with resolution III experiment designs). When interaction information is needed, it is best to increase the number of trials to capture this information. The descriptive insert to Table M1 (or Table 13.5) is useful, for example, to determine the resolution that is obtainable for six two-level factors when the test size is increased to 32 or 64 trials.

## 13.16. EXAMPLE 13-3: AUTOMOBILE TEST—FRACTIONAL FACTORIAL EXPERIMENT DESIGN

In Example 2-1 a failure rate criterion test was changed to a fractional factorial test strategy since this strategy would better meet the needs of the customer. Example 3-4 described the brainstorming process that was used to choose the experiment factors and their levels. This example discusses the creation of a fractional factorial experiment design for the factors and levels determined in example 3-4.

An eight-trial resolution III design alternative was chosen from Table M2 and is noted in Table 13.9 with the experiment factors and their levels. In this conceptual example the two-factor interactions would then be confounded with the main effects.

The output to each trial (response) could be one or more measurement considerations. For example, it could be the electronically measured response times of the vehicle and the driver to various obstacles placed in the path of the operator in a simulated test environment (similar to that given to airline pilots during training).

Instead of having a "random" sample of people drive automobiles under their "normal" operating conditions (as proposed in the original problem definition in Example 2-1), this test philosophy considers the range of operator

**TABLE 13.9. Example 13-3: An Eight-Trial Test Design**

| Number of Trial | A B C D E F | Where | (−) | (+) |
|---|---|---|---|---|
| 1 | + − − + − + | A = Weather | Wet | Dry |
| 2 | + + − − + − | B = Alcohol | None | Legal limit |
| 3 | + + + − − + | C = Speed | 40 mph | 70 mph |
| 4 | − + + + − − | D = Age of driver | 20–30 | 70–80 |
| 5 | + − + + + − | E = Vehicle | Current | New |
| 6 | − + − + + + | F = Road curvature | None | Curved |
| 7 | − − + − + + | | | |
| 8 | − − − − − − | | | |

EXAMPLE 13-3: AUTOMOBILE TEST–FACTORIAL EXPERIMENT DESIGN    **197**

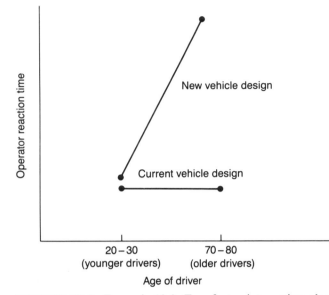

**FIGURE 13.2.** Example 13-3: Two-factor interaction plot.

types along with a range of operating conditions—the thought being that if there is satisfactory performance under extreme conditions (i.e., factor levels are set to "boundary" conditions), then there would probably be satisfactory performance under less extreme conditions.

Consider the hypothetical situation shown in Figure 13.2, where, unknown to the experimenter, the "age of driver" interacts with "vehicle design." Experiments are performed for the purpose of finding useful information that is true so that actions can be taken, as needed, in either the design or the manufacturing process. This plot indicates that elderly drivers have a high reaction time when operating the new vehicle design. Because of this type of information, a design change may then need to be made that improves the safety of this vehicle for elderly people. Detection of this type of problem is most important early in the development cycle, not after the new automobile design is in production. [Note: The automobile example used in this text is only a conceptual example to illustrate how a problem can be redefined for the purpose of do-it-smarter considerations. All "results" and "conclusions" from this "experiment" are fabricated for illustration purposes only.]

The resolution III designs, such as the one shown in Table 13.3, are not normally used to determine two-factor interactions; however, Table N3 can be used to show how the two-level factors are confounded with two-factor interactions. This confounding in the contrast columns (for the design shown in Table 13.9) is noted in Table 13.10.

In this experiment the age of the driver was factor $D$ and the vehicle design was $E$. The preceding $DE$ interaction effect would be described in contrast column 7. Consider that a probability plot of contrast column effects

**TABLE 13.10. Example 13-3: Two-Factor Interaction Confounding from Table N3[a]**

| Contrast Column Number | | | | | | |
|---|---|---|---|---|---|---|
| 1 | 2 | 3 | 4 | 5 | 6 | 7 |
| *A | *B | *C | AB | BC | ABC | AC |
| BD | AD | BE | *D | *E | CD | DE |
| EF | CE | DF | CF | AF | AE | BF |
| CG | FG | AG | EG | DG | *F | *G |
| | | | | | BG | |

[a] Main effects are denoted by *

(see Chapter 15) noted that absolute value effect from contrast column 7 was "significant" compared to the other effects. Since in this experiment there were only six factors (i.e., there was no *G* factor), there was not (by chance) confounding of this interaction effect with any main effects. If there were considerations that were (in fact) important, the experimenter at test completion might speculate that this interaction (or one of the other interactions in this column) were significant. Obviously any of the chosen theories would need to be verified in a confirmation experiment.

This automobile example was introduced early in this text as a conceptual example to illustrate the power of using fractional factorial tests versus a "random" test strategy. As noted previously, there are other practical concerns for this experiment design. For example, it would be unreasonable to assume that one elderly driver would accurately represent the complete population of elderly drivers. Generally several drivers should be considered for each trial assessment. Section 13.19 discusses the situation where the trial response for an experiment is an attribute, which is an alternative response for this type of test. To illustrate this situation, consider 3 out of 10 people having a reaction time that was not quick enough to avoid a simulated obstacle; hence, these people are classified as having an accident for this trial.

Example 18-1 illustrates another conceptual analysis possibility for this example. In this analysis the trials are considered to yield a "logic pass/fail" response.

## 13.17. FACTORIAL DESIGNS THAT HAVE MORE THAN TWO LEVELS

As previously noted, I recommend using either two-level fractional factorial or response surface designs (see Chapter 17). Other statistics books can be used to determine design matrices to use in situations where "many-level" factorials *must* be considered (see Section 13.5 and Example 22-4).

Tables M1 to M5 could be used to create designs that can be used for these test considerations. To do this the contrast columns of the designs in Tables M1 to M5 are combined for these test considerations (e.g., $--$ = source $W$, $-+$ = source $X$, $+-$ = source $Y$, $++$ = source $Z$). However, an additional contrast column needs to be preserved in the case of four levels, since there are three degrees of freedom with 4 levels (4 levels $-$ $1 = 3$ degrees of freedom) (Ross 1988). The contrast column to preserve is the contrast column that normally contains the two-factor interaction effect of the two contrast columns selected to represent the four levels. For example, from Table 13.3, if the $A$ and $B$ contrast columns were combined to define the levels, the $AB$ contrast column should not be assigned a factor. These three contrast columns contain the four-level main effect information. Analysis of the data resulting from this type of experiment can be handled using a computer routine in the manner described in Example 15-1 (e.g., Duncan's multiple range test in Table 15.3).

Again, I believe that for test efficiency most factor level considerations above the level of 2 should be reduced to the value of 2 during an "initial" fractional factorial experiment. Higher level considerations that cannot be eliminated from consideration can still be evaluated in a test strategy that consists of multiple experiments. When the number of factors that significantly affect a response is reduced to a manageable number (via a fractional factorial experiment), response surface analysis techniques (see Chapter 17) can be useful to find the factor levels that optimize a response.

## 13.18. SAMPLE SIZE: A SIMPLE STRATEGY FOR FRACTIONAL FACTORIAL EXPERIMENTS THAT HAVE A CONTINUOUS RESPONSE OUTPUT

Section C.4 of Appendix C discusses a mathematical approach to determine a sample size to use when conducting a fractional factorial experiment. Through the years I have found the following procedure and rationale satisfactory for many (if not most) industrial experiments that have a continuous response output.

I believe that many (if not most) industry experiments can be structured such that they have either 16 or 32 trials, normally with no trial replication and only two-level factor considerations. (Obviously if trials are "cheap" and time is not an issue more trials are better.)

The following discussion illustrates the logic for making this conclusion. With two-level experiment designs advantages are achieved relative to two-factor interaction assessments when the number of trials are $2^n$ (i.e., those containing the number of trials in Tables M1 to M5), where $n$ is a whole number. This will then yield 2, 4, 8, 16, 32, 64, 128, . . . trial experiment design alternatives. Experiments with 2, 4, and 8 trials are in general "too small" to give adequate confidence in the test results. Experiments with 64 and a higher number of trials are usually too expensive. Also, when larger experiments require much manual data collection, the person responsible for this work may become fatigued, causing sloppy data collection. Sloppy data collection can yield a high value for experimental error, which can mask factors that have a relatively small (but important) effect on the response. In addition, any individual trial mistake that goes undetected can jeopardize the accuracy of all conclusions. Sixteen and 32 trial fractional factorial designs are a more manageable design size that can usually address the number of factors of interest with sufficient accuracy. Consider also that a series of shorter tests that give quick feedback can sometimes be more desirable than one long test.

It is perhaps more important than getting a "large sample size" to do everything that is possible to achieve the lowest possible measurement error. Often experimental error can be reduced by simple operator awareness. For an individual experiment trade-offs typically need to be made between the number of factors, number of trials, experiment resolution, and number of possible follow-on experiments.

When someone is introduced to design experiment concepts, a 16-trial experiment may even appear to be "too much testing" to them. An 8-trial experiment can be a more viable alternative, which is still a much better approach than a one-at-a-time strategy (see Example 4-5).

## 13.19. FRACTIONAL FACTORIAL EXPERIMENT: ATTRIBUTE RESPONSE

The previous sections in this chapter dwelled on continuous response outputs. In some situations the appropriate response for a trial may be, for example, that there were 2 failures out of 300,000 tested solder joints (Agresti 1990).

If the sample size is the same for each trial, the attribute data can be analyzed using the proportion defect rate as a response for each trial; however, a data transformation may be needed when doing this analysis (see Section 15.4). The accuracy of such an analysis approach can become questionable whenever the sample size is such that many trials have no failures.

An alternative approach is to use a computer categorical data modeling routine such as SAS CATMOD. In some cases additional insight may be achieved by "looking at the data" after it is ranked (see Sections 14.7 and 18.10); however, an attribute test that should evaluate the proportion of failures for each trial should not begin with the intent of relying solely on such an analysis strategy.

## 13.20. FRACTIONAL FACTORIAL EXPERIMENT: RELIABILITY EVALUATIONS

In some situations it is beneficial when doing a reliability evaluation to build and test devices/systems using a fractional factorial experiment design approach. This strategy can be beneficial when deciding on what design changes should be implemented to fix a problem. This strategy could also be used to describe how systems are built/configured when running a generic reliability test during early stages of production.

In this type of test if all trials experience failures, a failure rate (or time of failure) could be the response that is used when doing the fractional factorial analysis, with the transformation considerations noted in Section 15.4. In general, however, it is considered more precise to analyze the data using a categorical routine that can handle such Poisson distribution considerations. When some trials have censored data, it can become difficult to draw precise solutions. Like the attribute considerations noted in Section 13.19, a search pattern strategy (see Section 18.10) then may be helpful to "look at the data."

## 13.21. MODELING EQUATION FORMAT FOR TWO-LEVEL FACTORIAL EXPERIMENTS

Previously this chapter illustrated the use of Tables M1 to M5 when making experiment design decisions that involve such considerations as the number of trials, number of factors, and experiment resolution. To this point, emphasis was given to determine which factor levels significantly affect a response.

If an experimenter has a situation where "lower is always better" or "higher is always better," the choice of the significant factor levels to use either in a conformation or follow-up experiment may be obvious by some simple data analysis, as described in Chapters 14 and 15. However, in some situations a mathematical model is needed for the purpose of estimating the response as a function of the factor level considerations.

To illustrate the construction of a model equation, consider the design matrix in Table 13.3. The two-level model for this structured experiment would take the form of Equation 17.1.

$$y = b_0 + b_1x_1 + b_2x_2 + b_3x_3 + b_4x_4 + b_5x_5 + b_6x_6 + b_7x_7$$

where $y$ is the response and $b_0$ would be the average of all the trials. In this equation $b_1$ to $b_7$ are half of the calculated effects of the factors $x_1$ (factor A) to $x_7$ (factor G) noting that $x_1$ to $x_7$ would take on values of $-1$ or $+1$. The reader should not confuse the $x_1$ to $x_7$ nomenclature used in the previous equation with the output response nomenclature shown previously in this chapter (e.g., in Table 13.1).

The model resulting from the experimental data in Table 13.4 would be

$$y = 250 + 0(x_1) + 0(x_2) + 0(x_3) + 0(x_4) + 250(x_5) + 0(x_6) + 0(x_7)$$

Since $b_5$ is the E factor (i.e., $x_5$ factor consideration) coefficient it would have a value of 250. This equation would reduce to $y = 250 + 250(x_5)$. We then note that whenever factor $E$ is high (i.e., $x_5 = 1$), the response $y$ would be equal to 500 and when $E$ is low (i.e., $x_5 = -1$) the response $y$ is equal to zero.

It should be noted that this equation form considers that the factor levels have a linear relationship with the response (e.g., there are no squared term considerations in the model). Center points may have been included in the basic experiment design to check this assumption (see Section 13.12). The results from one or more two-level fractional factorial experiments might lead a practitioner from having many factor considerations initially to a few factors that may need to be analyzed further using response surface techniques (see Chapter 17). Books on regression analysis (e.g., Draper and Smith 1966) address the more general situation of model building where the factor levels are not set within an experiment design structure.

## 13.22. VARIANCE COMPONENTS

Previous sections of this chapter dealt with fixed factor effects. In these sections a hypothesis was made about the mean response effect between factor levels. This section deals with random effects using variance components analysis, where the objective is to deduce the values of component variances that cannot be measured directly.

It was illustrated in Equation 4.3 how total variability in an experiment was the sum of the variance component pieces. An important use of variance components is the isolation of different sources of variability that affect product or system variability. This problem of product variability frequently arises in quality assurance, where the isolation of the sources for this variability can often be very difficult.

Because of the nature of the situation, a test to determine these variance components often has nesting. Example 13-4 illustrates a nested (hierarchical) design (Box et al. 1978), while example 13-5 illustrates another random effects design (Montgomery 1984). The references just cited discuss approach(es) to use for manual data analyses of these problems. In this text Examples 15-3 and 15-4 describe a computer analysis approach for the data analysis.

Additional discussion can be found on variance estimation in Box et al. (1978), Box and Tiao (1973), Kempthorne and Folks (1971), Montgomery (1984), and Searle (1971a, 1971b).

## 13.23. EXAMPLE 13-4: NESTED VARIANCE COMPONENTS

Consider that numerous batches of a pigment paste are sampled and tested once. The variation of the resulting moisture content is that shown pictorially in Figure 13.3 (Box et al 1978).

EXAMPLE 13-5: VARIANCE COMPONENTS    **203**

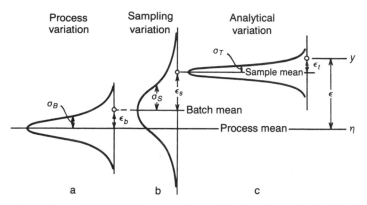

**FIGURE 13.3.** Example 13-4: Three components of variance in the final moisture reading. (a) Distribution of batch means about the process mean $\eta$. (b) Distribution of sample means about the batch mean. (c) Distribution of analytical test results about sample mean. [Reproduced with permission: G. E. P. Box, W. Hunter, and S. Hunter *Statistics for Experimenters*, John Wiley and Sons, 1978.]

In this figure $\eta$ is shown to be the long-run process mean for moisture content. In this figure process variation is shown to be the distribution of batch means about this process mean, sampling variation is shown to be the distribution of samples about the batch mean, and analytical variation is shown to be the distribution of analytical test results about the sample mean.

The overall error ($\epsilon = y - \eta$) will contain the three separate error components (i.e., $\epsilon = \epsilon_t + \epsilon_s + \epsilon_b$), where $\epsilon_t$ is the analytical test error, $\epsilon_s$ is the error made in taking the samples, and $\epsilon_b$ is the batch-to-batch error.

By these definitions the mean of the error components (i.e., $\epsilon_t$, $\epsilon_s$, and $\epsilon_b$) have zero means. The assumption is made that the samples are random (independent) from normal distributions with fixed variances $\sigma_t^2$, $\sigma_s^2$, and $\sigma_b^2$.

Figure 13.4 exemplifies a nested experiment design for this type of problem. Example 15-3 shows experimental data along with a computer analysis output that estimates the components of variance.

## 13.24. EXAMPLE 13-5: VARIANCE COMPONENTS

Fabric is woven on a large number of looms (Montgomery 1984). It is suspected that variation can occur both within samples from fabric from the same loom

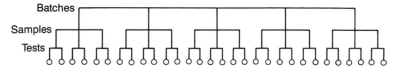

**FIGURE 13.4.** Example 13-4: A 5 × 3 × 2 hierarchical design. [Reproduced with permission: G. E. P. Box, W. Hunter, and S. Hunter, *Statistics for Experimenters*, John Wiley and Sons, 1978.]

and between different looms. To investigate this, four looms were randomly selected and four strength determinations were made on the fabric that was produced.

Example 15-4 shows experimental data along with a computer analysis output that estimates the components of variance.


## 13.25. DO-IT-SMARTER CONSIDERATIONS

With justification individuals can sometimes challenge a fractional factorial experimental design strategy chosen by engineers for lack of purity. Many "what ifs" can often be made about experimental designs proposed by "others." For example, a normal justified concern is the amount of interaction confounding in a fractional factorial experiment design. For this example perhaps the criticizing individual should consider the dilemma of engineers and that the product design/manufacturing process is "full of risks." In general, managed risks dealing with interactions that are confounded is a better experiment strategy than a one-at-a-time test approach—a common "alternative" to statistical design of experiment techniques.

Practitioners sometimes do not consider the "hidden" amount of information that might be prevalent from the data obtained when running a fractional factorial experiment, even when no factors are found significant. It is obvious that if no factors are found significant and a problem still exists, it may be helpful to consider having another brainstorming session to determine other factors to consider and/or how the measurement technique might be improved to give a more consistent response in another experiment. There are situations where looking at the trial response data can be very enlightening. Consider the following:

If all the response data is "good," then perhaps the experimenter is done with the specific task at hand.

A ranking of the fractional factorial trials according to the level of a response can sometimes yield additional insight to other interaction possibilities that may be prevelent (see Section 14.7).

If much of the response data is "bad" but a few trials were especially "good," unusual setup or other conditions should be investigated for these good trials so that these conditions might be mimicked.

If factors with levels consistent to that in the manufacturing process were not found significant, these factor tolerances could possibly be relaxed as part of a cost reduction effort.

A probability plot (see Chapter 5) of the raw experiment data could be useful to pictorially describe the variability of the overall response when the factors are varied within the levels described by the fractional factorial experiment (see Example 22-2).

A "sizing" for the process capability (see Section 19.15) could be made from the raw data information (see Figure 15.5).

[Note that the last two suggestions are for "sizings" only, since the data are not random from the process.]

In some instances it can be appropriate to use variance component analysis data collection techniques to determine a variance value that is used when making process capability calculations (see Section 19.15). With this approach information could be gained about a variance component that is a major contributor to a poor process capability index. It may be found from this analyses, for example, that the measurement procedure is causing much variability and needs to be improved.

It should be noted that it is not only important to decide upon an efficient test strategy. It is also important for the experimenter to become involved in the data collection. If this is not done, the data might be faulty because of a misunderstanding, which can lead to erroneous conclusions and/or a waste of resources (see Example 4-6).

Examples 22-1 to 22-6 illustrate more considerations utilizing fractional factorial experiment matrices. Cox (1958) has more discussion on planning an experiment.

# 14

# FACTORIAL EXPERIMENTS: BASIC ANALYSES

Recommended introductory reading: Chapters 1, 2, 3, 4, 5, and 13.

Examples are used in this chapter to illustrate basic approaches to the analysis of two-level fractional factorial experiment data (see Chapter 13). In this chapter methodologies are presented such that they can be manually implemented; however, the discussion is useful introductory material to Chapter 15, which covers analysis approaches that utilize computer programs.

In this chapter both probability plotting techniques (see Chapter 5) and *t* tests (see Table 9.1) are used to interpret two-level fractional factorial response data.

## 14.1. DETERMINING THE SIGNIFICANT EFFECTS AND A PROBABILITY PLOTTING PROCEDURE

Analysis of variance (ANOVA) (Box et al. 1978; Montgomery 1984) has traditionally been used to determine the significant effects in a fractional factorial experiment. However, when manually calculating the significance tests for two-level factorial experiment data, practitioners usually consider a *t*-test criterion approach more appealing (Diamond 1989). Hence, the *t*-test analysis approach is used in this chapter, while Chapter 15 includes ANOVA routines along with some computer analysis extensions to these concepts. Section 13.13 gives various strategies that can be used as part of these techniques to determine an estimated experimental error value that is used within the calculations.

EXAMPLE 14-1: RESOLUTION III FACTORIAL ANALYSIS    **207**

An alternative to a formal significance test is a probability plot (see Chapter 5) of the contrast column effects, $\Delta$'s, from the two-level fractional factorial matrix. These effects are the same as those that were conceptually described in Equation (13.1). For the two-level factorial designs included in this text, a contrast column effect can be determined from the equation

$$\Delta = \left( \sum_{i=1}^{n_{high}} \frac{x_{high\ i}}{n_{high}} \right) - \left( \sum_{i=1}^{n_{low}} \frac{x_{low\ i}}{n_{low}} \right) \tag{14.1}$$

where $x_{high\ i}$ and $x_{low\ i}$ are the response values of each of the $i$ responses from the total of $n_{high}$ and $n_{low}$ trials [for high (+) and low (−) factor level conditions, respectively]. A plot of the absolute values of the contrast column effects is an alternative plotting approach (i.e., a half normal probability plot) (Daniel 1959).

An effect (i.e., main effect or interaction effect) is said to be "significant" if its magnitude [from Equation (14.1)] is large relative to the other contrast column effects that can be determined from an experiment design. When the plot position of an effect is beyond the bounds of a "straight line" through the "insignificant" contrast column effects, this effect is thought to be "significant" (see Figure 14.1). Since this is not a rigorous approach, obviously there can be differences of opinions as to whether some effects are really significant.

Computer programs are available to create the probability plot; however, as illustrated in Chapter 5, the task can be done manually by using the percentage plot positions from Table P* and normal probability paper (Table Q1). The following example illustrates the mechanics behind the probability plot analysis approach.

## 14.2. EXAMPLE 14-1: ANALYSIS OF A RESOLUTION III FRACTIONAL FACTORIAL SCREENING EXPERIMENT

A 2-level, 16-trial resolution III screening experiment that had 15 factors was created in Example 13-2 (The analysis of example 13-1 is in Example 14-2). The factor designations ($A-O$) are shown in Table 14.1, along with the trial responses from the experiment.

If there is an estimate for experimental error (see Section 13.13), traditional ANOVA or $t$-test techniques could be used to determine factor significance. However, the experiment was a saturated resolution III design.

In general, an estimate for experimental error could be made by considering the contrast columns that are not under consideration in the model. The practitioner should remember that this estimate can be distorted because

---

* Tables A through R3 are located in Appendix D.

these contrast columns can contain information about two-factor or higher interactions that may exist. However, for this experiment there are no columns that could be used for this estimate since all 15 columns from the original design matrix (Table M) were used for factor level assignments.

As noted in Section 14.1, an alternative analysis approach to a formal significance test is to perform a probability plot of the mean contrast column effects. Again, many computer programs (see Section 2.3) are available to perform this task; however, in this example a manual procedure will be discussed that can utilize normal probability paper (Table Q1) with the percentage plot points ($F_i$) determined from Table P. The following discussion illustrates the mechanics of a procedure that can be used to manage the numbers when creating such a probability plot.

Table 14.2 is first created when the plus/minus signs of the experiment design are combined with the response value for each trial. Using Equation (14.1), the mean contrast column effect for factor $A$ (contrast column 1) is then, for example,

$$\frac{5.6 + 2.1 + 4.9 + \ldots}{8} - \frac{4.1 + 1.9 + 5.1}{8} = -0.188$$

**TABLE 14.1. Example 14-1: Design Matrix with Trial Responses**

| | | |
|---|---|---|
| $A\ B\ C\ D\ E\ F\ G\ H\ I\ J\ K\ L\ M\ N\ O$ | ⊢—— Factor designations | |
| $\quad\quad\quad\quad\quad\quad\quad\quad\ 1\ 1\ 1\ 1\ 1\ 1$ <br> $1\ 2\ 3\ 4\ 5\ 6\ 7\ 8\ 9\ 0\ 1\ 2\ 3\ 4\ 5$ | └—— Contrast column designations | |

| | A B C D E F G H I J K L M N O | Response |
|---|---|---|
| 1 | + − − − + − − + + − + − + + + | 5.6 |
| 2 | + + − − − + − − + + − + − + + | 2.1 |
| 3 | + + + − − − + − − + + − + − + | 4.9 |
| 4 | + + + + − − − + − − + + − + − | 4.9 |
| 5 | − + + + + − − − + − − + + − + | 4.1 |
| 6 | + − + + + + − − − + − − + + − | 5.6 |
| 7 | − + − + + + + − − − + − − + + | 1.9 |
| 8 | + − + − + + + + − − − + − − + | 7.2 |
| 9 | + + − + − + + + + − − − + − − | 2.4 |
| 10 | − + + − + − + + + + − − − + − | 5.1 |
| 11 | − − + + − + − + + + + − − − + | 7.9 |
| 12 | + − − + + − + − + + + + − − − | 5.3 |
| 13 | − + − − + + − + − + + + + − − | 2.1 |
| 14 | − − + − − + + − + − + + + + − | 7.6 |
| 15 | − − − + − − + + − + − + + + + | 5.5 |
| 16 | − − − − − − − − − − − − − − − | 5.3 |

↑ —— Number of Trial        ↑ —— Trial response

TABLE 14.2. Example 14-1: Experiment Response Values with Level Considerations and Contrast Column Totals

Contrast Column Number/Factor Designation

| | 1 A | 2 B | 3 C | 4 D | 5 E | 6 F | 7 G | 8 H | 9 I | 10 J | 11 K | 12 L | 13 M | 14 N | 15 O |
|---|---|---|---|---|---|---|---|---|---|---|---|---|---|---|---|
| | +5.6 | −5.6 | −5.6 | −5.6 | +5.6 | −5.6 | −5.6 | +5.6 | +5.6 | −5.6 | +5.6 | −5.6 | +5.6 | +5.6 | +5.6 |
| | +2.1 | +2.1 | −2.1 | −2.1 | −2.1 | +2.1 | −2.1 | −2.1 | +2.1 | +2.1 | −2.1 | +2.1 | −2.1 | +2.1 | +2.1 |
| | +4.9 | +4.9 | +4.9 | −4.9 | −4.9 | −4.9 | +4.9 | −4.9 | −4.9 | +4.9 | +4.9 | −4.9 | +4.9 | −4.9 | +4.9 |
| | +4.9 | +4.9 | +4.9 | +4.9 | −4.9 | −4.9 | −4.9 | +4.9 | −4.9 | −4.9 | +4.9 | +4.9 | −4.9 | +4.9 | −4.9 |
| | −4.1 | +4.1 | +4.1 | +4.1 | +4.1 | −4.1 | −4.1 | −4.1 | +4.1 | −4.1 | −4.1 | +4.1 | +4.1 | −4.1 | +4.1 |
| | +5.6 | −5.6 | +5.6 | +5.6 | +5.6 | +5.6 | −5.6 | −5.6 | −5.6 | +5.6 | −5.6 | −5.6 | +5.6 | +5.6 | −5.6 |
| | −1.9 | +1.9 | −1.9 | +1.9 | +1.9 | +1.9 | +1.9 | −1.9 | −1.9 | −1.9 | +1.9 | −1.9 | −1.9 | +1.9 | +1.9 |
| | +7.2 | −7.2 | +7.2 | −7.2 | +7.2 | +7.2 | +7.2 | +7.2 | −7.2 | −7.2 | −7.2 | +7.2 | −7.2 | −7.2 | +7.2 |
| | +2.4 | +2.4 | −2.4 | +2.4 | −2.4 | +2.4 | +2.4 | +2.4 | +2.4 | −2.4 | −2.4 | −2.4 | +2.4 | −2.4 | −2.4 |
| | −5.1 | +5.1 | +5.1 | −5.1 | +5.1 | −5.1 | +5.1 | +5.1 | +5.1 | +5.1 | −5.1 | −5.1 | −5.1 | +5.1 | −5.1 |
| | −7.9 | −7.9 | +7.9 | +7.9 | −7.9 | +7.9 | −7.9 | +7.9 | +7.9 | +7.9 | +7.9 | −7.9 | −7.9 | −7.9 | +7.9 |
| | +5.3 | −5.3 | −5.3 | +5.3 | +5.3 | −5.3 | +5.3 | −5.3 | +5.3 | +5.3 | +5.3 | +5.3 | −5.3 | −5.3 | −5.3 |
| | −2.1 | +2.1 | −2.1 | −2.1 | +2.1 | +2.1 | −2.1 | +2.1 | −2.1 | +2.1 | +2.1 | +2.1 | +2.1 | −2.1 | +2.1 |
| | −7.6 | −7.6 | +7.6 | −7.6 | −7.6 | +7.6 | +7.6 | −7.6 | +7.6 | −7.6 | +7.6 | +7.6 | +7.6 | +7.6 | −7.6 |
| | −5.5 | −5.5 | −5.5 | +5.5 | −5.5 | −5.5 | +5.5 | +5.5 | −5.5 | +5.5 | −5.5 | +5.5 | +5.5 | +5.5 | +5.5 |
| | −5.3 | −5.3 | −5.3 | −5.3 | −5.3 | −5.3 | −5.3 | −5.3 | −5.3 | −5.3 | −5.3 | −5.3 | −5.3 | −5.3 | −5.3 |
| Totals | −1.5 | −22.5 | +17.1 | −2.3 | −3.7 | −3.9 | +2.3 | +3.9 | +2.7 | −0.5 | +2.9 | +0.1 | −1.9 | −0.9 | +0.9 |

An alternative approach when using the two-level fractional factorial designs in Table M is to simply divide the contrast column summation from Table 14.2 by half the total sample size. For factor $A$ this would be

$$-1.5/8 = -0.188$$

Similarly, the mean effects for all 15 factors can be determined. These results are shown in Table 14.3. Next, the absolute values of these effects can be ranked and plotted with the percent plot positions noted from Table P to make a half normal probability plot. These ranked effects and corresponding plot coordinates are shown in Table 14.4.

A computer generated normal probability plot of these absolute values (half normal probability plot) is shown in Figure 14.1. The conclusion from this plot is that factors $B$ and $C$ (contrast column numbers 2 and 3) are significant. The "best estimates" for the magnitude of the difference (with no regard to sign) from a high level to low level for these factors are 2.813 for $B$ and 2.138 for $C$.

However, it must be remembered that this was a resolution III experiment since the main effects and two-factor interactions are confounded. A confirmation experiment is needed to verify the conclusion that two-factor interaction effects did not make these factors appear significant.

When deciding what should be done next, consider the real purpose of the experiment. If the primary objective was to determine whether a satisfactory output is achieved within the operational extremes of environmental and tolerance conditions and all the responses are "very good," the significance of effects may be of little practical importance. A probability plot (e.g., Figure 22.3 in Example 22-2) of the experimental outputs for each trial can be a "picture" to assess variabilities in this "operational space"—perhaps with only one prototype system. It should be noted, however, that this would not be a random sample (of future production); hence, the percentage of population values are not necessarily representative of the true population. But, this procedure can often give a more meaningful "picture" of how well a specification criterion will be met in future systems/devices than a "random" sample of a single lot of early production assemblies.

## 14.3. A SIGNIFICANCE TEST PROCEDURE FOR THESE TWO-LEVEL EXPERIMENTS

As noted earlier, if there is an estimate for the standard deviation of experimental error (see Section 13.13), $t$ tests can be used to determine if the change from a high to low level of a factor significantly affects a response. As was previously noted, contrast columns for high-factor interaction considerations can be used to determine an estimate for the experimental error.

**TABLE 14.3. Example 14-1: Mean Effects for Contrast Columns**

Contrast Column Number, Factor Designation, and Mean Effect

| 1 | 2 | 3 | 4 | 5 | 6 | 7 | 8 |
|---|---|---|---|---|---|---|---|
| A | B | C | D | E | F | G | H |
| −0.188 | −2.813 | +2.138 | −0.288 | −0.463 | −0.488 | +0.288 | +0.488 |

| 9 | 10 | 11 | 12 | 13 | 14 | 15 | |
|---|---|---|---|---|---|---|---|
| I | J | K | L | M | N | O | |
| +0.338 | −0.063 | +0.363 | +0.013 | −0.238 | −0.113 | +0.113 | |

**TABLE 14.4. Example 14-1: Ranking of Absolute Value of Mean Effects with Plot Positions**

| Contrast Column | Factor Designation | Mean Effect | Percentage Plot Position |
|---|---|---|---|
| 12 | L | 0.013 | 3.3 |
| 10 | J | 0.063 | 10.0 |
| 14 | N | 0.113 | 16.7 |
| 15 | O | 0.113 | 23.3 |
| 1 | A | 0.188 | 30.0 |
| 13 | M | 0.238 | 36.7 |
| 4 | D | 0.288 | 43.3 |
| 7 | G | 0.288 | 50.0 |
| 9 | I | 0.338 | 56.7 |
| 11 | K | 0.363 | 63.3 |
| 5 | E | 0.463 | 70.0 |
| 6 | F | 0.488 | 76.7 |
| 8 | H | 0.488 | 83.3 |
| 3 | C | 2.138 | 90.0 |
| 2 | B | 2.813 | 96.7 |

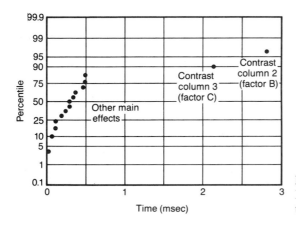

**FIGURE 14.1.** Example 14-1: Half normal probability plot of the contrast column effects.

**211**

To perform this significance test for the two-level factor designs in this text, Equation (14.2) can be used to determine a sum of squares (SS) contribution for a contrast column. (Section C.5 in Appendix C shows a derivation of this equation from a more general equation format typically found in most other texts.)

$$(SS)_j = \frac{\left[\sum_{i=1}^{n} w_i\right]^2}{n} \tag{14.2}$$

where $w_i$ is a trial response *preceded by either a + or − sign* for contrast column $j$, and $n$ denotes the number of trials (see data format shown in Table 14.2).

Next the sum of squares for the contrast columns that are being used to estimate error $(SS_e)$ are combined using Equation (14.3) to yield a mean square (MS) value.

$$MS = \frac{\sum_{j=1}^{q} (SS_e)_j}{q} \tag{14.3}$$

where $q$ is the number of contrast columns combined.

It then follows that the standard deviation estimate for the error $s_e$ (i.e., root mean square error) is

$$s_e = \sqrt{MS} \tag{14.4}$$

Contrast column effects are then considered significant if the magnitude of the effect from a high to low level [i.e., result from Equation (14.1)] is greater than the value determined from Equation (14.5) (see Table 9.1).

$$|\bar{x}_{\text{high}} - \bar{x}_{\text{low}}|_{\text{criterion}} = t_\alpha s_e \sqrt{1/n_{\text{high}} + 1/n_{\text{low}}} \tag{14.5}$$

where the $t_\alpha$ is taken from the double-sided Table E with the number of degrees of freedom equal to the number of contrast columns that were combined.

EXAMPLE 14-2: RESOLUTION V FACTORIAL ANALYSIS     **213**

## 14.4. EXAMPLE 14-2: ANALYSIS OF A RESOLUTION V FRACTIONAL FACTORIAL EXPERIMENT DESIGN

The following factors and level assignments were made in Example 13-1 for an experiment that was to give understanding of (with an intent to minimize) the settle-out time of a stepper motor when it was stopped.

| | | Levels | |
|---|---|---|---|
| Factors and Their Designations | | $(-)$ | $(+)$ |
| A: Motor temperature | (mot_temp) | Cold | Hot |
| B: Algorithm | (algor) | Current design | Proposed redesign |
| C: Motor adjustment | (mot_adj) | Low tolerance | High tolerance |
| D: External adjustment | (ext_adj) | Low tolerance | High tolerance |
| E: Supply voltage | (sup_volt) | Low tolerance | High tolerance |

From "Instructions: Creating a Test Design Matrix," located in Table M1, it is noted that a resolution V experiment yields unconfounded 2-factor information for the given 5 factors and 16 trials. Table 13.6 illustrated the procedure used to determine the factor level assignments as they were taken from Table M3.

The experiment yielded the trial responses shown in Table 14.5 along with the noted input factors levels. Note that these response values for each trial are the same as those shown in Table 14.1; hence, the numerical calculation for this example is similar to that shown in Example 14-1 relative to determining the contrast column effects (see Tables 14.3 and 14.6).

In general, standard ANOVA or $t$-test techniques could be used to determine the factors that are significant. However, if two-factor interactions are considered within the model, there are no columns remaining to assess experimental error.

A probability plot of the main and interaction effects (i.e., all the contrast column effects from Table M3) can be used to pictorially determine the "significant" effects. For this resolution V design, the interaction considerations for each contrast column are noted from Table N1. The mean effects from the contrast columns is shown in Table 14.6. Since each trial had the same response as that in Example 14-1, the values in Table 14.6 are the same as that shown in Table 14.3; however, two-factor interactions now replace some of the previous main effect considerations. A probability plot would indicate again that contrast columns 2 and 3 are significant [i.e., factors B (algor) and C (mot_adj) are significant]. Because of the procedure used to calculate the estimates, the +2.138 mean effect for mot_adj indicates that the low tolerance value [$(-)$ level for C] yields a smaller settle-out time for the motor by approximately 2.138 msec, while the $-2.812$ mean effect for the algorithm [$(+)$ level for B] indicates that the proposed algorithm redesign yields a

**TABLE 14.5. Example 14-2: Design Matrix with Outputs**

| | A | B | C | D | E | Output timing (m sec) |
|---|---|---|---|---|---|---|
| | | | Number of trial input factors | | | |
| | mot_temp | algor | mot_adj | ext_adj | sup_volt | |
| 1 | + | − | − | − | + | 5.6 |
| 2 | + | + | − | − | − | 2.1 |
| 3 | + | + | + | − | + | 4.9 |
| 4 | + | + | + | + | − | 4.9 |
| 5 | − | + | + | + | + | 4.1 |
| 6 | + | − | + | + | + | 5.6 |
| 7 | − | + | − | + | − | 1.9 |
| 8 | + | − | + | − | − | 7.2 |
| 9 | + | + | − | + | + | 2.4 |
| 10 | − | + | + | − | − | 5.1 |
| 11 | − | − | + | + | − | 7.9 |
| 12 | + | − | − | + | − | 5.3 |
| 13 | − | + | − | − | + | 2.1 |
| 14 | − | − | + | − | + | 7.6 |
| 15 | − | − | − | + | + | 5.5 |
| 16 | − | − | − | − | − | 5.3 |
| | 1 | 2 | 3 | 4 | 13 ─── | Table M3 contrast column numbers |

smaller settle-out time by approximately 2.812 msec. No other main effects or interactions were considered significant.

Since there appear to be no interaction terms, let's, for the purpose of illustration, leave all the main effects in the model and use the contrast columns to make an estimate of error. To do this manually, Table 14.7 is first constructed for these two-factor interaction contrasts.

**TABLE 14.6. Example 14-2: Mean Effects of Contrasts Columns**

Column Contrast Number, Factor Designation, and Mean Effect

| 1 | 2 | 3 | 4 | 5 | 6 | 7 | 8 |
|---|---|---|---|---|---|---|---|
| A | B | C | D | AB | BC | CD | CE |
| −0.188 | −2.813 | +2.138 | −0.288 | −0.463 | −0.488 | +0.288 | +0.488 |

| 9 | 10 | 11 | 12 | 13 | 14 | 15 | |
|---|---|---|---|---|---|---|---|
| AC | BD | DE | AE | E | BE | AD | |
| +0.338 | −0.063 | +0.363 | +0.013 | −0.238 | −0.113 | +0.113 | |

TABLE 14.7. Responses with Level Considerations for Two-Factor Interactions Along with Contrast Column Totals

| Number of Trial | 5 | 6 | 7 | 8 | 9 | 10 | 11 | 12 | 14 | 15 |
|---|---|---|---|---|---|---|---|---|---|---|
| 1 | +5.6 | -5.6 | -5.6 | +5.6 | +5.6 | -5.6 | +5.6 | -5.6 | +5.6 | +5.6 |
| 2 | -2.1 | +2.1 | -2.1 | -2.1 | +2.1 | +2.1 | -2.1 | +2.1 | +2.1 | +2.1 |
| 3 | -4.9 | -4.9 | +4.9 | -4.9 | -4.9 | +4.9 | +4.9 | -4.9 | -4.9 | +4.9 |
| 4 | -4.9 | -4.9 | -4.9 | +4.9 | -4.9 | -4.9 | +4.9 | +4.9 | +4.9 | -4.9 |
| 5 | +4.1 | -4.1 | -4.1 | -4.1 | +4.1 | -4.1 | -4.1 | +4.1 | -4.1 | +4.1 |
| 6 | +5.6 | +5.6 | -5.6 | -5.6 | -5.6 | +5.6 | -5.6 | -5.6 | +5.6 | -5.6 |
| 7 | +1.9 | +1.9 | +1.9 | -1.9 | -1.9 | -1.9 | +1.9 | -1.9 | +1.9 | +1.9 |
| 8 | +7.2 | +7.2 | +7.2 | +7.2 | -7.2 | -7.2 | -7.2 | +7.2 | -7.2 | +7.2 |
| 9 | -2.4 | +2.4 | +2.4 | +2.4 | +2.4 | -2.4 | -2.4 | -2.4 | -2.4 | -2.4 |
| 10 | +5.1 | -5.1 | +5.1 | +5.1 | +5.1 | +5.1 | -5.1 | -5.1 | +5.1 | -5.1 |
| 11 | -7.9 | +7.9 | -7.9 | +7.9 | +7.9 | +7.9 | +7.9 | -7.9 | -7.9 | +7.9 |
| 12 | +5.3 | -5.3 | +5.3 | -5.3 | +5.3 | +5.3 | +5.3 | +5.3 | -5.3 | -5.3 |
| 13 | +2.1 | +2.1 | -2.1 | +2.1 | -2.1 | +2.1 | +2.1 | +2.1 | -2.1 | -2.1 |
| 14 | -7.6 | +7.6 | +7.6 | -7.6 | +7.6 | -7.6 | +7.6 | +7.6 | +7.6 | -7.6 |
| 15 | -5.5 | -5.5 | +5.5 | +5.5 | -5.5 | +5.5 | -5.5 | +5.5 | +5.5 | +5.5 |
| 16 | -5.3 | -5.3 | -5.3 | -5.3 | -5.3 | -5.3 | -5.3 | -5.3 | -5.3 | -5.3 |
| Totals | -3.7 | -3.9 | +2.3 | +3.9 | +2.7 | -0.5 | +2.9 | +0.1 | -0.9 | +0.9 |

The SS value from Equation (14.2) for each contrast column is then

| 5 | 6 | 7 | 8 | 9 | 10 | 11 | 12 | 14 | 15 |
|------|------|------|------|------|------|------|------|------|------|
| 0.8556 | 0.9506 | 0.3306 | 0.9506 | 0.4556 | 0.0156 | 0.5256 | 0.0006 | 0.0506 | 0.0506 |

For example, for contrast column 5:

$$SS = \frac{(\Sigma w_i)^2}{16} = \frac{(-3.7)^2}{16} = 0.8556$$

Next, using Equation (14.3), it follows that the MS value is

$$MS = \frac{0.8556 + 0.9506 + \cdots + 0.0506 + 0.0506}{10}$$

$$= 0.4186$$

From Equation (14.4) it then follows that the standard deviation estimate for experimental error ($s_e$) is (with 10 degrees of freedom)

$$s_e = \sqrt{0.4186} = 0.647$$

The factors are then considered significant if the output effect from high to low is greater than that determined using Equation (14.5). From the double-sided $t$ table (Table E), the $t_\alpha$ values for various $\alpha$ values with 10 degrees of freedom are as follows, with the noted significance criteria calculations:

| $\alpha$ | $t_\alpha$ | $|\bar{x}_{high} - \bar{x}_{low}|$ criterion |
|------|------|------|
| 0.10 | 1.812 | 0.586[a] |
| 0.05 | 2.228 | 0.721 |
| 0.01 | 3.169 | 1.025 |

[a] $|\bar{x}_{high} - \bar{x}_{low}|$ criterion $= t_\alpha s_e \sqrt{1/n_{high} + 1/n_{low}}$

$$= 1.812(0.647) \sqrt{1/8 + 1/8} = 0.586$$

A comparison of the absolute values for the $A$, $B$, $C$, $D$, and $E$ mean effects from Table 14.6 ($-0.188$, $-2.813$, $2.138$, $-0.288$, and $-0.238$, respectively) to the preceding tabular values yields $B$ (algor) and $C$ (mot_adj) significant at the 0.01 level, while the other three main effects cannot be shown significant at the 0.10 level (see Section 13.4).

EXAMPLE 14-3: RESOLUTION III/TWO-FACTOR INTERACTION    **217**

## 14.5. EXAMPLE 14-3: ANALYSIS OF A RESOLUTION III EXPERIMENT WITH TWO-FACTOR INTERACTION ASSESSMENT

A resolution III experiment was conducted to determine if a product would give a desirable response under various design tolerance extremes and operating conditions. The experiment had 64 trials with 52 two-level factors ($A$–$Z$, $a$–$z$). The experiment design format from Table M5 was

Factors

$\longrightarrow$   $A B C D E F G H I J K L M N O P Q R S T U V W X Y Z\ a\ b\ c\ d\ e\ f\ g\ h\ i\ j\ k\ l\ m\ n\ o\ p\ q\ r\ s\ t\ u\ v\ w\ x\ y\ z$

Contrast $\longrightarrow$

```
Factors
        A B C D E F G H I J K L M N O P Q R S T U V W X Y Z a b c d e f g h i j k l m n o p q r s t u v w x y z
Contrast                   1 1 1 1 1 1 1 1 1 1 2 2 2 2 2 2 2 2 2 2 3 3 3 3 3 3 3 3 3 3 4 4 4 4 4 4 4 4 4 4 5 5 5
column       1 2 3 4 5 6 7 8 9 0 1 2 3 4 5 6 7 8 9 0 1 2 3 4 5 6 7 8 9 0 1 2 3 4 5 6 7 8 9 0 1 2 3 4 5 6 7 8 9 0 1 2

   1 + - - - - - + - - - - + + - - - + - + - - + + + + - +- - - + + + - + - - + - - + - + + - + + + - + + - - +
   2 + + - - - - - + - - - - + + - - - + - + - - + + + + - + - - - + + + - + - - + - - + - + + - + + + - + + - -
   3 + + + - - - - - + - - - - + + - - - + - + - - + + + + - + - - - + + + - + - - + - - + - + + - + + + - + + -
                                                    .
                                                    .
                                                    .
  63 - - - - + - - - - + + - - - + - + - - + + + + - + - - - + + + - + - - + - - + - + + - + + + - + + - - + +
  64 - - - - - - - - - - - - - - - - - - - - - - - - - - - - - - - - - - - - - - - - - - - - - - - - - - - - -
```

Consider that an analysis was conducted that indicated that the only factors found significant were contrast columns 6, 8, and 18, which implies that factors $F$, $H$, and $R$ are significant. However, if Table N3 is examined, it is noted that contrast column 6 (i.e., factor $F$) also contains the $HR$ interaction, while contrast column 8 (i.e., factor $H$) also contains the $FR$ interaction and contrast column 18 (i.e., factor $R$) also contains the $FH$ interaction. Hence, it could be that instead of the three factors each being significant one of three two-factor interactions might be making the third contrast column significant. To assess which of these scenarios is most likely from a technical point of view, interaction plots can be made of the possibilities assuming that each of them are true. Engineering judgment could possibly then be used to assess which interaction is most likely or whether the three factors individually is the most probable cause for significance.

It is important to note that this example only illustrates a procedure that can be used to give additional insight to possible sources of significance. A confirmation experiment is necessary to confirm or dispute any theories. There are many circumstances that can cause contrast column significance within a resolution III experiment. For example, any of the interaction considerations within a contrast column could be the sources for significance, without the main effect being significant. However, with the initial problem definition, if all the trial responses are well within a desirable output range, then it may not be important to have a precise analysis to determine which factor(s) are significant.

## 14.6. ANALYSIS OF MEANS

Section 9.13 discusses the application of analysis of means (ANOM) (Ott 1983) techniques when comparing samples. These same techniques can be used as a graphical alternative to the analysis of fractional factorial experiments.

ANOM charts may be most useful when there are factor considerations greater than 2. These charts often have appeal in a manufacturing area since they are similar in appearance to statistical process control (SPC) charts, which are discussed in Chapter 19. Nelson (1983a) and Ramig (1983) discuss adjustments that may be appropriate to the $h$ values that are used in these significance tests.

## 14.7. DO-IT-SMARTER CONSIDERATIONS

The mechanics of the manual fractional factorial data analysis techniques described in this chapter are basically simple; however, they can be laborious. A practitioner who anticipates doing experiments regularly should consider the advantage of using a commercially available computer program (see Section 2.3). Some of these computer programs can both reduce the amount of data analysis work and increase the amount of readily available information from the data.

In the past I have found that sorting fractional factorial experiment trials by the level of a response can be an effective tool when "looking at the data" for the purpose of gaining additional insight to that given by traditional statistical analyses. Diamond (1989) refers to this basic analysis approach as "Analysis of goodness." This informal approach can lead to the identification of factors or combination of factors that could affect the response and may not show significance in a formal analysis. In addition, this approach can lead to the identification of a "bad datum" point that distorted the formal statistical analysis. Obviously, conclusions from this type of evaluation usually need further consideration in a follow-up confirmation experiment.

Sections 13.25 and 15.8 contain additional design and analysis do-it-smarter considerations.

# 15

# FACTORIAL EXPERIMENTS AND VARIANCE COMPONENTS: COMPUTER ANALYSES

Recommended introductory reading: Chapters 2, 3, 4, 5, 13, and 14.

It can be laborious to perform the mechanics of manual analyses for fractional factorial and variance component experiments that were described in Chapter 13. Examples in this chapter extend upon the basic concepts discussed in Chapter 14 by showing analysis alternatives that are more readily performed using a statistical analysis program package. SAS (Statistical Analysis Systems 1985a, 1985b) was used in this text to illustrate these analysis alternatives. Appendix C has a detailed description about the interpretation of the computer outputs along with the program code that created these outputs. This appendix also includes some of the basic mathematical concepts for making many of the elementary program calculations.

Emphasis was given in Chapter 13 to design a most effective experiment with the fewest trials, while Chapter 14 illustrated some analysis techniques that can be performed manually. This chapter will emphasize additional approaches to get information out of limited experimental data.

It should be noted that all of the steps that are discussed in this chapter do not need to be considered in each experiment. A practitioner may choose only to use, for example, a computer probability plot of the contrast column effects.

## 15.1. CONSIDERATIONS WHEN ANALYZING FRACTIONAL FACTORIAL DATA

As discussed in Chapters 13 and 14, an estimate for experimental error is needed to formally determine factor significance (see Section 13.4); however, the source of this estimate can have various origins (see Section 13.13). Texts in the past have often suggested the replication of experiment trials to determine an estimate for error. This approach may yield a "good" estimate for statistical calculations; however, often experiment trials are expensive and time consuming to complete. The methods discussed in this chapter assume that experiment trials are expensive and that it is a requirement to minimize the amount of experiment effort.

Data from Example 13-1 was analyzed manually in Example 14-2. Example 15-1 in this chapter both duplicates and adds to this analysis using computer analysis routines. This example first considers that the original intent of the experiment was only to assess main effects. Significance levels are available in this analysis since the two-factor interaction effects can then be used as an estimate of error. Next, the magnitudes of the sum of squares are assessed for a model that has both main effect and two-factor interaction considerations. A probability plot of the design column contrasts effects (Daniel 1959) is then created (similar to that of Figure 14.1). This analysis is then followed by regression on all combinations of the factors (Mallows 1973). Upon completion of this analysis, conclusions are illustrated in graphical format for an easy-to-understand pictorial presentation to others. The general analysis process illustrated within this example may be used for resolution III as well as experimental designs that have replicated trials. In addition, the techniques are applicable to analyzing data that is not from balanced experimental design matrices. Example 15-2 extends the analysis of Example 15-1 to the identification and consideration of outlier data.

Some of the figures in this chapter highlight certain portions of the computer outputs. More descriptions about computer output formats are contained in Appendix C.*

## 15.2. EXAMPLE 15-1: COMPUTER ANALYSIS OF A RESOLUTION V FRACTIONAL FACTORIAL EXPERIMENT DESIGN

The experiment design from Example 13-1 yielded the results that are shown in Table 15.1. Section C.6 shows the computer program that generated the outputs shown in this example. Section C.6 also shows the manual recreation of some of the values that are given in the output.

Table 15.2 shows the computer main effect model analyses where the two-factor interaction columns of this resolution V experiment are used for error considerations when making significance tests of the factors. In this analyses the minus ($-$) factor levels were designated as a $-1$, while the plus ($+$) levels were designated as a $+1$. This table shows the results from two significance test analyses. ANOVA significance levels were determined using

* Sections beginning with the letter C, e.g., Section C.6, are located in Appendix C. Tables A–R3 are located in Appendix D.

EXAMPLE 15-1: ANALYSIS OF A RESOLUTION V DESIGN    **221**

**TABLE 15.1. Example 15-1: Experiment Design Trials and Responses**

| Number of Trial | Inputs | | | | | Response Timing (msec) |
|---|---|---|---|---|---|---|
| | mot_temp | algor | mot_adj | ext_adj | sup_volt | |
| 1 | + | − | − | − | + | 5.6 |
| 2 | + | + | − | − | − | 2.1 |
| 3 | + | + | + | − | + | 4.9 |
| 4 | + | + | + | + | − | 4.9 |
| 5 | − | + | + | + | + | 4.1 |
| 6 | + | − | + | + | + | 5.6 |
| 7 | − | + | − | + | − | 1.9 |
| 8 | + | − | + | − | − | 7.2 |
| 9 | + | + | − | + | + | 2.4 |
| 10 | − | + | + | − | − | 5.1 |
| 11 | − | − | + | + | − | 7.9 |
| 12 | + | − | − | + | − | 5.3 |
| 13 | − | + | − | − | + | 2.1 |
| 14 | − | − | + | − | + | 7.6 |
| 15 | − | − | − | + | + | 5.5 |
| 16 | − | − | − | − | − | 5.3 |

the $F$ distribution (see Sections 6.10 and C.6) and are shown in Table 15.2 under note ②. Levels of significance using the $t$ distribution (as was done in Example 14-2; see Sections 6.9 and C.6) were also conducted and are shown in Table 15.2 under note ③.

Lower $F$ probability levels (Table 15.2, note ②) indicate a greater significance level for the corresponding factor. For the given model, an $F$ value of 0.1 indicates a significance level of 0.10 that there is a difference in output caused by the differing levels of the corresponding factor (Table 15.2, note ①). If a 0.10 significance level were our preexperiment decision point criterion for making significance statements, then we would say that this factor was significant with a 1 in 10 probability of making this statement erroneously. Similarly, significance tests using the $t$ probability output (Table 15.2, note ③) yield a similar conclusion. The $F$ significance test uses the sum of squares (via ANOVA) to test for significance, while the $t$ significance test assesses the magnitude of "estimate" (see Table 15.2, note ⑦). This is analogous to the significance tests conducted on the contrast column effects in Example 14-2. For this model the factors algor and mot_adj are both significant at a significance level of 0.0001. The other three factors cannot be shown to be significant at the 0.10 level (see Section 13.4).

Other information worth highlighting in Table 15.2 is the allocation of degrees of freedom. Since each of the factors had two levels, the number of degrees of freedom per factor was 1 ($2 − 1 = 1$) (Table 15.2, note ④). With a 16-trial experiment the total number of degrees of freedom is 15

**TABLE 15.2. Example 15-1: Main Effect Model Analyses**

GENERAL LINEAR MODELS PROCEDURE

DEPENDENT VARIABLE: TIMING

| SOURCE | DF | SUM OF SQUARES | MEAN SQUARE | F VALUE | PR > F | R-SQUARE | C.V. |
|---|---|---|---|---|---|---|---|
| MODEL | 5 | 50.61312500 | 10.12262500 | 24.18 | 0.0001 | ⑥ 0.923608 | 13.3577 |
| ERROR | ⑤ 10 | 4.18625000 | 0.41862500 | | ROOT MSE | | TIMING MEAN |
| CORRECTED TOTAL | 15 | 54.79937500 | | | 0.64701236 | | 4.84375000 |

① ④

| SOURCE | DF | TYPE III SS | F VALUE | PR > F |
|---|---|---|---|---|
| | | | | ② |
| MOT_TEMP | 1 | 0.14062500 | 0.34 | 0.5750 |
| ALGOR | 1 | 31.64062500 | 75.58 | 0.0001 |
| MOT_ADJ | 1 | 18.27562500 | 43.66 | 0.0001 |
| EXT_ADJ | 1 | 0.33062500 | 0.79 | 0.3950 |
| SUP_VOLT | 1 | 0.22562500 | 0.54 | 0.4797 |

| PARAMETER | ESTIMATE | T FOR H0: PARAMETER=0 | PR > \|T\| ③ | STD ERROR OF ESTIMATE |
|---|---|---|---|---|
| | ⑦ | | | |
| INTERCEPT | 4.84375000 | 29.95 | 0.0001 | 0.16175309 |
| MOT_TEMP | -0.09375000 | -0.58 | 0.5750 | 0.16175309 |
| ALGOR | -1.40625000 | -8.69 | 0.0001 | 0.16175309 |
| MOT_ADJ | 1.06875000 | 6.61 | 0.0001 | 0.16175369 |
| EXT_ADJ | -0.14375000 | -0.89 | 0.3950 | 0.16175369 |
| SUP_VOLT | -0.11875000 | -0.73 | 0.4797 | 0.16175369 |

EXAMPLE 15-1: ANALYSIS OF A RESOLUTION V DESIGN    **223**

(16 − 1 = 15); hence, there are 10 degrees of freedom for error since the total number of degrees of freedom for the main effects model is 5 (Table 15.2, note ⑤). The $R^2$ value of 0.92 (Table 15.2, note ⑥) indicates that the model describes 92% of the experiment variability; however, care should be exercised when interpreting this value. $R^2$ can give a deceptively large number when the number of terms in the model approaches the number of trials minus one (see Table 15.5). The estimate values (Table 15.2, note ⑦) are the coefficients of the terms in the linear regression model (see Section 13.21). Since this experiment is balanced, this output format represents half the best estimate differences from −1 to +1 levels of the factors (see Section 13.21). For example, a −1 level for algor should yield an output that is approximately 2.81 msec higher than a +1 level for this factor (i.e., 1.40625 × 2 ≈ 2.81). When factor levels in a design are not balanced and interactions are considered, the user should beware that the magnitude of the regression coefficients can deceive the observer to making an erroneous conclusion about the magnitude of an effect.

Table 15.3 shows the means (Table 15.3, note ①) for each of the factor levels (Table 15.3, note ②). The Duncan option was exercised to test for significance between the factor levels (Table 15.3, note ③); again, the factors algor and mot_adj are significant (i.e., there are two "groupings" indicated, "A" and "B"). Multiple range tests such as Duncan are of more value whenever there are more than two levels of the factor. In this test a factor having four levels may indicate, for example, that level 1 is significantly different than 2 and 3, which is still different than 4. The $N$ output (Table 15.3, note ④) indicates that eight trials were performed at both the −1 and +1 levels of the factor. In this example the Duncan test was used for the significance test of the levels of the factors. Other multiple range tests that could similarly be determined are BonFerroni $t$ tests, Gabriel Multiple Comparison Procedure, Fisher's least significant difference test, Tukey's studentized range test, and Waller–Duncan $k$-Ratio $t$ test (SAS 1985b; Box, et al. 1978; Montgomery 1984). Each of these tests has unique advantages, which may be data sensitive.

The accuracy of the preceding significance test and best estimate assessments are dependent on the accuracy of the assumption that the errors are normal and independently distributed with mean zero and a constant but unknown variance. In reality, these assumptions are not generally exact; however, it is wise to ensure that there are not any large deviations from these assumptions. Violations of some basic assumptions can be investigated by examining the residuals of the model. The residual for each trial is the difference between the trial output and the model prediction value. If these assumptions are valid, the data has balanced scatter and no patterns. If there is much deviation from these assumptions, a data transformation (see Section 15.4) may be necessary to get a more accurate significance test.

Table 15.4 shows the original data along with the model prediction values and residuals. For this example a plot of the residuals against the predicted values is shown in Figure 15.1. This plot does not indicate any general

**TABLE 15.3. Example 15-1: Duncan's Multiple-Range Means Analysis**

```
              GENERAL LINEAR MODELS PROCEDURE
DUNCAN'S MULTIPLE RANGE TEST FOR VARIABLE: TIMING
NOTE: THIS TEST CONTROLS THE TYPE I COMPARISONWISE ERROR RATE,
     NOT THE EXPERIMENTWISE ERROR RATE

         ALPHA=0.05  DF=10  MSE=0.418625

            NUMBER OF MEANS        2
            CRITICAL RANGE    0.71952
```

MEANS WITH THE SAME LETTER ARE NOT SIGNIFICANTLY DIFFERENT.

| DUNCAN | GROUPING ③ | | MEAN ① | ④ N | MOT_TEMP ② |
|--------|------------|---|--------|-----|------------|
| | A | | 4.9375 | 8 | -1 |
| | A | | | | |
| | A | | 4.7500 | 8 | 1 |
| DUNCAN | GROUPING | | ⑤ MEAN | N | ALGOR |
| | A | * | 6.2500 | 8 | -1 |
| | B | | 3.4375 | 8 | 1 |
| DUNCAN | GROUPING | | ⑥ MEAN | N | MOT_ADJ |
| | A | ** | 5.9125 | 8 | 1 |
| | B | | 3.7750 | 8 | -1 |
| DUNCAN | GROUPING | | MEAN | N | EXT_ADJ |
| | A | | 4.9875 | 8 | -1 |
| | A | | | | |
| | A | | 4.7000 | 8 | 1 |
| DUNCAN | GROUPING | | MEAN | N | SUP_VOLT |
| | A | | 4.9625 | 8 | -1 |
| | A | | | | |
| | A | | 4.7250 | 8 | 1 |

```
*   3.4375 - 6.2500 = - 2.8125

**  5.9125 - 3.7750 = + 2.1375
```

curvature or change in the amount spread as a function of pred1; however, the datum point that has the $-1.36$ residual may need to be further investigated for accuracy since it appears to be an outlier from the model (Table 15.9). From Table 15.4 this point is noted to be for the number of trials which is 6 ($NT = 6$). Residuals plotted against factor levels, sequence of trials, and so forth should similarly not have trends.

A probability plot (see Chapter 5) is a convenient tool to assess the normality assumption of the residuals. The data plot in Figure 15.2 should approximately

**TABLE 15.4. Example 15-1: Experimental Data with Model Predictions and Residuals**

| OBS | NT | MOT_TEMP | ALGOR | MOT_ADJ | EXT_ADJ | SUP_VOLT | TIMING | PRED1 | RES1 |
|-----|----|----------|-------|---------|---------|----------|--------|--------|---------|
| 1 | 1 | 1 | -1 | -1 | -1 | 1 | 5.6 | 5.1125 | 0.4875 |
| 2 | 2 | 1 | 1 | -1 | -1 | -1 | 2.1 | 2.5375 | -0.4375 |
| 3 | 3 | 1 | 1 | -1 | -1 | -1 | 4.9 | 4.4375 | 0.4625 |
| 4 | 4 | -1 | 1 | 1 | 1 | 1 | 4.9 | 4.3875 | 0.5125 |
| 5 | 5 | -1 | -1 | 1 | 1 | 1 | 4.1 | 4.3375 | -0.2375 |
| 6 | 6 | 1 | -1 | 1 | 1 | 1 | 5.6 | 6.9625 | -1.3625 |
| 7 | 7 | -1 | -1 | -1 | -1 | -1 | 1.9 | 2.4375 | -0.5375 |
| 8 | 8 | 1 | -1 | -1 | -1 | -1 | 7.2 | 7.4875 | -0.2875 |
| 9 | 9 | -1 | 1 | 1 | 1 | -1 | 2.4 | 2.0125 | 0.3875 |
| 10 | 10 | -1 | 1 | -1 | -1 | -1 | 5.1 | 4.8625 | 0.2375 |
| 11 | 11 | -1 | 1 | 1 | 1 | -1 | 7.9 | 7.3875 | 0.5125 |
| 12 | 12 | -1 | 1 | -1 | 1 | -1 | 5.3 | 5.0625 | -0.2375 |
| 13 | 13 | -1 | 1 | -1 | -1 | 1 | 2.1 | 2.4875 | -0.3875 |
| 14 | 14 | -1 | 1 | -1 | -1 | 1 | 7.6 | 7.4375 | 0.1625 |
| 15 | 15 | -1 | 1 | 1 | 1 | 1 | 5.5 | 5.0125 | 0.4875 |
| 16 | 16 | -1 | -1 | -1 | -1 | -1 | 5.3 | 5.5375 | -0.2375 |

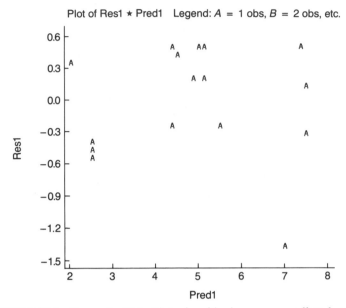

**FIGURE 15.1.** Example 15-1: Plot of residuals versus predicted values.

follow a straight line for this plot for the assumptions to be valid. However, the fit is not as good as we would like to see. A data transformation (see Section 15.4) in general can be considered when one is confronted with a nonlinear probability plot. In this plot the $-1.36$ residual appears again as a possible outlier. In Example 15-2 this experimental data is reanalyzed without the datum point Number 6, which was responsible for this residual.

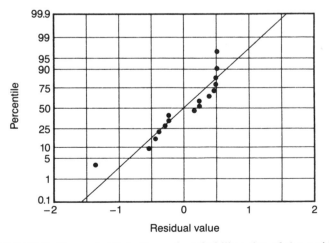

**FIGURE 15.2.** Example 15-1: Normal probability plot of the residuals.

**TABLE 15.5. Example 15-1: Main Effects and Interactions Model**

GENERAL LINEAR MODELS PROCEDURE

DEPENDENT VARIABLE: TIMING

| SOURCE | DF | SUM OF SQUARES | MEAN SQUARE | F VALUE | PR > F | R-SQUARE | C.V. |
|---|---|---|---|---|---|---|---|
| MODEL | 15 | 54.79937500 | 3.65329167 | . | . | 1.000000 | 0.0000 |
| ERROR | 0 | 0.00000000 | 0.00000000 | | ROOT MSE | | TIMING MEAN |
| CORRECTED TOTAL | 15 | 54.79937500 | | | 0.00000000 | | 4.84375000 |

| SOURCE ① | DF | TYPE III SS ② | F VALUE | PR > F |
|---|---|---|---|---|
| MOT_TEMP | 1 | 0.14062500 | . | . |
| ALGOR | 1 | 31.64062500 | . | . |
| MOT_ADJ | 1 | 18.27562500 | . | . |
| EXT_ADJ | 1 | 0.33062500 | . | . |
| SUP_VOLT | 1 | 0.22562500 | . | . |
| MOT_TEMP*ALGOR | 1 | 0.05562500 | . | . |
| MOT_TEMP*MOT_ADJ | 1 | 0.45562500 | . | . |
| MOT_TEMP*EXT_ADJ | 1 | 0.05062500 | . | . |
| MOT_TEMP*SUP_VOLT | 1 | 0.00062500 | . | . |
| ALGOR*MOT_ADJ | 1 | 0.95062500 | . | . |
| ALGOR*EXT_ADJ | 1 | 0.01562500 | . | . |
| ALGOR*SUP_VOLT | 1 | 0.05062500 | . | . |
| MOT_ADJ*EXT_ADJ | 1 | 0.33062500 | . | . |
| MOT_ADJ*SUP_VOLT | 1 | 0.95062500 | . | . |
| EXT_ADJ*SUP_VOLT | 1 | 0.52562500 | . | . |

227

The residual plots (see Figures 15.6 and 15.7) from this analysis have a more desirable appearance.

Again, this experiment is a resolution V design since there are 5 factors in 16 trials, and it follows a design matrix of Table M3. Because of this, a two-factor interaction model is then made to yield the regression output noted in Table 15.5.

From Table 15.5 the number of factors and corresponding interactions (Table 15.5, note ①) utilize all the columns of the matrix; hence, there are no interaction larger than two-factor contrast columns left to use to estimate experimental error. However, the values in the sum of squares column (Table 15.5, note ②) for algor and mot_adj are by far large numbers relative to the other factors and interactions sum of squares; hence, our previous model considering only main effects seems reasonable. It should be noted that for this situation where there is no estimate for error the model fits perfectly (i.e., $R^2 = 1$); hence, a residual plot for this situation would have no meaning.

As noted earlier, some computer software packages have an option for a probability plot of the contrast column effects. If this feature is not available, then the following procedure is a feasible alternative for these packages.

Table 15.6 indicates the output that was obtained by creating a model such that the interactions appear as newly defined "factors." To illustrate this, see Section C.6 for the program coding and note, for example, the creation of temalgo such that

| Temalgo | Mot_temp | algor |
|---------|----------|-------|
| +       | −        | −     |
| +       | +        | +     |
| −       | +        | −     |
| −       | −        | +     |

In this balanced design situation, the coefficient estimates are one-half (see Section 13.21) the effects for each of the contrast columns from the −1 to +1 levels (Table 15.6, note ①). Figure 15.3 illustrates a probability plot of the effects of each of the contrast columns. Since of the 15 data points the only 2 that do not appear to follow a straight line are algor and mot_adj, it is a fair assumption to assume that these are the only significant factors. From this plot it could be justifable for this balanced design to consider only a model of these two factors. The other terms could then be used in an estimate for experimental error.

Another approach to data analysis in general is the consideration of stepwise regression (Draper and Smith 1966) or taking all possible regressions of the data, when selecting the number of terms to include in a model. This approach can be most useful whenever data is from an experiment that does not have the experiment structure that is proposed by this text. However, experimenters

EXAMPLE 15-1: ANALYSIS OF A RESOLUTION V DESIGN    229

**TABLE 15.6. Example 15-1: Analysis Output for Normal Probability Plot Considerations**

GENERAL LINEAR MODELS PROCEDURE

DEPENDENT VARIABLE: TIMING

| SOURCE | DF | SUM OF SQUARES | MEAN SQUARE | F VALUE | PR > F | R-SQUARE | C.V. |
|--------|----|----------------|-------------|---------|--------|----------|------|
| MODEL | 15 | 54.79937500 | 3.65329167 | . | . | 1.000000 | 0.0000 |
| ERROR | 0 | 0.00000000 | 0.00000000 | | ROOT MSE | | TIMING MEAN |
| CORRECTED TOTAL | 15 | 54.79937500 | | | | 0.00000000 | 4.84375000 |

| SOURCE | DF | TYPE III SS | F VALUE | PR > F |
|--------|----|-------------|---------|--------|
| EMOT_TEM | 1 | 0.14062500 | . | . |
| EALGOR | 1 | 31.64062500 | . | . |
| EMOT_ADJ | 1 | 18.27562500 | . | . |
| EEXT_ADJ | 1 | 0.33062500 | . | . |
| ESUP_VOL | 1 | 0.22562500 | . | . |
| TEMALGO | 1 | 0.85562500 | . | . |
| TEMMADJ | 1 | 0.45562500 | . | . |
| TEMEADJ | 1 | 0.05062500 | . | . |
| TEMVOLT | 1 | 0.00062500 | . | . |
| ALGMADJ | 1 | 0.95062500 | . | . |
| ALGEADJ | 1 | 0.01562500 | . | . |
| ALGVOLT | 1 | 0.05062500 | . | . |
| MADJEADJ | 1 | 0.33062500 | . | . |
| MADJVOLT | 1 | 0.95062500 | . | . |
| EADJVOLT | 1 | 0.52562500 | . | . |

| PARAMETER | ①<br>ESTIMATE | T FOR H0:<br>PARAMETER=0 | PR > \|T\| | STD ERROR OF<br>ESTIMATE |
|-----------|----------|--------------------------|-----------|--------------------------|
| INTERCEPT | 5.77500000 | 99999.99 | . | 0 |
| EMOT_TEM | -0.18750000 | -99999.99 | . | 0 |
| EALGOR | -2.81250000 | -99999.99 | . | 0 |
| EMOT_ADJ | 2.13750000 | 99999.99 | . | 0 |
| EEXT_ADJ | -0.28750000 | -99999.99 | . | 0 |
| ESUP_VOL | -0.23750000 | -99999.99 | . | 0 |
| TEMALGO | 0.46250000 | 99999.99 | . | 0 |
| TEMMADJ | -0.33750000 | -99999.99 | . | 0 |
| TEMEADJ | -0.11250000 | -99999.99 | . | 0 |
| TEMVOLT | -0.01250000 | -99999.99 | . | 0 |
| ALGMADJ | 0.48750000 | 99999.99 | . | 0 |
| ALGEADJ | 0.06250000 | 99999.99 | . | 0 |
| ALGVOLT | 0.11250000 | 99999.99 | . | 0 |
| MADJEADJ | -0.28750000 | -99999.99 | . | 0 |
| MADJVOLT | -0.48750000 | -99999.99 | . | 0 |
| EADJVOLT | -0.36250000 | -99999.99 | . | 0 |

should be aware of the potential pitfalls from happenstance data (Box, et al. 1978).

Consider next an analysis of all possible regressions for the previous data. Table 15.7 illustrates a computer output with all possible regressions. This approach first considers only one factor within a model, then two, and so forth (Table 15.7, notes ① and ②). The $R^2$ value is then considered for each of the models (Table 15.7, note ③); only factor combinations containing the highest two $R^2$ values are shown in Table 15.7. For example, if one were to consider a model containing only one factor, the factor to consider would be algor. Likewise, if one were to consider a model containing only two factors, the factors to consider would be algor with mot_adj.

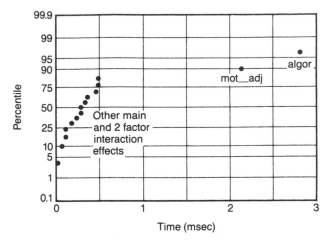

**FIGURE 15.3.** Example 15-1: Half normal probability plot of the contrast column effects.

Mallows' $C_p$ statistic [C(P) in Table 15.7, note ④] is useful to determine the minimum number of parameters that best fits the model. Technically this statistic measures the sum of the squared biases plus the squared random errors in $Y$ at all $n$ data points (Daniel and Wood 1980).

The minimum number of factors needed in the model is when the Mallows' $C_p$ statistic is a minimum. From this output the pertinent Mallows' $C_p$ statistic values under consideration as a function of numbers of factors within this model are

| Number in Model | Mallows' $C_p$[a] |
|:---:|:---:|
| 1 | 43.32 |
| 2 | 1.67 |
| 3 | 2.87 |
| 4 | 4.33 |
| 5 | 6.00 |

[a] The Mallows' $C_p$ is not related to the process indices $C_p$ in Chapter 19.

From this summary it is noted that the Mallows' $C_p$ statistic is minimized whenever there are two parameters in the model. The corresponding factors are algor and mot_adj. This conclusion is consistent with our previous analyses. The interaction terms from our previous analysis indicate that they are not significant; however, in general with a highly saturated design or unbalanced analyses using this analysis procedure, these interaction terms might also be initially included when determining the coefficients of the terms in a model.

EXAMPLE 15-1: ANALYSIS OF A RESOLUTION V DESIGN    **231**

**TABLE 15.7. Example 15-1: Summary from all Possible Regressions Analysis**

| N=16 | REGRESSION MODELS FOR DEPENDENT VARIABLE: TIMING MODEL: MODEL1 | | |
|---|---|---|---|
| NUMBER IN MODEL ① | R-SQUARE ③ | C(P) ④ | VARIABLES IN MODEL ② |
| 1 | 0.33350061 | 75.246939 | MOT_ADJ |
| 1 | 0.57739025 | 43.320991 | ALGOR |
| 2 | 0.58342362 | 44.531203 | ALGOR EXT_ADJ |
| 2 | 0.91009006 | 1.664676 | ALGOR MOT_ADJ |
| 3 | 0.91500815 | 3.125709 | ALGOR MOT_ADJ SUP_VOLT |
| 3 | 0.91692423 | 2.874888 | ALGOR MOT_ADJ EXT_ADJ |
| 4 | 0.91949041 | 4.538967 | ALGOR MOT_ADJ EXT_ADJ MOT_TEMP |
| 4 | 0.92104153 | 4.335921 | ALGOR MOT_ADJ EXT_ADJ SUP_VOLT |
| 5 | 0.92360771 | 6.000000 | ALGOR MOT_ADJ EXT_ADJ SUP_VOLT MOT_TEMP |

The initial purpose of the experiment was to determine whether a new algorithm should be used to move a stepper motor. The answer to this question is yes; the new algorithm can be expected to improve the motor settle-out time by approximately 2.81 msec. (See Table 15.3 note ⑤).

A couple of additional steps can be useful to address questions beyond the initial problem definition and put the data in better presentation form. Dissecting and presenting the data in a clear form can have hidden benefits. These additional considerations can be useful to reducing overall product costs. With these additional considerations perhaps a tolerance is discovered that should be tightened to reduce overall manufacturing variability, resulting in fewer customer failures and/or complaints. Another possibility is that a noncritical tolerance may be increased, causing another form of cost reduction.

Within this experiment the settle-out time was shown to be affected by motor adjustment (in addition to algorithm level); a +1 level of motor adjustment on the average increases the settle-out time by 2.1 msec (Table 15.3, note ⑥). To better understand this physical effect, determine from the raw data the mean values for the four combinations of algor and mot_adj, as indicated in Table 15.8. Assuming that the decision is made to convert to the new

**TABLE 15.8. Example 15-1: Overall Averages of algor and mot_adj**

| | ALGOR | MOT_ADJ | N | TIMING |
|---|---|---|---|---|
| NEW ALGORITHM | 1 | 1 | 4 | 4.75000000 |
| | 1 | -1 | 4 | 2.12500000 |
| OLD ALGORITHM | -1 | 1 | 4 | 7.07500000 |
| | -1 | -1 | 4 | 5.42500000 |

algorithm, a settle-out time of about 4.75 ms with the +1 level of the motor adjustment is expected, while this time should be about 2.12 ms with the −1 level of the factor (a settle-out time difference of 2.63 ms).

Obviously it is expected that it would be better if the mot_adj factor could always be adjusted near the −1 level. However, there may be some cost to reducing the adjustment from reaching the +1 level. To better understand the possible gain from recommending that the +1 mot_adj level should be targeted, a probability plot can yield a picture of the four scenario possibilities (Figure 15.4). This clearly indicates that combination 4 is superior. Similarly using the means and standard deviation values from each of the four combinations, a probability density function (Figure 15.5) can give a graphical sizing that illustrates the potential effects in another format. Care needs to be exercised when drawing specific conclusions from these graphs since the graphs only indicate trends from the calculated estimates and do not represent a random sample of a population with such characteristics.

The next action step depends on the settle-out time requirements for the product design. If a settle-out time less than 15 msec, for example, presents no chance of causing a machine failure, the best decision may be to simply accept the new algorithm with no special considerations about the motor adjustment. However, to obtain additional safety factor for unknown variabilities (e.g., motor to motor differences), a tightening of the motor adjustment tolerance toward the −1 level perhaps should be considered. If, however,

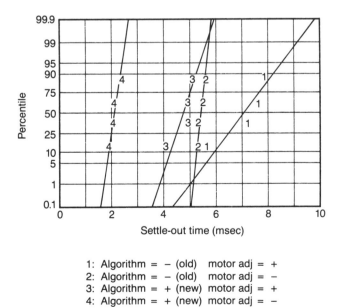

1: Algorithm = − (old)  motor adj = +
2: Algorithm = − (old)  motor adj = −
3: Algorithm = + (new)  motor adj = +
4: Algorithm = + (new)  motor adj = −

**FIGURE 15.4.** Example 15-1: Normal probability plots of the four combinations of algorithm and motor adjustment.

EXAMPLE 15-2: ANALYSIS/RESOLUTION V DESIGN WITH MISSING DATA    **233**

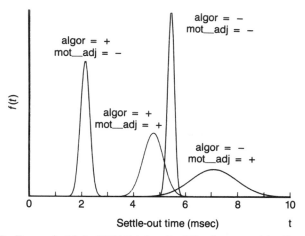

**FIGURE 15.5.** Example 15-1: PDF "sizings" of the four combinations of algorithm and motor adjustment.

the settle-out time requirement were less than 6 msec, for example, then another experiment seems appropriate to further assess other factors along with the other significant factor, mot_adj, to reduce this variability. Perhaps a further extremity than the −1 level for mot_adj could be considered. To bridge this new experiment proposal with the existing experiment, the same adjustment value for the −1 level of mot_adj could be used as a baseline level against a new adjustment value.

Example 19-14 continues the discussion on what could be done in the manufacturing environment to track the settle-out time of motors that are being built. In this example a CUSUM control chart is used to monitor for degradation of the motor's performance.

## 15.3. EXAMPLE 15-2: COMPUTER ANALYSIS OF A FRACTIONAL FACTORIAL EXPERIMENT DESIGN WITH MISSING DATA

Reconsider Example 15-1 given that higher response values are better. Consider also that additional investigation indicated that the questionable data point in Figure 15.4 was found to be in error and there was no way to repeat the test and get a valid response for this trial.

The following is an analysis where trial 6 is removed (see Table 15.1). The output from this computer analysis is shown in Table 15.9, which indicates that the decision about factor significance does not change from that of Example 15.1. Figure 15.6 contains a residual plot for this analysis that has a better random scatter pattern than Figure 15.1, while the normal probability plot of residuals in Figure 15.7 has a better linear pattern than Figure 15.2. For this analysis Table 15.10 shows a slightly different estimation of the

**TABLE 15.9. Example 15-2: Main Effects Model Without Bad Datum Point**

GENERAL LINEAR MODELS PROCEDURE

DEPENDENT VARIABLE: TIMING

| SOURCE | DF | SUM OF SQUARES | MEAN SQUARE | F VALUE | PR > F | R-SQUARE | C.V. |
|---|---|---|---|---|---|---|---|
| MODEL | 5 | 52.97333333 | 10.59466667 | 78.41 | 0.0001 | 0.977560 | 7.6685 |
| ERROR | 9 | 1.21600000 | 0.13511111 | | ROOT MSE | | TIMING MEAN |
| CORRECTED TOTAL | 14 | 54.18933333 | | | 0.36757463 | | 4.79333333 |

| SOURCE | DF | TYPE III SS | F VALUE | PR > F |
|---|---|---|---|---|
| MOT_TEMP | 1 | 0.02627273 | 0.19 | 0.6696 |
| ALGOR | 1 | 34.60809091 | 256.15 | 0.0001 |
| MOT_ADJ | 1 | 21.12036364 | 156.32 | 0.0001 |
| EXT_ADJ | 1 | 0.00081818 | 0.01 | 0.9397 |
| SUP_VOLT | 1 | 0.00445455 | 0.03 | 0.8599 |

| PARAMETER | ESTIMATE | T FOR H0: PARAMETER=0 | PR > |T| | STD ERROR OF ESTIMATE |
|---|---|---|---|---|
| INTERCEPT | 4.98000000 | 51.67 | 0.0001 | 0.09637888 |
| MOT_TEMP | 0.04250000 | 0.44 | 0.6696 | 0.09637888 |
| ALGOR | -1.54250000 | -16.00 | 0.0001 | 0.09637888 |
| MOT_ADJ | 1.20500000 | 12.50 | 0.0001 | 0.09637888 |
| EXT_ADJ | -0.00750000 | -0.08 | 0.9397 | 0.09637888 |
| SUP_VOLT | 0.01750000 | 0.18 | 0.8599 | 0.09637888 |

234

EXAMPLE 15-2: ANALYSIS/RESOLUTION V DESIGN WITH MISSING DATA **235**

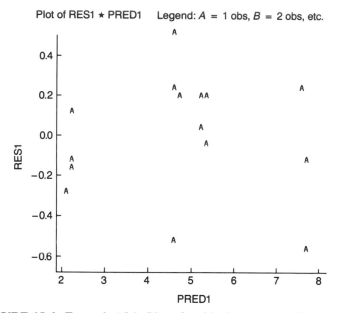

**FIGURE 15.6.** Example 15-2: Plot of residuals versus predicted values.

mean effects for the factors. If the probability plot of Figure 15.4 is reconstructed (not shown) for the −1 level of algor and the +1 level of mot_adj (i.e., Scenario Number 1), the fit for this scenario would be found better since the 5.6 msec data point for this scenario was the bad datum point that was removed from the analysis.

In Example 13-1 no interactions were found significant. However, if interactions are significant, their effects can be graphically displayed, as shown

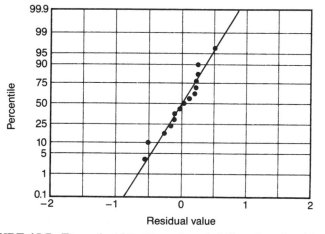

**FIGURE 15.7.** Example 15-2: Normal probability plot of residuals.

**TABLE 15.10. Example 15-2: Duncan Multiple-Range Means Analysis (without bad datum point)**

```
                    GENERAL LINEAR MODELS PROCEDURE

DUNCAN'S MULTIPLE RANGE TEST FOR VARIABLE: TIMING
NOTE: THIS TEST CONTROLS THE TYPE I COMPARISONWISE ERROR RATE,
      NOT THE EXPERIMENTWISE ERROR RATE

            ALPHA=0.05   DF=9   MSE=0.135111

        WARNING: CELL SIZES ARE NOT EQUAL.
                 HARMONIC MEAN OF CELL SIZES=7.46667

                NUMBER OF MEANS          2
                CRITICAL RANGE    0.429652

    MEANS WITH THE SAME LETTER ARE NOT SIGNIFICANTLY DIFFERENT.

        DUNCAN    GROUPING          MEAN      N  ALGOR

                    A              6.3429     7  -1

                    B              3.4375     8   1



                    GENERAL LINEAR MODELS PROCEDURE

DUNCAN'S MULTIPLE RANGE TEST FOR VARIABLE: TIMING
NOTE: THIS TEST CONTROLS THE TYPE I COMPARISONWISE ERROR RATE,
      NOT THE EXPERIMENTWISE ERROR RATE

            ALPHA=0.05   DF=9   MSE=0.135111

        WARNING: CELL SIZES ARE NOT EQUAL.
                 HARMONIC MEAN OF CELL SIZES=7.46667

                NUMBER OF MEANS          2
                CRITICAL RANGE    0.429652

    MEANS WITH THE SAME LETTER ARE NOT SIGNIFICANTLY DIFFERENT.

        DUNCAN    GROUPING          MEAN      N  MOT_ADJ

                    A              5.9571     7   1

                    B              3.7750     8  -1
```

in Figure 13.1. In addition, as noted in Chapter 13, a confirmation experiment should be considered before using the fractional factorial information in the manufacturing process. For the previous example a comparison experiment (see Chapter 9) might be appropriate using several motors (e.g., 10), where the settle-out time characteristics of old algorithm/motor adj = +1 is compared to new algorithm/motor adj = −1. In addition to statistically comparing mean and variance of the two situations, probability plots of the timings for the 10 "new" and "old" motors could be very enlightening (see Figure 22.7).

## 15.4. DATA TRANSFORMATIONS

Residual plots should show no structure relative to any factor including the fitted response; however, trends within the data may occur for various reasons. One phenomenon that may occur is inconsistent variance. One example of this situation is that the error of an instrument may increase with larger readings since this error could be a percentage of the scale reading. If this were the case, the residuals would increase as a function of scale reading. A data transformation could then be used to reduce this phenomenon within the residuals, which would yield a more precise significance test.

Another situation occurs when the output is count data, where a square root transformation may be appropriate, while a log-normal transformation is often appropriate if the trial outputs are standard deviation values and a logit might be helpful when there are upper and lower limits. A summary of common transformations is noted in Table 15.11.

As an alternative approach to the tabular considerations, Box (1988) and Fung (1986) describe a method to eliminate unnecessary coupling of dispersion effects and location effects by determining an approximate transformation using a lambda plot.

With transformations, one should note that the conclusions of the analysis apply to the transformed populations. Montgomery (1984) and Box et al. (1978) discuss transformations in additional depth.

**TABLE 15.11. Data Transformations**

| Data Characteristics | Data ($x_i$ or $p_i$) Transformation |
| --- | --- |
| $\sigma \propto$ constant | none |
| $\sigma \propto \mu^2$ | $\dfrac{1}{x_i}$ |
| $\sigma \propto \mu^{3/2}$ | $\dfrac{1}{\sqrt{x_i}}$ |
| $\sigma \propto \mu$, sample variance | $\log x_i$ |
| $\sigma \propto \sqrt{\mu}$, Poisson (count) data | $\sqrt{x_i}$ or $\sqrt{x_i + 1}$ |
| Binomial proportions[a] | $\sin^{-1}(\sqrt{p_i})$ |
| Upper and lower bounded data (e.g., $0 - 1$ probability of failure) (logit transformation) | $\log \dfrac{x_i - \text{lower limit}}{\text{upper limit} - x_i}$ |

[a] As noted in Section 13.19, proportion defective (i.e., $p$ from attribute data) fractional factorial information can often be more precisely analyzed using a categorical computer analysis routine.

## 15.5. VARIANCE COMPONENTS: ANALYSIS

Box et al. (1978) and Montgomery (1984) discuss the "analysis of variance method" when estimating variance components (see Section 4.8). In this procedure the expected mean squares of the analysis of variance table are equated to their observed value in the analysis of variance table and then solved for the variance components. In this text the SAS VARCOMP procedure is used for the analysis.

Occasionally variance components analyses yield negative estimates. Negative estimates are viewed with concern since it is obvious that by definition variance components cannot be negative. For these situations it has intuitive appeal to accept the negative estimate and use it as evidence that the true value is zero. This approach suffers from theoretical difficulties since using a zero in place of the negative estimates can affect the statistical properties of the other estimates. Another approach is to use alternate calculating technique that yields a nonnegative estimate [see SAS (1985b)]. Still another approach is to consider that this is evidence that the linear model is incorrect and the problem needs to be reexamined (Montgomery 1984).

Examples 15-3 and 15-4 illustrate the application of the SAS analysis procedure PROC VARCOMP to solving the variance components problems originally defined in Examples 13-4 and 13-5.

## 15.6. EXAMPLE 15-3: NESTED VARIANCE COMPONENTS ANALYSIS

Example 13-4 discussed three components of variance in the final moisture reading of pigment paste. Consider the experimental data shown in Table 15.12 (Box et al. 1978).

A variance components analysis for this set of experimental data is shown in Table 15.13. The programming steps used to generate this output is shown in Section C.7. The parenthesis around the names are used to indicate nesting. For example, Sample (Batch) indicates that the variable name "sample" is nested in "batch."

From this analysis output the variance component estimates are noted to be the following. (See Box et al. 1978 for the mechanics on how these estimates can be determined without the aid of a computer program.)

Analytical test variance = 0.92

Sample variance (within batches) = 28.5

Process variance (between batches) = 7.1

The square roots of these variances are estimates of the standard deviations that are pictorially compared in Figure 15.8.

These results indicate that the largest individual source for variation was the error arising in chemical sampling. Box et al. (1978) discuss how inves-

**TABLE 15.12. Example 15-3: Moisture Content of Pigment Pastes**

| Sample | Subsample | Batch | | | | | | | | | | | | | | |
|---|---|---|---|---|---|---|---|---|---|---|---|---|---|---|---|---|
| | | 1 | 2 | 3 | 4 | 5 | 6 | 7 | 8 | 9 | 10 | 11 | 12 | 13 | 14 | 15 |
| 1 | 1 | 40 | 26 | 29 | 30 | 19 | 33 | 23 | 34 | 27 | 13 | 25 | 29 | 19 | 23 | 39 |
| | 2 | 39 | 28 | 28 | 31 | 20 | 32 | 24 | 34 | 27 | 16 | 23 | 29 | 20 | 24 | 37 |
| 2 | 1 | 30 | 25 | 14 | 24 | 17 | 26 | 32 | 29 | 31 | 27 | 25 | 31 | 29 | 25 | 26 |
| | 2 | 30 | 26 | 15 | 24 | 17 | 24 | 33 | 29 | 31 | 24 | 27 | 32 | 30 | 25 | 28 |

**TABLE 15.13. Example 15-3: Computer Output**

VARIANCE COMPONENT ESTIMATION PROCEDURE

DEPENDENT VARIABLE: MOISTURE

| SOURCE | DF | TYPE I SS | TYPE I MS | EXPECTED MEAN SQUARE |
|---|---|---|---|---|
| BATCH | 14 | 1210.93333333 | 86.49523810 | VAR(ERROR) + 2 VAR(SAMPLE(BATCH)) + 4 VAR(BATCH) |
| SAMPLE(BATCH) | 15 | 869.75000000 | 57.98333333 | VAR(ERROR) + 2 VAR(SAMPLE(BATCH)) |
| ERROR | 30 | 27.50000000 | 0.91666667 | VAR(ERROR) |
| CORRECTED TOTAL | 59 | 2108.18333333 | | |

| VARIANCE COMPONENT | ESTIMATE |
|---|---|
| VAR(BATCH) | 7.12797619 |
| VAR(SAMPLE(BATCH)) | 28.53333333 |
| VAR(ERROR) | 0.91666667 |

EXAMPLE 15-4: VARIANCE COMPONENTS ANALYSIS    **241**

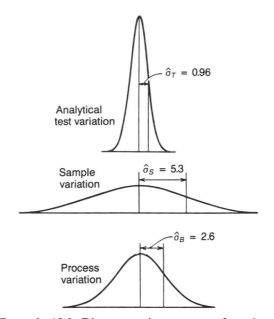

**FIGURE 15.8.** Example 15-3: Diagrammatic summary of results of experiment to determine components of variance. [Reproduced with permission: G. E. P. Box, W. Hunter, and S. Hunter, *Statistics for Experimenters*, John Wiley and Sons, 1978.]

tigators given this information then discovered and resolved the problem of operators not being aware of the correct sampling procedure.

## 15.7. EXAMPLE 15-4: VARIANCE COMPONENTS ANALYSIS

Example 13-5 discussed an experiment consideration where it was desired to investigate the variation in strength produced by a large number of looms in a textile company. The data from this experiment was as follows:

| Looms | Observations | | | |
|---|---|---|---|---|
| | 1 | 2 | 3 | 4 |
| 1 | 98 | 97 | 99 | 96 |
| 2 | 91 | 90 | 93 | 92 |
| 3 | 96 | 95 | 97 | 95 |
| 4 | 95 | 96 | 99 | 98 |

An output from the computer variance components analysis is shown in Table 15.14. The program code that generated this output is shown in Section C.8.

From this analysis output it is noted that the estimated variance component "between looms" is 6.96, while the "within loom estimate" is 1.90. The

**TABLE 15.14. Example 15-4: Computer Output**

VARIANCE COMPONENT ESTIMATION PROCEDURE

DEPENDENT VARIABLE: STRENGTH

| SOURCE | DF | TYPE I SS | TYPE I MS | EXPECTED MEAN SQUARE |
|---|---|---|---|---|
| LOOMS | 3 | 89.18750000 | 29.72916667 | VAR(ERROR) + 4 VAR(LOOMS) |
| ERROR | 12 | 22.75000000 | 1.89583333 | VAR(ERROR) |
| CORRECTED TOTAL | 15 | 111.93750000 | | |

| VARIANCE COMPONENT | ESTIMATE |
|---|---|
| VAR(LOOMS) | 6.95833333 |
| VAR(ERROR) | 1.89583333 |

variance of any observation on strength is 8.86 (6.96 + 1.90). The standard deviation consideration for this value would then be 2.977 (i.e., $\sqrt{8.86}$).

If the overall standard deviation of 2.977 is concluded to be too large resulting in too much fabric that is out of criterion, the differences between looms needs to be investigated for improvement opportunities. When making such quantifications relative to the specification limits, a process index $C_p$ calculation is often beneficial (see Section 19.15).

The Taguchi loss function (see Section 16.2) is a useful tool that can be used to consider the economic implications of not meeting a target even though all of the product produced may be within specification. Outputs from a variance components analysis could be used as inputs to the calculation of this loss function.

## 15.8. DO-IT-SMARTER CONSIDERATIONS

In some situations effort should be given to understanding the magnitude of the effects from significant factors. With this understanding follow-up experiments can be designed to yield additional insight toward an optimal solution. Understanding the levels of factors that did not affect the output significantly is also important since this knowledge can lead to relaxed tolerances that can be easier to achieve.

In many instances the overall understanding of the process through fractional factorial experiments can be combined with general cost considerations in order to determine the changes that are "best" in order to supply the customer with a high-quality/low-cost product. In other instances fractional factorial experiments can be used to structure a test strategy so that the test efficiently evaluates a product relative to meeting the needs of the customer.

Variability is often the elusive enemy of manufacturing processes. Variance components analysis can aid in the identification of the major contributors to this variability. Example 15-4 discusses the possibility of using the output from a variance components analysis to quantify variability relative to specification limits and economic considerations [via the process index $C_p$ (Section 19.15) and Taguchi loss function (Section 16.2)]. When variability in a product or process is too large and the source for this variability is understood, perhaps only a few simple changes are necessary to reduce its magnitude and improve quality. In other cases there may not be good insight on how a large detrimental variance component can be reduced. In this case it could be appropriate to next use a fractional factorial experiment design strategy that considers various factors that could contribute to the largest amount of variability in the area of concern; output from this experiment could lead to better insight to what changes should be made to the process for the purpose of reducing variability.

Examples 22-2 and 22-3, along with Section 13.25, contain additional do-it-smarter considerations.

# 16

# FACTORIAL EXPERIMENTS: TAGUCHI CONTRIBUTIONS

Recommended introductory reading: Chapters 2, 3, 4, and 13.

The experimentation procedures proposed by Genichi Taguchi (Taguchi and Konishi 1987) have experienced both acclaim and criticism. Some nonstatisticians like the practicality of the techniques, while statisticians have noted problems that can lead to erroneous conclusions. However, most statisticians will agree that Taguchi has increased visibility to the area of design of experiments. In addition, most statisticians and engineers will probably agree with Taguchi that more direct emphasis should have been given in the past to the reduction of process variability and the reduction of cost within product design and manufacturing processes.

This chapter gives a brief overview of the basic Taguchi philosophy as it relates to the concepts discussed in this text. The loss function also is discussed along with an approach that can be used to reduce variability in the manufacturing process.

## 16.1. TEST STRATEGIES

Published Taguchi (Taguchi and Konishi 1987) "orthogonal arrays and linear graphs" contain both two- and three-level experiment design matrices. As discussed in Chapter 13, I prefer a basic two-level factor strategy for most experiments with follow-up experiments that could address additional levels of a factor or factors. The response surface techniques described in Chapter 17 could also be used, in some cases, as part of that follow-up effort.

The basic two-level Taguchi design matrices are equivalent to those in Table M (Breyfogle, 1989e), where these basic matrices have $n$ trials with $n - 1$ contrast column considerations. For the two-level designs of 4, 8, 16, 32, and 64 trials, Table N contains the two-factor interaction confounding for the design matrices found in Table M (see Section 13.10).*

One suggested Taguchi test strategy consists of implementing one experiment (which could be rather large) with a confirmation experiment. Taguchi experiment analysis techniques do not normally dwell upon interaction considerations that are not anticipated before the start of test. If care is not taken during contrast column selection when choosing the experiment design matrix, an unnecessary or a messy interaction confounding structure may result, which can lead the experimenter to an erroneous conclusion (Box et al. 1988).

This text suggests first considering what initial experiment resolution (see Section 13.6) is needed and manageable with the number of two-level factors that are present. If a resolution is chosen that does not directly consider interactions, some interaction concerns can be managed by using the techniques described in Example 22-5. After this first experiment analysis, one of several actions may next be appropriate, depending on the analysis results. First, the test may yield dramatic conclusions that could answer the question of concern. For this situation a simple confirmation experiment may then be appropriate. The results from another experiment may lead testers to plan a follow-up experiment that considers other factors in conjunction with those factors that appear significant. Still another situation may suggest a follow-up experiment of significant factors at a higher resolution for interaction considerations.

Again, if interactions are not managed properly within an experiment, confusion and erroneous action plans can result. In addition, the management of these interactions is much more plausible when three-level factors are not involved in the fractional factorial experiment design.

## 16.2. LOSS FUNCTION

The loss function is a contribution of Genichi Taguchi (1978). This concept can bridge the language barrier between upper management and those involved in the technical details. Upper management best understands money, while those involved within the technical arena better understand product variability. Classical experiment design concepts traditionally do not directly emphasize the reduction of process variability and translate this need to economical considerations understood by all management.

---

* Tables A through R3 are located in Appendix D of the book.

The loss function describes the loss that occurs when a process does not produce a product that meets a target value. Loss is minimized when there is "no variability" and the "best" response is achieved in all areas of the product design.

Traditionally, manufacturing has considered all parts that are outside specification limits to be equally nonconforming, while all parts within specification are equally conforming. The loss function associated with this way of thinking is noted in Figure 16.1.

With the Taguchi approach it is not believed that loss relative to the specification limit is a step function. To understand this point, consider whether it is realistic, for example, to believe that there is no exposure of having any problems (i.e., loss) when a part is barely within the specification limit and if the maximum loss level is appropriate whenever the part is barely outside these limits. Most people would agree that this is not normally true.

Taguchi addresses variability within the process using a loss function. The loss function can take many forms. A common form is the quadratic loss function

$$L = k(y - m)^2 \tag{16.1}$$

where $L$ is the loss associated with a particular value of the independent variable $y$. The specification nominal value is $m$, while $k$ is a constant depending on the cost and width of the specification limits. Figure 16.2 illustrates this loss function graphically. When this loss function is applied to a situation more emphasis will be given toward achieving target as opposed to just meeting specification limits. This type of philosophy encourages, for example, a television manufacturer to continually strive to routinely manufacture prod-

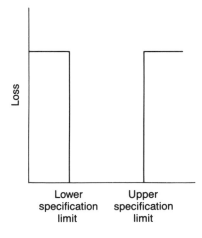

Lower specification limit   Upper specification limit

**FIGURE 16.1.** Traditional method of interpreting manufacturing limits.

EXAMPLE 16-1: LOSS FUNCTION    **247**

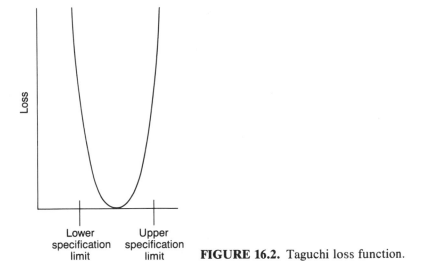

**FIGURE 16.2.** Taguchi loss function.

ucts that have a very high quality picture (i.e., a nominal specification value), as opposed to accepting and distributing a quality level that is "good enough."

### 16.3. EXAMPLE 16-1: LOSS FUNCTION

Given that the cost of scrapping a part is $10.00 when it exceeds a target by ±0.50 mm, from Equation (16.1), the quadratic loss function given $m$ (the nominal value) of 0.0 is

$$\$10.00 = k(0.5 - 0.0)^2$$

Hence

$$k = 10.00/0.25 = \$40.00 \text{ per mm}^2 \quad (\text{i.e., } \$25,806 \text{ per in.}^2)$$

This loss function then becomes

$$L = 40(y - 0)^2$$

As Ross (1988) notes, the loss function can yield different conclusions from decisions based on classical "goal post" specification limits. For example, a different decision can result relative to frequency of maintenance for a tool that wears within a manufacturing process. In addition, with this loss function economic decisions can now be made to determine whether expense should be incurred to implement a new process that can yield a tighter tolerance.

## 16.4. STANDARD DEVIATION AS A RESPONSE

Again, most practitioners of statistical techniques agree with Taguchi that it is important to reduce variability within the manufacturing process. To do this, Taguchi suggests using an inner and outer array (i.e., fractional factorial design structure) to address the issue. The inner array addresses the items that can be controlled (e.g., part tolerances), while the outer array addresses factors that cannot necessarily be controlled (e.g. ambient temperature and humidity). To analyze the data, he devised a signal to noise ratio technique, which Box et al. (1988) show can yield debatable results. However, Box (1988) states that it can be shown that use of the signal-to-noise ratio concept is equivalent to an analysis of the logarithm of the data (see Table 15.11).

The included fractional factorial designs in this text can be used to address the basic strategy of reducing manufacturing variability using the inner/outer array experimentation strategy. To do this simply categorize the factor listing into controllable and noncontrollable factors. The controllable factors would contain a design structure similar to that illustrated with the examples shown in Chapter 13, while the noncontrollable factors would be set to levels denoted by another fractional factorial design. All the noncontrollable factor experimental design trials would be performed for each trial of the controllable factor experimentation design. Note, however, that in using this inner/outer experimentation strategy a traditional design of 16 trials might now contain a total of 64 trials, if there is an outer experiment design containing 4 test trials.

Now, both a mean and standard deviation value can be obtained for each trial and analyzed independently. The trial mean value could be directly analyzed using the procedures noted in Chapters 14 and 15. The standard deviation for each trial would probably need to have a logarithm transformation within the analysis procedure (the transformation commonly used to normalize standard deviation data—see Table 15.11).

If the Taguchi experiment philosophy of using an inner and outer array were followed in the design of the stepper motor fractional factorial experiment (see Example 13-1), the temperature factor in the experiment would probably be considered within an outer array matrix. This could be done along with perhaps other parameters remembering that the mean value needs to be optimized (minimized to meet this particular test objective) in addition to minimizing variability considerations.

Obviously a practitioner is not required to use the inner/outer array experiment design approach when investigating the source of variability. It may be appropriate, for example, to construct an experiment design where each trial is replicated and the variance between replications is considered a trial response.

## 16.5. DO-IT-SMARTER CONSIDERATIONS

The mechanics of implementing some of the Taguchi concepts discussed in other texts is questionable. However, Taguchi has got management's attention on the importance of using design of experiment techniques. He has also got focus on the importance of reducing variability.

As noted in Section 19.15, the process index $C_p$ addresses the effects variability can have on the consistency of a process toward meeting specification objectives. Fractional factorial experiment concepts with standard deviation as a response can be used to improve $C_p$.

Example 22-1 addresses [with quality function deployment (QFD) concepts] tolerance and parameter considerations that are often addressed in other texts that elaborate more on specific Taguchi concepts.

# 17

# RESPONSE SURFACE AND MIXTURE DESIGNS

Recommended introductory reading: Chapters 2, 3, 4, and 13.

Response surface methods are used to determine how a response is affected by a set of quantitative variables/factors over some specified region. This information can be used to optimize the settings of a process to give, for example, a maximum or minimum response. With knowledge of the response surface, settings can possibly be chosen for a process such that day-to-day variations typically found in a manufacturing environment will have a minimum affect on the degradation of product quality.

For a given number of variables, response surface analysis techniques require more trials than the two-level fractional factorial design techniques discussed in Chapter 13; hence, the number of variables to consider within an experiment may first need to be reduced either through technical considerations or fractional factorial experiments.

This chapter shows the application of the central composite rotatable and Box–Behnken designs for determining the response surface analysis of variables. This chapter also discusses extreme vertices and simplex lattice designs along with computer algorithm designs for mixtures.

## 17.1. MODELING EQUATIONS

Chapters 13, 14, 15, and 16 on two-level fractional factorial experimentation considered main effects and interaction effects. For these designs the response was assumed to be linear between the level considerations for the factors. In these chapters the general philosophy is that several factor extremes are investigated to address many types of different problems expediently with a minimal number of test trials. This form of experimentation is adequate in itself to solve many types of problems. However, there are situations where a response needs to be optimized as a function of the levels of a few input factors/variables. This chapter focuses on such a situation.

The prediction equation for a two-factor linear main effect model without the consideration of interactions, as discussed in Section 13.21, takes the form

$$y = b_0 + b_1x_1 + b_2x_2 \qquad (17.1)$$

where $y$ is the response, $b_0$ is the $y$-axis intercept, and $(b_1, b_2)$ are the coefficients of the factors. For a balanced experiment design that had factor level considerations for $x_1$ and $x_2$, respectively equal to $-1$ and $+1$, the $b_1$ and $b_2$ coefficients equate to one-half of the effect determined using Equation (14.1) and $b_0$ is the overall average of all the responses. For a given set of experimental data, computer programs can determine these coefficients by such techniques as least-squares regression.

If there were an interaction consideration in a model, the equation would then take the form

$$y = b_0 + b_1x_1 + b_2x_2 + b_{12}x_1x_2 \qquad (17.2)$$

The number of terms in the equation describes the minimum number of experimental trials that are needed to determine the model. For example, Equation (17.2) has four terms; hence, a minimum of four experimental design trials are needed to calculate the coefficients. The two-level fractional factorial significance tests, as discussed in Section 13.4, were to determine which of the coefficient estimates were "large enough" to affect the response ($y$) "significantly" when changed from a low $(-1)$ level to a high level $(+1)$.

Center points can be added to the two-level fractional factorial design to determine the validity of the linearity assumption of the model (see Section 13.12). When using a regression program on the coded effects, the fractional factorial levels should take on symmetry values around zero (i.e., $-1$ and $+1$). To determine if the linearity assumption is valid, the average response of the center points can be compared to the overall average of the two-level fractional factorial experiment trials.

If the first-degree polynomial approximation does not fit the data when describing the process, a second-degree polynomial model may adequately describe the curvature of the response surface as a function of the input factors. For two factor consideration, this model takes the form

$$y = b_0 + b_1x_1 + b_2x_2 + b_{11}x_1^2 + b_{22}x_2^2 + b_{12}x_1x_2 \qquad (17.3)$$

See Section C.9 for additional discussion on lack of fit evaluations.

## 17.2. CENTRAL COMPOSITE DESIGN

To determine the additional coefficients of a second-degree polynomial, additional levels of the variables are needed between the end point levels. An efficient test approach to determine the coefficients of a second-degree polynomial is to use a central composite design. Figure 17.1 shows this design for the two-factor situation.

An experiment design is said to be rotatable if the variance of the predicted response at some point is a function of only the distance of the point from the center. The central composite design is made rotatable when $[a = (F)^{1/4}]$, where $F$ is the number of points used in the factorial part of the design. For two factors $F = 2^2 = 4$; hence $a = (4)^{1/4} = 1.414$. A useful property of the central composite design is that the additional axial points can be added to a two-level fractional factorial design as additional trials after the curvature is detected from the initial experimental data.

With a proper number of center points, the central composite design can be made such that the variance of the response at the origin is equal to the variance of the response at unit distance from the origin (i.e., a uniform precision design). This characteristic in the uniform precision design is important since it gives more protection against bias in the regression coefficients because of the presence of third-degree and higher terms in the true surface than orthogonal designs (Montgomery 1984). Table 17.1 shows the parameters needed to achieve a uniform precision design as a function of the number of variables within the experiment.

From Table 17.1 a design, for example, assessing five variables along with all two-factor interactions plus the curvature of all variables would be that shown in Table 17.2. Data is then analyzed using regression analysis techniques to determine the output response surface as a function of the input variables.

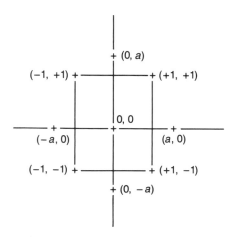

**FIGURE 17.1.** Central composite design for two factors.

**TABLE 17.1. Uniform Precision Central Composite Rotatable Designs**

| Number of Variables | Number of Factorial Trial | Number of Axial Trials | Number of Center Trials | $a$ | Total Number of Trials |
|---|---|---|---|---|---|
| 2 | 4 | 4 | 5 | 1.4142 | 13 |
| 3 | 8 | 6 | 6 | 1.6820 | 20 |
| 4 | 16 | 8 | 7 | 2.0000 | 31 |
| 5 | 16 | 10 | 6 | 2.0000 | 32 |
| 6 | 32 | 12 | 9 | 2.3780 | 53 |
| 7 | 64 | 14 | 14 | 2.8280 | 92 |

**TABLE 17.2. Response Surface Design Matrix for Five Variables**

| A | B | C | D | E | |
|---|---|---|---|---|---|
| +1 | −1 | −1 | −1 | +1 | |
| +1 | +1 | −1 | −1 | −1 | |
| +1 | +1 | +1 | −1 | +1 | |
| +1 | +1 | +1 | +1 | −1 | |
| −1 | +1 | +1 | +1 | +1 | |
| +1 | −1 | +1 | +1 | +1 | |
| −1 | +1 | −1 | +1 | −1 | |
| +1 | −1 | +1 | −1 | −1 | Fractional factorial design from Table M3 |
| +1 | +1 | −1 | +1 | +1 | |
| −1 | +1 | +1 | −1 | −1 | |
| −1 | −1 | +1 | +1 | −1 | |
| +1 | −1 | −1 | +1 | −1 | |
| −1 | +1 | −1 | −1 | +1 | |
| −1 | −1 | +1 | −1 | +1 | |
| −1 | −1 | −1 | +1 | +1 | |
| −1 | −1 | −1 | −1 | −1 | |
| −2 | 0 | 0 | 0 | 0 | |
| +2 | 0 | 0 | 0 | 0 | |
| 0 | −2 | 0 | 0 | 0 | |
| 0 | +2 | 0 | 0 | 0 | |
| 0 | 0 | −2 | 0 | 0 | Axial trials with levels consistent with Table 17.1 |
| 0 | 0 | +2 | 0 | 0 | |
| 0 | 0 | 0 | −2 | 0 | |
| 0 | 0 | 0 | +2 | 0 | |
| 0 | 0 | 0 | 0 | −2 | |
| 0 | 0 | 0 | 0 | +2 | |
| 0 | 0 | 0 | 0 | 0 | |
| 0 | 0 | 0 | 0 | 0 | |
| 0 | 0 | 0 | 0 | 0 | Center point trials consistent with table 17.1 |
| 0 | 0 | 0 | 0 | 0 | |
| 0 | 0 | 0 | 0 | 0 | |
| 0 | 0 | 0 | 0 | 0 | |

Cornell (1984), Montgomery (1984), and Box et al. (1978) discuss analytical methods to then determine maximum points on the response surface using the canonical form of the equation. The coefficients of this equation can be used to describe the shape of the surface (elipsoid, hyperboloid, etc.). An alternative approach is to understand the response surface by using a computer contour plotting program, as illustrated in the next example. From the understanding of a particular contour plot, perhaps, for example, process factors can be determined/changed to yield a desirable/improved response output that has minimal expected day-to-day variation.

## 17.3.  EXAMPLE 17-1: RESPONSE SURFACE DESIGN

A chemical engineer desires to determine the operating conditions that maximize the yield of a process. A previous two-level factorial experiment of many considerations indicated that reaction time and reaction temperature were the parameters that should be optimized. A central composite design was chosen and yielded the responses shown in Table 17.3 (Montgomery 1984). A second-degree model can be fitted using the natural levels of the variables (e.g., time = 80) or the coded levels (e.g., time = $-1$). A computer analysis of this data shows that the variables are significant.

Section C.9 shows and discusses the computer analysis outputs and input statements used to make the following conclusions, projections, and response

**TABLE 17.3.  Responses in Central Composite Design**

| Natural Variables | | Coded Variables | | |
|---|---|---|---|---|
| Reaction Time (min) | Reaction Temp. (°F) | Reaction Time | Reaction Temp. | Response Yield |
| $u_1$ | $u_2$ | $v_1$ | $v_2$ | $y$ |
| 80 | 170 | $-1$ | $-1$ | 76.5 |
| 80 | 180 | $-1$ | 1 | 77.0 |
| 90 | 170 | 1 | $-1$ | 78.0 |
| 90 | 180 | 1 | 1 | 79.5 |
| 92.07 | 175 | 1.414 | 0 | 78.4 |
| 77.93 | 175 | $-1.414$ | 0 | 75.6 |
| 85 | 182.07 | 0 | 1.414 | 78.5 |
| 85 | 167.93 | 0 | $-1.414$ | 77.0 |
| 85 | 175 | 0 | 0 | 79.9 |
| 85 | 175 | 0 | 0 | 80.3 |
| 85 | 175 | 0 | 0 | 80.0 |
| 85 | 175 | 0 | 0 | 79.7 |
| 85 | 175 | 0 | 0 | 79.8 |

surface plot. The output in Section C.9 also illustrates how a standard regression modeling program (e.g., SAS GLM) can be used in lieu of a response surface analysis program (e.g., SAS RSREG) to determine the model coefficients and the significance level of these coefficients. However, with this regression model lack of fit of data to the model surface has to be determined manually.

From this analysis the second-degree model using the natural levels of the variables noted in Table 17.3 is

$$\hat{y} = -1430.69 + 7.81u_1 + 13.27u_2 - 0.06u_1^2 + 0.01u_1u_2 - 0.04u_2^2$$

Also from this analysis the second-degree model using the coded levels of the variable noted in Table 17.3 is

$$\hat{y} = 79.940 + 0.995v_1 + 0.515v_2 - 1.376v_1^2 + 0.250v_1v_2 - 1.001v_2^2$$

These equations will yield the same response value for a given input data state. The advantage of using the coded levels is that the importance of each term can be compared somewhat by looking at the magnitude of the coefficients since the relative magnitude of the variable levels are brought to a single unit of measure.

When projections are made off a response surface, it is obviously important that the model fit the initial data satisfactorily. Erroneous conclusions can result where there is lack of fit. The computer analysis did not indicate that there was lack of fit; hence, the second-degree polynomial model is accepted. A response surface of this coded polynomial is shown in Figure 17.2.

The computer output in Section C.9 also notes for the coded variable level estimates that a maximum response level of 80.212 will be obtained when TIMECODE equals 0.389 and TEMPCODE equals 0.306, which is consistent with this response surface plot shown in Figure 17.2.

## 17.4. BOX–BEHNKEN DESIGNS

When estimating the first- and second-order terms of a response surface, Box and Behnken (1960) give an alternative to a central composite design approach. In their paper the authors present a list of 10 second-order rotatable designs covering 3, 4, 5, 6, 7, 9, 10, 11, 12, and 16 variables. However, in general these designs are not always rotatable nor are they block orthogonal.

One reason that an experimenter may choose to use this design over a central composite design is because of physical test constraints. This design requires only three levels of each variable, as opposed to five for the central composite design. Figure 17.3 shows the test points for this design approach given three design variables.

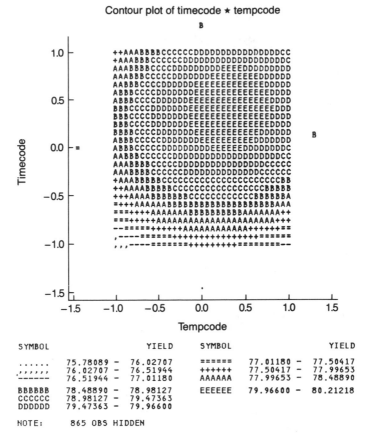

**Contour plot of timecode ⋆ tempcode**

| SYMBOL | YIELD | | SYMBOL | YIELD | |
|---|---|---|---|---|---|
| ...... | 75.78089 | − 76.02707 | ====== | 77.01180 | − 77.50417 |
| ,,,,,, | 76.02707 | − 76.51944 | ++++++ | 77.50417 | − 77.99653 |
| ------ | 76.51944 | − 77.01180 | AAAAAA | 77.99653 | − 78.48890 |
| BBBBBB | 78.48890 | − 78.98127 | EEEEEE | 79.96600 | − 80.21218 |
| CCCCCC | 78.98127 | − 79.47363 | | | |
| DDDDDD | 79.47363 | − 79.96600 | | | |

NOTE:     865 OBS HIDDEN

**FIGURE 17.2.** Example 17-1: Response for coded variables.

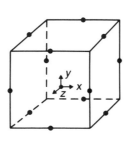

| | Experiment Trials | | |
|---|---|---|---|
| | $x$ | $y$ | $z$ |
| | +1 | +1 | 0 |
| | +1 | −1 | 0 |
| | −1 | +1 | 0 |
| | −1 | −1 | 0 |
| | +1 | 0 | +1 |
| | +1 | 0 | −1 |
| | −1 | 0 | +1 |
| | −1 | 0 | −1 |
| | 0 | +1 | −1 |
| | 0 | +1 | +1 |
| | 0 | −1 | −1 |
| | 0 | −1 | +1 |
| | 0 | 0 | 0 |
| | 0 | 0 | 0 |
| | 0 | 0 | 0 |

**FIGURE 17.3.** Box–Behnken design space for three factors.

## 17.5. MIXTURE DESIGNS

The experimenter designs discussed previously in this text were for discrete and/or continuous factors, where the levels of each factor was completely independent from the other factors. However, consider a chemist who mixes three ingredients together. If the chemist wishes to increase the content of one ingredient, the percentage of another ingredient must be adjusted accordingly. Mixture experiment designs are used for this situation, where the components (factors/variables) under consideration take levels that are a proportion of the whole.

For the practitioner of mixture designs, the discussion in the next few sections of this chapter explains the concepts. In practice a textbook experiment design approach to this type of problem is often not practical. Computer-generated designs and analyses are usually better for most realistic mixture problems (see Section 17.12).

In the general mixture problem the measured response depends only on the proportions of the components present in the mixture and does not depend on the total amount of the mixture, as noted in Equation (17.4) for three components:

$$x_1 + x_2 + x_3 = 1 \qquad (17.4)$$

To illustrate the application of this equation consider that a mixture consisted of 3 components: $A$, $B$, and $C$. If component $A$ was 20% and $B$ was 50%, $C$ would have to be 30% to give a total of 100% (i.e., $0.2 + 0.5 + 0.3 = 1$).

When three factors were considered in a two-level full factorial experiment ($2^3$), the factor space of interest is a cube. However, a three-component mixture experiment is represented by an equilateral triangle. The coordinate system for these problems is called a simplex coordinate system. Figure 17.4 shows the triangle for three components whose proportions are $x_1$, $x_2$, and $x_3$. A four-component would similarly take on the space of a tetrahedron.

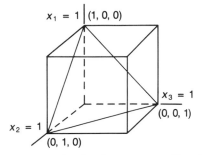

**FIGURE 17.4.** Three-component simplex factor space. [Reprinted with the permission of the American Society for Quality Control: John A. Cornell, *Volume 5: How to Run Mixture Experiments for Product Quality*, American Society for Quality Control, 1983.]

With three components coordinates are plotted on equilateral triangular graph paper that has lines parallel to the three sides of the triangle. Each vertex of the triangle represents 100% of one of the components in the mixture. The lines away from a vertex represent decreasing amounts of the component described by that vertex. The center of the equilateral triangle represents, for example, a mixture with equal proportions (i.e., $\frac{1}{3}$, $\frac{1}{3}$, $\frac{1}{3}$) from each of the components.

In a designed mixture experiment several combinations of components are chosen within the spatial extremes defined by the number of components (e.g., an equilateral triangle for three components). Within one experiment all possible combinations of the components can be considered as viable candidates to determine an "optimal" response. However, in many situations some combinations of the components are not reasonable or may even cause a dangerous response (e.g., an explosion).

Within this chapter simplex lattice designs will be used when all combinations of the components are under consideration, while extreme vertices designs will be used for the situation when there are restrictions placed in the test on the proportions of the components.

## 17.6. SIMPLEX LATTICE DESIGNS FOR EXPLORING THE WHOLE SIMPLEX REGION

The simplex lattice designs (Scheffé 1958) in this section address problems where there are no restrictions on the limits of the percentages when determining the total 100% composition.

A simplex lattice designs for $q$ components consists of points defined by the coordinates $(q, m)$, where the proportions assumed by each component take $m + 1$ equally spaced values from 0 to 1 and all possible combinations of the components are considered. Figure 17.5 illustrates pictorially the spatial test consideration of several lattice design alternatives for three and four components. Cornell (1983) notes that a general form of regression function that can be fitted easily to data collected at the points of a $(q, m)$ simplex lattice is the canonical form of the polynomial. This form is then derived by applying the restriction that the terms in a standard polynomial of a mixture design sum to 1. The simplified expression yields for three components the first-degree model form

$$y = b_1 x_1 + b_2 x_2 + b_3 x_3 \tag{17.5}$$

The second-degree model form is

$$y = b_1 x_1 + b_2 x_2 + b_3 x_3 + b_{12} x_1 x_2 + b_{13} x_1 x_3 + b_{23} x_2 x_3 \tag{17.6}$$

The special cubic polynomial form is

$$y = b_1 x_1 + b_2 x_2 + b_3 x_3 + b_{12} x_1 x_2 + b_{13} x_1 x_3 + b_{23} x_2 x_3 + b_{123} x_1 x_2 x_3$$
$$\tag{17.7}$$

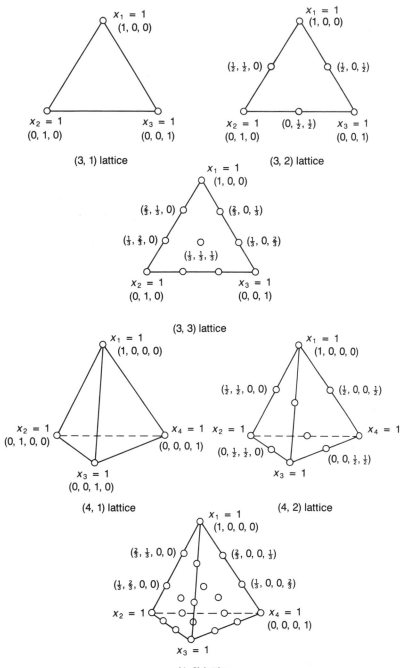

**FIGURE 17.5.** Some simplex lattice designs for three and four components. [Reprinted with the permission of the American Society for Quality Control: John A. Cornell, *Volume 5: How to Run Mixture Experiments for Product Quality*, American Society for Quality Control, 1983.]

**TABLE 17.4.  Example 17-2: Design Proportions of Solvents, and Byproduct Response**

| Trial | Methanol | Acetone | Trichloroethylene | By-product (%) |
|-------|----------|---------|-------------------|----------------|
| 1 | 1 | 0 | 0 | 6.2 |
| 2 | 0 | 1 | 0 | 8.4 |
| 3 | 0 | 0 | 1 | 3.9 |
| 4 | ½ | ½ | 0 | 7.4 |
| 5 | ½ | 0 | ½ | 2.8 |
| 6 | 0 | ½ | ½ | 6.1 |
| 7[a] | ⅓ | ⅓ | ⅓ | 2.2 |

[a]Center point.

## 17.7.  EXAMPLE 17-2: SIMPLEX-LATTICE DESIGNED MIXTURE EXPERIMENT

Any one combination of three solvents could be most effective in the solvent rinse of a contaminating by-product (Diamond 1989). A (3,2) simplex lattice with a center point was chosen for the initial evaluation. The design proportions with the by-product responses are shown in Table 17.4.

A plot of the results is shown in Figure 17.6. Regression analysis techniques could be used (as discussed in Example 17-3); however, in some cases, such as this example, the conclusions are obvious. For this example the best result is the center point composition; however, there is curvature and a still better response is likely in the vicinity of this point.

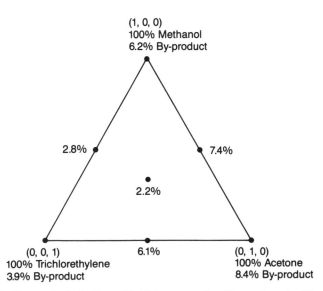

**FIGURE 17.6.** Example 17-2: Plot of initial test results. [Reproduced with permission: W. Diamond, *Practical Experiment Designs for Engineers and Scientists*, Van Nostrand Reinhold, New York, 1989.]

EXAMPLE 17-2: SIMPLEX LATTICE DESIGN **261**

**TABLE 17.5. Example 17-2: Experimental Points and Their Rationales**

| Experimental Point Number | Rationale |
| --- | --- |
| 8, 9, 10 | (3,1) simplex lattice design vertices around the best response with the noted diagonal relationship to the original data points. |
| 11 | Since point 5 is the second best result, another data point was added in that direction. |
| 12 | Repeat of the treatment combination that was the best in the previous experiment and is now the centroid of this follow-up experiment. |

To reduce the by-product content amount of 2.2%, more experimental trials are needed near this point to determine a better process optimum. Diamond (1989) chose to consider adding the following additional trials using the noted rationale. These points are spatially shown in Figure 17.7, where the lines decrease in magnitude of 0.05 for a variable from an initial proportion value of 1.0 at the apex. Table 17.5 illustrates these trials and their rationales.

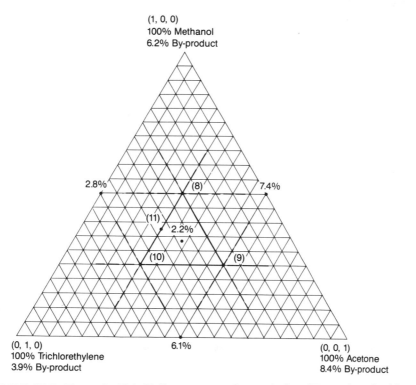

**FIGURE 17.7.** Example 17-2: Follow-up experiment design. [Reproduced with permission: W. Diamond, *Practical Experiment Designs for Engineers and Scientists*, Van Nostrand Reinhold, New York, 1989.]

**TABLE 17.6. Example 17-2: Results of Experimental Trials**

| Trial | Methanol | Acetone | Trichloroethylene | By-product (%) |
|-------|----------|---------|-------------------|----------------|
| 8 | ½ | ¼ | ¼ | 3.3 |
| 9 | ¼ | ½ | ½ | 4.8 |
| 10 | ¼ | ¼ | ½ | 1.4 |
| 11 | ⅜ | ¼ | ⅜ | 1.2 |
| 12 | ⅓ | ⅓ | ⅓ | 2.4 |

The results from these experimental trials are seen in Table 17.6. A plot of the data and an estimate of the response surface is shown in Figure 17.8. The apparent minimum (shown as the point with no number in Figure 17.8) along with the results from an additional trial setting at this value is as follows:

| Trial | Methanol | Acetone | Trichloroethylene | By-product (%) |
|-------|----------|---------|-------------------|----------------|
| 13 | 0.33 | 0.15 | 0.52 | 0.45 |

Additional simplex design trials around this point could yield a smaller amount of by-product. However, if the by-product percentage is "low enough," additional experimental trials might not serve any economic purpose.

## 17.8. MIXTURE DESIGNS WITH PROCESS VARIABLES

Consider the situation where a response is not only a function of a mixture but also a function of its process variables (e.g., cooking temperature and cooking time). For the situation where there are three components to a mixture and there are three process variables, the complex simplex-centroid design takes the form shown in Figure 17.9 (later applied in Example 17-3).

In general, the number of experimental trial possibilities can get very large when there are many variable considerations. Cornell and Gorman (1984) discuss fractional factorial design alternatives. Cornell (1990) discusses the embedding of mixture experiments inside factorial experiments. Algorithm designs, which are discussed later in Section 17.12, are another test alternative which can reduce the number of test trials.

## 17.9. EXAMPLE 17-3: MIXTURE EXPERIMENT WITH PROCESS VARIABLES

The data in Table 17.7 is the average of replicated texture reading in kilogram force required to puncture fish patty surfaces (Cornell 1981; Cornell and

EXAMPLE 17-3: MIXTURE EXPERIMENT WITH PROCESS VARIABLES **263**

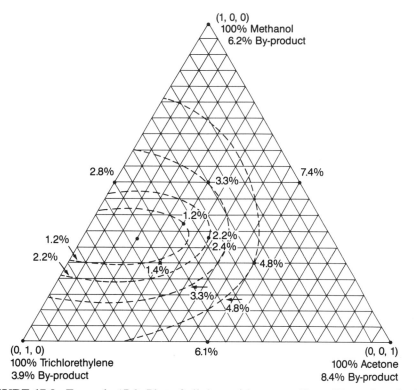

**FIGURE 17.8.** Example 17-2: Plot of all data with contour lines. [Reproduced with permission: W. Diamond, *Practical Experiment Designs for Engineers and Scientists*, Van Nostrand Reinhold, New York, 1989.]

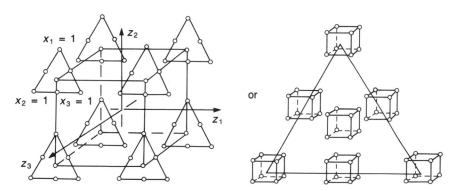

**FIGURE 17.9.** Complete simplex Centroid $\times$ $2^3$ factorial design. [Reprinted with the permission of the American Society for Quality Control: John A. Cornell and John W. Gorman, "Fractional Design Plans for Process Variables in Mixture Experiments," *Journal of Quality Technology*, **16**(1) 1984.]

Gorman 1984; Gorman and Cornell 1982) that were prepared under process conditions that had code values of $-1$ and $+1$ for

$z_1$: cooking temperature ($-1 = 375°F$, $+1 = 425°F$)
$z_2$: cooking time ($-1 = 25$ min, $+1 = 40$ min)
$z_3$: deep fat frying time ($-1 = 25$ sec, $+1 = 40$ sec)

The patty was composed of three types of fish that took on composition ratios of 0, $\frac{1}{3}$, $\frac{1}{2}$, or 1. The fish designations are

$x_1$: mullet
$x_2$: sheepshead
$x_3$: croaker

The desired range of fish texture (in the noted scaled units) for customer satisfaction is between 2.0 and 3.5; however, other characteristics (not discussed here) were also considered as responses within the actual experiment. A computer analysis of this data (shown in Section C.10) yielded the coefficient estimates shown in Table 17.8 (see Section 17.1). The standard error (SE) for this example was determined using all the original data and was taken from Cornell (1981).

In the data analysis of the averages, there were 54 data inputs and the same number of estimates; hence, a regression analysis cannot give any significance test on the variables. A half normal probability plot of the effects (see Figure 14.1) is not mathematically helpful since the standard error is not consistent between the estimates.

**TABLE 17.7. Example 17-3: Results of Mixture Experiment with Process Variables**

| | | | | | | Texture Readings | | | |
|---|---|---|---|---|---|---|---|---|---|
| Coded Process Variables | | | | | | Mixture Composition ($x_1$, $x_2$, $x_3$) | | | |
| $z_1$ | $z_2$ | $z_3$ | (1, 0, 0) | (0, 1, 0) | (0, 0, 1) | ($\frac{1}{2}$, $\frac{1}{2}$, 0) | ($\frac{1}{2}$, 0, $\frac{1}{2}$) | (0, $\frac{1}{2}$, $\frac{1}{2}$) | ($\frac{1}{3}$, $\frac{1}{3}$, $\frac{1}{3}$) |
| $-1$ | $-1$ | $-1$ | 1.84 | 0.67 | 1.51 | 1.29 | 1.42 | 1.16 | 1.59 |
| 1 | $-1$ | $-1$ | 2.86 | 1.10 | 1.60 | 1.53 | 1.81 | 1.50 | 1.68 |
| $-1$ | 1 | $-1$ | 3.01 | 1.21 | 2.32 | 1.93 | 2.57 | 1.83 | 1.94 |
| 1 | 1 | $-1$ | 4.13 | 1.67 | 2.57 | 2.26 | 3.15 | 2.22 | 2.60 |
| $-1$ | $-1$ | 1 | 1.65 | 0.58 | 1.21 | 1.18 | 1.45 | 1.07 | 1.41 |
| 1 | $-1$ | 1 | 2.32 | 0.97 | 2.12 | 1.45 | 1.93 | 1.28 | 1.54 |
| $-1$ | 1 | 1 | 3.04 | 1.16 | 2.00 | 1.85 | 2.39 | 1.60 | 2.05 |
| 1 | 1 | 1 | 4.13 | 1.30 | 2.75 | 2.06 | 2.82 | 2.10 | 2.32 |

EXAMPLE 17-3: MIXTURE EXPERIMENT WITH PROCESS VARIABLES    265

**TABLE 17.8. Example 17-3: Coefficient Estimates from Computer Analysis**

|  | Mean | $z_1$ | $z_2$ | $z_3$ | $z_1z_2$ | $z_1z_3$ | $z_2z_3$ | $z_1z_2z_3$ | SE |
|---|---|---|---|---|---|---|---|---|---|
| $x_1$ | 2.87* | 0.49* | 0.71* | −0.09 | 0.07 | −0.05 | 0.10 | 0.04 | 0.05 |
| $x_2$ | 1.08* | 0.18* | 0.25* | −0.08 | −0.03 | −0.05 | −0.03 | −0.04 | 0.05 |
| $x_3$ | 2.01* | 0.25* | 0.40* | 0.01 | 0.00 | 0.17* | −0.05 | −0.04 | 0.05 |
| $x_1x_2$ | −1.14* | −0.81* | −0.59 | 0.10 | −0.06 | 0.14 | −0.19 | −0.09 | 0.23 |
| $x_1x_3$ | −1.00* | −0.54 | −0.05 | −0.03 | −0.06 | −0.27 | −0.43 | −0.12 | 0.23 |
| $x_2x_3$ | 0.20 | −0.14 | 0.07 | −0.19 | 0.23 | −0.25 | 0.12 | 0.27 | 0.23 |
| $x_1x_2x_3$ | 3.18 | 0.07 | −1.41 | 0.11 | 1.74 | −0.71 | 1.77 | −1.33 | 1.65 |

* Individual estimates thought to be significant.

However, using the standard error terms (where the number of degrees of freedom for error is 56; i.e., $\nu_{error} = 56$) that were noted in Cornell (1981), the asterisk shows those items that are thought to be different from zero. To illustrate this, the effect level for significance for a variable with a standard error of 0.05 is as shown below (see Table E for interpolated t value):

$$\text{Effect level criterion} = (\text{SE})(t_{\alpha;\nu}) = (\text{SE}) (t_{0.01;56}) = 0.05 (2.667) = 0.13$$

Any of the effects noted in the table that have a standard error of 0.05 are significant at the 0.01 level if their magnitude is greater that 0.13. A highly significant probability level of 0.01 for this problem is appropriate since the parameter effect estimates are not independent; hence, the individual $t$ tests are not independent.

Various characteristics of fish patty hardness can be determined by evaluating the main effect and interaction considerations in the preceding table; however, another alternative to evaluate the characteristics is to isolate the individual blend characteristics at each of the eight process variable treatments.

The equation to consider, for example, is where $z_1 = -1$, $z_2 = -1$, and $z_3 = -1$ is

$$y = a_1x_1 + a_2x_1z_1 + \cdots = 2.87x_1 + 0.49x_1 (-1) \ldots$$

Various $x_1$, $x_2$, and $x_3$ values are then substituted to create a contour plot in a simplex coordinate system for each of the eight variable treatments, as noted in Figure 17.10.

The shaded area in Figure 17.10 shows when the desirable response range of 2.0 to 3.5 (nominal = 2.75) was achieved. This figure illustrates that a $z_2 = 1$ level (i.e., 40 min cooking time) is desirable; however, there are many other combinations of the other parameters at $z_2 = 1$ that can yield a satisfactory texture reading. However, to maximize customer satisfaction, effort should

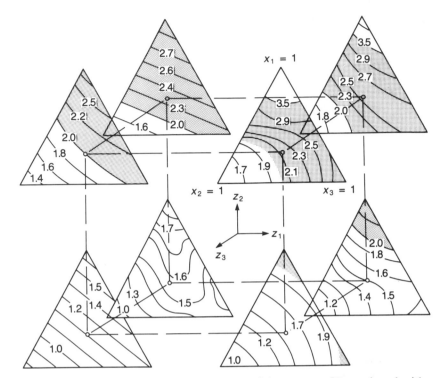

**FIGURE 17.10.** Example 17-3: Contour plots of the texture. [Reproduced with permission: J. Cornell, *Experiments with Mixtures: Designs, Models, and the Analysis of Mixture Data*, John Wiley and Sons, New York, 1981.]

be directed toward achieving the nominal criterion on the average with minimum variability between batches.

At this point in the analysis, perhaps other issues should be considered. For example, it may be desirable to make the composition of the fish patty so that its sensitivity is minimized relative to deep fat frying time. In the "real world" it may be relatively easy to control the cooking temperature; however, a person frying patties in a fast-food restaurant may be too busy to remove the patties immediately when the timer sounds. To address this concern, it appears that a $z_1 = -1$ level (i.e., 375°F cooking temperature) is most desirable with a relative high concentration of mullet in the fish patty composition.

Other considerations to make, for example, when determining the "best" composition and variable levels are economics (e.g., cost of each type of fish) and other experimental output response surface plots (e.g., taste evaluation of fish patties). To aid in the decision-making process, a similar output to that of Figure 17.10 could be made for a weighted (by importance) mathematical combination of the several responses.

EXAMPLE 17-4: EXTREME VERTICES MIXTURE EXPERIMENT    **267**

## 17.10. EXTREME VERTICES MIXTURE DESIGNS

Extreme vertices designs (Anderson and McLean 1974), can take on most of the nice properties of the previously discussed matrix designs (Diamond 1989). This design is explained in the following example.

## 17.11. EXAMPLE 17-4: EXTREME VERTICES MIXTURE EXPERIMENT

A chemist wishes to develop a floor wax product. The following range of proportions of three ingredients are under consideration along with the noted proportion percentage limitations. The response to this experiment takes on several values: level of shine, scuff resistance, and so forth.

Wax: 0–0.25   (i.e., 0%–25%)
Resin: 0–0.20   (i.e., 0%–20%)
Polymer: 0.70–0.90   (i.e., 70%–90%)

Again, mixture experiment trial combinations are determined by using a simplex coordinate system. This relationship is noted in Figure 17.11, where

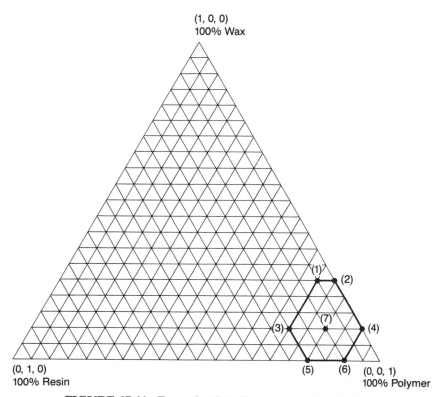

**FIGURE 17.11.** Example 17-4: Extreme vertices design.

**TABLE 17.9. Example 17-4: Test Trials Combinations**

| Trial | Wax ($x_1$) | Resin ($x_2$) | Polymer ($x_3$) | Response ($Y$) |
|-------|-------------|---------------|-----------------|----------------|
| 1     | 0.25        | 0.05          | 0.70            | $y_1$          |
| 2     | 0.25        | 0             | 0.75            | $y_2$          |
| 3     | 0.10        | 0.20          | 0.70            | $y_3$          |
| 4     | 0.10        | 0             | 0.90            | $y_4$          |
| 5     | 0           | 0.20          | 0.80            | $y_5$          |
| 6     | 0           | 0.10          | 0.90            | $y_6$          |
| $7^a$ | 0.10        | 0.10          | 0.80            | $y_7$          |

[a] Center point.

the lines leaving a vertex decrease in magnitude of 0.05 proportion from an initial proportion value of 1.

The space of interest is noted by the polygon shown in Figure 17.11. Table 17.9 shows test trials for the vertices along with a center point.

The logic used in Example 17-1 for follow-up experiments can similarly be applied to this problem in an attempt to better optimize the process using additional trials.

## 17.12. COMPUTER-GENERATED MIXTURE DESIGNS/ANALYSES

The concepts behind algorithm design were introduced by Wynn (1970) and Fedorov (1972). With these designs a computer program creates a list of possible trials to fit the model, calculates the standard deviation of the value predicted by the polynomial for each trial, and picks the trial with the largest standard deviation as the next trial to include in the design. The coefficients of the polynomial are then recalculated using this new trial and the process is repeated. The designs that are best are those having the largest variance proportional to the number of terms in the polynomial (B. Wheeler 1989).

Mixture design problems typically have physical constraints that make "textbook designs" impractical. Algorithm designs (see Section 17.14) are particularily helpful for mixture design problems. A practitioner that needs to perform a mixture experiment should consider utilizing a commercially available computer program that both creates an algorithm design and can analyze the results (see Section 2.3).

The following example illustrates the application of a computer program to generate a design matrix and then analyze the results.

## 17.13. EXAMPLE 17-5: COMPUTER-GENERATED MIXTURE DESIGN/ANALYSES

An improvement is needed in the paste used to attach electronic components when manufacturing surface-mounted printed circuit cards. Viscosity of the

EXAMPLE 17-5: COMPUTER-GENERATED MIXTURE DESIGN/ANALYSES    **269**

paste was one response that was desired as a function of the proportion composition of the five mixture components that had the following ranges:

| Component | Proportion |
|-----------|------------|
| Comp1 | 0.57–0.68 |
| Comp2 | 0.15–0.21 |
| Comp3 | 0.03–0.08 |
| Comp4 | 0.05–0.10 |
| Comp5 | 0.04–0.06 |

ECHIP, a computer program (B. Wheeler 1989), was used to create an algorithm design, given the above constraints. The mixture proportions for this resulting design along with the experimental viscosity measurement responses (in units of pascal-seconds) for the trials are shown in Table 17.10.

From the analysis three variables were found significant (Comp1, Comp2, and Comp3). Figure 17.12 shows three pictorial views that were then generated to better understand the relationship of these variables, where Comp4 was set to a proportion of 0.077 and Comp5 was set to a proportion of 0.050. It

**TABLE 17.10. Example 17-5: Input Variable Levels and Viscosity Response**

| | Comp1 | Comp2 | Comp3 | Comp4 | Comp5 | Viscosity |
|---|-------|-------|-------|-------|-------|-----------|
| 1[a] | 0.5700 | 0.2100 | 0.0800 | 0.1000 | 0.0400 | 7.6 |
| 2 | 0.6800 | 0.1500 | 0.0600 | 0.0500 | 0.0600 | 32.0 |
| 3 | 0.6700 | 0.2100 | 0.0300 | 0.0500 | 0.0400 | 20.5 |
| 4 | 0.6800 | 0.1500 | 0.0300 | 0.1000 | 0.0400 | 13.9 |
| 5 | 0.6000 | 0.2100 | 0.0300 | 0.1000 | 0.0600 | 12.2 |
| 6 | 0.6000 | 0.2100 | 0.0800 | 0.0500 | 0.0600 | 13.6 |
| 7 | 0.6100 | 0.1500 | 0.0800 | 0.1000 | 0.0600 | 15.8 |
| 8 | 0.6800 | 0.1500 | 0.0800 | 0.0500 | 0.0400 | 21.4 |
| 9 | 0.6200 | 0.2100 | 0.0300 | 0.1000 | 0.0400 | 12.5 |
| 10 | 0.6200 | 0.2100 | 0.0800 | 0.0500 | 0.0400 | 14.8 |
| 11 | 0.6300 | 0.1500 | 0.0800 | 0.1000 | 0.0400 | 7.0 |
| 12 | 0.6650 | 0.1800 | 0.0300 | 0.0650 | 0.0600 | 19.3 |
| 13 | 0.6750 | 0.1800 | 0.0550 | 0.0500 | 0.0400 | 15.2 |
| 14 | 0.6200 | 0.2100 | 0.0550 | 0.0750 | 0.0400 | 11.6 |
| 15 | 0.6600 | 0.2100 | 0.0300 | 0.0500 | 0.0500 | 16.4 |
| 16 | 0.5700 | 0.2100 | 0.0800 | 0.0800 | 0.0600 | 7.8 |
| 17 | 0.6600 | 0.1500 | 0.0300 | 0.1000 | 0.0600 | 19.3 |
| 18 | 0.5700 | 0.2100 | 0.0600 | 0.1000 | 0.0600 | 9.6 |
| 19 | 0.5900 | 0.1800 | 0.0800 | 0.1000 | 0.0500 | 6.8 |
| 20 | 0.6800 | 0.1500 | 0.0450 | 0.0750 | 0.0500 | 20.5 |
| 1[a] | 0.5700 | 0.2100 | 0.0800 | 0.1000 | 0.0400 | 7.8 |
| 2 | 0.6800 | 0.1500 | 0.0600 | 0.0500 | 0.0600 | 35.5 |
| 3 | 0.6700 | 0.2100 | 0.0300 | 0.0500 | 0.0400 | 20.7 |
| 4 | 0.6800 | 0.1500 | 0.0300 | 0.1000 | 0.0400 | 12.6 |
| 5 | 0.6000 | 0.2100 | 0.0300 | 0.1000 | 0.0600 | 11.0 |

[a]Note: Some variable level combinations are repeated.

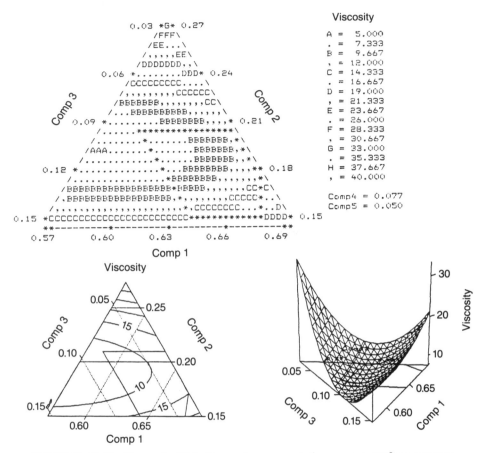

**FIGURE 17.12.** Example 17-5: Computer-generated response surface outputs.

should be noted that the program highlights the bounds of the levels of the variables used in the experiment so that the interpreter of the plots will know when to exercise caution because the predictions are extrapolated.

## 17.14. ADDITIONAL RESPONSE SURFACE DESIGN CONSIDERATIONS

When no linear relationship exists between the regressors they are said to be orthogonal. For these situations the following inferences can be made relatively easily:

1. Estimation and/or prediction.
2. Identification of relative effects of regressor variables.
3. Selection of a set of variables for the model.

However, inferences from the analysis of response surface designs can yield conclusions that may be misleading because of dependencies between the regressors. When near linear dependencies exist between the regressors, multicollinearity is said to be prevalent. Other texts [e.g., Montgomery and Peck (1982)] discuss diagnostic procedures for this problem (e.g., variance inflation factor) along with other procedures that are used to better understand the output from regression analyses (e.g., detecting influential observations).

Additional "textbook" design alternatives to that of the central composite and Box–Behnken designs are discussed in Cornell (1984), Montgomery (1984) and Khuri and Cornell (1987). "Algorithm" designs (see Section 7.12) can also be applied to nonmixture designs, as discussed in B. Wheeler (1989), where, as previously noted, algorithm designs are "optimized" to fit a particular model (e.g., linear or quadratic) with a given set of factor considerations.

## 17.15. DO-IT-SMARTER CONSIDERATIONS

If there are several response outputs to the trials, it may be necessary to compromise the optimum solution for each response to get an overall optimization. Several response outputs can be collectively weighted to yield a combined response output for consideration within the analyses.

An overall experiment implementation strategy for continuous response variables can be to first implement a linear model design (i.e., a two-level fractional factorial design for a nonmixture design) with center points. The center points are used to determine if there is adequate fit. If the model does not fit well and an "optimum" response is needed, then additional trials can be added in consideration of higher order model terms (e.g., second-order polynomial). After the initial test, factor considerations that were found not important can be removed to make the response surface experiment more manageable in size.

B. Wheeler (1989) notes that "boldness" should be used when choosing the levels of the variables so either the desired maximum or minimum is likely to be contained within the response surface design. A basic strategy when building a response surface is first to choose bold factor levels that are consistent with a simple model and then make lack of fit tests. If the model does not fit, additional trials can then be added to the original design consistent with the variable levels needed to add higher order terms to the model.

Perhaps an evaluation of the magnitude of the center points relative to the fractional factorial end points indicate that the initial selection of the magnitude of the variables did not have enough "boldness" to contain the optimum value. The surface outside these bounds can be quite different than the extrapolated value. A multiexperiment response surface test strategy may be needed to evaluate possible process improvements outside the bounds initially considered within the experiment. The variable levels to consider in the next experiment can be determined by evaluating the direction for improvement [i.e., the path of steepest ascent of the response curve, assuming higher numbers are better (Box et al. 1978; Cornell 1984; and Montgomery 1984)].

# 18

# PASS/FAIL FUNCTIONAL TESTING

Recommended introductory reading: Chapters 2, 3, 4, and 13.

In many instances it is impossible to test all possible combinations of input parameters when trying to assure that there is no combination that can cause a failure. This chapter illustrates an efficient test strategy where fractional factorial design matrices are used to design an efficient test of a *pass/fail logic* response for multiple combinational considerations (Breyfogle 1988). The strategy suggests that a small carefully selected subset of possible factor combinations can yield a satisfactory test of combinational effects (not to be confused with interaction effects). In addition, an expected "test coverage" is quantifiable for a given test matrix and factor considerations (Breyfogle and Aloia 1991).

## 18.1. THE CONCEPT OF PASS/FAIL FUNCTIONAL TESTING

Consider the situation where a product will be "put together" (i.e., configured) in many different ways by a customer. Because of possible design flaws, it is of interest to discover when things will not work together during an in-house test (i.e., a "logic" failure situation). If the number of configuration possibilities is not large, a test person should simply evaluate all possible combinations to assess whether there are any design problems. However, in some situations the number of combinational possibilities can be very large (e.g., tens of thousands). For these situations it becomes very difficult (if not impossible) to test all possible combinations.

This chapter describes a test strategy for the situation where the number of test scenarios needs to be much less than all possible combinations. This approach is used to identify a small subset of test configurations that will identify the types of problems that are found in many situations.

Consider, for example, the electomagnetic interference (EMI) emissions of a product. Compliance to government specifications is important since noncompliance can result in legal actions by the Federal Communications Commission (FCC). However, each EMI test setup and measurement can be very time consuming; hence, to test all possible configurations of a complex system can be a virtually impossible task.

To illustrate the type of EMI problem that this approach will capture, consider that (unknown to the experimenter) a new computer design only emits unacceptable high EMI levels whenever a certain type of display monitor is used in conjunction with a power supply that was manufactured by a certain vendor that had an optional "long size" cable.

In lieu of testing all possible combinations, an EMI test strategy that evaluates factors one at a time would probably not detect this type of combinational problem. A nonstructural test alternative that evaluates a few common "typical configurations" might miss important factor considerations because they are "not typical." In addition, with this second approach, there is typically no mention of test coverage at the completion of the test.

The test strategy discussed in this chapter is directed toward efficiently identifying circumstances where combinational problems exists. This identification focuses on how problems are often defined. In this problem a "group size" of three factor levels caused a combinational problem (a typical manner in which problems are often identified). Example 18-2 later illustrates a simple basic test design strategy for evaluating this "logic pass/fail situation" using only a minimal number of test scenarios. The example also addresses a measurement for the "test coverage" that is achieved when using such a test strategy.

## 18.2. EXAMPLE 18-1: AUTOMOBILE TEST—PASS/FAIL FUNCTIONAL TESTING CONSIDERATIONS

Example 2-1 changed a failure rate criterion test to a fractional factorial test strategy. Example 3-4 described the brainstorming process that was used to choose the experiment factors and their levels. Example 13-3 described the creation of a fractional factorial experiment. This example illustrates another test design alternative, if a pass/fail logic response is appropriate.

From Example 13-3, the experiment design is shown in Table 18.1. Consider now that there is a catastrophic failure situation involving the combination of three factor levels. Assume that it is fact that elderly drivers always caused accidents when driving this new vehicle design on curved roads. The question of concern is whether this experiment would detect this fact. The answer is

EXAMPLE 18-1: AUTOMOBILE TEST—PASS/FAIL CONSIDERATIONS    **275**

**TABLE 18.1. Example 18-1: Experimental Design for Automobile Test**

| Number of Trial | $ABCDEF$ | | $(-)$ | $(+)$ |
|---|---|---|---|---|
| 1 | $+--+-+$ | where | | |
| 2 | $++--+-$ | | | |
| 3 | $+++--+$ | $A$ = weather | Wet | Dry |
| 4 | $-+++--$ | $B$ = alcohol | None | Legal limit |
| 5 | $+-+++-$ | $C$ = speed | 40 mph | 70 mph |
| 6 | $-+-+++$ | $D$ = age of driver | 20–30 | 60–70 |
| 7 | $--+-++$ | $E$ = vehicle | Current | New |
| 8 | $------$ | $F$ = road curvature | None | Curved |

yes, since this combination is covered in trial 6 (elderly driver: $D = +$, new vehicle: $E = +$, road curved: $F = +$).

Most of the three-factor combinations of any of the factor levels (i.e., group size equaling three) are covered in this experiment. This level of "test coverage" is illustrated conceptually where all combinations of $DEF$ are included in the design matrix in Table 18.2. Section 18.3 and Example 18-2 discuss test coverage further.

The purpose of the automobile example in this text is to illustrate the importance of "answering the right question." In Example 2-1, the initial test strategy of verifying a criterion could easily end up as a test where individuals might "play games with the numbers" to certify one accident in 5-years as the failure criterion before "shipment" (e.g., what do you expect would be done if the day before shipment it is discovered that the automobile does not "meet" its failure criterion?). The examples that followed Example 2-1 describe a "customer-driven" test strategy that can combine the knowledge that exists within organizations toward a similar goal that can be done early in the development cycle.

These examples illustrate how a few early development models (or a simulator) could be used to evaluate a product design. This test could be

**TABLE 18.2. Example 18-1: Illustration of 3-Factor Coverage**

| $D\,E\,F$ | Trial Number |
|---|---|
| $---$ | 8 |
| $--+$ | 3 |
| $-+-$ | 2 |
| $-++$ | 7 |
| $+--$ | 4 |
| $+-+$ | 1 |
| $++-$ | 5 |
| $+++$ | 6 |

better than a larger "random" sample that was simply exercised against a failure rate criterion. With this approach multiple applications are assessed concurrently to assess interaction (Example 13-3 approach) or combinational affects (Example 18-1 approach), which are very difficult, if not impossible, to detect when assessing each factor individually (i.e., a one-at-a-time test strategy). Problems detected early in product development with this strategy can be resolved with less cost and schedule impacts. However, it must be reemphasized that often the original question needs redefinition. From this hypothetical example early detection of a high accident risk for "elderly drivers" could lead to a redesign resulting in increased safety for these drivers.

## 18.3.  A TEST APPROACH FOR PASS/FAIL FUNCTIONAL TESTING

Fractional factorial designs classically are used to assess continuous response outputs as a function of factor level considerations (see Section 13.10). However, there are instances where a more appropriate experimental task is to determine a *logic pass/fail* (binary) result that will *always* occur relative to machine function or configuration. This section illustrates how the structure of fractional factorial designs can also be used to give an efficient test strategy for this type of evaluation.

With pass/fail functional testing, test trials from a fractional factorial design are used to define configurations and/or experimental conditions, while test coverage is used to describe the percentage of all possible combinations of the factor levels ($C$) tested for various group sizes ($G$). In the EMI problem noted earlier in Section 18.1, the levels from a group size of three factors were identified (i.e., display type, power supply manufacturer, and power supply cable length). Using the strategy described in this chapter, Example 18-2 shows how a test coverage of 90% can be expected for a group of size three given a logic pass/fail output consideration of seven two-level factors in only eight test trials.

The desired output from a fractional factorial design matrix using this test strategy is that all experimental trial conditions pass. The percent coverage as a function of the group size and the number of test trials can be determined from Table O.* It should be noted, however, that whenever a trial fails there may be no statistical analysis technique that indicates the source of the problem. If additional engineering analyses do not identify the problem source, additional trials can be added to assist the experimenter in determining the cause of failure (see Section 18.10).

The percentage test coverage $C$ that is possible from a fractional factorial designed experiment, where $F$ two-level factors are assessed in $T$ trials is

---

* Tables A through R3 are found in Appendix D of the book.

$$C(F) = \frac{T}{2^F} \times 100 \qquad C(F) \leqslant 100\% \qquad (18.1)$$

This means, for example, that if $T = 32$, the maximum number of factors yielding complete coverage (i.e., $C = 100\%$) is $F = 5$.

Besides the total coverage of the experiment, it would be interesting to know the coverage of a particular subclass (or group) of $G$ factors chosen out of the total $F$ factors that comprise the experiment under consideration. Theoretically Equation (18.1) is still valid if $G$ replaced $F$, but actually for a generic group of $G$ factors, the fractional factorial design is not guaranteed against pattern repetitions. Therefore we expect to have

$$C(G) \leqslant \frac{T}{2^G} \times 100 \qquad G \leqslant T - 1 \qquad (18.2)$$

This relation gives us a theoretical maximum coverage value in a very general case. The mean percent coverage of all the possible $G$ groups from $F$ factors was calculated using a computer for a representative sample of resolution III fractional factorial design matrices for $2^n$ trials, where $n = 3$, 4, 5, and 6 (see Tables M1 to M5). Results from this study indicate that there is only a slight variation in the value of coverage ($C$) as a function of the number of factors ($F$), which, when ignored, graphically yields the percentage coverage noted in Table O. Note that in lieu of using a computer program to manually observe and calculate the observed coverage, the aliasing structure could have been examined to determine this coverage.

The number of $P$ possible $G$ groups of factors is determined from the binomial coefficient formula

$$P = \binom{F}{G} = \frac{F!}{G!\,(F - G)!} \qquad (18.3)$$

The $N$ total number of possible combinations of the two-level factors then becomes

$$N = 2^G \binom{F}{G} \qquad (18.4)$$

The value $C$ determined from Table O is the test percent coverage of the $N$ possible combinations of the factor levels for a group size $G$.

A step-by-step implementation approach to this procedure for two-level factor considerations is as follows (see Section 18.7 for factor levels greater than two).

1. List the number of two-level factors ($F$).
2. Determine the minimum number of trials ($T$) (i.e., 8, 16, 32, or 64 trials) that is at least one larger than the number of factors. Higher test

coverage can be obtained by using a fractional factorial design that has more trials.

3. Choose a fractional factorial design from Tables M1 to M5 (or some other source). Use Table O to determine the test percent coverage ($C$) for 3, 4, 5, 6, . . . two-level group sizes ($G$) with the number of trials ($T$).

4. Determine the number of possibilities for each group size ($G$) consideration using Equation (18.4).

5. Tabulate the percent coverage with possible combinational effects to understand better the effectiveness of the test.

Often determining the "right problem to solve" is more difficult than performing the mechanics of solving the problem. The next three examples have two purposes. The first purpose is to illustrate more applications of pass/fail functional testing. The second purpose is to illustrate some typical discussions that could be encountered when choosing factors and their levels. Even though the reader may not directly relate to a specific example for his or her job, hopefully this discussion will stimulate additional insight in how the technique may be applied.

## 18.4. EXAMPLE 18-2: A PASS/FAIL SYSTEM FUNCTIONAL TEST

A computer is to be tested where a *logic pass/fail* response is thought to be a function of the two-level considerations of seven factors shown in Table 18.3. A minimal number of test trials is needed while achieving high test coverage. (Note: A similar approach can be applied to the test situation where many more factors are involved. For example, 63 two-level factors could be assessed in a 64-trial design.)

Using the preceding procedure, this test can be performed using the following eight trials, taken from Table M2, shown in Table 18.4.

**TABLE 18.3. Example 18-2: Factors and Levels in Computer Test**

| Factor Designation | Contrast Column Level | |
|---|---|---|
| | ($-$) | ($+$) |
| $A$ | Display type X | Display type Y |
| $B$ | Memory size, small | Memory size, large |
| $C$ | Power supply vendor X | Power supply vendor Y |
| $D$ | Power cable length, short | Power cable length, long |
| $E$ | Printer type X | Printer type Y |
| $F$ | Hardfile size, small | Hardfile size, large |
| $G$ | Modem, yes | Modem, no |

EXAMPLE 18-2: A PASS/FAIL SYSTEM FUNCTIONAL TEST    **279**

**TABLE 18.4. Example 18-2: Test Matrix from Table M2**

| Number of Trial | $ABCDEFG$ |
|:---:|:---:|
| 1 | + − − + − + + |
| 2 | + + − − + − + |
| 3 | + + + − − + − |
| 4 | − + + + − − + |
| 5 | + − + + + − − |
| 6 | − + − + + + − |
| 7 | − − + − + + + |
| 8 | − − − − − − − |

From Table O and Equation (18.4) the information in Table 18.5 can be determined.

Note that with only eight trials there is 90% coverage for the number of groups of size three, which contains 280 possibilities! If this is not considered to be satisfactory test coverage, Table O can be referenced to determine the increase in coverage that will be obtained if the number of fractional factorial experimental trials is doubled, for example, to 16.

To illustrate the type of problem that this test would be able to detect, consider that the following failure condition exists (unknown to the test person):

Display type X: $A = -$
Power supply vendor Y: $C = +$
Power supply cable length, long: $D = +$

**TABLE 18.5. Example 18-2: Percent Coverage and Number of Possible Combinations**

|  | Number of Groups | | | | | |
|---|:---:|:---:|:---:|:---:|:---:|:---:|
|  | 2 | 3 | 4 | 5 | 6 | 7 |
| Percentage coverage | 100[a] | 90 | 50 | 25 | 12 | 6 |
| Number of possible combinations | 84 | 280[b] | 560 | 672 | 448 | 128 |

[a] Example coverage statement: 100% coverage of two combinations of the seven two-level factors.
[b] Example calculation: When the number of groups = 3 and the number of factors = 7, it is determined from Equation (18.3) that (where, e.g., $3! = 3 \times 2 \times 1$).

$$\binom{7}{3} = \frac{7!}{3!\,(7-3)!} = 35$$

From equation (18.4) it is then determined that the

$$\text{Number of possible combinations} = 2^3 \binom{7}{3} = 8(35) = 280$$

This combination of factor levels is noted to be contained in trial 4; hence, trial 4 (in this case) would be the only test trial to "fail." As noted earlier, an experimenter would not know from the pass/fail information of the trials (i.e., trial 4 was the only trial that failed) what specifically caused the failure (i.e., the *ACD* combination of $-++$ caused the failure). This information cannot be deduced since many combinations of factor levels could have caused the problem; however, with this test strategy, the tester was able to identify that a problem exists with a minimal number of test case scenarios. For the experimenter to determine the root cause of failure, a simple technical investigation may be the only additional work that is necessary. If the cause cannot be determined from such an investigation, additional trial patterns may need to be added to search for the root cause (see Section 18.10).

## 18.5. EXAMPLE 18-3: A PASS/FAIL HARDWARE/SOFTWARE SYSTEM FUNCTIONAL TEST

A company is considering buying several new personal computers to replace its existing equipment. The company has some atypical configurations for its computers; hence, the company wishes to have a "quick and dirty" test to verify that the product will work with its existing peripheral equipment and software.

The company believes that there will probably be no future problems if it can find no combination of the levels of three factors that cause a failure. The following discussion describes their test concerns.

Four different types of printers are used; however, it was believed that two of the four "special" printers could assess the "space" of the printer applications. Some of the companies' users had an application where two displays were concurrently used on one computer. Two different word processor packages were often used with two different database managers and two different spreadsheet programs. Some individuals used a plotter, while others did not. In addition, the company had two basic network systems interconnecting the computers.

The seven factors and associated levels can take the form shown in Table 18.6.

**TABLE 18.6. Example 18-3: Factors and Levels in Computer Assessment**

| Factor | $(-)$ | $(+)$ |
|--------|-------|-------|
| A | Printer X | Printer Y |
| B | One display | Two displays |
| C | Word processor X | Word processor Y |
| D | Database manager X | Database manager Y |
| E | Spreadsheet X | Spreadsheet Y |
| F | No plotter | Plotter |
| G | Network X | Network Y |

**TABLE 18.7. Example 18-3: Test Matrix from Table M2**

| Number of Trial | A B C D E F G |
|---|---|
| 1 | + − − + − + + |
| 2 | + + − − + − + |
| 3 | + + + − − + − |
| 4 | − + + + − − + |
| 5 | + − + + + − − |
| 6 | − + − + + + − |
| 7 | − − + − + + + |
| 8 | − − − − − − − |

Since $2^3 = 8$, an eight-trial experiment can then be used to test most of the combinational possibilities of group size three. From Tables M1 to M5, this test matrix is as shown in Table 18.7.

One approach to executing this experiment is to first build various "configurations" and applications and then perform test cases that exercise command sequences that "stress" the product application. As an addition to a pass/fail output scenario, one may include "performance" test cases that can realistically assess the amount of performance improvement that can be expected via the new computer.

The percentage test coverage of the factor levels for the test would be similar to that shown in Example 18-2; if no failures are noted, the company will probably feel more secure with the purchase. Example 18-5 illustrates a search methodology for determining the cause, if failures occur during test.

## 18.6. GENERAL CONSIDERATIONS WHEN ASSIGNING FACTORS

For a given test some groups of $G$ factors can have 100% coverage while others have 50% coverage for the $2^n$ trial designs in Tables M1 to M5. Instead of arbitrarily assigning factors, an experimenter may wish to make assignments so that factor combinational considerations that are thought important will have 100% test coverage. Combinational considerations to avoid for these factors are those that are identity elements (Diamond 1989; Box et al. 1978; Montgomery 1984) or a multiple of identity elements of the design matrix.

## 18.7. FACTOR LEVELS GREATER THAN 2

Two-level factors are generally desirable in a fractional factorial experiment; however, fractional factorial design matrices that contain levels greater than two levels can still be used to efficiently detect the type of functional problems discussed in this chapter. If there are no design matrices available to describe the desired number of factor levels of interest, a two-level fractional factorial matrix design can be used to create a design matrix, as noted in Section 13.17. For pass/fail functional testing I believe that contrast column selection is not as important as it is whenever the response is continuous (relative to addressing the problem of confounded effects). Because of this sometimes (e.g., when test resources are limited) I do not "preserve additional contrast columns" (see Section 13.17) when creating these greater-than-two-level designs from Tables M1–M5.

For this test situation the previous procedure using Tables M1 to M5 could be used with some modification to determine test coverage. However, in general, when there are several factors of differing multiple levels, it seems more applicable to randomly choose many differing configurations of a group size and examine whether these configurations were tested. The test percentage coverage ($C$) could then be calculated and plotted versus group size ($G$) to give a generalized pictorial representation of the coverage for the particular test (Breyfogle 1991).

## 18.8.  EXAMPLE 18-4: A SOFTWARE INTERFACE PASS/FAIL FUNCTIONAL TEST

A program was written so that a computer terminal could interface with a link that is attached to a computer network. A structured test strategy was desired to directly assess combinational problems with only a relatively few number of test cases and hardware configurations. The test cases need to check for combinational problems and abnormal situations that could occur and cause a problem in a situation that customers may encounter.

The following assumptions were made when creating the test cases. A basic test case scenario will be defined using a fractional factorial matrix design from Tables M1 to M5. The test case will be written to stress the level combinations of the factors.

- If two extreme levels of factors pass, the levels between these extremes will be assumed to pass.
- If an abnormal situation causes a failure, the trial will be reassessed without the abnormal situation.

The factors and factor levels considered within the experiment design are shown in Table 18.8. From Table M3 the experimental design matrix is shown in Table 18.9.

Coverage for tests that contain factors that are larger than two is discussed in Section 18.7, along with a philosophy for creating greater-than-two-level factor tests from Tables M1–M5.

EXAMPLE 18-4: SOFTWARE INTERFACE TEST     **283**

**TABLE 18.8. Example 18-4: Factors and Levels in Software Interface Test**

| Factors | Levels | |
|---|---|---|
| | (−) | (+) |
| A   Send data | Large data block (32K) | Small control message (8 bytes) |
| B   Receive data | Large data block (32K) | Small control message (8 bytes) |
| C   Interrupt | No | Yes |
| D   Link type | Switched circuit | Leased line |
| E   Type of cable interface between the terminal and modem | Slow Minimum baud rate | Fast Maximum baud rate |
| F   Throughput negotiations | No: use default baud rate | Yes: different baud rate then default rate |
| G   Loading/utilization of system | Multiple sessions | Single session |
| H   Personal computer processor type | Fast type | Slow type |
| I   Personal computer internal clock speed | Fastest | Slowest |
| J   Abnormal situations | None | Connection broken |
| M   Upstream link to mainframe computer | No | Yes |
| K and L   Network adapters | − −   Only one type X network adapter<br>− +   Two type X network adapters<br>+ −   One type X and one type Y network adapter<br>+ +   One type X and one type Z network adapter | |

**TABLE 18.9. Example 18-4: Test Matrix from Table M3**

| Number of Trial | $ABCDEFGHIJKLM$ |
|:---:|:---:|
| 1 | + - - - + - - + + - + - + |
| 2 | + + - - - + - - + + - + - |
| 3 | + + + - - - + - - + + - + |
| 4 | + + + + - - - + - - + + - |
| 5 | - + + + + - - - + - - + + |
| 6 | + - + + + + - - - + - - + |
| 7 | - + - + + + + - - - + - - |
| 8 | + - + - + + + + - - - + - |
| 9 | + + - + - + + + + - - - + |
| 10 | - + + - + - + + + + - - - |
| 11 | - - + + - + - + + + + - - |
| 12 | + - - + + - + - + + + + - |
| 13 | - + - - + + - + - + + + + |
| 14 | - - + - - + + - + - + + + |
| 15 | - - - + - - + + - + - + + |
| 16 | - - - - - - - - - - - - - |

## 18.9. A SEARCH PATTERN STRATEGY TO DETERMINE THE SOURCE OF FAILURE

When a failure occurs when using the preceding matrix test strategy, sometimes the problem source is obvious, from a physical point of view. However, sometimes a cause cannot be determined and a search pattern is needed to better understand the failure mode.

A diagnostic search pattern strategy can begin with first noting the trials that had a common failure mode. Next, factors that obviously do not affect the output are removed from consideration. A logical assessment of the previous combinational pass/fail conditions is done to determine additional test trials that should be conducted, or a good starting point for additional trials can be the reversal of the level states in the original matrix design (i.e., a fold over design; see Section 13.9). These two techniques are illustrated in the following example.

## 18.10. EXAMPLE 18-5: A SEARCH PATTERN STRATEGY TO DETERMINE THE SOURCE OF FAILURE

If there were no failures found in Example 18-3, the company would probably be comfortable in purchasing the product, since most three-factor combinations are considered in the test and there was no reason to expect any failure.

However, if a trial or trials did fail for an unknown reason, the experimenter, in general, may not understand the cause. The following illustrates, using

EXAMPLE 18-5: SEARCH PATTERN FOR FAILURE SOURCE    **285**

three different scenarios, a logic search pattern procedure to diagnose a *single-source combinational problem* of factor levels that results in a failure condition for certain trials.

Consider first that the experiment design had failures with trials 2, 3, 4, and 6, as noted with the x's:

| Number of Trial | $ABCDEFG$ | |
|:---:|:---:|:---:|
| 1 | $+--+-++$ | |
| 2 | $++--+-+$ | x |
| 3 | $+++--+-$ | x |
| 4 | $-+++--+$ | x |
| 5 | $+-+++--$ | |
| 6 | $-+-+++-$ | x |
| 7 | $--+-+++$ | |
| 8 | $-------$ | |

The trials with failures are noted to be

| Number of Trial | $ABCDEFG$ | |
|:---:|:---:|:---:|
| 2 | $++--+-+$ | x |
| 3 | $+++--+-$ | x |
| 4 | $-+++--+$ | x |
| 6 | $-+-+++-$ | x |

Assuming that problems originate from a single source, this pass/fail pattern leads us to conclude that the failure is caused by $B = +$, since the level of $B = -$ had no failures (i.e., the computer does not work with two displays). Consider now that trials 2 and 3 were the only two that had failures.

| Number of Trial | $ABCDEFG$ | |
|:---:|:---:|:---:|
| 1 | $+--+-++$ | |
| 2 | $++--+-+$ | x |
| 3 | $+++--+-$ | x |
| 4 | $-+++--+$ | |
| 5 | $+-+++--$ | |
| 6 | $-+-+++-$ | |
| 7 | $--+-+++$ | |
| 8 | $-------$ | |

The trials with failure are then noted to be

| Number of Trial | $ABCDEFG$ | |
|:---:|:---:|:---:|
| 2 | $++--+-+$ | x |
| 3 | $+++--+-$ | x |

This pass/fail pattern leads us to conclude initially that the failure could be caused by $ABD = ++-$. However, consider the subset of all possible combinations of $ABD$ that where exercised in this test.

| $A\,B\,D$ | Trial |
|---|---|
| $-\,-\,-$ | 7,8 |
| $-\,-\,+$ | |
| * $-\,+\,-$ | |
| $-\,+\,+$ | 4,6 |
| $+\,-\,-$ | |
| $+\,-\,+$ | 1,5 |
| $+\,+\,-$ | 2,3 |
| * $+\,+\,+$ | |

As noted earlier, not all combinations of three factors are covered within $2^3 = 8$ test trials. Approximately 90% of the all possible combinations are covered when there are seven two-level factors in eight trials. For this particular combination of factors ($ABD$), there is 50% coverage. Hence, to determine the cause of the failure, the other subset combinations of ABD need to be considered.

To determine whether the problem is from an $ABD = ++-$ effect or a combinational consideration that has one less factor, consider a test of the combinations that contain a "single-factor-level" change from the state of $++-$ to levels not previously tested. The two combinational considerations not previously tested that meet this "single-factor-level change" are noted by an *. If, for example, the problem was really caused by $AB = ++$, then the $ABD = +++$ trial would fail while the $ABD = -+-$ combination would pass. Further step reductions in the number of factors would not be necessary since these combinations have previously passed.

Consider now that trial 3 was the only trial that failed. The failure pattern for this trial is

| Number of Trial | $A\,B\,C\,D\,E\,F\,G$ |
|---|---|
| 3 | $+++--+-$    x |

There are many reasons why this one trial could have failed; hence, several test trials are needed to further assess the failure source.

Consider that the real cause was from the combinational effect $BCD$ of $++-$ (i.e., two displays with word processor Y and database manager X). However, the experimenter did not know the cause and wanted to determine the reason for failure.

Sometimes there are obvious factors that can be removed from further consideration, which can lead to a significant reduction in test effort. However,

EXAMPLE 18-5: SEARCH PATTERN FOR FAILURE SOURCE    **287**

let's assume in this example that there was no engineering/programming knowledge that could eliminate some of the factor considerations. A good beginning strategy to consider is using a fold-over design (see Section 13.9). In this approach all the levels are changed to the opposite level condition. These trials are then tested. The additional trials to execute then would be

| Number of Trial | $ABCDEFG$ | |
|:---:|:---:|:---:|
| 9 | $-++-+--$ | x |
| 10 | $--++-+-$ | |
| 11 | $---++-+$ | |
| 12 | $+---++-$ | |
| 13 | $-+---++$ | |
| 14 | $+-+---+$ | |
| 15 | $++-+---$ | |
| 16 | $+++++++$ | |

Trial 9 would now be the only failure since it is the only trial with $BCD = ++-$. The trials that failed collectively are now

| Number of Trial | $ABCDEFG$ | |
|:---:|:---:|:---:|
| 3 | $+++--+-$ | x |
| 9 | $-++-+--$ | x |

From the information obtained at this point of the experiment process, effects $A$, $E$, and $F$ can be removed from consideration since these factors occurred at both high and low levels for the failure conditions. The reduced combinational factor effect considerations are then

| Number of Trial | $BCDG$ | |
|:---:|:---:|:---:|
| 3 | $++--$ | x |
| 9 | $++--$ | x |

At this point it is not known where there is a $BCDG$ combinational relationship or a subset of these effects causing the failure. These trials can then be listed to determine which combinations were/were not exercised. By examination, the combinations of $BCDG$ shown in Table 18.10 were exercised by the noted trial(s) in the preceding two experiments.

To determine whether the problem is from an $BCDG = ++--$ effect or a subset that has one less factor level consideration, note the combinations that contain a single-factor-level change from the $BCDG$ state of $++--$ to those levels not previously tested. The four preceding combinational considerations not previously tested that meet this single-factor-level change are again

**TABLE 18.10. Example 18-5: Listing of**
**_BCDG_ Combinations and Trials**

| _B C D G_ | Trial(s) |
|---|---|
| − − − − | 8, 12 |
| − − − + | |
| − − + − | |
| − − + + | 1, 11 |
| * − + − − | |
| − + − + | 7, 14 |
| − + + − | 5, 10 |
| − + + + | |
| * + − − − | |
| + − − + | 2, 13 |
| + − + − | 6, 15 |
| + − + + | |
| + + − − | 3, 9[a] |
| * + + − + | |
| * + + + − | |
| + + + + | 4, 16 |

[a]9 was the previously failed scenario.

noted by an *. Since $BCD = ++-$ is the "real" problem, the $BCDG = ++-+$ combination would fail, while the other combinations would pass. Since all smaller "group sizes" of these factor levels were already tested without failure, the experimenter would then correctly conclude that the problem was originated by $BCD = ++-$ (i.e., two displays, word processor Y, and database manager X).

Note that for this last single failure scenario, this procedure was able to both structurally identify a three-level combinational problem in eight trials and then isolate the source of the problem in only 12 more trials, given the combinational possibilities of seven two-level factors.

It should be noted, in general, that it is good experimental practice to run a confirmation experiment since there are situations where multiple combinational effects or other experimental problems could cause an erroneous conclusion.

## 18.11. ADDITIONAL APPLICATIONS

Pass/fail functional testing procedures can also apply to the situation where a problem is noted within an assembly; suspected "bad" part components can be exchanged in a structured fashion with an assembly that has "good parts". The objective of this test then is to determine a particular part type or combination of part types that cause a problem. For this situation each part type becomes a factor with a level that indicates whether it was from either a "good" or "bad" assembly. However, with this type of situation, trial replication may be necessary to determine whether, for example, a consistent pass/fail response occurs for the combination consideration. This is important since the assembly process may be a major source of the problem.

Pass/fail search pattern can also be useful to get some insight to why some attribute fractional factorial trials are very good and others are not very good, even when attribute fractional factorial testing procedures (see Section 13.19) showed nothing to be significant in terms of the "mean" effect analysis (see Equation 14.1). Insight can sometimes be achieved by ranking the trials from goodness to badness. Sometimes there is an obvious change in the failure rate between the ranked trials. For example, trials 7 and 9 may have had no failures, while all the other trials had between 6 and 10 failures. Perhaps something unique can then be identified for these trials (e.g., a pass/fail logic condition) by looking at the patterns of $+$'s and $-$'s. Obviously any theories that are developed would need further evaluation in a confirmation experiment.

## 18.12. DO-IT-SMARTER CONSIDERATIONS

Obviously it is important when using a fractional factorial design strategy not to exclude factors or factor levels that are important relative to the response of interest. One major advantage to the test strategy discussed in this chapter is that this risk can be minimized if brainstorming techniques (see Section 21.3) are used to choose the test factors and factor levels. In addition, the concepts lend themselves to a structured pyramid test strategy that can be used in the development of products (see Figure 21.10).

It is often impossible to test all combinations of factor levels because of the potentially staggering number of combinational possibilities. However, by determining the number of factor groupings that realistically should be assessed and then testing the combinations of factor levels within a fractional factorial design structure, an "impossible" situation can become quite manageable, plus, the test coverage effectiveness can be reported.

The basic test strategy described in this chapter can also be used to assess software and microcode effectiveness where the number of factors and desired trials could exceed the matrix designs given in this text. Larger $2^n$ trial design matrices could be generated for this situation by combining the $+/-$ patterns of columns using the same approach as that shown in Section 13.7 and 13.8 (via a computer program). The methodology described in Section 18.7 could then be used to determine test coverage (Breyfogle 1991.)

It should be remembered fractional factorial design matrices can have more than one response. A pass/fail functional response in addition to multiple continuous response outputs can be a very powerful basic test strategy.

# 19

# ANALYSES OF PROCESSES

Recommended introductory reading: Chapters 2, 3, and 4.

It was noted in Section 3.3 that Juran classifies manufacturing process problems into two categories, sporadic and chronic. Similarly there was discussion about Deming's categorization of process situations that result from common causes and special causes. It was emphasized that corrective action can be very different depending on which of the two categories exists in a given situation. The process control charts discussed in this chapter are tools that can identify when a sporadic or chronic problem (common causes or special causes) exists so that the appropriate action can be taken.

The first sections of this chapter illustrate attribute and variables process control charts as a methodology to identify when sporadic problems occur and whether there are chronic problems (e.g., the mean of the process is unacceptably high or low). Also, process capability studies are illustrated as a procedure to determine whether a process is capable of consistently meeting design specifications. Pareto diagrams (see Figures 3.4 and 21.6) are then illustrated as a tool to help isolate the cause of chronic problems in a process.

The techniques covered in this chapter are normally associated with manufacturing processes. However, these analysis techniques can be used to assess parameters in other areas of the business (e.g., the time required to process an invoice).

## 19.1. MONITORING PROCESSES

Preproduction tests can assess the basic design of a product; however, the manufacturing process needs to be capable of mass producing a product with consistent quality. To assess this, manufacturing should first determine the measurements that need to be taken and the procedures to make these measurements with precision (see Section 4.8). A continuous monitoring strategy is needed to evaluate the product so that unexpected degradation within the process will be identified quickly. Corrective action can then be made in a timely fashion to limit the number of products manufactured with the degradation.

A process is said to be in statistical control when there are only common causes affecting variation. Process control systems are a tool to provide a statistical signal when there are special causes of variation within the process. Figure 19.1 illustrates both an "out-of-control" and "in-control" process condition.

However, a process can be in statistical control and not be capable of consistently producing product that is within specification limits, as shown in Figure 19.2. This can occur because the process mean is shifted excessively from the nominal target value, or because the variability is excessive. Process capability studies can be used to assess this situation.

When a process is identified that consistently does not meet specifications, major design changes may be necessary. A Pareto diagram (see Figures 19.14 and 21.6) can be useful to identify where focus should be given when considering design and/or process changes. It should be noted that the fractional factorial and response surface experiment techniques discussed in Chapters 13–17 can often be used to efficiently determine off-line which design change considerations are beneficial to the process.

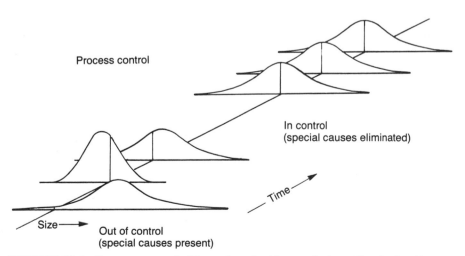

Process control

In control
(special causes eliminated)

Time

Size

Out of control
(special causes present)

**FIGURE 19.1.** Process control. [Reproduced with permission: *Continuing Process Control and Process Capability Improvement*, Ford Corporate Quality Education and Training Center, 1987.]

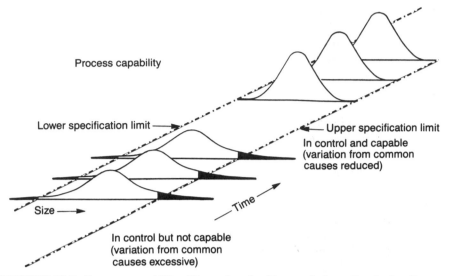

Process capability

Lower specification limit

Upper specification limit

In control and capable
(variation from common
causes reduced)

Size

Time

In control but not capable
(variation from common
causes excessive)

**FIGURE 19.2.** Process capability. [Reproduced with permission: *Continuing Process Control and Process Capability Improvement*, Ford Corporate Quality Education and Training Center, 1987.]

## 19.2. STATISTICAL PROCESS CONTROL CHARTS

Shewhart control charts (Shewhart 1931) track processes by plotting data over time in the form shown in Figure 19.3. This chart can track either variables or attribute process parameters. The variable types discussed within this text are process mean ($\bar{x}$), range ($R$), standard deviation ($s$), and individual values ($X$). The attribute types discussed are proportion nonconforming ($p$), number of nonconforming items ($np$), number of nonconformities ($c$), and nonconformities per unit ($u$).

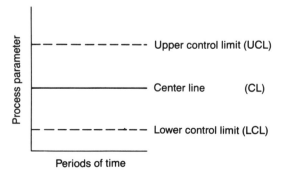

Process parameter

Upper control limit (UCL)

Center line        (CL)

Lower control limit (LCL)

Periods of time

**FIGURE 19.3.** Shewhart control chart format.

The typical control limits shown in Figure 19.3 are $3\sigma$ limits. When a point falls outside these limits, the process is said to be out of control. Other interpretations of control chart patterns are discussed in Section 19.12. It should be emphasized that the process (not the specification) determines the process control limits noted in the following sections.

## 19.3. $\bar{x}$ AND $R$ AND $\bar{x}$ AND $s$ CHARTS: MEAN AND VARIABILITY MEASUREMENTS

Consider that $m$ samples of size $n$ are taken over a period of time. The number of $m$ samples should be at least 20 to 25 where $n$ will often be smaller and either 4, 5, or 6. For each sample of size $n$ a mean [see Equation (4.1)] and range can be determined, where range is the difference between high and low readings.

For a process variable to be in statistical control, both the process's mean and range (or standard deviation) must be within control. For a new process typically the process mean ($\bar{\bar{x}}$) (center line of Figure 19.3) is not known; hence, it has to be calculated using the equation

$$\bar{\bar{x}} = \frac{\bar{x}_1 + \bar{x}_2 + \cdots + \bar{x}_m}{m} \tag{19.1}$$

Similarly the mean range value ($\bar{R}$) of the $m$ subgroups is

$$\bar{R} = \frac{R_1 + R_2 + \cdots + R_m}{m} \tag{19.2}$$

For small sample sizes a relatively good estimate for the population standard deviation ($\hat{\sigma}$) is (see Table J for factor $d_2$):

$$\hat{\sigma} = \frac{\bar{R}}{d_2} \tag{19.3}$$

In general, it is better to use the standard deviation from each subgroup instead of the range when tracking variability. This was more difficult in the past before the advent of on-line computers and calculators. However, when sample sizes for $n$ are of a magnitude of 4 to 6, the range approximation is satisfactory.

When the sample size $n$ for the subgroup is moderately large, say ($n > 10$ to 12), the range method for estimating $\sigma$ loses efficiency. In these situations it is best to consider using $\bar{x}$ and $s$ charts, where $s$ (the sample standard deviation) can be determined from Equation (4.2). For $m$ subgroups $\bar{s}$ can then be determined using the equation

$$\bar{s} = \frac{s_1 + s_2 + \cdots + s_m}{m} \quad \text{[for Equations (19.4) and (19.6)]}$$

The upper control limit (UCL) and lower control limit (LCL) around a center line (CL) for $\bar{x}$ and ($R$ or $s$) can be determined from the following equations, where the constants (e.g., $A_2$ and $D_3$) are taken from Table J.*

$$\bar{x}: \quad CL = \bar{\bar{x}} \qquad \begin{array}{ll} UCL = \bar{\bar{x}} + A_2\bar{R} & LCL = \bar{\bar{x}} - A_2\bar{R} \\ & \qquad\qquad\qquad \text{or} \\ UCL = \bar{\bar{x}} + A_3\bar{s} & LCL = \bar{\bar{x}} - A_3\bar{s} \end{array} \qquad (19.4)$$

$$R: \quad CL = \bar{R} \qquad UCL = D_4\bar{R} \qquad LCL = D_3\bar{R} \qquad (19.5)$$

$$s: \quad CL = \bar{s} \qquad UCL = B_4\bar{s} \qquad LCL = B_3\bar{s} \qquad (19.6)$$

If successive group values plotted on the $s$ or $R$ charts are in control, control statements can then be made relative to an $\bar{x}$ chart.

When it is possible to specify the standard values for the process mean ($\mu$) and standard deviation ($\sigma$), these standards could be used to establish the control charts without the analysis of past data. For this situation Equations (19.7) to (19.9) are used, where the constants are again taken from Table J.

$$\bar{x}: \quad CL = \mu \qquad UCL = \mu + A\sigma \qquad LCL = \mu - A\sigma \qquad (19.7)$$

$$R: \quad CL = d_2\sigma \qquad UCL = D_2\sigma \qquad LCL = D_1\sigma \qquad (19.8)$$

$$s: \quad CL = c_4\sigma \qquad UCL = B_6\sigma \qquad LCL = B_5\sigma \qquad (19.9)$$

Care must be exercised when using this approach since the standards may not be applicable to the process, which can result in many out-of-control signals.

### 19.4. EXAMPLE 19-1: $\bar{x}$ AND $R$ CHARTS

A grinding machine is to produce treads for a hydraulic system of an aircraft to a diameter of $0.4037 \pm 0.0013$ in. Go/no-go thread ring gages are currently used in a 100% test plan to reject parts that are not within tolerance. In an attempt to better understand the process variability so that the process can be improved, variables data were taken for the process. Measurements were taken every hour on five samples using a visual comparator that had an accuracy of 0.0001. The averages and ranges from this test are noted in Table 19.1 (Grant and Leavenworth 1980).

* Tables A–R3 are located in Appendix D of this book.

EXAMPLE 19-1: $\bar{x}$ AND $R$ CHARTS    295

**TABLE 19.1. Example 19-1: Data**

| Sample Number | Measurement on Each Item of Five Items per Hour[a] | | | | | Mean $\bar{x}$ | Range $R$ |
|---|---|---|---|---|---|---|---|
| 1 | 36 | 35 | 34 | 33 | 32 | 34.0 | 4 |
| 2 | 31 | 31 | 34 | 32 | 30 | 31.6 | 4 |
| 3 | 30 | 30 | 32 | 30 | 32 | 30.8 | 2 |
| 4 | 32 | 33 | 33 | 32 | 35 | 33.0 | 3 |
| 5 | 32 | 34 | 37 | 37 | 35 | 35.0 | 5 |
| 6 | 32 | 32 | 31 | 33 | 33 | 32.2 | 2 |
| 7 | 33 | 33 | 36 | 32 | 31 | 33.0 | 5 |
| 8 | 23 | 33 | 36 | 35 | 36 | 32.6 | 13 |
| 9 | 43 | 36 | 35 | 24 | 31 | 33.8 | 19 |
| 10 | 36 | 35 | 36 | 41 | 41 | 37.8 | 6 |
| 11 | 34 | 38 | 35 | 34 | 38 | 35.8 | 4 |
| 12 | 36 | 38 | 39 | 39 | 40 | 38.4 | 4 |
| 13 | 36 | 40 | 35 | 26 | 33 | 34.0 | 14 |
| 14 | 36 | 35 | 37 | 34 | 33 | 35.0 | 4 |
| 15 | 30 | 37 | 33 | 34 | 35 | 33.8 | 7 |
| 16 | 28 | 31 | 33 | 33 | 33 | 31.6 | 5 |
| 17 | 33 | 30 | 34 | 33 | 35 | 33.0 | 5 |
| 18 | 27 | 28 | 29 | 27 | 30 | 28.2 | 3 |
| 19 | 35 | 36 | 29 | 27 | 32 | 31.8 | 9 |
| 20 | 33 | 35 | 35 | 39 | 36 | 35.6 | 6 |
| | | | | | | $\bar{\bar{x}} = 33.6$ | $\bar{R} = 6.2$ |

[a] Values are expressed in units of 0.0001 in. in excess of 0.4000 in. Dimension is specified to be 0.4037 ±0.0013 in.

The $\bar{x}$ and $R$ chart parameters are determined from Equations (19.4) and (19.5) to be as follows (values are expressed in units of 0.0001 in. in excess of 0.4000 in.):

for the $\bar{x}$ chart:

$$\text{CL} = \bar{\bar{x}} = 33.6 \qquad \text{UCL} = \bar{\bar{x}} + A_2\bar{R} = 33.6 + 0.577(6.2) = 37.18$$

$$\text{LCL} = \bar{\bar{x}} - A_2\bar{R} = 33.6 - 0.577(6.2) = 30.02$$

for the $R$ chart:

$$\text{CL} = \bar{R} = 6.2$$

$$\text{UCL} = D_4\bar{R} = 2.114(6.2) = 13.1 \qquad \text{LCL} = D_3\bar{R} = 0(6.2) = 0$$

A computer-generated $\bar{x}$ control chart of the data is shown in Figure 19.4. The $R$ control chart is shown in Figure 19.5.

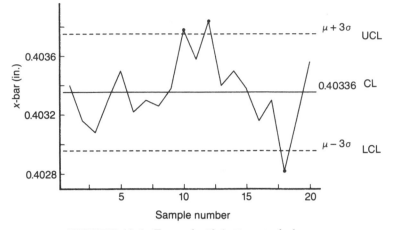

**FIGURE 19.4.** Example 19-1: $\bar{x}$ control chart.

Both the $\bar{x}$ (points 10, 12, and 18) and $R$ (points 9 and 13) charts show lack of control. These points should have an assignable cause for being outside the control limits; however, in general, determining the real cause after some period of time may be impossible. In addition, often not much can be done about these past causes beside creating some awareness of trying to prevent a certain type of problem in the future; however, this chart gives evidence that there is opportunity to reduce the variability of the current process. For this example the previously noted abnormal variation in the mean was determined to be from the machine setting, while abnormal variation in the range was determined to be from operator carelessness. After isolating special causes, these points should then, in general, be removed from the data to create new control charts with new limits.

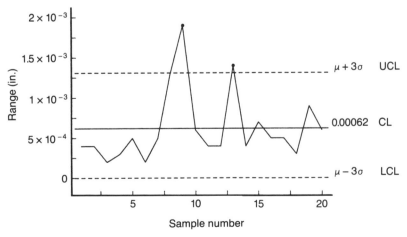

**FIGURE 19.5.** Example 19-1: $R$ control chart.

Assuming an average range value of 0.0006, it indicates that the tolerance of ±0.0013 could be consistently obtainable with a stable process that is centered within the specification, if there are no operator and machine problems. However, Figure 19.4 indicates that the process mean is shifted from the nominal specification. Example 19-5 will later quantify this measurement of process capability.

Whenever natural tolerances are found to be consistently within specification limits, consideration should be given to replacing a 100% inspection plan with periodic variable measurements of samples. For this example this can mean the replacement of the 100% go/no-go test with periodic measurements and control charting of the actual dimensions of five samples, as long as the control chart is in control and has an acceptable level of process capability. Often this change can yield both a significant savings and improvement in quality, since the process is better understood.

## 19.5. *X* CHART: INDIVIDUAL MEASUREMENTS

The control criteria in Section 9.3 considered sample sizes greater than one within the sampling groups. For some situations, such as chemical batch processes, only a sample size of one is achievable. Individual measurements of this type can be monitored using *X* charts.

For this situation the process average is simply the mean of the $n$ data points, which is

$$\bar{x} = \frac{\sum\limits_{i=1}^{n} x_i}{n} \tag{19.10}$$

The moving ranges (MRs) are determined from the data using the equations

$$MR_1 = |x_2 - x_1| \quad MR_2 = |x_3 - x_2|, \ldots \tag{19.11}$$

The charting parameters are

$$CL = \bar{x} \quad UCL = \bar{x} + 2.66(\overline{MR}) \quad LCL = \bar{x} - 2.66(\overline{MR}) \tag{19.12}$$

where the average moving range ($\overline{MR}$) is the average MR value for the $n$ values as shown in Equation (19.13). An explanation for the 2.66 factor can be found in ASTM (1976).

$$\overline{MR} = \frac{\sum\limits_{i=1}^{m} MR_i}{m} = \frac{(MR_1) + (MR_2) + (MR_3), \ldots, (MR_m)}{m} \tag{19.13}$$

Many of the conditions detected with $\bar{x}$ and $R$ (or $s$) charts can be detected with an $X$ chart that has reduced sensitivity. However, the validity of an $X$ chart is more sensitive to the data's not being from a normal distribution.

Although a moving range chart can be constructed (ASTM STP15D), Messina (1987) notes that it is not recommended because

1. All the information that can be obtained from the moving range is contained in the $X$ chart.
2. The moving ranges are correlated. For example, $MR_1$(i.e., $x_2 - x_1$) and $MR_2$(i.e., $x_3 - x_2$) both contain the point $x_2$, and this correlation can induce patterns of runs or cycles (see Section 19.12) on the chart that may not really exist in the data.

## 19.6. EXAMPLE 19-2: $X$ CHART

The viscosity of a chemical mixing process has the centipoise (cP) measurements noted in Table 19.2 for 20 batches (Messina 1987).

The MRs are determined by using Equation (19.11), where, for example, the moving range for batch 2 is $75.2 - 70.1 = 5.10$. The process average

**TABLE 19.2. Example 19-2: Data on Batch Viscosity**

| Batch Number | Viscosity (cP) | Moving Range (MR) |
|---|---|---|
| 1 | 70.10 | — |
| 2 | 75.20 | 5.10 |
| 3 | 74.40 | 0.80 |
| 4 | 72.07 | 2.33 |
| 5 | 74.70 | 2.63 |
| 6 | 73.80 | 0.90 |
| 7 | 72.77 | 1.03 |
| 8 | 78.17 | 5.40 |
| 9 | 70.77 | 7.40 |
| 10 | 74.30 | 3.53 |
| 11 | 72.90 | 1.40 |
| 12 | 72.50 | 0.40 |
| 13 | 74.60 | 2.10 |
| 14 | 75.43 | 0.83 |
| 15 | 75.30 | 0.13 |
| 16 | 78.17 | 2.87 |
| 17 | 76.00 | 2.17 |
| 18 | 73.50 | 2.50 |
| 19 | 74.27 | 0.77 |
| 20 | 75.05 | 0.73 |
| | $\bar{\bar{x}} = 74.197$ | $\overline{MR} = 2.264$ |

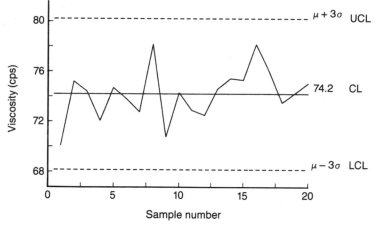

**FIGURE 19.6.** Example 19-2: $X$ chart.

and moving range average are determined using Equations (19.12). Using these values along with Equation (19.13) yields the following chart parameters:

$$CL = \bar{x} \qquad UCL = \bar{x} + 2.66(\overline{MR}) \qquad LCL = \bar{x} - 2.66(\overline{MR})$$

$$CL = 74.197 \quad UCL = 74.197 + 2.66(2.264) \quad LCL = 74.197 - 2.66(2.264)$$

$$UCL = 80.219 \qquad\qquad LCL = 68.175$$

There is no indication of an out-of-control condition in the control chart plot shown in Figure 19.6. If we consider that the 20 batch readings are a random sample of the process, we could make a probability plot (see Chapter 5) of the raw data to determine the expected range in viscosities that will be experienced by the customer.

## 19.7. *p* CHART: FRACTION NONCONFORMING MEASUREMENTS

The fraction nonconforming ($p$) is defined as

$$p = \frac{x}{n} \tag{19.14}$$

where $x$ is the number of nonconforming items and $n$ is the sample size. The process average nonconforming $\bar{p}$ for $m$ subgroups is

$$\bar{p} = \frac{\sum\limits_{i=1}^{m} p_i}{m} \tag{19.15}$$

where in general $m$ should be at least 20 to 25. The chart parameters for this binomial scenario are

$$\text{CL} = \bar{p} \qquad \text{UCL} = \bar{p} + 3\sqrt{\frac{\bar{p}(1 - \bar{p})}{n}}$$

$$\text{LCL} = \bar{p} - 3\sqrt{\frac{\bar{p}(1 - \bar{p})}{n}} \tag{19.16}$$

The preceding $p$-charting techniques can still be used whenever the sizes of the samples are not equal; however, $\bar{p}$ would most typically be determined as the total number of defects from all the samples divided by the total number of samples that are taken. Note that the control limits either need to be adjusted for each sample or an overall averaging of the sample sizes can be adequate, if there is not much difference between the sample sizes. Montgomery (1985) and Messina (1987) discuss variable sample size $p$ charts in more depth. If possible, it is best to use a strategy where the sample sizes are equal.

## 19.8. EXAMPLE 19-3: $p$ CHART

A machine manufactures the cardboard can used to package frozen orange juice. Cans are then inspected to determine whether they will leak when filled with orange juice. A $p$ chart is initially established by taking 30 samples of 50 cans at half hour intervals within the manufacturing process, as summarized in Table 19.3 (Montgomery 1985).

From Equation (19.15) the process average is

$$\bar{p} = \sum_{i=1}^{m} \frac{p_i}{m} = \frac{0.24 + 0.30 + 0.16, \dots}{30} = 0.2313$$

From Equation (19.16) the chart parameters are

$$\text{CL} = 0.2313 \qquad \text{UCL} = 0.2313 + 3\sqrt{\frac{0.2313(1 - 0.2313)}{50}} = 0.4102$$

$$\text{LCL} = 0.2313 - 3\sqrt{\frac{0.2313(1 - 0.2313)}{50}} = 0.0524$$

The $p$ chart of the data with the control limits is shown in Figure 19.7. Sample 15 and 23 are above the limits in the control chart; hence, the process is considered "not in control." If investigation indicates that these two points were caused by an adverse condition (e.g., a new batch of raw material or an inexperienced operator), the process control limits can be recalculated

**TABLE 19.3. Example 19-3: Data on Orange Juice**

| Sample Number | Number of Nonconformances | Sample Nonconforming Fraction |
|:---:|:---:|:---:|
| 1 | 12 | 0.24 |
| 2 | 15 | 0.30 |
| 3 | 8 | 0.16 |
| 4 | 10 | 0.20 |
| 5 | 4 | 0.08 |
| 6 | 7 | 0.14 |
| 7 | 16 | 0.32 |
| 8 | 9 | 0.18 |
| 9 | 14 | 0.28 |
| 10 | 10 | 0.20 |
| 11 | 5 | 0.10 |
| 12 | 6 | 0.12 |
| 13 | 17 | 0.34 |
| 14 | 12 | 0.24 |
| 15 | 22 | 0.44 |
| 16 | 8 | 0.16 |
| 17 | 10 | 0.20 |
| 18 | 5 | 0.10 |
| 19 | 13 | 0.26 |
| 20 | 11 | 0.22 |
| 21 | 20 | 0.40 |
| 22 | 18 | 0.36 |
| 23 | 24 | 0.48 |
| 24 | 15 | 0.30 |
| 25 | 9 | 0.18 |
| 26 | 12 | 0.24 |
| 27 | 7 | 0.14 |
| 28 | 13 | 0.26 |
| 29 | 9 | 0.18 |
| 30 | 6 | 0.12 |

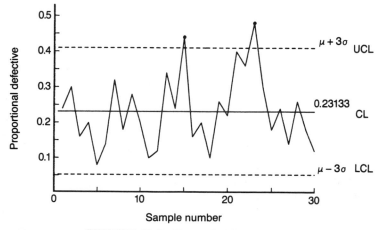

**FIGURE 19.7.** Example 19-3: $p$ chart.

without the data points. Whenever out of control conditions exist that cannot be explained, these data points should typically not be removed from the control limit computations. If this initial process control chart also does not have any abnormal patterns, as discussed previously, then the control limits are used to monitor the current production on a continuing basis.

For a stable process the magnitude of the average failure rate (i.e., 0.23133) should be examined for acceptability. A reduction in the overall average typically requires a more involved overall process or design change (i.e., see chronic problems and common causes in Section 3.3). The Pareto diagram (see Section 19.17) in conjunction with fractional factorial techniques (see Chapter 13) is a powerful approach to aid in determining which changes are beneficial to improving the process.

### 19.9. *np* CHART: NUMBER OF NONCONFORMING ITEMS

An alternative to the *p* chart when the sample size (*n*) is constant is a *np* chart. In this chart the number of nonconforming items is plotted instead of the fraction nonconforming (*p*). The chart parameters are

$$\text{CL} = n\bar{p} \quad \text{UCL} = n\bar{p} + 3\sqrt{n\bar{p}(1 - \bar{p})} \quad \text{LCL} = n\bar{p} - 3\sqrt{n\bar{p}(1 - \bar{p})}$$

(19.17)

where $\bar{p}$ is determined from Equation (19.15).

### 19.10. *c* CHART: NUMBER OF NONCONFORMITIES

In some cases the number of nonconformities per unit is a more appropriate unit of measure than the fraction nonconforming. An example of this situation is where a printed circuit board is tested. If the inspection process considered the board as a pass/fail entity, then a *p* chart or *np* chart would be appropriate. However, a given printed circuit board can have multiple failures; hence, it may be better to track the total number of defects per unit of measure. For a printed circuit board the unit of measure could be the number of solder joints in 100 cards, while the unit of measure when manufacturing cloth could be the number of blemishes per 100 square yards.

The *c* chart can be used to monitor these processes, if the Poisson distribution is an appropriate model. As noted earlier, the Poisson distribution (see Section 6.4) can be used for various analysis considerations if the number of opportunities for nonconformities are sufficiently large and the probability of occurrence of a nonconformity at a location is small and constant. The chart parameters for the $c$ chart are

$$CL = \bar{c} \quad UCL = \bar{c} + 3\sqrt{\bar{c}} \quad LCL = \bar{c} - 3\sqrt{\bar{c}} \quad (19.18)$$

where $\bar{c}$ is the mean of the occurrences and the LCL is set to zero if the calculations yield a negative number.

## 19.11. $u$ CHART: NONCONFORMITIES PER UNIT

A $u$ chart can be used in lieu of a $c$ chart when the rationale subgroup is not constant. This occurs for subgroups that are based on time (e.g., the number of defects produced during a shift where the production volume varies). For a sample size $n$ that has a total number of nonconformities $c$, $u$ is defined as

$$u = c/n \quad (19.19)$$

The control chart parameters for the $u$ chart are then

$$CL = \bar{u} \quad UCL = \bar{u} + 3\sqrt{\bar{u}/n} \quad LCL = \bar{u} - 3\sqrt{\bar{u}/n} \quad (19.20)$$

where $\bar{u}$ is the mean of the occurrences.

## 19.12. INTERPRETATION OF CONTROL CHART PATTERNS

When a process is in control, the control chart pattern should exhibit "natural characteristics" as if it were from random data (Western Electric 1956). Unnatural patterns involve the absence of one or more of the characteristics of a natural pattern. Some example unnatural patterns are mixture, stratification, and/or instability.

Unnatural patterns classified as mixture have an absence of points near the center line. These patterns can be the combination of two different patterns on one chart—one at a high level and one at a low level. Unnatural patterns classified as stratification have up-and-down variations that are very small in comparison to the control limits. This pattern can occur when samples are taken consistently from widely different distributions. Unnatural patterns classified as instability have points outside the control limits. This pattern indicates that something has changed within the process (either "goodness" or "badness").

Consider further the analysis approach to determine whether there is instability in the process. It should be remembered that whenever the process is stated to be out of control there is a chance that the statement was made

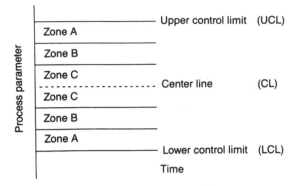

**FIGURE 19.8.** Shewhart control chart zones.

in error because there is a chance that either abnormally "good" or "bad" samples were drawn. This chance of error increases with the introduction of more criteria when analyzing the charts. When using the following pattern criteria, this chance of error should be considered before making a process out-of-control statement.

Since the upper and lower control limits each are $3\sigma$, consider a control chart that is subdivided into three $\sigma$ regions, as noted in Figure 19.8. Tests for out-of-control conditions relative to these zones are:

1. One point beyond zone A.
2. Two out of three points in zone A or beyond.
3. Four out of five points in zone B or beyond.
4. Eight points in zone C or beyond.

In Figure 19.9 the out-of-control data points are replaced with the applicable condition number.

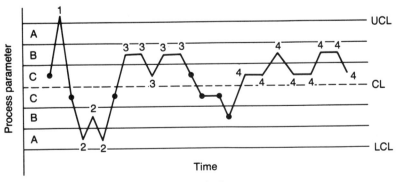

**FIGURE 19.9.** Control charts—zone tests.

Another test is the runs test, which indicates that the process has shifted. Sequential data is evaluated relative to the center line (Messina 1987). A shift has occurred if:

1. At least 10 out of 11 sequential data points are on the same side of the center line.
2. At least 12 out of 14 sequential data points are on the same side of the center line.
3. At least 14 out of 17 sequential data points are on the same side of the center line.
4. At least 16 out of 20 sequential data points are on the same side of the center line.

Other patterns within a control chart can tell a story. For example, a cyclic pattern that has a large amplitude relative to the control limits may indicate that samples are being taken from two different distributions. This could occur because of operator or equipment differences.

## 19.13.  CUSUM CHART: CUMULATIVE SUM OF MEASUREMENTS

An alternative to Shewhart control charts is the cumulative sum (CUSUM) control chart. CUSUM charts can detect small process shifts faster than Shewhart control charts. The form of a CUSUM charts can be "v mask" or "decision intervals." The decision intervals approach will be discussed in this text.

The following scenario is for the consideration where smaller numbers are better (single-sided case). For a double-sided situation, two single-sided intervals are run concurrently. The three parameters considered in CUSUM analyses are $n$, $k$, and $h$, where $n$ is the sample size of the subgroup, $k$ is the reference value, and $h$ is the decision interval.

Consider a situation where it is desirable for a process to operate at a target value $\mu$ [an acceptable quality level (AQL)] with desired protection against an upper shift of the mean to a reject quality level (RQL). The chart is obtained by plotting $s_m$, the CUSUM value for the $m$th subgroup.

$$s_m = \sum_{i=1}^{m} (\bar{x}_i - k) \qquad (19.21)$$

where $\bar{x}_i$ is the average of the $i$th subgroup of a total $m$ subgroups and $k$ is the reference value, which is usually chosen to be half way between the AQL and RQL values.

Since Equation (19.21) is written in a one-sided form where only high numbers can cause problems, the process is assumed to be in control and no chart even needs to be generated if the values for $\bar{x}_i$ are less than $k$. However, whenever $s_m$ exceeds $h$, the process should be investigated to determine if a problem exists within the process. The procedure to determine $h$ is discussed later in this section. Note that for a two-sided decision interval, two single-sided intervals are examined concurrently (one for the upper limit and one for the lower limit).

CUSUM charting is not in general a direct substitute for Shewhart charting since this procedure often tests the process to a quantifiable shift in the process mean or directly to acceptable/rejectable limits determined from specifications or from a preproduction design of experiment test. Because of this direct comparison to limits, the CUSUM chart setup procedure differs from that of a Shewhart chart.

When samples are taken frequently within a process and tested against a criterion, there are two types of sampling problems. First, when the threshold to detect problems is large, small process perturbations and shifts can take a "long" time to detect. Second, when many samples are taken within a process, eventually false alarms will occur because of chance. The design of a CUSUM chart addresses these problems directly using average run length (ARL) as a design input, where $L_r$ is the ARL at the reject quality level (RQL) and $L_a$ is the ARL at the accept quality level (AQL).

When first considering a CUSUM test procedure, the selection of $L_a$ and $L_r$ values can appear to be difficult. Items to consider when selecting these parameters are:

1. High frequency of sampling. (For example, $L_r$ should usually be higher with a high-volume process that is checked hourly than with a process that is checked monthly.)
2. Low frequency of sampling. (For example, $L_a$ should usually be lower for a sampling plan that has infrequent sampling than that which has frequent sampling.)
3. Other process charting. (For example, $L_r$ should usually be higher when a product has many process control charts that have frequent test intervals because the overall chance of false alarms can increase dramatically.)
4. Importance of specification. (For example, $L_a$ should usually be lower when the specification limit is important to product safety and reliability.)

The final input requirement to the design of a CUSUM chart is the process standard deviation ($\sigma$). The output from a preproduction designed experiment is a possible source for this information. Note that after the CUSUM test is begun it may be necessary to readjust the sampling plan because of an erroneous assumption or an improvement (hopefully), with time, of the parameter of concern.

The nomogram in Figure 19.10 can now be used to design the sampling plan. By placing a ruler across the nomogram corresponding to $L_a$ and $L_r$, values for the following can be determined

EXAMPLE 19-4: CUSUM CHART    **307**

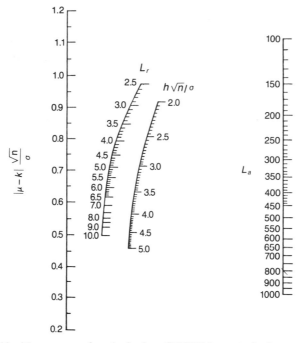

**FIGURE 19.10.** Nomogram for designing CUSUM control charts. (The labeling reflects the nomenclature used in this text.) [From K. W. Kemp, "The use of cumulative sums for sampling inspection schemes," *Applied Statistics*, **11** (1962), reprinted by permission of the Royal Statistical Society.]

$$|\mu - k| \frac{\sqrt{n}}{\sigma} \tag{19.22}$$

$$\frac{h\sqrt{n}}{\sigma} \tag{19.23}$$

At the reject quality level, $\mu - k$ is a known parameter; hence, $n$ can then be determined from Equation (19.22). With this $n$ value Equation (19.23) can then be used to yield the value of $h$. The data are then plotted using Equation (19.21) with the control limit $h$.

## 19.14. EXAMPLE 19-4: CUSUM CHART

The settle-out time of a selection motor was analyzed during preproduction using fractional factorial experimentation techniques (see Example 15-1). Figure 15.4 was instrumental in determining that an algorithm change was important (which had no base machine implementation costs), along with an inexpensive reduction in a motor adjustment tolerance. Because of this work and other analyses, it was determined that there would be no functional problems if the motors did not experience a settle-out time greater than 8 msec. A CUSUM control charting scheme was desired to monitor the production process to assess this criterion on a continuing basis.

If we consider the 8-msec tolerance a single-sided $3\sigma$ upper limit, we need to subtract the expected $3\sigma$ variability from 8 to get an upper mean limit for our CUSUM chart. Hence, given an expected production $3\sigma$ value of 2 (i.e., $\sigma = \frac{2}{3}$), the upper accepted mean criterion could be assigned a value of 6 $(8 - 2 = 6)$. However, because of the importance of this machine criterion and the previous test results pictorially illustrated in Figure 15.4, the designers decided to set the upper AQL to 5 along with an RQL set to 4. The value for $k$ is then determined to be 4.5, which is the midpoint between these extremes.

Given a $L_r$ of 3 and a $L_a$ of 800, from Figure 19.10 the result for Equation (19.22) is

$$|\mu - k| \frac{\sqrt{n}}{\sigma} = 1.11$$

Substitution yields

$$|5.0 - 4.5| \frac{\sqrt{n}}{2/3} = 1.11 \quad \text{so} \quad n = 2.19$$

Being conservative, $n$ should be rounded up to give a sample size of 3. In addition, from Figure 19.10 the result for Equation (19.23) is

$$\frac{h\sqrt{n}}{\sigma} = 2.3$$

Substitution yields

$$\frac{h\sqrt{3}}{2/3} = 2.3 \quad \text{so} \quad h = 0.89$$

Summarizing, the overall design is as follows. The inputs were an RQL of 4.0 with an associated $L_r$ (ARL) of 3, an AQL of 4.0 with an associated $L_a$ (ARL) of 800, and a process standard deviation of $\frac{2}{3}$. Rationale subgroups samples of size 3 should be taken where a change in the process is declared whenever the cumulative sum above 4.5 exceeds 0.88. That is, from Equation (19.21), whenever

$$s_m = \left[ \sum_{i=1}^{m} (\bar{x}_i - 4.5) \right] > 0.89$$

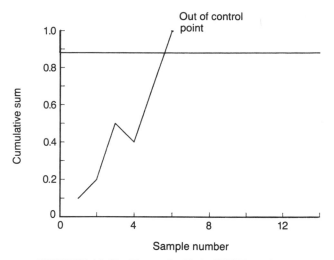

**FIGURE 19.11.** Example 19-4: CUSUM chart.

A typical conceptual plot of this information is shown in Figure 19.11. In time enough data can be collected to yield a more precise estimate for the standard deviation, which can be used to adjust the preceding procedural computations. In addition, it may be appropriate to adjust the $k$ value to the mean of the sample that is being assessed, which can yield an earlier indicator to determine when there is a process change occurring.

Other supplemental tests can be useful when the process in stable to better understand the data and yield earlier problem detection. For example, a probability plot (see Chapter 5) of data by lots could be used to visually assess whether there appears to be a percentage of population differences that can be detrimental. If no differences are noted, one probability plot might be made of all collected data over time to better determine the percentage of population as a function of a control parameter.

## 19.15. PROCESS CAPABILITY STUDIES

As mentioned earlier, a process may be in statistical control; however, it may still not be capable of consistently meeting target criteria. After a process is determined to be in control, process capability studies can then be performed to address whether the process will consistently produce an output that meets specification limits.

The process capability index $C_p$ in Equation 19.24 can be used to measure the allowable tolerance spread to the actual spread of the data when the data follow a normal distribution.

$$C_p = \frac{\text{USL} - \text{LSL}}{6\sigma} \tag{19.24}$$

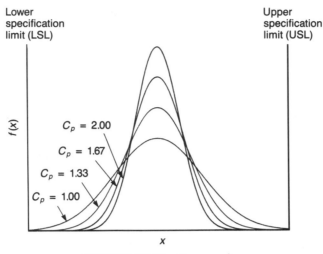

**FIGURE 19.12.** $C_p$ examples.

where USL and LSL are the upper specification limit and lower specification limit, respectively, and $6\sigma$ describes the range or spread of the process.

Figure 19.12 illustrates graphically various $C_p$ values relative to specification limits; $C_p$ addresses only the spread of the process; $C_{pk}$ is used to concurrently to consider the spread and mean shift of the process as graphically illustrated in Figure 19.13. Mathematically $C_{pk}$ can be represented as the minimum value of two quantities:

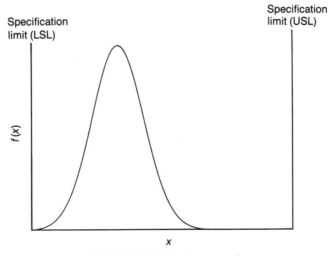

**FIGURE 19.13.** $C_{pk}$ example.

EXAMPLE 19-5: PROCESS CAPABILITY     311

$$C_{pk} = \min \left[ \frac{\text{USL} - \mu}{3\sigma} , \frac{\mu - \text{LSL}}{3\sigma} \right] \qquad (19.25)$$

The following equation relates $C_{pk}$ to $C_p$

$$C_{pk} = C_p(1 - k) \qquad (19.26)$$

where the $k$ factor quantifies the amount by which the process is off center and equates to

$$k = \frac{|m - \mu|}{(\text{USL} - \text{LSL})/2} \qquad (19.27)$$

where $m = [(\text{USL} + \text{LSL})/2]$ is the midpoint of the specification range and $0 \leqslant k \leqslant 1$.

A minimum acceptable process capability index often recommended (Juran, Gryna, and Bingham 1976) is 1.33 ($4\sigma$); however, Motorola, in its Six Sigma program, proposes directing efforts toward obtaining a minimum individual process step $C_p$ value of 2.0 and a $C_{pk}$ value of 1.5 (see Section 21.1).

Note that care must be exercised when determining a value for $\sigma$ to be used in the preceding calculations. The total error from a variance components analysis (see Example 15-4) could be used to determine this estimate. Another alternative is to use the average of process variances from a control chart that has been shown to be stable over time. Or, in general, historical data from various sources ($g$) with degrees of freedom $v_g$ could be combined using Equation (19.28) to give an estimate $s_t^2$ for the variance. The estimate will have $v_t$ degrees of freedom.

$$s_t^2 = \frac{v_1 s_1^2 + v_2 s_2^2 + v_3 s_3^2 + \cdots + v_g s_g^2}{v_1 + v_2 + v_3 + \cdots v_g} \qquad (19.28)$$

where $v_t = v_1 + v_2 + v_3 + \cdots v_g$

## 19.16. EXAMPLE 19-5: PROCESS CAPABILITY

From Example 19-1 determine the process capability that is possible if samples 8, 9, 10, 12, 13, and 18 were removed from the data set, for the purpose of establishing future process control limits. Assume that for each of these data points circumstances for an out-of-control response were identified and will be avoided in future production.

The $\bar{\bar{x}}$ of the remaining samples from Table 19.1 is then 33 (i.e., 0.4033 in. is an estimate for $\mu$), while $\bar{R}$ is 4.6 (i.e., 0.00046 in.). The process capability index for the specification tolerance of 0.4037 ±0.0013 in. (i.e., 0.4024 to 0.4050 in.) is determined using the following procedure.

First convert the $\overline{R}$ into $\sigma$ using Equation (19.3). [Note: Equation (19.28) could have been used to get a more precise estimate.]

$$\hat{\sigma} = \overline{R}/d_2 = 0.00046/2.326 = 0.00020 \text{ in.}$$

From Equation (19.24)

$$C_p = \frac{\text{USL} - \text{LSL}}{6\sigma} = \frac{0.4050 - 0.4024}{6(0.00020)} = 2.17$$

From Equation (19.25)

$$C_{pk} = \min \left[ \frac{\text{USL} - \mu}{3\sigma} , \frac{\mu - \text{LSL}}{3\sigma} \right]$$

$$= \min \left[ \frac{0.4050 - 0.4031}{3(0.00020)} , \frac{0.4031 - 0.4024}{3(0.00020)} \right]$$

$$= \min [3.17 , 1.17] = 1.17$$

When special causes are removed the current process variability is low enough such that the process appears to be currently capable of producing parts consistently within specification (i.e., $C_p = 2.17$). However, the process capability index $C_{pk}$ indicates that the current process mean is far enough away from the center of the tolerance such that the percentage of parts produced outside of specification could be considered excessive (i.e., $C_{pk}$ = 1.17). Hence, it appears that the grinding machine should be readjusted to make a larger mean diameter. However, if there is no feedback in the manufacturing process, a drift in the mean could occur because of wear in the grinding wheel. For this situation a process control chart could then be used to monitor this shift to help optimize the frequency of machine adjustments and adjustment setting. At the same time thought should be given to any process changes that could be made to reduce the process variability, which would reduce the sensitivity of the process to this adjustment precision and frequency of calibration. The fractional factorial testing strategies discussed in Chapter 13 can be used to evaluate the effectiveness of these possible changes. These fractional factorial techniques can help avoid the implementation of process changes that perhaps in theory sound good from a "one-at-a-time" experiment but, in general, may not be helpful or could in fact be detrimental to the quality of the process.

Indices $C_p$ and $C_{pk}$ are discussed further in Section 21.1 as part of Motorola's Six Sigma program for quality improvement. Example 22-7 combines process index considerations with statistical tolerancing.

EXAMPLE 19-6: PARETO DIAGRAM     **313**

## 19.17. PARETO DIAGRAMS

Pareto diagrams are a tool that can be helpful to identify the source of chronic problems/common causes in a manufacturing process. The Pareto principle basically states that a "vital few" of the manufacturing process characteristics cause most of the quality problems on the line, while a "trivial many" of the manufacturing process characteristics cause only a small portion of the quality problems.

A procedure to construct a Pareto diagram is as follows:

1. Define the problem and process characteristics to use in the diagram.
2. Define the period of time for the diagram. For example, weekly, daily, or shift. Quality improvements over time can later be made from the information determined within this step.
3. Total the number of times each characteristic occurred.
4. Rank the characteristics according to the totals from step 3.
5. Plot the number of occurrences of each characteristic in descending order in bar graph form along with a cumulative plot of the magnitudes from the bars (e.g., a Pareto diagram is shown in Figure 21.6, and Figure 19.14 shows a Pareto diagram without a cumulative percentage overlay).
6. Trivial columns can be lumped under one column designation; however, care must be exercised not to forget a small but important item.

Note that a Pareto chart may need to consider data from different perspectives. For example, a Pareto chart of defects by machine may not be informative while a Pareto chart of defects by manufacturing shifts could illustrate a trend.

## 19.18. EXAMPLE 19-6: PARETO DIAGRAM

A $p$ chart (see Figure 3.5) indicated a process was in control, however, it was producing a high percentage of printed circuit boards that either had to be reworked or scrapped. During a week's production, 3200 printed circuit boards were observed to have the following failures (Messina 1987):

|     |                    |
|-----|--------------------|
| 440 | Insufficient solder |
| 120 | Blow holes         |
| 80  | Unwetted           |
| 64  | Unsoldered         |
| 56  | Pinholes           |
| 40  | Shorts             |
| 800 |                    |

From the Pareto diagram of the solder defects shown in Figure 19.14, it becomes obvious that the insufficient solder characteristic should be "attacked

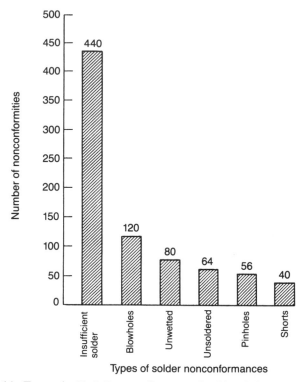

**FIGURE 19.14.** Example 19-6: Pareto diagram of solder defects [Reproduced with permission: William S. Messina, *Statistical Quality Control for Manufacturing Managers*, John Wiley and Sons, New York, 1987.]

first." Technical individuals that are familiar with the process should be consulted using the aid of brainstorming techniques, to determine if there are any obvious changes that should be made to reduce the magnitude of this failure characteristic. Again, fractional factorial testing (see Chapter 13) is an efficient technique to determine which of these changes help reduce the magnitude of this failure characteristic. This group of technical individuals can perhaps also determine a continuous response to use in addition to or in lieu of the preceding attribute response consideration. One can expect that a continuous response output would require a much smaller sample size.

After changes are made to the process and improvements are demonstrated on the control charts, a new Pareto diagram can then be created. Perhaps the improvements will be large enough to the insufficient solder characteristic that blow holes may now be the largest of the "vital few" to be attacked next. Process control charts could also be used to track insufficient solder individually so that process degradation from the "fix level" can be identified quickly.

Pareto diagram techniques were also used in Examples 3-1 and 3-2 in this text.

## 19.19. IMPLEMENTATION CONSIDERATIONS

With time the process mean of a Shewhart chart may appear to shift. Hopefully, this apparent shift in the process is an improvement, perhaps caused by a change resulting from a fractional factorial experiment or better operator awareness. The techniques in Chapter 9 can be used to determine whether there is a significant amount of shift. Example 9-5 discusses an approach to do this test for the orange juice packaging example discussed in Example 19-3.

The $\bar{x}$ and $R$ or $\bar{x}$ and $s$ charts are preferable over $p$ charts because there can be a considerable reduction in sample size required while yielding more information. CUSUM charting, as discussed in Section 19.13, has some basic differences from Shewhart charts. Additional considerations for Shewhart versus CUSUM chart selection are: (1) When choosing a control chart strategy using Shewhart techniques, variable sample sizes can be difficult to manage when calculating control limits, while this is not a concern with CUSUM techniques. (2) Shewhart charts handle number of nonconforming items via $p$ charts, while CUSUM can consider this a continuous variable (e.g., number of "good" samples selected before a "bad" sample is found). (3) CUSUM charting does not use many rules to define an out-of-control condition, which can, in the case of Shewhart charting, lead to an increase in false alarms (Yashchin 1989).

Additional information on control charts and their interpretation is contained in Messina (1987), Affourtit (1986), Oakland (1986), Montgomery (1985), Nelson (1984, 1985), Flynn and Bolcar (1984), Flynn (1983), Deming (1982), Grant and Leavenworth (1980), Duncan (1986), and Western Electric (1956).

## 19.20. DO-IT-SMARTER CONSIDERATIONS

It is unfortunate that many manufacturing organizations in the past have plotted data in control chart form just for information. SPC charts should be used in real time as a tool to identify unusual events and determine if there is a need to improve the process. Commercially available computer programs (see Section 2.3) can be used to expedite this process.

Several do-it-smarter considerations were discussed in this chapter, primarily in the illustrated examples. A summary of a few of these points follows:

1. $p$ Charting can often require very large samples. Control charting of variables has much more statistical power. Transition from a $p$ chart to an $\bar{x}$ and $R$ chart may require an "innovative alternative response," such as stress level to failure.
2. CUSUM charting may be a favorable alternative to Shewhart charts.
3. Pareto diagrams are useful to identify the vital few areas that should be focused upon when making major changes to a process and/or design.

4. Fractional factorial experiment techniques (see Chapters 13, 14, 15, and 16) are a valuable tool to aid with improving both process mean and variability.

5. Probability plots (see Chapter 5) of data can be a supplementary tool for a better understanding of the effects of process variability.

Within manufacturing in the electronics industry, systems or components are often run-in or burned-in (i.e. screened) to capture early-life failures before the product reaches the customer's office. When the time of failure during this test is known, the techniques discussed in Example 11-6 are useful to determine the duration of this test on a repairable system, where the same concepts can similarly be applied to nonrepairable systems using the Weibull distribution (see Chapter 12). However, it is not reasonable to expect that this test will capture all problem escapes of the manufacturing process before a product reaches the customer, although, if the product does experience an early-life failure mode, it is reasonable to expect that the quality experienced by the customer will be better because of the burn-in/run-in test.

After a burn-in/run-in test time is determined, a *p* chart can be beneficial to monitor over time the proportion that fails during the test. When special causes are identified in the chart, it is reasonable to expect that the customer will also have an increased failure rate because, as noted earlier, all individual machine problems will not normally be captured during this test. In a stable process over some period of time, a list of failure causes can be generated and presented in a Pareto diagram. Reduction of the vital few causes could then be addressed using fractional factorial experiment techniques or perhaps by making some obvious changes to the process. Significant improvements that reduce the number of the causes in the manufacturing process should later be detected as an out-of-control condition (for the better) in the overall failure rate *p* chart of the burn-in station. This procedure could then be repeated for further improvements.

In time it would be desirable to get enough improvement in the basic manufacturing process such that a dramatic, consistent reduction in the *p*-chart overall failure rate is shown. If this happens it might be appropriate to change the 100% burn-in/run-in procedure to a sampling plan for the detection of special causes. It should be noted, however, that even though the burn-in/run-in (i.e., screen) test may experience *no* failures, a customer may be having many difficulties. A Pareto chart of the cause of field problems can be illuminating. Perhaps the burn-in/run-in test is evaluating the wrong things and missing many of the problems experienced by customers. The tester function may, for example, need to be changed to capture these types of problems.

# PART III

# COMBINING VARIOUS STATISTICAL CONCEPTS AND OTHER IMPLEMENTATION TOOLS

This part of the text includes a structured methodology where employees work with customers to determine what issues should be addressed in the development of future products.

There is also discussion about a 10-step approach toward process improvement; in this approach, emphasis is given toward reducing product variability, which should result in fewer product defects. For each of these 10 steps, application tools are listed. Many previously discussed statistical methodologies are included in these lists.

There is also discussion of an approach where a hierarchy of fractional factorial design matrices can be used to test a complex system during its development cycle. When brainstorming techniques are used to develop these designs, there can be an improvement in test effectiveness with a reduction in the amount of test effort.

Finally, there is a chapter that contains examples that either extend upon or bridge the concepts discussed previously in this text.

# 20

# DETERMINING THE NEEDS
# OF THE CUSTOMER

Recommended introductory reading: Chapters 2 and 3.

In the past some companies have not given adequate focus to "meeting the needs of the customer." Companies now, in general, realize that addressing these needs is very important. But, how do the needs of the customer get communicated to the right people so that these needs will be fulfilled when creating the design requirements of a product? Quality function deployment (QFD) is a formal methodology that addresses this need. This chapter gives an overview of QFD along with an example.

Unfortunately a formal QFD evaluation on some products can be a very large and time-consuming task. In this chapter there is also discussion on a simplified alternative to a formal QFD approach. Some practitioners will find that this approach is a viable alternative (or supplement) to QFD.

## 20.1. MEETING THE NEEDS OF THE CUSTOMER

Consider products that a customer has purchased that do not meet his or her expectations. Perhaps a product has a lot of "bells and whistles"; however, it does not meet his or her basic needs. Or, perhaps the product is not user friendly. Will a customer take the time to complain about the product or service? Will the customer avoid purchasing products from that company in the future?

When addressing the needs of customers, it should be emphasized that the end user of a product is not the only customer. For example, a vendor that manufactures a component part of a larger assembly has a customer relationship with the company responsible for the larger assembly. Procedures to determine the needs of customers can also be useful to define such business procedural tasks as office physical layout, accounting procedures, internal organization structure, and product test procedures. Focusing on the needs of customers goes hand in hand with "answering the right question" and "do-it-smarter" consideration concepts discussed throughout this text.

QFD can be used in many different areas of the business (e.g., planning, testing, engineering, manufacturing, distribution, marketing, and service). However, it must be understood that a large amount of effort can be required to perform a formal QFD evaluation. If the amount of work is thought to be excessive, the methodology discussed in Section 20.4 may be a viable alternative (or supplemental) approach.

## 20.2. QUALITY FUNCTION DEPLOYMENT (QFD)

Quality function deployment or the "house of quality" (a term coined in QFD because of the shape of its matrix) is a tool that can be used to give direction on what should be done to meet the needs of the customer. It is a tool that can aid with this process and translate customer requirements into basic requirements that have direction. It is a communication tool that uses a team concept where many organizations (e.g., sales, manufacturing, development) can break down barriers so that product definition and efforts have direct focus toward the needs of the customer. A QFD chart can be used to organize, preserve, and provide for the transfer of knowledge. It can also be used in conjunction with fractional factorial experiments (see Example 22-1).

It should be noted that many problems can be encountered when conducting a QFD. If extreme care is not exercised, wrong conclusions can result from the effort. For example, bias can easily be injected into a survey through the way the questions were asked, the procedure that was used to conduct the survey, or the type of people who were asked questions. Practitioners might ask themselves if they would expect to get the same results if the survey were conducted again (i.e., perhaps the experimental error in the results is too high and a forced comparison survey procedure should have been utilized). Another way in which an erroneous conclusion can be made is through the data analysis. For example, the technical importance calculations that are made in step 7 (see Section 20.3) are generic procedures. In a given situation it may be more important to weight responses by the importance of overall secondary or primary customer requirements. Perhaps the most important benefit that can result from creating a QFD is via personal interviews with customers. The comments resulting from these discussions can perhaps give the best (although not numerically tangible) direction [Brown (1991)].

An overall product QFD implementation strategy involves first listing the customer expectations (voice of the customer). These WHATs are then

**TABLE 20.1. QFD Matrices: An Example About Car Durability**

| QFD Matrix | Example Matrix Outputs |
|---|---|
| Customer requirement | Years of durability |
| Design requirement | No visible exterior rust in 3 yr |
| Part characteristics | Paint weight: 2–2.5 g/m$^2$ |
| | Crystal size: 3 maximum |
| Manufacturing operations | Dip tank |
| | 3 coats |
| Production requirements | Time: 2.0 min minimum |
| | Acidity: 15–20 |
| | Temperature: 48–55°C |

tabulated along with the listing of design requirements related to meeting these customers' expectations (HOWs). The important HOWs can then be transferred to WHATs of another QFD matrix within a complete QFD matrix-to-matrix process flow. For example, consider the customer requirement of increasing the years of durability for a car. This matrix-to-matrix flow is exemplified in Table 20.1.

The needs of the customer are dynamic. Product features that were considered "wow" features in the past are now taken for granted. For example, a person seeing for the first time a car that does not need a "crank start" would consider this a "wow" change; however, electronic starters are now taken for granted. Kano's (1984) description of this is illustrated conceptually in Figure 20.1.

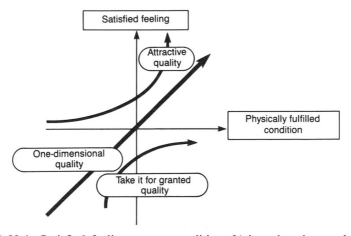

**FIGURE 20.1.** Satisfied feeling versus condition. [Adapted and reproduced with permission: Bob King, *Better Designs in Half the Time*, GOAL/QPC, Methuen, MA, 1989.]

The arrow in the middle, "one-dimensional quality," shows the situation where the customers tell the producer what they want and the producer supplies this need. The lower arrow represents the items that are expected. Customers are less likely to mention them; however, they are dissatisfied if they do not receive them. Safety is an example in this category. The top arrow represents wow quality. These are the items that a normal customer will not mention. Innovative individuals within the producers' organization or "leading edge" users need to anticipate these items, which must be satisfiers (not dissatisfiers).

To determine accurate WHATs for the requirement matrix (i.e., accurate one-dimensional quality projections and anticipated attractive quality additions), personal interviews with customers may first be appropriate. Surveys should use the words of the customer when determining these WHAT items. These WHATs can then be compiled into primary, secondary, and even tertiary requirements. Follow-up surveys can then be done using test summaries to get importance ratings (e.g., 1–5) for each WHAT item. Opinions about competitive products can also be compiled during these surveys.

The WHATs for the other matrices may be determined from internal inputs in addition to pass down information from higher state matrices. These WHATs are often more efficiently determined when the QFD team begins with tertiary WHATs and then summarizes these into a shorter list of secondary WHATs followed by another summary into the primary WHATs.

The following is a step-by-step QFD matrix creation process, as it relates to Figure 20.2. The steps are applied in Example 20-1. The steps are written around the development of a design requirement matrix (see Table 20.1); however, the basic procedural flow is similar for other matrices. With this procedure equations, weights, specific parameters, and step sequence may be altered to better identify important items that need emphasis for a particular situation.

**1.** A list of customer requirements (WHATs) is made in primary, secondary, and tertiary sequence. Applicable government regulation items should also be contained within this list.

**2.** The importance of each WHAT item can similarly be determined from a survey using a rating scale (e.g., 1–5, where 5 is the most important). Care must be exercised when quantifying these values since the action of the customer may not accurately reflect their perceived importance. For example, a customer may purchase a product more because of packaging than characteristics of the product within the package.

**3.** Customer ratings should be obtained for both the competition and the existing design for each of the WHAT item. It is important to identify and quantify the important WHATs in which a design of a competitor exceeds the current design so that design changes can focus upon these areas. The WHATs should be identified where the existing product is preferred so that these items can be protected within future design considerations.

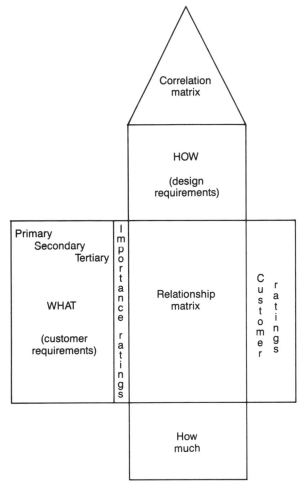

**FIGURE 20.2.** A QFD chart format.

**4.** Engineering first compiles a list of design requirements that are necessary to achieve the market-driven WHATs. The design team lists across the top of the matrix the design requirements (HOWs) that affect one or more of the customer attributes. Each design requirement should describe the product in measurable terms and should directly affect customer perceptions. For example, within a design requirements matrix, the closing force of a car door may be noted, in contrast to the thickness of the metal within the door, which may be noted within a future parts characteristics matrix. The arrow at the top of the design requirements listing indicates the direction for improvement (e.g., a downward pointing error indicates a lower value is better, while a zero indicates a target is desired). Each WHAT item is systematically assessed for specific measurement requirements. Vague and trivial characteristics should be avoided.

**5.** Cell strengths within the matrix are quantified to the importance of each HOW item relative to getting each WHAT item. Symbols describing these relationships include ⊙, which indicates much importance or a strong relationship, ○, which indicates some importance or relationship, △, which indicates a small importance or relationship, and no mark, which indicates no relationship or importance.

The symbols are later replaced by weights (e.g., 9, 3, 1, and 0) to give the relationship value needed to make the technical importance calculations. Initially, the symbols are used to clarify the degree of importance attributed to the relationships and weightings. From this visual representation, it is easier to determine where to place critical resources. If a current quality control measurement does not affect any customer attribute, this current quality control measurement is either not necessary or a WHAT item is missing. HOW items may need to be added such that there is at least one HOW item for each WHAT requirement.

**6.** From technical tests of both competitive products and our existing product design, objective measurements are added to the bottom of the house beneath each HOW item. Note that if the customer perception WHAT of the competition does not correlate to the HOW engineering characteristic competition measurement, either the measurements are in error, the HOW measurement characteristic is not valid for this WHAT, or a product has an image perception problem.

**7.** The technical importance of each design requirement is determined by using the following equations. The two sets of calculations are made for each HOW consideration given a total of $n$ WHATs affecting the relationship matrix. An equation to determine an absolute measurement for technical importance is

$$\text{Absolute} = \sum_{i=1}^{n} \text{relationship value} \times \text{customer importance} \quad (20.1)$$

To get a relative technical importance number, rank the responses from Equation (20.1), where 1 is the highest ranking. It should be noted that other equations and/or procedures found in textbooks or articles may be more appropriate for a given situation (e.g. for each HOW determine an overall percentage value of the total of all absolute technical importances).

**8.** The technical difficulty of each HOW design requirement is documented on the chart so focus can be given to important HOWs that may be difficult to achieve.

**9.** The correlation matrix is established to determine the technical inter-relationships between the HOWs. These relationships can be denoted by the following symbols: ⊕, high positive correlation; +, positive correlation; ⊖, high negative correlation; −, negative correlation, and a blank, no correlation (see Fig. 20.3).

EXAMPLE 20-1: CREATING A QFD CHART     **325**

**10.** New target values are, in general, determined from the customer ratings and information within the correlation matrix. Trend charts and snapshots are very useful tools to determine target objective values for key items. Fractional factorial techniques are useful to determine targets that need to be compromised between HOWs.

**11.** Areas that need concentrated effort are selected. Key elements are identified for follow-up matrix activity. The technical importance and technical difficulty areas are useful to identify these elements.

As previously noted, this discussion was written around a design requirement matrix. Information within the "how much" (see Figure 20.2) area can vary depending on the type of matrix. For example, the matrix may or may not have adjusted target specification values for the HOWs, technical analyses of competitive products, and/or degree of technical difficulty.

## 20.3.  EXAMPLE 20-1: CREATING A QFD CHART

A fraction of one QFD chart is directed toward determining the design requirements for a car door. The following describes the creation of a QFD chart for this design (Hauser and Clausing 1988).

Customer surveys and personal interviews led to the QFD chart inputs noted in items 1 to 3 in Section 20.2. The remaining items were the steps used to determine the technical aspects of achieving these WHATs.

1. A partial list of customer requirements (WHATs) for the car door is noted in Table 20.2. A government impact resistance requirement was also a WHAT item, but it is not shown in this list.
2. In Figure 20.3 an importance rating to the customer is noted for each WHAT item. For example, the ease of closing the door from the outside was given an importance rating of 5.
3. A rating (1–5, where 5 is best) of two competitor products and the current design is noted in Figure 20.3 for each WHAT item. For example, the customer perceives our existing design to be the worst (i.e., 1.5) of the three evaluated in the area of "easy to close"; however, when making any design changes to change this rating, care must be given to protect the favorable opinion customers have about our current design in the area of road noise.
4. The engineering team addresses the design requirements (HOWs) necessary to achieve the market-driven WHATs for the car door. For example, "Energy to close door" is a HOW to address the WHAT, "Easy to close from outside." The arrow indicates that a lower energy is better.

5. The relationship of the HOWs in meeting the customer's requirements (WHATs) is noted. For example, an important measurement (⊙) to address the customer WHAT, "Easy to close from outside" is the HOW, "Torque to close door."
6. Objective measurements are noted for both customer requirements and our existing product (i.e., a competitive survey). For example, our car door currently measures 11 ft-lb closing torque.
7. Absolute technical importance of the design requirements is determined within the HOW MUCH area by using Equation (20.1). For example, the absolute technical importance (see Fig. 20.3, second to last row)

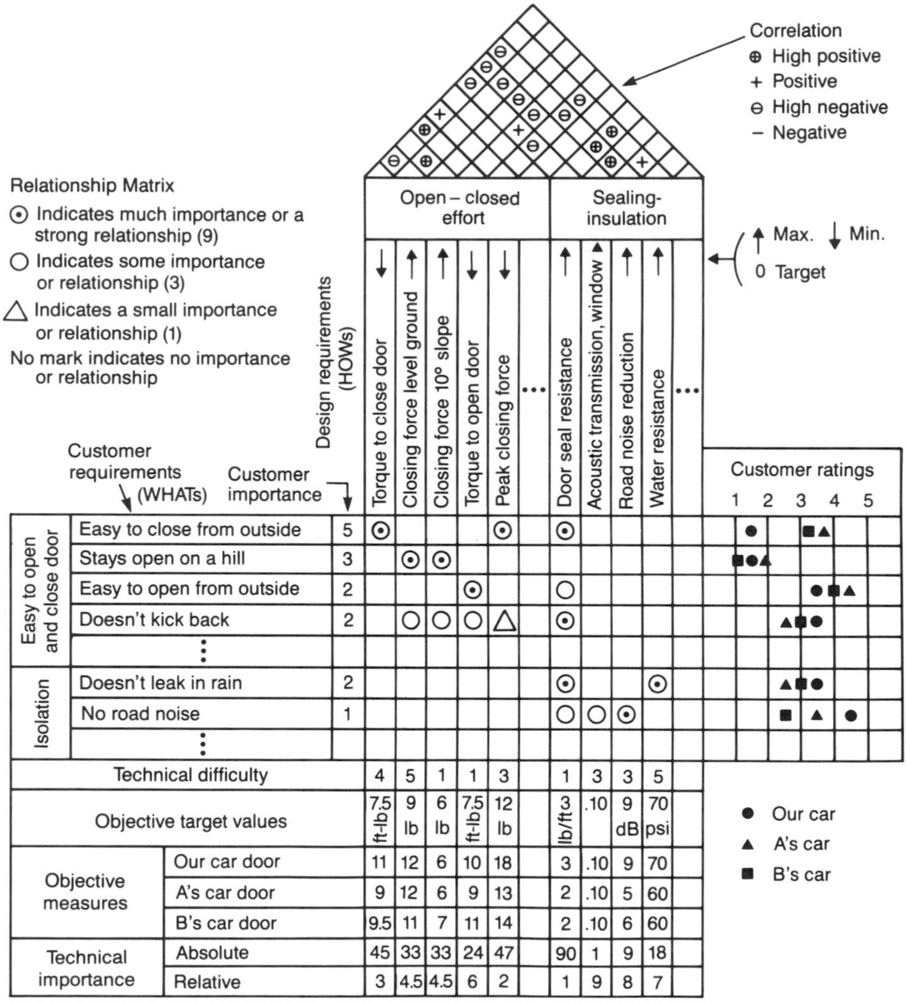


| | | Customer importance | Torque to close door | Closing force level ground | Closing force 10° slope | Torque to open door | Peak closing force | ... | Door seal resistance | Acoustic transmission, window | Road noise reduction | Water resistance | ... |
|---|---|---|---|---|---|---|---|---|---|---|---|---|---|
| Technical difficulty | | | 4 | 5 | 1 | 1 | 3 | | 1 | 3 | 3 | 5 | |
| Objective target values | | | 7.5 ft-lb | 9 lb | 6 lb | 7.5 ft-lb | 12 lb | | 3 lb/ft | .10 | 9 dB | 70 psi | |
| Objective measures | Our car door | | 11 | 12 | 6 | 10 | 18 | | 3 | .10 | 9 | 70 | |
| | A's car door | | 9 | 12 | 6 | 9 | 13 | | 2 | .10 | 5 | 60 | |
| | B's car door | | 9.5 | 11 | 7 | 11 | 14 | | 2 | .10 | 6 | 60 | |
| Technical importance | Absolute | | 45 | 33 | 33 | 24 | 47 | | 90 | 1 | 9 | 18 | |
| | Relative | | 3 | 4.5 | 4.5 | 6 | 2 | | 1 | 9 | 8 | 7 | |

where lb = pounds ft-lb = foot-pounds dB = decibels psi = pounds per square inch

**FIGURE 20.3.** Example 20-1: QFD chart.

EXAMPLE 20-1: CREATING A QFD CHART    **327**

**TABLE 20.2. Example 20-1: List of WHATs for Car Door**

| Primary | Secondary | Tertiary |
|---------|-----------|----------|
| Good operation and use | Easy to open and close door | Stays open on hill |
| | | Easy to open from inside |
| | | Easy to open from outside |
| | | Easy to close from inside |
| | | Easy to close from outside |
| | | Doesn't kick back |
| | Isolation | Doesn't leak |
| | | No road noise |
| | | No wind noise |
| | | Doesn't rattle |
| | | Crash impact resistance |
| Good appearance | Arm rest | Soft |
| | | Correct position |
| | | Durable |
| | Interior trim | Material won't fade |
| | | Attractive |
| | Clean | Easy to clean |
| | | No grease from door |

of door seal resistance would be 5(9)+2(3)+2(9)+1(3) = 90 (see Fig. 20.3, seventh column from left). Since this was the highest of those numbers shown, it had the highest ranking; hence, it is given a "1" relative ranking since it was the most import HOW in meeting the needs of the customer.

8. The technical difficulty requirements are determined. For example, the technical difficulty of water resistance is assessed the most difficult and is given a rating of 5.

9. The correlation matrix is established to determine the technical interrelationships between the HOWs. For example, the ⊖ symbol indicates that there is a high negative correlation between "Torque to close door" and "Closing force on level ground." The customer wants the door to be easy to close from outside along with being able to stay open on a hill (i.e., two opposite design requirement needs).

10. Because our car door had a relatively poor customer rating for the WHAT "Easy to close from outside," a target value was set that was better than the measured values of the competition (i.e., 7.5 ft-lb). Trade-offs may be necessary when determining targets to address relationships within the correlation matrix and relative importance ratings.

11. Important issues can be carried forward to WHATs of another "house" that is concerned with the detailed product design. For example, the engineering requirement of minimizing the torque (ft-lb) to close the door is important and can become a WHAT for another matrix that leads to part characteristics such as weather stripping properties or hinge design.

## 20.4. A SIMPLE METHODOLOGY TO ASSESS THE NEEDS OF CUSTOMERS

The mechanics of QFD can be very laborious and time consuming. However, some situations do not necessarily require all the outputs from a formal QFD. (Note: A lengthy, accurate QFD investigation can be useless if it is not conducted and compiled in a timely fashion.)

This section describes an approach that utilizes brainstorming techniques along with surveys to quantify the needs of customers. The following steps describe an approach to first determine the questions to ask and then quantify and prioritize needs, as perceived by the customer.

1. Conduct brainstorming session(s) (see Section 3.5) where a "wish list" of features, problem resolutions, and so forth are identified.

2. If there are many different brainstorming sessions that contain too many ideas to consider collectively in a single survey, it may be necessary to rank the individual brainstorming session items. A secret ballot rating for each topic by the attendees could be done during or after the sessions. The items that have the highest rankings from each brainstorming session are then considered as a survey question consideration.

3. A set of questions is then determined and worded from a positive point of view. Obviously, care needs to be exercised with the wording of these questions so as not to interject bias. The respondent to the question is asked to give an importance statement and a satisfaction statement relative to the question. The question takes the form shown in Table 20.3. Note that this survey is soliciting the same type of information from customers as that was done in a QFD. In Figure 20.3 the "customer satisfaction rating" and "customer importance" both were a numerical query issue for each WHAT item.

4. The information from this type of survey can be plotted in a perceptual map (Urban and Hasser 1980) format.

**TABLE 20.3. Example Questionnaire Format That Can Give a Perceptual Map Response**

The products produced by our company are reliable. (Please comment on any specific changes that you believe are needed)

| What is the importance of this requirement to you? | What is your level of satisfaction that this requirement is met? |
|---|---|
| 5  Very important | 5  Very satisfied |
| 4  Important | 4  Satisfied |
| 3  Neither important nor unimportant | 3  Neither satisfied nor unsatisfied |
| 2  Unimportant | 2  Unsatisfied |
| 1  Very unimportant | 1  Very unsatisfied |

Response: _____                                Response _____

Comments:

A plot of this type can be created for each respondent to the survey, where the plot point that describes a particular question could be identified as its survey question number (see Figure 20.4). Areas that need work are those areas that are judged important with low satisfaction (i.e., questions 8 and 4).

The average question response could similarly be plotted; however, with any analysis approach of this type care must be exercised not to lose individual response information that might be very important. An expert may rate something completely differently than the rest of the group because he or she has much more knowledge of an area. Some effort needs to be given to

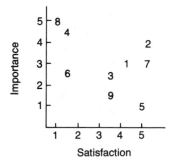

**FIGURE 20.4.** Coordinate system and example data for a perceptual map.

identify these people so that they can be asked more questions individually for additional insight that could later prove to be very valuable (i.e., let's not miss the important issues by "playing games" with the numbers).

Determining the areas that need focus from such a plot would not be rigorous since the response has two dimensional considerations (importance and satisfaction). To address a more rigorous approach, consider first the extreme situation where a question is thought to be very important (a 5) with low satisfaction (a 1). The difference between the importance and satisfaction numbers could be used to create a number that is used for the purpose of determining which areas have the largest opportunity for improvement. A large number difference (i.e., 4) indicates an area that has a large amount of potential for improvement, while lower numbers have less potential (a negative number is perhaps meaningless) (Wheeler 1990). These differences could then be ranked. From this ranking there can result a better understanding of where opportunities exist for improvement. Perhaps also from this ranking important questions can be grouped to get a better idea of what areas should have the most focus for change.

This survey procedure is usually associated with determining the needs and wishes of the end users of a product. However, good customer–supplier relationships should exist within a company. Consider, for example, two steps of a process in a manufacturing line. People involved with the second step of the process are customers of the people who are involved with the first step of the process.

A customer–supplier relationship can also be considered to exist between the employees of an organization and the procedures that they use, for example, to develop a product. The methodology described in this section could be used to identify bureaucratic procedures that hamper productive activities of employees. After these areas are identified additional brainstorming sessions could be conducted to improve the areas of processes that need to be changed.

## 20.5. DO-IT-SMARTER CONSIDERATIONS

For illustration purposes consider the development cycle of high-technology products. If this cycle time is long (e.g., 3 years), design requirements can frequently change in a reactionary mode to competitive announcement pressures. A goal for product development should be to contain the develop cycle time to a short period of time (e.g., one year from start to finish). With a reduced product cycle time, a manufacturer does not have to constantly change target values and requirements in a reactionary mode to these pressures. New requirements that may not have been anticipated initially are added to the next product development cycle.

Eliminating changes to design requirements during the development cycle will permit better internal planning and can help dramatically reduce a product's development cycle time. This strategy in conjunction with the application of other do-it-smarter considerations can make a seemingly impossible reduction in the development cycle time become a manageable reality. These efforts can result in delivering a high-quality product that is "great" in the eyes of the customer.

# 21

# DEVELOPMENT AND MANUFACTURING PROCESS IMPROVEMENT "TOOLS"

Recommended introductory reading: Chapters 2, 3, 13, 18, and 19.

Chapter 3 discussed the philosophy of quality management along with steps for effective decision making and such tools as brainstorming and cause-and-effect diagraming.

This chapter discusses additional "tools" to aid with the process of developing and manufacturing a quality product. This chapter includes a 10-step procedure from Motorola that is a guide for continuous improvement toward "Six Sigma" quality. Discussed also is a project development test strategy that uses fractional factorial test matrices.

## 21.1. MOTOROLA'S SIX SIGMA PROGRAM

A Six Sigma program was described by Motorola, Inc., as part of the work that they did when they received the Malcolm Baldrige National Quality Award in 1988. Much of the following information in this section was taken from a booklet by Motorola that describes 10 steps for continuous improvement towards Six Sigma quality. The basic procedure described in this booklet can be used as a road-map to give direction toward improving quality. The statistical community may note that the statistical procedures suggested in the 10 steps are not new; however, the program name has increased the awareness of upper-level management to the value of using statistical concepts.

Figures 21.1 to 21.3 illustrate various aspects of a normal distribution as it applies to Six Sigma. Figure 21.1 illustrates the basic measurement concept of Six Sigma where parts are to be manufactured consistently and well within

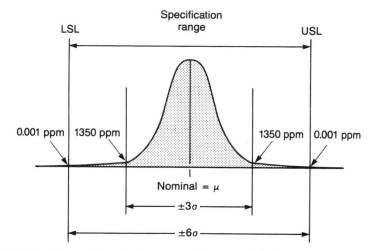

**FIGURE 21.1.** Normal distribution curve illustrates the Three Sigma and Six Sigma parametric conformance. [Copyright of Motorola, Inc., used with permission.]

their specification range. Figure 21.2 shows the number of parts per million that would be outside the specification limits if the data were centered within these limits and had various standard deviations. Figure 21.3 extends figure 21.2 to non-central data relative to specification limits, where the mean of the data is shifted by $1.5\sigma$. This basic philosophy of Six Sigma then translates to setting a $C_p$ and $C_{pk}$ requirement of 2.0 and 1.5 respectively (see section 19.15).

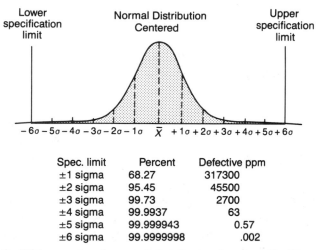

| Spec. limit | Percent | Defective ppm |
|---|---|---|
| ±1 sigma | 68.27 | 317300 |
| ±2 sigma | 95.45 | 45500 |
| ±3 sigma | 99.73 | 2700 |
| ±4 sigma | 99.9937 | 63 |
| ±5 sigma | 99.999943 | 0.57 |
| ±6 sigma | 99.9999998 | .002 |

**FIGURE 21.2.** With a centered normal distribution between Six Sigma limits only two devices per billion fail to meet the specification target. [Copyright of Motorola, Inc., used with permission.]

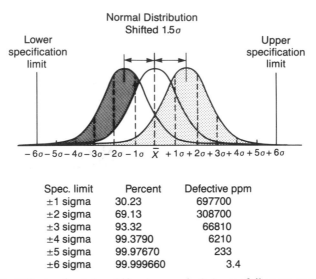

| Spec. limit | Percent | Defective ppm |
|---|---|---|
| ±1 sigma | 30.23 | 697700 |
| ±2 sigma | 69.13 | 308700 |
| ±3 sigma | 93.32 | 66810 |
| ±4 sigma | 99.3790 | 6210 |
| ±5 sigma | 99.97670 | 233 |
| ±6 sigma | 99.999660 | 3.4 |

**FIGURE 21.3.** Effects of a 1.5 $\sigma$ shift where only 3.4 ppm fail to meet specification. [Copyright of Motorola, Inc., used with permission.]

A basic goal of a Six Sigma program (see Figure 21.3) might be to produce at least 99.99966% "quality" at the "process step" and part level within an assembly (i.e., no more than 3.4 parts per million defective). If, for example, there was on the average 1 defect for an assembly that contained 100 parts and 61 process steps, practitioners might consider that the Six Sigma measurement level for the assembly would be 4 sigma, since the number of defects in parts per million is: $(1/161)(1 \times 10^6) \approx 6210$. However, various questions can arise when trying to implement a Six Sigma program. One question might be: For *my* product, how am I going to count the steps (remembering that we do not want to "play games" with the numbers)? Another issue of concern is that this approach addresses the concept as an attribute consideration, which can lead to tough (if not impossible) testing scenarios (see Section 8.2).

An intent of a Six Sigma program is to improve quality by reducing product variability. However, the term itself can be misleading in that the concept can be used to address much more than just increasing the process indices $C_p$ and $C_{pk}$ to values of 2.0 and 1.5, respectively (see Section 19.15).

Various steps have been proposed by oganizations to adopt a Six Sigma type program for *their* situation. Figures 21.4 − 21.7 show a set of steps and methodologies that Motorola used for continuous improvement toward Six Sigma quality. I like this set of steps since process improvement is encouraged and many statistical methodologies are suggested in the steps. I included these figures to illustrate the basic approach suggested by Motorola, not to dwell on the precise company definitions for all terms and techniques that are described in the document.

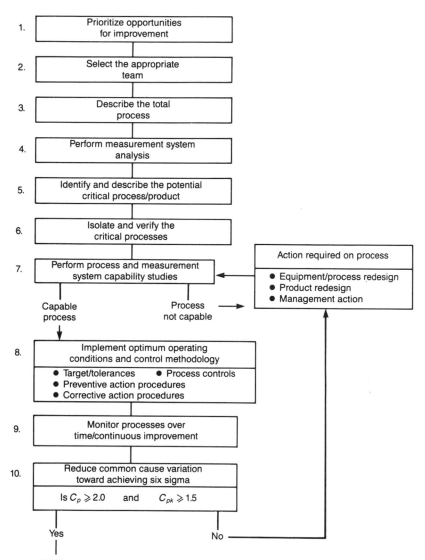

**FIGURE 21.4.** Product/process improvement flow diagram. [Copyright of Motorola, Inc., used with permission.]

### Scatter Diagrams

- These diagrams are used to study the relationship between one variable and another.
- A measure of the strength of the relationship may be obtained.
- Used to determine a cause and effect relationship between the input and output parameters of a process.
- These are individual data points, not averages.

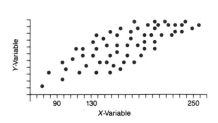

**Scatter Diagram.** Used to Study the Relationship Between Variables

### Multi-vari Charts

This type of chart allows insight into the component parts of the variations. The chart is useful for the following:

- Monitor the product variation.
- View and analyze the relationship between two variables.
- View and assess the variations that occur within part, between parts, and across time.
- Simultaneously analyze multiple parameters.
- Study natural or artificially induced variations.
- Study a process without any alterations or interruptions to it.

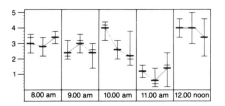

**Multi-vari Chart.** Allows Insight into the Nature of Variations

### Control Charts

| TYPE | USAGE |
|---|---|
| X bar & R | Variables Data |
| X bar & S | Variables Data |
| "P" | Binary Data |
| 'C' | Count Data |
| X & $R_M$ | Batch Processes |

- Illustrates when special cause variation is present (process needs attention.)
- Illustrates when only common cause variation is present (predictable & stable).
- For use on critical process parameters
- May be used to determine process capability.

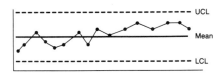

**Control Chart.** Used as a Continuous Indicator of Process Control and Capability

**FIGURE 21.5.** Graphical tools for continuous improvement. [Copyright of Motorola, Inc., used with permission.]

## Pareto Diagrams

- 80 % of the costs are associated with approximately 20 % of the defect types.
- These diagrams are used to indicate which problems we should solve first.

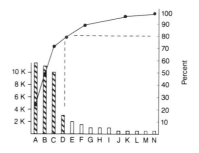

**Pareto Diagram.** Represents the Basis for Project Improvement Studies

## Cause and Effect Diagrams

- This diagram is most effectively used for brainstorming using the " six M's ".
- Rank order (prioritize) potential problems and/or group them for investigation or experimentation.
- This type of diagram may be combined with a process flow diagram to form a process cause and effects problem-solving flow diagram.
- This is a powerful tool in the early stages of problem-solving.

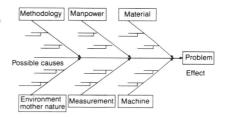

**Cause and Effect Diagram.** Powerful Tool for Early Stages of Problem Solving (Brainstorming)

## Process Flow Charts

This type of diagram graphically illustrates:
- Sequential process steps
- Relationship between process steps
- Problem areas
- Unnecessary loops and complexity
- Where simplification is possible
- May be used in conjunction with a cause and effect diagram for problem-solving.
- Material Flow

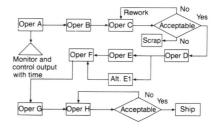

**Process Flow Chart.** Shows Sequential Process Steps for Isolation of Problem Areas

**FIGURE 21.6.** Graphical tools for continuous improvement. [Copyright of Motorola, Inc., used with permission.]

The discussion about these Six Sigma process steps is from a manufacturing perspective; however, the basic flow is applicable to many other areas of a business. For example, this basic process flow could be used to decrease development cycle time and reduce the chance of design problems escaping to manufacturing (i.e., better meet the needs of the customer). Section 21.2 discusses steps that can be used in the development process. This set of steps notes the importance of basic education by including it as a subject topic.

The philosophy of Six Sigma summarized in Figure 21.7 is consistent with the objectives of this text. The following examples considered "prioritizing opportunities for improvement" (i.e. step 1) as an integral part of the solution to a specific problem.

| Example Number | Identified "Opportunity for Improvement" |
|---|---|
| Example 2-1 | Automobile test—answering the right question |
| Example 3-1 | Improving a process with subjective information |
| Example 3-2 | Reducing the total cycle time of a process |
| Example 3-3 | Improving a process that has defects |
| Example 22-2 | A reliability and functional test of an assembly |

## 21.2. A SIX SIGMA APPROACH TO PRODUCT DEVELOPMENT

This section gives a more specific road map to how the previously discussed Six Sigma philosophy can be applied to product development (Lorenzen 1990). Again, the examples shown in Chapters 2 and 3 are consistent with the intent of this philosophy.

**1.** Provide education in statistical methodologies. The fundamental methodologies of statistical process control, fractional factorial experiments, brainstorming, and quality function deployment type activity must be used by large numbers of individuals to develop, manufacture, and deliver the best possible products to customers at competitive prices.

**2.** Identify and optimize key process and product parameters. Defining all processes and creating flowcharts that describe the steps of the process can give enlightening insight that may not be otherwise apparent. The list of processes needs to include existing basic internal processes in the development process. Brainstorming (see Section 3.5) and Pareto analysis (see Section 19.17) techniques can be helpful to determine which processes need to be changed and how these processes can be improved. For example, a brainstorming session may identify a source as "simple" as the current procurement procedure for standard components as the major contibutor to "long" development cycles (see Example 3-2). Another brainstorming session that bridges departmental barriers may then indicate the changes that are

## Flow

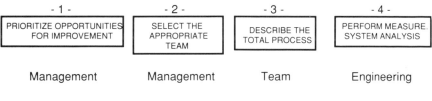

|  - 1 -  |  - 2 -  |  - 3 -  |  - 4 -  |
| --- | --- | --- | --- |
| PRIORITIZE OPPORTUNITIES FOR IMPROVEMENT | SELECT THE APPROPRIATE TEAM | DESCRIBE THE TOTAL PROCESS | PERFORM MEASURE. SYSTEM ANALYSIS |
| Management | Management | Team | Engineering |

## Description

Quantify any known or perceived opportunities for improvement. Specify the problems in quantifiable terms such as how much, when, where, and how. Indicate which impact the customer, reliability, product quality and yields. Identify potential cost savings to the customer and Motorola.

Select a small group of people with the product / process knowledge, experience, technical discipline, authority, time and skill in the specific area of concern. Establish and identify the role of the team and each member. Identify a "Champion" (in addition to the team leader) who can assist the team and can ensure that the teams recommendations are carried out. The team must decide what and how much it can accomplish.

Utilize a process flow diagram to illustrate the possible variations and alternatives of the process. Include all equipment, manpower, methods, tools, piece parts and measurement instruments in the process description. **Identify all of the known** input / output relationships. Highlight any of the alternative work procedures and flows.

Determine precision, accuracy, repeatability and reproducibility of each instrument or gauge used in order to ensure that they are capable. Ensure that the measurement precision is at least ten times better than the magnitude that is to be discerned

## Tools

• Pareto Analysis
• Reliability Reports
• Yield Loss Reports
• Cost of Quality
• Graphic Illustrations

• Select
  Champion
  Leader
  Advisors
• Identify Correct
  Number of
  Participants
• Ensure Cross-
  functional
  Membership

• Flow Diagram
• Pareto Analysis
• Historical Data
• Process Definitions
• C & E Diagrams
• Trend Charts

• Calibration
• Measurement
  System Error
  Study

**FIGURE 21.7a.** The Motorola guide to implementation of SPC. [Copyright of Motorola, Inc., used with permission.] Figure is continued on next page.

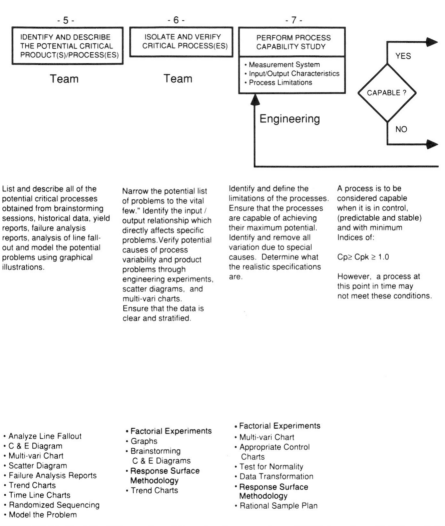

**FIGURE 21.7b.** The Motorola guide to implementation of SPC (continued). [Copyright of Motorola, Inc., used with permission.]

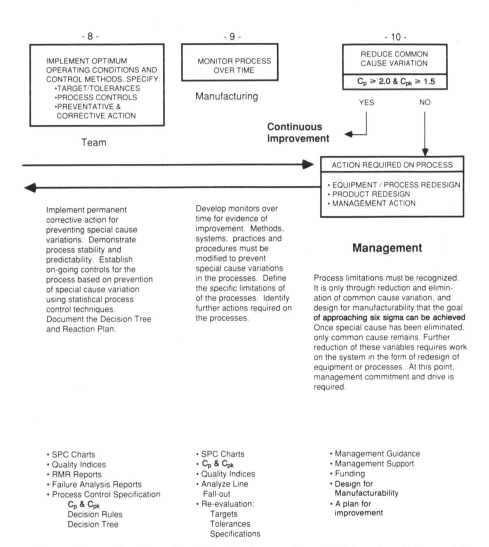

FIGURE 21.7c.  The Motorola guide to implementation of SPC (continued). [Copyright of Motorola, Inc., used with permission.]

needed to improve this process so that it better meets the overall needs of the business. It is also important to establish processes that can identify the parameters that affect product performance and quality early in the design and development phase. Fractional factorial experiments (see Chapter 13), response surface experiments (see Chapter 17), and pass/fail functional testing (see Chapter 18) are tools that need to be considered as an integral part of these processes.

**3.** Define tolerances on key parameters. Quality function deployment is a tool that can be helpful when defining limits relative to meeting the needs of the customer. Fractional factorial experiment (see Example 22-1) and statistical tolerancing techniques (see Section 7.10) can also be useful tools to determine tolerance levels. For example, a fractional factorial experiment on one prototype early in the development cycle could indicate that the tolerancing of only one of four areas under consideration needed to be closely monitored in the manufacturing process (see Example 15-1).

**4.** Construct control charts, establish control limits, and determine process capability indices. The initial identification and tracking procedures for key parameters need to begin in development. Continuous response outputs should be used wherever possible. The initial data collection should begin as part of the development process.

**5.** Implement statistical process controls in the development line with a management system to assure compliance. Functional statistical process control (SPC, not just the existence of control charts) is a tool that can monitor the key product parameters as a function of time (see Chapter 19). An implementation process is needed to address both sporadic/special (i.e., out-of control) conditions and chronic/common conditions (e.g., the number of defects is consistent from day-to-day; however, the amount of defects is too high). An implementation process (see Figure 21.4) must be created that encourages continual process improvement, as opposed to "fixing all the problems" via "firefighting" techniques.

**6.** Demonstrate process capability indices for key processes. For an accurate quantification, the process capability indices (see Section 19.15) need to be calculated from data that was taken from a stable process over time. However, it is beneficial to make an estimate of the process capabilities for key parameters and their tolerances with early data. Results from this activity can yield a priority list of work that needs to be done with a starting point where robust designed experiments (i.e., fractional factorial experiment strategy) are used for optimization and the reduction of product variability. To meet variability reduction needs, it may be necessary in some cases to change the design or process. Additional key parameters can be identified from the knowledge gained from this work. Periodic review and updates need to be made for the parameters and their tolerances.

**7.** Transfer the responsibility for continuing process improvement to manufacturing. The manufacturing organization should be given inputs to all these development activities; however, in most organizations there is some point in time when the ownership of these processes needs to be transferred to a manufacturing organization. SPC charting needs to be conducted on all key parameters with an emphasis of making continual process improvements where required (see Figure 21.4).

## 21.3. A PROCESS TO MANAGE PRODUCT DEVELOPMENT WITH FRACTIONAL FACTORIAL EXPERIMENTS

Competitive pressures within many industries are driving for improved quality and reduced costs, while requiring state-of-the-art technology with a shorter development cycle time. Historical product development processes are not adequate to create a product that is competitive.

Consider a product development strategy where a product is to be conceived by developers and then tested by a "design test" organization. After the test is complete the product design is then given to the manufacturing organization that will mass produce the product under the supervision of a quality department. Information flow with this approach is graphically depicted in Figure 21.8.

This review approach may be satisfactory with small projects that are not on aggressive development and build programs. However, it is impractical for a test organization of a complex product to know as much detail about the product as the developers and to choose a reasonable test approach without the aid of the developers. However, each developer cannot define a thorough test strategy alone since he or she can become "too close" to the design and may not have insight to potential problems that can exist when the design interfaces with the designs of other developers.

Organizations might state that Figure 21.8 does not represent their situation since the testing and manufacturing organizations review the work plans of the previous group. I do not believe that the review of plans is often as effective as one would like to believe. Let's consider the question: How might a review/test process structure be improved upon so as to increase its effectiveness between organizations such that a higher quality product will be produced more expediently?

A common language to aid communication between all organizations should be used to remove any walls between both test activities and organization

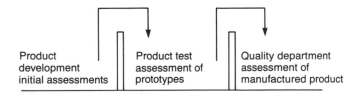

**FIGURE 21.8.** Information flow in a product development cycle.

function. To yield the best overall test strategy, all organizations might need to input (e.g., brainstorming) to a basic test strategy and limiting assumptions that assess the product performance relative to needs of the customer. This language needs be at a "high enough" level for effective communication and still "low enough" to give adequate test details within the experiment(s).

The techniques illustrated in Part II of this text are useful after the basic problem is defined; however, determining the best test strategy is often both more important and difficult then "analyzing the data." This challenge increases when developing a complex product since consideration should be made of how to institute a multiple experimental test strategy that promotes both test efficiency and early problem detection.

This "guide" encourages the use of fractional factorial experiment design matrices whenever possible to address questions that may initially take a different form, since this powerful approach to problem solving assesses several factors (i.e., variables) within one experiment. In addition, these designs have a format that can aid in bridging the communication barriers that can exist between departments within an organization.

The experimental strategy that is illustrated in the following example contains a layering of planned fractional factorial experiments within the product development cycle. The fractional factorial experiments can have structural inputs from other organizations (via brainstorming and cause-and-effect diagrams) to improve the effectiveness of the experiment and to achieve maximum coverage and early problem detection within the product development cycle.

## 21.4. EXAMPLE 21-1: MANAGING PRODUCT DEVELOPMENT USING FRACTIONAL FACTORIAL EXPERIMENTS

Consider the design cycle and integration testing of a complex computer system. Figure 21.9 pictorially illustrates an approach where example concerns are expressed from each organization to yield a collaborative general test strategy that can utilize brainstorming concepts (see Section 3.5) to evaluate the development of the computer (see Example 18-3).

This unified test strategy can reduce a products development cycle time, resource requirements and solution costs while achieving improved test effectiveness. Product cycles and resource requirements can be reduced by eliminating redundant testing and by improved test efficiency, while solution costs are reduced by earlier problem detection and minimizing the chance of problem escapes.

Inputs for test consideration should place emphasis on directing efforts toward meeting the needs of the customer with less emphasis on criteron validation of noncritical areas (that are currently being performed because

EXAMPLE 21-1: MANAGING PRODUCT DEVELOPMENT    **345**

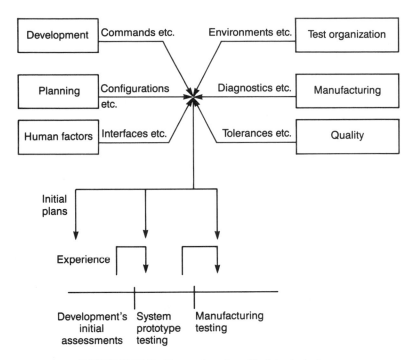

**FIGURE 21.9.** Example: A unified test strategy.

"that is the way it has been done in the past"). For this to be a reality, the original test objective may need reassessment and redefinition.

Figure 21.10 illustrates a basic experiment design building process for this product development cycle. The product is first broken down into functional areas that will have individual fractional factorial experiments. Also at this time plans should be made for pyramiding functional area experiments to assess the interrelationships between areas. Initial "rough" factor plans should be made at this time for experimental designs at all levels of the pyramid. Factor selection for higher level pyramid designs should consider those factors and levels that can cause interrelationship problems, since lower level designs should have previously considered the factors as independent entities. However, the higher level design factors and levels will be subject to change because information from earlier experiments can be combined with initial thoughts on these selections.

The following steps should be considered for this process flow:

1. Assemble representatives of affected areas to determine the functional area and hierarchical structure, as noted in the Figure 21.10.

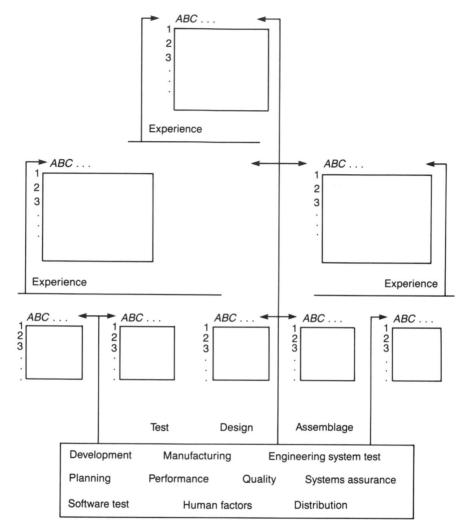

**FIGURE 21.10.** A structured test strategy.

2. Use brainstorming techniques to determine for each functional area (see Table 3.5) the
   a. Test objective
   b. Limiting assumptions
   c. Outputs
   d. Factors with respective levels
3. Perform experiments and analyze results.
4. Draw conclusions with assemblage and then publish results.

5. Adjust other higher hierarchical structure experimental plans, which may change depending on previous experiments.

6. Repeat the process as needed throughout the hierarchy of experiments.

## 21.5. OTHER TOOLS

Failure mode, effect, and criticality analysis (FMECA) (Juran and Grynn 1980; Juran 1988) is a technique that provides a methodical way to examine a proposed design for possible ways that a failure can occur. With this approach, first the failure modes for a proposed design are listed (note that the failure mode is the symptom of the failure, as opposed to the cause of failure). For each of the failure modes, the effect on the overall system or components is then studied. A review is then made of the action that is (will be) taken to minimize the probability of failure or to minimize the effect of failure. FMECA can be done to study the effects of maintenance, safety, down time, and inspection planning. Block diagrams can also be used within an FMECA analysis. US MIL STD 1629A (U.S. Department of Defense 1980) more precisely quantifies the criticality using probability and other considerations.

Fault tree analysis (Juran 1988; Juran and Grynn 1980; Barlow et al. 1975) is the reverse of FMECA. In this technique a supposition is made that an accident or failure occurs. Consideration is then given to the possible direct causes that could lead to the accident or failure. Next, the possible origins of these causes are considered. Finally, ways are visualized to avoid the origins and causes. Standard logic symbols are used in fault tree diagrams. The basic analysis can be extended by adding estimates of probability. A computer program can then be used to calculate the probability for various paths. From this information, priorities can then be established for further work.

Evolutionary operation (EVOP) (Box et al. 1978; Juran and Grynn 1980) is an analytical approach targeted at securing data from a manufacturing process where process conditions are varied in a planned pattern (e.g., fractional factorial experiment trials) from one lot to another without jeopardizing the manufactured product. Analytical techniques are then used to determine what process changes to make for product improvement.

A decision tree (Moody 1983) is another opportunity to blend statistical experiments with decision-making tools. For a problem this graphical decision-making tool integrates both uncertainties and cost with the alternatives to help in choosing the "best" alternative. Uncertainties typically take on values of probabilities that are opinions. For some situations a fractional factorial experiment could be used to get a better assessment of these input probability levels.

The Delphi technique (Moody 1983) is a method of predicting the future by surveying experts in the problem area. Like the cause-and-effect diagram, this tool could also be used as a methodology for getting wise inputs to an experiment strategy.

## 21.6. DO-IT-SMARTER CONSIDERATIONS

Previous chapters discuss the mechanics of solving many types of problems using statistical techniques. This chapter discusses management philosophy along with tools that can help with problem solving and decision making. No one of the concepts discussed in this text is right for all situations. Practitioners can often receive the most benefit when the procedure and statistical tools are creatively combined to do what is "right" for the customer.

# 22

# EXAMPLES WITH DO-IT-SMARTER CONSIDERATIONS

Recommended introductory reading: Chapters 2, 3, 4, 5, 7, 13, 14, and 20.

The discussion and examples in this chapter contain additional applications that further illustrate and combine the concepts discussed in various sections of this text with an emphasis on do-it-smarter considerations. Alternative approaches are discussed where the situations under consideration involve complex problems that need to be solved with limited resources.

## 22.1. EXAMPLE 22-1: A QFD EVALUATION WITH FRACTIONAL FACTORIAL EXPERIMENTATION

A company (the customer) purchased metalized glass plates from a vendor for additional processing in an assembly (Lorenzen 1989). The quality of these parts was unsatisfactory. The current vendor process of sputtering chrome/copper/chrome thin films onto these glass substrates caused yields that were too low and costs that were too high. It should be noted that the information for this example was taken from an experiment that was conducted in the early 1980s before QFD (see Section 20.2) and Taguchi concepts (see Chapter 16) became popular; hence, some of the analyses cannot be recreated with the procedural rigor suggested within the procedure.

There are many trade-offs to consider when attempting to improve this process. For this example a QFD approach (see Section 20.2) is used to address this type of situation. The discussion that follows addresses how some of the information that is contained in Figure 22.1 was determined.

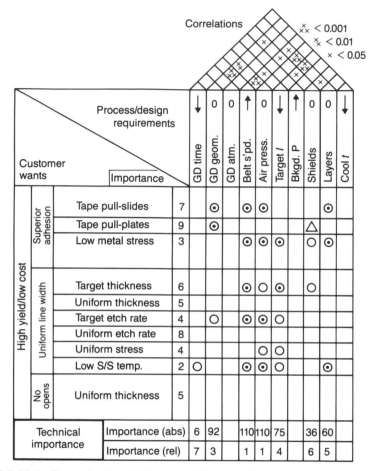

**FIGURE 22.1.** Example 22-1: QFD chart. GD, glow discharge; Belt s'pd., belt speed; Target 1, target current; Bkgd.P, background pressure; Cool $t$, plate cool-down time.

The primary QFD WHAT of the customer was first determined to be high yield/low cost. The secondary customer WHATs addressed the type of problems encountered in meeting these primary desires. These secondary WHAT considerations were then determined to be superior adhesion to eliminate peeling lines, uniform line widths to improve electrical operating margins, and no electrical open circuit paths. Tertiary WHATs then follow, addressing these desires along with an importance rating. The process/design requirements thought necessary to meet these tertiary WHAT items are then listed as the HOWs across the top of this matrix (Figure 22.1). The following discussion will give the thought process used to determine the other parameters of this "house of quality."

The next step that can be taken is to define the relationship between the WHATs and HOWs. One option is to assign a value from a known or assumed

EXAMPLE 22-1: QFD EVALUATION WITH FACTORIAL EXPERIMENTATION  **351**

relationship of fundamental principles; however, this relationship may be invalid. Another approach is to use a fractional factorial experiment. When taking this second approach, consider a WHAT (e.g., "target thickness") as output to a fractional factorial experiment with the 10 HOW factors and levels, as shown in Table 22.1.

One glass substrate would be manufactured according to a fractional factorial design matrix that sets the 10 factor levels for each sample that is produced. The 64-trial experiment design shown in Table 22.2 (which was created from Table M5) gives unconfounded information about the main effects with two-factor interactions; however, the two-factor interactions are confounded with each other (i.e., a resolution IV design).

For purpose of illustration, consider the "target thickness" WHAT that had a value of 1600 angstroms, with a customer tolerance of 300 angstroms. This thickness measurement response is noted in Table 22.2 for each of the 64 trials. The other WHATs can similarly have an output level for each trial.

The results from a computer analysis is shown in Table 22.3 (see Chapter 15), where the factors and interactions are noted as contrasts columns (i.e., cont1–cont63). It should be noted that this nomenclature is consistent with Table N2 and that the contrast columns not noted in the computer output were used by the SAS program to estimate experimental error (since only factors $A - J$ and their two-factor interaction contrast columns were defined in this resolution IV experiment design model.) The computer program steps used to create this output are noted in Section C.11.

For this design the interaction effects are confounded. Table 22.3 includes the results of the engineering judgment that was used to determine which of the interactions noted from Table N2 probably caused the contrast column to be significant. A confirmation experiment will later be needed to assess the validity of these assumptions.

Results from this data analysis shown in Table 22.3 provide quantitative information on the nature of the relationships between the customer WANTs

**TABLE 22.1. Example 22-1: HOWs for Glass Plates**

| | | Level | |
|---|---|---|---|
| Factor | | $(-)$ | $(+)$ |
| A. | Belt speed | 2.2 rpm | 1.1 rpm |
| B. | Argon sputter pressure | 4 mTorr | 14 mTorr |
| C. | Glow discharge atmosphere | Dry | Wet |
| D. | Target current | 4 amperes | 8 amperes |
| E. | Glow discharge plate geometry | Flat | Edge |
| F. | Background pressure | $8 \times 10^{-6}$ Torr | $5 \times 10^{-5}$ Torr |
| G. | Plate cool-down time | 2 min | 10 min |
| H. | Shields | With | Without |
| I. | Number of layers | 1 | 3 |
| J. | Glow discharge time | 10 min | 20 min |

**TABLE 22.2. Example 22-1: A WHAT Output versus HOW Factors**

| Number of Trial | (HOWs) Factors A B C D E F G H I J | (WHAT) Thickness | Number of Trial | (HOWs) Factors A B C D E F G H I J | (WHAT) Thickness |
|---|---|---|---|---|---|
| 1 | + − − − − − + + − + | 1405 | 33 | + + − − + − − + + + | 1300 |
| 2 | + + − − − − − − + − | 1122 | 34 | + + + − − + + − + + | 1074 |
| 3 | + + + − − − − − − − | 895 | 35 | − + + + − − + + − − | 1070 |
| 4 | + + + + − − − − − + | 1915 | 36 | − − + + + − − + + − | 1360 |
| 5 | + + + + + − − + − − | 2060 | 37 | − − − + + + + + + + | 1340 |
| 6 | + + + + + + + + + + | 1985 | 38 | + − − − + + − − + + | 1530 |
| 7 | − + + + + + − − + − | 1050 | 39 | − + − − − + − + − − | 870 |
| 8 | + − + + + + − − − − | 2440 | 40 | + − + − − − + + + + | 1480 |
| 9 | − + − + + + − − − − | 960 | 41 | + + − + − − − − + + | 1920 |
| 10 | + − + − + + − − − + | 1260 | 42 | + + + − + − − + − + | 975 |
| 11 | − + − + − + − + − + | 1110 | 43 | + + + + − + + − + − | 2130 |
| 12 | + − + − + − + − + − | 1495 | 44 | − + + + + − + − − + | 770 |
| 13 | + + − + − + + − − − | 1810 | 45 | − − + + + + + + − + | 1210 |
| 14 | − + + − + − + − − − | 482 | 46 | + − − + + + − − + − | 1800 |
| 15 | − − + + − + + − − − | 1040 | 47 | − + − − + + − − − + | 450 |
| 16 | + − − + + − + − − + | 2620 | 48 | + − + − − + − + − − | 1380 |
| 17 | + + − − + + + + − − | 910 | 49 | − + − + − − + + + − | 1360 |
| 18 | − + + − − + − + + − | 545 | 50 | − − + − + − − + + + | 840 |
| 19 | + − + + − − + + + − | 3650 | 51 | − − − + − + + − + − | 1020 |
| 20 | + + − + + − − + + − | 2430 | 52 | + − − − + − + − − − | 1180 |
| 21 | + + + − + + + + + − | 1065 | 53 | + + − − − + + − − + | 980 |
| 22 | − + + + − + − + + + | 1260 | 54 | − + + − − − + + − + | 470 |
| 23 | + − + + + − + − + + | 1976 | 55 | − − + + − − − − + + | 770 |
| 24 | + + − + + + + + − + | 2000 | 56 | − − − + + − − + − − | 1320 |
| 25 | − + + − + + − − + + | 430 | 57 | − − − − + + + + + − | 820 |
| 26 | + − + + − + − + − + | 2070 | 48 | + − − − − + − + + − | 1424 |
| 27 | − + − + + − + − + + | 780 | 59 | − + − − − − + + + + | 620 |
| 28 | − − + − + + + + − − | 570 | 60 | − − + − − − − − + − | 500 |
| 29 | + − − + − + − + + + | 3600 | 61 | − − − + − − − − − + | 1010 |
| 30 | − + − − + − + − + − | 495 | 62 | − − − − + − − + − + | 545 |
| 31 | − − + − − + + − − + | 620 | 63 | − − − − − + + − + + | 600 |
| 32 | + − − + − − + + − − | 2520 | 64 | − − − − − − − − − − | 590 |

and the HOWs for the process/design requirements noted in Figure 22.1 (see Section 20.2). When computing importance (see Equation 20.1), a 5 (⊙) was used to indicate a very strong relationship (Pr < 0.001), a 3 (○) represented a strong relationship (Pr < 0.01), and a 1 (△) indicated a weak relationship (Pr < 0.05). A ↑ indicated from the range of factor levels used in this experiment that the value of the customer WANT improves as the process requirement increased, while ↓ indicated lower values are better and ○ indicated that there was a preferred target value. Significant interactions are indicated in the correlation matrix with the noted significance levels (see "roof of house" in Fig. 22.1).

# TABLE 22.3. Example 22-1: Computer Output (significance calculations)

ANALYSIS OF VARIANCE PROCEDURE

DEPENDENT VARIABLE: THICKNES

| SOURCE | DF | SUM OF SQUARES | MEAN SQUARE | F VALUE | PR > F | R-SQUARE | C.V. |
|---|---|---|---|---|---|---|---|
| MODEL | 41 | 30235649.12500000 | 737454.85670732 | 11.12 | 0.0001 | 0.953963 | 19.7919 |
| ERROR | 22 | 1459141.81250000 | 66324.62784091 | | | ROOT MSE | THICKNES MEAN |
| CORRECTED TOTAL | 63 | 31694790.93750000 | | | | 257.53568266 | 1301.21875000 |

| SOURCE | DF | ANOVA SS | F VALUE | PR > F | |
|---|---|---|---|---|---|
| CONT1 | 1 | 13619790.25000000 | 205.35 | 0.0001 | ← A: Belt Speed |
| CONT2 | 1 | 1180482.25000000 | 17.80 | 0.0004 | ← B: Argon Sputter Pressure |
| CONT3 | 1 | 40200.25000000 | 0.61 | 0.4445 | |
| CONT4 | 1 | 10107630.56250000 | 152.40 | 0.0001 | ← D: Target Current |
| CONT5 | 1 | 88655.06250000 | 1.34 | 0.2600 | |
| CONT6 | 1 | 5112.25000000 | 0.08 | 0.7839 | |
| CONT7 | 1 | 530348.06250000 | 8.00 | 0.0098 | ← A*B: Belt Speed * Argon Pressure |
| CONT8 | 1 | 1207.56250000 | 0.02 | 0.8939 | |
| CONT9 | 1 | 110.50000000 | 0.00 | 0.9678 | |
| CONT10 | 1 | 57960.56250000 | 0.87 | 0.3600 | |
| CONT11 | 1 | 17030.56250000 | 0.26 | 0.6174 | |
| CONT12 | 1 | 529.00000000 | 0.01 | 0.9296 | |
| CONT13 | 1 | 637.56250000 | 0.01 | 0.9228 | |
| CONT14 | 1 | 39006.25000000 | 0.59 | 0.4513 | |
| CONT15 | 1 | 5256.25000000 | 0.08 | 0.7809 | |
| CONT16 | 1 | 11025.00000000 | 0.17 | 0.6874 | |
| CONT17 | 1 | 962851.56250000 | 14.52 | 0.0010 | ← H: Target Shields |
| CONT18 | 1 | 284089.00000000 | 4.28 | 0.0504 | ← I: Number of Metal Layers |
| CONT19 | 1 | 6.25000000 | 0.00 | 0.9923 | |
| CONT20 | 1 | 25680.25000000 | 0.39 | 0.5402 | |
| CONT21 | 1 | 249750.06250000 | 3.77 | 0.0652 | |
| CONT22 | 1 | 32761.00000000 | 0.49 | 0.4895 | |
| CONT23 | 1 | 378840.25000000 | 5.71 | 0.0258 | ← H*I: Target Shields * Number of Layers |
| CONT25 | 1 | 83810.25000000 | 1.26 | 0.2731 | |
| CONT26 | 1 | 3937.56250000 | 0.06 | 0.8098 | |
| CONT31 | 1 | 57600.56250000 | 0.87 | 0.3615 | |
| CONT33 | 1 | 1400672.25000000 | 21.12 | 0.0001 | ← A*D: Belt Speed * Target Current |
| CONT34 | 1 | 2070.25000000 | 0.03 | 0.8614 | |
| CONT35 | 1 | 5365.56250000 | 0.08 | 0.7787 | |
| CONT39 | 1 | 362705.06250000 | 5.47 | 0.0289 | ← D*H: Target Current * Target Shields |
| CONT40 | 1 | 88209.00000000 | 1.33 | 0.2612 | |
| CONT42 | 1 | 85.56250000 | 0.00 | 0.9717 | |
| CONT43 | 1 | 15813.06250000 | 0.24 | 0.6302 | |
| CONT45 | 1 | 65025.00000000 | 0.98 | 0.3329 | |
| CONT48 | 1 | 127627.56250000 | 1.92 | 0.1793 | |
| CONT52 | 1 | 5550.25000000 | 0.08 | 0.7751 | |
| CONT55 | 1 | 38220.25000000 | 0.58 | 0.4558 | |
| CONT56 | 1 | 8742.25000000 | 0.13 | 0.7200 | |
| CONT59 | 1 | 226338.06250000 | 3.41 | 0.0782 | |
| CONT61 | 1 | 15067.56250000 | 0.23 | 0.6383 | |
| CONT63 | 1 | 89850.06250000 | 1.35 | 0.2569 | |

A strategy could now be taken to evaluate parameter and tolerance design considerations from a "target thickness" point of view. In general, the model parameter coefficients could be used to determine target parameters for each design requirement (see Section 13.21). However, in lieu of this procedure, consider the summary of significant interacting factors shown in Table 22.4. When significant main effects are involved in interactions, the main effects must be discussed in terms of other factors, as was illustrated in Figure 13.1 (e.g., the average of all the 16 thickness responses where $A = 1$ and $B = 1$ was 1535.68750). Of these interactions first consider the $A*B$ interaction (Table 22.4, note 1). Given the target objective of 1300 to 1900 (i.e., 1600 $\pm$ 300), it is inferred that the process should have $A$ and $B$ both near the $+1$ level (* combination in Table 22.4). From the $A*D$ interaction (Table 22.4, note 2), $A$ should be near the $+1$ level with $D$ approximately half way between its two test extremes. From the $H*I$ interaction (Table 22.4, note 3), $H$ should be at a level near the $+1$ level with $I$ also at a $+1$ level. Finally, the $D*H$ interaction (Table 22.4, note 4) information does not dispute the conclusions for our previously selected factor levels.

**TABLE 22.4. Example 22-1: Results from a Computer Output (Mean Interaction Effects from Data)**

| | | | | *Note 1: A*B Interaction* |
|---|---|---|---|---|
| $A$ | $B$ | $N^a$ | Thickness | |
| 1 | 1 | 16 | 1535.68750 | * Conclude that $A$ and $B$ should be near $+1$ level. |
| 1 | $-1$ | 16 | 1989.37500 | |
| $-1$ | 1 | 16 | 795.12500 | |
| $-1$ | $-1$ | 16 | 884.68750 | |

| | | | | *Note 2: A*D Interaction* |
|---|---|---|---|---|
| $A$ | $D$ | $N$ | Thickness | |
| 1 | 1 | 16 | 2307.87500 | * Conclude $D$ should be near half way point |
| 1 | $-1$ | 16 | 1217.18750 | between $-1$ and $+1$ levels given $A = +1$. |
| $-1$ | 1 | 16 | 1089.37500 | |
| $-1$ | $-1$ | 16 | 590.43750 | |

| | | | | *Note 3: H*I Interaction* |
|---|---|---|---|---|
| $H$ | $I$ | $N$ | Thickness | |
| 1 | 1 | 16 | 1567.43750 | * Conclude that $H$ and $I$ should be near $+1$ level. |
| 1 | $-1$ | 16 | 1280.31250 | |
| $-1$ | 1 | 16 | 1168.25000 | |
| $-1$ | $-1$ | 16 | 1188.87500 | |

| | | | | *Note 4: D*H Interaction* |
|---|---|---|---|---|
| $D$ | $H$ | $N$ | Thickness | |
| 1 | 1 | 16 | 1896.56250 | * Conclude previous $D$ and $H$ levels look |
| 1 | $-1$ | 16 | 1500.68750 | reasonable. |
| $-1$ | 1 | 16 | 951.18750 | |
| $-1$ | $-1$ | 16 | 856.43750 | |

[a] $N$ is the number of trials that were averaged to get the Thickness response.

EXAMPLE 22-1: QFD EVALUATION WITH FACTORIAL EXPERIMENTATION    **355**

A summary of the conclusions are: $A = +$, $B = +$, $D = $ half way between high and low, $H = +$, and $I = +$. From the raw data consider now the thickness output for the trials that had the preceding combination levels:

| Trial | ABDHI |  |  |  |  |
|-------|-------|---|---|---|---|
| 6 | +++++ | 1985 | | | We would |
| 20 | +++++ | 2430 | average 2007.5 | if D | expect |
| | | | | were halfway | an output |
| 21 | ++−++ | 1065 | average 1183 | | of approx. |
| 33 | ++−++ | 1300 | | | 1595.25 |

The expected value of 1595.25 is close to the desired target value of 1600. A confirmation experiment should be performed to verify this conclusion. A response surface design (see Chapter 17) could also be used to gain more information about the sensitivity of the factor levels to the output response.

Note that these are the target considerations given that thickness tolerance is the only output. There may be conflict between WHAT items, causing a compromise for these levels.

The preceding thought process parallels the intent of what some other texts on Taguchi techniques call parameter design. The next step when using a Taguchi strategy would be a tolerance design (i.e., an experiment design that is to determine the tolerance of the parameters). It can be easy to assign a tolerance value to the nonsignificant factors. From the previous analysis for thickness and other WHAT analyses not discussed, the cooling time from 2 min (the experimental low level) to 10 min (the high level) had no affect on the WHAT items. Hence, it is probably safe to use the test extremes as tolerance extremes. Likewise, the background pressure can vary from its experimental level settings of 8 to $5 \times 10^{-5}$ Torr and the glow discharge atmosphere can be wet or dry. However, to speculate about a reasonable tolerance for these other critical parameters from the given data could yield questionable conclusions. Hence, more information would be needed to determine satisfactory tolerance limits for these factors.

We believe that the five parameters noted earlier affect thickness individually and through two-factor interaction considerations. Let's consider economics first. I suggest first determining what tolerance can be maintained without any additional expenditures to the process. An experiment can then be conducted similar to that shown around the "new" nominal values. From Table M3 we can get a 16-trial experiment that can be used to assess all two-factor interactions of five factors. A 16-trial test where the two factors are evaluated at their tolerance extremes represent the "space" (i.e., assessment of boundary conditions) of the tolerances expected. If these data are plotted on probability paper (see Chapter 5), a picture of the extreme operating range can be determined. If this plot is centered and the 0.1–99.9% probability plot positions are well within the tolerance extremes, then it would be rea-sonable to conclude that the tolerances are adequate (see $C_p$ in Section

19.15). If this is not true, then the fractional factorial information needs to be analyzed again using the preceding logic so that the tolerance of critical factors can be tightened while less important factors maintain their loose tolerance limits. A response surface design approach, as shown in Chapter 17, can be used to optimize complex process parameters.

After the process parameters are determined, statistical process control (SPC) charting techniques (see Chapter 19) should be used to monitor the important process factors noted in the manufacturing process. In addition, sampling should be performed as necessary along with SPC charting to monitor all the other primary and secondary WHAT factors.

## 22.2. EXAMPLE 22-2: A RELIABILITY AND FUNCTIONAL TEST OF AN ASSEMBLY

A power supply has sophisticated design requirements. In addition, the specification indicates an aggressive MTBF (mean time between failures) criterion of $10 \times 10^6$ hr. A test organization is to evaluate the reliability and function of the nonrepairable power supply.

Tests of this type seem to be directed toward emphasizing testing the failure rate criterion by exercising enough units long enough to verify the criterion. Considering that the failure rate of the units is constant with age, as the criterion implies, Table K can yield a factor that is used to determine the total number of test hours needed (see Section 11.7). If we desire 90% confidence with a test design that allows no failures, then the factor would be 2.303, which would yield a total test time of

$$T = 2.303 (10 \times 10^6) = 23.03 \times 10^6 \text{ hr}$$

The number of units could range from $23.03 \times 10^6$ units for one hour or one unit for $23.03 \times 10^6$ hr. Relative to the single-unit test length, it may be unlikely that many products would survive this much usage without failure because of some type of wear-out mechanism. And, in reality, it is not very important that a single product would last this long, since for continual customer usage it would require 114 years to accumulate one million hours of usage. Hence, for this test a single product would need to survive 2636 years without failure before "passing" the test. This test approach is a "little" ridiculous.

In addition, the wording of this criterion is deceptive from another point of view. Whenever a nonrepairable device fails, it needs to be replaced. The wording for the above criterion implies a repairable device (mean time between failures). What is probably intended by the criterion is that the failure rate for each hour should not exceed 0.0000001 failures/hour (i.e., $1/[10 \times 10^6 \text{ hours/failure}]$). From a customer point of view, where the annual usage is expected to be 5000 hr and there is a 5-year expected life, this would equate

EXAMPLE 22-2: RELIABILITY AND FUNCTIONAL TEST OF ASSEMBLY    **357**

to 0.05% of the assemblies failing after 1 year's usage and 0.25% of the assemblies after 5 year's usage. If the criterion were quoted with percentages of this type, there would be no confusion about the reliability objectives of the product.

In general, it seems that two percentage values, for example, are often adequate for this type criterion, where the first percentage value is directed toward a maximum fail percentage value within a warranty period, while the second percentage value is directed toward a maximum fail percentage value during the expected product life.

Consider that the expected annual number of power-on hours for the power supply is 5000 hr, and each unit is tested to this expected usage. This test would require 4605 (i.e., $23.026 \times 10^6/5000 = 4605$) units, while a 5-year test would require 921 units [i.e., $23.026 \times 10^6/(5000)(5) = 921$]). For most scenarios involving complex assemblies, neither of these two test alternatives are reasonable since the unit costs would be prohibitive, the test facilities would be very large, the test would be too long, and information obtained late in the test would probably be "too late" for any "value added." Accelerated test alternatives (see Section 10.5) can be helpful to reduce test duration; however, the same basic problems still exist with less magnitude.

Even if the time and resources are spent to do this test and no failure occurs, customer reliability problems can still exist. Two basic assumptions are often overlooked with the preceding test strategy. The first assumption is that the sample is a random sample of the population. If this test were performed early in the manufacturing process, the "sample" may be the first units built, which is not a random sample of future builds that will go to the customer. Problems can occur later in the manufacturing process causing field problems, which this test will not detect since test samples were from an earlier production vintage. The second assumption is that the test replicates customer usage. If a test does not closely replicate customer situations, real problems may not be detected. For example, if the customer turns off a system unit that contains the power supply each evening and our test units are just exercised continuously, the test may miss some thermal cycling component fatigue failures. Or, another example could be that the customer puts more electrical load on the system than was done on the test system. The test may again miss a failure mode caused by this additional loading. Perhaps a fractional factorial test strategy (see Chapter 13) could better define how the power supplies should be loaded and exercised when trying to identify customer reliability problems.

It is easy to get in the trap of "playing games" when testing to verify a failure rate criterion. Let's consider do-it-smarter alternatives. Let's reflect on problems of other products that were found during previous tests or in the user environment. Tests should be designed to give the *customer* the best possible product.

Single-lot testing that gives primary emphasis to initial production testing where the product is considered as a "black box" can yield a large test effort where important problems are not detected. To maximize test efforts, consider the following: Should more emphasis be placed on monitoring the component selection/design considerations as opposed to "running them and counting the number of failures?" Should more emphasis be given to the monitoring of the manufacturing process (i.e., control charting, process capability, etc.)? Should more fractional factorial experiments be used within the internal design process of the mechanism, with stress to failure considerations as an output?

Consider also the real purpose of a reliability test. For the product test criterion, what should really happen if a zero failure test plan had one, two, three, . . . failures? Hopefully the process or design would be "fixed" so that the failures did not occur again. It is doubtful that time would permit another sample of the "new design/process" every time a failure was detected. Hence, typically the test-stated objective may be to verify a criterion; however, the real intent of the test may be to determine and then fix problems.

Now, if the real objective is to identify and fix problems (instead of playing games with numbers), test efforts should be directed to do this *efficiently*. An efficient test would not probably be to turn on 4605 units for a 5000 hr test and once a week monitor them to see if any failures occur. An efficient approach, for example, can include querying the experts for the types of failure expected and monitoring historical field data so that test efforts can be directed toward these considerations and new technology risks. For example, a test without power on/off switching and heating/cooling effects does not make sense if previous power supplies experience 70% of their field failures during the power-on cycling (i.e., a light bulb failure mode) or if 10% of the time the power supply does not start the first time it is used because handling during shipment caused "out-of-box" failures.

Using do-it-smarter considerations it may be found appropriate to use more fractional factorial experiments within the development process. Then, for a preproduction test, the experimenter may decide to test only three units at an elevated temperature for as long as possible to determine if there are any wear-out "surprises." The person who conducts the test may also plan to exercise some units within a thermal cycle chamber and thermal shock chamber. Plans may also consider a shipping test and a out-of-box vibration stress to failure test for some units.

In addition, the experimenter should work with the manufacturing group to obtain time-of-failure information during the production preshipment run-in tests. Data from this test could be used to determine early-life characteristics of the product, which could possibly be projected into the customer environment. The experimenter also would like to ensure that any run-in test time focus on in manufacturing is optimized (see Example 11-6).

A good reliability test strategy has a blend of test considerations that focus on efficiently capturing the types of failures that would be experienced by the customer. It is not a massive test effort that "plays games with numbers."

EXAMPLE 22-2: RELIABILITY AND FUNCTIONAL TEST OF ASSEMBLY    **359**

In addition to the reliability considerations, the experimenter needs to also address functional considerations within the customer environment. Fractional factorial testing is an efficient method to meet these needs.

For the preceding test, one preproduction unit could be functionally tested at the extremes of its operating environment using a fractional factorial test strategy. The following is such a strategy where input factors are evaluated for their effect on the various important output characteristic requirements of the power supply; it is summarized in Table 22.5.

From Table M4 a 32-trial resolution IV design was chosen. With this design the main effects would not be confounded with two-factor interactions; however, there would be confounding of two-factor interactions with each other. The 11 contrast columns from Table M4 were assigned alphabetical factor designations from left to right ($A-K$). These test trials along with two of the experimental trial outputs ($-12$ and 3.4 voltage level outputs) are noted in Table 22.6.

As illustrated in Equation (14.1), the effect of the $-12$-V loading (factor $F$), for example, on the $-12$-V output level is simply the difference in average output response for the trials at the high load to those at low load, which is

**TABLE 22.5.  Example 22-2: Summary of Strategy**

| | Inputs | | |
|---|---|---|---|
| | | Levels | |
| | Factors | $(-)$ | $(+)$ |
| $A$ | Ambient temperature | 47°C | 25°C |
| $B$ | Input ac voltage range | 110 V | 220 V |
| $C$ | Mode on programmable output | 3.4 V | 5.1 V |
| $D$ | ac line voltage (within range in $B$) | Min | Max |
| $E$ | Frequency at ac input | Min | Max |
| $F$ | Load on $-12$ V output | Min | Max |
| $G$ | Load on $-5$ V output | Min | Max |
| $H$ | Load on 12 V output | Min | Max |
| $I$ | Load on 5.1 V output | Min | Max |
| $J$ | Load on 3.4 V output | Min | Max |
| $K$ | Load on programmable output | Min | Max |

| Outputs |
|---|
| Output voltage on each output ($-12$ V, $-5$ V, 12 V, 5.1 V, 3.4 V, programmable volt output) |
| Ripple/noise |
| Noise |
| Input (power factor) |
| Efficiency |
| Line current |
| Line power |

**TABLE 22.6. Example 22-2: Fractional Factorial Experiment Design with Two of the Output Responses**

| Number of Trial | Input Matrix ABCDEFGHIJK | Outputs −12 V | 3.4 V |
|---|---|---|---|
| 1 | +−−−++++−+− | −11.755 | 3.1465 |
| 2 | ++−−−++−+−− | −11.702 | 3.3965 |
| 3 | +++−−−++−++ | −12.202 | 3.1470 |
| 4 | ++++−+−++−− | −11.813 | 3.4038 |
| 5 | +++++++++++ | −11.761 | 3.1537 |
| 6 | −++++−+−++− | −12.200 | 3.1861 |
| 7 | −−+++−−+−++ | −12.325 | 3.1902 |
| 8 | +−−++−−++−+ | −12.292 | 3.3980 |
| 9 | ++−−++−−+++ | −11.872 | 3.1498 |
| 10 | −++−−++−−+− | −11.819 | 3.1914 |
| 11 | +−++−++−−−+ | −11.685 | 3.4084 |
| 12 | −+−++++++−−+ | −11.763 | 3.4217 |
| 13 | −−+−+++++−− | −11.780 | 3.4249 |
| 14 | +−−+−−++++− | −12.223 | 3.1403 |
| 15 | −+−−+−−+++− | −12.344 | 3.1782 |
| 16 | −−+−−+−++++ | −11.909 | 3.1972 |
| 17 | −−−+−++−+++ | −11.834 | 3.1902 |
| 18 | −−−−+−+−−++ | −12.181 | 3.1847 |
| 19 | +−−−−+−+−−+ | −11.801 | 3.4063 |
| 20 | −+−−−−+++−+ | −12.146 | 3.4184 |
| 21 | +−+−−−−−++− | −12.355 | 3.1401 |
| 22 | −+−+−+−+−+− | −11.891 | 3.1826 |
| 23 | +−+−+−+−+−+ | −12.146 | 3.4044 |
| 24 | ++−+−−−−−++ | −12.337 | 3.1435 |
| 25 | +++−+−−+−−− | −12.280 | 3.3975 |
| 26 | −+++−−−+−+ | −12.275 | 3.4230 |
| 27 | +−+++−+−−+− | −11.852 | 3.1459 |
| 28 | ++−++−+−−−− | −12.131 | 3.3900 |
| 29 | −++−++−−−−+ | −11.819 | 3.4281 |
| 30 | −−++−−++−−− | −12.134 | 3.4193 |
| 31 | −−−+++−−+−− | −11.846 | 3.4226 |
| 32 | −−−−−−−−−− | −12.261 | 3.4203 |

Average effect
on −12-V output
by −12-V load
($F$ effect)

$$= \frac{(-11.755 - 11.702, \cdots)}{16} - \frac{(-12.202 - 12.200, \cdots)}{16}$$

$$= -0.43 \text{ V}$$

The main effect and interaction considerations (given the confounding that is noted in Table N2) plotted on normal probability paper is shown in

EXAMPLE 22-2: RELIABILITY AND FUNCTIONAL TEST OF ASSEMBLY    **361**

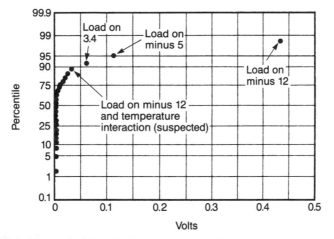

**FIGURE 22.2.** Example 22-2: Half normal probability plot of the contrast column effects (−12-V output).

Figure 22.2 (see Section 14.1). The −0.43-V effect is a large outlier from any linear relationships; hence, it is concluded that the loading of the −12-V output significantly affects the −12-V output (best estimate value of 0.43 V). Other less significant effects are similarly noted.

The results of statistical analyses are commonly presented as significance statements. However, a practitioner may be interested in the overall affects relative to specification limits. One approach *to size* this consideration is to make a probability plot of the outputs of the 32 trials and include the specification limits on the plot (note that this plot is not a true random sample plot of a population). Figure 22.3 illustrates such a plot for the −12-V source,

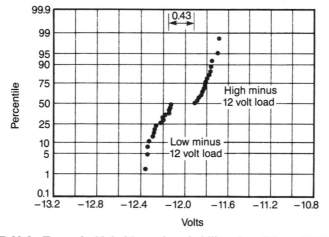

**FIGURE 22.3.** Example 22-2: Normal probability plot of the −12-V responses.

where the magnitude of the loading effect is noticeable as a discontinuity in the line. This plot reflects the variability of one machine given various worst-case loading scenarios. Since the distribution tails are within the noted specification limits, it might be concluded that there are no major problems (if the variability from machine to machine is not large and there is not a degradation with usage).

Consider now the 3.4-V output. A probability plot of the 3.4-V effects is shown in Figure 22.4. The 3.4-V loading effect appears most significant when followed by the temperature effect. The third most significant effect is noted to be a suspicion of an interaction between this loading and temperature.

This interaction effect is suspected because two-factor interactions are confounded with this resolution IV experiment design. This probability point is in reality contrast column 15 (see the design matrix in Table M4). Table N2 indicates that contrast 15, in general, has many interactions that are confounded. However, the number of interaction possibilities is reduced since this experiment had only 11 factors (designated $A$ through $K$); hence, the number of possibilities is reduced to $EF$, $GH$, $AJ$, and $BK$. Engineering then technically considered which of these interaction possibilities [frequency at ac input/load on $-12$-V output ($EF$), load on $-5$-V output/load on 12-V output ($GH$), ambient temperature/load on 3.4-V output ($AJ$), and input ac voltage range/load on programmable output ($BK$)] would be the most likely to affect the $-12$-V output level. Engineering concluded that the most likely interaction was temperature/load on $-12$-V output ($AJ$). Obviously, if it is important to be certain about this contrast column effect, then a confirmation experiment would later need to be conducted.

Similarly to the $-12$-V analyses, a probability plot of the 32 trial outputs is shown in Figure 22.5. This plot illustrates the previously suspected two-

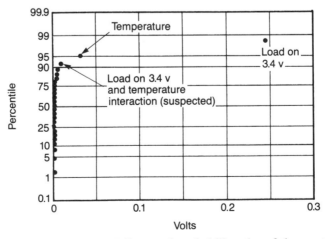

**FIGURE 22.4.** Example 22-2: Half normal probability plot of the contrast column effects (3.4-V output).

EXAMPLE 22-2: RELIABILITY AND FUNCTIONAL TEST OF ASSEMBLY    **363**

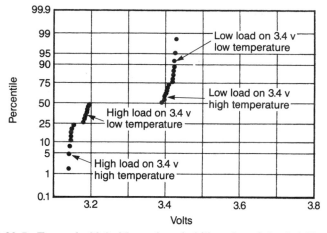

**FIGURE 22.5.** Example 22-2: Normal probability plot of the 3.4-V responses.

factor interaction by the grouping of the data. However, some of the data points fall below the lower specification limit. It appears that the vendor is adjusting the power supply to a 3.4-V output under a low-load condition. However, with additional load, the output decreases to a value that is close to the specification limit. It is apparent from the out-of-specification condition that the voltage adjustment procedure at the vendor should be changed to "center" the high/low loading conditions within the specification limits.

Figure 22.6 shows an estimate for the PDFs that describe the four different scenarios. With this format the findings from the experiment might possibly

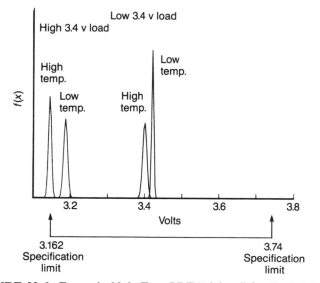

**FIGURE 22.6.** Example 22-2: Four PDF "sizings" for the 3.4-V output.

be more easily presented to others who are not familiar with probability plots (noting that this is a very rough estimate since the data was not a random sample consisting of many units).

The next question of concern is whether there are any other parameters that should be considered. One possible addition to the variability conditions is circuitry drift with component age. Another is variability between power supply assembly units.

To address the between assemblies condition, multiple units could have been used for these analyses. However, the test duration and resource requirements could be much larger. An alternative is to consider an addition derived from historical information; however, this information is not often available. Another alternative is to evaluate a sample of parts held at constant conditions to assess the magnitude of this variability. This effort can also serve as a confirmation experiment to assess whether the conclusions that were drawn from the fractional factorial experiment are valid.

In Figure 22.7 the test data for 10 power supply assemblies is plotted. The test data consists of two points for each assembly (taken at low and high load on the 3.4-V output and at low temperature). The plot indicates that approximately 99.8% of the population variability is within a 0.1-V range. Therefore, assuming the same machine-to-machine variability at high temperatures, allowance should be made for this 0.1-V variation in the 3.4-V analyses. Note that this type of plot should be constructed for each level of voltage since the variation probably will be different for these other outputs.

After the power supply qualification test process is completed satisfactorily, information from this test can be used to determine which parameters need

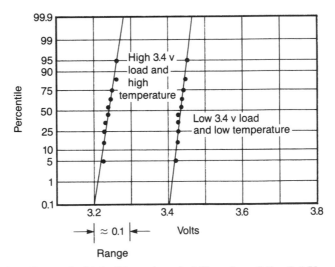

**FIGURE 22.7.** Example 22-2: Normal probability plot of the 3.4-V output on 10 machines under 2 different conditions.

EXAMPLE 22-3: SYSTEM STRESS TO FAIL TEST     **365**

to be monitored within the manufacturing process using process control chart techniques (see Chapter 19).


## 22.3. EXAMPLE 22-3: A SYSTEM FRACTIONAL FACTORIAL STRESS TO FAIL TEST

During the development of a new computer a limited amount of test hardware is available to evaluate the overall design of the product. Four test systems are available along with three different card/adapter types (designated as card A, card B, and adapter) that are interchangeable between the systems.

A "quick and dirty" fractional factorial test approach is desired to evaluate the different combinations of the hardware along with the temperature and humidity extremes typically encountered in a customer's office. One obvious response for the experimental trial configurations is whether the combination of hardware "worked" or "did not work" satisfactorily. However, more information was desired from the experiment than just a binary response. In the past it was shown that the "system design safety factor" can be quantified by noting the 5-V power supply output level values (both upward and downward) at which the system begins to perform unsatisfactorily. A probability plot is then made of these voltage values to estimate the number of systems from the population that would not perform satisfactorily outside the 4.7 to 5.3 tolerance range of the 5-V power supply.

Determining a "low-voltage" failure value could easily be accomplished for this test procedure since this type of system failure was not catastrophic (i.e., the system would still perform satisfactorily again if the voltage level were increased). However, if a failure did not occur at 6.00, previous experience indicates that additional stressing might destroy one or more components. Because of this nonrecoverable scenario, it was decided that the system voltage stressing would be suspended at 6.00 V.

A 16-trial test matrix is shown in Table 22.7 along with measured voltage levels. Note that the trial fractional factorial levels of this type can be created from Tables M1 to M5 where four levels of the factors are created by combining contrast columns (e.g., $-- = 1$, $-+ = 2$, $+- = 3$, and $++ = 4$). It should be noted that the intent of the experiment was to do "a quick and dirty test" at the boundaries of the conditions to assess the range of response that might be expected when parts are assembled in different patterns. Because of this, no special care was taken when picking the contrast columns to create the four levels of factors; hence, there will be some confounding of the effects (see Section 13.17). Obviously a practitioner would need to take more care when choosing a design matrix (see Box et al. 1978; Montgomery 1984) if he or she wishes to make an analysis that addresses these effect considerations.

From Table 22.7 it is noted that the system 3 planar board was changed during the experiment (denoted by a postscript $a$). Changes of this type

**TABLE 22.7. Example 22-3: Experiment Data**

| Temp. (°F) | Hum. (%) | Sys. (#) | Card A (#) | Card B (#) | Adapter (#) | 5 V (error types[a], voltages) | |
|---|---|---|---|---|---|---|---|
| | | | | | | Elevated voltage | Lowered voltage |
| 95 | 50 | 1 | 4 | 1** | 4 | E1 5.92 | E2 4.41 |
| 95 | 50 | 3* | 3 | 3 | 2 | sus 6.00 | E3 4.60 |
| 95 | 50 | 4 | 1 | 2 | 1 | sus 6.00 | E2 4.50 |
| 95 | 50 | 2 | 2 | 4 | 3 | sus 6.00 | E2 4.41 |
| 55 | 20 | 1 | 4 | 1** | 1 | sus 6.00 | E2 4.34 |
| 55 | 20 | 2 | 1 | 4 | 2 | sus 6.00 | E2 4.41 |
| 55 | 20 | 3a*** | 2 | 3 | 3 | sus 6.00 | E2 4.45 |
| 55 | 20 | 4 | 3 | 2 | 4 | sus 6.00 | E2 4.51 |
| 55 | 85 | 1 | 1 | 2 | 2 | sus 6.00 | E2 4.52 |
| 55 | 85 | 2 | 4 | 3 | 1 | sus 6.00 | E2 4.45 |
| 55 | 85 | 3* | 2 | 4 | 4 | sus 6.00 | E3 4.62 |
| 55 | 85 | 4 | 3 | 1** | 3 | E1 5.88 | E2 4.58 |
| 95 | 20 | 1 | 1 | 2 | 3 | sus 6.00 | E2 4.51 |
| 95 | 20 | 2 | 3 | 3 | 4 | sus 6.00 | E2 4.44 |
| 95 | 20 | 3a*** | 4 | 4 | 1 | sus 6.00 | E2 4.41 |
| 95 | 20 | 4 | 2 | 1** | 2 | E1 5.98 | E2 4.41 |

[a] sus = suspended test at noted voltage.

* lowering 5 V caused an E3 error.

** lowering 5 V caused a different error type (i.e., E1) three out of four times when card B = 1.

*** 3a = new system planar board installed.

EXAMPLE 22-3: SYSTEM STRESS TO FAIL TEST    **367**

should be avoided during test; however, if an unexpected event mandates a change, the change should be documented.

It is noted from Table 22.7 that the trials containing system 3 with the original system planar resulted in a different error message when the 5-V power supply was lowered to failure. It is also noted that the only "elevated voltage" failures occurred (three out of four times) when card B number 1 was installed. Generalities made from observations of this type must be made with extreme caution since aliasing and experimental measurement errors can lead to erroneous conclusions. Additional investigation beyond the original experiment needs to be performed for the purpose of either confirming or rejecting such theories.

Since the failures only occurred whenever the voltage was varied outside its limits, some people might conclude that there is "no problem." It is true that these observations and failure voltage levels may not be indicative of future production problems. However, the basic strategy behind this type of experiment is to assess the amount of "safety factor" before failure with a limited amount of hardware. A design that has a small margin of safety may experience problems in the future if the manufacturing process experiences any slight change. In addition, it is good general practice to make other appropriate evaluations on any cards and devices that have peculiar failures for the purpose of assessing whether there is a potential design problem.

A probability plot of the trial responses in Figure 22.8 gives some idea of the amount of safety factor that is prevalent in the design (note that this is

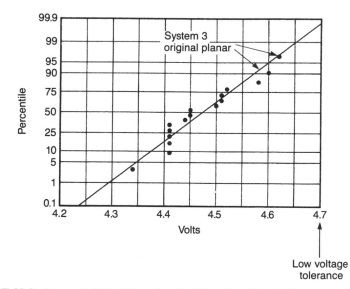

**FIGURE 22.8.** Example 22-3: Normal probability plot of the 5-V stress to fail responses (first design test).

not a probability plot of random data). From this plot a best estimate projection is that about 99.9% of the systems will perform at the low-voltage tolerance value of 4.7.

Consider next that another similar experiment is performed with a new level of hardware. The results from this experiment are shown in Table 22.8. From Table 22.8 it is noted that abnormalities from the previous test did not occur. A probability plot of the low-voltage stress values is again made and is shown in Figure 22.9.

One of the points in the Figure 22.9 probability plot could be an outlier. This data measurement should be investigated for abnormalities. Another observation from Figure 22.9 is that there is a larger percentage projection at the 4.7-V specification limit than from the earlier set of data (see Figure 22.8); hence, this later design appears to have a larger safety factor. Figure 22.10 gives a pictorial presentation of this comparison using the estimated normal PDFs functions from each set of data.

From Figure 22.10 it is noted that the average value of the density functions are approximately the same; however, there was a reduction in measurement variability in the later design level. This is "goodness"; however, if the situation were reversed and the newer design had greater variability, then there might be concern that things could degrade more in the future.

In manufacturing it is feasible that the preceding basic test strategy could be repeated periodically. Data could then be monitored on $\bar{x}$ and $R$ control charts for degradation/improvement as a function of time (see Section 19.3).

## 22.4. EXAMPLE 22-4: CREATING A TWO-LEVEL FRACTIONAL FACTORIAL EXPERIMENT STRATEGY FROM A "MANY-LEVEL" FULL FACTORIAL INITIAL PROPOSAL

As suggested in Section 13.5, factorial experiments should be at two-level considerations wherever possible. However, how to make the change from an experiment design of "many-level" considerations to two-level considerations is sometimes not very obvious. The purpose of this example is to illustrate a basic thought process that can be used when addressing this transition.

An experiment is proposed that considers an output as a function of the following factors with various level considerations.

| Factors | Number of Levels |
|---------|------------------|
| A | 4 |
| B | 3 |
| C | 2 |
| D | 2 |
| E | 2 |
| F | 2 |

**TABLE 22.8. Example 22-3: Experiment Data with New Hardware**

| Temp. (°F) | Hum. (%) | Sys. (#) | Card A (#) | Card B (#) | Adapter (#) | 5 V (error types[a], voltages) | |
| --- | --- | --- | --- | --- | --- | --- | --- |
| | | | | | | Elevated voltage | Lowered voltage |
| 95 | 20 | 1 | 4 | 1 | 1 | sus 6.00 | E2 4.48 |
| 95 | 20 | 2 | 1 | 4 | 2 | sus 6.00 | E2 4.48 |
| 95 | 20 | 3 | 2 | 3 | 3 | sus 6.00 | E2 4.45 |
| 95 | 20 | 4 | 3 | 2 | 4 | sus 6.00 | E2 4.42 |
| 55 | 85 | 1 | 1 | 2 | 2 | sus 6.00 | E2 4.56 |
| 55 | 85 | 2 | 4 | 3 | 1 | sus 6.00 | E2 4.46 |
| 55 | 85 | 3 | 2 | 4 | 4 | sus 6.00 | E2 4.45 |
| 55 | 85 | 4 | 3 | 1 | 3 | sus 6.00 | E2 4.43 |
| 55 | 20 | 1 | 1 | 2 | 3 | sus 6.00 | E2 4.45 |
| 55 | 20 | 2 | 3 | 3 | 4 | sus 6.00 | E2 4.46 |
| 55 | 20 | 3 | 4 | 4 | 1 | sus 6.00 | E2 4.42 |
| 55 | 20 | 4 | 2 | 1 | 2 | sus 6.00 | E2 4.48 |
| 95 | 50 | 1 | 4 | 1 | 4 | sus 6.00 | E2 4.45 |
| 95 | 50 | 3 | 2 | 4 | 3 | sus 6.00 | E2 4.49 |
| 95 | 50 | 4 | 3 | 3 | 2 | sus 6.00 | E2 4.45 |
| 95 | 50 | 2 | 1 | 2 | 1 | sus 6.00 | E2 4.49 |

[a]sus = suspended test at noted voltage.

369

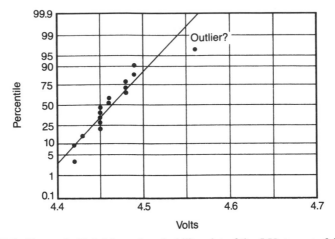

**FIGURE 22.9.** Example 22-3: Normal probability plot of the 5-V stress to fail responses (second design test).

where the $A$ factor may be temperature at four temperature levels and $B$ to $F$ may consider the effects from other process or design factor tolerances.

To use an experiment design that considers all possible combinations of the factors (i.e., a full factorial experiment), there would need to be 192 experiment trials ($4 \times 3 \times 2 \times 2 \times 2 \times 2 = 192$). In reality, this experiment would probably never be performed since the number of trials would make the experiment too expensive and time consuming to perform for most industrial situations.

Again, an experiment that considers all possible combinations of the factors typically contains more information than is needed for engineering decisions.

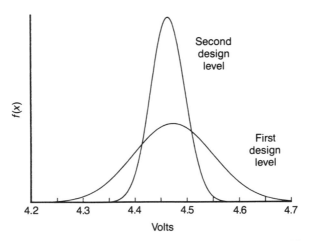

**FIGURE 22.10.** Example 22-3: Two PDF "sizings" that illustrate a difference between the first and second design.

EXAMPLE 22-5: RESOLUTION III EXPERIMENT    **371**

By changing all factors to two levels and reducing the amount of interaction output information, a design alternative can be determined by using Tables M1 to M5. This experiment could then be performed in 8, 16, or 32 trials depending on the desired experimental resolution.

The first of two basic arguments against restructuring this example is that the factor levels cannot be changed to two levels. In some cases a reduction to a two-level experiment is not possible; however, in many situations an experiment can be reduced to two-level considerations. For example, perhaps only two temperatures are initially assessed, and then if significance is found perhaps more investigation is appropriate for other temperature effects via another experiment. The specific temperature values to use in an experiment can be dependent on the test objectives. If the test is to determine whether a product is to have a satisfactory output within a temperature range, the levels of temperature may be the two tolerance extremes. However, if a test is to determine the sensitivity of a process to a temperature input, a smaller difference in temperature range may be appropriate. Even factors that appear impossible to change to a two-level consideration can often initially be made two levels with the understanding that if factor significance is found additional investigation of the other levels will be made via another experiment.

The second argument is the what-if doldrums. These questions can take numerous basic forms. Limiting assumptions should be listed and critiqued before performing experiments so appropriate modifications suggested by others can be incorporated into the initial experiment strategy (see Example 2-1).

If reasonable limiting assumptions are not made, a "test-all-combinations" strategy will probably prove to be "too large" and will not be done. A one-at-a-time test strategy can then occur, which is inefficient and may in the end require more test time than a fractional factorial experiment. In addition, a one-at-a-time strategy will, in general, have a higher risk of not yielding the desired information (see Example 4-5).

A strategy using a series of two-level experiments (with perhaps a screening experiment) is in general a more efficient basic test strategy, where in this strategy an experiment resolution is chosen such that two-factor interactions may be confounded but are managed. After the significant parameters are identified, a follow-up experiment is made at a resolution that better assesses main effects and the two-factor interactions of these factors.

## 22.5. EXAMPLE 22-5: FRACTIONAL FACTORIAL SCREENING (RESOLUTION III) EXPERIMENT WITH INTERACTION CONSIDERATION

An experimenter wants to assess the effects of 14 two-level factors $(A-N)$ on an output. Two of these factors are temperature and humidity. Each test trial is very expensive; hence, only a 16-trial resolution III screening experiment is planned. However, the experimenter is concerned that temperature and humidity may interact.

From Table M3 it is noted that for a 14-factor experiment, the 15th contrast column is not needed for any main effect consideration. This column could be used to estimate experimental error or the temperature–humidity interaction that is of concern. To make the temperature–humidity interaction term appear within this column, the factor assignments must be managed such that the temperature and humidity assignments are consistent with an interaction noted within this column. From Table N3 it is noted that there are several assignment alternatives (i.e., *AD*, *BH*, *GI*, *EJ*, *KL*, *FM*, and *CN*). For example, temperature could be assigned an *A* while humidity is assigned a *D*, or humidity could be assigned a *B* while temperature is assigned an *H*.

Note that the methodology in Example 13-2 could be extended to address more than one interaction consideration for both resolution III and IV designs, as long as the total number of two-level factors and interaction contrast column considerations does not exceed one less than the number of trials.

## 22.6. EXAMPLE 22-6: A DEVELOPMENT STRATEGY FOR A CHEMICAL PRODUCT

A chemist needs to develop a floor polish that is equal to or better than the competitions' floor polish in 20 areas of measurement (e.g., slip resistance, scuff resistance, visual gloss, and buffability).

Example 17-4 illustrated an extreme vertices design approach that used response surface design techniques to "optimize" the amount of mixture components of wax, resin, and polymer to create a quality floor polish. Consider from this experiment that the conclusion was that a good-quality floor finish would be obtained with the mixture proportions of wax (0.08–0.12) and resin (0.10–0.14), where polymer was the remaining proportion.

Consider now that this previous experiment was performed with only one source for each of the mixture components. Consider that there is now another source for the materials that claims higher quality with reduced costs. A fractional factorial test is now desired to compare the alternate sources for the mixture components.

It was believed that the range of mixture proportions previously determined needed consideration as factor level effects. The factors and levels were assigned as noted in the following for consideration in a 16-trial, resolution V design (see Section 13.14), where the amount of polymer used within a mixture trial would be the amount necessary to achieve a total proportion of 1.0 with the given proportions of resin and wax specified for each trial listed below.

From Table M3 the design matrix for five factors would be as shown in Table 22.9.

EXAMPLE 22-6: DEVELOPING A CHEMICAL PRODUCT    **373**

| Factors | Levels | |
|---|---|---|
| | (−) | (+) |
| A   Polymer brand | Original source | New source |
| B   Wax brand | Original source | New source |
| C   Wax proportion amount | 0.08 | 0.12 |
| D   Resin brand | New source | Original source |
| E   Resin proportion amount | 0.14 | 0.10 |

From Table M3 the design matrix for five factors would be as shown in Table 22.9. From this design two-factor interaction effects can be determined. After the 16 formulations are prepared, the test environment and trial responses could also be considered. Do we expect the response to vary as a function of the weather (temperature and humidity), application equipment, application techniques, and/or type of flooring? If so, we could chose a Taguchi strategy (see Section 16.4) of using these factors within an outer array. This inner/outer array test strategy would require more trials; however, it can help us avoid developing a product that works well in a laboratory environment but not well in a customer situation. Or, as an alternative to an inner/outer array strategy, these considerations can be managed as factors within the experiment design considerations.

Another concern that can be addressed is the relationship of our new product composition to that of the competition. To make a competitive

**TABLE 22.9. Example 22-6**
**Design Matrix for 16-Trial Test**

| Number of Trial | A B C D E |
|---|---|
| 1 | + − − − + |
| 2 | + + − − − |
| 3 | + + + − + |
| 4 | + + + + − |
| 5 | − + + + + |
| 6 | + − + + + |
| 7 | − + − + − |
| 8 | + − + − − |
| 9 | + + − + + |
| 10 | − + + − − |
| 11 | − − + + − |
| 12 | + − − + − |
| 13 | − + − − + |
| 14 | − − + − + |
| 15 | − − − + + |
| 16 | − − − − − |

assessment, competitive products could be evaluated in a similar "outer array" test environment during initial testing. From this information comparisons can be made during and after the final chemical composition is selected.

After the chemical composition is determined, stability is needed within the manufacturing process so that a quality product is produced on a continuing basis. An $X$ chart (see Section 19.5) is a tool that is useful to monitor key parameters within a batch chemical manufacturing process.

## 22.7. EXAMPLE 22-7: A PROCESS CAPABILITY STUDY

Management has given the mandate that process steps are to have process indices of $C_p \geq 2.0$ and $C_{pk} \geq 1.5$ (see Sections 21.1 and 19.15). Consider the five parts in Figure 22.11 that are to be manufactured and then assembled. The tolerances of the dimensions on the parts were believed achievable using conventional manufacturing practices.

For purposes of final measurements, should each dimension be considered a process step? Should equivalent effort be given to monitoring all the dimensions relative to the process indices? Should manufacturing steps also meet this criterion? After these questions are addressed, what procedure will then be followed to correct manufacturing processes if the parts are shown not to meet the process capability objective? Since quality cannot be measured into a product, would it be better to rephrase the initial question to address how the philosophy of Figure 21.4 can be used to better meet the needs of the customer? Let's consider the following discussion when addressing what is to be done.

Measurements from an in-control process over an extended period of time are needed to determine the precise process indices for a process step. Measurements that are considered should include other parameters besides just the final characteristics of the part (e.g., final part dimension considerations). Effort should be made to create a process that consistently produces products as close to the nominal specification as possible (not ones that just meet specification—see Section 16.2).

The cost to determine many capability indices in a process over time can become very expensive. Often it may be more important to monitor a key process parameter (e.g., a pressure that was prevalent in a manufacturing tool) than the final specification considerations of the manufactured part. This basic manufacturing philosophy can result in the detection of process degradation shifts before a large volume of "bad" parts is produced.

If the philosophy of striving for nominal considerations during development is stressed, the chance of meeting the desired process capability indices initially will be higher. For this example effort should be given to make tools and identify economical processes that manufacture the parts with precision

EXAMPLE 22-7: A PROCESS CAPABILITY STUDY    **375**

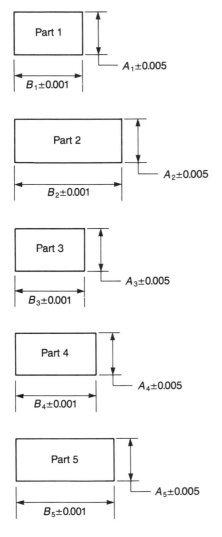

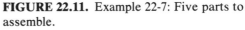

**FIGURE 22.11.** Example 22-7: Five parts to assemble.

and consistency along with the emphasis of continual process improvement in the areas that are important from the perspective of the customer.

Let's now get back to the initial question of concern. It may not be necessary, from a customer's point of view, to collect enough dimensions to calculate the process indices for all dimensions. Assume that the 0.005 tolerance (in inches) is easy to achieve consistently with the current process, if the manufacturing processes is initially shown via a tool sample to produce this dimension well within specification. For this dimension only periodic measurements may be needed over time.

However, the tolerance of the $B$ dimensions may require a special operation that is more difficult to achieve on a continuing basis. For the process that was chosen initially, assume that the $B$ dimensions are shown to be in control over time for all the $B$ value considerations. For the purpose of illustration consider also that the processes had a mean value equal to the nominal specification (i.e., $C_{pk} = C_p$); however, the $C_p$ values for these dimensions ranged from 1.0 to 1.33 for the five parts. A brainstorming session was then conducted since the $C_p$ values were less than the objective of 2.0. The consensus of opinion from this session was that a new, expensive process would be required to replace the existing process in order to achieve a higher $C_p$ value.

The question of concern is now whether this new process should be developed in order to reduce the $B$-dimensional variability. Before making this decision, the group considered first how these parts are used when they are assembled. The important dimension from a customer's perspective is the overall dimensional consideration of $B$, which after the assembly process is pictorially shown in Figure 22.12.

Consider that the manufactured $B$ dimensions conformed to a straight line when plotted on normal probability paper (i.e., the parts are distributed normally). In addition, the mean value for each part equaled the nominal specification value and a $3\sigma$ limit equaled the tolerance of 0.001 (i.e., $C_p = C_{pk} = 1.0$).

When these parts are assembled in series, a low dimension for $B_1$ can be combined with a high dimension for $B_2$, and so on; hence, it would not be reasonable to just add the tolerance considerations of the individual parts to get the overall tolerance consideration. Since the individual part dimensions are normally distributed, it is noted from Equation (7.5) that the overall assembled expected tolerance for $B$ would be

$$B \text{ tolerance } = \pm (0.001^2 + 0.001^2 + 0.001^2 + 0.001^2 + 0.001^2)^{1/2}$$

$$= \pm 0.00224$$

Since 0.00224 describes $3\sigma$, from Equation (19.24) we can see that

$$C_p = \frac{\text{USL} - \text{LSL}}{6\sigma} - = \frac{0.010}{2(0.00224)} = 2.23$$

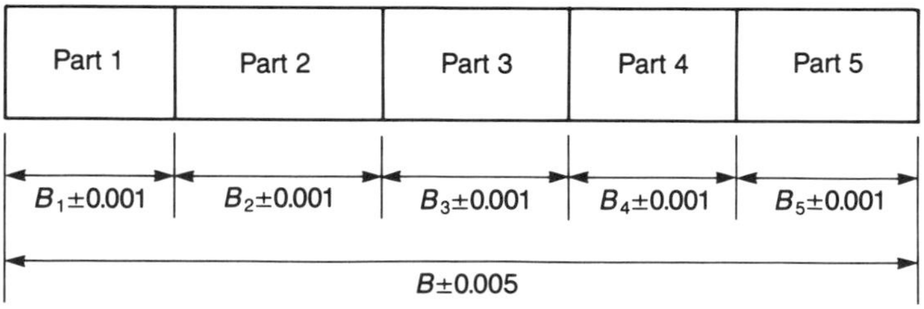

| Part 1 | Part 2 | Part 3 | Part 4 | Part 5 |
|--------|--------|--------|--------|--------|

$B_1 \pm 0.001$    $B_2 \pm 0.001$    $B_3 \pm 0.001$    $B_4 \pm 0.001$    $B_5 \pm 0.001$

$B \pm 0.005$

(where $B = B_1 + B_2 + B_3 + B_4 + B_5$)

**FIGURE 22.12.** Example 22-7: Five assembled parts.

EXAMPLE 22-7: A PROCESS CAPABILITY STUDY    **377**

Since the $C_p \geq 2.0$, this process index target is met on the overall dimension even though the individual measurements do not meet the target of 2.0.

The purpose of this example is to illustrate that care must be taken not to spend resources unwisely by striving for the tightening of tolerances that may not have much benefit to the customer. There are many ways to determine which parameters should be tracked (e.g., experience, history data, or the factorial approach discussed in Example 22-1). Efforts must also be directed toward continually improving processes in those areas that benefit the customer the most. Playing games with the numbers should be avoided.

# APPENDIX A

# EQUATIONS FOR THE DISTRIBUTIONS

This appendix contains equations associated with many of the distributions discussed in this text. In this text $t$ replaces $x$ when the independent variable considered is time. In the following equations $f(x)$ is used to describe the PDF, $F(x)$ is used to describe the CDF, and Pr is used to describe probability. The relationship of $F(x)$ and $\Pr(x)$ to $f(x)$ is

$$F(x) = \Pr(X \leq x) = \int_{-\infty}^{x} f(x)\, dx$$

where the capital letter $X$ denotes the distribution, which is also loosely called a random variable (Nelson 1982).

## A.1. NORMAL DISTRIBUTION

The normal PDF (see Figure 6.1) is

$$f(x) = \frac{1}{\sigma\sqrt{2\pi}} \exp\left[-\frac{(x-\mu)^2}{2\sigma^2}\right] \qquad -\infty \leq x \leq +\infty \qquad \text{(A.1)}$$

where $\mu$ = mean and $\sigma$ = standard deviation. The CDF (see Figure 6.2) is

$$F(x) = \int_{-\infty}^{x} \frac{1}{\sigma\sqrt{2\pi}} \exp\left[-\frac{(x-\mu)^2}{2\sigma^2}\right] dx \qquad \text{(A.2)}$$

## A.2.. BINOMIAL DISTRIBUTION

The probability of exactly $x$ defects in $n$ binomial trials with probability of defect equal to $p$ is (see Figure 6.4)

$$\Pr(X = x) = \binom{n}{x} p^x(1 - p)^{n-x} \qquad x = 0,1,2, \cdots, n \qquad (A.3)$$

where

$$\binom{n}{x} = \frac{n!}{x!(n - x)!} \qquad (A.4)$$

The mean ($\mu$) and standard deviation ($\sigma$) of the distribution are

$$\mu = np \qquad (A.5)$$

$$\sigma = \sqrt{np(1 - p)} \qquad (A.6)$$

The probability of observing $a$ or fewer defects (see Figure 6.5) is

$$\Pr(X \leq a) = \sum_{x=0}^{a} \Pr(X = x) \qquad (A.7)$$

## A.3. HYPERGEOMETRIC DISTRIBUTION

The probability of observing exactly $x$ defects when $n$ items are sampled without replacement from a population of $N$ items containing $D$ defects is given by the hypergeometric distribution [see Equation (A.4) format]

$$\Pr(X = x) = \frac{\binom{D}{x}\binom{N - D}{n - x}}{\binom{N}{n}} \qquad x = 0, 1, 2, \cdots, n \qquad (A.8)$$

The probability of observing $a$ or fewer defects is

$$\Pr(X \leq a) = \sum_{x=0}^{a} \Pr(X = x) \qquad (A.9)$$

## A.4. POISSON DISTRIBUTION

The probability of observing exactly $x$ events in the Poisson situation is given by the Poisson PDF (see Figure 6.6)

$$\Pr(X = x) = \frac{e^{-\lambda}\lambda^x}{x!} \qquad x = 0,1,2,3, \cdots \tag{A.10}$$

The mean and standard deviation are, respectively,

$$\mu = \lambda \tag{A.11}$$

$$\sigma = \sqrt{\lambda} \tag{A.12}$$

The probability of observing $a$ or fewer events (see Figure 6.7) is

$$\Pr(X \leq a) = \sum_{x=0}^{a} \Pr(X = x) \tag{A.13}$$

## A.5. EXPONENTIAL DISTRIBUTION

The PDF of the exponential distribution (see Figure 6.8) is

$$f(x) = (1/\theta)e^{-x/\theta} \tag{A.14}$$

The exponential distribution has only one parameter $(\theta)$, which is also the mean. The exponential CDF (see Figure 6.9) is

$$F(x) = \int_0^x (1/\theta)e^{-x/\theta} \, dx \tag{A.15}$$

$$= 1 - e^{-x/\theta} \tag{A.16}$$

For the exponential distribution substitution into the hazard rate Equation (6.5) ($t$ is replaced by an $x$) yields a constant hazard rate of

$$\lambda = \frac{f(x)}{1 - F(x)} = \frac{(1/\theta)e^{-x/\theta}}{1 - (1 - e^{-x/\theta})} = \frac{1}{\theta} \tag{A.17}$$

## A.6. WEIBULL DISTRIBUTION

The PDF of the three-parameter Weibull is

$$f(x) = \left[ \frac{b}{k - x_0} \left( \frac{x - x_0}{k - x_0} \right)^{b-1} \right] \left\{ \exp\left[ -\left( \frac{x - x_0}{k - x_0} \right)^b \right] \right\} \tag{A.18}$$

and the CDF is

$$F(x) = 1 - \exp\left[-\left(\frac{x - x_0}{k - x_0}\right)^b\right] \qquad (A.19)$$

The three-parameter Weibull distribution reduces to the two-parameter distribution when $x_0$ (i.e., location parameter) equals zero, as is commonly done in reliability analysis. The PDF of the two-parameter Weibull (see Figure 6.10) is

$$f(x) = \left[\frac{b}{k}\left(\frac{x}{k}\right)^{b-1}\right]\left\{\exp\left[-\left(\frac{x}{k}\right)^b\right]\right\} \qquad (A.20)$$

and the CDF (see Figure 6.11) is

$$F(x) = 1 - \exp\left[-\left(\frac{x}{k}\right)^b\right] \qquad (A.21)$$

For the two-parameter Weibull distribution the probability that a device will fail at the characteristic life $k$ or less is 0.632, as illustrated when making the following substitution:

$$F(k) = 1 - \exp\left[-\left(\frac{k}{k}\right)^b\right] = 1 - \frac{1}{e} = 0.632$$

Another way of stating this phenomenon is that the characteristic life ($k$) of a device is the usage probability plot coordinate value that corresponds to the percentage less than the value of 63.2%.

The characteristic life ($k$) in Equation (A.21) is also related to the median life ($B_{50}$) since the CDF at $B_{50} = 0.5$ is

$$F(B_{50}) = 0.50 = 1 - \exp\left[-\left(\frac{B_{50}}{k}\right)^b\right]$$

or

$$0.5 = \exp\left[-\left(\frac{B_{50}}{k}\right)^b\right]$$

which gives

$$\ln 2 = \left(\frac{B_{50}}{k}\right)^b$$

and finally

$$k = \frac{B_{50}}{(0.693)^{1/b}}$$

It can also be shown that the characteristic life $k$ relates to the Weibull mean ($T_d$) by the equation (Nelson 1982)

$$k = \frac{T_d}{\Gamma(1 + 1/b)} \tag{A.22}$$

where the gamma function value $\Gamma(1 + 1/b)$ is determined from Table H.

Equation (6.5) (with $t$ replaced by $x$) shows that the hazard rate of the two-parameter Weibull distribution is

$$\lambda = \frac{f(x)}{1 - F(x)} = \frac{b}{k^b}(x)^{b-1} \tag{A.23}$$

When the shape parameter $b$ equals 1 this reduces to a constant failure rate $\lambda = 1/k$. Since the Weibull with $b = 1$ is an exponential distribution, we can use the relationship in Equation (A.17) to show that $\lambda = 1/k = 1/\theta$ for the exponential distribution. From Equation (A.23) the values of $b$ less than 1 are noted to have a hazard rate that decreases with $x$ (early-life failures), while $b$ values greater than 1 have a hazard rate that increases with $x$ (wear-out failures). The classical reliability bathtub curve illustrated in Figure 6.17 describes this characteristic.

# APPENDIX B

# HISTOGRAM CREATION, PROBABILITY PLOTTING, AND LACK OF FIT

This appendix extends the discussion found earlier on histogram and probability plotting (see Sections 4.2 and 5.4, respectively). Included is a discussion on the details of manual histogram plotting. The theoretical concept of probability plotting is also discussed along with alternative probability plotting positions to that of Equation (5.1).

Probability plots can be determined either manually or by using a computer package. Relative to each of these approaches, this appendix also discusses how to determine the best-fit probability line and how to determine if this line (i.e., the estimated PDF) adequately represents the data.

## B.1. CREATING HISTOGRAMS MANUALLY

As noted in Section 4.2, when making a histogram of response data that is not continuous, the data needs first to be placed into groups (i.e., cells). Many computer programs internally handle this grouping; however, a practitioner may have to manually create this grouping if no program is available.

For manual data plotting it should be noted that the group size is an important detail to give meaningful results to the plot. King (1981) suggests grouping data according to the Sturges's rule (Freund 1960). This rule gives a method of determining the number of groups, cells, to use when tallying the results for a graphical summary. Using this rule, the "optimum" number of cells for sample size $N$ is first calculated to be

$$\text{Number of cells} = 1 + 3.3 \log N \tag{B.1}$$

From the range of data the number of measurement units to be assigned each cell is then determined to be

$$\text{Number of units per cell} = \frac{\text{range in units}}{\text{number of cells}} \qquad \text{(B.2)}$$

Example B-1 illustrates the application of these equations.

## B.2. EXAMPLE B-1: HISTOGRAM PLOT

From Example 4-1 a sample yielded the following 24 ranked (low to high value) data points:

> 2.2 2.6 3.0 4.3 4.7 5.2 5.2 5.3 5.4 5.7 5.8 5.8 5.9 6.3 6.7
> 7.1 7.3 7.6 7.6 7.8 7.9 9.3 10.0 10.1

To create a histogram, Equation (B.1) yields a starting point for grouping of

$$\text{Number of cells} = 1 + 3.3 \log N = 1 + 3.3 \log (24) = 5.55$$

Hence, for a sample of 24, the number of cells falls between 5 and 6. The range of data is 7.9 ($10.1 - 2.2 = 7.9$). With a basic unit size of 0.1, this range is 79 units. Equation (B.2) then yields

Using 5 cells:

$$\text{Number of units} = \frac{79}{5} = 15.8 \quad \text{(16 rounded off)}$$

Using 6 cells:

$$\text{Number of units} = \frac{79}{6} = 13.2 \quad \text{(13 rounded off)}$$

Either number of units is acceptable. The number of cells after this rounding off calculates to be

Using 16 units:

$$\text{Number of cells} = \frac{79}{16} = 4^+$$

Using 13 units:

$$\text{Number of cells} = \frac{79}{13} = 6^+$$

Consider now positioning the cell boundaries by balancing the end points. The number of units required to display the range is 80 units (i.e., 79 + 1). If we choose 13 units per cell, then 7 cells would take 91 units (i.e., 7 × 13 = 91). There would be 11 units (i.e., 91 − 80 = 11) that need to be split between the two end points. Five or 6 units could then be subtracted from the lowest value to begin the increment sequencing. If we subtracted 6 units from the lowest point to get the first minimum cell value (i.e., 2.2 − 0.6 = 1.6), the increments would then be

Minimum cell values = 1.6, 2.9, 4.2, 5.5, 6.8, 8.1, 9.4

Since the cell size is 1.3 (i.e., 13 units per cell with a basic unit size of 0.1), it then follows from these values that

Maximum cell values = 2.9, 4.2, 5.5, 6.8, 8.1, 9.4, 10.7

A histogram of this data is shown in Figure 4.2. Even with the rigorous procedure used within this example, the practitioner should note that another increment could yield a better histogram pictorial representation of the data. This procedure should perhaps be considered when determining a "starting point" before doing a more traditional "select and view" procedure.

## B.3. THEORETICAL CONCEPT OF PROBABILITY PLOTTING

Consider the Weibull CDF Equation (6.3):

$$F(x) = 1 - \exp\left[-(x/k)^b\right] \tag{B.3}$$

The rearrangement and transformation of this equation yields

$$\frac{1}{1 - F(x)} = \exp\left(\frac{x}{k}\right)^b$$

$$\ln\left(\frac{1}{1 - F(x)}\right) = \left(\frac{x}{k}\right)^b$$

$$\ln\ln\left(\frac{1}{1 - F(x)}\right) = b \ln x - b \ln k \tag{B.4}$$

Equation (B.4) is in the form of a straight line $[Y = mX + c]$ where

$$Y = \ln \ln \frac{1}{1 - F(x)} \tag{B.5}$$

$$m = b \tag{B.6}$$

$$X = \ln x \tag{B.7}$$

$$c = -b \ln k \tag{B.8}$$

Weibull probability paper has incorporated the $X$ and $Y$ transformations noted in Equations (B.7) and (B.5). Hence, data plotted on Weibull probability paper that follow a straight line can be assumed to be from a unimodal Weibull density function.

The unknown parameters for the population ($k$ and $b$ for the Weibull distribution) can also be estimated from the plot. Since the $X$ axis in Equation (B.4) has the transform of Equation (B.7), Equation (B.6) indicates that the slope of the curve yields an estimate for $b$ (Weibull shape parameter). Given the $Y$ axis intercept ($c$) and shape parameter ($b$), Equation (B.8) can yield the other unknown parameter $k$ (characteristic life) for Equation (B.3).

Similar transformations are made to create the scale for the probability axes for other functions such as the normal and log-normal distributions.

## B.4. PLOTTING POSITIONS

An equation to determine the "midpoint" plotting position on probability paper for an $i$th-ranked datum point is noted in Equation (5.1) to be

$$F_i = \frac{100(i - 0.5)}{n} \qquad i = 1, 2, \cdots, n \tag{B.9}$$

Nelson (1982) describes the motivation for using the equation; however, he also notes that different plotting positions have been zealously advanced. Some of these alternative plotting positions are as follows.

The "mean" plotting position is a popular alternative, which is

$$F_i = \frac{100i}{n + 1} \qquad i = 1, 2, \cdots, n \tag{B.10}$$

King (1971) suggests using the equation noted by Cunnane (1978):

$$F_i = \frac{100(i - a)}{n + 1 - 2a} \qquad i = 1, 2, \cdots, n \tag{B.11}$$

where $a$ is a distribution-related constant with values of

0.375 for the normal and logarithmic normal distributions
0.44 for the type I extreme value distributions
0.5 for types II and III (Weibull) extreme value distributions
0.4 as a compromise for other nonnormal distributions

Johnson (1964) advocates and tabulates median plotting positions that are well approximated by

$$F_i \approx \frac{100(i - 0.3)}{n + 0.4} \qquad i = 1, 2, \cdots, n \qquad (B.12)$$

Nelson (1982) states that plotting positions differ little compared with the randomness of the data. For convenience, I chose to use and tabulate (i.e., Table P) the plotting positions determined from Equation (B.9), which is consistent with Nelson. However, a reader may choose to use another set of plotting positions and still apply the concepts described in this text.

## B.5. MANUAL ESTIMATION OF A BEST-FIT PROBABILITY PLOT LINE*

There are inconsistencies when determining the best-fit line when manually plotting data. To get consist results for a given set of data, King (1981) promotes the following technique.

Ferrell (1958) proposed the use of a "median regression line" to be fitted to a set of data points plotted on probability paper in order to characterize the data in a manner that allows subsequent estimation of the distribution parameters directly from the probability plot. The Ferrell best-fit line divides the data plot into two halves in which half of the data points are above the fitted line and half are below the line, which is a classical definition of a median. It is obtained as follows:

**1.** Divide the data set into two parts to obtain a "lower half" and an "upper half," as indicated in Figure B.1. If the number of points is even, then each half is unique and distinct such that no overlap occurs. When the number of points is odd, the middle point is plotted on the 50% vertical line and it is not clear to which half the odd point belongs. There are two choices: (a) Ignore the odd point or (b) treat the odd point as though it belongs to each half until a preference can be determined. We recommend choice (b).

**2.** Place a sharp pencil on the lowest point of the plot, as shown in Figure B.1. Then, place a transparent straightedge against the pencil point and rotate

* Reproduced from King (1981) with permission of author.

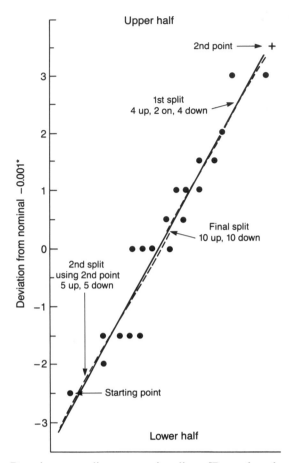

**FIGURE B.1.** Drawing a median regression line. [Reproduced with permission: James R. King, *Probability Charts for Decision Making*, Technical Aids for Management (TEAM), Tamworth, NH, 1981.]

the straightedge until the upper half of the data points are subdivided into two equal parts. This is accomplished simply by counting until 50% of the upper points are above the edge of the straightedge.

**3.** Mark a second reference point on the graph somewhere beyond the highest plotted point. Transfer the pencil to this point and, again, rotating the straightedge against the pencil, divide the lower half of the data points into two equal halves.

**4.** Make another reference point toward the lower left corner of the plot and repeat steps 2 and 3 until both the upper and lower halves of the data points are equally divided by the same position of the straightedge. Using this final split, draw in the best-fit line.

Lack of fit of the line to the data can be then be assessed by the following technique (King 1981): After a Ferrell median regression line is obtained, the fit of this line is checked by two simple tests. The first test is to check the accuracy with which the lower and upper halves of the data set were divided by counting the number of points above the median regression line and the number of points below it. The difference in the number of points on either side of the line should not exceed $|2|$, otherwise the line should be redrawn.

If the count difference is satisfactory, the second test is to count the number of runs above and below the line. A "run" is any group of consecutive points on the same side of the line. Any point which lies on the fitted line counts as the end of a run. After the number of runs is determined, refer to Table B.1, which was adapted from Dixon (1957). This table gives the approximate 95% confidence limits for the number of runs to be expected from different sample sizes assuming that only random sampling variation occurs in the sample. Limits for sample sizes not given may be approximated by simple linear interpolation.

When the number of runs above and below the fitted line are too few, there is good evidence that the data are not homogeneous, that is, that they did not come from a stable or consistent process when it is known that the data are plotted on an appropriate probability paper. Such knowledge usually comes from prior experience or from technical considerations. If one is not sure that the appropriate probability paper is being used, a simple test of the data is to place a straightedge across the lowest and highest points on the plot. If all remaining data points fall on either side of the straightedge, then it is likely that the wrong probability paper has been used. When this occurs, also place the straightedge across the second lowest and the second highest points. If all the remaining points are still on the same side of the straightedge, then it is highly likely that the wrong paper was used.

On a second check, if some points now fall on either side of the straightedge, there may be a problem due to the incomplete data caused by such activities as inspection, sorting, and/or test used to remove certain portions of the

**TABLE B.1. Approximate 95% Confidence Limits for the Number of Runs Above and Below the Median Regression Line**

| Sample Size | Limits | Sample Size | Limits | Sample Size | Limits |
|---|---|---|---|---|---|
| 20 | 7–14 | 50 | 18–33 | 120 | 49–72 |
| 25 | 7–19 | 60 | 22–39 | 160 | 68–93 |
| 30 | 10–21 | 70 | 27–40 | 180 | 77–104 |
| 35 | 11–25 | 80 | 31–50 | 200 | 85–115 |
| 40 | 14–27 | 90 | 36–55 | | |
| 45 | 16–30 | 100 | 40–59 | | |

Reproduced with permission from King (1981).

original or intrinsic population for special uses or for failure to conform to a governing specification.

Finally, if there are too many runs above and below the line, then there is evidence that the sample was not randomly selected and that the sampling procedures should be reviewed to prevent similar results in the future.

## B.6. COMPUTER-GENERATED PLOTS AND LACK OF FIT

As part of a computer-generated plot, a best-fit line can be determined by using approaches that can be computationally intensive (e.g., maximum likelihood). In these programs lack-of-fit calculations of the line fit to the data may be available on the program package. The program could use statistical tests such as chi-square goodness of fit (Duncan 1986; Tobias 1986), Kolmogorov–Smirnov (KS) [Massey 1951; Jenson 1982—constant hazard rate test], Cramer–Von Misses (Crow 1974), and Shapiro–Wilk (Shapiro and Wilk 1965). More information is contained in D'Agostino and Stephens (1986).

When determining if a model is adequate using these techniques, the data are assumed to fit the model until proven otherwise by a lack-of-fit significance test. Risks when making a "nonfit" statement have type I error (e.g., $\alpha$ risk at a level of 0.05).

Another approach is to examine the $r^2$ (correlation coefficient squared) value of the best-fit line on a probability plot. If this value were 0.9, then 90% of the variability is explained by the model (Kroehling 1990).

If the distribution test is for data normality, a "skewness' calculation can be made to measure the "sidedness" of the distribution, while a kurtosis calculation can be used to measure heaviness of tails (Duncan 1986; Ramsey and Ramsey 1990).

Much discussion has been made over the years about lack-of-fit tests. Each test has benefits under certain situations; however, there is no one universal "best test." In addition, some tests can require more than 30 to 50 data points to be "valid" and can be quite conservative.

# APPENDIX C

# FRACTIONAL FACTORIAL AND RESPONSE SURFACE ANALYSES

This appendix contains a more detailed description of some of the SAS output listing formats shown earlier in this text. Included is also a listing of the SAS programs written to solve problems discussed earlier in this text. One derivation is also included along with discussion about sample size and the mechanics of both computer and manual analysis techniques.

## C.1. COMPUTER OUTPUT DESCRIPTION: ANALYSIS OF VARIANCE

Table C.1 exemplifies SAS's PROC ANOVA output. Descriptions for each of the outputs are noted.

**TABLE C.1. SAS Analysis of Variance Output Example**

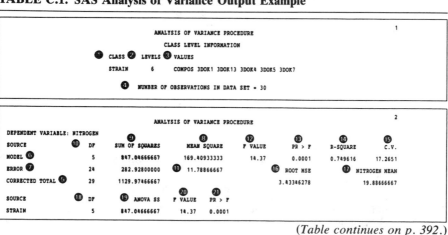

*(Table continues on p. 392.)*

**TABLE C.1.** (*Continued*)

ANOVA first prints a table that includes:

1. the name of each variable in the CLASS statement
2. the number of different values or LEVELS of the CLASS variables
3. the VALUES of the CLASS variables
4. the number of observations in the data set and the number of observations excluded from the analysis because of missing values, if any.

ANOVA then prints an analysis-of-variance table for each dependent variable in the MODEL statement. This table breaks down:

5. the CORRECTED TOTAL sum of squares for the dependent variable
6. into the portion attributed to the MODEL
7. and the portion attributed to ERROR.
8. the MEAN SQUARE term is the
9. SUM OF SQUARES divided by the
10. DEGREES OF FREEDOM (DF).
11. the MEAN SQUARE for ERROR is an example of $\sigma^2$, the variance of the true errors.
12. the F VALUE is the ratio produced by dividing MS(MODEL), the mean square for the model, by the MS(ERROR), the mean square for error. It tests how well the model as a whole (adjusted for the mean) accounts for the dependent variable's behavior. This $F$ test is a test that all parameters except the intercept are zero.
13. the significance probability associated with the $F$ statistic, labeled PR>F.
14. R-SQUARE, $R^2$, measures how much variation in the dependent variable can be accounted for by the model. $R^2$, which can range from 0 to 1, is the ratio of the sum of squares for the model divided by the sum of squares for the corrected total. In general, the larger the $R^2$ value, the better the model fits the data.
15. C.V., the coefficient of variation, is often used to describe the amount of variation in the population. The C.V. is 100 times the standard deviation of the dependent variable, STD DEV, divided by the MEAN. The coefficient of variation is often a preferred measure because it is unitless.
16. ROOT MSE estimates the standard deviation of the dependent variable and is computed as the square root of MS(ERROR), the mean square of the error term.
17. the MEAN of the dependent variable.

For each effect (or source of variation) in the model, ANOVA then prints:

18. DF, degrees of freedom
19. ANOVA SS, the sum of squares
20. the F VALUE for testing the hypothesis that the group means for that effect are equal
21. PR>F, the significance probability value associated with the F VALUE.

Reproduced with permission: SAS Institute Inc., *SAS User's Guide: Statistics, Version 5 Edition*, Cary, NC: SAS Institute Inc., 1985, pp. 125–127.

## C.2. COMPUTER OUTPUT DESCRIPTION: GENERAL LINEAR MODEL

Table C.2 exemplifies SAS's PROC GLM output. Descriptions for each of the outputs are noted.

**TABLE C.2. SAS General Linear Model Output Example**

```
                                                                            2
                          GENERAL LINEAR MODELS PROCEDURE

DEPENDENT VARIABLE: STEMLENG
                             ⑥
SOURCE              DF      ⑤                ④              ⑧         ⑨         ⑩           ⑪
                         SUM OF SQUARES   MEAN SQUARE    F VALUE   PR > F    R-SQUARE      C.V.

MODEL                8   ② 142.18857143    17.77357143    10.80     0.0002   0.878079     3.9397

ERROR               12  ③  19.74285714   ⑦ 1.64523810              ⑰ ROOT MSE          STEMLENG MEAN ⑬

CORRECTED TOTAL     20  ① 161.93142857                              1.28266835          32.55714286

                             ⑭                                        ⑮          ⑯
SOURCE              DF      TYPE I SS    F VALUE   PR > F   DF    TYPE III SS   F VALUE   PR > F

TYPE                 6    103.15142857    10.45    0.0004    6    103.15142857   10.45    0.0004
BLOCK                2     39.03714286    11.86    0.0014    2     39.03714286   11.86    0.0014
```

```
                          NUMBER OF OBSERVATIONS IN DATA SET = 21

                          GENERAL LINEAR MODELS PROCEDURE

DEPENDENT VARIABLE: STEMLENG

SOURCE              DF      SUM OF SQUARES   MEAN SQUARE    F VALUE   PR > F    R-SQUARE      C.V.

MODEL                8      142.18857143    17.77357143    10.80     0.0002   0.878079     3.9397

ERROR               12       19.74285714     1.64523810              ROOT MSE           STEMLENG MEAN

CORRECTED TOTAL     20      161.93142857                             1.28266835          32.55714286


SOURCE              DF      TYPE I SS    F VALUE   PR > F   DF    TYPE III SS   F VALUE   PR > F

TYPE                 6    103.15142857    10.45    0.0004    6    103.15142857   10.45    0.0004
BLOCK                2     39.03714286    11.86    0.0014    2     39.03714286   11.86    0.0014


CONTRAST            DF          SS       F VALUE   PR > F

COMPOST VS OTHERS    1      29.24198413    17.77    0.0012
RIVER SOILS VS.NON   2      48.26944444    14.66    0.0006
GLACIAL VS DRIFT     1      22.14083333    13.46    0.0032
CLARION VS WEBSTER   1       1.70666667     1.04    0.3285
KNOX VS ONEILL       1       1.81500000     1.10    0.3143

                                       ⑱            ⑲            ⑳
                                     T FOR HO:     PR > |T|    STD ERROR OF
PARAMETER     ⑰         ESTIMATE    PARAMETER=0                 ESTIMATE

INTERCEPT              29.35714286 B    34.96       0.0001     0.83970354
TYPE    CLARION         1.06666667 B     1.02       0.3285     1.04729432
        CLINTON        -0.80000000 B    -0.76       0.4597     1.04729432
        KNOX            3.80000000 B     3.63       0.0035     1.04729432
        O'NEILL         2.70000000 B     2.58       0.0242     1.04729432
        COMPOST        -1.43333333 B    -1.37       0.1962     1.04729432
        WABASH          4.86666667 B     4.65       0.0006     1.04729432
        WEBSTER         0.00000000 B      .           .            .
BLOCK   1               3.32857143 B     4.85       0.0004     0.68561507
        2               1.90000000 B     2.77       0.0169     0.68561507
        3               0.00000000 B      .           .            .

NOTE: THE X'X MATRIX HAS BEEN DEEMED SINGULAR AND A GENERALIZED INVERSE HAS BEEN EMPLOYED TO SOLVE THE NORMAL EQUATIONS.
      THE ABOVE ESTIMATES REPRESENT ONLY ONE OF MANY POSSIBLE SOLUTIONS TO THE NORMAL EQUATIONS. ESTIMATES FOLLOWED BY
      THE LETTER B ARE BIASED AND DO NOT ESTIMATE THE PARAMETER BUT ARE BLUE FOR SOME LINEAR COMBINATION OF PARAMETERS
      (OR ARE ZERO). THE EXPECTED VALUE OF THE BIASED ESTIMATORS MAY BE OBTAINED FROM THE GENERAL FORM OF ESTIMABLE
      FUNCTIONS. FOR THE BIASED ESTIMATORS, THE STD ERR IS THAT OF THE BIASED ESTIMATOR AND THE T VALUE TESTS
      HO: E(BIASED ESTIMATOR) = 0. ESTIMATES NOT FOLLOWED BY THE LETTER B ARE BLUE FOR THE PARAMETER.
```

The GLM procedure produces the following printed output by default:

1. The overall analysis-of-variance table breaks down the CORRECTED TOTAL sum of squares for the dependent variable
2. into the portion attributed to the MODEL
3. and the portion attributed to ERROR.
4. The MEAN SQUARE term is the
5. SUM OF SQUARES divided by the
6. DEGREES OF FREEDOM (DF).

(*Table continues on p. 394.*)

**TABLE C.2.** (*Continued*)

7. The MEAN SQUARE for ERROR, (MS(ERROR)), is an estimate of $\sigma^2$, the variance of the true errors.

8. The F VALUE is the ratio produced by dividing MS(MODEL) by MS(ERROR). It tests how well the model as a whole (adjusted for the mean) accounts for the dependent variable's behavior. An $F$ test is a joint test that all parameters except the intercept are zero.

9. A small significance probability, PR>F, indicates that some linear function of the parameters is significantly different from zero.

10. R-SQUARE, $R^2$, measures how much variation in the dependent variable can be accounted for by the model. $R^2$, which can range from 0 to 1, is the ratio of the sum of squares for the model divided by the sum of squares for the corrected total. In general, the larger the value of $R^2$, the better the model's fit.

11. C.V., the coefficient of variation, which describes the amount of variation in the population, is 100 times the standard deviation estimate of the dependent variable, ROOT MSE, divided by the MEAN. The coefficient of variation is often a preferred measure because it is unitless.

12. ROOT MSE estimates the standard deviation of the dependent variable (or equivalently, the error term) and equals the square root of MS(ERROR).

13. MEAN is the sample mean of the dependent variable.

These tests are used primarily in analysis-of-variance applications:

14. The TYPE I SS measures incremental sums of squares for the model as each variable is added.

15. The TYPE III SS is the sum of squares that results when that variable is added last to the model.

16. The F VALUE and PR>F values for TYPE III tests in this section of the output.

17. This section of the output gives the ESTIMATES for the model PARAMETERs—the intercept and the coefficients.

18. T FOR $H_0$: PARAMETER = 0 is the Student's $t$ value for testing the null hypothesis that the parameter (if it is estimable) equals zero.

19. The significance level, PR>|T|, is the probability of getting a larger value of $t$ if the parameter is truly equal to zero. A very small value for this probability leads to the conclusion that the independent variable contributes significantly to the model.

20. The STD ERROR OF ESTIMATE is the standard error of the estimate of the true value of the parameter.

## C.3. COMPUTER OUTPUT DESCRIPTION: RESPONSE SURFACE REGRESSION

Table C.3 exemplifies SAS's PROC RSREG output. Descriptions for each of the outputs are noted.

**TABLE C.3. SAS Response Surface Regression Output Example**

```
                                                                                         1
RESPONSE SURFACE FOR VARIABLE Y

      ①  RESPONSE MEAN              15.2
      ②  ROOT MSE              22.47851
      ③  R-SQUARE             0.8819895
      ④  COEF OF VARIATION    1.478849


      ⑤  REGRESSION     ⑥ DF  ⑦ TYPE I SS   ⑧ R-SQUARE ⑨ F-RATIO ⑩ PROB

          LINEAR           3   7143.25000      0.3337    4.71  0.0641
          QUADRATIC        3  11445.23333      0.5346    7.55  0.0264
          CROSSPRODUCT     3    293.50000      0.0137    0.19  0.8965
          TOTAL REGRESS    9  18881.98333      0.8820    4.15  0.0657

          RESIDUAL        DF           SS  MEAN SQUARE  F-RATIO    PROB

          LACK OF FIT      3   2485.75000    828.58333   40.750  0.0240
          PURE ERROR       2  40.66666667  20.33333333
      ⑪  TOTAL ERROR      5   2526.41667    505.28333  ⑫

                                    ⑭            ⑮          ⑯        ⑰
          PARAMETER       DF     ESTIMATE      STD DEV  T-RATIO    PROB

          INTERCEPT        1  -30.66666667  12.97797279    -2.36  0.0645
          X1               1  -12.12500000   7.94735281    -1.53  0.1876
          X2               1  -17.00000000   7.94735281    -2.14  0.0854
          X3               1  -21.37500000   7.94735281    -2.69  0.0433
          X1*X1            1   32.08333333  11.69818659     2.74  0.0407
          X2*X1            1    8.25000000  11.23925413     0.73  0.4959
          X2*X2            1   47.83333333  11.69818659     4.09  0.0095
          X3*X1            1    1.50000000  11.23925413     0.13  0.8990
          X3*X2            1   -1.75000000  11.23925413    -0.16  0.8824
          X3*X3            1    6.08333333  11.69818659     0.52  0.6252

          FACTOR          DF           SS  MEAN SQUARE  F-RATIO    PROB    ⑲

          X1               4     5258.016     1314.504     2.60  0.1613 TEMPERATURE
          X2               4      11044.6     2761.151     5.46  0.0454 GAS-LIQUID RATIO
      ⑱  X3               4     3813.016      953.254     1.89  0.2510 PACKING HEIGHT
```

```
                                                                                         2
SOLUTION FOR OPTIMUM RESPONSE

        FACTOR CRITICAL VALUE

        X1        0.12191255
        X2        0.19957464
        X3        1.77052494

PREDICTED VALUE AT OPTIMUM    -52.0246


EIGENVALUES    EIGENVECTORS
                        X1           X2           X3
  48.85881      0.2380908    0.9711161   -0.0156903
  31.10346      0.9706958   -0.237384    0.03739919
  6.037732     -0.0325943    0.02413488   0.9991772

SOLUTION WAS A MINIMUM
```

**Printed Output**

All estimates and hypothesis tests depend on the correctness of the model and the error distributed according to classical statistical assumptions.

The individual items in the output from RSREG are

1. RESPONSE MEAN is the mean of the response variable in the sample.
2. ROOT MSE estimates the standard deviation of the response variable by the square root of the TOTAL ERROR mean square.
3. R-SQUARE is $R^2$, or the coefficient of determination. $R^2$ measures the portion of the variation in the response that is attributed to the model rather than to random error.

(*Table continues on p. 396.*)

**TABLE C.3.** (*Continued*)

4. COEF OF VARIATION is the coefficient of variation, which is equal to 100*rootmse/mean for the response variable.
5. Terms are brought into the regression in four steps: (1) INTERCEPT and COVARIATES (not shown), (2) LINEAR terms like X1 AND X2, (3) QUADRATIC terms like X1*X1 or X2*X2, and (4) CROSSPRODUCT terms like X1*X2.
6. DF indicates degree of freedom and should be the same as the number of parameters unless one or more of the parameters are not estimable.
7. TYPE I SS, also called the sequential sums of squares, measure the reduction in the error sum of squares as terms are added to the model individually (LINEAR, QUADRATIC, and so forth).
8. These R-SQUAREs measure the portion of total $R^2$ contributed as each set of terms (LINEAR, QUADRATIC, and so forth) is added to the model.
9. Each F-RATIO tests the hypothesis that all parameters in the term are zero using the TOTAL ERROR mean square as the denominator. This item is a test of a TYPE I hypothesis, containing the usual F test numerator, conditional on the effects of subsequent variables not being in the model.
10. PROB is the significance value or probability of obtaining at least as great an F ratio given that the hypothesis is true. When PROB<.05, the effect is usually termed significant.
11. The TOTAL ERROR sum of squares can be partitioned into LACK OF FIT and PURE ERROR. When LACK OF FIT is significantly different from PURE ERROR, then there is variation in the model not accounted for by random error.
12. The TOTAL ERROR MEAN SQUARE estimates $\sigma^2$, the variance.
13. If an effect is a linear combination of previous effects, the parameter for it is not estimable. When this happens, the DF is zero, the parameter estimate is set to zero, and the estimates and tests on other parameters are conditional on this parameter being zero (not shown).
14. The ESTIMATE column contains the parameter estimates.
15. The STD DEV column contains the estimated standard deviations of the parameter estimates.
16. The T-RATIO column contains *t* values of a test of the hypothesis that the true parameter is zero.
17. PROB gives the significance value or probability of a greater absolute *t* ratio given that the hypothesis is true.
18. The test on a factor, say X1, is a joint test on all the parameters involving that factor. For example, the test for X1 tests the hypothesis that the parameters for X1, X1*X1, and X1*X2 are all zero.
19. The CRITICAL VALUEs for the factor variables are solved to find the factor combinations that yield the optimum response. The critical values can be at a minimum, maximum, or saddle point.
20. The EIGENVALUES and EIGENVECTORS are from the matrix of quadratic parameter estimates that determine the curvature of the response surface.

## C.4. SAMPLE SIZE: FRACTIONAL FACTORIAL EXPERIMENT WITH A CONTINUOUS RESPONSE OUTPUT—MATHEMATICAL CONSIDERATIONS

Section 13.18 discussed a simplified approach to determining a sample size for a fractional factorial experiment that has a continuous response. This section addresses a more rigorous strategy to calculate sample size.

Sample size is a common question encountered when designing a fractional factorial experiment. Unfortunately there is no general agreed-upon approach to address the question. Even though there is no procedure to determine the "right" sample size for a given situation, the question is still a real issue for the practitioner. The following methodology and discussion is based on an approach discussed in Diamond (1989).

Chapters 14 and 15 illustrate approaches to test for factor significance where there is an estimate for error. The following was noted in Section 13.4 relative to the meaning of factor significance statements. If a factor is significant, the statement is made at an $\alpha$ risk of being wrong (i.e., the null hypothesis is rejected). However, the inverse is not true about factors not found to be significant. In other words there is *not* an $\alpha$ risk of being wrong when these factors are *not* significant. The reason for this is that the second statement relates to a $\beta$ risk (i.e., acceptance of the null hypothesis, which is a function of the sample size and $\delta$) (see Section 4.5).

To make a statement relative to the risk of being in error when it is stated that there is no significant difference (between the levels of factors), consider $e$, which is defined as the ratio of an acceptable amount of uncertainty to the standard deviation.

$$e = \delta/\sigma \tag{C.1}$$

where $\delta$ is an amount that may be of importance in making $\beta$ risk statements and $\sigma$ is the standard deviation of error $(s_e)$. If the parameter $(e)$ is "too large," then additional trials should be considered for the experiment design.

Diamond (1989) multiplies Equation (7.2) by 2 to determine a total number of trials to use in a two-level fractional factorial experiment at each level. Substitution of Equation (C.1) with this equation yields:

$$n = 2(t_\alpha + t_\beta)^2 \frac{\sigma^2}{\delta^2} = 2(t_\alpha + t_\beta)^2 \frac{\sigma^2}{(e\sigma)^2} \tag{C.2}$$

Solving for $e$ yields

$$e = \frac{[2(t_\alpha + t_\beta)^2]^{1/2}}{\sqrt{n}}$$

Reducing

$$e = \frac{1.414(t_\alpha + t_\beta)}{\sqrt{n}} \tag{C.3}$$

Consider the situation where $\alpha = 0.1$, $\beta = 0.1$, and $n_{high} = n_{low} = 8$ (i.e., 8 trials are conduced at the high level and 8 trials at the low level of the factors). For 7 degrees of freedom, $t_\beta = 1.415$ (from Table D) and $t_\alpha = 1.895$ (from Table E), respectively, then yields

$$e = \frac{1.414(1.415 + 1.895)}{\sqrt{8}} = 1.65$$

Because of the given assumptions and analyses, the risk is 0.10 that the "nonsignificant" factor levels do not alter the response by 1.65 times the standard deviation ($s_e$). For comparison, consider the amount $e$ would decrease if there were 32 trials instead of 16 (i.e., 16 at each factor level). Then $e$ would become

$$e = \frac{1.414(1.341 + 1.753)}{\sqrt{16}} = 1.09$$

It could then be stated that doubling the number of trials from 16 to 32 improves the nonsignificance statements by about 34% {i.e., 100 [(1.65 − 1.09)/1.65]}. Increasing the sample size may be necessary to get better resolution when setting up an experiment to evaluate interactions; however, the cost to double the sample size from 16 to 32 using trial replications to get a more accurate response is often not justifiable. Instead of striving to get a larger sample size, it may be more feasible, in some cases, for a practitioner to work at getting a measurement scheme that yields a smaller amount error relative to the amount of change considered important. As noted earlier in this text, a test strategy of several information building "small" factorial experiments is often more advantageous than a "large" factorial experiment that may technically have a "better" sample size.

## C.5. DERIVATION OF EQUATION FOR CONTRAST COLUMN SS

Equation (14.2) was used in this text to manually determine the sum of squares of the column contrasts for the two-level fractional factorial unreplicated designs originating from Tables M1–M5. The following discussion illustrates how a more typical format found in other texts reduces to the simplified format in this equation (for the fractional factorial test design approach proposed in this text).

Sometimes the contrast column sum of squares (SS) that is used when creating an analysis of variance table is described as having a crude treatment SS that is adjusted by a correction factor to yield a desired between-treatment SS. This can be expressed as

$$\text{SS (between-treatment)} = \sum_{t=1}^{k} \frac{T_t^2}{n_t} - \frac{(\Sigma x)^2}{n} \qquad \text{(C.4)}$$

where $T_t$ is the total for each treatment (i.e., factor level), $n_t$ is the number of observations (i.e., responses) comprising this total, $x$ is the observations, $n$ is the total number of observations, and $k$ is the number of treatment classifications (i.e., number of levels).

For a two-level fractional factorial consideration where half of the trials are at a "high" level and the other half are at a "low" level, Equation (C.4) can be rewritten in the following form:

$$\text{SS (contrast column)} = \left( \frac{T_{\text{high}}^2}{n/2} + \frac{T_{\text{low}}^2}{n/2} \right) - \frac{(T_{\text{high}} + T_{\text{low}})^2}{n}$$

where for a contrast column $T_{\text{high}}$ and $T_{\text{low}}$ is the totals of the responses at the high and low levels, respectively, and $n$ is the total number of trials. This equation then can be rearranged to the form

$$\text{SS (contrast column)} = \frac{2T_{\text{high}}^2 + 2T_{\text{low}}^2 - T_{\text{high}}^2 - 2T_{\text{low}}T_{\text{high}} - T_{\text{low}}^2}{n}$$

which reduces to

$$\text{SS (contrast column)} = \frac{(T_{\text{high}} - T_{\text{low}})^2}{n}$$

This equation is equal to the following Equation (14.2) format:

$$(\text{SS})_j = \frac{\left[ \sum_{i=1}^{n} w_i \right]^2}{n}$$

given that $w_i$ is the trial response values preceded by either a + or − sign, depending on the level designation that is in the contrast column $j$ (i.e., a high + or a low − level).

## C.6.  EXAMPLE 15-1: COMPUTER ANALYSIS PROGRAM STEPS AND MANUAL CALCULATIONS

The SAS program to create the outputs shown for Examples 15-1 and 15-2 is as follows:

```
* NOTE, THE LOGIC FLOW OF THE FOLLOWING PROGRAM STEPS WERE WRITTEN FOR;
* THE PURPOSE OF DOING A STATISTICAL ANALYSIS ON DATA FROM A FACTORIAL;
* EXPERIMENT DESIGN.  PROGRAM STEPS WERE ADDED TO OUTPUT INFORMATION;
* THAT COULD BE USED EXTERNALLY FROM THE PROGRAM TO CREATE PROBABILITY;
* PLOTS EITHER MANUALLY OR VIA A DIFFERENT COMPUTER PROGRAM ROUTINE.;

* ---- CREATING A DATA SET OF INPUTS AND OUTPUTS -----;
* "DATA" FOLLOWED BY A NAME CHOSEN FOR THE CREATED DATA SET;
DATA MOTOR;
* "INPUT" FOLLOWED BY THE NAMES OF COLUMNS AFTER COMMAND "CARDS";
INPUT NT MOT_TEMP ALGOR MOT_ADJ EXT_ADJ SUP_VOLT TIMING;
* "CARDS" FOLLOWED BY THE DATA AS RELATED TO "INPUT" NAMES;
  CARDS;
   1   1 -1 -1 -1   1 5.6
   2   1  1 -1 -1  -1 2.1
   3   1  1  1 -1   1 4.9
   4   1  1  1 -1   1 4.9
   5  -1  1  1  1   1 4.1
   6   1 -1  1  1   1 5.6
   7  -1  1 -1  1  -1 1.9
   8   1 -1  1 -1  -1 7.2
   9   1  1 -1  1   1 2.4
  10  -1  1 -1 -1  -1 5.1
  11  -1 -1  1  1  -1 7.9
  12   1 -1 -1  1  -1 5.3
  13  -1  1 -1 -1   1 2.1
  14  -1 -1  1 -1   1 7.6
  15  -1 -1 -1  1   1 5.5
  16  -1 -1 -1 -1  -1 5.3
;
* -- THE DATA ARE NOW ANALYZED USING VARIOUS PROCEDURES, (I.E."PROC" --);
* "PROC GLM" IS NOW DONE FOR "DATA=" MOTOR.  A "PROC ANOVA" COULD;
* BE DONE AS AN ALTERNATIVE SINCE THE DESIGN NOW HAS BALANCE;

PROC GLM DATA=MOTOR;
* "MODEL" IS FOLLOWED BY THE OUTPUT (TIMING) AS A FUNCTION OF THE;
* INPUT FACTORS TO CONSIDER IN THE MODEL.  THE SAS OPTIONS SHOWN;
* AFTER THE "/" SIGN WERE USED TO OUTPUT ONLY THE TYPE 3 SUM OF SQUARES;
* AND "SOLUTION" WOULD YIELD THE COEFFICIENTS ALONG WITH A T-TEST;
MODEL TIMING = MOT_TEMP ALGOR MOT_ADJ EXT_ADJ SUP_VOLT /SS3 SOLUTION;
* A RESIDUAL PLOT IS USEFUL TO ASSESS HOW WELL THE DATA POINTS FIT;
* THE MODEL. TO CREATE A RESIDUAL PLOT THE FOLLOWING STEPS ARE DONE;
* "OUTPUT" FOLLOWED BY "OUT=" A NEW DATA SET NAMED "D1" WHICH;
* CONTAINS "RESIDUAL=" THE RESIDUALS DEFINED AS "RES1";
* AND THE "PREDICTED=" DEFINED AS "PRED1";
OUTPUT OUT=D1 RESIDUAL=RES1 PREDICTED=PRED1;
* "PROC PRINT" "DATA=" WILL OUTPUT THE NEWLY CREATED DATA SET;
PROC PRINT DATA=D1;
* "PROC PLOT" WILL PLOT DATA FROM "DATA=" AS SPECIFIED IN THE FOLLOWING
* STEPS;
PROC PLOT DATA=D1;
* "PLOT" IS FOLLOWED BY THE ORDINATE FACTOR "*" THE ABSCISSA FACTOR;
PLOT RES1*PRED1 / VPOS=30 HPOS=50;
PLOT RES1*MOT_TEMP;
PLOT RES1*ALGOR;

PLOT RES1*MOT_ADJ;
PLOT RES1*EXT_ADJ;
PLOT RES1*SUP_VOLT;
* "PROC UNIVARIATE" WITH THE NOTED OPTIONS CAN BE USED TO CREATE;
* A NORMAL PROBABILITY PLOT.  NOTE THAT SINCE THIS PRINT PLOT;
* IS SMALL, THE ILLUSTRATION SHOWN IN THE TEXT WAS CREATED FROM
* A DIFFERENT SOFTWARE PACKAGE.;
PROC UNIVARIATE FREQ PLOT NORMAL DATA=D1;
* "VAR" IS FOLLOWED BY THE FACTOR THAT IS TO BE PLOTTED;
VAR RES1;
* -----THE FOLLOWING STEPS ARE USED SIMILARLY AS NOTED ABOVE ---- ;
* -----HOWEVER, INTERACTION TERMS ARE ADDED TO THE MODEL -----;
```

```
PROC GLM DATA=MOTOR;
   MODEL TIMING = MOT_TEMP ALGOR MOT_ADJ EXT_ADJ SUP_VOLT
      MOT_TEMP*ALGOR MOT_TEMP*MOT_ADJ MOT_TEMP*EXT_ADJ
      MOT_TEMP*SUP_VOLT ALGOR*MOT_ADJ ALGOR*EXT_ADJ
      ALGOR*SUP_VOLT MOT_ADJ*EXT_ADJ MOT_ADJ*SUP_VOLT
      EXT_ADJ*SUP_VOLT
      /SS3 SOLUTION;
   OUTPUT OUT=D2 RESIDUAL=RES2 PREDICTED=PRED2;
PROC PLOT DATA=D2;
   PLOT RES2*PRED2/VPOS=30 HPOS=50;
   PLOT RES2*MOT_TEMP;
   PLOT RES2*ALGOR;
   PLOT RES2*MOT_ADJ;
   PLOT RES2*EXT_ADJ;
   PLOT RES2*SUP_VOLT;
PROC PRINT DATA=D2;
PROC UNIVARIATE FREQ PLOT NORMAL;
   VAR RES2;
* -- "PROC RSQUARE" WITH MALLOWS "CP" OPTION IS USED FOR ALL POSSIBLE--;
* -- REGRESSIONS OF THE FACTORS IN AN ATTEMPT TO FIND THE MINIMUM --;
* -- NUMBER OF FACTORS TO CONSIDER IN THE MODEL (CP IS A MINIMUM) --;
* -- THIS OPTION CAN BE USED TO EXPLORE DATA THAT DOES NOT HAVE A --;
* -- FACTORIAL BALANCE STRUCTURE.--- ;
PROC RSQUARE CP SELECT=2 DATA=MOTOR;
MODEL TIMING = MOT_TEMP ALGOR MOT_ADJ EXT_ADJ SUP_VOLT;
* --- GIVEN KNOWLEDGE OF THE INTERACTION STRUCTURE OF THE EXPERIMENT,--;
* --- THE NEXT STEPS CALCULATE THE EFFECTS FOR ALL THE EXPERIMENTAL ---;
* --- CONTRASTS. THESE EFFECTS CAN BE USED TO CREATE A PROBABILITY ---;
* --- PLOT EXTERNAL TO THIS PROGRAM. ----;
DATA MODIFIED;
   SET MOTOR;
      EMOT_TEM = MOT_TEMP=1;
      EALGOR = ALGOR=1;
      EMOT_ADJ = MOT_ADJ=1;
      EEXT_ADJ = EXT_ADJ=1;
      ESUP_VOL = SUP_VOLT=1;
      TEMALGO = MOT_TEMP=ALGOR;
      TEMMADJ = MOT_TEMP=MOT_ADJ;
      TEMEADJ = MOT_TEMP=EXT_ADJ;
      TEMVOLT = MOT_TEMP=SUP_VOLT;
      ALGMADJ = ALGOR=MOT_ADJ;
      ALGEADJ = ALGOR=EXT_ADJ;
      ALGVOLT = ALGOR=SUP_VOLT;

      MADJEADJ = MOT_ADJ=EXT_ADJ;
      MADJVOLT = MOT_ADJ=SUP_VOLT;
      EADJVOLT = EXT_ADJ=SUP_VOLT;
PROC GLM DATA = MODIFIED;
   MODEL TIMING = EMOT_TEMP EALGOR EMOT_ADJ EEXT_ADJ ESUP_VOLT
      TEMALGO TEMMADJ TEMEADJ TEMVOLT ALGMADJ ALGEADJ ALGVOLT
      MADJEADJ MADJVOLT EADJVOLT/ SS3 SOLUTION;
* --- REMOVE OUTLIER TRIAL NUMBER 6 AND REANALYZE -- ;
DATA MOTORNO6;
   SET MOTOR;
   IF NT ¬=6;
PROC PRINT DATA=MOTORNO6;
PROC GLM DATA=MOTORNO6;
   MODEL TIMING = MOT_TEMP ALGOR MOT_ADJ EXT_ADJ SUP_VOLT
      /SS3 SOLUTION;
   OUTPUT OUT=D1 RESIDUAL=RES1 PREDICTED=PRED1;
PROC PRINT DATA=D1;
PROC PLOT;
   PLOT RES1*PRED1 / VPOS=30 HPOS=50 ;
   PLOT RES1*MOT_TEMP;
   PLOT RES1*ALGOR;
   PLOT RES1*MOT_ADJ;
   PLOT RES1*EXT_ADJ;
   PLOT RES1*SUP_VOLT;
PROC UNIVARIATE FREQ PLOT NORMAL;
   VAR RES1;
* -- THE FOLLOWING IS STATEMENTS WERE USED TO CREATE THE DUNCAN --;
* -- MULTIPLE RANGE TEST OUTPUTS -- ;
* NOTE THAT THE ABOVE ANALYSIS COULD HAVE BEEN DONE WITH A "CLASS";
* STATEMENT, HOWEVER THE OUTPUT FOR THE MODEL COEFFICIENTS NEED;
* DIFFERENT CONSIDERATION;
PROC GLM DATA=MOTOR;
* "CLASS" IS FOLLOWED BY FACTORS THAT HAVE QUALITATIVE LEVELS;
```

```
CLASS MOT_TEMP ALGOR MOT_ADJ EXT_ADJ SUP_VOLT;
MODEL TIMING = MOT_TEMP ALGOR MOT_ADJ EXT_ADJ SUP_VOLT /SS3 SOLUTION;
* "MEANS" GIVE THE MEAN EFFECTS FROM EACH "CLASS" FACTOR. THE "DUNCAN";
* OPTION FOLLOWS THE "/" SIGN.  THE "DUNCAN" AND OTHER SIMILAR;
* TYPE TESTS COMPARE THE LEVELS OF THE NOTED FACTORS. THIS TYPE
* OF OPTION IS MORE USEFUL WHEN THERE ARE SEVERAL LEVELS FOR THE FACTORS;
MEANS MOT_TEMP ALGOR MOT_ADJ EXT_ADJ SUP_VOLT/DUNCAN;
PROC GLM DATA=MOTOR;
    CLASS MOT_TEMP ALGOR MOT_ADJ EXT_ADJ SUP_VOLT;
    MODEL TIMING = MOT_TEMP ALGOR MOT_ADJ EXT_ADJ SUP_VOLT
        MOT_TEMP*ALGOR MOT_TEMP*MOT_ADJ MOT_TEMP*EXT_ADJ
        MOT_TEMP*SUP_VOLT ALGOR*MOT_ADJ ALGOR*EXT_ADJ
        ALGOR*SUP_VOLT MOT_ADJ*EXT_ADJ MOT_ADJ*SUP_VOLT
        EXT_ADJ*SUP_VOLT
        /SS3 SOLUTION;
    MEANS  MOT_TEMP*ALGOR MOT_TEMP*MOT_ADJ MOT_TEMP*EXT_ADJ
        MOT_TEMP*SUP_VOLT ALGOR*MOT_ADJ ALGOR*EXT_ADJ
        ALGOR*SUP_VOLT MOT_ADJ*EXT_ADJ MOT_ADJ*SUP_VOLT
        EXT_ADJ*SUP_VOLT;
PROC GLM DATA = MODIFIED;
    CLASS MOT_TEMP ALGOR MOT_ADJ EXT_ADJ SUP_VOLT
        TEMALGO TEMMADJ TEMEADJ TEMVOLT ALGMADJ ALGEADJ ALGVOLT
        MADJEADJ MADJVOLT EADJVOLT;
    MODEL TIMING = MOT_TEMP ALGOR MOT_ADJ EXT_ADJ SUP_VOLT
        TEMALGO TEMMADJ TEMEADJ TEMVOLT ALGMADJ ALGEADJ ALGVOLT
        MADJEADJ MADJVOLT EADJVOLT/ SS3 SOLUTION;
    MEANS MOT_TEMP ALGOR MOT_ADJ EXT_ADJ SUP_VOLT
        TEMALGO TEMMADJ TEMEADJ TEMVOLT ALGMADJ ALGEADJ ALGVOLT
        MADJEADJ MADJVOLT EADJVOLT;
* --- REMOVE OUTLIER TRIAL NUMBER 6 AND REANALYZE;
PROC GLM DATA=MOTORNO6;
    CLASS MOT_TEMP ALGOR MOT_ADJ EXT_ADJ SUP_VOLT;
    MODEL TIMING = MOT_TEMP ALGOR MOT_ADJ EXT_ADJ SUP_VOLT
        /SS3 SOLUTION;
    MEANS MOT_TEMP ALGOR MOT_ADJ EXT_ADJ SUP_VOLT/DUNCAN;
* --- SORT DATA TO LOOK FOR PATTERNS IN DATA;
PROC SORT DATA=MOTOR;
    BY TIMING;
PROC PRINT;
```

Two different analysis approaches (i.e., analysis of variance and $t$ test) are shown in the computer output that is in Table 15.2. These techniques yield the same conclusions about the significance of effects. Analysis of variance techniques tend to be more often considered; however, the results from $t$ tests can sometimes be easier to physically understand.

The following example illustrates how much of the computer output shown in Table 15.2 could be created manually. To begin this illustration, the low factor levels (i.e., $-$ levels) for the trial factors were first designated with parenthesis and put in Table C.4 along with response timing output.

The following discussion exemplifies calculations for the algorithm effect (i.e., algor); the same procedure is applicable to the other factors. In this discussion algor$^+$ is used to represent trials that are conducted at a high level (i.e., those trials with no parentheses) and algor$^-$ are those at a low level (i.e., those trials within parentheses). Algor represents a mean calculation. The total number of trials ($n$) is 16.

To determine the mean effect of algor, the following can be done:

$$\Sigma(\text{algor}^+) = 2.1 + 4.9 + 4.9 + 4.1 + 1.9 + 2.4 + 5.1 + 2.1 = 27.5$$

$$\Sigma(\text{algor}^-) = 5.6 + 5.6 + 7.2 + 7.9 + 5.3 + 7.6 + 5.5 + 5.3 = 50.0$$

$$\overline{\text{algor}^+} = 27.5/8 = 3.4375 \qquad \overline{\text{algor}^-} = 50.0/8 = 6.25$$

$$\Delta\ \overline{\text{algor}} = \overline{\text{algor}^+} - \overline{\text{algor}^-} = 3.4375 - 6.25 = -2.8125$$

Since the computer model output had factor level designations of $-1$ and $+1$, this $-2.8125$ algor effect value is double the $-1.40625$ algor coefficient estimate shown under note 7 of Table 15.2.

To determine the type III sum of squares value for algor shown in Table 15.2, Equation (C.4) yields

$$\text{Correction factor} = \frac{(\Sigma x_i)^2}{n} = \frac{[(\Sigma \text{algor}^+) + (\Sigma \text{algor}^-)]^2}{n}$$

$$= \frac{[27.5 + 50.0]^2}{16} = 375.390625$$

$$\text{SS (algor uncorrected)} = \frac{(\Sigma \text{algor}^+)^2 + (\Sigma \text{algor}^-)^2}{8} = \frac{27.5^2 + 50^2}{8}$$

$$= 407.03125$$

$$\text{SS (algor corrected)} = \text{SS (algor uncorrected)} - \text{correction factor}$$

$$= 407.03125 - 375.390625 = 31.640625$$

**TABLE C.4. Example 15-1: Main Effects Contrast Columns Considerations**

| Number of Trial | Inputs | | | | | Response Timing |
|---|---|---|---|---|---|---|
| | mot_temp | algor | mot_adj | ext_adj | sup_volt | |
| 1 | 5.6 | (5.6) | (5.6) | (5.6) | 5.6 | 5.6 |
| 2 | 2.1 | 2.1 | (2.1) | (2.1) | (2.1) | 2.1 |
| 3 | 4.9 | 4.9 | 4.9 | (4.9) | 4.9 | 4.9 |
| 4 | 4.9 | 4.9 | 4.9 | 4.9 | (4.9) | 4.9 |
| 5 | (4.1) | 4.1 | 4.1 | 4.1 | 4.1 | 4.1 |
| 6 | 5.6 | (5.6) | 5.6 | 5.6 | 5.6 | 5.6 |
| 7 | (1.9) | 1.9 | (1.9) | 1.9 | (1.9) | 1.9 |
| 8 | 7.2 | (7.2) | 7.2 | (7.2) | (7.2) | 7.2 |
| 9 | 2.4 | 2.4 | (2.4) | 2.4 | 2.4 | 2.4 |
| 10 | (5.1) | 5.1 | 5.1 | (5.1) | (5.1) | 5.1 |
| 11 | (7.9) | (7.9) | 7.9 | 7.9 | (7.9) | 7.9 |
| 12 | 5.3 | (5.3) | (5.3) | 5.3 | (5.3) | 5.3 |
| 13 | (2.1) | 2.1 | (2.1) | (2.1) | 2.1 | 2.1 |
| 14 | (7.6) | (7.6) | 7.6 | (7.6) | 7.6 | 7.6 |
| 15 | (5.5) | (5.5) | (5.5) | 5.5 | 5.5 | 5.5 |
| 16 | (5.3) | (5.3) | (5.3) | (5.3) | (5.3) | 5.3 |

**TABLE C.5. Example 15-1: Calculations**

| Effect | Sums High | Sums Low | Average High | Average Low | Δ | SS | df |
|--------|------|-----|------|------|-------|-----|----|
| mot_temp | 38.0 | 39.5 | 4.7500 | 4.9375 | −0.188 | 0.140625 | 1 |
| algor | 27.5 | 50.0 | 3.4375 | 6.2500 | −2.813 | 31.640625 | 1 |
| mot_adj | 47.3 | 30.2 | 5.9125 | 3.7750 | 2.138 | 18.275625 | 1 |
| ext_adj | 37.6 | 39.9 | 4.7000 | 4.9875 | −0.288 | 0.330625 | 1 |
| sup_volt | 37.8 | 39.7 | 4.725 | 4.9625 | −0.238 | 0.225625 | 1 |
|  |  |  |  |  | For model | 50.613125 | 5 |

Note that this value of 31.640625 is the same as that listed under the type III sum of squares for algor in Table 15.2. When this procedure is performed for the other effects, Table C.5 can be generated (which is consistent with the computer output shown in Table 15.2).

The total SS value of 50.613125 in Table C.5 is the same as the sum of squares for the model shown in Table 15.2. A minus sign for Δ indicates that a higher response was determined on the average for the negative level of the factor.

The degrees of freedom for the model is shown in Table C.5 to be 5. The total degrees of freedom is df(total) $= n - 1 = 16 - 1 = 15$. The degrees of freedom for algor is df(algor) $= (2 \text{ levels} - 1) = 1$.

The corrected total sum of squares of 54.79938 in Table 15.2 can be manually generated by performing the following calculations:

$$\text{SS (total)} = \Sigma x_i^2 - \text{correction factor} = (5.6^2 + 2.1^2 + \cdots) - 375.390625$$
$$= 430.19 - 375.390625 = 54.799375$$

The "corrected error" considerations described in Table 15.2 is consistent with the following calculations:

$$\text{SS(error)} = \text{SS(total)} - \text{SS(model)} = 54.799375 - 50.613125 = 4.18625$$

$$\text{df(error)} = \text{df(total)} - \text{df(model)} = 15 - 5 = 10$$

$$\text{MS(error)} = \text{SS(error)/df(error)} = 4.18625/10 = 0.418625$$

$$s_e = \text{root MS(error)} = \sqrt{\text{MS(error)}}$$

$$= \sqrt{0.418625} = 0.64701236$$

It can also be noted that this is the same SS value that was determined using the manual approach that was described in Example 14-2.

The ANOVA procedure for testing significance utilizes the $F$ distribution as shown for unreplicated experiment trials:

$$F = \frac{SS(\text{effect})}{MS(\text{error})} = \frac{SS(\text{algor})}{MS(\text{error})} = \frac{31.640625}{0.418625} = 75.58$$

From the $F$ table (i.e., Table F) the variance ratio criteria for significance is as follows (when an effect level has 1 degree of freedom and the error estimate has 10 degrees of freedom):

| Probability Level | Variance Ratio Criterion |
|:---:|:---:|
| 0.10 | 3.28 |
| 0.05 | 4.96 |
| 0.01 | 10.0 |

Since $75.58 > 10.0$, algor is significant at a level of 0.01 (see Table 15.2). Note that the computer output extends this significance level to 0.0001 level, which was beyond the range of Table F.

Another alternative is to use the $t$ statistic to assess the mean changes for the effect levels. The equation for this test (see Table 9.1) for algor is

$$t = \frac{|\Delta\text{algor}|}{s_e\sqrt{1/n_{\text{high}} + 1/n_{\text{low}}}} = \frac{2.8125}{0.64701236\sqrt{1/8 + 1/8}} = 8.69$$

From the double-sided $t$ table (Table E), a value of 4.587 is determined for the significance level of 0.001 and 10 degrees of freedom. Since $8.69 > 4.587$, algor is significant at the 0.001 level.

Rather than calculate the $t$ value for each factor effect, the required ($|\bar{x}_{\text{high}} - \bar{x}_{\text{low}}|_{\text{criterion}}$) value for significance could have been determined for various significance levels [see Equation (14.5)]. For example, from Table E the two-sided $t$ value given 10 degrees of freedom and a significance level of 0.001 is 4.587. Hence, the criterion for a 0.001 significance test is

$$|x_{\text{high}} - x_{\text{low}}|_{\text{criterion}} = t_\alpha(s_e)\sqrt{1/n_{\text{high}} + 1/n_{\text{low}}}$$

$$= 4.587\,(0.64701236)\,\sqrt{1/8 + 1/8} = 1.484$$

In Table C.5 the only two $\Delta$ values exceeding the magnitude of this criterion of 1.484 are algor and mot_adj; hence, the other factors are not considered significant at a level of 0.001.

## C.7. EXAMPLE 15-3: COMPUTER ANALYSIS PROGRAM STEPS

The SAS program to create the outputs shown for Example 15-3 is as follows. Reference Section C.6 for a more detailed explanation on frequently used SAS coding commands.

```
* DATA INPUT STATEMENTS;
DATA PIGMENT;
  INPUT BATCH SAMPLE SUBSAMPL MOISTURE aa;
  CARD;
   1  1 1 40
   1  1 2 39
   1  2 1 30
   1  2 2 30    2  1 1 26    2  1 2 28    2  2 1 25    2  2 2 26    3  1 1 29
   3  1 2 28    3  2 1 14    3  2 2 15    4  1 1 30    4  1 2 31    4  2 1 24
   4  2 2 24    5  1 1 19    5  1 2 20    5  2 1 17    5  2 2 17    6  1 1 33
   6  1 2 32    6  2 1 26    6  2 2 24    7  1 1 23    7  1 2 24    7  2 1 32
   7  2 2 33    8  1 1 34    8  1 2 34    8  2 1 29    8  2 2 29    9  1 1 27
   9  1 2 27    9  2 1 31    9  2 2 31   10  1 1 13   10  1 2 16   10  2 1 27
  10  2 2 24   11  1 1 25   11  1 2 23   11  2 1 25   11  2 2 27   12  1 1 29
  12  1 2 29   12  2 1 31   12  2 2 32   13  1 1 19   13  1 2 20   13  2 1 29
  13  2 2 30   14  1 1 23   14  1 2 24   14  2 1 25   14  2 2 25   15  1 1 39
  15  1 2 37   15  2 1 26   15  2 2 28
  ;
* VARIANCE COMPONENTS ANALYSIS PROCEDURE;
PROC VARCOMP METHOD=TYPE1;
  CLASS BATCH SAMPLE SUBSAMPL;
  MODEL MOISTURE= BATCH SAMPLE(BATCH) ;
```

## C.8. EXAMPLE 15-4: COMPUTER ANALYSIS PROGRAM STEPS

The SAS program to create the outputs shown for Example 15-4 is as follows. See Section C.6 for a more detailed explanation on frequently used SAS coding commands.

```
* DATA INPUT STATEMENTS;
DATA LOOM;
  INPUT LOOMS OBSERV STRENGTH aa;
  CARDS;
  1 1 98
  1 2 97    1 3 99    1 4 96    2 1 91    2 2 90    2 3 93    2 4 92
  3 1 96    3 2 95    3 3 97    3 4 95    4 1 95    4 2 96    4 3 99    4 4 98
  ;
* VARIANCE COMPONENTS ANALYSIS PROCEDURE;
PROC VARCOMP METHOD=TYPE1;
  CLASS LOOMS OBSERV;
  MODEL STRENGTH = LOOMS;
```

## C.9. EXAMPLE 17-1: COMPUTER ANALYSIS PROGRAM STEPS AND LACK OF FIT ASSESSMENTS

Figure 17.2 contains a contour plot that was created as an output from the SAS program steps shown in Table C.6. Included also in this section is discussion on other response surface analysis outputs; footnotes in Tables

C.7 and C.8 are included as part of the output for explanation purposes. Both response surface (PROC RSREG) [see Tables C.7 and C.9] and regression (PROC REG) [see Tables C.8 and C.10] outputs are discussed using both coded and natural variable level factor inputs. See Section C.6 for a more detailed explanation on frequently used SAS coding commands.

Lack of fit for a model can be assessed by dividing the mean square value for pure error into the mean square value for lack of fit. An $F$ test is then done to determine if the ratio is large enough to show that the model does not adequately fit the data. If the ratio is not shown to be significant, then the model is said to "fit" the data.

To show this procedure with the information from the regression output shown in Table C.10, consider the following numerical illustration. As noted from this regression output, the total sum of squares for error is equal 0.496. This error consists of both lack of fit and pure error. For this example there are five replications of the center point that is used to determine the pure error sum of squares. In determining this pure error sum of squares, the mean of the five readings is first determined to be

$$\frac{79.9 + 80.3 + 80.0 + 79.7 + 79.8}{5} = 79.94$$

Using this mean value along with the measured values yield a pure error sum of squares of

$$SS(\text{pure error}) = (79.9 - 79.94)^2 + (80.3 - 79.94)^2 + (80.0 - 79.94)^2$$
$$+ (79.7 - 79.94)^2 + (79.8 - 79.94)^2 = 0.212$$

The lack-of-fit sum of squares is then

$$SS(\text{lack of fit}) = 0.496 - 0.212 = 0.284$$

Since the mean square error equates to the sum of squares divided by its number of degrees, the mean square errors are determined to be

$$MS(\text{pure error}) = 0.212/4 = 0.053$$
$$MS(\text{lack of fit}) = 0.284/3 = 0.095$$

Note that the number of degrees of freedom for the MS(pure error) [i.e., $\nu_{\text{pure error}}$] equals number of samples at the center point (five) minus one (i.e., $5 - 1 = 4$) and the number of degrees of freedom for MS(lack of fit) [i.e., $\nu_{\text{lack of fit}}$] equals the number of degrees of freedom for total error (seven) minus the four for the MS(error) (i.e., $7 - 4 = 3$).

**TABLE C.6. Example 17-1: Computer Analysis Program Steps**

```
* DATA INPUT STATEMENTS;
 DATA A;
  INPUT TIME TEMP TIMECODE TEMPCODE YIELD;
  TIMESQ = TIME*TIME;
* TIMESQ = 'TIME SQUARE';
  TEMPSQ = TEMP*TEMP;
* TEMPSQ = 'TEMP SQUARE';
  TIMETEMP = TIME*TEMP;
* TIMETEMP = 'INTERACTION OF TIME AND TEMP';
  TIMCODSQ = TIMECODE*TIMECODE;
* TIMCODSQ = 'TIMECODE SQUARED';
  TEMCODSQ = TEMPCODE*TEMPCODE;
* TEMCODSQ = 'TEMPCODE SQUARED';
  TIMTEMCD = TIMECODE*TEMPCODE;
* TIMTEMCD = 'INTERACTION OF TIMECODE AND TEMPCODE';
  CARDS;
     80     170      -1       -1      76.5
     80     180      -1        1      77.0
     90     170       1       -1      78.0
     90     180       1        1      79.5
     92.07 175       1.414     0      78.4
     77.93 175      -1.414     0      75.6
     85     182.07   0        1.414   78.5
     85     167.93   0       -1.414   77.0
     85     175       0        0      79.9
     85     175       0        0      80.3
     85     175       0        0      80.0
     85     175       0        0      79.7
     85     175       0        0      79.8
 PROC PRINT;
* RESPONSE SURFACE MODEL USING NATURAL VARIABLE LEVELS;
 PROC SORT DATA=A; BY TIME TEMP;
 PROC RSREG;
  MODEL YIELD = TIME  TEMP/LACKFIT;
* REGRESSION MODEL USING NATURAL VARIABLE LEVELS;
 PROC REG DATA=A;
  MODEL YIELD = TIME TIMESQ TEMP TEMPSQ TIMETEMP / INFLUENCE;
* RESPONSE SURFACE MODEL USING CODED VARIABLE LEVELS;
 PROC SORT DATA=A; BY TIMECODE TEMPCODE;
 PROC RSREG ;
  MODEL YIELD = TIMECODE TEMPCODE/LACKFIT;
* REGRESSION MODEL USING CODED VARIABLE LEVELS;
 PROC REG DATA=A;
  MODEL YIELD = TIMECODE TIMCODSQ TEMPCODE TEMCODSQ
        TIMTEMCD/ INFLUENCE ;
  OUTPUT OUT=PREDICTE PREDICTED=PREDICT RESIDUAL=RESIDUAL;
 PROC PRINT DATA=PREDICTE;
* CONTOUR PLOT OF THE RESPONSE SURFACE OF THE CODED VARIABLES;
DATA B;
*  ---    ACTUAL VALUES ---;
  SET A END=EOF;
  OUTPUT;
* --- FOLLOWED BY A TIMECODE*TEMPCODE GRID FOR PLOTTING --;
  IF EOF THEN DO; YIELD=.;
  DO TIMECODE= -1 TO 1 BY .05;
    DO TEMPCODE= -1 TO 1 BY .05;
       OUTPUT;
       END;
    END;
  END;
PROC RSREG DATA=B OUT=C NOPRINT;
  MODEL YIELD= TIMECODE TEMPCODE / PREDICT NOPRINT;
DATA D; SET C;
PROC PLOT DATA=D;
  PLOT TIMECODE*TEMPCODE=YIELD / CONTOUR=10 HPOS=50 VPOS=36
    S1='.' S2=',' S3='-' S4='=' S5 ='+' S6='A' S7='B' S8='C'
    S9='D' S10='E';
```

408

**TABLE C.7. Response Surface Model Output Using Natural Variable Levels**

```
RESPONSE SURFACE FOR VARIABLE YIELD
```

| | | | RESPONSE MEAN | 78.47692 | | |
|---|---|---|---|---|---|---|
| | | | ROOT MSE | 0.2662903 | | |
| | | | R-SQUARE | 0.9827307 | | |
| | | | COEF OF VARIATION | 0.00339323 | | |

| REGRESSION | DF | TYPE I SS | R-SQUARE | F-RATIO | PROB ② |
|---|---|---|---|---|---|
| LINEAR | 2 | 10.04295469 | 0.3494 | 70.81 | 0.0001 |
| QUADRATIC | 2 | 17.95374874 | 0.6246 | 126.59 | 0.0001 |
| CROSSPRODUCT | 1 | 0.25000000 | 0.0087 | 3.53 | 0.1025 |
| TOTAL REGRESS | 5 | 28.24670343 | 0.9827 | 79.67 | 0.0001 |

| RESIDUAL | DF | SS | MEAN SQUARE | F-RATIO | PROB ① |
|---|---|---|---|---|---|
| LACK OF FIT | 3 | 0.28437350 | 0.09479117 | 1.789 | 0.2886 |
| PURE ERROR | 4 | 0.21200000 | 0.05300000 | | |
| TOTAL ERROR | 7 | 0.49637350 | 0.07091050 | | |

| PARAMETER | DF | ESTIMATE ④ | STD DEV | T-RATIO | PROB ③ |
|---|---|---|---|---|---|
| INTERCEPT | 1 | -1430.68844 | 152.85133 | -9.36 | 0.0001 |
| TIME | 1 | 7.80886518 | 1.15782322 | 6.74 | 0.0003 |
| TEMP | 1 | 13.27174453 | 1.48460608 | 8.94 | 0.0001 |
| TIME×TIME | 1 | -0.05505797 | 0.004039367 | -13.63 | 0.0001 |
| TEMP×TIME | 1 | 0.010000000 | 0.005325805 | 1.88 | 0.1025 |
| TEMP×TEMP | 1 | -0.04005344 | 0.004039367 | -9.92 | 0.0001 |

| FACTOR | DF | SS | MEAN SQUARE | F-RATIO | PROB |
|---|---|---|---|---|---|
| TIME | 3 | 21.34401 | 7.114669 | 100.33 | 0.0001 |
| TEMP | 3 | 9.345251 | 3.115084 | 43.93 | 0.0001 |

```
SOLUTION FOR OPTIMUM RESPONSE

           FACTOR  CRITICAL VALUE
           TIME     86.94615216
           TEMP    176.52923

PREDICTED VALUE AT OPTIMUM     80.21239

EIGENVALUES    EIGENVECTORS ⑤
                    TIME          TEMP
 -0.0385399      0.2897174     0.9571122
 -0.0565715      0.9571122    -0.289717

SOLUTION WAS A MAXIMUM
```

1. A model is assumed to be valid until proven otherwise. For this case, the quadratic model is presumed to be adequate since the probability level is not "low." If, for example, this probability were 0.05, then we would normally reject the model fit at the 0.05 level.

2. The quadratic model is significant at 0.0001 level.

3. All terms (except one) in the model are significant at the 0.001 level.

4. The model equation coefficients are noted as "estimate".

5. Eigenvalues and Eigenvectors are from the matrix of quadratic parameter estimates that determine the curvature of the response surface. To determine if the solution of critical values is a maximum or minimum look at the eigenvalues

| if eigenvalues | then solution is |
|---|---|
| are all negative | maximum |
| are all positive | minimum |
| have mixed signs | saddle-point |
| contain zeros | in a flat area |

The eigenvector for the largest eigenvalue gives the direction of steepest ascent, if positive, or steepest descent, if negative. The eigenvectors corresponding to small or zero eigenvalues point in directions of relative flatness.

## TABLE C.8. Regression Model Output Using Natural Variable Levels

```
DEP VARIABLE: YIELD                        ANALYSIS OF VARIANCE

                                    SUM OF         MEAN
                   SOURCE    DF    SQUARES        SQUARE     F VALUE      PROB>F

                   MODEL      5   28.24670343   5.64934069   79.669      0.0001
                   ERROR      7    0.49637350   0.07091050
                   C TOTAL   12   28.74307692

                   ROOT MSE      0.2662903    R-SQUARE     0.9827
                   DEP MEAN     78.47692      ADJ R-SQ     0.9704
                   C.V.          0.339323

                                    PARAMETER ESTIMATES

                            PARAMETER ②      STANDARD     T FOR H0:
            VARIABLE   DF     ESTIMATE         ERROR     PARAMETER=0    PROB > |T|  ①

            INTERCEP    1   -1430.68844     152.85133       -9.360      0.0001
            TIME        1       7.80886518    1.15782322     6.744      0.0003
            TIMESQ      1      -0.05505797    0.004039367  -13.630      0.0001
            TEMP        1      13.27174453    1.48460608     8.940      0.0001
            TEMPSQ      1      -0.04005344    0.004039367   -9.916      0.0001
            TIMETEMP    1       0.010000000   0.005325805    1.878      0.1025
```

1. All terms (except one) in the model are significant at the 0.001 level.
2. Model coefficients are noted as "estimate."

## TABLE C.9. Response Surface Model Output Using Coded Variable Levels

```
RESPONSE SURFACE FOR VARIABLE YIELD ①

                          RESPONSE MEAN        78.47692
                          ROOT MSE              0.2662903
                          R-SQUARE              0.9827307
                          COEF OF VARIATION     0.00339323

             REGRESSION      DF     TYPE I SS    R-SQUARE    F-RATIO     PROB

             LINEAR           2   10.04295469     0.3494     70.81      0.0001
             QUADRATIC        2   17.95374874     0.6246    126.59      0.0001
             CROSSPRODUCT     1    0.25000000     0.0087      3.53      0.1025
             TOTAL REGRESS    5   28.24670343     0.9827     79.67      0.0001

             RESIDUAL        DF           SS    MEAN SQUARE   F-RATIO    PROB

             LACK OF FIT      3    0.28437349    0.09479116    1.789     0.2886
             PURE ERROR       4    0.21200000    0.05300000
             TOTAL ERROR      7    0.49637349    0.07091050

             PARAMETER       DF     ESTIMATE      STD DEV    T-RATIO     PROB

             INTERCEPT        1   79.93995461    0.11908862  671.26     0.0001
             TIMECODE         1    0.99505025    0.09415493   10.57     0.0001
             TEMPCODE         1    0.51520280    0.09415493    5.47     0.0009
             TIMECODE*TIMECODE 1  -1.37644928    0.10098417  -13.63     0.0001
             TEMPCODE*TIMECODE 1   0.25000000    0.13314513    1.88     0.1025
             TEMPCODE*TEMPCODE 1  -1.00133600    0.10098417   -9.92     0.0001

             FACTOR          DF           SS    MEAN SQUARE   F-RATIO    PROB

             TIMECODE         3   21.34401      7.114669     100.33     0.0001
             TEMPCODE         3    9.345251     3.115084      43.93     0.0001

SOLUTION FOR OPTIMUM RESPONSE

             FACTOR CRITICAL VALUE

             TIMECODE   0.38923043
             TEMPCODE   0.30584659

PREDICTED VALUE AT OPTIMUM       80.21239

EIGENVALUES    EIGENVECTORS
                 TIMECODE      TEMPCODE
  -0.963499     0.2897174     0.9571122
  -1.41429      0.9571122    -0.289717

SOLUTION WAS A MAXIMUM
```

1. See Table C.7 for output interpretations.

**TABLE C.10. Regression Model Output Using Coded Variable Levels**

DEP VARIABLE: YIELD

ANALYSIS OF VARIANCE

| SOURCE | DF | SUM OF SQUARES | MEAN SQUARE | F VALUE | PROB>F |
|--------|-----|------|------|------|------|
| MODEL | 5 | 28.24670343 | 5.64934069 | 79.669 | 0.0001 |
| ERROR | 7 | 0.49637349 | 0.07091050 | | |
| C TOTAL | 12 | 28.74307692 | | | |

| | | | |
|-----|------|------|------|
| ROOT MSE | 0.2662903 | R-SQUARE | 0.9827 |
| DEP MEAN | 78.47692 | ADJ R-SQ | 0.9704 |
| C.V. | 0.339323 | | |

PARAMETER ESTIMATES

| VARIABLE | DF | PARAMETER ESTIMATE | STANDARD ERROR | T FOR H0: PARAMETER=0 | PROB > |T| |
|--------|-----|------|------|------|------|
| INTERCEP | 1 | 79.93995461 | 0.11908862 | 671.264 | 0.0001 |
| TIMECODE | 1 | 0.99505025 | 0.09415493 | 10.568 | 0.0001 |
| TIMCODSQ | 1 | -1.37644928 | 0.10098417 | -13.630 | 0.0001 |
| TEMPCODE | 1 | 0.51520280 | 0.09415493 | 5.472 | 0.0009 |
| TEMCODSQ | 1 | -1.00133600 | 0.10098417 | -9.916 | 0.0001 |
| TIMTEMCD | 1 | 0.25000000 | 0.13314513 | 1.878 | 0.1025 |

The $F$ test ratio is then

$$F = 0.095/0.053 = 1.79$$

From Table F the $F$ value is noted to be

$$F_{(\nu \text{ lack-of-fit});(\nu \text{ pure-error});0.1} = F_{3;4;0.1} = 4.19$$

Since $1.79 < 4.19$, the conclusion is that the model fits.

Note that these lack of fit calculations from the SAS regression analysis output in Table C.10 are consistent with the output from the response surface SAS analysis shown in Table C.9. Note also that the general equations associated with this test can be found in many statistical texts (Cornell 1984).

## C.10.  EXAMPLE 17-3: COMPUTER ANALYSIS PROGRAM STEPS

The SAS program to create the outputs shown for Example 17-3 is shown in Table C.11. See Section C.6 for a more detailed explanation on frequently used SAS coding commands. The computer output is shown in Table C.12.

## C.11.  EXAMPLE 22-1: COMPUTER ANALYSIS PROGRAM STEPS

The SAS program to create the outputs shown for Example 22-1 is shown in Table C.13. See Section C.6 for a more detailed explanation on frequently used SAS coding commands.

**TABLE C.11. Example 17-3: SAS Program Steps**

```
DATA PATTY;
 INPUT Z1 Z2 Z3 X1 X2 X3 TEXTURE;
CARDS;
 -1 -1 -1  1    0    0   1.84        -1 -1  1  1    0    0   1.65
 -1 -1 -1  0    1    0    .67        -1 -1  1  0    1    0   0.58
 -1 -1 -1  0    0    1   1.51        -1 -1  1  0    0    1   1.21
 -1 -1 -1  .5   .5   0   1.29        -1 -1  1  .5   .5   0   1.18
 -1 -1 -1  .5   0    .5  1.42        -1 -1  1  .5   0    .5  1.45
 -1 -1 -1  0    .5   .5  1.16        -1 -1  1  0    .5   .5  1.07
 -1 -1 -1  .33333 .33333 .33333 1.59 -1 -1  1  .33333 .33333 .33333 1.41
  1 -1 -1  1    0    0   2.86
  1 -1 -1  0    1    0   1.10         1 -1  1  1    0    0   2.32
  1 -1 -1  0    0    1   1.60         1 -1  1  0    1    0   0.97
  1 -1 -1  .5   .5   0   1.53         1 -1  1  0    0    1   2.12
  1 -1 -1  .5   0    .5  1.81         1 -1  1  .5   .5   0   1.45
  1 -1 -1  0    .5   .5  1.50         1 -1  1  .5   0    .5  1.93
  1 -1 -1  .33333 .33333 .33333 1.68  1 -1  1  0    .5   .5  1.28
                                      1 -1  1  .33333 .33333 .33333 1.54
 -1  1 -1  1    0    0   3.01
 -1  1 -1  0    1    0   1.21        -1  1  1  1    0    0   3.04
 -1  1 -1  0    0    1   2.32        -1  1  1  0    1    0   1.16
 -1  1 -1  .5   .5   0   1.93        -1  1  1  0    0    1   2.00
 -1  1 -1  .5   0    .5  2.57        -1  1  1  .5   .5   0   1.85
 -1  1 -1  0    .5   .5  1.83        -1  1  1  .5   0    .5  2.39
 -1  1 -1  .33333 .33333 .33333 1.94 -1  1  1  0    .5   .5  1.60
                                     -1  1  1  .33333 .33333 .33333 2.05
  1  1 -1  1    0    0   4.13
  1  1 -1  0    1    0   1.67         1  1  1  1    0    0   4.13
  1  1 -1  0    0    1   2.57         1  1  1  0    1    0   1.30
  1  1 -1  .5   .5   0   2.26         1  1  1  0    0    1   2.75
  1  1 -1  .5   0    .5  3.15         1  1  1  .5   .5   0   2.06
  1  1 -1  0    .5   .5  2.22         1  1  1  .5   0    .5  2.82
  1  1 -1  .33333 .33333 .33333 2.60  1  1  1  0    .5   .5  2.10
                                      1  1  1  .33333 .33333 .33333 2.32
                                 ;
            PROC PRINT;
            PROC GLM;
            MODEL TEXTURE =
             X1 X1*Z1 X1*Z2 X1*Z3 X1*Z1*Z2 X1*Z1*Z3 X1*Z2*Z3 X1*Z1*Z2*Z3
             X2 X2*Z1 X2*Z2 X2*Z3 X2*Z1*Z2 X2*Z1*Z3 X2*Z2*Z3 X2*Z1*Z2*Z3
             X3 X3*Z1 X3*Z2 X3*Z3 X3*Z1*Z2 X3*Z1*Z3 X3*Z2*Z3 X3*Z1*Z2*Z3
             X1*X2 X1*X2*Z1 X1*X2*Z2 X1*X2*Z3 X1*X2*Z1*Z2 X1*X2*Z1*Z3
               X1*X2*Z2*Z3 X1*X2*Z1*Z2*Z3
             X1*X3 X1*X3*Z1 X1*X3*Z2 X1*X3*Z3 X1*X3*Z1*Z2 X1*X3*Z1*Z3
               X1*X3*Z2*Z3 X1*X3*Z1*Z2*Z3
             X2*X3 X2*X3*Z1 X2*X3*Z2 X2*X3*Z3 X2*X3*Z1*Z2 X2*X3*Z1*Z3
               X2*X3*Z2*Z3 X2*X3*Z1*Z2*Z3
             X1*X2*X3 X1*X2*X3*Z1 X1*X2*X3*Z2 X1*X2*X3*Z3 X1*X2*X3*Z1*Z2
               X1*X2*X3*Z1*Z3 X1*X2*X3*Z2*Z3 X1*X2*X3*Z1*Z2*Z3
            /SS3 SOLUTION NOINT;
```

**TABLE C.12. Example 17-3: SAS Program Computer Output**

GENERAL LINEAR MODELS PROCEDURE

DEPENDENT VARIABLE: TEXTURE

| SOURCE | DF | SUM OF SQUARES | MEAN SQUARE | F VALUE | PR > F | R-SQUARE | C.V |
|---|---|---|---|---|---|---|---|
| MODEL | 56 | 233.41400000 | 4.16810714 | . | . | 1.000000 | 0.000 |
| ERROR | 0 | 0.00000000 | 0.00000000 | | | | |
| UNCORRECTED TOTAL | 56 | 233.41400000 | | | | | |

| | | | ROOT MSE | | | TEXTURE MEA |
|---|---|---|---|---|---|---|
| | | | 0.00000000 | | | 1.9053571 |

| SOURCE | DF | TYPE III SS | F VALUE | PR > F |
|---|---|---|---|---|
| X1 | 1 | 66.01005000 | . | . |
| X1*Z1 | 1 | 1.90125000 | . | . |
| X1*Z2 | 1 | 3.97620000 | . | . |
| X1*Z3 | 1 | 0.06125000 | . | . |
| X1*Z1*Z2 | 1 | 0.03380000 | . | . |
| X1*Z1*Z3 | 1 | 0.01805000 | . | . |
| X1*Z2*Z3 | 1 | 0.07220000 | . | . |
| X1*Z1*Z2*Z3 | 1 | 0.01280000 | . | . |
| X2 | 1 | 9.37445000 | . | . |
| Z1*X2 | 1 | 0.29205000 | . | . |
| Z2*X2 | 1 | 0.51005000 | . | . |
| Z3*X2 | 1 | 0.05120000 | . | . |
| Z1*Z2*X2 | 1 | 0.06605000 | . | . |
| Z1*Z3*X2 | 1 | 0.01620000 | . | . |
| Z2*Z3*X2 | 1 | 0.00500000 | . | . |
| Z1*Z2*Z3*X2 | 1 | 0.00980000 | . | . |
| X3 | 1 | 32.32080000 | . | . |
| Z1*X3 | 1 | 0.50000000 | . | . |
| Z2*X3 | 1 | 1.28000000 | . | . |
| Z3*X3 | 1 | 0.00080000 | . | . |
| Z1*Z2*X3 | 1 | 0.00000000 | . | . |
| Z1*Z3*X3 | 1 | 0.21780000 | . | . |
| Z2*Z3*X3 | 1 | 0.01620000 | . | . |
| Z1*Z2*Z3*X3 | 1 | 0.01280000 | . | . |
| X1*X2 | 1 | 0.42940833 | . | . |
| X1*Z1*X2 | 1 | 0.21600833 | . | . |
| X1*Z2*X2 | 1 | 0.11603333 | . | . |
| X1*Z3*X2 | 1 | 0.00333333 | . | . |
| X1*Z1*Z2*X2 | 1 | 0.00120000 | . | . |
| X1*Z1*Z3*X2 | 1 | 0.00653333 | . | . |
| X1*Z2*Z3*X2 | 1 | 0.01140833 | . | . |
| X1*Z1*Z2*Z3*X2 | 1 | 0.00240833 | . | . |
| X1*X3 | 1 | 0.33000833 | . | . |
| X1*Z1*X3 | 1 | 0.07540833 | . | . |
| X1*Z2*X3 | 1 | 0.00083333 | . | . |

(Table continues on p. 414.)

413

TABLE C.12. (Continued)

| SOURCE | DF | TYPE III SS | F VALUE | PR > F |
|---|---|---|---|---|
| X1*Z3*X3 | 1 | 0.00020833 | . | . |
| X1*Z1*Z2*X3 | 1 | 0.00120000 | . | . |
| X1*Z1*Z3*X3 | 1 | 0.02340833 | . | . |
| X1*Z2*Z3*X3 | 1 | 0.06163333 | . | . |
| X1*Z1*Z2*Z3*X3 | 1 | 0.00480000 | . | . |
| X2*X3 | 1 | 0.01267500 | . | . |
| Z1*X2*X3 | 1 | 0.00607500 | . | . |
| Z2*X2*X3 | 1 | 0.00140833 | . | . |
| Z3*X2*X3 | 1 | 0.01203333 | . | . |
| Z1*Z2*X2*X3 | 1 | 0.01687500 | . | . |
| Z1*Z3*X2*X3 | 1 | 0.02083333 | . | . |
| Z2*Z3*X2*X3 | 1 | 0.00480000 | . | . |
| Z1*Z2*Z3*X2*X3 | 1 | 0.02430000 | . | . |
| X1*X2*X3 | 1 | 0.06827686 | . | . |
| X1*Z1*X2*X3 | 1 | 0.00003418 | . | . |
| X1*Z2*X2*X3 | 1 | 0.01345774 | . | . |
| X1*Z3*X2*X3 | 1 | 0.00007961 | . | . |
| X1*Z1*Z2*X2*X3 | 1 | 0.02047642 | . | . |
| X1*Z1*Z3*X2*X3 | 1 | 0.00338288 | . | . |
| X1*Z2*Z3*X2*X3 | 1 | 0.02100737 | . | . |
| X1*Z1*Z2*Z3*X2*X3 | 1 | 0.01193437 | . | . |

| PARAMETER | ESTIMATE | T FOR H0: PARAMETER=0 | PR > \|T\| | STD ERROR OF ESTIMATE |
|---|---|---|---|---|
| X1 | 2.87250000 | 99999.99 | 0.0001 | 0 |
| X1*Z1 | 0.48750000 | 99999.99 | 0.0001 | 0 |
| X1*Z2 | -0.70500000 | 99999.99 | 0.0001 | 0 |
| X1*Z3 | -0.08750000 | -99999.99 | 0.0001 | 0 |
| X1*Z1*Z2 | -0.06500000 | -99999.99 | 0.0001 | 0 |
| X1*Z1*Z3 | -0.04750000 | -99999.99 | 0.0001 | 0 |
| X1*Z2*Z3 | 0.04000000 | 99999.99 | 0.0001 | 0 |
| X1*Z1*Z2*Z3 | 1.08250000 | 99999.99 | 0.0001 | 0 |
| X2 | 0.17750000 | 99999.99 | 0.0001 | 0 |
| Z1*X2 | 0.25250000 | 99999.99 | 0.0001 | 0 |
| Z2*X2 | -0.08000000 | -99999.99 | 0.0001 | 0 |
| Z3*X2 | -0.02750000 | -99999.99 | 0.0001 | 0 |
| Z1*Z2*X2 | -0.04500000 | -99999.99 | 0.0001 | 0 |
| Z2*Z3*X2 | -0.02500000 | -99999.99 | 0.0001 | 0 |

| Term | Coefficient | | |
|---|---|---|---|
| Z1*Z2*Z3*X2 | -0.03500000 | -99999.99 | 0.0001 |
| X3 | -2.01000000 | 99999.99 | 0.0001 |
| Z1*X3 | 0.25000000 | 99999.99 | 0.0001 |
| Z2*X3 | 0.40000000 | 99999.99 | 0.0001 |
| Z3*X3 | -0.01000000 | -99999.99 | 0.0001 |
| Z1*Z2*X3 | -0.16500000 | -99999.99 | 0.0001 |
| Z1*Z3*X3 | -0.04500000 | -99999.99 | 0.0001 |
| Z2*Z3*X3 | -0.04000000 | -99999.99 | 0.0001 |
| Z1*Z2*Z3*X3 | -1.13500000 | -99999.99 | 0.0001 |
| X1*X2 | -0.80500000 | -99999.99 | 0.0001 |
| X1*Z1*X2 | -0.59000000 | -99999.99 | 0.0001 |
| X1*Z2*X2 | -0.10000000 | -99999.99 | 0.0001 |
| X1*Z3*X2 | -0.16000000 | -99999.99 | 0.0001 |
| X1*Z1*Z2*X2 | -0.06000000 | -99999.99 | 0.0001 |
| X1*Z1*Z3*X2 | -0.18500000 | -99999.99 | 0.0001 |
| X1*Z2*Z3*X2 | -0.08500000 | -99999.99 | 0.0001 |
| X1*Z1*Z2*Z3*X2 | -0.53500000 | -99999.99 | 0.0001 |
| X1*X3 | -0.05000000 | -99999.99 | 0.0001 |
| X1*Z1*X3 | -0.02500000 | -99999.99 | 0.0001 |
| X1*Z2*X3 | -0.06000000 | -99999.99 | 0.0001 |
| X1*Z3*X3 | -0.26500000 | -99999.99 | 0.0001 |
| X1*Z1*Z2*X3 | -0.43000000 | -99999.99 | 0.0001 |
| X1*Z1*Z3*X3 | -0.12000000 | -99999.99 | 0.0001 |
| X1*Z2*Z3*X3 | -0.19500000 | -99999.99 | 0.0001 |
| X1*Z1*Z2*Z3*X3 | -0.13500000 | -99999.99 | 0.0001 |
| X2*X3 | -0.06500000 | -99999.99 | 0.0001 |
| Z1*X2*X3 | -0.19000000 | 99999.99 | 0.0001 |
| Z2*X2*X3 | -0.22500000 | 99999.99 | 0.0001 |
| Z3*X2*X3 | -0.25000000 | 99999.99 | 0.0001 |
| Z1*Z2*X2*X3 | -0.12000000 | 99999.99 | 0.0001 |
| Z1*Z3*X2*X3 | 0.27000000 | 99999.99 | 0.0001 |
| Z2*Z3*X2*X3 | 3.18426628 | 99999.99 | 0.0001 |
| Z1*Z2*Z3*X2*X3 | -1.07124599 | 99999.99 | 0.0001 |
| X1*X2*X3 | -1.41370474 | 99999.99 | 0.0001 |
| X1*Z1*X2*X3 | 1.10873219 | 99999.99 | 0.0001 |
| X1*Z2*X2*X3 | 1.74381199 | 99999.99 | 0.0001 |
| X1*Z3*X2*X3 | -0.70878724 | -99999.99 | 0.0001 |
| X1*Z1*Z2*X2*X3 | -1.76627554 | -99999.99 | 0.0001 |
| X1*Z1*Z3*X2*X3 | -1.33128919 | -99999.99 | 0.0001 |
| X1*Z2*Z3*X2*X3 | | | |
| X1*Z1*Z2*Z3*X2*X3 | | | |

# TABLE C.13. Example 22-1: SAS Program

```
* THE FOLLOWING STATEMENTS GIVE THE DATA SET NAME AND ASSIGNS THE FACTOR;
* NAMES (A-H) THAT IS LOCATED IN COLUMNS NUMBERED (6-15). THE OUTPUT;
* "THICKNES" IS ALSO ASSIGNED A VALUE;
DATA ORIGINAL;
INPUT TRIAL A B C D E F G H I J THICKNES;
* THE FOLLOWING STATEMENTS USE THE RESOLUTION IV, 64 TRIAL TABLE;
* TO DEFINE THE CONTRAST COLUMNS THAT WILL BE CONSIDERED WITHIN;
* THIS MODEL;
  CONT1=A;  CONT2=B;  CONT3=C;  CONT4=D;  CONT5=E;  CONT6=F;  CONT7=A*B;
  CONT8=B*C;  CONT9=C*D;  CONT10=D*E;  CONT11=E*F;  CONT12=G;  CONT13=A*C;
  CONT14=B*D;  CONT15=C*E;  CONT16=D*F;  CONT17=H;  CONT18=I;  CONT19=A*B*C*D;
  CONT20=B*C*D*E;  CONT21=C*D*E*F;  CONT22=A*B*D*E*F;  CONT23=A*C*E*F;
  CONT24=A*D*F;  CONT25=A*E;  CONT26=B*F;  CONT27=A*B*C;  CONT28=B*C*D;
  CONT29=C*D*E;  CONT30=D*E*F;  CONT31=A*B*E*F;  CONT32=A*C*F;  CONT33=A*D;
  CONT34=B*E;  CONT35=C*F;  CONT36=A*B*D;  CONT37=B*C*E;  CONT38=C*D*F;
  CONT39=A*B*D*E;  CONT40=B*C*E*F;  CONT41=A*B*C*D*F;  CONT42=A*C*D*E;
  CONT43=B*D*E*F;  CONT44=A*B*C*E*F;  CONT45=A*C*D*F;  CONT46=A*D*E;
  CONT47=B*E*F;  CONT48=A*B*C*F;  CONT49=A*C*D;  CONT50=B*D*E;  CONT51=C*E*F;
  CONT52=A*B*D*F;  CONT53=A*C*E;  CONT54=B*D*F;  CONT55=A*B*E*C;
  CONT56=B*C*D*F;  CONT57=A*B*C*D*E;  CONT58=B*C*D*E*F;  CONT59=A*B*C*D*E*F;
  CONT60=A*C*D*E*F;  CONT61=A*D*E*F;  CONT62=A*E*F;  CONT63=A*F;
* THE INPUT FACTOR LEVELS AND OUTPUT (THICKNE) IS ENTERED;
CARDS;
  1    1 -1 -1 -1 -1 -1  1  1 -1  1       1405
  2    1  1 -1 -1 -1 -1 -1 -1  1 -1       1122
  3    1  1  1 -1 -1 -1 -1 -1 -1 -1        895
  4    1  1  1  1 -1 -1 -1 -1 -1 -1       1915
  5    1  1  1  1  1 -1 -1  1 -1 -1       2060
  6    1  1  1  1  1  1  1  1  1  1       1985
  7   -1  1  1  1  1  1  1 -1  1 -1       1050
  8    1 -1  1  1  1  1 -1 -1 -1 -1       2440
  9   -1 -1 -1  1  1  1 -1 -1 -1 -1        960
 10   -1 -1 -1 -1  1  1 -1 -1 -1 -1       1260
 11   -1 -1 -1 -1 -1  1 -1 -1 -1 -1       1110
 12   -1 -1 -1 -1 -1  1 -1 -1 -1 -1       1495
 13   -1 -1 -1 -1 -1 -1 -1 -1 -1 -1       1810
 14   -1 -1  1 -1 -1 -1 -1 -1 -1 -1        482
 15   -1 -1  1  1 -1 -1 -1 -1 -1 -1       1040
 16   -1 -1  1  1  1 -1 -1 -1 -1 -1       2620
 17    1 -1  1  1 -1 -1 -1 -1 -1 -1        910
 18   -1 -1 -1  1 -1 -1 -1 -1 -1 -1        545
 19   -1 -1  1 -1 -1 -1  1 -1 -1 -1       3650
 21   -1 -1  1  1  1 -1 -1 -1 -1 -1       2430
 21   -1 -1  1  1  1  1 -1 -1 -1 -1       1065
 22   -1 -1  1  1  1 -1  1 -1  1  1       1260
 23    1 -1  1 -1 -1 -1 -1  1  1  1       1976
 24    1 -1  1  1  1 -1  1 -1  1  1       2000
 25   -1 -1  1 -1  1 -1 -1 -1  1 -1        430
 26   -1 -1  1  1  1 -1 -1  1 -1  1       2070
 27   -1 -1 -1  1  1 -1  1 -1  1 -1        780
 28   -1 -1 -1  1 -1 -1  1 -1 -1 -1        570
 29   -1 -1  1 -1 -1 -1 -1 -1 -1 -1       3600
 31   -1 -1  1 -1 -1 -1 -1 -1 -1 -1        495
 31   -1 -1  1 -1  1 -1 -1 -1 -1 -1        620
 32    1 -1  1 -1  1 -1  1 -1  1  1       2520
 33    1 -1  1 -1 -1  1 -1 -1 -1  1       1300
 34   -1  1  1 -1 -1 -1 -1 -1 -1 -1       1074
 35   -1 -1  1  1  1 -1  1 -1 -1 -1       1070
 36   -1 -1  1  1  1 -1 -1 -1 -1 -1       1360
 37   -1 -1 -1  1 -1  1 -1 -1 -1 -1       1340
 38   -1 -1 -1  1 -1 -1  1 -1 -1 -1       1530
 39   -1 -1 -1  1 -1 -1 -1 -1 -1 -1        870
 40    1 -1  1 -1 -1 -1 -1  1 -1 -1       1480
 41    1  1  1 -1 -1 -1 -1 -1 -1 -1       1920
 42    1 -1  1 -1  1 -1 -1  1 -1 -1        975
 43   -1 -1  1  1  1 -1 -1  1 -1 -1       2130
 44   -1  1 -1  1  1  1 -1 -1 -1 -1        770
 45   -1 -1  1  1  1  1 -1 -1 -1 -1       1210
 46   -1 -1 -1  1  1  1 -1 -1 -1 -1       1800
 47   -1 -1 -1  1  1  1  1 -1 -1 -1        450
 48    1 -1 -1 -1  1 -1  1 -1 -1 -1       1380
 49   -1 -1 -1 -1  1 -1  1 -1 -1 -1       1360
 51   -1 -1 -1 -1 -1  1  1 -1  1 -1        840
 51   -1 -1 -1 -1 -1 -1  1 -1  1 -1       1020
 51    1 -1 -1 -1 -1 -1  1  1 -1 -1       1180
 52    1 -1 -1 -1 -1 -1  1 -1 -1 -1        980
 53    1 -1  1 -1 -1 -1  1 -1 -1  1        470
 54   -1  1  1 -1 -1 -1  1 -1 -1  1        770
 55   -1  1  1 -1 -1 -1  1 -1 -1  1       1320
 56   -1 -1 -1  1  1 -1 -1  1 -1 -1        820
 57   -1 -1  1 -1  1 -1  1  1  1 -1       1424
 58    1 -1 -1 -1 -1  1 -1  1  1 -1        620
 59   -1  1 -1 -1 -1 -1  1  1  1  1        500
 61   -1 -1  1 -1 -1 -1 -1 -1  1 -1       1010
 61   -1 -1  1 -1 -1 -1 -1 -1  1  1        545
 62   -1 -1 -1 -1  1 -1 -1 -1  1  1        545
 63   -1 -1 -1  1 -1 -1 -1 -1  1  1        600
 64   -1 -1 -1 -1 -1 -1 -1 -1 -1 -1        590
;
* SAS ANALYSIS OF VARIANCE ROUTINE IS USED DEFINING THE INPUT RANGE OF;
* CLASS FACTORS TO BE CONT1, CONT2, .... CONT63;
PROC ANOVA;
CLASS CONT1-CONT63 A B C D E F G H I J;
* THE MODEL STATEMENT NOTES THE OUTPUT (THICKNES) AND FACTORS CONSIDERED;
MODEL THICKNES = CONT1-CONT23 CONT25 CONT26 CONT31 CONT33 CONT34
       CONT35 CONT39 CONT40 CONT42 CONT43 CONT45 CONT48 CONT52 CONT55
       CONT56 CONT59 CONT61 CONT63;
* THE MEANS STATEMENT WILL GIVE AN OPTIONAL LEAST SQUARES DIFFERENCE(LSD)
* T-TEST FOR SIGNIFICANCE OF THE FACTORS IN THE MODEL AND AMOUNT OF;
* DIFFERENCE;
MEANS A B C A*B H I H*I A*D D*H/LSD;
MEANS CONT1-CONT23 CONT25 CONT26 CONT31 CONT33 CONT34 CONT35
       CONT39 CONT40 CONT42 CONT43 CONT45 CONT48 CONT52 CONT55 CONT56
       CONT59 CONT61 CONT63/ LSD CLDIFF;
```

# APPENDIX D

# REFERENCE TABLES

**TABLE A.  Area under the Standardized Normal Curve**

| $z_\alpha$ | .00 | .01 | .02 | .03 | .04 | .05 | .06 | .07 | .08 | .09 |
|---|---|---|---|---|---|---|---|---|---|---|
| 0.0 | .5000 | .4960 | .4920 | .4880 | .4840 | .4801 | .4761 | .4721 | .4681 | .4641 |
| 0.1 | .4602 | .4562 | .4522 | .4483 | .4443 | .4404 | .4364 | .4325 | .4286 | .4247 |
| 0.2 | .4207 | .4168 | .4129 | .4090 | .4052 | .4013 | .3974 | .3936 | .3897 | .3859 |
| 0.3 | .3821 | .3783 | .3745 | .3707 | .3669 | .3632 | .3594 | .3557 | .3520 | .3483 |
| 0.4 | .3446 | .3409 | .3372 | .3336 | .3300 | .3264 | .3228 | .3192 | .3156 | .3121 |
| 0.5 | .3085 | .3050 | .3015 | .2981 | .2946 | .2912 | .2877 | .2843 | .2810 | .2776 |
| 0.6 | .2743 | .2709 | .2676 | .2643 | .2611 | .2578 | .2546 | .2514 | .2483 | .2451 |
| 0.7 | .2420 | .2389 | .2358 | .2327 | .2296 | .2266 | .2236 | .2206 | .2177 | .2146 |
| 0.8 | .2119 | .2090 | .2061 | .2033 | .2005 | .1977 | .1949 | .1922 | .1894 | .1867 |
| 0.9 | .1841 | .1814 | .1788 | .1762 | .1736 | .1711 | .1685 | .1660 | .1635 | .1611 |
| 1.0 | .1587 | .1562 | .1539 | .1515 | .1492 | .1469 | .1446 | .1243 | .1401 | .1379 |
| 1.1 | .1357 | .1335 | .1314 | .1292 | .1271 | .1251 | .1230 | .1210 | .1190 | .1170 |
| 1.2 | .1151 | .1131 | .1112 | .1093 | .1075 | .1056 | .1038 | .1020 | .1003 | .0985 |
| 1.3 | .0968 | .0951 | .0934 | .0918 | .0901 | .0885 | .0869 | .0853 | .0838 | .0823 |
| 1.4 | .0808 | .0793 | .0778 | .0764 | .0749 | .0735 | .0721 | .0708 | .0694 | .0681 |
| 1.5 | .0668 | .0655 | .0643 | .0630 | .0618 | .0606 | .0594 | .0582 | .0571 | .0559 |
| 1.6 | .0548 | .0537 | .0526 | .0516 | .0505 | .0495 | .0485 | .0475 | .0465 | .0455 |
| 1.7 | .0446 | .0436 | .0427 | .0418 | .0409 | .0401 | .0392 | .0384 | .0375 | .0367 |
| 1.8 | .0359 | .0351 | .0344 | .0336 | .0329 | .0322 | .0314 | .0307 | .0301 | .0294 |
| 1.9 | .0287 | .0281 | .0274 | .0268 | .0262 | .0256 | .0250 | .0244 | .0239 | .0233 |
| 2.0 | .0228 | .0222 | .0217 | .0212 | .0207 | .0202 | .0197 | .0192 | .0188 | .0183 |
| 2.1 | .0179 | .0174 | .0170 | .0166 | .0162 | .0158 | .0154 | .0150 | .0146 | .0143 |
| 2.2 | .0139 | .0136 | .0132 | .0129 | .0125 | .0122 | .0119 | .0116 | .0113 | .0110 |
| 2.3 | .0107 | .0104 | .0102 | .00990 | .00964 | .00939 | .00914 | .00889 | .00866 | .00842 |
| 2.4 | .00820 | .00798 | .00776 | .00755 | .00734 | .00714 | .00695 | .00676 | .00657 | .00639 |
| 2.5 | .00621 | .00604 | .00587 | .00570 | .00554 | .00539 | .00523 | .00508 | .00494 | .00480 |
| 2.6 | .00466 | .00453 | .00440 | .00427 | .00415 | .00402 | .00391 | .00379 | .00368 | .00357 |
| 2.7 | .00347 | .00336 | .00326 | .00317 | .00307 | .00298 | .00289 | .00280 | .00272 | .00264 |
| 2.8 | .00256 | .00248 | .00240 | .00233 | .00226 | .00219 | .00212 | .00205 | .00199 | .00193 |
| 2.9 | .00187 | .00181 | .00175 | .00169 | .00164 | .00159 | .00154 | .00149 | .00144 | .00139 |

**TABLE A.** (*Continued*)

| $z_\alpha$ | .0 | .1 | .2 | .3 | .4 | .5 | .6 | .7 | .8 | .9 |
|---|---|---|---|---|---|---|---|---|---|---|
| 3 | .00135 | $.0^3988$ | $.0^3687$ | $.0^3483$ | $.0^3337$ | $.0^3233$ | $.0^3159$ | $.0^3108$ | $.0^4723$ | $.0^4481$ |
| 4 | $.0^4317$ | $.0^4207$ | $.0^4133$ | $.0^5854$ | $.0^5541^*$ | $.0^5340$ | $.0^5211$ | $.0^5130$ | $.0^6793$ | $.0^6479$ |
| 5 | $.0^6287$ | $.0^6170$ | $.0^7996$ | $.0^7579$ | $.0^7333$ | $.0^7190$ | $.0^7107$ | $.0^8599$ | $.0^8332$ | $.0^8182$ |
| 6 | $.0^9987$ | $.0^9530$ | $.0^9282$ | $.0^9149$ | $.0^{10}777$ | $.0^{10}402$ | $.0^{10}206$ | $.0^{10}104$ | $.0^{11}523$ | $.0^{11}260$ |

\* $.0^5541$ means .00000541.

Reference: Frederick E. Croxton, *Elementary Statistics with Applications in Medicines*, Prentice-Hall, Inc., Englewood Cliffs, NJ, 1953.

Note 1: The same information can be obtained from Tables B and C; however, this table format is different.

Note 2: In this text the tabular value corresponds to $Z_\alpha$, where $\alpha$ is the value of probability associated with the distribution area pictorially represented as

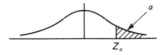

**TABLE B. Probability Points of the Normal Distribution: Single Sided ($\sigma^2$ known)**

| ($\alpha$ or $\beta$) | $U$ | ($\alpha$ or $\beta$) | $U$ |
|---|---|---|---|
| 0.001 | 3.090 | 0.100 | 1.282 |
| 0.005 | 2.576 | 0.150 | 1.036 |
| 0.010 | 2.326 | 0.200 | 0.842 |
| 0.015 | 2.170 | 0.300 | 0.524 |
| 0.020 | 2.054 | 0.400 | 0.253 |
| 0.025 | 1.960 | 0.500 | 0.000 |
| 0.050 | 1.645 | 0.600 | −0.253 |

Reproduced with permission: W. Diamond, *Practical Experiment Designs for Engineers and Scientists*, Van Nostrand Reinhold, New York, 1989.

Note 1: The same information can be obtained from Table A; however, the table format is different.

Note 2: In this text the tabular value corresponds to $U_\alpha$, where $\alpha$ is the value of probability associated with the distribution area pictorially represented as

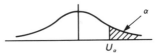

**TABLE C. Probability Points of the Normal Distribution: Double Sided ($\sigma^2$ known)**

| ($\alpha$ only) | $U$ | ($\alpha$ only) | $U$ |
|---|---|---|---|
| 0.001 | 3.291 | 0.100 | 1.645 |
| 0.005 | 2.807 | 0.150 | 1.440 |
| 0.010 | 2.576 | 0.200 | 1.282 |
| 0.015 | 2.432 | 0.300 | 1.036 |
| 0.020 | 2.326 | 0.400 | 0.842 |
| 0.025 | 2.241 | 0.500 | 0.675 |
| 0.050 | 1.960 | 0.600 | 0.524 |

Reproduced with permission: W. Diamond, *Practical Experiment Designs for Engineers and Scientists*, Van Nostrand Reinhold, New York, 1989.

Note 1: The same information can be obtained from Table A; however, the table format is different.

Note 2: In this text the tabular value corresponds to $U_\alpha$, where $\alpha$ is the value of probability associated with the distribution area pictorially represented as

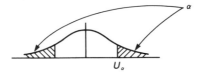

# TABLE D. Probability Points of the $t$ Distribution: Single Sided

| $\nu$ | .40 | .30 | .20 | .10 | .050 | .025 | .010 | .005 | .001 | .0005 |
|---|---|---|---|---|---|---|---|---|---|---|
| 1 | .325 | .727 | 1.376 | 3.078 | 6.314 | 12.71 | 31.82 | 63.66 | 318.3 | 636.6 |
| 2 | .289 | .617 | 1.061 | 1.886 | 2.920 | 4.303 | 6.965 | 9.925 | 22.33 | 31.60 |
| 3 | .277 | .584 | .978 | 1.638 | 2.353 | 3.182 | 4.541 | 5.841 | 10.22 | 12.94 |
| 4 | .271 | .569 | .941 | 1.533 | 2.132 | 2.776 | 3.747 | 4.604 | 7.173 | 8.610 |
| 5 | .267 | .559 | .920 | 1.476 | 2.015 | 2.571 | 3.365 | 4.032 | 5.893 | 6.859 |
| 6 | .265 | .553 | .906 | 1.440 | 1.943 | 2.447 | 3.143 | 3.707 | 5.208 | 5.959 |
| 7 | .263 | .549 | .896 | 1.415 | 1.895 | 2.365 | 2.998 | 3.499 | 4.785 | 5.405 |
| 8 | .262 | .546 | .889 | 1.397 | 1.860 | 2.306 | 2.896 | 3.355 | 4.501 | 5.041 |
| 9 | .261 | .543 | .883 | 1.383 | 1.833 | 2.262 | 2.821 | 3.250 | 4.297 | 4.781 |
| 10 | .260 | .542 | .879 | 1.372 | 1.812 | 2.228 | 2.764 | 3.169 | 4.144 | 4.587 |
| 11 | .260 | .540 | .876 | 1.363 | 1.796 | 2.201 | 2.718 | 3.106 | 4.025 | 4.437 |
| 12 | .259 | .539 | .873 | 1.356 | 1.782 | 2.179 | 2.681 | 3.055 | 3.930 | 4.318 |
| 13 | .259 | .538 | .870 | 1.350 | 1.771 | 2.160 | 2.650 | 3.012 | 3.852 | 4.221 |
| 14 | .258 | .537 | .868 | 1.345 | 1.761 | 2.145 | 2.624 | 2.977 | 3.787 | 4.140 |
| 15 | .258 | .536 | .866 | 1.341 | 1.753 | 2.131 | 2.602 | 2.947 | 3.733 | 4.073 |
| 16 | .258 | .535 | .865 | 1.337 | 1.746 | 2.120 | 2.583 | 2.921 | 3.686 | 4.015 |
| 17 | .257 | .534 | .863 | 1.333 | 1.740 | 2.110 | 2.567 | 2.898 | 3.646 | 3.965 |
| 18 | .257 | .534 | .862 | 1.330 | 1.734 | 2.101 | 2.552 | 2.878 | 3.611 | 3.922 |
| 19 | .257 | .533 | .861 | 1.328 | 1.729 | 2.093 | 2.539 | 2.861 | 3.579 | 3.883 |
| 20 | .257 | .533 | .860 | 1.325 | 1.725 | 2.086 | 2.528 | 2.845 | 3.552 | 3.850 |
| 21 | .257 | .532 | .859 | 1.323 | 1.721 | 2.080 | 2.518 | 2.831 | 3.527 | 3.819 |
| 22 | .256 | .532 | .858 | 1.321 | 1.717 | 2.074 | 2.508 | 2.819 | 3.505 | 3.792 |
| 23 | .256 | .532 | .858 | 1.319 | 1.714 | 2.069 | 2.500 | 2.807 | 3.485 | 3.767 |
| 24 | .256 | .531 | .857 | 1.318 | 1.711 | 2.064 | 2.492 | 2.797 | 3.467 | 3.745 |
| 25 | .256 | .531 | .856 | 1.316 | 1.708 | 2.060 | 2.485 | 2.787 | 3.450 | 3.725 |
| 26 | .256 | .531 | .856 | 1.315 | 1.706 | 2.056 | 2.479 | 2.779 | 3.435 | 3.707 |
| 27 | .256 | .531 | .855 | 1.314 | 1.703 | 2.052 | 2.473 | 2.771 | 3.421 | 3.690 |
| 28 | .256 | .530 | .855 | 1.313 | 1.701 | 2.048 | 2.467 | 2.763 | 3.408 | 3.674 |
| 29 | .256 | .530 | .854 | 1.311 | 1.699 | 2.045 | 2.462 | 2.756 | 3.396 | 3.659 |
| 30 | .256 | .530 | .854 | 1.310 | 1.697 | 2.042 | 2.457 | 2.750 | 3.385 | 3.646 |
| 40 | .255 | .529 | .851 | 1.303 | 1.684 | 2.021 | 2.423 | 2.704 | 3.307 | 3.551 |
| 50 | .255 | .528 | .849 | 1.298 | 1.676 | 2.009 | 2.403 | 2.678 | 3.262 | 3.495 |
| 60 | .254 | .527 | .848 | 1.296 | 1.671 | 2.000 | 2.390 | 2.660 | 3.232 | 3.460 |
| 80 | .254 | .527 | .846 | 1.292 | 1.664 | 1.990 | 2.374 | 2.639 | 3.195 | 3.415 |
| 100 | .254 | .526 | .845 | 1.290 | 1.660 | 1.984 | 2.365 | 2.626 | 3.174 | 3.389 |
| 200 | .254 | .525 | .843 | 1.286 | 1.653 | 1.972 | 2.345 | 2.601 | 3.131 | 3.339 |
| 500 | .253 | .525 | .842 | 1.283 | 1.648 | 1.965 | 2.334 | 2.586 | 3.106 | 3.310 |
| $\infty$ | .253 | .524 | .842 | 1.282 | 1.645 | 1.960 | 2.326 | 2.576 | 3.090 | 3.291 |

*Source*: Taken with permission from E. S. Pearson and H. O. Hartley (Eds.) (1958), *Biometrika Tables for Statisticans*, Vol. 1, Cambridge University Press. Parts of the table are also taken from Table III of Fisher and Yates: *Statistical Tables for Biological, Agricultural and Medical Research*, published by Longman Group Ltd., London (previously published by Oliver and Boyd, Edinburgh), by permission of the authors and publishers.

*Note*: In this text the tabular value corresponds to $t_{\alpha;\nu}$, where $\nu$ is the number of degrees of freedom and $\alpha$ is the value of probability associated with the distribution area pictorially represented as

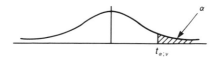

421

**TABLE E. Probability Points of the $t$ Distribution: Double Sided**

| Degrees of Freedom | Probability of a Larger Value, Sign Ignored | | | | | | | | |
|---|---|---|---|---|---|---|---|---|---|
| | 0.500 | 0.400 | 0.200 | 0.100 | 0.050 | 0.025 | 0.010 | 0.005 | 0.001 |
| 1 | 1.000 | 1.376 | 3.078 | 6.314 | 12.706 | 25.452 | 63.657 | | |
| 2 | .816 | 1.061 | 1.886 | 2.920 | 4.303 | 6.205 | 9.925 | 14.089 | 31.598 |
| 3 | .765 | .978 | 1.638 | 2.353 | 3.182 | 4.176 | 5.841 | 7.453 | 12.941 |
| 4 | .741 | .941 | 1.533 | 2.132 | 2.776 | 3.495 | 4.604 | 5.598 | 8.610 |
| 5 | .727 | .920 | 1.476 | 2.015 | 2.571 | 3.163 | 4.032 | 4.773 | 6.859 |
| 6 | .718 | .906 | 1.440 | 1.943 | 2.447 | 2.969 | 3.707 | 4.317 | 5.959 |
| 7 | .711 | .896 | 1.415 | 1.895 | 2.365 | 2.841 | 3.499 | 4.029 | 5.405 |
| 8 | .706 | .889 | 1.397 | 1.860 | 2.306 | 2.752 | 3.355 | 3.832 | 5.041 |
| 9 | .703 | .883 | 1.383 | 1.833 | 2.262 | 2.685 | 3.250 | 3.690 | 4.781 |
| 10 | .700 | .879 | 1.372 | 1.812 | 2.228 | 2.634 | 3.169 | 3.581 | 4.587 |
| 11 | .697 | .876 | 1.363 | 1.796 | 2.201 | 2.593 | 3.106 | 3.497 | 4.437 |
| 12 | .695 | .873 | 1.356 | 1.782 | 2.179 | 2.560 | 3.055 | 3.428 | 4.318 |
| 13 | .694 | .870 | 1.350 | 1.771 | 2.160 | 2.533 | 3.012 | 3.372 | 4.221 |
| 14 | .692 | .868 | 1.345 | 1.761 | 2.145 | 2.510 | 2.977 | 3.326 | 4.140 |
| 15 | .691 | .866 | 1.341 | 1.753 | 2.131 | 2.490 | 2.947 | 3.286 | 4.073 |
| 16 | .690 | .865 | 1.337 | 1.746 | 2.120 | 2.473 | 2.921 | 3.252 | 4.015 |
| 17 | .689 | .863 | 1.333 | 1.740 | 2.110 | 2.458 | 2.898 | 3.222 | 3.965 |
| 18 | .688 | .862 | 1.330 | 1.734 | 2.101 | 2.445 | 2.878 | 3.197 | 3.922 |
| 19 | .688 | .861 | 1.328 | 1.729 | 2.093 | 2.433 | 2.861 | 3.174 | 3.883 |
| 20 | .687 | .860 | 1.325 | 1.725 | 2.086 | 2.423 | 2.845 | 3.153 | 3.850 |
| 21 | .686 | .859 | 1.323 | 1.721 | 2.080 | 2.414 | 2.831 | 3.135 | 3.819 |
| 22 | .686 | .858 | 1.321 | 1.717 | 2.074 | 2.406 | 2.819 | 3.119 | 3.792 |
| 23 | .685 | .858 | 1.319 | 1.714 | 2.069 | 2.398 | 2.807 | 3.104 | 3.767 |
| 24 | .685 | .857 | 1.318 | 1.711 | 2.064 | 2.391 | 2.797 | 3.090 | 3.745 |
| 25 | .684 | .856 | 1.316 | 1.708 | 2.060 | 2.385 | 2.787 | 3.078 | 3.725 |
| 26 | .684 | .856 | 1.315 | 1.706 | 2.056 | 2.379 | 2.779 | 3.067 | 3.707 |
| 27 | .684 | .855 | 1.314 | 1.703 | 2.052 | 2.373 | 2.771 | 3.056 | 3.690 |
| 28 | .683 | .855 | 1.313 | 1.701 | 2.048 | 2.368 | 2.763 | 3.047 | 3.674 |
| 29 | .683 | .854 | 1.311 | 1.699 | 2.045 | 2.364 | 2.756 | 3.038 | 3.659 |
| 30 | .683 | .854 | 1.310 | 1.697 | 2.042 | 2.360 | 2.750 | 3.030 | 3.646 |
| 35 | .682 | .852 | 1.306 | 1.690 | 2.030 | 2.342 | 2.724 | 2.996 | 3.591 |
| 40 | .681 | .851 | 1.303 | 1.684 | 2.021 | 2.329 | 2.704 | 2.971 | 3.551 |
| 45 | .680 | .850 | 1.301 | 1.680 | 2.014 | 2.319 | 2.690 | 2.952 | 3.520 |
| 50 | .680 | .849 | 1.299 | 1.676 | 2.008 | 2.310 | 2.678 | 2.937 | 3.496 |
| 55 | .679 | .849 | 1.297 | 1.673 | 2.004 | 2.304 | 2.669 | 2.925 | 3.476 |

**TABLE E.** (*Continued*)

| Degrees of Freedom | Probability of a Larger Value, Sign Ignored | | | | | | | | |
|---|---|---|---|---|---|---|---|---|---|
| | 0.500 | 0.400 | 0.200 | 0.100 | 0.050 | 0.025 | 0.010 | 0.005 | 0.001 |
| 60 | .679 | .848 | 1.296 | 1.671 | 2.000 | 2.299 | 2.660 | 2.915 | 3.460 |
| 70 | .678 | .847 | 1.294 | 1.667 | 1.994 | 2.290 | 2.648 | 2.899 | 3.435 |
| 80 | .678 | .847 | 1.293 | 1.665 | 1.989 | 2.284 | 2.638 | 2.887 | 3.416 |
| 90 | .678 | .846 | 1.291 | 1.662 | 1.986 | 2.279 | 2.631 | 2.878 | 3.402 |
| 100 | .677 | .846 | 1.290 | 1.661 | 1.982 | 2.276 | 2.625 | 2.871 | 3.390 |
| 120 | .677 | .845 | 1.289 | 1.658 | 1.980 | 2.270 | 2.617 | 2.860 | 3.373 |
| ∞ | .6745 | .8416 | 1.2816 | 1.6448 | 1.9600 | 2.2414 | 2.5758 | 2.8070 | 3.2905 |

Reprinted from adapted material from G. W. Snedecor and W. G. Cochran, *Statistical Methods*, 8th ed., © 1989 by Iowa State University Press, Ames, IA 50010.

Note: In this text the tabular value corresponds to $t_{\alpha;\nu}$, where $\nu$ is the number of degrees of freedom and $\alpha$ is the value of probability associated with the distribution area, pictorially represented as

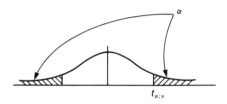

# TABLE F. Probability Points of the Variance Ratio (*F* Distribution)

| Probability point | $v_2$ | Numerator ($v_1$) | | | | | | | | | | | | | | | | | | |
|---|---|---|---|---|---|---|---|---|---|---|---|---|---|---|---|---|---|---|---|---|
| | | 1 | 2 | 3 | 4 | 5 | 6 | 7 | 8 | 9 | 10 | 12 | 15 | 20 | 24 | 30 | 40 | 60 | 120 | ∞ |
| 0.1 | 1 | 39.9 | 49.5 | 53.6 | 55.8 | 57.2 | 58.2 | 58.9 | 59.4 | 59.9 | 60.2 | 60.7 | 61.2 | 61.7 | 62.0 | 62.3 | 62.5 | 62.8 | 63.1 | 63.3 |
| 0.05 | | 161 | 199 | 216 | 225 | 230 | 234 | 237 | 239 | 241 | 242 | 244 | 246 | 248 | 249 | 250 | 251 | 252 | 253 | 254 |
| 0.01 | | 4052 | 4999 | 5403 | 5625 | 5764 | 5859 | 5928 | 5982 | 6022 | 6056 | 6106 | 6157 | 6209 | 6235 | 6261 | 6287 | 6313 | 6339 | 6366 |
| 0.1 | 2 | 8.53 | 9.00 | 9.16 | 9.24 | 9.29 | 9.33 | 9.35 | 9.37 | 9.38 | 9.39 | 9.41 | 9.42 | 9.44 | 9.45 | 9.46 | 9.47 | 9.47 | 9.48 | 9.49 |
| 0.05 | | 18.5 | 19.0 | 19.2 | 19.2 | 19.3 | 19.3 | 19.4 | 19.4 | 19.4 | 19.4 | 19.4 | 19.4 | 19.4 | 19.5 | 19.5 | 19.5 | 19.5 | 19.5 | 19.5 |
| 0.01 | | 98.5 | 99.0 | 99.2 | 99.2 | 99.3 | 99.3 | 99.4 | 99.4 | 99.4 | 99.4 | 99.4 | 99.4 | 99.4 | 99.5 | 99.5 | 99.5 | 99.5 | 99.5 | 99.5 |
| 0.1 | 3 | 5.54 | 5.46 | 5.39 | 5.34 | 5.31 | 5.28 | 5.27 | 5.25 | 5.24 | 5.23 | 5.22 | 5.20 | 5.18 | 5.18 | 5.17 | 5.16 | 5.15 | 5.14 | 5.13 |
| 0.05 | | 10.1 | 9.55 | 9.28 | 9.12 | 9.01 | 8.94 | 8.89 | 8.85 | 8.81 | 8.79 | 8.74 | 8.70 | 8.66 | 8.64 | 8.62 | 8.59 | 8.57 | 8.55 | 8.53 |
| 0.01 | | 34.1 | 30.8 | 29.5 | 28.7 | 28.2 | 27.9 | 27.7 | 27.5 | 27.3 | 27.2 | 27.1 | 26.9 | 26.7 | 26.6 | 26.5 | 26.4 | 26.3 | 26.2 | 26.1 |
| 0.1 | 4 | 4.54 | 4.32 | 4.19 | 4.11 | 4.05 | 4.01 | 3.98 | 3.95 | 3.94 | 3.92 | 3.90 | 3.87 | 3.84 | 3.83 | 3.82 | 3.80 | 3.79 | 3.78 | 3.76 |
| 0.05 | | 7.71 | 6.94 | 6.59 | 6.39 | 6.26 | 6.16 | 6.09 | 6.04 | 6.00 | 5.96 | 5.91 | 5.86 | 5.80 | 5.77 | 5.75 | 5.72 | 5.69 | 5.66 | 5.63 |
| 0.01 | | 21.2 | 18.0 | 16.7 | 16.0 | 15.5 | 15.2 | 15.0 | 14.8 | 14.7 | 14.5 | 14.4 | 14.2 | 14.0 | 13.9 | 13.8 | 13.7 | 13.7 | 13.6 | 13.5 |
| 0.1 | 5 | 4.06 | 3.78 | 3.62 | 3.52 | 3.45 | 3.40 | 3.37 | 3.34 | 3.32 | 3.30 | 3.27 | 3.24 | 3.21 | 3.19 | 3.17 | 3.16 | 3.14 | 3.12 | 3.10 |
| 0.05 | | 6.61 | 5.79 | 5.41 | 5.19 | 5.05 | 4.95 | 4.88 | 4.82 | 4.77 | 4.74 | 4.68 | 4.62 | 4.56 | 4.53 | 4.50 | 4.46 | 4.43 | 4.40 | 4.36 |
| 0.01 | | 16.3 | 13.3 | 12.1 | 11.4 | 11.0 | 10.7 | 10.5 | 10.3 | 10.2 | 10.1 | 9.89 | 9.72 | 9.55 | 9.47 | 9.38 | 9.29 | 9.20 | 9.11 | 9.02 |
| 0.1 | 6 | 3.78 | 3.46 | 3.29 | 3.18 | 3.11 | 3.05 | 3.01 | 2.98 | 2.96 | 2.94 | 2.90 | 2.87 | 2.84 | 2.82 | 2.80 | 2.78 | 2.76 | 2.74 | 2.72 |
| 0.05 | | 5.99 | 5.14 | 4.76 | 4.53 | 4.39 | 4.28 | 4.21 | 4.15 | 4.10 | 4.06 | 4.00 | 3.94 | 3.87 | 3.84 | 3.81 | 3.77 | 3.74 | 3.70 | 3.67 |
| 0.01 | | 13.7 | 10.9 | 9.78 | 9.15 | 8.75 | 8.47 | 8.26 | 8.10 | 7.98 | 7.87 | 7.72 | 7.56 | 7.40 | 7.31 | 7.23 | 7.14 | 7.06 | 6.97 | 6.88 |
| 0.1 | 7 | 3.59 | 3.26 | 3.07 | 2.96 | 2.88 | 2.83 | 2.78 | 2.75 | 2.72 | 2.70 | 2.67 | 2.63 | 2.59 | 2.58 | 2.56 | 2.54 | 2.51 | 2.49 | 2.47 |
| 0.05 | | 5.59 | 4.74 | 4.35 | 4.12 | 3.97 | 3.87 | 3.79 | 3.73 | 3.68 | 3.64 | 3.57 | 3.51 | 3.44 | 3.41 | 3.38 | 3.34 | 3.30 | 3.27 | 3.23 |
| 0.01 | | 12.2 | 9.55 | 8.45 | 7.85 | 7.46 | 7.19 | 6.99 | 6.84 | 6.72 | 6.62 | 6.47 | 6.31 | 6.16 | 6.07 | 5.99 | 5.91 | 5.82 | 5.74 | 5.65 |
| 0.1 | 8 | 3.46 | 3.11 | 2.92 | 2.81 | 2.73 | 2.67 | 2.62 | 2.59 | 2.56 | 2.54 | 2.50 | 2.46 | 2.42 | 2.40 | 2.38 | 2.36 | 2.34 | 2.32 | 2.29 |
| 0.05 | | 5.32 | 4.46 | 4.07 | 3.84 | 3.69 | 3.58 | 3.50 | 3.44 | 3.39 | 3.35 | 3.28 | 3.22 | 3.15 | 3.12 | 3.08 | 3.04 | 3.01 | 2.97 | 2.93 |
| 0.01 | | 11.3 | 8.65 | 7.59 | 7.01 | 6.63 | 6.37 | 6.18 | 6.03 | 5.91 | 5.81 | 5.67 | 5.52 | 5.36 | 5.28 | 5.20 | 5.12 | 5.03 | 4.95 | 4.86 |
| 0.1 | 9 | 3.36 | 3.01 | 2.81 | 2.69 | 2.61 | 2.55 | 2.51 | 2.47 | 2.44 | 2.42 | 2.38 | 2.34 | 2.30 | 2.28 | 2.25 | 2.23 | 2.21 | 2.18 | 2.16 |
| 0.05 | | 5.12 | 4.26 | 3.86 | 3.63 | 3.48 | 3.37 | 3.29 | 3.23 | 3.18 | 3.14 | 3.07 | 3.01 | 2.94 | 2.90 | 2.86 | 2.83 | 2.79 | 2.75 | 2.71 |
| 0.01 | | 10.6 | 8.02 | 6.99 | 6.42 | 6.06 | 5.80 | 5.61 | 5.47 | 5.35 | 5.26 | 5.11 | 4.96 | 4.81 | 4.73 | 4.65 | 4.57 | 4.48 | 4.40 | 4.31 |

| | | | | | | | | | | | | | | | | | | | | |
|---|---|---|---|---|---|---|---|---|---|---|---|---|---|---|---|---|---|---|---|---|
| 10 | 0.1 | 3.28 | 2.92 | 2.73 | 2.61 | 2.52 | 2.46 | 2.41 | 2.38 | 2.35 | 2.32 | 2.28 | 2.24 | 2.20 | 2.18 | 2.16 | 2.13 | 2.11 | 2.08 | 2.06 |
| | 0.05 | 4.96 | 4.10 | 3.71 | 3.48 | 3.33 | 3.22 | 3.14 | 3.07 | 3.02 | 2.98 | 2.91 | 2.84 | 2.77 | 2.74 | 2.70 | 2.66 | 2.62 | 2.58 | 2.54 |
| | 0.01 | 10.0 | 7.56 | 6.55 | 5.99 | 5.64 | 5.39 | 5.20 | 5.06 | 4.94 | 4.85 | 4.71 | 4.56 | 4.41 | 4.33 | 4.25 | 4.17 | 4.08 | 4.00 | 3.91 |
| 11 | 0.1 | 3.23 | 2.86 | 2.66 | 2.54 | 2.45 | 2.39 | 2.34 | 2.30 | 2.27 | 2.25 | 2.21 | 2.17 | 2.12 | 2.10 | 2.08 | 2.05 | 2.03 | 2.00 | 1.97 |
| | 0.05 | 4.84 | 3.98 | 3.59 | 3.36 | 3.20 | 3.09 | 3.01 | 2.95 | 2.90 | 2.85 | 2.79 | 2.72 | 2.65 | 2.61 | 2.57 | 2.53 | 2.49 | 2.45 | 2.40 |
| | 0.01 | 9.65 | 7.21 | 6.22 | 5.67 | 5.32 | 5.07 | 4.89 | 4.74 | 4.63 | 4.54 | 4.40 | 4.25 | 4.10 | 4.02 | 3.94 | 3.86 | 3.78 | 3.69 | 3.60 |
| 12 | 0.1 | 3.18 | 2.81 | 2.61 | 2.48 | 2.39 | 2.33 | 2.28 | 2.24 | 2.21 | 2.19 | 2.15 | 2.10 | 2.06 | 2.04 | 2.01 | 1.99 | 1.96 | 1.93 | 1.90 |
| | 0.05 | 4.75 | 3.89 | 3.49 | 3.26 | 3.11 | 3.00 | 2.91 | 2.85 | 2.80 | 2.75 | 2.69 | 2.62 | 2.54 | 2.51 | 2.47 | 2.43 | 2.38 | 2.34 | 2.30 |
| | 0.01 | 9.33 | 6.93 | 5.95 | 5.41 | 5.06 | 4.82 | 4.64 | 4.50 | 4.39 | 4.30 | 4.16 | 4.01 | 3.86 | 3.78 | 3.70 | 3.62 | 3.54 | 3.45 | 3.36 |
| 13 | 0.1 | 3.14 | 2.76 | 2.56 | 2.43 | 2.35 | 2.28 | 2.24 | 2.20 | 2.16 | 2.14 | 2.10 | 2.05 | 2.01 | 1.98 | 1.96 | 1.93 | 1.90 | 1.88 | 1.85 |
| | 0.05 | 4.67 | 3.81 | 3.41 | 3.18 | 3.03 | 2.92 | 2.83 | 2.77 | 2.71 | 2.67 | 2.60 | 2.53 | 2.46 | 2.42 | 2.38 | 2.34 | 2.30 | 2.25 | 2.21 |
| | 0.01 | 9.07 | 6.70 | 5.74 | 5.21 | 4.86 | 4.62 | 4.44 | 4.30 | 4.19 | 4.10 | 3.96 | 3.82 | 3.66 | 3.59 | 3.51 | 3.43 | 3.34 | 3.25 | 3.17 |
| 14 | 0.1 | 3.10 | 2.73 | 2.52 | 2.39 | 2.31 | 2.24 | 2.19 | 2.15 | 2.12 | 2.10 | 2.05 | 2.01 | 1.96 | 1.94 | 1.91 | 1.89 | 1.86 | 1.83 | 1.80 |
| | 0.05 | 4.60 | 3.74 | 3.34 | 3.11 | 2.96 | 2.85 | 2.76 | 2.70 | 2.65 | 2.60 | 2.53 | 2.46 | 2.39 | 2.35 | 2.31 | 2.27 | 2.22 | 2.18 | 2.13 |
| | 0.01 | 8.86 | 6.51 | 5.56 | 5.04 | 4.69 | 4.46 | 4.28 | 4.14 | 4.03 | 3.94 | 3.80 | 3.66 | 3.51 | 3.43 | 3.35 | 3.27 | 3.18 | 3.09 | 3.00 |
| 15 | 0.1 | 3.07 | 2.70 | 2.49 | 2.36 | 2.27 | 2.21 | 2.16 | 2.12 | 2.09 | 2.06 | 2.02 | 1.97 | 1.92 | 1.90 | 1.87 | 1.85 | 1.82 | 1.79 | 1.76 |
| | 0.05 | 4.54 | 3.68 | 3.29 | 3.06 | 2.90 | 2.79 | 2.71 | 2.64 | 2.59 | 2.54 | 2.48 | 2.40 | 2.33 | 2.29 | 2.25 | 2.20 | 2.16 | 2.11 | 2.07 |
| | 0.01 | 8.68 | 6.36 | 5.42 | 4.89 | 4.56 | 4.32 | 4.14 | 4.00 | 3.89 | 3.80 | 3.67 | 3.52 | 3.37 | 3.29 | 3.21 | 3.13 | 3.05 | 2.96 | 2.87 |
| 16 | 0.1 | 3.05 | 2.67 | 2.46 | 2.33 | 2.24 | 2.18 | 2.13 | 2.09 | 2.06 | 2.03 | 1.99 | 1.94 | 1.89 | 1.87 | 1.84 | 1.81 | 1.78 | 1.75 | 1.72 |
| | 0.05 | 4.49 | 3.63 | 3.24 | 3.01 | 2.85 | 2.74 | 2.66 | 2.59 | 2.54 | 2.49 | 2.42 | 2.35 | 2.28 | 2.24 | 2.19 | 2.15 | 2.11 | 2.06 | 2.01 |
| | 0.01 | 8.53 | 6.23 | 5.29 | 4.77 | 4.44 | 4.20 | 4.03 | 3.89 | 3.78 | 3.69 | 3.55 | 3.41 | 3.26 | 3.18 | 3.10 | 3.02 | 2.93 | 2.84 | 2.75 |
| 17 | 0.1 | 3.03 | 2.64 | 2.44 | 2.31 | 2.22 | 2.15 | 2.10 | 2.06 | 2.03 | 2.00 | 1.96 | 1.91 | 1.86 | 1.84 | 1.81 | 1.78 | 1.75 | 1.72 | 1.69 |
| | 0.05 | 4.45 | 3.59 | 3.20 | 2.96 | 2.81 | 2.70 | 2.61 | 2.55 | 2.49 | 2.45 | 2.38 | 2.31 | 2.23 | 2.19 | 2.15 | 2.10 | 2.06 | 2.01 | 1.96 |
| | 0.01 | 8.40 | 6.11 | 5.18 | 4.67 | 4.34 | 4.10 | 3.93 | 3.79 | 3.68 | 3.59 | 3.46 | 3.31 | 3.16 | 3.08 | 3.00 | 2.92 | 2.83 | 2.75 | 2.65 |
| 18 | 0.1 | 3.01 | 2.62 | 2.42 | 2.29 | 2.20 | 2.13 | 2.08 | 2.04 | 2.00 | 1.98 | 1.93 | 1.89 | 1.84 | 1.81 | 1.78 | 1.75 | 1.72 | 1.69 | 1.66 |
| | 0.05 | 4.41 | 3.55 | 3.16 | 2.93 | 2.77 | 2.66 | 2.58 | 2.51 | 2.46 | 2.41 | 2.34 | 2.27 | 2.19 | 2.15 | 2.11 | 2.06 | 2.02 | 1.97 | 1.92 |
| | 0.01 | 8.29 | 6.01 | 5.09 | 4.58 | 4.25 | 4.01 | 3.84 | 3.71 | 3.60 | 3.51 | 3.37 | 3.23 | 3.08 | 3.00 | 2.92 | 2.84 | 2.75 | 2.66 | 2.57 |
| 19 | 0.1 | 2.99 | 2.61 | 2.40 | 2.27 | 2.18 | 2.11 | 2.06 | 2.02 | 1.98 | 1.96 | 1.91 | 1.86 | 1.81 | 1.79 | 1.76 | 1.73 | 1.70 | 1.67 | 1.63 |
| | 0.05 | 4.38 | 3.52 | 3.13 | 2.90 | 2.74 | 2.63 | 2.54 | 2.48 | 2.42 | 2.38 | 2.31 | 2.23 | 2.16 | 2.11 | 2.07 | 2.03 | 1.98 | 1.93 | 1.88 |
| | 0.01 | 8.18 | 5.93 | 5.01 | 4.50 | 4.17 | 3.94 | 3.77 | 3.63 | 3.52 | 3.43 | 3.30 | 3.15 | 3.00 | 2.92 | 2.84 | 2.76 | 2.67 | 2.58 | 2.49 |

(*Table continues on p. 426.*)

**TABLE F.** (*Continued*)

| Probability point | $v_2$ | \| | 1 | 2 | 3 | 4 | 5 | 6 | 7 | 8 | 9 | 10 | 12 | 15 | 20 | 24 | 30 | 40 | 60 | 120 | ∞ |
|---|---|---|---|---|---|---|---|---|---|---|---|---|---|---|---|---|---|---|---|---|---|
| | | | | | | | | | | | | | | | Numerator ($v_1$) | | | | | | |
| 0.1 | 20 | | 2.97 | 2.59 | 2.38 | 2.25 | 2.16 | 2.09 | 2.04 | 2.00 | 1.96 | 1.94 | 1.89 | 1.84 | 1.79 | 1.77 | 1.74 | 1.71 | 1.68 | 1.64 | 1.61 |
| 0.05 | | | 4.35 | 3.49 | 3.10 | 2.87 | 2.71 | 2.60 | 2.51 | 2.45 | 2.39 | 2.35 | 2.28 | 2.20 | 2.12 | 2.08 | 2.04 | 1.99 | 1.95 | 1.90 | 1.84 |
| 0.01 | | | 8.10 | 5.85 | 4.94 | 4.43 | 4.10 | 3.87 | 3.70 | 3.56 | 3.46 | 3.37 | 3.23 | 3.09 | 2.94 | 2.86 | 2.78 | 2.69 | 2.61 | 2.52 | 2.42 |
| 0.1 | 21 | | 2.96 | 2.57 | 2.36 | 2.23 | 2.14 | 2.08 | 2.02 | 1.98 | 1.95 | 1.92 | 1.87 | 1.83 | 1.78 | 1.75 | 1.72 | 1.69 | 1.66 | 1.62 | 1.59 |
| 0.05 | | | 4.32 | 3.47 | 3.07 | 2.84 | 2.68 | 2.57 | 2.49 | 2.42 | 2.37 | 2.32 | 2.25 | 2.18 | 2.10 | 2.05 | 2.01 | 1.96 | 1.92 | 1.87 | 1.81 |
| 0.01 | | | 8.02 | 5.78 | 4.87 | 4.37 | 4.04 | 3.81 | 3.64 | 3.51 | 3.40 | 3.31 | 3.17 | 3.03 | 2.88 | 2.80 | 2.72 | 2.64 | 2.55 | 2.46 | 2.36 |
| 0.1 | 22 | | 2.95 | 2.56 | 2.35 | 2.22 | 2.13 | 2.06 | 2.01 | 1.97 | 1.93 | 1.90 | 1.86 | 1.81 | 1.76 | 1.73 | 1.70 | 1.67 | 1.64 | 1.60 | 1.57 |
| 0.05 | | | 4.30 | 3.44 | 3.05 | 2.82 | 2.66 | 2.55 | 2.46 | 2.40 | 2.34 | 2.30 | 2.23 | 2.15 | 2.07 | 2.03 | 1.98 | 1.94 | 1.89 | 1.84 | 1.78 |
| 0.01 | | | 7.95 | 5.72 | 4.82 | 4.31 | 3.99 | 3.76 | 3.59 | 3.45 | 3.35 | 3.26 | 3.12 | 2.98 | 2.83 | 2.75 | 2.67 | 2.58 | 2.50 | 2.40 | 2.31 |
| 0.1 | 23 | | 2.94 | 2.55 | 2.34 | 2.21 | 2.11 | 2.05 | 1.99 | 1.95 | 1.92 | 1.89 | 1.85 | 1.80 | 1.74 | 1.72 | 1.69 | 1.66 | 1.62 | 1.59 | 1.55 |
| 0.05 | | | 4.28 | 3.42 | 3.03 | 2.80 | 2.64 | 2.53 | 2.44 | 2.37 | 2.32 | 2.27 | 2.20 | 2.13 | 2.05 | 2.00 | 1.96 | 1.91 | 1.86 | 1.81 | 1.76 |
| 0.01 | | | 7.88 | 5.66 | 4.76 | 4.26 | 3.94 | 3.71 | 3.54 | 3.41 | 3.30 | 3.21 | 3.07 | 2.93 | 2.78 | 2.70 | 2.62 | 2.54 | 2.45 | 2.35 | 2.26 |
| 0.1 | 24 | | 2.93 | 2.54 | 2.33 | 2.19 | 2.10 | 2.04 | 1.98 | 1.94 | 1.91 | 1.88 | 1.83 | 1.78 | 1.73 | 1.70 | 1.67 | 1.64 | 1.61 | 1.57 | 1.53 |
| 0.05 | | | 4.26 | 3.40 | 3.01 | 2.78 | 2.62 | 2.51 | 2.42 | 2.36 | 2.30 | 2.25 | 2.18 | 2.11 | 2.03 | 1.98 | 1.94 | 1.89 | 1.84 | 1.79 | 1.73 |
| 0.01 | | | 7.82 | 5.61 | 4.72 | 4.22 | 3.90 | 3.67 | 3.50 | 3.36 | 3.26 | 3.17 | 3.03 | 2.89 | 2.74 | 2.66 | 2.58 | 2.49 | 2.40 | 2.31 | 2.21 |
| 0.1 | 25 | | 2.92 | 2.53 | 2.32 | 2.18 | 2.09 | 2.02 | 1.97 | 1.93 | 1.89 | 1.87 | 1.82 | 1.77 | 1.72 | 1.69 | 1.66 | 1.63 | 1.59 | 1.56 | 1.52 |
| 0.05 | | | 4.24 | 3.39 | 2.99 | 2.76 | 2.60 | 2.49 | 2.40 | 2.34 | 2.28 | 2.24 | 2.16 | 2.09 | 2.01 | 1.96 | 1.92 | 1.87 | 1.82 | 1.77 | 1.71 |
| 0.01 | | | 7.77 | 5.57 | 4.68 | 4.18 | 3.86 | 3.63 | 3.46 | 3.32 | 3.22 | 3.13 | 2.99 | 2.85 | 2.70 | 2.62 | 2.54 | 2.45 | 2.36 | 2.27 | 2.17 |
| 0.1 | 26 | | 2.91 | 2.52 | 2.31 | 2.17 | 2.08 | 2.01 | 1.96 | 1.92 | 1.88 | 1.86 | 1.81 | 1.76 | 1.71 | 1.68 | 1.65 | 1.61 | 1.58 | 1.54 | 1.50 |
| 0.05 | | | 4.23 | 3.37 | 2.98 | 2.74 | 2.59 | 2.47 | 2.39 | 2.32 | 2.27 | 2.22 | 2.15 | 2.07 | 1.99 | 1.95 | 1.90 | 1.85 | 1.80 | 1.75 | 1.69 |
| 0.01 | | | 7.72 | 5.53 | 4.64 | 4.14 | 3.82 | 3.59 | 3.42 | 3.29 | 3.18 | 3.09 | 2.96 | 2.82 | 2.66 | 2.58 | 2.50 | 2.42 | 2.33 | 2.23 | 2.13 |
| 0.1 | 27 | | 2.90 | 2.51 | 2.30 | 2.17 | 2.07 | 2.00 | 1.95 | 1.91 | 1.87 | 1.85 | 1.80 | 1.75 | 1.70 | 1.67 | 1.64 | 1.60 | 1.57 | 1.53 | 1.49 |
| 0.05 | | | 4.21 | 3.35 | 2.96 | 2.73 | 2.57 | 2.46 | 2.37 | 2.31 | 2.25 | 2.20 | 2.13 | 2.06 | 1.97 | 1.93 | 1.88 | 1.84 | 1.79 | 1.73 | 1.67 |
| 0.01 | | | 7.68 | 5.49 | 4.60 | 4.11 | 3.78 | 3.56 | 3.39 | 3.26 | 3.15 | 3.06 | 2.93 | 2.78 | 2.63 | 2.55 | 2.47 | 2.38 | 2.29 | 2.20 | 2.10 |
| 0.1 | 28 | | 2.89 | 2.50 | 2.29 | 2.16 | 2.06 | 2.00 | 1.94 | 1.90 | 1.87 | 1.84 | 1.79 | 1.74 | 1.69 | 1.66 | 1.63 | 1.59 | 1.56 | 1.52 | 1.48 |
| 0.05 | | | 4.20 | 3.34 | 2.95 | 2.71 | 2.56 | 2.45 | 2.36 | 2.29 | 2.24 | 2.19 | 2.12 | 2.04 | 1.96 | 1.91 | 1.87 | 1.82 | 1.77 | 1.71 | 1.65 |
| 0.01 | | | 7.64 | 5.45 | 4.57 | 4.07 | 3.75 | 3.53 | 3.36 | 3.23 | 3.12 | 3.03 | 2.90 | 2.75 | 2.60 | 2.52 | 2.44 | 2.35 | 2.26 | 2.17 | 2.06 |

| | | | | | | | | | | | | | | | | | | | | |
|---|---|---|---|---|---|---|---|---|---|---|---|---|---|---|---|---|---|---|---|---|
| 29 | 0.1 | 2.89 | 2.50 | 2.28 | 2.15 | 2.06 | 1.99 | 1.93 | 1.89 | 1.86 | 1.83 | 1.78 | 1.73 | 1.68 | 1.65 | 1.62 | 1.58 | 1.55 | 1.51 | 1.47 |
| | 0.05 | 4.18 | 3.33 | 2.93 | 2.70 | 2.55 | 2.43 | 2.35 | 2.28 | 2.22 | 2.18 | 2.10 | 2.03 | 1.94 | 1.90 | 1.85 | 1.81 | 1.75 | 1.70 | 1.64 |
| | 0.01 | 7.60 | 5.42 | 4.54 | 4.04 | 3.73 | 3.50 | 3.33 | 3.20 | 3.09 | 3.00 | 2.87 | 2.73 | 2.57 | 2.49 | 2.41 | 2.33 | 2.23 | 2.14 | 2.03 |
| 30 | 0.1 | 2.88 | 2.49 | 2.28 | 2.14 | 2.05 | 1.98 | 1.93 | 1.88 | 1.85 | 1.82 | 1.77 | 1.72 | 1.67 | 1.64 | 1.61 | 1.57 | 1.54 | 1.50 | 1.46 |
| | 0.05 | 4.17 | 3.32 | 2.92 | 2.69 | 2.53 | 2.42 | 2.33 | 2.27 | 2.21 | 2.16 | 2.09 | 2.01 | 1.93 | 1.89 | 1.84 | 1.79 | 1.74 | 1.68 | 1.62 |
| | 0.01 | 7.56 | 5.39 | 4.51 | 4.02 | 3.70 | 3.47 | 3.30 | 3.17 | 3.07 | 2.98 | 2.84 | 2.70 | 2.55 | 2.47 | 2.39 | 2.30 | 2.21 | 2.11 | 2.01 |
| 40 | 0.1 | 2.84 | 2.44 | 2.23 | 2.09 | 2.00 | 1.93 | 1.87 | 1.83 | 1.79 | 1.76 | 1.71 | 1.66 | 1.61 | 1.57 | 1.54 | 1.51 | 1.47 | 1.42 | 1.38 |
| | 0.05 | 4.08 | 3.23 | 2.84 | 2.61 | 2.45 | 2.34 | 2.25 | 2.18 | 2.12 | 2.08 | 2.00 | 1.92 | 1.84 | 1.79 | 1.74 | 1.69 | 1.64 | 1.58 | 1.51 |
| | 0.01 | 7.31 | 5.18 | 4.31 | 3.83 | 3.51 | 3.29 | 3.12 | 2.99 | 2.89 | 2.80 | 2.66 | 2.52 | 2.37 | 2.29 | 2.20 | 2.11 | 2.02 | 1.92 | 1.80 |
| 60 | 0.1 | 2.79 | 2.39 | 2.18 | 2.04 | 1.95 | 1.87 | 1.82 | 1.77 | 1.74 | 1.71 | 1.66 | 1.60 | 1.54 | 1.51 | 1.48 | 1.44 | 1.40 | 1.35 | 1.29 |
| | 0.05 | 4.00 | 3.15 | 2.76 | 2.53 | 2.37 | 2.25 | 2.17 | 2.10 | 2.04 | 1.99 | 1.92 | 1.84 | 1.75 | 1.70 | 1.65 | 1.59 | 1.53 | 1.47 | 1.39 |
| | 0.01 | 7.08 | 4.98 | 4.13 | 3.65 | 3.34 | 3.12 | 2.95 | 2.82 | 2.72 | 2.63 | 2.50 | 2.35 | 2.20 | 2.12 | 2.03 | 1.94 | 1.84 | 1.73 | 1.60 |
| 120 | 0.1 | 2.75 | 2.35 | 2.13 | 1.99 | 1.90 | 1.82 | 1.77 | 1.72 | 1.68 | 1.65 | 1.60 | 1.54 | 1.48 | 1.45 | 1.41 | 1.37 | 1.32 | 1.26 | 1.19 |
| | 0.05 | 3.92 | 3.07 | 2.68 | 2.45 | 2.29 | 2.18 | 2.09 | 2.02 | 1.96 | 1.91 | 1.83 | 1.75 | 1.66 | 1.61 | 1.55 | 1.50 | 1.43 | 1.35 | 1.25 |
| | 0.01 | 6.85 | 4.79 | 3.95 | 3.48 | 3.17 | 2.96 | 2.79 | 2.66 | 2.56 | 2.47 | 2.34 | 2.19 | 2.03 | 1.95 | 1.86 | 1.76 | 1.66 | 1.53 | 1.38 |
| ∞ | 0.1 | 2.71 | 2.30 | 2.08 | 1.94 | 1.85 | 1.77 | 1.72 | 1.67 | 1.63 | 1.60 | 1.55 | 1.49 | 1.42 | 1.38 | 1.34 | 1.30 | 1.24 | 1.17 | 1.00 |
| | 0.05 | 3.84 | 3.00 | 2.60 | 2.37 | 2.21 | 2.10 | 2.01 | 1.94 | 1.88 | 1.83 | 1.75 | 1.67 | 1.57 | 1.52 | 1.46 | 1.39 | 1.32 | 1.22 | 1.00 |
| | 0.01 | 6.63 | 4.61 | 3.78 | 3.32 | 3.02 | 2.80 | 2.64 | 2.51 | 2.41 | 2.32 | 2.18 | 2.04 | 1.88 | 1.79 | 1.70 | 1.59 | 1.47 | 1.32 | 1.00 |

Table F is taken from Table V of Fisher and Yates': *Statistical Tables for Biological, Agricultural and Medical Research*, Longman Group U.K. Ltd. London (previously published by Oliver and Boyd Ltd., Edinburgh) and by permission of the authors and publishers. (The labeling reflects the nomenclature used in this text)

Note: The tabular value corresponds to $F_{\alpha;v1;v2}$, where $v1$ is the number of degrees of freedom of the larger value in the numerator, $v2$ is the number of degrees of freedom of the smaller value in the denominator, and $\alpha$ is the value of probability associated with the distribution area pictorially represented as

427

**TABLE G.** Cumulative Distribution of $\chi^2$

| Degrees of Freedom | Probability of a Greater Value | | | | | | | | | | | | |
|---|---|---|---|---|---|---|---|---|---|---|---|---|---|
| | 0.995 | 0.990 | 0.975 | 0.950 | 0.900 | 0.750 | 0.500 | 0.250 | 0.100 | 0.050 | 0.025 | 0.010 | 0.005 |
| 1 | ... | ... | ... | ... | 0.02 | 0.10 | 0.45 | 1.32 | 2.71 | 3.84 | 5.02 | 6.63 | 7.88 |
| 2 | 0.01 | 0.02 | 0.05 | 0.10 | 0.21 | 0.58 | 1.39 | 2.77 | 4.61 | 5.99 | 7.38 | 9.21 | 10.60 |
| 3 | 0.07 | 0.11 | 0.22 | 0.35 | 0.58 | 1.21 | 2.37 | 4.11 | 6.25 | 7.81 | 9.35 | 11.34 | 12.84 |
| 4 | 0.21 | 0.30 | 0.48 | 0.71 | 1.06 | 1.92 | 3.36 | 5.39 | 7.78 | 9.49 | 11.14 | 13.28 | 14.86 |
| 5 | 0.41 | 0.55 | 0.83 | 1.15 | 1.61 | 2.67 | 4.35 | 6.63 | 9.24 | 11.07 | 12.83 | 15.09 | 16.75 |
| 6 | 0.68 | 0.87 | 1.24 | 1.64 | 2.20 | 3.45 | 5.35 | 7.84 | 10.64 | 12.59 | 14.45 | 16.81 | 18.55 |
| 7 | 0.99 | 1.24 | 1.69 | 2.17 | 2.83 | 4.25 | 6.35 | 9.04 | 12.02 | 14.07 | 16.01 | 18.48 | 20.28 |
| 8 | 1.34 | 1.65 | 2.18 | 2.73 | 3.49 | 5.07 | 7.34 | 10.22 | 13.36 | 15.51 | 17.53 | 20.09 | 21.96 |
| 9 | 1.73 | 2.09 | 2.70 | 3.33 | 4.17 | 5.90 | 8.34 | 11.39 | 14.68 | 16.92 | 19.02 | 21.67 | 23.59 |
| 10 | 2.16 | 2.56 | 3.25 | 3.94 | 4.87 | 6.74 | 9.34 | 12.55 | 15.99 | 18.31 | 20.48 | 23.21 | 25.19 |
| 11 | 2.60 | 3.05 | 3.82 | 4.57 | 5.58 | 7.58 | 10.34 | 13.70 | 17.28 | 19.68 | 21.92 | 24.72 | 26.76 |
| 12 | 3.07 | 3.57 | 4.40 | 5.23 | 6.30 | 8.44 | 11.34 | 14.85 | 18.55 | 21.03 | 23.34 | 26.22 | 28.30 |
| 13 | 3.57 | 4.11 | 5.01 | 5.89 | 7.04 | 9.30 | 12.34 | 15.98 | 19.81 | 22.36 | 24.74 | 27.69 | 29.82 |
| 14 | 4.07 | 4.66 | 5.63 | 6.57 | 7.79 | 10.17 | 13.34 | 17.12 | 21.06 | 23.68 | 26.12 | 29.14 | 31.32 |
| 15 | 4.60 | 5.23 | 6.27 | 7.26 | 8.55 | 11.04 | 14.34 | 18.25 | 22.31 | 25.00 | 27.49 | 30.58 | 32.80 |
| 16 | 5.14 | 5.81 | 6.91 | 7.96 | 9.31 | 11.91 | 15.34 | 19.37 | 23.54 | 26.30 | 28.85 | 32.00 | 34.27 |
| 17 | 5.70 | 6.41 | 7.56 | 8.67 | 10.09 | 12.79 | 16.34 | 20.49 | 24.77 | 27.59 | 30.19 | 33.41 | 35.72 |
| 18 | 6.26 | 7.01 | 8.23 | 9.39 | 10.86 | 13.68 | 17.34 | 21.60 | 25.99 | 28.87 | 31.53 | 34.81 | 37.16 |
| 19 | 6.84 | 7.63 | 8.91 | 10.12 | 11.65 | 14.56 | 18.34 | 22.72 | 27.20 | 30.14 | 32.85 | 36.19 | 38.58 |
| 20 | 7.43 | 8.26 | 9.59 | 10.85 | 12.44 | 15.45 | 19.34 | 23.83 | 28.41 | 31.41 | 34.17 | 37.57 | 40.00 |

| ν | | | | | | | | | | | | | |
|---|---|---|---|---|---|---|---|---|---|---|---|---|---|
| 21 | 8.03 | 8.90 | 10.28 | 11.59 | 13.24 | 16.34 | 20.34 | 24.93 | 29.62 | 32.67 | 35.48 | 38.93 | 41.40 |
| 22 | 8.64 | 9.54 | 10.98 | 12.34 | 14.04 | 17.24 | 21.34 | 26.04 | 30.81 | 33.92 | 36.78 | 40.29 | 42.80 |
| 23 | 9.26 | 10.20 | 11.69 | 13.09 | 14.85 | 18.14 | 22.34 | 27.14 | 32.01 | 35.17 | 38.08 | 41.64 | 44.18 |
| 24 | 9.89 | 10.86 | 12.40 | 13.85 | 15.66 | 19.04 | 23.34 | 28.24 | 33.20 | 36.42 | 39.36 | 42.98 | 45.56 |
| 25 | 10.52 | 11.52 | 13.12 | 14.61 | 16.47 | 19.94 | 24.34 | 29.34 | 34.38 | 37.65 | 40.65 | 44.31 | 46.93 |
| 26 | 11.16 | 12.20 | 13.84 | 15.38 | 17.29 | 20.84 | 25.34 | 30.43 | 35.56 | 38.89 | 41.92 | 45.64 | 48.29 |
| 27 | 11.81 | 12.88 | 14.57 | 16.15 | 18.11 | 21.75 | 26.34 | 31.53 | 36.74 | 40.11 | 43.19 | 46.96 | 49.64 |
| 28 | 12.46 | 13.56 | 15.31 | 16.93 | 18.94 | 22.66 | 27.34 | 32.62 | 37.92 | 41.34 | 44.46 | 48.28 | 50.99 |
| 29 | 13.12 | 14.26 | 16.05 | 17.71 | 19.77 | 23.57 | 28.34 | 33.71 | 39.09 | 42.56 | 45.72 | 49.59 | 52.34 |
| 30 | 13.79 | 14.95 | 16.79 | 18.49 | 20.60 | 24.48 | 29.34 | 34.80 | 40.26 | 43.77 | 46.98 | 50.89 | 53.67 |
| 40 | 20.71 | 22.16 | 24.43 | 26.51 | 29.05 | 33.66 | 39.34 | 45.62 | 51.80 | 55.76 | 59.34 | 63.69 | 66.77 |
| 50 | 27.99 | 29.71 | 32.36 | 34.76 | 37.69 | 42.94 | 49.33 | 56.33 | 63.17 | 67.50 | 71.42 | 76.15 | 79.49 |
| 60 | 35.53 | 37.48 | 40.48 | 43.19 | 46.46 | 52.29 | 59.33 | 66.98 | 74.40 | 79.08 | 83.30 | 88.38 | 91.95 |
| 70 | 43.28 | 45.44 | 48.76 | 51.74 | 55.33 | 61.70 | 69.33 | 77.58 | 85.53 | 90.53 | 95.02 | 100.42 | 104.22 |
| 80 | 51.17 | 53.54 | 57.15 | 60.39 | 64.28 | 71.14 | 79.33 | 88.13 | 96.58 | 101.88 | 106.63 | 112.33 | 116.32 |
| 90 | 59.20 | 61.75 | 65.65 | 69.13 | 73.29 | 80.62 | 89.33 | 98.64 | 107.56 | 113.14 | 118.14 | 124.12 | 128.30 |
| 100 | 67.33 | 70.06 | 74.22 | 77.93 | 82.36 | 90.13 | 99.33 | 109.14 | 118.50 | 124.34 | 129.56 | 135.81 | 140.17 |

$$\chi^2_{\alpha;\nu}$$

Reprinted from material adapted from G. W. Snedecor and W. G. Cochran, *Statistical Methods*, 8th ed., © 1989 by Iowa State University Press, Ames, IA 50010.

Note: In this text the tabular value corresponds to $\chi^2_{\alpha;\nu}$, where $\nu$ is the number of degrees of freedom and $\alpha$ is the value of probability associated with the distribution area pictorially represented as

## TABLE H. Gamma Function

*Tabulation of value of Γ(n) versus n*

| n | Γ(n) | n | Γ(n) | n | Γ(n) | n | Γ(n) |
|---|------|---|------|---|------|---|------|
| 1.00 | 1.00000 | 1.25 | .90640 | 1.50 | .88623 | 1.75 | .91906 |
| 1.01 | .99433 | 1.26 | .90440 | 1.51 | .88659 | 1.76 | .92137 |
| 1.02 | .98884 | 1.27 | .90250 | 1.52 | .88704 | 1.77 | .92376 |
| 1.03 | .98355 | 1.28 | .90072 | 1.53 | .88757 | 1.78 | .92623 |
| 1.04 | .97844 | 1.29 | .89904 | 1.54 | .88818 | 1.79 | .92877 |
| 1.05 | .97350 | 1.30 | .89747 | 1.55 | .88887 | 1.80 | .93138 |
| 1.06 | .96874 | 1.31 | .89600 | 1.56 | .88964 | 1.81 | .93408 |
| 1.07 | .96415 | 1.32 | .89464 | 1.57 | .89049 | 1.82 | .93685 |
| 1.08 | .95973 | 1.33 | .89338 | 1.58 | .89142 | 1.83 | .93969 |
| 1.09 | .95546 | 1.34 | .89222 | 1.59 | .89243 | 1.84 | .94261 |
| 1.10 | .95135 | 1.35 | .89115 | 1.60 | .89352 | 1.85 | .94561 |
| 1.11 | .94739 | 1.36 | .89018 | 1.61 | .89468 | 1.86 | .94869 |
| 1.12 | .94359 | 1.37 | .88931 | 1.62 | .89592 | 1.87 | .95184 |
| 1.13 | .93993 | 1.38 | .88854 | 1.63 | .89724 | 1.88 | .95507 |
| 1.14 | .93642 | 1.39 | .88785 | 1.64 | .89864 | 1.89 | .95838 |
| 1.15 | .93304 | 1.40 | .88726 | 1.65 | .90012 | 1.90 | .96177 |
| 1.16 | .92980 | 1.41 | .88676 | 1.66 | .90167 | 1.91 | .96523 |
| 1.17 | .92670 | 1.42 | .88636 | 1.67 | .90330 | 1.92 | .96878 |
| 1.18 | .92373 | 1.43 | .88604 | 1.68 | .90500 | 1.93 | .97240 |
| 1.19 | .92088 | 1.44 | .88580 | 1.69 | .90678 | 1.94 | .97610 |
| 1.20 | .91817 | 1.45 | .88565 | 1.70 | .90864 | 1.95 | .97988 |
| 1.21 | .91558 | 1.46 | .88560 | 1.71 | .91057 | 1.96 | .98374 |
| 1.22 | .91311 | 1.47 | .88563 | 1.72 | .91258 | 1.97 | .98768 |
| 1.23 | .91075 | 1.48 | .88575 | 1.73 | .91466 | 1.98 | .99171 |
| 1.24 | .90852 | 1.49 | .88595 | 1.74 | .91683 | 1.99 | .99581 |
| | | | | | | 2.00 | 1.00000 |

$$\Gamma(n) = \int_0^\infty e^{-x} x^{n-1} \, dx$$

$$\Gamma(n + 1) = n\Gamma(n)$$

$$\Gamma(1) = 1$$

$$\Gamma\left(\frac{1}{2}\right) = \sqrt{\pi}$$

$$\Gamma\left(\frac{n}{2}\right) = \left(\frac{n}{2} - 1\right)! = \begin{cases} \left(\dfrac{n}{2} - 1\right)\left(\dfrac{n}{2} - 2\right) \cdots (3) \cdot (2) \cdot (1) & \text{for } n \text{ even and } n > 2 \\ \left(\dfrac{n}{2} - 1\right)\left(\dfrac{n}{2} - 2\right) \cdots \left(\dfrac{3}{2}\right)\left(\dfrac{1}{2}\right)\sqrt{\pi} & \text{for } n \text{ odd and } n > 2 \end{cases}$$

Reproduced with permission: Charles Lipson and Narendra Sheth, *Statistical Design and Analysis of Engineering Experiments*, McGraw-Hill Publishing Company, New York, 1973.

# TABLE I. Exact Critical Values for Use with the Analysis of Means

Exact Critical Values $h_{0.10}$ for the Analysis of Means
Significance Level = 0.10
Number of Means, $k$

| DF | 3 | 4 | 5 | 6 | 7 | 8 | 9 | 10 | 11 | 12 | 13 | 14 | 15 | 16 | 17 | 18 | 19 | 20 | DF |
|----|---|---|---|---|---|---|---|----|----|----|----|----|----|----|----|----|----|----|----|
| 3 | 3.16 | | | | | | | | | | | | | | | | | | 3 |
| 4 | 2.81 | 3.10 | | | | | | | | | | | | | | | | | 4 |
| 5 | 2.63 | 2.88 | 3.05 | | | | | | | | | | | | | | | | 5 |
| 6 | 2.52 | 2.74 | 2.91 | 3.03 | | | | | | | | | | | | | | | 6 |
| 7 | 2.44 | 2.65 | 2.81 | 2.92 | 3.02 | | | | | | | | | | | | | | 7 |
| 8 | 2.39 | 2.59 | 2.73 | 2.85 | 2.94 | 3.02 | | | | | | | | | | | | | 8 |
| 9 | 2.34 | 2.54 | 2.68 | 2.79 | 2.88 | 2.95 | 3.01 | | | | | | | | | | | | 9 |
| 10 | 2.31 | 2.50 | 2.64 | 2.74 | 2.83 | 2.90 | 2.96 | 3.02 | | | | | | | | | | | 10 |
| 11 | 2.29 | 2.47 | 2.60 | 2.70 | 2.79 | 2.86 | 2.92 | 2.97 | 3.02 | | | | | | | | | | 11 |
| 12 | 2.27 | 2.45 | 2.57 | 2.67 | 2.75 | 2.82 | 2.88 | 2.93 | 2.98 | 3.02 | | | | | | | | | 12 |

(Table continues on p. 432.)

## TABLE I. (Continued)

Exact Critical Values $h_{0.10}$ for the Analysis of Means

Significance Level = 0.10

Number of Means, $k$

| DF | 3 | 4 | 5 | 6 | 7 | 8 | 9 | 10 | 11 | 12 | 13 | 14 | 15 | 16 | 17 | 18 | 19 | 20 | DF |
|---|---|---|---|---|---|---|---|---|---|---|---|---|---|---|---|---|---|---|---|
| 13 | 2.25 | 2.43 | 2.55 | 2.65 | 2.73 | 2.79 | 2.85 | 2.90 | 2.95 | 2.99 | 3.03 | | | | | | | | 13 |
| 14 | 2.23 | 2.41 | 2.53 | 2.63 | 2.70 | 2.77 | 2.83 | 2.88 | 2.92 | 2.96 | 3.00 | 3.03 | | | | | | | 14 |
| 15 | 2.22 | 2.39 | 2.51 | 2.61 | 2.68 | 2.75 | 2.80 | 2.85 | 2.90 | 2.94 | 2.97 | 3.01 | 3.04 | | | | | | 15 |
| 16 | 2.21 | 2.38 | 2.50 | 2.59 | 2.67 | 2.73 | 2.79 | 2.83 | 2.88 | 2.92 | 2.95 | 2.99 | 3.02 | 3.05 | | | | | 16 |
| 17 | 2.20 | 2.37 | 2.49 | 2.58 | 2.65 | 2.72 | 2.77 | 2.82 | 2.86 | 2.90 | 2.93 | 2.97 | 3.00 | 3.03 | 3.05 | | | | 17 |
| 18 | 2.19 | 2.36 | 2.47 | 2.56 | 2.64 | 2.70 | 2.75 | 2.80 | 2.84 | 2.88 | 2.92 | 2.95 | 2.98 | 3.01 | 3.03 | 3.06 | | | 18 |
| 19 | 2.18 | 2.35 | 2.46 | 2.55 | 2.63 | 2.69 | 2.74 | 2.79 | 2.83 | 2.87 | 2.90 | 2.94 | 2.96 | 2.99 | 3.02 | 3.04 | 3.06 | | 19 |
| 20 | 2.18 | 2.34 | 2.45 | 2.54 | 2.62 | 2.68 | 2.73 | 2.78 | 2.82 | 2.86 | 2.89 | 2.92 | 2.95 | 2.98 | 3.00 | 3.03 | 3.05 | 3.07 | 20 |
| 24 | 2.15 | 2.32 | 2.43 | 2.51 | 2.58 | 2.64 | 2.69 | 2.74 | 2.78 | 2.82 | 2.85 | 2.88 | 2.91 | 2.93 | 2.96 | 2.98 | 3.00 | 3.02 | 24 |
| 30 | 2.13 | 2.29 | 2.40 | 2.48 | 2.55 | 2.61 | 2.66 | 2.70 | 2.74 | 2.77 | 2.81 | 2.84 | 2.86 | 2.89 | 2.91 | 2.93 | 2.96 | 2.98 | 30 |
| 40 | 2.11 | 2.27 | 2.37 | 2.45 | 2.52 | 2.57 | 2.62 | 2.66 | 2.70 | 2.73 | 2.77 | 2.79 | 2.82 | 2.85 | 2.87 | 2.89 | 2.91 | 2.93 | 40 |
| 60 | 2.09 | 2.24 | 2.34 | 2.42 | 2.49 | 2.54 | 2.59 | 2.63 | 2.66 | 2.70 | 2.73 | 2.75 | 2.78 | 2.80 | 2.82 | 2.84 | 2.86 | 2.88 | 60 |
| 120 | 2.07 | 2.22 | 2.32 | 2.39 | 2.45 | 2.51 | 2.55 | 2.59 | 2.62 | 2.66 | 2.69 | 2.71 | 2.74 | 2.76 | 2.78 | 2.80 | 2.82 | 2.84 | 120 |
| $\infty$ | 2.05 | 2.19 | 2.29 | 2.36 | 2.42 | 2.47 | 2.52 | 2.55 | 2.59 | 2.62 | 2.65 | 2.67 | 2.69 | 2.72 | 2.74 | 2.76 | 2.77 | 2.79 | $\infty$ |

Exact Critical Values $h_{0.05}$ for the Analysis of Means

Significance Level = 0.05

Number of Means, $k$

| DF | 3 | 4 | 5 | 6 | 7 | 8 | 9 | 10 | 11 | 12 | 13 | 14 | 15 | 16 | 17 | 18 | 19 | 20 | DF |
|----|----|----|----|----|----|----|----|----|----|----|----|----|----|----|----|----|----|----|----|
| 3 | 4.18 | | | | | | | | | | | | | | | | | | 3 |
| 4 | 3.56 | 3.89 | | | | | | | | | | | | | | | | | 4 |
| 5 | 3.25 | 3.53 | 3.72 | | | | | | | | | | | | | | | | 5 |
| 6 | 3.07 | 3.31 | 3.49 | 3.62 | | | | | | | | | | | | | | | 6 |
| 7 | 2.94 | 3.17 | 3.33 | 3.45 | 3.56 | | | | | | | | | | | | | | 7 |
| 8 | 2.86 | 3.07 | 3.21 | 3.33 | 3.43 | 3.51 | | | | | | | | | | | | | 8 |
| 9 | 2.79 | 2.99 | 3.13 | 3.24 | 3.33 | 3.41 | 3.48 | | | | | | | | | | | | 9 |
| 10 | 2.74 | 2.93 | 3.07 | 3.17 | 3.26 | 3.33 | 3.40 | 3.45 | | | | | | | | | | | 10 |
| 11 | 2.70 | 2.88 | 3.01 | 3.12 | 3.20 | 3.27 | 3.33 | 3.39 | 3.44 | | | | | | | | | | 11 |
| 12 | 2.67 | 2.85 | 2.97 | 3.07 | 3.15 | 3.22 | 3.28 | 3.33 | 3.38 | 3.42 | | | | | | | | | 12 |
| 13 | 2.64 | 2.81 | 2.94 | 3.03 | 3.11 | 3.18 | 3.24 | 3.29 | 3.34 | 3.38 | 3.42 | | | | | | | | 13 |
| 14 | 2.62 | 2.79 | 2.91 | 3.00 | 3.08 | 3.14 | 3.20 | 3.25 | 3.30 | 3.34 | 3.37 | 3.41 | | | | | | | 14 |
| 15 | 2.60 | 2.76 | 2.88 | 2.97 | 3.05 | 3.11 | 3.17 | 3.22 | 3.26 | 3.30 | 3.34 | 3.37 | 3.40 | | | | | | 15 |

(Table continues on p. 434.)

# TABLE I. (*Continued*)

Exact Critical Values $h_{0.05}$ for the Analysis of Means

Significance Level = 0.05

Number of Means, $k$

| DF | 3 | 4 | 5 | 6 | 7 | 8 | 9 | 10 | 11 | 12 | 13 | 14 | 15 | 16 | 17 | 18 | 19 | 20 | DF |
|----|---|---|---|---|---|---|---|----|----|----|----|----|----|----|----|----|----|----|----|
| 16 | 2.58 | 2.74 | 2.86 | 2.95 | 3.02 | 3.09 | 3.14 | 3.19 | 3.23 | 3.27 | 3.31 | 3.34 | 3.37 | 3.40 | | | | | 16 |
| 17 | 2.57 | 2.73 | 2.84 | 2.93 | 3.00 | 3.06 | 3.12 | 3.16 | 3.21 | 3.25 | 3.28 | 3.31 | 3.34 | 3.37 | 3.40 | | | | 17 |
| 18 | 2.55 | 2.71 | 2.82 | 2.91 | 2.98 | 3.04 | 3.10 | 3.14 | 3.18 | 3.22 | 3.26 | 3.29 | 3.32 | 3.35 | 3.37 | 3.40 | | | 18 |
| 19 | 2.54 | 2.70 | 2.81 | 2.89 | 2.96 | 3.02 | 3.08 | 3.12 | 3.16 | 3.20 | 3.24 | 3.27 | 3.30 | 3.32 | 3.35 | 3.37 | 3.40 | | 19 |
| 20 | 2.53 | 2.68 | 2.79 | 2.88 | 2.95 | 3.01 | 3.06 | 3.11 | 3.15 | 3.18 | 3.22 | 3.25 | 3.28 | 3.30 | 3.33 | 3.35 | 3.37 | 3.40 | 20 |
| 24 | 2.50 | 2.65 | 2.75 | 2.83 | 2.90 | 2.96 | 3.01 | 3.05 | 3.09 | 3.13 | 3.16 | 3.19 | 3.22 | 3.24 | 3.27 | 3.29 | 3.31 | 3.33 | 24 |
| 30 | 2.47 | 2.61 | 2.71 | 2.79 | 2.85 | 2.91 | 2.96 | 3.00 | 3.04 | 3.07 | 3.10 | 3.13 | 3.16 | 3.18 | 3.20 | 3.22 | 3.25 | 3.27 | 30 |
| 40 | 2.43 | 2.57 | 2.67 | 2.75 | 2.81 | 2.86 | 2.91 | 2.95 | 2.98 | 3.01 | 3.04 | 3.07 | 3.10 | 3.12 | 3.14 | 3.16 | 3.18 | 3.20 | 40 |
| 60 | 2.40 | 2.54 | 2.63 | 2.70 | 2.76 | 2.81 | 2.86 | 2.90 | 2.93 | 2.96 | 2.99 | 3.02 | 3.04 | 3.06 | 3.08 | 3.10 | 3.12 | 3.14 | 60 |
| 120 | 2.37 | 2.50 | 2.59 | 2.66 | 2.72 | 2.77 | 2.81 | 2.84 | 2.88 | 2.91 | 2.93 | 2.96 | 2.98 | 3.00 | 3.02 | 3.04 | 3.06 | 3.08 | 120 |
| $\infty$ | 2.34 | 2.47 | 2.56 | 2.62 | 2.68 | 2.72 | 2.76 | 2.80 | 2.83 | 2.86 | 2.88 | 2.90 | 2.93 | 2.95 | 2.97 | 2.98 | 3.00 | 3.02 | $\infty$ |

Exact Critical Values $h_{0.01}$ for the Analysis of Means

Significance Level = 0.01

Number of Means, $k$

| DF | 3 | 4 | 5 | 6 | 7 | 8 | 9 | 10 | 11 | 12 | 13 | 14 | 15 | 16 | 17 | 18 | 19 | 20 | DF |
|---|---|---|---|---|---|---|---|---|---|---|---|---|---|---|---|---|---|---|---|
| 3 | 7.51 | | | | | | | | | | | | | | | | | | 3 |
| 4 | 5.74 | 6.21 | | | | | | | | | | | | | | | | | 4 |
| 5 | 4.93 | 5.29 | 5.55 | | | | | | | | | | | | | | | | 5 |
| 6 | 4.48 | 4.77 | 4.98 | 5.16 | | | | | | | | | | | | | | | 6 |
| 7 | 4.18 | 4.44 | 4.63 | 4.78 | 4.90 | | | | | | | | | | | | | | 7 |
| 8 | 3.98 | 4.21 | 4.38 | 4.52 | 4.63 | 4.72 | | | | | | | | | | | | | 8 |
| 9 | 3.84 | 4.05 | 4.20 | 4.33 | 4.43 | 4.51 | 4.59 | | | | | | | | | | | | 9 |
| 10 | 3.73 | 3.92 | 4.07 | 4.18 | 4.28 | 4.36 | 4.43 | 4.49 | | | | | | | | | | | 10 |
| 11 | 3.64 | 3.82 | 3.96 | 4.07 | 4.16 | 4.23 | 4.30 | 4.36 | 4.41 | | | | | | | | | | 11 |
| 12 | 3.57 | 3.74 | 3.87 | 3.98 | 4.06 | 4.13 | 4.20 | 4.25 | 4.31 | 4.35 | | | | | | | | | 12 |
| 13 | 3.51 | 3.68 | 3.80 | 3.90 | 3.98 | 4.05 | 4.11 | 4.17 | 4.22 | 4.26 | 4.30 | | | | | | | | 13 |
| 14 | 3.46 | 3.63 | 3.74 | 3.84 | 3.92 | 3.98 | 4.04 | 4.09 | 4.14 | 4.18 | 4.22 | 4.26 | | | | | | | 14 |
| 15 | 3.42 | 3.58 | 3.69 | 3.79 | 3.86 | 3.92 | 3.98 | 4.03 | 4.08 | 4.12 | 4.16 | 4.19 | 4.22 | | | | | | 15 |
| 16 | 3.38 | 3.54 | 3.65 | 3.74 | 3.81 | 3.87 | 3.93 | 3.98 | 4.02 | 4.06 | 4.10 | 4.14 | 4.17 | 4.20 | | | | | 16 |
| 17 | 3.35 | 3.50 | 3.61 | 3.70 | 3.77 | 3.83 | 3.89 | 3.93 | 3.98 | 4.02 | 4.05 | 4.09 | 4.12 | 4.14 | 4.17 | | | | 17 |
| 18 | 3.33 | 3.47 | 3.58 | 3.66 | 3.73 | 3.79 | 3.85 | 3.89 | 3.94 | 3.97 | 4.01 | 4.04 | 4.07 | 4.10 | 4.12 | 4.15 | | | 18 |
| 19 | 3.30 | 3.45 | 3.55 | 3.63 | 3.70 | 3.76 | 3.81 | 3.86 | 3.90 | 3.94 | 3.97 | 4.00 | 4.03 | 4.06 | 4.08 | 4.11 | 4.13 | | 19 |
| 20 | 3.28 | 3.42 | 3.53 | 3.61 | 3.67 | 3.73 | 3.78 | 3.83 | 3.87 | 3.90 | 3.94 | 3.97 | 4.00 | 4.02 | 4.05 | 4.07 | 4.09 | 4.12 | 20 |
| 24 | 3.21 | 3.35 | 3.45 | 3.52 | 3.58 | 3.64 | 3.69 | 3.73 | 3.77 | 3.80 | 3.83 | 3.86 | 3.89 | 3.91 | 3.94 | 3.96 | 3.98 | 4.00 | 24 |
| 30 | 3.15 | 3.28 | 3.37 | 3.44 | 3.50 | 3.55 | 3.59 | 3.63 | 3.67 | 3.70 | 3.73 | 3.76 | 3.78 | 3.81 | 3.83 | 3.85 | 3.87 | 3.89 | 30 |
| 40 | 3.09 | 3.21 | 3.29 | 3.36 | 3.42 | 3.46 | 3.50 | 3.54 | 3.58 | 3.60 | 3.63 | 3.66 | 3.68 | 3.70 | 3.72 | 3.74 | 3.76 | 3.78 | 40 |
| 60 | 3.03 | 3.14 | 3.22 | 3.29 | 3.34 | 3.38 | 3.42 | 3.46 | 3.49 | 3.51 | 3.54 | 3.56 | 3.59 | 3.61 | 3.63 | 3.64 | 3.66 | 3.68 | 60 |
| 120 | 2.97 | 3.07 | 3.15 | 3.21 | 3.26 | 3.30 | 3.34 | 3.37 | 3.40 | 3.42 | 3.45 | 3.47 | 3.49 | 3.51 | 3.53 | 3.55 | 3.56 | 3.58 | 120 |
| ∞ | 2.91 | 3.01 | 3.08 | 3.14 | 3.18 | 3.22 | 3.26 | 3.29 | 3.32 | 3.34 | 3.36 | 3.38 | 3.40 | 3.42 | 3.44 | 3.45 | 3.47 | 3.48 | ∞ |

(Table continues on p. 436.)

**TABLE I.** *(Continued)*

Exact Critical Values $h_{0.001}$ for the Analysis of Means
Significance Level = 0.001
Number of Means, $k$

| DF | 3 | 4 | 5 | 6 | 7 | 8 | 9 | 10 | 11 | 12 | 13 | 14 | 15 | 16 | 17 | 18 | 19 | 20 | DF |
|---|---|---|---|---|---|---|---|---|---|---|---|---|---|---|---|---|---|---|---|
| 3 | 16.4 | | | | | | | | | | | | | | | | | | 3 |
| 4 | 10.6 | 11.4 | | | | | | | | | | | | | | | | | 4 |
| 5 | 8.25 | 8.79 | 9.19 | | | | | | | | | | | | | | | | 5 |
| 6 | 7.04 | 7.45 | 7.76 | 8.00 | | | | | | | | | | | | | | | 6 |
| 7 | 6.31 | 6.65 | 6.89 | 7.09 | 7.25 | | | | | | | | | | | | | | 7 |
| 8 | 5.83 | 6.12 | 6.32 | 6.49 | 6.63 | 6.75 | | | | | | | | | | | | | 8 |
| 9 | 5.49 | 5.74 | 5.92 | 6.07 | 6.20 | 6.30 | 6.40 | | | | | | | | | | | | 9 |
| 10 | 5.24 | 5.46 | 5.63 | 5.76 | 5.87 | 5.97 | 6.05 | 6.13 | | | | | | | | | | | 10 |
| 11 | 5.05 | 5.25 | 5.40 | 5.52 | 5.63 | 5.71 | 5.79 | 5.86 | 5.92 | | | | | | | | | | 11 |
| 12 | 4.89 | 5.08 | 5.22 | 5.33 | 5.43 | 5.51 | 5.58 | 5.65 | 5.71 | 5.76 | | | | | | | | | 12 |
| 13 | 4.77 | 4.95 | 5.08 | 5.18 | 5.27 | 5.35 | 5.42 | 5.48 | 5.53 | 5.58 | 5.63 | | | | | | | | 13 |
| 14 | 4.66 | 4.83 | 4.96 | 5.06 | 5.14 | 5.21 | 5.28 | 5.33 | 5.38 | 5.43 | 5.48 | 5.51 | | | | | | | 14 |
| 15 | 4.57 | 4.74 | 4.86 | 4.95 | 5.03 | 5.10 | 5.16 | 5.21 | 5.26 | 5.31 | 5.35 | 5.39 | 5.42 | | | | | | 15 |
| 16 | 4.50 | 4.66 | 4.77 | 4.86 | 4.94 | 5.00 | 5.06 | 5.11 | 5.16 | 5.20 | 5.24 | 5.28 | 5.31 | 5.34 | | | | | 16 |
| 17 | 4.44 | 4.59 | 4.70 | 4.78 | 4.86 | 4.92 | 4.98 | 5.03 | 5.07 | 5.11 | 5.15 | 5.18 | 5.22 | 5.25 | 5.28 | | | | 17 |
| 18 | 4.38 | 4.53 | 4.63 | 4.72 | 4.79 | 4.85 | 4.90 | 4.95 | 4.99 | 5.03 | 5.07 | 5.10 | 5.14 | 5.16 | 5.19 | 5.22 | | | 18 |
| 19 | 4.33 | 4.47 | 4.58 | 4.66 | 4.73 | 4.79 | 4.84 | 4.88 | 4.93 | 4.96 | 5.00 | 5.03 | 5.06 | 5.09 | 5.12 | 5.14 | 5.17 | | 19 |
| 20 | 4.29 | 4.42 | 4.53 | 4.61 | 4.67 | 4.73 | 4.78 | 4.83 | 4.87 | 4.90 | 4.94 | 4.97 | 5.00 | 5.03 | 5.05 | 5.08 | 5.10 | 5.12 | 20 |
| 24 | 4.16 | 4.28 | 4.37 | 4.45 | 4.51 | 4.56 | 4.61 | 4.65 | 4.69 | 4.72 | 4.75 | 4.78 | 4.81 | 4.83 | 4.86 | 4.88 | 4.90 | 4.92 | 24 |
| 30 | 4.03 | 4.14 | 4.23 | 4.30 | 4.35 | 4.40 | 4.44 | 4.48 | 4.51 | 4.54 | 4.57 | 4.60 | 4.62 | 4.64 | 4.67 | 4.69 | 4.71 | 4.72 | 30 |
| 40 | 3.91 | 4.01 | 4.09 | 4.15 | 4.20 | 4.25 | 4.29 | 4.32 | 4.35 | 4.38 | 4.40 | 4.43 | 4.45 | 4.47 | 4.49 | 4.50 | 4.52 | 4.54 | 40 |
| 60 | 3.80 | 3.89 | 3.96 | 4.02 | 4.06 | 4.10 | 4.14 | 4.17 | 4.19 | 4.22 | 4.24 | 4.27 | 4.29 | 4.30 | 4.32 | 4.33 | 4.35 | 4.37 | 60 |
| 120 | 3.69 | 3.77 | 3.84 | 3.89 | 3.93 | 3.96 | 4.00 | 4.03 | 4.05 | 4.07 | 4.09 | 4.11 | 4.13 | 4.15 | 4.16 | 4.17 | 4.19 | 4.21 | 120 |
| ∞ | 3.58 | 3.66 | 3.72 | 3.76 | 3.80 | 3.84 | 3.87 | 3.89 | 3.91 | 3.93 | 3.95 | 3.97 | 3.99 | 4.00 | 4.02 | 4.03 | 4.04 | 4.06 | ∞ |

Reprinted with the permission of the American Society for Quality Control: Lloyd S. Nelson, "Exact Critical Values for Use with the Analysis of Means," *Journal of Quality Technology*, **15**(1) January 1983, 40–42.

# TABLE J. Factors for Constructing Variables Control Charts

| Observations in Sample $n$ | Chart for Averages — Factors for Control Limits | | | Chart for Standard Deviations — Factors for Central Line | | Factors for Control Limits | | | | Factors for Central Line | | | Chart for Ranges — Factors for Control Limits | | | |
|---|---|---|---|---|---|---|---|---|---|---|---|---|---|---|---|---|
| | $A$ | $A_2$ | $A_3$ | $c_4$ | $1/c_4$ | $B_3$ | $B_4$ | $B_5$ | $B_6$ | $d_2$ | $1/d_2$ | $d_3$ | $D_1$ | $D_2$ | $D_3$ | $D_4$ |
| 2  | 2.121 | 1.880 | 2.659 | 0.7979 | 1.2533 | 0     | 3.267 | 0     | 2.606 | 1.128 | 0.8865 | 0.853 | 0     | 3.686 | 0     | 3.267 |
| 3  | 1.732 | 1.023 | 1.954 | 0.8862 | 1.1284 | 0     | 2.568 | 0     | 2.276 | 1.693 | 0.5907 | 0.888 | 0     | 4.358 | 0     | 2.574 |
| 4  | 1.500 | 0.729 | 1.628 | 0.9213 | 1.0854 | 0     | 2.266 | 0     | 2.088 | 2.059 | 0.4857 | 0.880 | 0     | 4.698 | 0     | 2.282 |
| 5  | 1.342 | 0.577 | 1.427 | 0.9400 | 1.0638 | 0     | 2.089 | 0     | 1.964 | 2.326 | 0.4299 | 0.864 | 0     | 4.918 | 0     | 2.114 |
| 6  | 1.225 | 0.483 | 1.287 | 0.9515 | 1.0510 | 0.030 | 1.970 | 0.029 | 1.874 | 2.534 | 0.3946 | 0.848 | 0     | 5.078 | 0     | 2.004 |
| 7  | 1.134 | 0.419 | 1.182 | 0.9594 | 1.0423 | 0.118 | 1.882 | 0.113 | 1.806 | 2.704 | 0.3698 | 0.833 | 0.204 | 5.204 | 0.076 | 1.924 |
| 8  | 1.061 | 0.373 | 1.099 | 0.9650 | 1.0363 | 0.185 | 1.815 | 0.179 | 1.751 | 2.847 | 0.3512 | 0.820 | 0.388 | 5.306 | 0.136 | 1.864 |
| 9  | 1.000 | 0.337 | 1.032 | 0.9693 | 1.0317 | 0.239 | 1.761 | 0.232 | 1.707 | 2.970 | 0.3367 | 0.808 | 0.547 | 5.393 | 0.184 | 1.816 |
| 10 | 0.949 | 0.308 | 0.975 | 0.9727 | 1.0281 | 0.284 | 1.716 | 0.276 | 1.669 | 3.078 | 0.3249 | 0.797 | 0.687 | 5.469 | 0.223 | 1.777 |
| 11 | 0.905 | 0.285 | 0.927 | 0.9754 | 1.0252 | 0.321 | 1.679 | 0.313 | 1.637 | 3.173 | 0.3152 | 0.787 | 0.811 | 5.535 | 0.256 | 1.744 |
| 12 | 0.866 | 0.266 | 0.886 | 0.9776 | 1.0229 | 0.354 | 1.646 | 0.346 | 1.610 | 3.258 | 0.3069 | 0.778 | 0.922 | 5.594 | 0.283 | 1.717 |
| 13 | 0.832 | 0.249 | 0.850 | 0.9794 | 1.0210 | 0.382 | 1.618 | 0.374 | 1.585 | 3.336 | 0.2998 | 0.770 | 1.025 | 5.647 | 0.307 | 1.693 |
| 14 | 0.802 | 0.235 | 0.817 | 0.9810 | 1.0194 | 0.406 | 1.594 | 0.399 | 1.563 | 3.407 | 0.2935 | 0.763 | 1.118 | 5.696 | 0.328 | 1.672 |
| 15 | 0.775 | 0.223 | 0.789 | 0.9823 | 1.0180 | 0.428 | 1.572 | 0.421 | 1.544 | 3.472 | 0.2880 | 0.756 | 1.203 | 5.741 | 0.347 | 1.653 |
| 16 | 0.750 | 0.212 | 0.763 | 0.9835 | 1.0168 | 0.448 | 1.552 | 0.440 | 1.526 | 3.532 | 0.2831 | 0.750 | 1.282 | 5.782 | 0.363 | 1.637 |
| 17 | 0.728 | 0.203 | 0.739 | 0.9845 | 1.0157 | 0.466 | 1.534 | 0.458 | 1.511 | 3.588 | 0.2787 | 0.744 | 1.356 | 5.820 | 0.378 | 1.622 |
| 18 | 0.707 | 0.194 | 0.718 | 0.9854 | 1.0148 | 0.482 | 1.518 | 0.475 | 1.496 | 3.640 | 0.2747 | 0.739 | 1.424 | 5.856 | 0.391 | 1.608 |
| 19 | 0.688 | 0.187 | 0.698 | 0.9862 | 1.0140 | 0.497 | 1.503 | 0.490 | 1.483 | 3.689 | 0.2711 | 0.734 | 1.487 | 5.891 | 0.403 | 1.597 |
| 20 | 0.671 | 0.180 | 0.680 | 0.9869 | 1.0133 | 0.510 | 1.490 | 0.504 | 1.470 | 3.735 | 0.2677 | 0.729 | 1.549 | 5.921 | 0.415 | 1.585 |
| 21 | 0.655 | 0.173 | 0.663 | 0.9876 | 1.0126 | 0.523 | 1.477 | 0.516 | 1.459 | 3.778 | 0.2647 | 0.724 | 1.605 | 5.951 | 0.425 | 1.575 |
| 22 | 0.640 | 0.167 | 0.647 | 0.9882 | 1.0119 | 0.534 | 1.466 | 0.528 | 1.448 | 3.819 | 0.2618 | 0.720 | 1.659 | 5.979 | 0.434 | 1.566 |
| 23 | 0.626 | 0.162 | 0.633 | 0.9887 | 1.0114 | 0.545 | 1.455 | 0.539 | 1.438 | 3.858 | 0.2592 | 0.716 | 1.710 | 6.006 | 0.443 | 1.557 |
| 24 | 0.612 | 0.157 | 0.619 | 0.9892 | 1.0109 | 0.555 | 1.445 | 0.549 | 1.429 | 3.895 | 0.2567 | 0.712 | 1.759 | 6.031 | 0.451 | 1.548 |
| 25 | 0.600 | 0.153 | 0.606 | 0.9896 | 1.0105 | 0.565 | 1.435 | 0.559 | 1.420 | 3.931 | 0.2544 | 0.708 | 1.806 | 6.056 | 0.459 | 1.541 |

For $n > 25$

$$A = \frac{3}{\sqrt{n}}, \quad A_3 = \frac{3}{c_4\sqrt{n}}, \quad c_4 \simeq \frac{4(n-1)}{4n-3}$$

$$B_3 = 1 - \frac{3}{c_4\sqrt{2(n-1)}}, \quad B_4 = 1 + \frac{3}{c_4\sqrt{2(n-1)}}, \quad B_5 = c_4 - \frac{3}{\sqrt{2(n-1)}}, \quad B_6 = c_4 + \frac{3}{\sqrt{2(n-1)}}$$

Reprinted by permission: D. C. Montgomery, *Introduction to Statistical Quality Control*, John Wiley and Sons, New York, 1985.

**TABLE K. Poisson Distribution Factors**

| Decimal Conf. Level (c) | Poisson Distribution Confidence Factor B — Number of failures (r) | | | | | | | | | | | |
|---|---|---|---|---|---|---|---|---|---|---|---|---|
| | 0 | 1 | 2 | 3 | 4 | 5 | 6 | 7 | 8 | 9 | 10 | |
| .999 | 6.908 | 9.233 | 11.229 | 13.062 | 14.794 | 16.455 | 18.062 | 19.626 | 21.156 | 22.657 | 24.134 | .001 |
| .99 | 4.605 | 6.638 | 8.406 | 10.045 | 11.604 | 13.108 | 14.571 | 16.000 | 17.403 | 18.783 | 20.145 | .01 |
| .95 | 2.996 | 4.744 | 6.296 | 7.754 | 9.154 | 10.513 | 11.842 | 13.148 | 14.435 | 15.705 | 16.962 | .05 |
| .90 | 2.303 | 3.890 | 5.322 | 6.681 | 7.994 | 9.275 | 10.532 | 11.771 | 12.995 | 14.206 | 15.407 | .10 |
| .85 | 1.897 | 3.372 | 4.723 | 6.014 | 7.267 | 8.495 | 9.703 | 10.896 | 12.078 | 13.249 | 14.411 | .15 |
| .80 | 1.609 | 2.994 | 4.279 | 5.515 | 6.721 | 7.906 | 9.075 | 10.232 | 11.380 | 12.519 | 13.651 | .20 |
| .75 | 1.386 | 2.693 | 3.920 | 5.109 | 6.274 | 7.423 | 8.558 | 9.684 | 10.802 | 11.914 | 13.020 | .25 |
| .70 | 1.204 | 2.439 | 3.616 | 4.762 | 5.890 | 7.006 | 8.111 | 9.209 | 10.301 | 11.387 | 12.470 | .30 |
| .65 | 1.050 | 2.219 | 3.347 | 4.455 | 5.549 | 6.633 | 7.710 | 8.782 | 9.850 | 10.913 | 11.974 | .35 |
| .60 | 0.916 | 2.022 | 3.105 | 4.175 | 5.237 | 6.292 | 7.343 | 8.390 | 9.434 | 10.476 | 11.515 | .40 |
| .55 | 0.798 | 1.844 | 2.883 | 3.916 | 4.946 | 5.973 | 7.000 | 8.021 | 9.043 | 10.064 | 11.083 | .45 |
| .50 | 0.693 | 1.678 | 2.674 | 3.672 | 4.671 | 5.670 | 6.670 | 7.669 | 8.669 | 9.669 | 10.668 | .50 |
| .45 | 0.598 | 1.523 | 2.476 | 3.438 | 4.406 | 5.378 | 6.352 | 7.328 | 8.305 | 9.284 | 10.264 | .55 |
| .40 | 0.511 | 1.376 | 2.285 | 3.211 | 4.148 | 5.091 | 6.039 | 6.991 | 7.947 | 8.904 | 9.864 | .60 |
| .35 | 0.431 | 1.235 | 2.099 | 2.988 | 3.892 | 4.806 | 5.727 | 6.655 | 7.587 | 8.523 | 9.462 | .65 |
| .30 | 0.357 | 1.097 | 1.914 | 2.764 | 3.634 | 4.517 | 5.411 | 6.312 | 7.220 | 8.133 | 9.050 | .70 |

| | 1 | 2 | 3 | 4 | 5 | 6 | 7 | 8 | 9 | 10 | 11 | Decimal Conf. Level |
|---|---|---|---|---|---|---|---|---|---|---|---|---|
| .25 | 0.288 | 0.961 | 1.727 | 2.535 | 3.369 | 4.219 | 5.083 | 5.956 | 6.838 | 7.726 | 8.620 | .75 |
| .20 | 0.223 | 0.824 | 1.535 | 2.297 | 3.090 | 3.904 | 4.734 | 5.576 | 6.428 | 7.289 | 8.157 | .80 |
| .15 | 0.162 | 0.683 | 1.331 | 2.039 | 2.785 | 3.557 | 4.348 | 5.154 | 5.973 | 6.802 | 7.639 | .85 |
| .10 | 0.105 | 0.532 | 1.102 | 1.745 | 2.432 | 3.152 | 3.895 | 4.656 | 5.432 | 6.221 | 7.021 | .90 |
| .05 | 0.051 | 0.355 | 0.818 | 1.366 | 1.970 | 2.613 | 3.285 | 3.981 | 4.695 | 5.425 | 6.169 | .95 |
| .01 | 0.010 | 0.149 | 0.436 | 0.823 | 1.279 | 1.786 | 2.330 | 2.906 | 3.508 | 4.130 | 4.771 | .99 |
| .001 | 0.001 | 0.045 | 0.191 | 0.429 | 0.740 | 1.107 | 1.521 | 1.971 | 2.453 | 2.961 | 3.492 | .999 |
| | | | | | Number of Failures (r) | | | | | | | ← |

Poisson Distribution Confidence Factor A

*Applications of Table K*

Total test time: $T = B_{r;c}/\rho_a$    for $\rho \leq \rho_a$ where $\rho_a$ is a failure rate criterion, $r$ is allowed number of test failures, and $c$ is a confidence factor.

Confidence interval statements (time-terminated test): $\rho \leq B_{r;c}/T$    $\rho \geq A_{r;c}/T$

Examples: 1 failure test for a 0.0001 failures/hour criterion (i.e., 10,000 hr MTBF)

    95% confidence test: Total test time = 47,440 hr (i.e., 4.744/0.0001)

  5 failures in a total of 10,000 hr

    95% confident: $\rho \leq 0.0010513$ failures/hour (i.e., 10.513/10,000)

    95% confident: $\rho \geq 0.0001970$ failures/hour (i.e., 1.970/10,000)

    90% confidence: $0.0001970 \leq \rho \leq 0.0010513$

**TABLE L. Weibull Mean: Percentage Fail Value for Given Weibull Slope**

| Weibull Slope | Percent Failed at the Mean | Weibull Slope | Percent Failed at the Mean |
|:---:|:---:|:---:|:---:|
| 0.1 | 98.9 | 2.1 | 53.9 |
| 0.2 | 92.6 | 2.2 | 53.5 |
| 0.3 | 85.8 | 2.3 | 53.1 |
| 0.4 | 80.1 | 2.4 | 52.7 |
| 0.5 | 75.7 | 2.5 | 52.4 |
| 0.6 | 72.1 | 2.6 | 52.0 |
| 0.7 | 69.2 | 2.7 | 51.7 |
| 0.8 | 66.9 | 2.8 | 51.4 |
| 0.9 | 64.9 | 2.9 | 51.2 |
| 1.0 | 63.2 | 3.0 | 50.9 |
| 1.1 | 61.8 | 3.1 | 50.7 |
| 1.2 | 60.5 | 3.2 | 50.5 |
| 1.3 | 59.4 | 3.3 | 50.3 |
| 1.4 | 58.4 | 3.4 | 50.1 |
| 1.5 | 57.6 | 3.5 | 49.9 |
| 1.6 | 56.8 | 3.6 | 49.7 |
| 1.7 | 56.1 | 3.7 | 49.5 |
| 1.8 | 55.5 | 3.8 | 49.4 |
| 1.9 | 54.9 | 3.9 | 49.2 |
| 2.0 | 54.4 | 4.0 | 49.1 |

## TABLE M1. Two-Level Full and Fractional Factorial Designs, 4 Trials

```
            1 2 3  ← Contrast column numbers

R     V⁺  * 2
E
S     V   * * 3
O                        Applicable contrast columns
L                        for factors as a function of
U     IV                 experiment resolution
T
I
O     III
N
```

```
            1 2 3  ← Contrast column numbers

T    1    + − +
R    2    + + −
I    3    − + +
A    4    − − −
L
S
```

```
            1 2 3  ← Contrast column numbers
```

(*Table continues on p. 441.*)

**TABLE M1.** (*Continued*)

### *Instructions for Tables M1-M5: Creating a Two-Level Factorial Test Design Matrix[a]*

1. Choose for the given number of two-level factors a table (i.e., M1–M5) such that the number of test trials yields the desired resolution, which is defined to be

   $V^+$: Full two-level factorial

   V: All main effects and two-factor interactions are not confounded with other main effects or two-factor interactions.

   IV: All main effects are not confounded by two-factor interactions. Two-factor interactions are confounded with each other.

   III: Main effects confounded with two-factor interactions.

   The maximum number of factors for each trial matrix resolution is noted in the following:

   | | Experiment Resolution | | | |
   |---|---|---|---|---|
   | Number of Trials | $V^+$ | V | IV | III |
   | 4 | 2 | 3 | | |
   | 8 | 3 | | 4 | 5–7 |
   | 16 | 4 | 5 | 6–8 | 9–15 |
   | 32 | 5 | 6 | 7–16 | 17–31 |
   | 64 | 6 | 7–8 | 9–32 | 33–63 |

2. Look at the row of *'s and numerics within the selected table corresponding to the desired resolution.

3. Begin from the left identifying columns designated by either a * or numeric until the number of selected contrast columns equals the number of factors.

4. Record for each contrast column identified within step number three, the level states for each trial. Columns are included only if they have the * or numeric resolution designator. A straightedge can be helpful to align the contrast numbers tabulated within the columns.

[a] See Example 13-1.

**TABLE M2. Two-Level Full and Fractional Factorial Designs, 8 Trials[a]**

1 2 3 4 5 6 7 ← Contrast column numbers

```
R    V+  * * 3
E
S    V
O
L                          Applicable contrast columns
U    IV  * * *     4   ──  for factors as a function of
T                          experiment resolution
I
O    III * * * * 5 6 7
N
```

1 2 3 4 5 6 7 ← Contrast column numbers

| | | 1 | 2 | 3 | 4 | 5 | 6 | 7 |
|---|---|---|---|---|---|---|---|---|
| T | 1 | + | − | − | + | − | + | + |
| R | 2 | + | + | − | − | + | − | + |
| I | 3 | + | + | + | − | − | + | − |
| A | 4 | − | + | + | + | − | − | + |
| L | 5 | + | − | + | + | + | − | − |
| S | 6 | − | + | − | + | + | + | − |
|   | 7 | − | − | + | − | + | + | + |
|   | 8 | − | − | − | − | − | − | − |

1 2 3 4 5 6 7 ← Contrast column numbers

[a]Table usage instructions are noted after Table M1.

The 8, 16, 32, and 64 trial matrices in Tables M2–M5 were created from a computer program described by Diamond (1989).

**TABLE M3. Two-Level Full and Fractional Factorial Designs, 16 Trials[a]**

```
                              1 1 1 1 1 1
        1 2 3 4 5 6 7 8 9 0 1 2 3 4 5     ← Contrast column numbers

R  V+   * * * 4
E
S  V    * * * *                 5
O
L
U  IV   * * * *         *       6 7   8
T
I                       1 1 1 1 1 1
O  III  * * * * * * * * 9 0 1 2 3 4 5
N
```

(Applicable contrast columns for factors as a function of experiment resolution)

|         |                              1 1 1 1 1 1 |
| Contrast column numbers → | 1 2 3 4 5 6 7 8 9 0 1 2 3 4 5 |

| Trial | 1 | 2 | 3 | 4 | 5 | 6 | 7 | 8 | 9 | 10 | 11 | 12 | 13 | 14 | 15 |
|---|---|---|---|---|---|---|---|---|---|---|---|---|---|---|---|
| 1 | + | − | − | − | + | − | − | + | + | − | + | − | + | + | + |
| 2 | + | + | − | − | − | + | − | − | + | + | − | + | − | + | + |
| 3 | + | + | + | − | − | − | + | − | − | + | + | − | + | − | + |
| 4 | + | + | + | + | − | − | − | + | − | − | + | + | − | + | − |
| 5 | − | + | + | + | + | − | − | − | + | − | − | + | + | − | + |
| 6 | + | − | + | + | + | + | − | − | − | + | − | − | + | + | − |
| 7 | − | + | − | + | + | + | + | − | − | − | + | − | − | + | + |
| 8 | + | − | + | − | + | + | + | + | − | − | − | + | − | − | + |
| 9 | + | + | − | + | − | + | + | + | + | − | − | − | + | − | − |
| 10 | − | + | + | − | + | − | + | + | + | + | − | − | − | + | − |
| 11 | − | − | + | + | − | + | − | + | + | + | + | − | − | − | + |
| 12 | + | − | − | + | + | − | + | − | + | + | + | + | − | − | − |
| 13 | − | + | − | − | + | + | − | + | − | + | + | + | + | − | − |
| 14 | − | − | + | − | − | + | + | − | + | − | + | + | + | + | − |
| 15 | − | − | − | + | − | − | + | + | − | + | − | + | + | + | + |
| 16 | − | − | − | − | − | − | − | − | − | − | − | − | − | − | − |

|         |                              1 1 1 1 1 1 |
| Contrast column numbers → | 1 2 3 4 5 6 7 8 9 0 1 2 3 4 5 |

[a] Table usage instructions are noted in Table M1.

**TABLE M4. Two-Level Full and Fractional Factorial Designs, 32 Trials**[a]

$\leftarrow$ Contrast column numbers

Applicable contrast
columns for factors
as a function of
experiment resolution

| | | Contrast column numbers |
|---|---|---|
| | | 1 2 3 4 5 6 7 8 9 10 11 12 13 14 15 16 17 18 19 20 21 22 23 24 25 26 27 28 29 30 31 |
| R | V+ | * * * * *   5 |
| E | V | * * * * * *   6 |
| S | | |
| O | | |
| L | IV | * * * * * *     *7 8 9 10 11 12 13 14 15 16 |
| U | | |
| T | | |
| I | III | * * * * * * * * * * * * * * * * *7 8 9 10 11 12 13 14 15 16 17 18 19 20 21 22 23 24 25 26 27 28 29 30 31 |
| O | | |
| N | | |

$\leftarrow$ Contrast column numbers

Contrast column numbers: 1 2 3 4 5 6 7 8 9 10 11 12 13 14 15 16 17 18 19 20 21 22 23 24 25 26 27 28 29 30 31

| Run | Contrast columns 1–31 |
|---|---|
| 1 | + − − − + − + − + + − − + + − + − + + − − + + − − + + + − + + |
| 2 | + + + − − − − + + + + − − + + − − + + − − − − + + + + + + + − − |
| 3 | + + + + + + + − − − − − − + + + + + + + + − − − − − − + + + + + |
| 4 | + + + + − + − − + + − + + − − − + − + − + − + + − + − − + − + + |
| 5 | + − + + − + + + − + − + − + + − + − + + − + − + − − + + + − − − |
| 6 | − + − + + + + − + − − + + + − − − + + + − + − − + + + − − + + − |
| 7 | − − − + − + + − + − − + + − + − + + − − − + + + + − − + − − + + |
| 8 | + − + − + + − + − − + − + − + + − + − + + − − − − + − + − + + + |

|   | 1 | 2 | 3 | 4 | 5 | 6 | 7 | 8 | 9 | 10 | 11 | 12 | 13 | 14 | 15 | 16 | 17 | 18 | 19 | 20 | 21 | 22 | 23 | 24 | 25 | 26 | 27 | 28 | 29 | 30 | 31 |
|---|---|---|---|---|---|---|---|---|---|----|----|----|----|----|----|----|----|----|----|----|----|----|----|----|----|----|----|----|----|----|----|
| 9 | + | + | − | − | + | + | + | + | + | + | + | + | + | + | + | − | − | − | + | + | − | − | − | − | − | − | − | − | − | − | − |
| 10 | + | − | + | + | + | + | + | − | − | − | − | − | − | − | + | + | + | + | − | − | − | − | − | − | − | − | − | + | + | − | + |
| 11 | + | + | − | + | − | − | − | − | − | − | + | + | + | + | − | − | + | + | − | − | + | + | + | + | + | + | + | + | + | + | − |
| 12 | − | + | + | − | + | + | + | − | − | + | + | − | − | + | + | − | + | − | − | + | − | + | + | − | − | + | + | − | − | + | − |
| 13 | + | − | + | + | − | − | + | + | + | − | − | + | + | − | + | + | − | − | + | − | + | − | − | + | + | − | − | + | + | − | + |
| 14 | + | − | − | + | + | + | − | − | + | + | − | + | − | + | − | + | + | − | − | + | + | − | + | + | − | − | + | − | − | + | − |
| 15 | + | + | − | + | + | − | − | + | + | − | + | − | + | − | + | + | − | + | + | − | − | + | − | − | + | + | − | + | + | − | − |
| 16 | − | − | − | − | − | − | − | − | − | − | − | − | − | − | − | − | − | − | − | − | − | − | − | − | − | − | − | − | − | − | − |
| 17 | + | + | + | + | + | + | + | + | + | + | + | + | + | + | + | + | + | + | + | + | + | + | + | + | + | + | + | + | + | + | + |

**TABLE M5. Two-Level Full and Fractional Factorial Designs 64 Trials**[a]

| Contrast | | 1 | 2 | 3 | 4 | 5 | 6 | 7 | 8 | 9 | 1 0 | 1 1 | 1 2 | 1 3 | 1 4 | 1 5 | 1 6 | 1 7 | 1 8 | 1 9 | 2 0 | 2 1 | 2 2 | 2 3 | 2 4 | 2 5 | 2 6 | 2 7 | 2 8 | 2 9 | 3 0 | 3 1 | 3 2 | 3 3 | 3 4 | 3 5 | 3 6 | 3 7 | 3 8 | 3 9 | 4 0 | 4 1 | 4 2 | 4 3 | 4 4 | 4 5 | 4 6 | 4 7 | 4 8 | 4 9 | 5 0 | 5 1 | 5 2 | 5 3 | 5 4 | 5 5 | 5 6 | 5 7 | 5 8 | 5 9 | 6 0 | 6 1 | 6 2 | 6 3 |
|---|---|---|---|---|---|---|---|---|---|---|---|---|---|---|---|---|---|---|---|---|---|---|---|---|---|---|---|---|---|---|---|---|---|---|---|---|---|---|---|---|---|---|---|---|---|---|---|---|---|---|---|---|---|---|---|---|---|---|---|---|---|---|---|---|

**RESOLUTION**

| | | 1 | 2 | 3 | 4 | 5 | 6 | 7 | 8 | 9 | 10 | 11 | 12 | 13 | 14 | 15 | 16 | 17 | 18 | 19 | 20 | 21 | 22 | 23 | 24 | 25 | 26 | 27 | 28 | 29 | 30 | 31 | 32 | 33 | 34 | 35 | 36 | 37 | 38 | 39 | 40 | 41 | 42 | 43 | 44 | 45 | 46 | 47 | 48 | 49 | 50 | 51 | 52 | 53 | 54 | 55 | 56 | 57 | 58 | 59 | 60 | 61 | 62 | 63 |
|---|---|---|---|---|---|---|---|---|---|---|---|---|---|---|---|---|---|---|---|---|---|---|---|---|---|---|---|---|---|---|---|---|---|---|---|---|---|---|---|---|---|---|---|---|---|---|---|---|---|---|---|---|---|---|---|---|---|---|---|---|---|---|---|---|
| V⁺ | $V^+$ | * | * | * | * | * | 6 | | | | | | | | | | | | | | | | | | | | | | | | | | | | | | | | | | | | | | | | | | | | | | | | | | | | | | | | | |
| V | V | * | * | * | * | * | * | | | | | | | | | | | | | | 7 | | | 8 | | | | | | | | | | | | | | | | | | | | | | | | | | | | | | | | | | | | | | | | |
| IV | IV | * | * | * | * | * | * | | | | | | * | | | | | | *9 | | | 1 0 | 1 1 | | | 1 2 | 1 3 | 1 4 | 1 5 | | 1 6 | | | | 1 7 | 1 8 | 1 9 | | 2 0 | | | 2 1 | | 2 2 | 2 3 | | 2 4 | 2 5 | 2 6 | | 2 7 | 2 8 | | | 2 3 | | 3 0 | 3 1 | | 3 2 | | | |
| III | III | * | * | * | * | * | * | * | * | * | * | * | * | * | * | * | * | * | * | * | * | * | * | * | * | * | * | * | * | * | * | * | * | 3 4 | 3 5 | 3 6 | 3 7 | 3 8 | 3 9 | 4 0 | 4 1 | 4 2 | 4 3 | 4 4 | 4 5 | 4 6 | 4 7 | 4 8 | 4 9 | 5 0 | 5 1 | 5 2 | 5 3 | 5 4 | 5 5 | 5 6 | 5 7 | 5 8 | 5 9 | 6 0 | 6 1 | 6 2 | 6 3 | |

| Contrast | | 1 | 2 | 3 | 4 | 5 | 6 | 7 | 8 | 9 | 1 0 | 1 1 | 1 2 | 1 3 | 1 4 | 1 5 | 1 6 | 1 7 | 1 8 | 1 9 | 2 0 | 2 1 | 2 2 | 2 3 | 2 4 | 2 5 | 2 6 | 2 7 | 2 8 | 2 9 | 3 0 | 3 1 | 3 2 | 3 3 | 3 4 | 3 5 | 3 6 | 3 7 | 3 8 | 3 9 | 4 0 | 4 1 | 4 2 | 4 3 | 4 4 | 4 5 | 4 6 | 4 7 | 4 8 | 4 9 | 5 0 | 5 1 | 5 2 | 5 3 | 5 4 | 5 5 | 5 6 | 5 7 | 5 8 | 5 9 | 6 0 | 6 1 | 6 2 | 6 3 |
|---|---|---|---|---|---|---|---|---|---|---|---|---|---|---|---|---|---|---|---|---|---|---|---|---|---|---|---|---|---|---|---|---|---|---|---|---|---|---|---|---|---|---|---|---|---|---|---|---|---|---|---|---|---|---|---|---|---|---|---|---|---|---|---|---|

| Row | 1 | 2 | 3 | 4 | 5 | 6 | 7 | 8 | 9 | 10 | 11 | 12 | 13 | 14 | 15 | 16 | 17 | 18 | 19 | 20 | 21 | 22 | 23 | 24 | 25 | 26 | 27 | 28 | 29 | 30 | 31 | 32 | 33 | 34 | 35 | 36 | 37 | 38 | 39 | 40 | 41 | 42 | 43 | 44 | 45 | 46 | 47 | 48 | 49 | 50 | 51 | 52 | 53 | 54 | 55 | 56 | 57 | 58 | 59 | 60 | 61 | 62 | 63 |
|---|---|---|---|---|---|---|---|---|---|---|---|---|---|---|---|---|---|---|---|---|---|---|---|---|---|---|---|---|---|---|---|---|---|---|---|---|---|---|---|---|---|---|---|---|---|---|---|---|---|---|---|---|---|---|---|---|---|---|---|---|---|---|---|---|
| 1 | + | − | − | − | − | + | − | − | − | − | + | + | − | − | + | − | + | − | − | + | + | + | − | + | − | − | + | + | − | − | + | + | + | − | + | − | − | + | − | + | − | + | + | + | − | + | − | − | + | + | − | + | − | + | − | + | − | + | + | + | + | + |
| 2 | + | + | − | − | − | − | + | − | − | − | − | + | + | − | − | + | − | + | − | − | + | + | + | − | + | − | − | + | + | − | − | + | + | + | − | + | − | − | + | − | + | − | + | + | + | − | + | − | − | + | + | − | + | − | + | − | + | − | + | + | + | + |
| 3 | + | + | + | − | − | − | − | + | − | − | − | − | + | + | − | − | + | − | + | − | − | + | + | + | − | + | − | − | + | + | − | − | + | + | + | − | + | − | − | + | − | + | − | + | + | + | − | + | − | − | + | + | − | + | − | + | − | + | − | + | + | + |
| 4 | + | + | + | + | − | − | − | − | + | − | − | − | − | + | + | − | − | + | − | + | − | − | + | + | + | − | + | − | − | + | + | − | − | + | + | + | − | + | − | − | + | − | + | − | + | + | + | − | + | − | − | + | + | − | + | − | + | − | + | − | + | + |
| 5 | + | + | + | + | + | − | − | − | − | + | − | − | − | − | + | + | − | − | + | − | + | − | − | + | + | + | − | + | − | − | + | + | − | − | + | + | + | − | + | − | − | + | − | + | − | + | + | + | − | + | − | − | + | + | − | + | − | + | − | + | − | + |
| 6 | + | + | + | + | + | + | − | − | − | − | + | − | − | − | − | + | + | − | − | + | − | + | − | − | + | + | + | − | + | − | − | + | + | − | − | + | + | + | − | + | − | − | + | − | + | − | + | + | + | − | + | − | − | + | + | − | + | − | + | − | + | − |
| 7 | − | + | + | + | + | + | + | − | − | − | − | + | − | − | − | − | + | + | − | − | + | − | + | − | − | + | + | + | − | + | − | − | + | + | − | − | + | + | + | − | + | − | − | + | − | + | − | + | + | + | − | + | − | − | + | + | − | + | − | + | − | + |
| 8 | + | − | + | + | + | + | + | + | − | − | − | − | + | − | − | − | − | + | + | − | − | + | − | + | − | − | + | + | + | − | + | − | − | + | + | − | − | + | + | + | − | + | − | − | + | − | + | − | + | + | + | − | + | − | − | + | + | − | + | − | + | − |

TRIALS 9–32

Contrast: 1 2 3 4 5 6 7 8 9 0 1 1 1 1 1 1 1 1 1 1 2 2 2 2 2 2 2 2 2 2 3 3 3 3 3 3 3 3 3 3 4 4 4 4 4 4 4 4 4 4 5 5 5 5 5 5 5 5 5 5 6 6 6 6 6 6

(Table continues on p. 448.)

448

## TABLE M5. Two-Level Full and Fractional Factorial Designs 64 Trials[a] (Continued)

| Contrast → | | 1 2 3 4 5 6 7 8 9 | 1 1 1 1 1 1 1 1 1 1 2 2 2 2 2 2 2 2 2 2 3 2 3 3 3 3 3 3 3 3 4 4 4 4 4 4 4 4 4 5 5 5 5 5 5 5 5 5 5 6 6 6 6 0 1 2 3 4 5 6 7 8 9 0 1 2 3 4 5 6 7 9 0 0 1 2 3 4 5 6 7 8 9 0 1 2 3 4 5 6 7 8 9 0 1 2 3 4 5 6 7 8 9 0 1 2 3 |
|---|---|---|---|

**RESOLUTION**

| | $V^+$ | * * * * * 6 |
|---|---|---|

| | V | * * * * * *  ... 7 ... 8 |
|---|---|---|

| | IV | * * * * * *  ... *  ... * 9  ... 1 0 ... 1 1 ... 1 1 1 1 2 3 4 5 ... 1 6 ... 1 1 1 7 8 9 ... 2 0 ... 2 1 ... 2 2 2 3 ... 2 2 2 4 5 6 ... 2 2 7 8 ... 2 3 9 0 ... 3 1 ... 3 2 |
|---|---|---|

| | III | * * * * * * * * * * * * * * * * * * * * * * * * * * * * * * * * * 3 3 3 3 3 3 3 4 4 4 4 4 4 4 4 4 5 5 5 5 5 5 5 5 5 5 6 6 6 6 3 4 5 6 7 8 9 0 1 2 3 4 5 6 7 8 9 0 1 2 3 4 5 6 7 8 9 0 1 2 3 |
|---|---|---|

| Contrast → | | 1 2 3 4 5 6 7 8 9 0 | 1 1 1 1 1 1 1 1 1 2 2 2 2 2 2 2 2 2 2 3 3 3 3 3 3 3 3 3 4 4 4 4 4 4 4 4 4 5 5 5 5 5 5 5 5 5 5 6 6 6 6 1 2 3 4 5 6 7 8 9 0 1 2 3 4 5 6 7 8 9 0 1 2 3 4 5 6 7 8 9 0 1 2 3 4 5 6 7 8 9 0 1 2 3 |
|---|---|---|

| 33 | + + − + − + − + + + − + + + − − + + − + − + − + + + + + + + − − − − − − − − − + + − − − + − + − + + + + − + − − − + |
| 34 | + + + − − + − + − + + − + + + − − + + − + − + − + − + + + + + + − − − − − − − + + − − − + − + − + − + + + + − + − − − + |
| 35 | − + + + − − + − + − + + − + + + − − + + − + − + − + − + + + + + + − − − − − − − + + − − − + − + − + − + + + + − + − − − |
| 36 | − − + + + − − + − + − + + − + + + − − + + − + − + − + − + + + + + + − − − − − − − + − − − − + − − + + − + − + − + + + + − + − |
| 37 | − − − + + + − − + − + − + + − + + + − − + + − + − + − + − + + + + + + − − − − − + − − − − + + − − + + − − + − + − − + + + + − + |
| 38 | + − − − + + + − − + − + − + + − + + + − − + + − + − + − + − + + + + + + − − − − − + + − − − + + + − − − + + − − + + − + − + − − + + + + − |
| 39 | − + − − − + + + − − + − + − + + − + + + − − + + − + − + − + + + + + + + − − − − − + + + − − − + + − − − + + + − − − + − + − − + + + + |
| 40 | + − + − − − + + + − − + − + − + + − + + + − − + + − + − + − + + + + + + + − − − − − + + + − − − + + − − − − + − + − − + − + − − + + + |
| 41 | + + − + − − − + + + − − + − + − + + − + + + − − + + − + − + − + + + + + + − − − − − + + + − − − − + − − − + + − − + + − − + − + − − + + |
| 42 | + + + − + − − − + + + − − + − + − + + − + + + − − + + − + − + − + + + + + + − − − − − + + + − − − − − + − − −·+ + − − + − + − − + + + |

TRIALS

| | Contrast |
|---|---|
| 43 | |
| 44 | |
| 45 | |
| 46 | |
| 47 | |
| 48 | |
| 49 | |
| 50 | |
| 51 | |
| 52 | |
| 53 | |
| 54 | |
| 55 | |
| 56 | |
| 57 | |
| 58 | |
| 59 | |
| 60 | |
| 61 | |
| 62 | |
| 63 | |
| 64 | |

Contrast — 1 2 3 4 5 6 7 8 9 0 1 2 3 4 5 6 7 8 9 0 1 2 3 4 5 6 7 8 9 0 1 2 3 4 5 6 7 8 9 0 1 2 3 4 5 6 7 8 9 0 1 2 3 4 5 6 7 8 9 0 1 2 3

[a]Table usage instructions are noted within Table M1.

# TABLE N1. Two-Factor Interaction Confounding in the Contrast Columns of the Tables M1-M5 Resolution V Fractional Factorial Designs[a]

**4 Trials**

| 1 | 2 | 3 |
|---|---|---|
| *A | *B | AB |

**8 Trials**

Not Applicable

**16 Trials**

| 1 | 2 | 3 | 4 | 5 | 6 | 7 | 8 | 9 | 10 | 11 | 12 | 13 | 14 | 15 |
|---|---|---|---|---|---|---|---|---|----|----|----|----|----|----|
| *A | *B | *C | *D | AB | BC | CD | ABD / CE | AC | BD | ABC / DE | BCD / AE | ABCD / *E | ACD / BE | AD |

**32 Trials**

| 1 | 2 | 3 | 4 | 5 | 6 | 7 | 8 | 9 | 10 | 11 | 12 | 13 | 14 | 15 | 16 | 17 | 18 | 19 | 20 | 21 |
|---|---|---|---|---|---|---|---|---|----|----|----|----|----|----|----|----|----|----|----|----|
| *A | *B | *C | *D | *E | AC | BD | CE | ACD | BDE | AE | ABC | BCD | CDE | ACDE / BF | ABCDE / *F | ABDE / CF | ABE | AB | BC | CD |

| 22 | 23 | 24 | 25 | 26 | 27 | 28 | 29 | 30 | 31 |
|----|----|----|----|----|----|----|----|----|----|
| DE | ACE | ABCD / EF | BCDE / AF | ADE | ABCE / DF | ABD | BCE | AD | BE |

**64 Trials**

| 1 | 2 | 3 | 4 | 5 | 6 | 7 | 8 | 9 | 10 | 11 | 12 | 13 | 14 | 15 | 16 | 17 | 18 | 19 | 20 | 21 |
|---|---|---|---|---|---|---|---|---|----|----|----|----|----|----|----|----|----|----|----|----|
| *A | *B | *C | *D | *E | *F | AB | BC | CD | DE | EF | ABF | AC | BD | CE | DF | ABE | BCF | ABCD / *G | BCDE | CDEF |

| 22 | 23 | 24 | 25 | 26 | 27 | 28 | 29 | 30 | 31 | 32 | 33 | 34 | 35 | 36 | 37 | 38 | 39 | 40 | 41 | 42 |
|----|----|----|----|----|----|----|----|----|----|----|----|----|----|----|----|----|----|----|----|----|
| ABDEF / GH | ACEF / *H | ADF | AE | BF | ABC / DG | BCD / AG | CDE | DEF | ABEF | ACF / EH | AD | BE | CF | ABD / CG | BCE | CDF | ABDE | BCEF | ABCDF / FG | ACDE |

| 43 | 44 | 45 | 46 | 47 | 48 | 49 | 50 | 51 | 52 | 53 | 54 | 55 | 56 | 57 | 58 | 59 | 60 | 61 | 62 | 63 |
|----|----|----|----|----|----|----|----|----|----|----|----|----|----|----|----|----|----|----|----|----|
| BDEF / GH | ABCEF / BH | ACDF | ADE | BEF | ABCF | ACD / BG | BDE | CEF / AH | ABDF | ACE / FH | BDF | ABCE | BCDF | ABCDE / EG | BCDEF | ABCDEF | ACDEF / DH | ADEF / DH | AEF / CH | AF |

[a]The higher order terms were used when generating the design. Main effects are denoted by *. See Example 13-1.

# TABLE N2. Two-Factor Interaction Confounding in the Contrast Columns of the Tables M1–M5 Resolution IV Fractional Factorial Designs[a]

## 8 Trials

| 1 | 2 | 3 | 4 | 5 | 6 | 7 |
|---|---|---|---|---|---|---|
| *A | *B | *C | AB | BC | ABC | AC |
|    |    |    | CD | AD | *D  | BD |

## 16 Trials

| 1 | 2 | 3 | 4 | 5 | 6 | 7 | 8 | 9 | 10 | 11 | 12 | 13 | 14 | 15 |
|---|---|---|---|---|---|---|---|---|----|----|----|----|----|----|
| *A | *B | *C | *D | AB | BC | CD | ABD | AC | BD | ABC | BCD | ABCD | ACD | AD |
|    |    |    |    | DE | AF | EF | *E  | BF | AE | *F  | *G  | CE   | *H  | BE |
|    |    |    |    | CF | DG | BG |     | EG | CG |     |     | DF   |     | FG |
|    |    |    |    | GH | EH | AH |     | DH | FH |     |     | AG   |     | CH |
|    |    |    |    |    |    |    |     |    |    |     |     | BH   |     |    |

## 32 Trials

| 1 | 2 | 3 | 4 | 5 | 6 | 7 | 8 | 9 | 10 | 11 | 12 | 13 | 14 | 15 | 16 | 17 | 18 | 19 | 20 | 21 |
|---|---|---|---|---|---|---|---|---|----|----|----|----|----|----|----|----|----|----|----|----|
| *A | *B | *C | *D | *E | AC | BD | CE | ACD | BDE | AE | ABC | BCD | CDE | ACDE | ABCDE | ABDE | ABE | AB | BC | CD |
|    |    |    |    |    | DF | EG | GI | *F  | *G  | FJ | *H  | *I  | *J  | EF   | *K    | AG   | *L  | CH | AH | AF |
|    |    |    |    |    | BH | FH | DJ |     |     | IK |     |     |     | GH   |       | HJ   |     | FI | DI | BL |
|    |    |    |    |    | GK | CI | HL |     |     | BL |     |     |     | AJ   |       | CK   |     | JK | GJ | EJ |
|    |    |    |    |    | EM | KM | AM |     |     | CM |     |     |     | BK   |       | DL   |     | EL | LM | KL |
|    |    |    |    |    | JN | LN | FN |     |     | DN |     |     |     | IL   |       | IM   |     | GN | KN | MN |
|    |    |    |    |    | IO | AO | KO |     |     | GO |     |     |     | DM   |       | BN   |     | DO | FO | HO |
|    |    |    |    |    | LP | JP | BP |     |     | HP |     |     |     | CN   |       | EO   |     | MP | EP | GP |
|    |    |    |    |    |    |    |    |     |     |    |     |     |     | OP   |       | FP   |     |    |    |    |

| 22 | 23 | 24 | 25 | 26 | 27 | 28 | 29 | 30 | 31 |
|----|----|----|----|----|----|----|----|----|----|
| DE | ACE | ABCD | BCDE | ADE | ABCE | ABD | BCE | AD | BE |
| BG | *M  | BF   | CG   | *N  | FG   | *O  | *P  | CF | DG |
| CJ |     | DH   | EI   |     | EH   |     |     | HI | IJ |
| HK |     | AI   | BJ   |     | DK   |     |     | GL | FK |
| FM |     | EK   | AK   |     | CL   |     |     | JM | AL |
| AN |     | JL   | FL   |     | BM   |     |     | EN | HM |
| LO |     | GM   | HN   |     | IN   |     |     | BO | NO |
| IP |     | CO   | MO   |     | JO   |     |     | KP | CP |
|    |     | NP   | DP   |     | AP   |     |     |    |    |

(Table continues on p. 452.)

## TABLE N2. Two-Factor Interaction Confounding in the Contrast Columns of the Tables M1–M5 Resolution IV Fractional Factorial Designs (*Continued*)

**64 Trials**

| 1 | 2 | 3 | 4 | 5 | 6 | 7 | 8 | 9 | 10 | 11 | 12 | 13 | 14 | 15 | 16 | 17 | 18 | 19 | 20 | 21 |
|---|---|---|---|---|---|---|---|---|----|----|----|----|----|----|----|----|----|----|----|----|
| *A | *B | *C | *D | *E | *F | AB | BC | CD | DE | EF | ABF | AC | BD | CE | DF | ABE | BCF | ABCD | BCDE | CDEF |
| | | | | | | FG | FI | BM | GJ | GH | *G | GI | GK | HL | HJ | *H | *I | IK | EM | JL |
| | | | | | | EH | AL | EN | CN | DO | | BL | CM | DN | AK | | | DL | BN | FN |
| | | | | | | CL | DM | KP | FO | JQ | | FP | AQ | BR | IM | | | AM | IO | CO |
| | | | | | | JO | GP | LQ | HQ | IR | | MQ | NR | OS | EO | | | HN | JP | ES |
| | | | | | | IP | ER | FS | MR | NS | | HR | IS | JT | GQ | | | CQ | DR | HT |
| | | | | | | DQ | KT | GT | TU | LU | | KS | PT | GU | CS | | | GS | KU | QU |
| | | | | | | ST | QX | JU | AV | KV | | NV | HV | IW | LT | | | FT | LV | PV |
| | | | | | | MX | NY | AX | BY | BW | | UW | OW | VX | PX | | | OU | SW | MW |
| | | | | | | VY | WZ | RY | SZ | CZ | | DX | LX | MY | WY | | | RV | HX | IY |
| | | | | | | UZ | Ha | OZ | Xa | Pa | | Ea | EY | FZ | NZ | | | BX | CY | DZ |
| | | | | | | Ra | Sb | Va | Wb | Yb | | Tb | Fb | Aa | Bb | | | JZ | Qa | Ka |
| | | | | | | Kb | Vc | Ib | Lc | Tc | | Yc | ac | Qc | Uc | | | Ya | Zb | Rb |
| | | | | | | Nc | Od | Hc | Id | Md | | Jd | Zd | bd | Rd | | | Pb | Ac | Gc |
| | | | | | | de | Je | Wd | Pe | Xe | | Oe | Ue | Ke | ae | | | Ec | Fd | Bd |
| | | | | | | Wf | Uf | ef | Kf | Af | | Zf | Jf | Pf | Vf | | | We | Ge | Ae |
| | | | | | | | | | | | | | | | | | | df | Tf | Xf |

| 22 | 23 | 24 | 25 | 26 | 27 | 28 | 29 | 30 | 31 | 32 | 33 | 34 | 35 | 36 | 37 | 38 | 39 | 40 | 41 | 42 |
|----|----|----|----|----|----|----|----|----|----|----|----|----|----|----|----|----|----|----|----|----|
| ABDEF | ACEF | ADF | AE | BF | ABC | BCD | CDE | DEF | ABEF | ACF | AD | BE | CF | ABD | BCE | CDF | ABDE | BCEF | ABCDF | ACDE |
| *J | HI | *K | BH | AG | *L | *M | *N | *O | EG | *P | FK | AH | BI | *Q | *R | *S | DH | EI | *T | IJ |
| | JM | | KO | CI | | | | | FH | | LM | JK | GL | | | | FJ | MO | | HM |
| | KN | | LR | LP | | | | | DI | | BQ | MN | NO | | | | LN | HP | | AN |
| | EP | | IU | KQ | | | | | OQ | | PS | CR | AP | | | | GO | FR | | OP |
| | GR | | DV | MS | | | | | PR | | IT | PU | DS | | | | EQ | AU | | QR |
| | BU | | GW | JV | | | | | NT | | EV | QV | QT | | | | SU | TV | | CV |

Alias table for the design columns 43–63. Columns denoted by `*` are main effects; the other columns are higher‑order terms, each shown with the effects that are aliased with it.

| Column | Alias generator | Designation |
|---|---|---|
| 43 | BDEF | |
| 44 | ABCEF | *U |
| 45 | ACDF | |
| 46 | ADE | *v |
| 47 | BEF | *w |
| 48 | ABCF | |
| 49 | ACD | *X |
| 50 | BDE | *Y |
| 51 | CEF | *Z |
| 52 | ABDF | |
| 53 | ACE | *a |
| 54 | BDF | *b |
| 55 | ABCE | |
| 56 | BCDF | |
| 57 | ABCDE | *c |
| 58 | BCDEF | *d |
| 59 | ABCDEF | |
| 60 | ACDEF | *e |
| 61 | ADEF | |
| 62 | AEF | *f |
| 63 | AF | |

Aliased effects for the higher‑order columns:

- **43 (BDEF):** SV, LW, OX, TY, AZ, Fa, bc, Qd, De, Cf, AJ, HK, IN, BO, RS, GV, DW, UX, FY, MZ, Ta, Eb, Pc, Cd, Le, Qf
- **45 (ACDF):** NX, QY, PZ, Ca, Jb, Mc, Td, Se, Ff, CK, GM, DP, IQ, JR, AS, BT, FX, UY, VZ, Oa, Lb, Wc, Hd, Ee, Nf
- **48 (ABCF):** EW, TX, OY, RZ, Ua, Db, Nd, ce, Hf, CG, AI, FL, KM, JN, BP, QS, DT, EU, HZ, Wa, Xb, Oc, Vd, Ye, Rf
- **52 (ABDF):** CU, AW, KY, LZ, Ia, Vb, Sc, Xd, Me, Bf, DG, EJ, BK, HO, MP, FQ, LS, CT, NU, VW, IX, Ab, Zc, ad, Re, Yf
- **55 (ABCE):** JW, CX, HY, Na, Gb, Rc, Ud, Ze, Oe, Gf, CH, EL, NQ, AR, JS, OT, FU, MV, PW, XY, GZ, Ba, Dc, Kd, be, If
- **56 (BCDF):** FW, DY, IZ, La, Ob, Xc, Sd, Te, Gf, DI, KL, FM, PQ, OR, BS, AT, UV, NW, GX, YZ, Ja, Cb, Ed, He, cf
- **59 (ABCDEF):** HU, RW, KX, EZ, Mb, Jc, Yd, Ve, af, CJ, GN, LO, KR, HS, ET, DU, IV, WX, PY, QZ, ab, Fc, Ad, Be, Mf
- **61 (ADEF):** BV, KW, RX, AY, TZ, Ma, Cc, Pd, Ie, bf, BJ, EK, AO, NP, RT, MU, FV, QW, GY, XZ, Sa, Hb, Ic, Ld, Ce, Df
- **63 (AF):** CW, JX, SY, BZ, Ga, Nb, Kc, Dd, Qe, If, TW, EX, LY, KZ, Da, Ub, Bc, Gd, Fe, Sf, BG, DK, IL, CP, MT, RU, OV, HW, SX, JY, Za, Qb, cd, Ne, Ef

ᵃThe higher order terms were used when generating the design. Main effects are denoted by *. See Example 13-1.

# TABLE N3. Two-Factor Interaction Confounding in the Contrast Columns of the Tables M1–M5 Resolution III Fractional Factorial Designs[a]

**8 Trials**

| 1 | 2 | 3 | 4 | 5 | 6 | 7 |
|---|---|---|---|---|---|---|
| *A | *B | *C | *D | *E | ABC | AC |
| BD | AD | BE | AB | BC | CD | DE |
| EF | CE | DF | CF | AF | AE | BF |
| CG | FG | AG | EG | DG | *F | *G |
| | | | | | BG | |

**16 Trials**

| 1 | 2 | 3 | 4 | 5 | 6 | 7 | 8 | 9 | 10 | 11 | 12 | 13 | 14 | 15 |
|---|---|---|---|---|---|---|---|---|----|----|----|----|----|----|
| *A | *B | *C | *D | AB | BC | CD | ABD | AC | BD | ABC | BCD | ABCD | ACD | AD |
| BE | AE | BF | CG | *E | *F | *G | DE | EF | FG | CE | DF | EG | AG | BH |
| CI | CF | DG | EH | DH | EI | FJ | *H | *I | AH | AF | BG | CH | FH | GI |
| HJ | DJ | AI | BJ | FI | GJ | HK | AJ | BK | *J | GH | HI | IJ | DI | EJ |
| FK | IK | EK | FL | CK | AK | BL | GK | HL | CL | BI | CJ | DK | JK | KL |
| LM | GL | JL | KM | GM | DL | EM | IL | JM | IM | *K | *L | AL | EL | FM |
| GN | MN | HM | IN | LN | HN | AN | CM | DN | KN | DM | AM | *M | BM | CN |
| DO | HO | NO | AO | JO | MO | IO | FN | GO | EO | JN | EN | BN | *N | *O |
| | | | | | | | BO | | | LO | KO | FO | CO | |

**32 Trials**

| 1 | 2 | 3 | 4 | 5 | 6 | 7 | 8 | 9 | 10 | 11 | 12 | 13 | 14 | 15 | 16 | 17 | 18 | 19 | 20 | 21 |
|---|---|---|---|---|---|---|---|---|----|----|----|----|----|----|----|----|----|----|----|----|
| *A | *B | *C | *D | *E | AC | BD | CE | ACD | BDE | AE | ABC | BCD | CDE | ACDE | ABCDE | ABDE | ABE | AB | BC | CD |
| CF | DG | AF | BG | CH | *F | *G | *H | DF | EG | FH | BF | CG | DH | EI | FJ | AJ | BK | CL | AL | AI |
| EK | FL | EH | FI | GJ | DI | EJ | FK | *I | *J | *K | GI | HJ | IK | JL | KM | GK | HL | IM | DM | BM |
| NO | OP | GM | HN | AK | HK | IL | JM | GL | HM | IN | *L | *M | *N | AN | BO | LN | MO | NP | JN | EN |
| JQ | KR | PQ | QR | IO | BL | CM | DN | KN | LO | MP | JO | KP | AO | *O | *P | CP | DQ | ER | OQ | KO |

(*Table continues on p. 456.*)

| BS | AS | LS | MT | RS | JP | KQ | LR | EO | FP | GQ | NQ | OR | LQ | BP | CQ | *Q | *R | *S | FS | PR |
|----|----|----|----|----|----|----|----|----|----|----|----|----|----|----|----|----|----|----|----|----|
| LT | CT | BT | CU | NU | ST | TU | UV | MS | AQ | BR | HR | IS | PS | MR | NS | DR | ES | FT | *T | GT |
| IU | MU | DU | EV | DV | OV | PW | AW | AU | NT | OU | CS | DT | JT | QT | RU | OT | PU | QV | GU | *U |
| HW | JV | NV | OW | FW | EW | FX | QX | VW | BV | CW | AT | BU | EU | KU | LV | SV | TW | UX | RW | HV |
| MX | NY | KW | LX | PX | GX | HY | GY | BX | WX | XY | PV | QW | CV | FV | GW | MW | NX | OY | VY | SX |
| PY | QZ | JY | KZ | MY | QY | RZ | IZ | RY | CY | DZ | DX | AX | RX | DW | EX | HX | IY | JZ | PZ | WZ |
| VZ | Wa | OZ | Pa | La | NZ | Oa | Sa | HZ | SZ | Ta | YZ | EY | BY | SY | AY | FY | GZ | Ha | Ka | Qa |
| Gb | Hc | Ra | Sb | Qb | Mb | Ab | Pb | Ja | Ia | Jb | Ea | YZ | FZ | CZ | TZ | BZ | Ca | Db | Ib | Lb |
| ac | bd | Xb | Yc | Tc | Rc | Nc | Bc | Tb | Kb | Lc | Ub | Za | ab | Ga | Da | Ua | Vb | Wc | Ec | Jc |
| Dd | Ee | Id | Ad | Zd | Ud | Sd | Od | Qc | Uc | Vd | Kc | Fb | Gc | bc | Hb | Eb | Fc | Gd | Xd | Fd |
| Re |    | ce | Je | Be | ae | Ve | Te | Cd | Rd | Se | Md | Vc | Wd | Hd | cd | Ic | Jd | Ke | He | Ye |
|    |    |    |    |    |    |    |    | Pe | De |    | We | Ld | Me | Xe | Ie | de | Ae |    |    |    |
|    |    |    |    |    |    |    |    |    |    |    |    | Ne |    |    |    |    |    |    |    |    |

| 22 | 23 | 24 | 25 | 26 | 27 | 28 | 29 | 30 | 31 |
|----|----|----|----|----|----|----|----|----|----|
| DE | ACE | ABCD | BCDE | ADE | ABCE | ABD | BCE | AD | BE |
| BJ | EF | FG | GH | HI | IJ | JK | KL | LM | DJ |
| CN | AH | BI | CJ | DK | EL | FM | GN | HO | MN |
| FO | CK | DL | EM | FN | GO | HP | IQ | JR | IP |
| LP | DO | AM | BN | CO | DP | EQ | FR | GS | AR |
| QS | GP | EP | AP | BQ | CR | DS | ET | FU | KS |
| HU | MQ | HQ | FQ | GR | HS | IT | JU | KV | HT |
| *V | RT | NR | IR | JS | KT | LU | MV | NW | GV |
| IW | IV | SU | OS | PT | QU | RV | SW | TX | LW |
| TY | *W | JW | TV | AV | BW | CX | DY | EZ | OX |
| AZ | JX | *X | KX | UW | VX | WY | XZ | Ya | UY |
| Xa | UZ | KY | *Y | LY | MZ | Na | Aa | Bb | Fa |
| Rb | Ba | Va | LZ | *Z | *a | *b | Ob | Pc | Zb |
| Mc | Yb | Cb | Wb | Ma | Nb | Oc | *c | *d | Cc |
| Kd | Sc | Zc | Dc | Xc | Ac | Bd | Pd | Qe | Qd |
| Ge | Nd | Td | ad | Ed | Yd | Ze | Ce |    | *e |
|    | Le | Oe | Ue | be | Fe |    |    |    |    |

## TABLE N3. Two-Factor Interaction Confounding in the Contrast Columns of the Tables M1–M5 Resolution III Fractional Factorial Designs (*Continued*)

*64 Trials*

| 1 | 2 | 3 | 4 | 5 | 6 | 7 | 8 | 9 | 10 | 11 | 12 | 13 | 14 | 15 | 16 | 17 | 18 | 19 | 20 | 21 |
|---|---|---|---|---|---|---|---|---|----|----|-----|----|----|----|----|-----|-----|------|------|------|
| *A | *B | *C | *D | *E | *F | AB | BC | CD | DE | EF | ABF | AC | BD | CE | DF | ABE | BCF | ABCD | BCDE | CDEF |
| BG | AG | BH | CI | DJ | EK | *G | *H | *I | *J | *K | FG | GH | HI | IJ | JK | EG | FH | GI | HJ | IK |
| CM | CH | DI | EJ | FK | GL | FL | GM | HN | IO | JP | *L | *M | *N | *O | *P | *Q | *R | MN | NO | OP |
| PX | DN | AM | BN | CO | DP | HM | IN | JO | KP | LQ | KQ | LR | MS | NT | OU | PV | QW | *S | *T | *U |
| EY | QY | EO | FP | AY | HR | IS | FR | GS | HT | MW | MR | NS | OT | PU | QV | RW | SX | TY | UZ | TZ |
| LZ | FZ | RZ | GQ | Tb | BZ | Ca | JT | KU | LV | Dd | JV | KW | IU | MY | AX | BY | CZ | Da | Eb | Va |
| Ha | Ma | Ga | Sa | Ic | Uc | Vd | Aa | Bb | Cc | Ge | NX | OY | LX | Qa | NZ | CZ | Pb | Ab | Bc | Fc |
| Sb | Ib | Nb | Hb | Pd | Jd | Ke | Db | Ec | Fd | Zh | AZ | Ba | PZ | Dc | Rb | Pb | Td | Qc | Rd | Cd |
| Dg | Tc | Jc | Oc | Le | Qe | Rj | We | Mg | Yg | Oi | Ee | Ff | Cb | Hh | Ed | Sc | Gf | Ue | Vf | Se |
| Qh | Eh | Ud | Kd | Wf | Mf | Ng | Xf | Th | Ui | Vj | Hf | Ig | Gg | Ki | Ii | Td | Bi | Hg | Ih | Wg |
| ji | Ri | Fi | Ve | Bh | Xg | Yh | Sg | Pi | Qj | Rk | ai | bj | Jh | Bk | Lj | Fe | Kk | Cj | Dk | Ji |
| Nj | gj | Sj | Ag | Hk | Ci | Dj | Oh | qj | bk | cl | Pj | Qk | Aj | dl | Cl | Ah | Nl | Ll | Mm | El |
| cp | Ok | hk | Gj | Ul | Il | Jm | Zi | bk | Gm | Hn | Wk | Xl | ck | Sm | em | Jj | En | Om | Pn | Nn |
| Vq | dq | Pl | Tk | jm | Vm | Wn | Ek | Fl | Mp | Nq | SI | Tm | Rl | Zn | Tn | Mk | go | Fo | Gp | Qo |
| nr | Wr | er | il | Rn | kn | lo | Kn | Lo | Zq | ar | dm | en | Ym | Vo | ao | Dm | Vp | hp | iq | Hq |
| ls | os | Xs | Qm | gt | So | Tp | Xo | Yp | or | ps | lo | Jp | Un | gp | Wp | fn | cq | Wq | Xr | jr |
| Jt | mt | pt | fs | Zu | hu | iv | mp | nq | Ws | Xt | Or | Ps | fo | Lr | hq | Uo | Yr | dr | es | Ys |
| eu | Ku | nu | Yt | rv | av | bw | Uq | Vr | At | Bu | bs | ct | Kq | Ru | Ms | bp | js | Zs | at | ft |
| Rv | fv | Lv | qu | pw | sw | tx | jw | Aw | Bx | Cy | qt | ru | Qt | ev | Sv | Xq | Ou | kt | lu | bu |
| Iw | Sw | gw | ov | Nx | Oy | ry | cx | kx | ly | mz | Yu | Zv | du | tw | fw | ir | Av | lu | Qw | mv |
| mx | Jx | Tx | Mw | iy | jz | Pz | uy | dy | ez | fa | Cv | Dw | sv | bx | ux | Ni | Ux | Pv | Cx | Rx |
| Wy | ny | Ky | kx | Vz | Wa | ka | sz | vz | wa | xβ | Dz | Ea | aw | Fy | cy | Tw | hy | Bw | Wz | Dy |
| Oa | Xz | oz | Uy | Ma | Nβ | Xβ | Qa | ta | uβ | vγ | na | oβ | Ex | Aα | Gz | gx | wz | Vy | ja | Xa |
| zβ | Pβ | Ya | Lz | qβ | rγ | Oγ | lβ | Rβ | Sγ | Tδ | gβ | hγ | FB | Gγ | Bβ | vy | eα | iz | yβ | kβ |
| kγ | αγ | Zβ | pa | aγ | bδ | sδ | Yγ | mγ | nδ | oε | yγ | zδ | PY | qδ | qδ | dz | IB | xα | xα | jγ |
| oδ | lδ | βδ | Zβ | Se | Tζ | cε | Pδ | Zδ | aε | bζ | wδ | iε | iδ | jε | re | Ha | Dδ | jβ | Kδ | Yδ |
| Tε | pe | me | Rδ | δζ | eη | Uζ | te | Qε | Rζ | Sη | Ue | xζ | αε | Bζ | kζ | ea | Fζ | iγ | Aε | hε |
| ζη | Uζ | qζ | γε | oη | pθ | ζθ | dζ | uζ | vη | wθ | pζ | yη | yζ | zη | γη | Cy | εη | Eε | Fζ | Lζ |
| Uθ | ηθ | Vη | nζ | sθ | tι | qι | Vθ | eη | wθ | gι | cη | qθ | Wη | Xθ | aθ | Iε | mθ | Kη | Lθ | Gη |
| dι | Vι | θι | rη | Xι | Yκ | uκ | ηι | θι | gι | Aκ | Tθ | dι | rθ | sι | Yι | sζ | eι | uθ | uθ | Aθ |
| Kκ | eκ | Wκ | Wθ | fκ | sλ | ZA | rκ | θκ | Xκ | YA | xι | yκ | eι | fκ | ικ | Zκ | γκ | nι | vι | Mι |
| Fλ | Lλ | fλ | Xλ | Lλ | Aλ | Zλ | vλ | sλ | uλ | Yλ | hκ | iλ | Vκ | WA | gA | aλ | yλ | ζκ | oκ | pλ |

456

| 22 | 23 | 24 | 25 | 26 | 27 | 28 | 29 | 30 | 31 | 32 | 33 | 34 | 35 | 36 | 37 | 38 | 39 | 40 | 41 | 42 |
|---|---|---|---|---|---|---|---|---|---|---|---|---|---|---|---|---|---|---|---|---|
| ABDEF | ACEF | ADF | AE | BF | ABC | BCD | CDE | DEF | ABEF | ACF | AD | BE | CF | ABD | BCE | CDF | ABDE | BCEF | ABCDF | ACDE |
| JL | KM | LN | MO | NP | CG | DH | EI | FJ | GK | HL | IM | JN | KO | DG | EH | FI | GJ | HK | IL | JM |
| PQ | QR | AP | BQ | AL | AH | BI | CJ | DK | EL | FM | GN | HO | IP | AN | BO | CP | DQ | ER | FS | GT |
| *V | *W | RS | ST | CR | BM | CN | DO | EP | FQ | GR | HS | AQ | BR | LP | MQ | NR | OS | PT | QU | RV |
| Ua | Vb | *X | *Y | TU | OQ | PR | QS | RT | SU | TV | UW | IT | JU | JQ | KR | LS | MT | NU | OV | PW |
| Wb | Xc | Wc | Xd | *Z | DS | AS | BT | CU | DV | EW | FX | VX | WY | CS | DT | EU | FV | GW | HX | IY |
| Gd | He | Yd | Ze | Ye | UV | ET | FU | GV | HW | IX | JY | GY | HZ | KV | LW | MX | NY | OZ | Pa | Qb |
| De | Ef | If | Jg | af | *a | VW | WX | XY | YZ | Za | ab | KZ | La | XZ | Ya | Zb | ac | bd | ce | Ac |
| TJ | Ug | Fg | Gh | Kh | Zf | *b | *c | *d | *e | *f | *g | bc | cd | Ia | Jb | Kc | Ld | Me | Nf | df |
| Xh | Yi | Vh | Wi | Hi | bg | ag | bh | ci | dj | ek | Bj | *h | Af | Mb | Nc | Od | Pe | Qf | Rg | Og |
| Kj | Lk | Zj | ak | Xj | Li | ch | di | ej | fk | gl | fl | Ck | *i | de | ef | fg | gh | hi | ij | sn |
| Fm | Gn | Ml | Nm | bl | ij | Mj | Nk | Ol | Pm | Qn | hm | gm | Dl | Bg | Ch | Di | Ej | Fk | Gl | jk |
| Oo | Pp | Ho | Ip | On | Yk | Jk | Kl | Lm | Mn | No | Ro | in | hn | *j | *k | *l | *m | *n | *o | Hm |
| Rp | Sq | Qq | Rr | Jq | cm | Zl | am | bn | co | dp | Op | Sp | jo | Em | Fn | Go | Hp | lq | Jr | *p |
| Aq | Br | Tr | Us | Ss | Po | dn | eo | fp | gq | hr | eq | Pq | Tq | io | jp | kq | lr | Ar | Bs | Ks |
| Ir | Js | Cs | Dt | Vt | Kr | Qp | Ap | Bq | Cr | Ds | is | fr | Qr | kp | lq | mr | ns | ms | nt | Ci |
| ks | lt | Kt | Lu | Eu | Tt | Ls | Rq | Sr | Ts | Ut | Et | ji | gs | Ur | Vs | As | Bt | ot | pu | ou |
| Zt | au | mu | nv | Mv | Wu | Uu | Mt | Nu | Au | Bv | Vu | Fu | ku | Rs | Sr | Wt | Xu | Cu | Dv | qv |
| gu | hv | bv | cw | ow | Fv | Xv | Vv | Ww | Ov | Pw | Cw | Wv | Gv | ht | iu | Tu | Uv | Yv | Zw | Ew |
| cv | dw | iw | jx | dx | Nw | Gw | Yw | Zx | Xx | Yy | Qx | Dx | Xw | lv | mw | jv | kw | Vw | Wx | ax |
| nw | ox | ex | fy | ky | px | Ox | Hx | ly | ay | bz | Zz | Ry | Ey | Hw | Ix | nx | Ax | lx | my | Xy |
| Sy | Ay | py | qz | gz | ey | qy | rz | Qz | Jz | Ka | cα | aα | Sz | Yx | Zy | Jy | oy | By | Cz | nz |
| Ez | Tz | Bz | Cα | ra | lz | fz | ga | sα | Ra | Sβ | Lβ | dβ | bβ | Fz | Ga | az | Kz | pz | qa | Da |
| YB | Fα | Uα | Vβ | Dβ | ha | ma | nβ | hβ | tβ | uγ | Ty | Mγ | eγ | Ta | Uβ | Hβ | ba | La | Mβ | rβ |
| Iγ | Zγ | Gβ | Hγ | Wγ | sβ | iβ | jγ | oγ | iγ | jδ | vδ | Uδ | Nδ | cγ | Aγ | Vγ | lγ | cβ | dγ | Ny |
| aδ | mδ | aδ | be | lδ | Ey | ty | uδ | kδ | pδ | qe | ke | we | Ve | fδ | dδ | Bδ | Wδ | Jδ | Aδ | eδ |
| ie | βε | nε | oζ | cζ | Xδ | Fδ | Ge | ve | le | mζ | rζ | lζ | xζ | Oe | ge | ee | Ce | Xe | Ke | Be |
| Mζ | jζ | γζ | δη | pη | Je | Ye | Zζ | Hζ | wζ | xη | nη | sη | mη | Wζ | Pζ | hζ | fζ | Dζ | Yζ | Lζ |
| Cη | Nη | kη | lθ | eθ | dη | Kζ | Lη | aη | Iη | Jθ | yθ | oθ | tθ | yη | Xη | Qη | iη | gη | Eη | Zη |
| Hθ | Dθ | Oθ | Pι | mι | qθ | eθ | fι | Mθ | bθ | cι | Kι | zι | pι | nθ | zθ | Yθ | Rθ | jθ | hθ | Fθ |
| Bι | lι | Eι | Fκ | Qκ | ζι | rι | sκ | Aι | Nι | Oκ | dκ | Lκ | ax | uι | oι | aι | Zι | aκ | kι | iι |
| Nκ | Cκ | Jκ | KA | GA | nκ | ηκ | θλ | gκ | Bκ | CA | PA | eA | MA | qκ | vκ | pκ | βκ | γλ | Tκ | lκ |
| xλ | OA | DA |  |  | RA | oλ |  | tλ | hλ |  |  |  |  | βA | rA | wA | qλ |  | bλ | UA |

(*Table continues on p. 458.*)

# TABLE N3. Two-Factor Interaction Confounding in the Contrast Columns of the Tables M1–M5 Resolution III Fractional Factorial Designs (Continued)

**64 Trials (continued)**

| 43 | 44 | 45 | 46 | 47 | 48 | 49 | 50 | 51 | 52 | 53 | 54 | 55 | 56 | 57 | 58 | 59 | 60 | 61 | 62 | 63 |
|---|---|---|---|---|---|---|---|---|---|---|---|---|---|---|---|---|---|---|---|---|
| BDEF | ABCEF | ACDF | ADE | BEF | ABCF | ACD | BDE | CEF | ABDF | ACE | BDF | ABCE | BCDF | ABCDE | BCDEF | ABCDEF | ACDEF | ADEF | AEF | AF |
| KN | LO | MP | AJ | BK | CL | AI | BJ | CK | DL | EM | FN | GO | HP | IQ | JR | KS | LT | MU | AK | BL |
| HU | IV | JW | NQ | OR | AR | DM | EN | FO | GP | AO | BP | CQ | DR | ES | FT | GU | AU | BV | NV | OW |
| AV | BW | CX | KX | LY | PS | BS | CT | DU | EV | HQ | IR | JS | KT | AT | BU | CV | HV | IW | CW | DX |
| SW | TX | UY | DY | EZ | MZ | QT | RU | SV | TW | FW | GX | HY | IZ | LU | MV | NW | DW | EX | JX | KY |
| QX | RY | SZ | VZ | Wa | Fa | Na | Ob | AW | BX | UX | VY | WZ | Xa | Ja | Kb | Lc | OX | PY | FY | GZ |
| JZ | Ka | Lb | Ta | Ub | Xb | Gb | Hc | Pc | Qd | CY | DZ | Ea | Fb | Yb | Zc | ad | Md | Ad | QZ | Ra |
| Rc | Sd | Te | Mc | Nd | Vc | Yc | Zd | Id | Je | Re | Sf | Tg | Yh | Gc | Hd | Ie | be | Ne | Be | CJ |
| Bd | Ce | Df | Uf | Ae | Oe | Wd | Xe | ae | bf | Kf | Lg | Mh | Ni | Vi | Wj | Xk | Jf | cf | Of | Pg |
| eg | fh | gi | Eg | Vg | Bf | Pf | Qg | Rh | Zg | ah | bi | ci | fj | gk | hl | im | Yl | Kg | dg | eh |
| Ph | Qi | Rj | hj | Fh | Wh | Cg | Dh | Ei | Si | Tj | Uk | Vl | dk | el | fm | gn | im | Zm | Lh | Mi |
| Ti | Uj | Vk | Sk | ik | Gi | Xi | Yj | Zk | Fj | Gk | Hl | Im | Bl | Cm | Dn | Eo | Rm | Sn | an | bo |
| kl | lm | Al | Wl | Tl | jl | Hj | Ik | Jl | al | bm | cn | do | Wm | Xn | Yo | Zp | jn | ko | To | Up |
| ln | An | Bo | Bm | Xm | Um | km | Am | Bn | Km | Ln | Mo | Np | Ao | Ko | Lp | Mq | Eo | ip | lp | mq |
| *q | Jo | Kp | no | Cn | Yn | Vn | Wo | mo | Co | Dp | Eq | Fr | ep | Bp | Cq | Dr | ho | Gq | jq | kr |
| Lt | *r | *s | Cp | op | Do | Zo | ap | Xp | np | oq | pr | qs | Oq | fq | gr | hs | aq | br | Hr | ls |
| Du | Mu | Nv | Lq | Dq | pq | Ep | Fq | bq | Yq | Zr | as | bt | Gs | Pr | Qs | Rt | Nr | Os | cs | dt |
| pv | Ev | Fw | *t | Mr | Er | qr | rs | Gr | cr | ds | et | fu | rt | Ht | Iu | Jv | Es | Ft | Pt | Qu |
| rw | qw | rx | Ow | *u | *v | Fs | Gt | st | tu | It | Ju | Kv | cu | su | tv | uw | it | ju | Gu | Hv |
| Fx | sx | ty | Gx | Px | Qy | Ot | Pu | Hu | Iv | uv | vw | wx | gv | dv | ew | fx | Su | Tv | kv | lw |
| by | Gy | Hz | sy | Hy | Iz | *w | *x | Qv | Rw | Sx | Kx | Ly | Lw | Mx | Ny | Oz | Kw | Lx | Uw | Vx |
| Yz | cz | da | uz | tz | ua | Rz | Sa | *y | *z | *a | Ty | Uz | xy | yz | za | aβ | vx | wy | My | Nz |
| oα | Za | aβ | Ia | va | wβ | Ja | Kβ | Tβ | Aβ | Bγ | Az | Ba | Mz | Na | Ob | Py | gy | hz | xz | ya |
| Eβ | pβ | qγ | eβ | Jβ | Kγ | vβ | wγ | Lγ | Uγ | Vδ | *β | *γ | Va | Wβ | Xγ | Yδ | kz | lα | ia | jβ |
| sγ | Fγ | Gδ | bγ | fγ | gδ | xγ | yδ | xδ | Mδ | Ne | Cδ | Dε | Cβ | Dγ | Eδ | Fε | Pa | QΒ | mβ | nγ |
| Oδ | tδ | Qε | rδ | cδ | de | Lδ | Me | ze | ye | zζ | We | Xζ | *δ | *ε | *ζ | *η | αβ | γδ | Rγ | Sδ |
| fε | Pε | hζ | He | se | tζ | he | iζ | Nζ | aζ | βη | Oζ | Pη | Eζ | Fη | Aη | Bθ | βγ | Rε | δε | eζ |
| Cζ | gζ | Rη | vζ | Iζ | Jη | eζ | fη | jη | Oη | Pθ | aη | βθ | Yη | Zθ | Gθ | Hι | γδ | Re | Sζ | Tη |
| Mη | Dη | iθ | Rη | lη | xθ | uη | vθ | gθ | kθ | lι | γθ | &ι | Qθ | Rι | aι | bκ | Bη | aζ | bη | cθ |
| aθ | Nθ | Fι | iθ | wθ | Sθ | Kθ | Kι | lι | hι | ικ | Qι | Rκ | γι | δκ | Sκ | TΛ | *θ | Hη | Iθ | Jι |
| Gι | bι | Oι | Fι | Sι | Tι | yι | Lκ | Mκ | xκ | yλ | &κ | nλ | εκ | ζΛ | eΛ |  | Cι | Cθ | Dι | Eκ |
| jκ | Hκ | cκ | Pκ | jκ | kκ | Uκ | zκ | aλ | Nλ |  | mκ |  | SΛ |  |  |  | Iκ | Dκ | *κ | *λ |
| mλ | kλ | lλ | dλ | Qλ | Hλ | lλ | Vλ |  | NA |  | jΛ |  |  |  |  |  | cλ | JΛ | EΛ |  |

[a] The higher order terms were used when generating the design. Main effects are denoted by *. See Example 13-1.

**TABLE O.  Pass/Fail Functional Test Matrix Coverage**

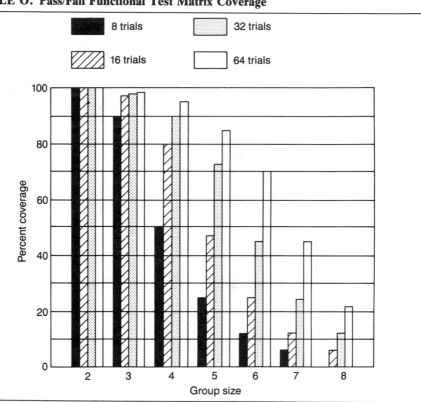

TABLE P. Generic Percent Plot Positions ($F_i$) for Probability Papers [$F_i = 100(i - 0.5)/n$]

| Ranking Number $i$ | Sample Size ($n$) | | | | | | | | | | | | |
|---|---|---|---|---|---|---|---|---|---|---|---|---|---|
| | 1 | 2 | 3 | 4 | 5 | 6 | 7 | 8 | 9 | 10 | 11 | 12 | 13 |
| 1 | 50.0 | 25.0 | 16.7 | 12.5 | 10.0 | 8.3 | 7.1 | 6.3 | 5.6 | 5.0 | 4.5 | 4.2 | 3.8 |
| 2 | | 75.0 | 50.0 | 37.5 | 30.0 | 25.0 | 21.4 | 18.8 | 16.7 | 15.0 | 13.6 | 12.5 | 11.5 |
| 3 | | | 83.3 | 62.5 | 50.0 | 41.7 | 35.7 | 31.3 | 27.8 | 25.0 | 22.7 | 20.8 | 19.2 |
| 4 | | | | 87.5 | 70.0 | 58.3 | 50.0 | 43.8 | 38.9 | 35.0 | 31.8 | 29.2 | 26.9 |
| 5 | | | | | 90.0 | 75.0 | 64.3 | 56.3 | 50.0 | 45.0 | 40.9 | 37.5 | 34.6 |
| 6 | | | | | | 91.7 | 78.6 | 68.8 | 61.1 | 55.0 | 50.0 | 45.8 | 42.3 |
| 7 | | | | | | | 92.9 | 81.3 | 72.2 | 65.0 | 59.1 | 54.2 | 50.0 |
| 8 | | | | | | | | 93.8 | 83.3 | 75.0 | 68.2 | 62.5 | 57.7 |
| 9 | | | | | | | | | 94.4 | 85.0 | 77.3 | 70.8 | 65.4 |
| 10 | | | | | | | | | | 95.0 | 86.4 | 79.2 | 73.1 |
| 11 | | | | | | | | | | | 95.5 | 87.5 | 80.8 |
| 12 | | | | | | | | | | | | 95.8 | 88.5 |
| 13 | | | | | | | | | | | | | 96.2 |

Sample Size (n)

| Ranking Number i | 14 | 15 | 16 | 17 | 18 | 19 | 20 | 21 | 22 | 23 | 24 | 25 | 26 |
|---|---|---|---|---|---|---|---|---|---|---|---|---|---|
| 1 | 3.6 | 3.3 | 3.1 | 2.9 | 2.8 | 2.6 | 2.5 | 2.4 | 2.3 | 2.2 | 2.1 | 2.0 | 1.9 |
| 2 | 10.7 | 10.0 | 9.4 | 8.8 | 8.3 | 7.9 | 7.5 | 7.1 | 6.8 | 6.5 | 6.3 | 6.0 | 5.8 |
| 3 | 17.9 | 16.7 | 15.6 | 14.7 | 13.9 | 13.2 | 12.5 | 11.9 | 11.4 | 10.9 | 10.4 | 10.0 | 9.6 |
| 4 | 25.0 | 23.3 | 21.9 | 20.6 | 19.4 | 18.4 | 17.5 | 16.7 | 15.9 | 15.2 | 14.6 | 14.0 | 13.5 |
| 5 | 32.1 | 30.0 | 28.1 | 26.5 | 25.0 | 23.7 | 22.5 | 21.4 | 20.5 | 19.6 | 18.8 | 18.0 | 17.3 |
| 6 | 39.3 | 36.7 | 34.4 | 32.4 | 30.6 | 28.9 | 27.5 | 26.2 | 25.0 | 23.9 | 22.9 | 22.0 | 21.2 |
| 7 | 46.4 | 43.3 | 40.6 | 38.2 | 36.1 | 34.2 | 32.5 | 31.0 | 29.5 | 28.3 | 27.1 | 26.0 | 25.0 |
| 8 | 53.6 | 50.0 | 46.9 | 44.1 | 41.7 | 39.5 | 37.5 | 35.7 | 34.1 | 32.6 | 31.3 | 30.0 | 28.8 |
| 9 | 60.7 | 56.7 | 53.1 | 50.0 | 47.2 | 44.7 | 42.5 | 40.5 | 38.6 | 37.0 | 35.4 | 34.0 | 32.7 |
| 10 | 67.9 | 63.3 | 59.4 | 55.9 | 52.8 | 50.0 | 47.5 | 45.2 | 43.2 | 41.3 | 39.6 | 38.0 | 36.5 |
| 11 | 75.0 | 70.0 | 65.6 | 61.8 | 58.3 | 55.3 | 52.5 | 50.0 | 47.7 | 45.7 | 43.8 | 42.0 | 40.4 |
| 12 | 82.1 | 76.7 | 71.9 | 67.6 | 63.9 | 60.5 | 57.5 | 54.8 | 52.3 | 50.0 | 47.9 | 46.0 | 44.2 |
| 13 | 89.3 | 83.3 | 78.1 | 73.5 | 69.4 | 65.8 | 62.5 | 59.5 | 56.8 | 54.3 | 52.1 | 50.0 | 48.1 |
| 14 | 96.4 | 90.0 | 84.4 | 79.4 | 75.0 | 71.1 | 67.5 | 64.3 | 61.4 | 58.7 | 56.3 | 54.0 | 51.9 |
| 15 |  | 96.7 | 90.6 | 85.3 | 80.6 | 76.3 | 72.5 | 69.0 | 65.9 | 63.0 | 60.4 | 58.0 | 55.8 |
| 16 |  |  | 96.9 | 91.2 | 86.1 | 81.6 | 77.5 | 73.8 | 70.5 | 67.4 | 64.6 | 62.0 | 59.6 |
| 17 |  |  |  | 97.1 | 91.7 | 86.8 | 82.5 | 78.6 | 75.0 | 71.7 | 68.8 | 66.0 | 63.5 |
| 18 |  |  |  |  | 97.2 | 92.1 | 87.5 | 83.3 | 79.5 | 76.1 | 72.9 | 70.0 | 67.3 |
| 19 |  |  |  |  |  | 97.4 | 92.5 | 88.1 | 84.1 | 80.4 | 77.1 | 74.0 | 71.2 |
| 20 |  |  |  |  |  |  | 97.5 | 92.9 | 88.6 | 84.8 | 81.3 | 78.0 | 75.0 |
| 21 |  |  |  |  |  |  |  | 97.6 | 93.2 | 89.1 | 85.4 | 82.0 | 78.8 |
| 22 |  |  |  |  |  |  |  |  | 97.7 | 93.5 | 89.6 | 86.0 | 82.7 |
| 23 |  |  |  |  |  |  |  |  |  | 97.8 | 93.8 | 90.0 | 86.5 |
| 24 |  |  |  |  |  |  |  |  |  |  | 97.9 | 94.0 | 90.4 |
| 25 |  |  |  |  |  |  |  |  |  |  |  | 98.0 | 94.2 |
| 26 |  |  |  |  |  |  |  |  |  |  |  |  | 98.1 |

TABLE Q1. Normal Probability Paper

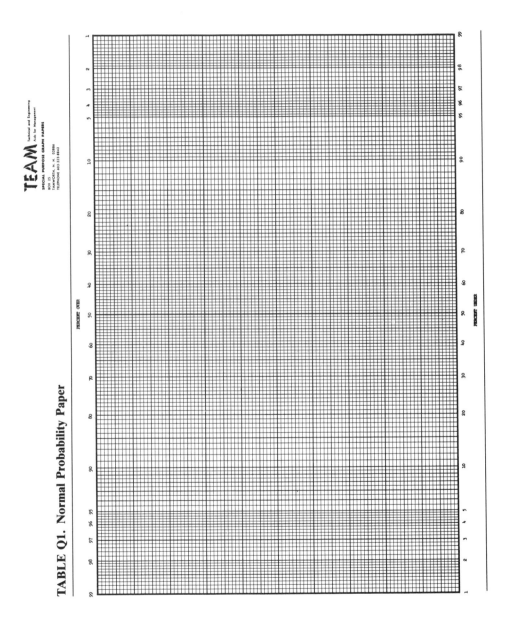

## TABLE Q2. Log-normal Probability Paper

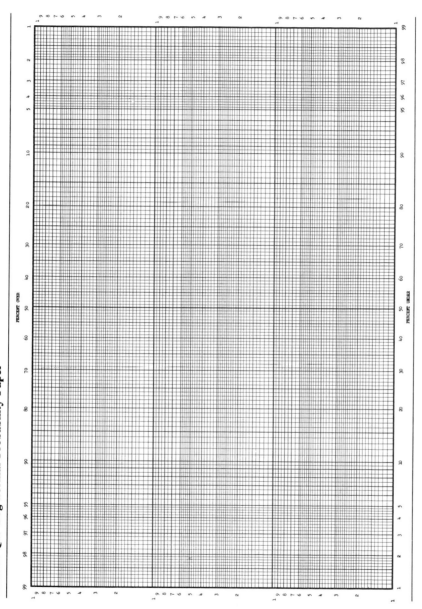

## TABLE Q3. Weibull Probability Paper

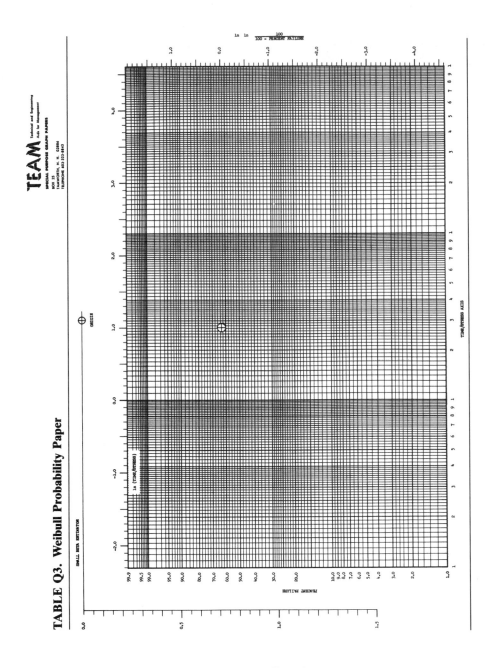

464

## TABLE R1. Normal Hazard Paper

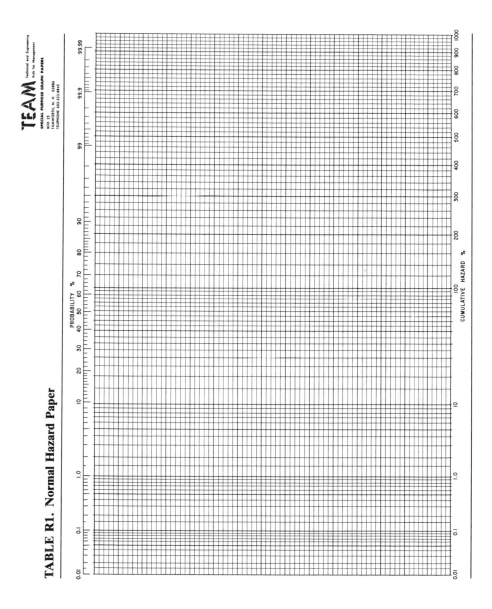

PROBABILITY %

CUMULATIVE HAZARD %

TEAM Technical and Engineering
Aids for Management

SPECIAL PURPOSE GRAPH PAPERS
BOX 25
TAMWORTH, N. H. 03886
TELEPHONE 603-323-8843

## TABLE R2. Log-normal Hazard Paper

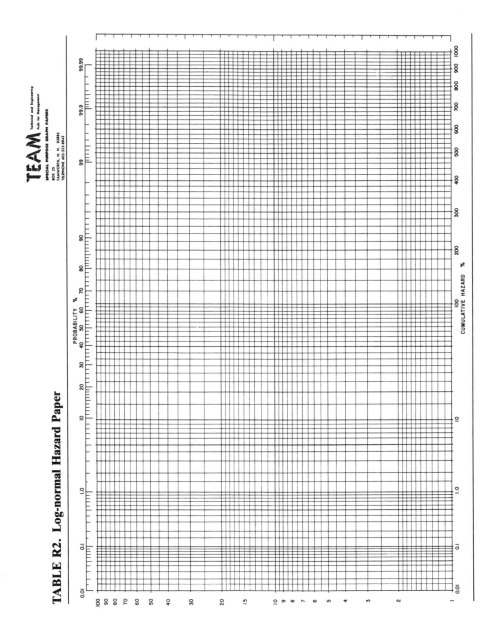

PROBABILITY %

CUMULATIVE HAZARD %

# TABLE R3. Weibull Hazard Paper

SHAPE PARAMETER

PROBABILITY %

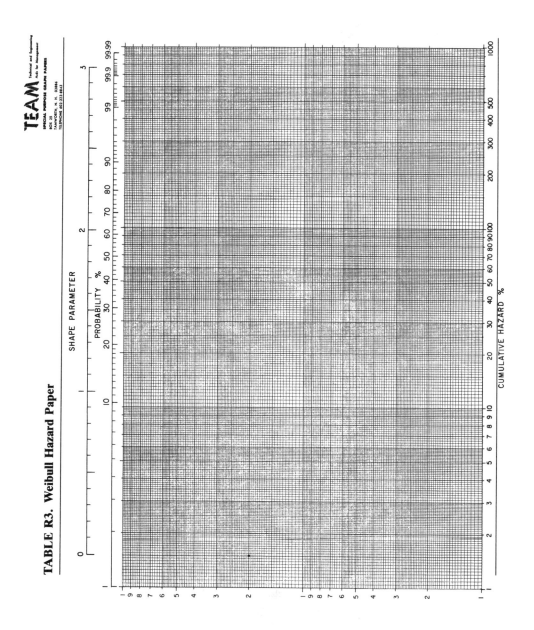

CUMULATIVE HAZARD %

467

# APPENDIX E

# LIST OF SYMBOLS

Symbols used locally in the text are not shown.

| | |
|---|---|
| $A_{r;c}$ | Factor from the Poisson distribution that is tabulated in Table K |
| ANOM | Analysis of means |
| ANOVA | Analysis of variance |
| AQL | Accept quality level |
| ARL | Average run length |
| ASQC | American Society for Quality Control |
| ASTM | American Society for Testing and Materials |
| $A_t$ | Acceleration test factor |
| $B_{r;c}$ | Factor from the Poisson distribution tabulated in Table K |
| $b$ | Weibull distribution shape parameter (slope of a Weibull probability plot); a parameter used in the NHPP with Weibull intensity model |
| $c$ | Confidence factor used in Table K |
| $c$ chart | Control chart for nonconformities |
| °C | Centigrade temperature |
| CL | Center line in a SPC chart |
| CDF | Cumulative distribution function |
| $C_p$ | Process capability index; the Mallows' $C_p$ statistic |
| $C_{pk}$ | Process capability index |
| cP | Centipoise (measure of fluid viscosity) |
| CUSUM | Cumulative sum (control chart approach) |
| $C_4$ | Controlled collapse chip connection (joints within electronic chip components) |

| | |
|---|---|
| C&E | Cause and effect (diagram) |
| $d$ | Discrimination ratio (Poisson distribution sequential testing) |
| df | degrees of freedom |
| DFM | Design for manufacturability |
| DOA | Dead on arrival |
| DOE | Design of experiments |
| $dt$ | Calculus expression used to describe an infinitesimally small increment of time $t$ |
| EVOP | Evolutionary operation |
| $\exp(x)$ | $= e^x = 2.71^x$ |
| °F | Fahrenheit temperature |
| $F_0$ | Test criterion value from the $F$ distribution (Table F) |
| $F_{\alpha;v1;v2}$ | Value from the $F$ distribution for $\alpha$ risk and $v_1$ and $v_2$ degrees of freedom (Table F) |
| $F_i$ | Probability plot positions determined from Table P |
| FMECA | Failure mode, effect, and criticality analysis |
| $F(x)$ | Describes the CDF where the independent variable is $x$ |
| $f(x)$ | Describes the PDF where the independent variable is $x$ |
| GLM | General linear modeling |
| $H_0$ | Null hypothesis |
| $H_a$ | Alternative hypothesis |
| HPP | Homogeneous Poisson process |
| in. | inches |
| K | Temperature in degrees Kelvin (273.16 + °C); Boltzmann's constant |
| $k$ | Characteristic life or scale parameter in the Weibull distribution |
| $L_a$ | Length run for AQL (in CUSUM charting) |
| LCL | Lower control limit (in SPC) |
| LDL | Lower decision level (in ANOM) |
| ln | $\log_e = \log_{2.718}$ |
| log | $\log_{10}$ |
| $L_r$ | Length run for RQL (in CUSUM charting) |
| mph | Miles per hour |
| MR | Moving range (in SPC) |
| MS | Mean square |
| msec | milliseconds |
| MTBF | Mean time between failures |
| $n$ | Sample size |
| $np$ (chart) | SPC chart of number of nonconforming items |
| NHPP | Nonhomogeneous Poisson process |
| $p$ (chart) | SPC chart of fraction nonconforming |
| $P$ | Test performance ratio ($\rho_t/\rho_a$) |
| PDF | Probability density function |
| ppm | Parts per million (defect rate) |
| Pr | probability |

| | |
|---|---|
| P/T | Precision to tolerance ratio |
| QFD | Quality function deployment |
| RQL | Reject quality level |
| $R$ | Range (in SPC) |
| RMR | Rejected material review |
| RSM | Response Surface Methodology |
| $r$ | Number of failures |
| $r(t)$ | System failure rate at time ($t$) for the NHPP model |
| $s$ | Standard deviation of a sample |
| SAS | Statistical Analysis Systems computer program, Trademark of SAS Institute, Cary, NC |
| SPC | Statistical process control |
| SS | Sum of squares |
| $T$ | Total test time used in Table K |
| $t$ | time |
| $t_0$ | Test criterion value from the $t$ distribution (Tables D or E) |
| $T_q$ | $q\%$ of the population is expected to be below this value for a population. |
| $t_{\alpha;\nu}$ | Value from the $t$ distribution for $\alpha$ risk and $\nu$ degrees of freedom (Tables D and E) |
| UCL | Upper control limit (SPC) |
| UDL | Upper decision level (ANOM) |
| $U_0$ | Test criterion value from the normal distribution (Table B or C) |
| $U_\alpha$ | Value from the normal distribution for $\alpha$ risk (Table B or C) |
| $U_\beta$ | Value from the normal distribution for $\beta$ risk (Table B or C) |
| $u$ (chart) | SPC chart of number of nonconformities per unit |
| $X$ (chart) | SPC chart of individual measurements |
| $x_0$ | Three-parameter Weibull distribution location parameter |
| $\overline{x}$ | Mean of a variable $x$ |
| $\overline{x}$ chart | SPC chart of means (i.e., $x$-bar chart) |
| $Z_\alpha$ | Normal distribution value for $\alpha$ risk (Table A) |
| $\alpha$ | Alpha, risk of rejecting the null hypothesis (accepting alternate hypothesis) in error. |
| $\beta$ | Beta, risk of accepting the null hypothesis in error. |
| $\Delta$ | Delta, effect of contrast column [see Equation (14.1)] |
| $\delta$ | Delta, an acceptable amount of uncertainty |
| $\theta$ | Theta, the parameter in the exponential distribution equation (mean of the distribution) |
| $\lambda$ | Lambda, hazard rate; intensity term in the NHPP equation. |
| $\mu$ | Mu, true mean of a population |
| $\nu$ | Nu, degrees of freedom |
| $\rho$ | Rho, actual failure rate of population |
| $\rho_a$ | A single failure rate test criterion |

| | |
|---|---|
| $\rho_t$ | The highest failure rate that is to be exhibited by the samples in a time-terminated test before a "pass test" statement can be given |
| $\rho_1$ | Higher failure rate (failures/unit time) to certify with $\beta$ risk in Poisson sequential testing (typically assigned equality to failure rate criterion $\rho_a$) |
| $\rho_0$ | Lower failure rate (failures/unit time) to certify with $\alpha$ risk in Poisson sequential testing |
| $\rho_\alpha$ | Used when calculating sample size for a fixed length test; the failure rate at which $\alpha$ is to apply |
| $\rho_\beta$ | Used when calculating sample size for a fixed length test; the failure rate at which $\beta$ is to apply |
| $\Sigma$ | Mathematical summation |
| $\chi^2_{\alpha;\nu}$ | Chi-square value from the chi-square distribution for $\alpha$ risk and $\nu$ degrees of freedom (Table G) |
| $\chi^2_0$ | Test criterion value from the chi-square distribution (Table G) |
| $\| \|$ | Mathematical symbol used to denote the absolute value of a quantity |

# APPENDIX F

# GLOSSARY

**Abscissa:** The coordinate representing the distance from the $y$ axis in a two-dimensional plot.

**Accelerated testing:** The testing of equipment in an environment so that the time will be shortened for failures to occur. For example, high temperature is often used to create failures sooner during a reliability test of electronic components. The acceleration test factor $(A_t)$ is the test time used to perform the accelerated testing divided into the expected "normal usage time" that the test is putting on the device under test.

**Accept quality level (AQL):** In a sampling plan the maximum proportion of defective units that can be considered satisfactory as the process average.

**Activation energy $(E_a)$:** A constant in the Arrhenius equation that is a function of the type of failure mechanism during a high-temperature accelerated test of electrical components.

**Alias:** *See* Confounded.

**Algorithm design:** A methodology to choose experiment design trials when fitting a model (e.g., quadratic). With these designs a computer creates a list of candidate trials and then calculates the standard deviation of the value predicted by the polynomial for each trial. The trial with the largest standard deviation is picked as the next trial to include in the design. The coefficients of the polynomial are next recalculated using this new trial and the process is repeated.

**Alpha ($\alpha$) risk:** The probability that the null hypothesis will be rejected when it is in fact true. It is also called type I error or producer's risk.

**Alternative hypothesis $(H_a)$:** *See* Hypothesis testing.

**Analysis of goodness:** The ranking of fractional factorial experiment trials according to the level of a response. An attempt is then made to identify factors or combination of factors that potentially affect the response.

**Analysis of means (ANOM):** A graphical analysis approach to compare the means of several groups of size $n$.

**Analysis of variance (ANOVA):** A statistical procedure that can be used to determine the significant effects in an factorial experiment.

**Arrhenius equation:** A common model that is used to describe the test acceleration on electronic components in a high-temperature environment.

**Attribute data:** The presence or absence of some characteristic in each device under test (e.g., proportion nonconforming in a pass/fail test).

**Average:** *See* Mean.

**Average run length (ARL):** The average number of points required before an out-of-control process condition is indicated.

**Balanced (design):** A fractional factorial experiment design where for each factor an equal number of trials is performed at each level state.

**Bar charts:** Horizontal or vertical bars that graphically illustrate the magnitude of multiple situations.

**Bathtub curve:** A curve used to describe the life cycle of a system/device as a function of usage. When the curve has its initial downward slope, the failure rate is decreasing with usage. This is the early-life region where manufacturing problems are typically encountered. The failure rate is constant during the flat part of the curve. When the curve begins sloping upward, the failure rate is increasing with usage. This region describes wear-out of a product.

**Best estimate:** A value where there is a 50% chance that the true reading is higher/lower than the estimate.

**Beta ($\beta$) risk:** The probability of accepting the null hypothesis ($H_0$) when it is false (i.e., the alternative hypothesis is true). Also called type II error or consumer's risk.

**Bias:** An error that is persistent or systematic as opposed to a random error.

**Bimodal distribution:** A distribution that is a combination of two different distributions resulting in two distinct peaks.

**Binomial distribution:** A distribution that is useful to describe discrete variables or attributes that have two possible outcomes (e.g., a pass/fail proportion test, heads/tails outcome from flipping a coin, defect/no defect present).

**Blocking:** A technique that is used to account for "nuisance" variables when structuring fractional factorial experiment test trials.

**Boldness:** The term used to choose the magnitude of the variable levels to use within a response surface design. The concept suggests that the magnitudes of variables should be large enough to capture the minimum and maximum responses of the process under test.

**Boltzmann's constant:** A constant of $8.617 \times 10^{-5}$ eV/K used in the Arrhenius equation for high-temperature accelerated testing.

**Brainstorming:** Consensus building among experts about a problem or issue using group discussion.

**Bugs:** A slang term used to describe problems that may occur in a process or in the use of a product. These problems can result from errors in the design or the manufacturing process.

**Burn-in:** Stress screen at perhaps high temperature or elevated voltages conducted on a product for the purpose of capturing failures inside the manufacturing facility and minimizing early-life field failures. *See* Screen.

**Canonical form:** A transformed form of a response surface equation to a new coordinate system such that the origin is at the maximum, minimum, or saddle point and the axis of the system is parallel to the principal axis of the fitted quadratic response surface.

**Cause-and-effect diagram (C&E diagram):** This is a technique that is useful in problem solving using brainstorming sessions. With this technique possible causes from such sources as materials, equipment, methods, and personnel are typically identified as a starting point to begin discussion. The technique is sometimes called an Ishikawa diagram or fishbone diagram.

**Cell:** A grouping of data that, for example, comprises a bar in a histogram.

**Censored datum:** The sample has not failed at a usage or stress level.

**Central composite rotatable design:** A type of response surface experiment design.

**Central Limit Theorem:** The means of samples from a population will tend to be normally distributed around the population mean.

**Certification:** A test to determine whether, for example, a product is expected to meet or be better than its failure rate criterion.

**Characteristic life ($k$):** A parameter that is contained in the Weibull distribution. In a reliability test, the value of this parameter equates to the usage when 63.2% of the devices will fail.

**Chronic problem:** A description of the situation where a process SPC chart may be in control; however, the overall response is not satisfactory (i.e., common causes yield an unsatisfactory response). For example, a manufacturing process has a consistent "yield" over time; however, the average yield number is not satisfactory.

**Class variables:** Factors that have discrete levels.

**Coded effects:** Regression analysis of factorial or response surface data can be performed where the levels are described in the natural levels of the factors (e.g., 5.5 and 4.5 V) or the coded levels of the factors (e.g., $-1$ and $+1$).

**Coefficient:** *See* Regression analysis.

**Collinearity:**  A problem in regression analysis where there are nearly linear dependencies between the regressors.

**Combinational problem:**  A term used in this text to describe a type of problem where the occurrences of a combination of factor levels cause a *logic* failure. Pass/fail functional testing is a suggested procedure to identify whether such a problem exists in a unit under test. This term is very different from the term "interaction."

**Common Causes:**  *See* Chronic problem.

**Component:**  A device that is one of many parts of a system. Within this text components are considered to be nonrepairable devices.

**Confidence interval:**  The region containing the limits or band of a parameter with an associated confidence level that the bounds are large enough to contain the true parameter value. The bands can be single sided to describe an upper/lower limit or double sided to describe both upper and lower limits.

**Confounded:**  Two factor effects that are represented by the same comparison are aliases of one another (i.e., different names for the same computed effect). Two effects that are aliases of one another are confounded (or confused) with one another. Although the word "confounded" is commonly used to describe aliases between factorial effects and block effects, it can more generally be used to describe any effects that are aliases of one another.

**Consumer's risk:**  *See* Beta risk.

**Continuous distribution:**  A distribution used in describing the probability of a response when the output is continuous (*See* Response).

**Continuous response:**  *See* Response.

**Contrast column effects:**  The effect of a contrast column, which might have considerations that are confounded.

**Control chart:**  A procedure used to track a process with time for the purpose of determining if sporadic or chronic problems (common or special causes) exist.

**Control:**  The term "in control" is used in process control charting to describe when the process indicates that there are no special causes. "Out of control" indicates that there is a special cause.

**Cost of quality charts:**  The cost of scrap, rework, and loss due to errors, which is charted as cost to total sales.

**Coverage:**  *See* Test coverage.

**Cumulative distribution function (CDF) [$F(x)$]:**  The calculated integral of the PDF from minus infinity to $x$. This integration takes on a characteristic "percentage less than" or "percentile" when plotted against $x$.

**Cumulative sum (CUSUM) (control chart):**  An alternative control charting technique to Shewhart control charting. CUSUM control charts can detect small process shifts faster than Shewhart control charts can.

**Customer:** Someone for whom work or a service is performed. The end user of a product is a customer to the employees within a company that manufactures the product. There are also internal customers in a company. When an employee does work or performs a service for someone else in the company, the person who receives this work is a customer to this employee.

**Dead on arrival (DOA):** A product that does not work the first time it is used or tested. The binomial distribution can often be used to statistically evaluate DOA (i.e., it works or does not work) scenarios.

**Decision tree:** A graphical decision-making tool that integrates for a defined problem both uncertainties and cost with the alternatives to decide on the "best" alternative.

**Defective:** A part or system containing at least one defect, which will cause failure to meet an established quality level.

**Degrees of freedom (df or $v$):** Number of measurements that are independently available for estimating a population parameter. For a random sample from a population, the number of degrees of freedom is equal to the sample size minus one.

**Delphi technique:** A method of "predicting" the future by surveying experts in the area of concern.

**Design of experiments (DOE):** *See* Fractional factorial experiment and Full factorial experiment.

**Discrete distribution:** A distribution function that describes the probability for a random discrete variable.

**Discrete random variable:** A random variable that can only assume discrete values.

**Discrimination ratio ($d$):** Poisson sequential testing relationship of failure rate considerations ($\rho_1/\rho_0$).

**Distribution:** A pattern that randomly collected numbers from a population follow. The normal, Weibull, Poisson, binomial, and log-normal distributions discussed in this text are applicable to the modeling of various industrial situations.

**Do-it-smarter considerations:** Using statistically based concepts while determining the "best" question to answer from the point of view of the customer. This includes noting that there are usually better questions to ask (to protect the "customer") than "What sample do I need?" or "What one thing should I do next to fix this problem?" (i.e., a one-at-a-time approach). Do-it-smarter may involve putting together what often traditionally are considered "separated statistical techniques" in a "smart" fashion to address various problems.

**Double-sided test:** A statistical consideration where, for example, the mean of a population is to be within a $\pm$ bound, as stated in a null hypothesis.

**Early-life failures:** *See* Bathtub curve.

**Effect:** The main effect of a factor in a two-level factorial experiment is the mean difference in responses between the two levels of the factor, which is averaged over all levels of the other factors.

**Error (experimental):** Ambiguities during data analysis caused from such sources as measurement bias, random measurement error, and unintentional mistake.

**Evolutionary operation (EVOP):** An analytical approach where process conditions are changed structurally in a manufacturing process (e.g., using a fractional factorial experiment design matrix) for the purpose of analytically determining changes to make for product improvement.

**Experiment:** A process undertaken to determine something that is not already known.

**Experimental error:** Variations in the experimental response under identical test conditions. Also called "residual error."

**F test:** A statistical test that utilizes tabular values from the $F$ distribution to assess significance.

**Factorial experiment:** *See* Full factorial experiment and Fractional factorial experiment.

**Factors:** Variables that are varied to different levels within a factorial designed experiment or response surface experiment.

**Failure:** A device is said to fail when it no longer performs its intended function satisfactorily.

**Failure mode, effect, and criticality analysis (FMECA):** Analytical approach directed toward problem prevention through the prioritization of potential problems and their resolution. Opposite of fault tree analysis.

**Failure rate:** Failures/unit time or failures/units of usage (i.e., 1/MTBF). Sample failure rates are: 0.002 failures/hour, 0.0003 failures/auto miles traveled, 0.01 failures/1000 parts manufactured. Failure rate criterion ($\rho_a$) is a failure rate value that is not to be exceeded in a product. Tests to determine if a failure rate criterion is met can be fixed or sequential in duration. With fixed length test plans, the test design failure rate ($\rho_t$) is the sample failure rate that cannot be exceeded in order to certify the criterion ($\rho_a$) at the boundary of the desired confidence level. With sequential test plans, failure rates $\rho_1$ and $\rho_0$ are used to determine the test plans.

**Fault tree analysis:** A schematic picture of possible failure modes and associated probabilities. Opposite of failure mode effects analysis.

**Fire fighting:** An expression used to describe the process of performing emergency fixes to problems.

**Fixed effects model:** A factorial experiment where the levels of the factors are specifically chosen by the experimenter (as opposed to a random effects or components of variance model).

**Fold over:** Resolution IV designs can be created from resolution III designs by the process of fold over. To fold over a resolution III design, simply add to the original fractional factorial design matrix a second fractional factorial design matrix with all the signs reversed.

**Fractional factorial experiment:** A designed experiment strategy that assesses several factors/variables simultaneously in one test, where only a partial set of all possible combinations of factor levels are tested to more efficiently identify important factors. This type of test is much more efficient than a traditional one-at-a-time test strategy.

**Freak distribution:** A set of substandard products that are produced by random occurrences in a manufacturing process.

**Full factorial experiment:** Factorial experiment where all combinations of factor levels are tested.

**Gauge capability study:** The evaluation of measuring instruments to determine their capability to yield a precise response. Error in a gauge measurement can be from several sources. Gauge accuracy is the difference between the average of measurements and the true average taken using precision instruments. Gauge repeatability is the variation in measurements using one part and one operator. Gauge reproducibility is the variation between operators measuring one part.

**General linear modeling (GLM):** A statistical procedure used to fit data to a general model using, for example, least squares.

**Goodness of fit:** *See* Lack of fit.

**Go/no-go:** A technique often used in manufacturing where a device is tested with a gauge that is to evaluate the device against its upper/lower specification limit. A decision is made that the device either meets or does not meet the criterion.

**Group size:** A term used in this text to describe how many factors are considered when making a combinational "test coverage" statement within a pass/fail functional test.

**Half normal probability plot:** A normal probability plot where the absolute data measurements are plotted.

**Hazard paper:** Specialized graph paper (*See* Tables R1 to R3 in Appendix D) that yields information about populations similar to that of probability paper. In this text this paper is used to plot data that contains censored information.

**Hazard rate ($\lambda$):** The probability that a device will fail between times $x$ and $x + dx$, after it has survived time (usage) $x$ (i.e., a conditional probability of failure given survival to that time). At a given point in time, the hazard rate and instantaneous failure rate are equivalent.

**Histogram:** A graphical representation of the sample frequency distribution that describes the occurrence of grouped items.

**Homogeneous Poisson process (HPP):** A model that considers that failure rate does not change with time.

**Hypergeometric distribution:** A distribution that has a similar use to that of the binomial distribution; however, the sample size is "large" relative to the population size (e.g., sample size is greater than 10% of the size of the population).

**Hypothesis testing:** Testing to decide whether a criterion is met. The null hypothesis ($H_0$) is the mathematical statement of acceptance with $\beta$ risk of error. The alternate hypothesis ($H_a$) is the mathematical statement of rejection with $\alpha$ risk of error.

**Inner array:** The structuring in a Taguchi style fractional factorial experiment of the factors that can be controlled in a process (as opposed to an outer array).

**In control:** The description of a process where variation is consistent over time (i.e., only common causes exist).

**Intensity function:** A function that was used to describe failure rate as a function of time (usage) in the NHPP.

**Interaction:** Two or more factors "working together" to affect the average response (e.g., there is a degradation in performance when both temperature and humidity are elevated in unison).

**Lack of fit:** A value determined by using one of many statistical techniques stating probabilistically whether data can be shown not to fit a model. Lack of fit is used to assess the goodness of fit of a model to data.

**Lambda plot:** A technique to determine a data transformation when analyzing the results from a factorial experiment.

**Least squares:** A method used in regression to estimate the equation coefficients and constant so that the sum of squares of the differences between the individual responses and the fitted model is a minimum.

**Levels:** The settings of factors in a factorial experiment (e.g., high and low levels of temperature).

**Location parameter ($x_0$):** A parameter in the three-parameter Weibull distribution that equates to the minimum value for the distribution.

**Logic pass/fail response:** *See* Response.

**Logit (transformation):** A type of data transformation sometimes advantageous in factorial analysis when data has a upper and lower bound restriction (e.g., 0–1 proportion defective).

**Loss function:** A continuous "Taguchi" function that measures the cost implications of product variability.

**Main distribution:** The main distribution is centered around an expected value of strengths, while a smaller freak distribution describes a smaller set of substandard products that are produced by random occurrences in a manufacturing process.

**Main effect:** The effect in a factorial experiment of a factor acting individually from one level to another.

**Mallows $C_p$ Statistic:** A regression parameter that is used to determine the smallest number of parameters that should be used when building a model. The number of parameters corresponding to the minimum of this statistic is the minimum number of parameters to include during the model-building process.

**Mean:** The mean of a sample ($\bar{x}$) is the sum of all the responses divided by the sample size. The mean of a population ($\mu$) is the sum of all responses of the population divided by the population size. In a random sample of a population, $\bar{x}$ is an estimate of the $\mu$ of the population.

**Mean square:** Sum of squares divided by degrees of freedom.

**Mean time between failure (MTBF):** A term that can be used to describe the frequency of failures in a repairable system with a constant failure rate. MTBF is the average time that is expected between failures. MTBF = 1/failure rate.

**Measurement systems studies and analysis:** *See* Gauge capability study.

**Median:** For a sample the number that is in the middle when all observations are ranked in magnitude. For a population the value at which the cumulative distribution function is 0.5.

**Mixture experiments:** Variables are expressed as proportions of the whole and sum to unity. Measured responses are assumed to depend only on the proportions of the ingredients and not on the amount of the mixture.

**Multicollinearity:** When there exists near linear dependencies between regressors, the problem of multicollinearity is said to exist. *See* Variance inflation factor.

**Multimodal distribution:** A combination of more than one distribution that has more than one distinct peak.

**Multi-var chart:** A chart that is constructed to display the variance within units, between units, between samples, and between lots.

**Nested data:** An experiment design where the trials are not fully randomized sets. In lieu of full randomization, trials are structured such that some factor considerations are randomized within other factor considerations.

**Nonhomogenous Poisson process (NHPP) with Weibull intensity:** A mathematical model that can often be used to describe the failure rate of a repairable system that has a decreasing, constant, or increasing rate.

**Nonrepairable device:** A term used to describe something that is discarded after it fails to function properly. Examples of a nonrepairable device are a tire, spark plug, and the water pump in an automobile (if it is not rebuilt after a failure).

**Normal distribution:** A bell-shaped distribution that is often useful to describe various physical, mechanical, electrical, and chemical properties.

**Null hypothesis ($H_0$):** *See* Hypothesis testing.

**One-at-a-time experiment:** An individual tries to fix a problem by making a change and then executing a test. Depending on the findings, something else may need to be tried. This cycle is repeated indefinitely.

**One-sided test:** *See* Single-sided test.

**Ordinate:** The coordinate representing the distance from the $x$ axis in a two-dimensional plot.

**Orthogonal:** The property of a fractional factorial experiment that ensures that effects can be determined separately without entanglement.

**Outlier:** A data point that does not fit a model because of an erroneous reading or some other abnormal situation.

**Outer array:** The structuring in a Taguchi style fractional factorial experiment of the factors that cannot be controlled in a process (as opposed to an inner array).

**Pareto diagram:** A graphical technique used to quantify problems so that effort can be expended in fixing the "vital few" causes, as opposed to the "trivial many." Named after Wilfredo Pareto, an European economist.

**Pareto principle:** 80% of the trouble comes from 20% of the problems (i.e., the vital few problems).

**Pass/fail functional test:** A test strategy described in this text to determine whether a failure will occur given that the response is a logic pass/fail situation. *See* Response.

**Path of steepest ascent:** A methodology used to determine different factor levels to use in a follow-up experiment (e.g., fractional factorial) such that the expected response will be larger than previous responses.

***p* chart:** A process control chart of fraction nonconforming.

**Point estimate:** An estimate calculated from sample data without a confidence interval.

**Poisson distribution:** A distribution that is useful to design reliability tests, where the failure rate is considered to be constant as a function of usage.

**Population:** A number of items that have a similar characteristic.

**Precision to tolerance ratio:** Indicates the amount of tolerance spread that could be used up in measurement error.

**Probability (Pr):** A numerical expression for the likelihood of an occurrence.

**Probability density function (PDF) [$f(x)$]:** A mathematical function that can model the probability density reflected in a histogram.

**Probability paper:** Various types of graph papers (see Tables Q1 to Q3 in Appendix D) where a particular CDF will plot as a straight line.

**Probability plot:** Data is plotted on a selected probability paper coordinate system (e.g. Tables Q1 to Q3) to determine if a particular distribution is appropriate (i.e., the data plots as a straight line) and to make statements about percentiles of the population.

**Problem solving:** The process of determining the cause from a symptom and then choosing an action to improve a process or product.

**Process:** A method to make or do something that involves a number of steps. A mathematical model such as the HPP (homogeneous Poisson process).

**Process capability indices ($C_p$ and $C_{pk}$):** $C_p$ is a measurement of the allowable tolerance spread divided by the actual $6\sigma$ data spread. $C_{pk}$ has a similar ratio to that of $C_p$ except that this ratio considers the shift of the mean relative to the central specification target.

**Process flow diagram (chart):** Path of steps of work used to produce or do something.

**Producer's risk:** *See* Alpha risk.

**Qualitative factor:** A factor that has discrete levels. For example, product origination where the factor levels are vendor A, vendor B, and vendor C.

**Quantitative factor:** A factor that is continuous. For example, a product can be manufactured with a process temperature factor between 50°C and 80°C.

**Quality function deployment (QFD):** A technique that is used, for example, to get the "voice of the customer" in the design of a product.

**Randomizing:** The procedure used in statistics to avoid possible bias due to the influence of systematic disturbances that are either known or unknown.

**Random:** Having no specific pattern.

**Random effects (or components of variance) model:** A factorial experiment where the variance of factors is investigated (as opposed to a fixed effects model).

**Random variable:** A variable that can be any value from a set of values.

**Range:** For a set of numbers, the arithmetic difference between the largest and smallest value.

**Ranked sample values:** Sample data that is listed in order relative to magnitudes.

**Regression analysis:** Data collected from an experiment is used to empirically quantify through a mathematical model the relationship that exists between the response variable and influencing factors. In a simple linear regression model $y = b_0 + b_1x + \epsilon$, $x$ is the regressor, $y$ is the expected response, $b_0$ and $b_1$ are coefficients, and $\epsilon$ is random error.

**Regressor:** *See* Regression analysis.

**Reject quality level (RQL):** The level of quality that is considered unsatisfactory when developing a test plan.

**Reliability:** The proportion surviving at some point in time during the life of a device. A generic description of tests evaluating failure rates.

**Repairable system:** A system that is repaired after experiencing a failure.

**Replication:** Test trials that are made under identical conditions.

**Residuals:** In an experiment the differences between experimental responses and predicted values that are determined from a model.

**Residual error:** Experimental error.

**Resolution III:** A fractional factorial designed experiment where main effects and two-factor interaction effects are confounded.

**Resolution IV:** A fractional factorial designed experiment where the main effects and two-factor interaction effects are not confounded; however, two-factor interaction effects are confounded with each other.

**Resolution V:** A fractional factorial designed experiment where all main effects and two-factor interaction effects are not confounded with other main effects or two-factor interaction effects.

**Resolution V$^+$:** Full factorial designed experiment.

**Response:** In this text three basic types of responses (i.e., outputs) are addressed: continuous, attribute, and logic pass/fail. A response is said to be continuous if any value can be taken between limits (e.g., 2, 2.0001, and 3.00005). A response is said to be attribute if the evaluation takes on a pass/fail proportion output (e.g., 999 out of 1000 sheets of paper on the average can be fed through a copier without a jam). In this text a response is said to be logic pass/fail if combinational considerations are involved that are said to either always cause an event to pass or fail (e.g., a computer display design will not work in combination with a particular keyboard design and software package).

**Response surface methodology (RSM):** The empirical study of relationships between one or more responses and input variable factors. The technique is used to determine the "best" set of input variables to optimize a response and/or gain a better understanding of the overall system response.

**Robust:** A description of a procedure that is not sensitive to deviations from some of its underlying assumptions.

**Robust design:** A term sometimes used to describe the application of Taguchi philosophy (i.e., reducing variability).

**Rotatable:** A term used in response surface designs. A design is said to be rotatable if the variance of the predicted response at some point is a function of only the distance of the point from the center.

**Run:** A consecutive number of points, for example, that are consistently decreasing, increasing, or on one side of the central line in an SPC chart.

**Run-in:** A procedure to put usage on a machine within the manufacturing facility for the purpose of capturing early-life failures before shipment. *See* Screen.

**Sample:** A random selection of items from a population.

**Sampling distribution:** A distribution derived from a parent distribution by random sampling.

**Sample size:** The number of observations made from a population when performing a test.

**Scale parameter:** *See* Characteristic life.

**Scatter diagram:** A plot to study possible relationships between two variables.

**Screening experiment:** The first step of a multiple factorial experiment strategy, where the experiment primarily assesses the significance of main effects. Two-factor interactions are normally considered in the experiments that follow a screening experiment. Screening experiments should typically consume only 25% of the monies that are allotted for the total experiment effort to solve a problem.

**Screen (in manufacturing):** A process step in the manufacturing process that is used to capture marginal product performance problems before the product is "shipped" to a customer. A burn-in or run-in test is a test that could be considered a screen for an electro-mechanical device.

**Sequential testing:** A procedure where items are tested in sequence. Decisions are "continually" made to determine whether the test should be continued or stopped (with either a pass or fail decision). Decision points of the tests are dependent on the test criteria and the $\alpha$ and $\beta$ risks selected.

**Shape parameter ($b$):** A parameter used in the Weibull distribution that describes the shape of the distribution and is equal to the slope of a Weibull probability plot.

**Shewhart control chart:** *See* Control chart. CUSUM and Shewhart control charting techniques are discussed in this text.

**Sigma:** The Greek letter ($\sigma$) that is often used to describe the standard deviation of data.

**Significance:** A statistical statement indicating that the level of a factor causes a difference in a response with a certain degree of risk of being in error.

**Single-sided test:** A statistical consideration where, for example, a test is conducted to determine if the mean of a population is less than or equal to a criterion value, as stated in a null hypothesis.

**Simplex lattice design:** A triangular spatial design space used for variables that are mixture ingredients.

**Six Sigma:** A term coined by Motorola that emphasizes the improvement of processes for the purpose of reducing variability and making general improvements.

**Space (functional):** A description of the range of factor levels that describe how a product will be used in customer applications.

**Special causes:** *See* Sporadic problem.

**Specification:** A criterion that is to be met by a part or product.

**Sporadic problem:** A problem that occurs in a process because of an unusual condition (i.e., from special causes). An out-of-control condition in a process control chart.

**Standard deviation ($\sigma$, $s$):** A mathematical quantity that describes the variability of a response. It equals the square root of variance. The standard deviation of a sample ($s$) is used to estimate the standard deviation of a population ($\sigma$).

**Standard error:** The confidence interval equation, for example, for a population mean is $\mu = \bar{x} \pm t_\alpha (s/\sqrt{n})$; $s/\sqrt{n}$ is sometimes called the standard error.

**Statistical process control (SPC):** The application of statistical techniques in the control of processes. SPC is often considered a subset of SQC, where the emphasis in SPC is on the tools associated with the process but not product acceptance techniques.

**Statistical quality control (SQC):** The application of statistical techniques in the control of quality. SQC includes the use of regression analysis, tests of significance, acceptance sampling, control charts, distributions, etc.

**Stress test:** A test of devices outside usual operating conditions in an attempt to find marginal design parameters.

**Subcause:** In a cause-and-effect diagram the specific items or difficulties that are identified as factual or potential causes of the problem.

**Sum of squares (SS):** The summation of the squared deviations relative to zero, to level means, or the grand mean of an experiment.

**System:** Devices that collectively perform a function. Within this text systems are considered repairable, where a failure is caused by failure of a devices(s). System failure rates can either be constant or change as a function of usage (time).

**Taguchi philosophy:** This text supports G. Taguchi's basic philosophy of reducing product/process variability for the purpose of improving quality and decreasing the loss to society; however, the procedures used to achieve this objective often are different.

**Test coverage:** The percent of possible combinations of group sizes (e.g., 3) evaluated in an pass/fail functional test (e.g., for a given test, there might be 90% test coverage of the levels of three factor combinational considerations).

**Test performance ratio ($\rho$):** For a reliability test using the Poisson distribution, the ratio of the sample failure rate to the criterion ($\rho_t/\rho_a$).

**Testing:** A means to determine whether an item is capable of meeting specified requirements by subjecting the item to a set of physical, environmental, chemical, or operating actions/conditions.

**Time-line chart:** Identification of the specific start, finish, and amount of time required to complete an activity.

**Trend chart:** A chart to view the resultant effect of a known variable on the response of a process. *See* Scatter diagram.

**Trial:** One of the observations within a fractional factorial experiment.

***t* test:** A statistical test that utilizes tabular values from the *t* distribution to assess, for example, whether two population means are different.

**Type I error:** *See* Alpha risk.

**Type II error:** *See* Beta risk.

**Type III error:** Answering the wrong question.

**Two-sided test:** *See* double-sided test.

**Uncensored data:** All sample data has failed or has a reading.

**Uncertainty (δ):** An acceptable amount of change from a criterion. The parameter is used when considering β risk in sample size calculation.

**Uniform precision design:** A type of central composite response surface design where the number of center points is chosen such that there is more protection against bias in the regression coefficients.

**Unimodal:** A distribution that is from one population and has one peak.

**Usage:** During a life test, the measure of time on test. This measurement could, for example, be in units of power-on hours, test days, or system operations.

**Variable data:** Data that can assume a range of numerical responses on a continuous scale, as opposed to data that can assume only discrete levels.

**Variables:** Factors within a fractional factorial designed experiment or response surface experiment.

**Variance ($\sigma^2$, $s^2$):** Standard deviation squared. *See* Standard deviation.

**Variance inflation factor (VIF):** A calculated quantity for each term in a regression model that measures the combined effect of the dependencies among the regressors on the variance of that term. One or more large VIFs can indicate multicollinearity.

**Vendor:** A supplier to a company.

**Verification:** The act of establishing and documenting whether processes, items, services, or documents conform to a specified requirement.

**Wear-out failures:** *See* Bathtub curve.

**Weibull distribution:** This distribution has a density function that has many possible shapes. The two-parameter distribution is described by the shape parameter ($b$) and the location parameter ($k$). This distribution has an $x$-intercept value at the low end of the distribution that approaches zero (i.e., zero probability of a lower value). The three-parameter has, in addition to the other parameters, the location parameter ($x_0$), which is the lowest $x$-intercept value.

**Weibull slope ($b$):** *See* Shape parameter.

**Worst-case tolerance:** The overall tolerance that can be expected if all mating components were at worst-case conditions.

# REFERENCES

Affourtit, B. B. (1986), "Statistical Process Control (SPC) Implementation Common Misconceptions," *Proc. 39th Ann Quality Cong.*, American Society for Quality Control, pp. 440–445.

Agresti, Alan (1990), *Categorical Data Analysis*, Wiley, New York.

Anderson, V. L., and R. A. McLean (1974), *Design of Experiments*, Marcel Dekker, New York.

American Society of Testing Metals (1976), *ASTM Manual on Presentation of Data and Control Charts Analysis STP15D*, ASTM, Philadelphia, PA.

Ball, R. A., and S. P. Barney (1982), *Quality Circle Project Manual*, Rawsonville, MI: UAW-Ford Employee Involvement.

Barlow, Richard E., Jerry B. Fussell, and Nozer D. Singpurwalla (1975), *Reliability and Fault Tree Analysis: Theoretical and Applied Aspects of System Reliability and Safety Assessment*, Society for Industrial and Applied Mathematics, Philadelphia, PA.

Bisgaard, Soren (1988), *A Practical Aid for Experimenters*, Starlight Press, Madison WI.

Box, G. E. P. (1988), "Signal to Noise Ratios, Performance Criteria and Transformations," *Technometrics* **30**(1): 1–40 (with discussion).

Box, G. E. P. and D. W. Behnken (1960), "Some New Three Level Designs for the Study of Quantitative Variables," *Technometrics*, **2**(4): 455–475.

Box, G. E. P. and G. C. Tiao (1973), *Bayesian Inference in Statistical Analysis*, Addison Wesley, Reading, MA.

Box, George, Soren Bisgaard, and Conrad Fung (1988), "An Explanation and Critique of Taguchi Contributions to Quality Engineering," *Quality and Reliability Engineering International*, **4**(2): 123–131.

Box, G. E. P., William G. Hunter, and Stuwart J. Hunter (1978), *Statistics for Experimenters*, Wiley, New York.

Breyfogle, F. W. (1988), "An Efficient Pass/Fail Functional Test Strategy," IBM Technical Report Number TR 51.0485.

Breyfogle, F. W. (1989a), "Software Test Process," *IBM Technical Disclosure Bulletin*, **31**(8): 155–157.

Breyfogle, F. W. (1989b), "Random Failure Graphical Analysis," *IBM Technical Disclosure Bulletin*, **31**(8): 321–322.

Breyfogle, F. W. (1989c), "Stress Test Scenario Assessment Process," *IBM Technical Disclosure Bulletin*, **31**(8): 355–356.

Breyfogle, F. W. (1989d), "Method to Provide a Software Overview Assessment," *IBM Technical Disclosure Bulletin*, **31**(10): 278–282.

Breyfogle, F. W. (1989e), "Comparing Hadamard and Taguchi Matrices," IBM Technical Report Number TR51.0527.

Breyfogle, F. W. (1991), "An Efficient Generalized Pass/Fail Functional Test Procedure," IBM Reliability and Applied Statistics Conference, East Fishkill, New York, pp. 67–74.

Breyfogle, F. W. and A. Aloia, (1991), "Pass/Fail Functional Testing and Associated Coverage," *Quality Engineering*, **4**(2): 227–234.

Breyfogle, F. W. and J. H. Davis (1988), "Worst Case Product Performance Verification with Electromagnetic Interference Test Applications," *Quality and Reliability Engineering International*, **4**(2): 183–187.

Breyfogle, F. W. and F. L. Steely (1988), "Statistical Analysis with Interaction Assessment," *IBM Technical Disclosure Bulletin*, **30**(10): 234–236.

Breyfogle, F. W. and S. Wheeler (1987), "Realistic Random Failure Criterion Certification," *IBM Technical Disclosure Bulletin*, **30**(6): 103–105.

Breyfogle, F. W., T. N. Le, and L. J. Record (1989), "Processor Verification Test Process," *IBM Technical Disclosure Bulletin*, **31**(10): 324–325.

Brown, D. K. (1991), personal communication.

Brush, Gary G. (1988), *How to Choose the Proper Sample Size*, American Society for Quality Control, Milwaukee, WI.

Burkland, G., P. Heidelberger, M. Schatzoff, P. Welch, and L. Wu (1984), "An APL System for Interactive Scientific-Engineering Graphics and Data Analysis," APL84 Proceedings, pp. 95–102, Helsinki.

Clopper, C. J. and E. S. Pearson (1934), "The Use of Confidence or Fiducial Limits Illustrated in the Use of the Binomial," *Biometrika*, **26**:404.

Cochran, William G. (1977), *Sampling Techniques*, Wiley, New York.

Coffin, Jr., L. F. (1954), "A Study of the Effects of Cyclic Thermal Stresses on a Ductile Metal," *Trans. ASME*, **76**:923–950.

Coffin, Jr., L. F. (1974), "Fatigue at High Temperature—Prediction and Interpretation," James Clayton Memorial Lecture, *Proc. Inst. Mech. Eng. (London)*, 188, 109–127.

Cornell, J. (1981), *Experiments with Mixtures: Designs, Models, and the Analysis of Mixture Data*, Wiley, New York.

Cornell, J. A. (1983), *How to Run Mixture Experiments for Product Quality*, American Society for Quality Control, Milwaukee, WI.

Cornell, J. (1984), *How to Apply Response Surface Methodology*, American Society for Quality Control, Milwaukee, WI.

Cornell, J. (1990), "Embedding Mixture Experiments inside Factorial Experiment," *JQT*, **22**(4): 265–276.

Cornell, J. A. and J. W. Gorman (1984), "Fractional Design Plans for Process Variables in Mixture Experiments," *Journal of Quality Technology*, **16**(1).

Cox, D. R. (1958), *Planning of Experiments*, Wiley, New York.

Crocker, O. L., J. S. L. Chiu, and C. Charney (1984), *Quality Circle a guide to participation and productivity*, Facts on File, New York.

Crow, Larry H. (1974), "Reliability Analysis for Complex, Repairable Systems, Reliability and Biometry, Statistical Analysis of Lifelength," *SIAM*, 379–410.

Crow, Larry H. (1975), "On Tracking Reliability Growth," *Proceedings 1975 Annual Reliability and Maintainability Symposium*, IEEE, New York, NY 1292 75RM079.

Cunnane, C. (1978), "Unbiased Plotting Positions—A Review," *Journal of Hydrology*, **37**, 205–222.

D'Agostino, Ralph B. and Michael A. Stephens, Eds. (1986), *Goodness-of-Fit Techniques*, Marcel Dekker, New York.

Daniel, C. (1959), "Use of Half-Normal Plots in Interpreting Factorial Two-Level Experiment," *Technometrics*, **1**(4): 311–341.

Daniel, C. (1976), *Applications of Statistics to Industrial Experimentation*, Wiley, New York.

Daniel, C. and F. S. Wood (1980), *Fitting Equations to Data*, 2nd ed. Wiley, New York.

Davies, O. L. (1967), *Design & Analysis of Industrial Experiments*, 2nd ed., Hafner Publishing, New York.

Deming, W. E. (1982), *Quality, Productivity and Competitive Position*, MIT Center for Advanced Engineering Study, Cambridge, MA.

Deming, W. E. (1986), *Out of the Crisis*, Massachusetts Institute of Technology, Cambridge, MA.

Dewar, D. L. (1980), *Leader Manual and Instructional Guide*, Quality Circle Institute, Reb Bluff, CA.

Diamond, William J. (1989), *Practical Experiment Designs for Engineers and Scientists*, Van Nostrand Reinhold, New York.

Dixon, W. J. (1957) and F. J. Massey, *Introduction to Statistical Analysis*, 2nd ed., McGraw-Hill, New York.

Dixon, W. J. and F. J. Massey, Jr. (1969), *Introduction to Statistical Analysis*, 3rd ed., McGraw-Hill, New York, pp. 246, 324.

Draper, N. R. and H. Smith (1966), *Applied Regression Analysis*, Wiley, New York.

Duane, J. T. (1964), "Learning Curve Approach to Reliability Monitoring," *IEEE Transactions on Aerospace*, **2**(2): April 1964.

Duncan, A. J. (1986), *Quality Control and Industrial Statistics*, 5th ed., Irwin, Homewood, IL.

Engelmaier, W. (1985), "Functional Cycles and Surface Mounting Attachment Reliability," *Circuit World*, **11**(3): 61–72.

Environmental Sciences (1984), "Environmental Stress Screening Guidelines for Assemblies," Institute of Environmental Sciences, Mount Prospect IL.

Fedorov, V. V. (1972), *Theory of Optimal Experiments*, Academic Press, New York.

Ferrell, E. B. (1958), "Probability Paper for Plotting Experimental Data," *Industrial Quality Control*, **XV**(1):

Flynn, M. F. (1983), "What Do Control Charts Really Mean?" Proc. 37th Ann. Quality Cong., American Society for Quality Control, Milwaukee, WI, pp. 448–453.

Flynn, M. F. and J. A. Bolcar (1984), "The Road to Hell," Proc. 38th Ann. Quality Cong., American Society for Quality Control, Milwaukee, WI, pp. 192–197.

Freund, J. E. (1960), *Modern Elementary Statistics*, 2nd ed. Prentice-Hall, New York.

Goldmann, L. S. (1969), "Geometric Optimization of Controlled Collapse Interconnections," *IBM J. Res Develop.*, **13**: 251.

Gorman, John W. and John A. Cornell (1982), "A Note on Model Reduction for Experiments with both Mixture Components and Process Variables," *Technometrics*, **24**(3): 243–247.

Grant, E. L. and R. S. Leavenworth (1980), *Statistical Quality Control*, 5th ed., McGraw-Hill, New York.

Halpern, Siegmund (1978), *The Assurance Sciences—An Introduction to Quality Control & Reliability*, Prentice-Hall, Englewood Cliff, NJ.

Hauser, John R. and Don Clausing (1988), "The House of Quality," *Harvard Business Review*, May–June, 63–73.

Heidelberger, P., P. Welch, and L. Wu (1983), "Application of Dual Screen Graphics and APL to Interactive Data Analysis," Computer Science and Statistics: Proceedings of the 14th Symposium on the Interface, Heiner et al., Eds., Springer-Verlag, RPI, Troy, NY, pp. 20–29.

Ireson, W. Grant (1966), *Reliability Handbook*, Ed., McGraw-Hill, New York.

Jensen, Finn and Niels Erik Petersen (1982), *Burn-in: An Engineering Approach to the Design and Analysis of Burn-in Procedures*, Wiley, New York.

John, Peter W. M. (1990), *Statistical Methods in Engineering and Quality Assurance*, Wiley, New York.

Johnson, L. G. (1964), *The Statistical Treatment of Fatigue Experiments*, Elsevier, New York.

Juran, J. M. (1988), *Juran's Quality Control Handbook*, 4th ed., McGraw-Hill, New York.

Juran, J. M. and F. R. Grynn (1980), *Quality Planning & Analysis*, 3rd ed., McGraw-Hill, New York.

Juran, J. M., F. M. Gryna, and R. S. Bingham (1976), *Quality Control Handbook*, 3rd ed., McGraw-Hill, New York.

Kano, Noritaki, Nobuhiro Seraku, Fumio Takashashi, and Shinichi Tsuji (1984), "Attractive Quality and Must be Quality", Nippon QC Gakka, 12th annual meeting, **14**(2): 39–48.

Kempthorne, O. and J. L. Folks (1971), *Probability, Statistics and Data Analysis*, Iowa State University Press, Ames, IA.

Kepner, Charles H. and Benjamin B. Tregoe (1981), *The New Rational Manager*, Kepner-Tregoe, Inc. Princeton, NJ.

King, Bob (1980a), *Better Designs in Half the Time, Implementing QFD in America*, Goal/QPC, Methuen, MA.

King, James R. (1980b), *Frugal Sampling Schemes*, Technical Aids for Management (TEAM), Tamworth, NH.

King, James R. (1981), *Probability Charts for Decision Making*, Technical Aids for Management (TEAM), Tamworth, NH.

Kroehling, Hugh (1990), "Tests for Normality," ASQC—Electronics Division, *Technical Supplement* Issue 14, Winter.

Khuri, A. I. and John A. Cornell (1987), *Response Surfaces Design and Analyses*, Marcel Dekker, New York.

Lane, T. and P. Welch (1987), "The Integration of a Menu-Oriented Graphical Statistical System with Its Underlying General Purpose Language," Computer Science and Statistics: Proceeding of the 19th Symposium on the Interface, 267–273, Philadelphia, PA.

Lentner, C. (1982), *Geigy Scientific Tables*, Vol. 2, Ciba-Geigy Limited, Basle, Switzerland.

Lipson, Charles and Narendra J. Sheth (1973), *Statistical Design & Analysis of Engineering Experiments*, McGraw-Hill, New York.

Lloyd, David K. and Myron Lipow (1976), *Reliability: Management, Methods, and Mathematics*, 2nd ed., Prentice-Hall, Englewood Cliffs, NJ.

Lorenzen (1989), personal communications.

Lorenzen (1990), personal communications.

Mallows, C. L. (1973), "Some Comments on $C(p)$", *Technometrics*, **15**(4): 661–675.

Mann, Nancy R., Ray E. Schafer, and Nozer D. Singpurwalia (1974), *Methods for Statistical Analysis of Reliability and Life Data*, Wiley, New York.

Manson, S. S. (1953), "Behavior of Materials under Conditions of Thermal Stress," NACA-TN-2933 from NASA, Lewis Research Center, Cleveland, OH.

Manson, S. S. (1966), *Thermal Stress and Low-Cycle Fatigue*, McGraw-Hill, New York.

Marwah, B. S. "A General Model for Reliability Testing," IBM Toronto Technical Report 74.027.

Massey, Frank J. Jr. (1951), The Kolmogorov–Smirnov Test for Goodness of Fit," *Journal of the American Statistical Association*, **46**: 68–78.

Mauritzson, B. H. (1971), "Cost Cutting with Statistical Tolerances," *Machine Design*, November 25, pp. 78–81.

McWilliams, Thomas P. (1990), "Acceptance Sampling Plans Based on the Hypergeometric Distribution," *JQT*, **22**(4): 319–327.

Messina, W. S. (1987), *Statistical Quality Control for Manufacturing Managers*, Wiley, New York.

Miller, Irwin and John Freund (1965), *Probability & Statistics for Engineers*, Prentice-Hall, Englewood Cliffs, NJ.

Montgomery, D. C. (1984), *Design and Analysis of Experiments*, Wiley, New York.

Montgomery D. C. (1985), *Introduction to Statistical Quality Control*, Wiley, New York.

Montgomery, D. C. and E. A. Peck (1982), *Introduction to Linear Regression Analysis*, Wiley, New York.

Moody, P. E. (1983), *Decision Making: Proven Methods for Better Decisions*, McGraw-Hill, New York.

Morris, Max D. and Toby J. Mitchell (1988), "Two-Level Multifactor Designs for Detecting the Presence of Interactions," *Technometrics*, 25(4): 345–355.

Motorola, *Statistical Process Control—The Motorola Guide to Statistical Process Control for Continuous Improvement Towards Six Sigma Quality*, BR392/D, Motorola, Phoenix, AZ.

Nachlas, J. A. (1986), "A General Model for Age Acceleration During Thermal Cycling," *Quality and Reliability Engineering International*, 2, 3–6.

Natrella, Mary Gibbons (1966), *Experimental Statistics*, National Bureau of Standards Handbook 91, Washington, D.C.

Navy (1979), "Navy Manufacturing Screening Program," NAVMAT P-9492, May.

NBS (1957), "Fractional Factorial Experiment Designs for Factors at Two Levels," U.S. Department of Commerce, National Bureau of Standards Applied Mathematics Series 48, Washington, D.C.

NBS (1959), "Fractional Factorial Experiment Designs for Factors at Three Levels," U.S. Department of Commerce, National Bureau of Standards Applied Mathematics Series 54, Washington, D.C.

NBS (1961), "Fractional Factorial Designs for Experiments with Factors at Two and Three Levels," U.S. Department of Commerce, National Bureau of Standards Applied Mathematics Series 58, Washington, D.C.

Nelson, L. S. (1990), "Comments on Significance Tests and Confidence Intervals," *JQT*, 22(4): 328–330.

Nelson, Lloyd S. (1983a), "Exact Critical Values for Use with the Analysis of Means," *Journal of Quality Technology*, 15(1): 40–44.

Nelson, Lloyd S. (1983b), "Transformations for Attribute Data," *Journal of Quality Technology*, 15(1): 55–56.

Nelson, L. S. (1984), "The Shewhart Control Chart-Test for Special Causes," *J. Qual. Tech.*, 16(4): 237–239.

Nelson, L. S. (1985), "Interpreting Shewhart $\overline{X}$ Control Charts," *J. Qual. Tech.*, 17: 114–116.

Nelson, Wayne (1982), *Applied Life Data Analysis*, Wiley, New York.

Nelson, Wayne (1990), *Accelerated Testing: Statistical Models, Test Plans, and Data Analyses*, Wiley, New York.

Nishimura, A., A. Tatemichi, H., Miura, and T. Sakamoto (1987), "Life Estimation of IC Plastic Packages under Temperature Cycling Based on Fracture Mechanics," *IEEE Trans. Comp., Hybrids, and Mfg. Tech.*, **CHMT-12**: 637–642.

Norris, K. C. and A. H. Landzberg (1969), "Reliability of Controlled Collapse Interconnections," *IBM Journal of Research*, May.

Oakland, John S. (1986), *Statistical Process Control, A practical guide*, Wiley, New York.

Ott, Ellis R. (1983), "Analysis of Means—A Graphical Procedure," *Journal of Quality Technology*, 15(1) (reproduced from August 1967 issue of *Industrial Quality Control*).

Pearson, E. S. and H. O. Hartley (1966), *Tables for Statisticians, Biometrika*, Vol. 1, 3rd ed., Cambridge University Press, England.

Peck, D. S. and Trapp, O. D. (1978), "Accelerated Testing Handbook," Technology Associates, Portola Valley, CA.

Plackett, R. L. and Burman, J. P. (1946), "Design of Optimal Multifactorial Experiments," *Biometrika*, **23**: 305–325.

Ramig, Pauline F. (1983), "Applications of the Analysis of Means," *Journal of Quality Technology*, **15**(1): 19–25.

Ramsey, Patricia P. and Philip H. Ramsey (1990), "Simple Tests of Normality in Small Samples," *JQT*, **22**(2): 299–309.

Ross, Philip J. (1988), *Taguchi Techniques for Quality Engineering*, McGraw-Hill, New York.

Saari, A. E., R. E. Schafer, and S. J. VanDenBerg (1982), "Stress Screening of Electronic Hardware," RADC-TR-82-87, Hughes Aircraft Company, Rome Air Development Center Griffiss Air Force Base, NY.

SAS (1985a), *SAS® User's Guide: Basics*, Version 5 Edition, SAS® Institute, Cary NC.

SAS (1985b), *SAS® User's Guide: Statistics*, SAS Institute, Cary NC.

Scheffé, H. (1958), "Experiments with Mixtures," *Journal of Royal Statistical Society*, (B). 344–360.

Scholtes, P. R. (1988), *The Team Handbook: How to use teams to improve quality*, Joiner Associates Inc., Madison WI.

Searle, S. R. (1971a), *Linear Models*, Wiley, New York.

Searle, S.R. (1971b), "Topics in Variance Component Estimation." *Biometrics*, **27**: 1–76.

Shapiro, S. S. and M. B. Wilk (1965), "Analysis of Variance Test of Normality (Complete Samples)," *Biometrika*, **52**: 591–611.

Shewhart, W. A. (1931), *Economic Control of Quality of Manufactured Product*, Van Nostrand, New York.

Snedecor, George W. and William G. Cochran (1967), *Statistical Methods*, 6th ed., Iowa State University Press, Ames, IA.

*Sporting News* (1989), July 3, p. 7.

Sutterland, R. R. and I. D. E. Videlo (1985), "Accelerated Life Testing of Small-Geometry Printed Circuit Boards," *Circuit World*, **11**(3): 35–40.

Taguchi, G. (1978), "Off-line and On-line Quality Control Systems," Proc. International Conference Quality Control, Tokyo Japan, pp. B4-1–B4-5.

Taguchi, G. and S. Konishi (1987), *Taguchi Methods® Orthogonal Arrays and Linear Graphics*, American Supplier Institute Inc., Center for Taguchi Methods®, Dearborn, MI.

TEAM, Technical and Engineering Aids for Management, Box 25 Tamworth, NH 03886.

Tobias, Paul A. and Trindade, David (1986), *Applied Reliability*, Van Nostrand Reinhold, New York.

Traver, Robert W. (1989), *Industrial Problem Solving*, Hitchcock Publishing Company, Carol Stream, IL.

Tummala, Rao R. and Eugene J. Rymaszewski (1989), *Microelectronics Packaging Handbook*, Van Nostrand Reinhold, New York.

U.S. Department of Defense (1957), "Sampling Procedures and Tables for Inspection by Variables for Percent Defective," MIL-STD 414, U.S. Government Printing Office, Washington, D.C.

U.S. Department of Defense (1963), "Sampling Procedures and Tables for Inspection by Attributes," MIL-STD 105D, U.S. Government Printing Office, Washington, DC.

U.S. Department of Defense (1978), "Military Standard—Reliability Growth Testing," MIL-STD-1635(EC), U.S. Government Printing Office, Washington, D.C., 3 February.

U.S. Department of Defense (1980), "Procedures for Performing Failure Mode Effects and Criticality," US MIL STD 1629A, Naval Publications and Forms Center, Philadelphia, PA.

U.S. Department of Defense (1981a), "Military Handbook—Reliability Growth Management," MIL-HDBK-189, U.S. Government Printing Office, Washington D.C., 13 February.

U.S. Department of Defense (1981b), "Single- and Multi-Level Continuous Sampling Procedures and Tables for Inspection by Attributes," MIL-STD 1235B, U.S. Government Printing Office, Washington, D.C.

U.S. Department of Defense (1986), "Military Standard—Reliability Testing for Engineering Development, Qualification, and Productions," MIL-STD-781D, U.S. Government Printing Office, Washington, D.C., 17 October.

U.S. Department of Defense (1987), "Military Handbook—Reliability Test Methods, Plans, and Environments for Engineering Development, Qualification, and Productions," MIL-HDBK-781, U.S. Government Printing Office, Washington D.C., 14 July.

Urban, Glen L. and John R. Hasser (1980), *Design and Marketing of New Products*, Prentice-Hall, Englewood Cliffs, NJ.

Wald, Abraham (1947), *Sequential Analysis*, Wiley, New York.

Western Electric (1956), *Statistical Quality Control Handbook*, Western Electric Co.

Wheeler, Bob (1989), *E-CHIP® Course Text*, ECHIP INC, Hockessin, DE.

Wheeler, Stan G. (1990), personal communications.

Wynn, Henry P. (1970), "The Sequential Generation of D-Optimum Experimental Designs," *Ann. Math. Statist.*, **41**: 1655–1664.

Yashchin, E. (1989), personal communications.

# AUTHOR INDEX

Affourtit B. B., 315
Alan, Agresti, 200
Aloia, A., 273
American Society for Quality Control (ASQC), 13
Anderson, V. L., 267

Ball, R. A., 25, 26
Barlow, Richard E., 347
Barney, S. P., 25, 26
Behnken, D. W., 255
Bingham, R. S., 311
Bisgaard, Soren, (Box et al.), 178, 190, 248
Bolcar, J. A., 315
Box, G. E. P., 54, 188, 202, 203, 206, 223, 237, 238, 241, 248, 254, 255, 272, 281, 347, 365
Breyfogle, F. W., 245, 273, 282, 289
Brown, D. K., 320
Brush, Gary G., 92, 106, 115
Burman, J. P., 182

Charney, C., 25
Chiu, J. S. L., 25
Clausing, Don, 326
Clopper C. J., 107
Cochran, William G., 92, 423, 429
Coffin, Jr., L. F., 137

Cornell, J. A., 254, 257, 258, 259, 262–266, 271
Cox, D. R., 205
Crocker, O. L., 25
Crow, Larry H., 133, 156, 390
Croxton, Frederick E., 419
Cunnane, C., 386

D'Agostino, Ralph B., 390
Daniel, C. 195, 220, 230
Davies, O. L., 47
Deming, W. E., 15–17, 22, 26, 160, 290, 315
Dewar, D. L., 24
Diamond, William J., 92, 106, 115–117, 147, 188, 191, 206, 218, 260, 261, 263, 281, 420, 442
Dixon, W. J., 86, 389
Draper, N. R., 202, 227
Duane, J. T., 133
Duncan, A. J., 315, 390

Engelmaier, W., 138

Fedorov, V. V., 268
Ferrell, E. B., 387
Fisher, Ronald A., 421, 427

Flynn, M. F., 315
Folks, J. L., 202
Ford, 291
Freund, John, 74, 86
Fung, Conrad, (Box et al.), 248
Fussell, Jerry B., 347

Goldmann, L. S., 138
Gorman, J. W., 262, 264
Grant, E. L., 294, 315
Gryna, F. M., 23, 311, 347

Halpern, Siegmund, 147
Hartley, H. O., 421
Hasser, John R., 328
Hunter, Stuwart J. (Box et. al), 54, 188,
    190, 202, 203, 206, 223, 237, 238, 241,
    248, 254, 272, 281, 347, 365
Hunter, William G. (Box et al.), 54, 188,
    190, 202, 203, 206, 223, 237, 238, 241,
    248, 254, 272, 281, 347, 365

Ireson, W. Grant, 112
Ishikawa, Karoru, 25

Jensen, Finn, 134, 135, 136, 169, 390
Johnson L. G., 387
Juran, J. M., 15, 23, 290, 311, 347

Kano, Noritaki, 321
Kemp, K. W. 307
Kempthorne, O., 202
Kepner, Charles H., 24
Khuri, A. I., 271
King, Bob, 321
King, James R., 67, 386, 387, 389
Konishi, S., 195, 244
Kroehling, Hugh, 390

Landzberg, A. H., 138
Leavenworth, R. S., 294, 315
Lentner, C., 70
Lipson, Charles, 430
Lorenzen J., 349

Mallows, C. L., 220
Mann, Nancy R., 69

Manson, S. S., 137
Massey, F. J., 86, 390
Mauritzson, B. H., 100
McLean, R. A., 267
McWilliams, Thomas P., 74
Messina, William S. 34, 112, 117, 298, 305,
    313–315
Miller, Irwin, 74, 86
Mitchell, Toby J., 178
Miura, H., (Nishimura et al.), 138
Montgomery, D. C., 117, 123, 190, 202,
    203, 206, 237, 238, 252, 254, 271, 272,
    281, 300, 365, 437
Moody, P. E., 24, 347, 348
Morris, Max D., 178
Motorola, 311, 312, 332–337, 339–341

Nachlas, J. A., 138
National Bureau of Standards, 178
Natrella, Mary Gibbons, 92, 98, 106, 115,
    116, 122
Navy, 169
Nelson, Lloyd. S., 46, 125, 218, 315, 436
Nelson, Wayne, 58, 62, 63, 67, 136–139,
    170, 173, 382, 386, 387
Nishimura, A., 138
Norris, K. C., 138

Oakland, John S., 315
Ott, Ellis R., 123, 218

Pearson, E. S., 107, 421
Peck, D. S., 135
Peck, E. A., 271
Petersen, Niels Erik, 134–136, 169, 390
Plackett, R. L., 182

Quality Progress, 13

Ramig, Pauline F., 123, 124, 218
Ramsey, Patricia P., 390
Ramsey, Philip H., 390
Ross, Philip J., 247
Rymaszewski, Eugene J., 138

Saari, A. E., 138
Sakamoto, T., (Nishimura et al.), 138
Sangster, Bill, 73
SAS, 200, 219, 238, 391–396, 411

Schafer, R. E., 138
Schafer, R. E., (Mann et al. and Saari et al.), 69
Scheffé, H., 258
Scholtes, P. R., 15
Searle, S. R., 202
Shapiro, S. S., 390
Sheth, Narendra J., 430
Shewhart, W. A., 292
Singpurwalla, Nozer D., 347
Singpurwalia, Nozer D., (Mann et al.), 69
Smith, H., 202, 227
Snedecor, George W., 423, 429
*Sporting News*, The, 7
Stephens, Michael A., 390
Sutterland, R. R., 136

Taguchi, G., 183, 195, 178, 243–249, 349, 355, 373
Tatemichi, A., (Nishimura et al.), 138
TEAM, Technical and Engineering Aids for Management, 58, 462–467
Tiao, G. C., 202
Tobias, Paul A., 133, 135–139, 173
Trapp, O. D., 135

Tregoe, Benjamin B., 24
Trindade, David, 133, 135–139, 173
Tummala, Rao R., 138

United States Department of Defense, 112, 133, 142, 143, 144, 347
Urban, Glen L., 328

VanDenBerg, S. J., (Saari et al.), 138
Videlo, I. D. E., 136

Wald, Abraham, 112
Western Electric, 303, 315
Wheeler, Bob, 268, 269, 271
Wheeler, Stan G., 330
Wilk, M. B., 390
Wood, F. S., 230
Wynn, Henry P., 268

Yashchin, E., 315
Yates, Frank, 421, 427

# SUBJECT INDEX

Accelerated testing, 3, 128, 133–136, 472
  Arrhenius model, 134, 137, 473
  application of, 53, 156, 163, 357
  Coffin–Manson model, 137
  considerations, 12, 173, 357
  example, high temperature test, 136
  Eyring model, 136
  high temperature, 134
  precision, 12
  model selection, 138
  step stress, 139, 173
  thermal cycling, 137
Acceptable quality level (AQL), 305, 468,
  472
Acceptance testing, See Criterion evaluation
Activation energy, 134, 472
Algorithm design, 250, 262, 268, 269, 271,
  472
Alias, 187, 472, 475, See also Factorial
  experiment (confounded)
Alpha (α) risk, 43, 472
  hypothesis test, 93, 479
  factorial experiment, 180
  sample size
    attribute response data, 106, 110–111
    continuous response data, 92–93
    factorial experiment, 397
    sequential testing, Poisson distribution,
      144–146

total test time, reliability evaluation, 146,
  148, 150
Alternative hypothesis, 42, 472, 479, See
  also hypothesis tests
American Society for Quality Control
  (ASQC), 13
Analysis of goodness, 218, 473
Analysis of means (ANOM), 114, 123–126,
  218, 468, 473
  tables, 431–436
Analysis paralysis, 11, 13, 179
Analysis of variance (ANOVA), 206, 208,
  220, 391, 402, 405, 468, 473, See also
  Factorial experiments
Answering the right question, 9, 89, 320,
  See also Do-it-smarter considerations,
  example, Automobile test, 9, 34, 196, 274
Approximations, distribution
  binomial for hypergeometric, 86
  normal for binomial, 86, 106, 107
  Poisson for binomial, 86, 110, 147
Arrhenius acceleration model, 134, 137, 473
Assumptions, See also Robust
  constant failure rate, 142
  customer usage, 357
  errors, normal and independently
    distributed, 54, 223
  experiment, 371
  independence, 45

Assumptions (*Continued*)
  linearity, 190
  normality, 54, 98, 101, 114, 223
  random sample, 54, 139, 143, 357
  sample size to population size, 143
  stability, process, 55, 112, 143
Attribute response, 105–113, 473
  alternative, continuous response data,
    105, 113, 180
  alternatives, test, 72, 112
  application, 198
  comparing two populations, 122–123
  control charts for, *See* Control chart (p)
  criterion test, 105, 110
  distribution considerations, 72, 86
  do-it-smarter considerations, 56, 112
  example
    comparing two proportions, 122
    Pareto, 314
    reduced sample size, 110–112
    sample size, 107
    factorial experiments, 176, 180
    sample size, 106
    reduced, 110
  sampling, 105
  sequential test plans, 112
  six sigma program, 334
  test performance ratio, 112
Average, *See* Mean

Bar charts, 473
Basic concepts, 3, 5, 37–55
Bathtub curve, 82, 128–129, 473
  early life failures, 142, 159, 164, 169, 173,
    316, 382
  wear out failures, 142, 164, 173, 382
Beta (β) risk, 43, 473
  hypothesis test, 93
  factorial experiment, 180
  sample size
    attribute response data, 106, 110–111
    continuous response data, 92–93
    factorial experiment, 397
    sequential testing, Poisson distribution,
      144–146
    total test time, reliability evaluation, 146,
      148, 150
Bias, 47, 179, 189, 473
Big-picture, 11
  application, 100
  example, reducing cycle time, 29
Bimodal distribution, 87, 99, 473
Binomial distribution, 72, 379, 473

application, 69, 72, 84, 106
Clopper and Pearson charts for attributes,
  108–109
comparison test, attribute, 114
confidence interval, attribute, 107
criterion, attribute test, 86, 107, 110
hypergeometric, in lieu of, 86, 105
normal distribution alternative, 86, 106
Poisson distribution alternative, 86, 106,
  110
properties of, 106, 379
sample size, attribute test, 106, 146–147
Table K, application of, 111, 438–439
Blocking, 473, *See* Factorial experiment
Boltzmann's constant, 134, 138
Box–Behnken Design, 255
Brainstorming, 9, 474
  application, 28, 99, 155, 204, 332, 338, 376
  conducting, 24
  customer needs, 328
  development process, 344
  example
    automobile test, 34
    development process improvement, 33
    factorial experiment, 178
    Pareto diagram, 314
    process improvement, 28, 33
    product development, 344
    reducing cycle time, 32
    reducing defects in a process, 33
  factorial experiment, 25, 178, 179, 191,
    196, 204, 317
  pass/fail functional testing, 289
  product development, 317, 344
  six sigma program, 338, 344
  voice of customer, 328
Break through sequence, 22
Burn-in, 316, 474, *See also* Screen

Canonical form, 254, 474
Capability measurement tool, 48
Categorical data analysis, 200–201, 237
Cause-and-effect diagram, 25, 337, 340
  applications, 24, 33, 34, 178, 344, 473, 474
*c* chart, *See* Control charts
Cell, 39, 59, 383, 474
Censored data, 60, 167, 201, 474
  example, hazard plot, 64, 167
  hazard plot, 58, 63
Center points,
  factorial experiment, 180, 190, 251, 271,
    407

mixture experiment, 260
response surface methodology, 251
Central composite design, 252–255, 474
Central limit theorem, 46, 68, 70, 93, 474
Certification, criterion, 474, *See also*
    Criterion evaluation
Characteristic life parameter, 474, *See also*
    Weibull distribution
Chemical experiments, 3, *See also* Mixture
    experiments
Chemists, 372, *See also* Engineers,
    Scientists, and Technicians
Chi-square ($\chi^2$) distribution, 80
    comparing two proportions, 122
    failure rate confidence interval, 147
    sequential test, Poisson distribution, 145
    standard deviation confidence interval, 96,
      97
    table, 428–429
Chronic problems, 160, 290, 474, *See*
    Common Causes
    Deming's 14 points, 17–21
    example, 302
    Juran's breakthrough sequence, 22
    six sigma program, 342
Clopper and Pearson charts, 108–109
Coffin–Manson model, 137
Combinational problem, 475, *See* Pass/fail
    functional testing
Common causes, 20, 22, 290–291, 302, 475,
    *See* Chronic problems
    example, process improvement, 26, 33
    six sigma program, 342
Communications, 19, 343
Comparison tests, 55, 114–127
    application, 191
    do-it-smarter considerations, 56, 126
    example
      comparing means, 116, 124
      comparing two proportions, 122
      comparing two variances, 118
      paired, 120
      probability plotting, 118
    factorial confirmation, 179, 236
    means, 115, 123
    paired, 119
    probability plot, 118
    proportions, 122
    sample size, 115
    variances, 117
Competition
    evaluation, 374
    pressures, 343

product opinions, 322, 325
Computer, application of
    analysis of variance (ANOVA) output, 391
      –392
    example programs, 400–402, 406, 408–416
    factorial experiments, 188, 190, 206–209,
      218–220, 227, 251, 351, 391–396
    fault tree analysis, 347
    general linear model (GLM) output, 220–
      236, 393–394, 400–405
    histograms, 39
    lack of fit, 173, 255, 390, 411
    mixture experiments, 257, 264, 268
    packages, 13
    probability plots, 58, 62, 164, 173
    response surface regression output, 255,
      395–396
    variance components, 238, 241
Confidence interval, 3, 37, 45, 475
    accelerated testing, 12, 139
    assumptions, 55, 112, 143
    attribute data, 105, 107, 111
    chi-square distribution, 80
    Clopper and Pearson charts, 108–109
    considerations, 38, 42, 55, 91
    double-sided, 45
    example
      attribute failure rate, 110
      mean, 95
      mean life of a device, 171
      standard deviation, 97
      system failure rate, 147, 149, 151, 155
    failure rate evaluations of repairable
      systems, 147–161, 477
    mean, 45, 81, 93, 218
    mean life of a device, 171
    single-sided, 45
    standard deviation, 80, 96
Confirmation experiment
    example, comparing two means, 116, 236
    example, process improvement, 34
    factorial experiment, 179, 180, 188, 201,
      217, 236, 362, 364
    pass/fail functional testing, 288, 289
Confounded, *See* Factorial experiment
Consumer's risk, 475, *See* Beta risk
Continuous response data, 55, 91–104, 475,
    *See also* Factorial experiments, mean,
    mixture, percentile statements,
    probability plotting, response surface
    methodology, standard deviation,
    variance components
    attribute data, alternative for, 105, 180

Continuous response data (*Continued*)
do-it-smarter considerations, 103
Contrast columns, *See* Factorial experiments
Control charts 1, 3, 290–309, 336, 475, *See also* Chronic problems, common causes, special causes, sporadic problems
acceptance of, 13
application, 100, 312
improvement, 21, 33
manufacturing, 48, 160–161, 175, 314–316, 356, 365, 368, 374
*p* chart, 123
process stability, 103, 112
stress to fail, 510
*X* chart, 374
*c* chart, 302
CUSUM, 305–309, 315
do-it-smarter considerations, 315
example
CUSUM, 307, 475
*p* chart, 300, 481
*p* chart with process improvement, 33
$\bar{x}$ and *R* chart, 294
*X* chart, 298
implementation considerations, 315
interpretation, 292, 303
*np* chart, 302
*p* chart, 123, 299, 315–316, 481
process, monitoring of, 89, 290–292
*R* chart, 293, 315
*s* chart, 293, 315
six sigma program, 338, 341, 342
stability of process, 103, 112, 309, 316
table for constructing, 437
types of, 292
*u* chart, 303
vendor qualification, 126–127
*X* chart, 297, 374
$\bar{x}$ chart, 293
replacement for go/no go, 294, 315
Control, in/out, 291, 300, 303, 475, *See also* Control charts
Control sequence, 22
Coverage, test, 485, *See also* Pass/fail functional testing
$C_p$, Mallows', 220, 230, 480
$C_p$, *See* Process capability indices
$C_{pk}$, *See* Process capability indices
Criterion evaluation, 43, *See also* Examples, sample size, specification
attribute response, 105, 110
considerations

post-test, 9, 104
pre-test, 38, 91, 97, 356, 374
system reliability test, 143
continuous response
mean, 92–96
percent of population, 97–100
customer needs, 11
do-it-smarter considerations, 103, 112, 126, 139, 160, 173
factorial experiment, 179, 191, 196, 344
hypothesis test, 37, 43
"playing games", 357
repairable system with changing failure rate, 155–160
repairable system with constant failure rate, 132, 141, 148–155, 357
sequential testing, Poisson distribution, 144
Taguchi contributions, 103
tolerance analysis, 100–103
Cumulative distribution function (CDF), 57, 64, 475
binomial, 73, 379
example, PDF, CDF, then a probability plot, 58
exponential, 77, 380
hypergeometric, 379
log-normal, 79
normal, 70, 378
Poisson, 75, 380
probability plotting, 58, 64
Weibull, 78, 131, 381
Curvature, *See* Factorial experiments, response surface methodology
Customer, 3, 476
big picture, 11
Deming's 14 points, 21
factorial experiment, 177, 231, 243, 344, 359
failure rate criterion test considerations, 11, 111, 140, 275, 357
needs of, 319, 321, 328
process improvement, 377
QFD, 349
quotas, measurement, 16
response surface methodology, 265
satisfaction, 9, 11
screen, manufacturing, 160
six sigma program, 375
statistical tools, 348
surveying needs, 328–330
test usage, 164, 357
types of, 319, 330

CUSUM chart 475, *See also* Control charts

Data
  looking at, 45, 200, 201, 218
  PDF, CDF, then a probability plot, 58
  presentation, 39, 336–337
Dead on arrival, 170, 476
Decision making, 3, 15, 23, 348
Decision tree, 347, 476
Degrees of freedom, 41, 470, 476, 499
  analysis of means, 124
  analysis of variance, 392
  chi-square distribution, 122, 145
  confidence interval, mean, 94
  factorial experiment, 221, 398, 404–405
  general linear modeling, 393
  response surface analysis, 396, 407–411
  *t* distribution, 81, 93, 117, 121, 216
  variances
    combining, 311
    comparing two, 117–118
Delphi technique, 348, 476
Delta ($\delta$), 43, 470
  hypothesis test, 93–94
  sample size
    continuous response data, 92–93
    factorial experiment, 397
Deming, W. E., 15, 17, *See also* Common
    causes, special causes
  do-it-smarter considerations, 15
  14 points, 17
  improving process, 26
  quota, 15–16, 20, 26
Descriptive statistics, 37–55
Design of Experiments (DOE), *See also*
    Factorial experiments
Development
  cycle time, 330–331
  design requirements, 323
  do-it-smarter considerations, advantages
    of, 11, 358
  example
    automobile, 275
    factorial experiment, 191, 197
    mixture experiment, 372
    post reliability test statements, 155
    reducing cycle time, 29
  factorial experiment factors, choosing,
    177, 343, 358
  factorial experiments, hierarchy of, 317,
    345
  information flow, 343–347

six sigma program, 338, 344
test group relationship, 150
test strategy, pyramid, 289
variability considerations, 12
wear out, system reliability testing for,
    142
Discrimination ratio, 144–145, 476
Distributions, 3, 68–87, 476, *See also*
    Binomial distribution, chi-square
    distribution, exponential distribution,
    hypergeometric distribution, lack of fit,
    log-normal distribution, normal
    distribution, Poisson distribution,
    Tables (*F* distribution and *t*
    distribution), Weibull distribution
  applications, 68–70, 84–85
  approximations, one-to-another, 86
  bimodal, 87, 99, 101
  combining, 169
  discrete, 86, 476
  equations for, 378–382
  freak, 169, 478
  main, 169, 479
  multinomial, 86
  PDF to CDF, 58–60
  residuals, 224, 233
  sampling, 483
  $\bar{x}$, *See* Central limit theorem
Do-it-smarter considerations, 2, 11, 89, 349–
    377, 476
  application advantages, 7
  attribute tests, 19, 55, 112
  comparative tests, 126
  continuous response data, 103
  control charts, 315
  customer, for, 320
  development cycle time, 330
  example
    automobile test, 9, 34, 196, 274
    development of chemical product, 372
    process capability study, 374
    QFD with factorial experiment, 349
    reliability and functional test, 356
    resolution III design with interaction
        assessment, 371
    system test, 365
    two-level from many-level factorial
        design, 368
  factorial experiments, 204, 218, 243, 249
    probability plot of trials, 232, 355, 361–
        368
  failure rate criterion, certification of, 357
  improvement, process, 19

Do-it-smarter considerations (*Continued*)
  management, 1, 15, 348
  overview, 11
  pass/fail functional testing, 289
  QFD, 328
  reliability testing, 139, 141, 160, 173, 358
  sampled data, 55, 103
  variability assessments, 205, 243, 249
Double-sided, 476, *See also* hypothesis
    testing
  attribute response data, 107, 111
  confidence interval, 45
  continuous response data, 92
  CUSUM chart, 306
  example, confidence interval on mean, 95
  failure rate evaluations, 147, 148
  hypothesis test, 43, 147
  normal distribution, 70
  Poisson distribution, 148
  *t* distribution, 81, 216

Early-life failures, *See* bathtub curve
Education, 21, 338, *See also* Training
Eigenvalues, 396, 409
Eigenvectors, 396, 409
Engineers, 1, 3, 9
  belief, 7
  knowledge of concepts, 8
  judgement, 11
  training needs, 7
Error, *See* alpha and beta
  bias, 179
  contributors, 47
  control charts, wrong decision with a, 303–
    304
  experimental, 46–48, 205, 477
  factorial experiment, 179–180, 190, 200,
    208, 214, 219–223, 477
  mean square, 392, 394, 396, 404, 407
  measurement, 46
  mistake, 18, 47
  root mean square, 392, 394, 395, 404
  sources of, 47
  standard, 265, 485
  sum of squares, 392, 394, 396, 403, 404,
    407
  traps, 37, 49–54
  type I, 45, 485
  type II, 44, 485
  type III, 23, 485
Evolutionary Operation (EVOP), 347, 477
Examples
  analysis of means, 124

attribute test, reduced sample size, 110
automobile test
  answering the right question, 9
  brainstorming for test considerations, 34
  fractional factorial experiment design,
    196
  pass/fail functional testing, 274
chemical product development, 372
confidence intervals
  attribute evaluation, 107
  mean, 95
  standard deviation, 97
comparison
  means of two samples, 116
  paired samples, 120
  proportions from two samples, 112
  samples using a probability plot, 118
  two variances, 117
computer programs, 400–416
control chart
  CUSUM, 307
  *p*, 299
  *X*, 297
  $\bar{x}$ and *R*, 294
experimentation errors, 48
experimentation trap
  confused effects, 50
  interaction of factors, 51
  lack of randomization, 49
  not monitoring experiment, 52
factorial design,
  two-level from many-level, 368
  stress to fail, 365
fractional factorial experiment analysis
  resolution III, 208
  resolution III with two-factor
    interaction assessment, 217
  resolution V, 213
fractional factorial experiment computer
    analysis, resolution V, 220
fractional factorial experiment computer
    analysis with missing datum point,
    resolution V, 233
fractional factorial experiment design
  resolution III, 194
  resolution V, 191
functional test, reliability and, 356
improvement
  process with defects, 33
  process with subjective information, 26
  reduction in cycle time, 29
high temperature accelerated test, 136
histogram creation, 384
histogram, 40

loss function, 247
management, project development, 344
mean of a sample, 41
mixture experiment design, extreme-vertices, 267
mixture experiment design/analysis
    computer, 268
    with process variables, 262
    simplex lattice, 260
Pareto diagram, 313
pass/fail functional test
    hardware/software system, 280
    with search pattern strategy, 284
    software interface, 282
    system, 278
PDF, CDF, then probability plot, 58
percent of population statement, 98
process capability, 311
QFD chart, 326
QFD with fractional factorial design, 349
reliability and functional test, 356
reliability device test
    log-normal probability plot for, 173
    hazard plot with censored data for, 167
    Weibull probability plot for, 165
    Weibull zero fail strategy for, 171
reliability system test
    changing failure rate, 156
    fixed time, 147
    post test evaluation of, 154
    reduced sample size, 149
    sequential, 145
    test performance considerations for, 151
reliability test with do-it-smarter considerations, 356
response surface design, 254
sample size
    attribute criterion test, 107
    mean criterion test, 92
standard deviation of a sample, 41
tolerance analysis, 101
variability, 48
variance components design, 202, 203
variance components analysis 238, 241
Experiment, *See* attribute, factorial, philosophy, mean, mixture experiment, probability plotting, reliability testing, response surface methodology, pass/fail functional testing, standard deviation
Experimentation traps, 3, 37, 49
    example
        conducting an experiment, 52
        confused effects, 50
        interaction of factors, 51
        lack of randomization, 49
Exponential distribution, 74
    application, 76, 85, 171
    hazard rate, 83–84, 380
    Poisson distribution, 85
    properties of, 380
Eyring model, 136

*F* distribution, 81, 469
    factorial analysis, 221, 392, 394, 405, 411
    response surface analysis, 396, 411
    table, 424–427, 469
    variances, comparing two, 117–118
Factorial experiments, full and fractional, 1, 3, 176–249, 477
    advantage of, 10, 176–177
    algorithm designs, 268, 271
    alias, 187, 472, 475
    analysis, 190, 206, 219
    analysis of goodness, 218
    analysis of variance, 206, 208, 213
    analysis paralysis, 179
    ANOM, 218
    application, 161, 338, 347
        design process, 102, 116, 177, 325, 359, 377
        manufacturing, 13, 140, 161, 177, 302
        process improvement, 99, 111, 155, 160, 243, 291, 312, 316
        product/vendor certification, 12, 127
        project development, 332, 343
        sampling plans, 100, 104, 113
    attribute response, 180, 200, 237, 289
    best estimate, 181, 209, 473
    bias, 189
    blocking, 179, 180, 189, 473
    brainstorming, 25, 178, 179, 191, 196, 204, 317
    center points, 180, 190, 251, 271, 407
    check list, 179
    coefficients, 201, 227, 251
    communications, 344
    comparison tests, 114
    computer output description, 391–396
    computer programs, 400–416
    confirmation experiment, 179, 180, 188, 201, 217, 236, 362, 364
    confounded, 185–187, 194, 197, 198, 204, 209
    considerations, 178–182, 245
    contrast columns, 185, 189, 191–193, 197–199, 207–217, 475

Factorial experiments (*Continued*)
  curvature, 180, 190
  customer considerations, 177, 231, 243, 344, 359
  determining tolerances, 355
  designs, two-level, 176, 186, 442–449
  do-it-smarter considerations, 204, 218, 243, 249
  error, 179–180, 190, 200, 208, 214, 219–223, 477
  estimating the response, 201
  evolutionary operation (EVOP), 347, 477
  example
    automobile test, 9, 34, 196
    confirmation experiment, 116
    confused effects, 50
    comparing sources, 372
    creating two-level from many-level full factorial, 368
    CUSUM factorial follow-up, 307
    factorial and reliability test with do-it-smarter considerations, 356
    managing project development, 344
    process improvement, 33
    QFD with factorial, 349
    resolution III, screening, 208
    resolution III with interactions, 217, 371
    resolution IV, 349, 356
    resolution V, 191, 213, 220, 233
    stressing to failure, 365
  experimentation traps, 50, 51, 52
  factors, considerations of, 177, 181, 355, 477
  factors, level considerations, 368–371
  $F$ test, 221, 392, 394, 405, 411
  fold-over design, 188, 287, 477
  fractional, 182, 187, 193, 196, 198–199, 204, 478
  full, 182, 187, 193, 257, 478
  half normal probability plot, 209
  hierarchy of designs, 317, 345
  implementation strategy, 177–182, 219–220, 271, 289
  inner/outer array, 248, 479, 481
  interactions, 179–190, 213, 479
    confounded, 185, 204
    considerations, 245, 371–372
    effects, two-factor, 183, 217, 250
    error, estimation of, 180, 190–191, 219
    example
      analysis considerations, 191, 213, 217, 220, 349, 356
      automobile, 196
    management of, 245, 360–362, 371–373

  model, 227, 251
    interpretation, 197, 235
    resolution III designs, in, 195, 371
  levels, 181, 197, 479
  many-level, 198
    two-level to, 179, 181, 371
  mean square, 392, 394, 396, 404, 407
  model, 201, 251
  multiple range tests, 223–224, 233–236
  obstacle, 177
  path of steepest assent, 272, 481
  planning for, 177–180
  probability plot of effects, 62, 180, 191, 206, 209, 213, 220, 227, 361–362
  probability plot of trials, 127, 204, 232, 355, 361–363, 365–367
  random sampling, in lieu of, 104, 113, 198, 211, 232
  random trial sequence, 178–180
  ranking of trials' magnitude, 204, 218
  reliability testing, 140, 200
  residual analysis, 54, 223–226, 233–235
  resolution, 180, 182, 187–188, 190, 245
    III, 182, 187, 188, 194, 195, 196, 208, 217, 371, 483
    IV, 182, 187, 188, 195, 351, 359, 483
    V, 182, 187, 191, 483
    $V^+$, 187, 483
  resolution III to IV, *See* Fold over
  $R^2$, 223–227, 393–396
  sample size, 180, 199, 397
  saturated two-level factorial, 185
  screening design, 187, 195, 484, *See* resolution III and IV
  search pattern strategy, 289
  significance, 180, 184, 186, 191, 211, 213, 219–221, 235, 397, 402, 405
    criterion for, 212, 216
  six sigma program, 340–341, 342, 344
  standard deviation, response of, 248
  stress to fail, 365
  sum of squares, 392, 394, 396, 403, 404, 407
  tables, design, 440–458
  $t$ test, 206, 208, 212, 213, 221, 402, 405
  transformations, 140, 223, 237
  why they "work", 182
Failure Mode Effect and Criticality Analysis (FMECA), 347, 477
Failure rate evaluations, 477
  accelerated testing, 133–139
  attribute response data, 106–112
  bathtub curve, 82, 128–129, 473
  constant rate evaluation, 141–155

do-it-smarter considerations, 112, 126, 139, 160, 173
early life, 142, 159, 164, 169, 173, 316, 382
example
  attribute response data, 107, 110
  automobile test, 9, 34, 196, 274
  post-reliability system test evaluation, 154
  reliability test with do-it-smarter considerations, 356
  system reliability test with changing failure rate, 156
  system reliability test with constant failure rate, 145, 149, 151
factorial experiment, 140
manufacturing start-up test, 103
nomenclatures, 477
sequential testing, 144–146
trend, lower criterion, 9
wear out, 142, 164, 173, 382
Fault tree analysis, 347, 477
"Fire fighting", 11, 21, 342, 477
Fishbone diagram, 25, *See also* Cause-and-effect diagram
Fixed effect model, 55, 176, 477
Flow chart, 21, 337, 338
example
  process improvement, 26
  reducing cycle time, 29
Fold-over design, 188, 287, 477
Forecasting, 54
Fourteen points, Deming's, 17
Fractional factorial experiment, *See* Factorial experiment
Full factorial experiment, *See* Factorial experiment

Gage capability study, 478, *See also* Variance components
Gamma Function, 171, 382, 478
General linear modeling, 393, 478, *See also* Factorial
Getting Started in text, 1–3
Glossary, 473
Goals, 20, 21
Goodness of fit, *See* Lack of fit

Happenstance data, 229
Hazard plotting, 3, 57, 63, 163, 478
example, plot, 64, 167
log-normal paper, 466
normal paper, 465

Weibull paper, 66, 168, 467
Hazard rate, 68, 82, 478
exponential distribution, 380
intensity HPP, 84
Weibull distribution, 382
Histogram, 41, 58, 64, 478
cells, 39, 59, 383, 474
creating manually, 383
example, histogram plot, 40, 59, 384
Homogeneous Poisson Process (HPP), 68, 69, 84, 85, 478
Hypergeometric distribution, 74, 479
application, 69, 84, 112
binomial distribution alternative, 86
properties of, 379
Hypothesis tests, 42, 479
attribute, 105–110
considerations, 37, 55
criterion, test, 94
do-it-smarter considerations, 103, 112, 126
factorial experiment, 180
sample size
  attribute evaluation, 106, 147
  comparing two means, 115
  mean evaluation, 92
total test time, system reliability test, 146

Improvement, 15–20, 330–335, 377
Inferences
  attribute response data, 105–113
  continuous response data, 91–104
  comparisons, 114–127
Inner array, 248, 373, 479
Inspection plans, 18, 112
Intensity function, 69, 83, 479
  exponential distribution, 84
  example, NHPP, 158
  system reliability testing, 142
Interactions, *See* Factorial experiments, mixture experiments, Response surface methodology
Ishikawa Diagram, 25

Judgement, Engineering, 11
Juran, J. M., 15, 22, *See also* Sporadic problems, chronic problems

K-factors, 98

Lack of fit, 133, 271, 479
  example, computer program, 406

Lack of fit (*Continued*)
  factorial experiment curvature, *See* Center
    points
  probability plot, 62–63, 98, 173, 389, 390
    computer generated, 173
    manual, 387
  response surface model, 251, 255, 271,
    406–411
Lambda plot, 237, 479
Leadership, 16, 19
Logic pass/fail response, 273–274, 479, *See*
  pass/fail functional testing
Log-normal distribution, 78, 128
  accelerated testing, 173
  application, 69, 79, 85
  censored data, 58
  do-it-smarter considerations, 173
  example, nonrepairable device, 173
  hazard paper, 466
  nonrepairable device, 132, 162, 172
  probability paper, 463
  probability plot, 62
logarithmic transformation, 237, 248
Loss Function, 243, 244, 245, 479


Mallows' $C_p$, 220, 230, 480
Management, 1, 3, 15, 19
  appreciation, 11
  breakthrough sequence, 22
  control sequence, 22
  Deming's 14 points, 17
  employee barriers, 20
  employee merit rating, 21
  example, reducing cycle time, 29
  factorial experiment factors, 178
  loss function, 245
  philosophy, 5
  posttest reliability test assessments, 111,
    152
  quality leadership, 16
  structure, 15
  Taguchi contributions, 249
  training needs, 7
Manufacturing, 3
  assumption, random sample, 367
  burn-in, 316, 474, *See also* Screen
    (manufacturing)
  capability indices, 374
  control chart, application of, 48, 160–161,
    175, 314–316, 356, 365, 368, 374
  customer relationships, 330
  cycle time, 330
  development, interface with, 342–343

do-it-smarter considerations, 12
example
  CUSUM chart, 307–309
  mixture experiment, 268
  *p* chart, 300
  post reliability test statements, 155
  $\bar{x}$ and *R* chart, 294
factorial experiment
  application of, 358
  factors for, 177, 197, 204
  in lieu of sampling, 113, 127
loss function, 245
processes, 290, 312, 342, 358
process improvement, 111, 113, 334
quality, 290
reliability testing alternative, 143
run-in, 358, *See also* burn-in
sample, start-up, 103, 143
screen, *See* Screen
six sigma program, 338
stress testing, 368
test group relationship, 150
variability considerations, 12, 38, 248
vendor, 126–127, 319, 486
Mean, 480
  ANOM, 123
  application, SPC, 100
  binomial distribution, 379
  central limit theorem, 46, 68, 70, 93, 474
  comparing two populations, 114–117
  confidence interval, 93–96
  control chart, 293
  criterion evaluation, 92–96
  example
    ANOM, 124
    comparing two, 116
  exponential distribution, 380
  log-normal distribution, 80
  normal distribution, 378
  Poisson distribution, 380
  population specification alternative, 97
  probability plot, 118, 126
  sample, 40, 45
  *t* distribution, 81
  Weibull distribution, 382
Mean time between failures (MTBF), 480,
    *See also* Reliability testing
  criterion test, 132, 141, 148–155, 357
  example
    automobile test, 9
    reliability test with do-it-smarter
      considerations, 356
  repairable versus non-repairable, 130
Measurement errors, 46

Median, 42, 480
  probability plotting, 58
  Weibull distribution, 381
Military standards, 112, 347
Mistakes, 18, 47
Mixture experiments, 250, 257–271, 480
  algorithm design, 262, 268
  center points, 260
  computer generated, 268
  example
    algorithm design, 268
    development strategy, 372
    extreme-vertices, 267
    simplex-lattice, 260
    with process variables, 262, 411–415
  extreme-vertices, 267
  interactions, 265
  process variables, with, 262
  simplex lattice, 258
Models, *See* exponential distribution,
    variance components, Weibull
    distribution
  accelerated criterion test, 133, 138
  Arrhenius, 134, 138, 475
  Coffin–Manson, 137
  dependence, 54
  Eyring, 136
  factorial, two-level, 201, 251
  mixture, 268
  response surface, 251, 255
  time series, 54
Multicollinearity, 271, 480
Multinomial distribution, 86
Multiple range tests, 223, 233
Multi-vari chart, 336, 340, 480


Nested design, 202, 480
Nonhomogeneous Poisson process (NHPP),
    83, 480
  application, 69, 85, 161
  reliability testing, system, 143, 155
Nonrepairable device reliability testing, 3,
    131, 480, *See* Reliability testing
  application, 161
  considerations, 69, 128, 162
  do-it-smarter considerations, 139, 173
  example, do-it-smarter, 356
  hazard plot, 66, 163, 467
  log-normal distribution, 78, 132, 162, 172,
    *See* log-normal distribution
  probability plot, 163, 172
  repairable system, versus, 130
  strategy, 139

Weibull distribution, 76, *See* Weibull
    distribution
Nomenclature, 14
Normal distribution, 70, 333–334, *See*
    Approximations
  application, 69, 70, 84, 376
  binomial distribution, in lieu of, 86, 106,
    107
  central limit theorem, 46, 68, 70, 93
  comparison tests, 114
  example
    confidence interval of population mean,
      95
    PDF, CDF and then a probability plot,
      58
    probability plot, 98, 118, 120
    tolerance analysis, 101
  hazard paper, 465
  lack of fit, 98, 390, 479
  mean, confidence interval of population,
    93
  percent of population, *K*-factors, 98
  probability paper, 462
  probability plot, 58, 62
  properties of, 72, 378
  sample data from, 44
  six sigma program, 332
  tables, 418–420
  tolerance analysis, 100
*np* chart, *See* Control charts
Null Hypothesis, *See* Hypothesis testing
Numbers game, 9


One-at-a-time experiment, 177, 200, 204, 481
  example
    automobile, 276
    interaction of factors, 51
  factorial experiment alternative, 11, 177,
    178, 204, 312, 371
  pass/fail functional test, 276
One-sided, *See* single-sided
Outer array, 248, 373, 481
Outlier, 118, 481
  factorial experiment, 220, 368
  probability plot, 62, 98, 119, 125


Paired comparison, 119–121
Pareto diagram, 313, 337, 481
  application, 23, 28, 155, 160, 290, 315, 339
  example
    creation of, 313
    defect rate, 33, 313

Pareto diagram (*Continued*)
  process improvement, 26, 33
  reducing cycle time, 30
  factorial experiment, 23
  six sigma program, 338–339
Pass/fail functional testing, 3, 89, 273–289,
    481
  applications, 288–289
  approach, step-by-step, 277
  configurations, test, 273–274, 281
  confirmation experiment, 288, 289
  coverage, test, 273–277, 281, 289, 485
  design, large number of factors, 289
  do-it-smarter considerations, 289
  example
    automobile, 274
    hardware/software system functional
      test, 280
    search pattern strategy, 284
    software interface, 282
    system functional test, 278
  factor assignment, 281
  factor levels greater than two, 281
  search pattern strategy, 284–288
  six sigma program, 342
  test strategy, 276, 344
Path of steepest accent, 272, 481
*p* chart, *See* control chart
Percentile statements and criteria, 57–67,
    *See* Probability plotting
  application, 97, 113, 126, 191
  confidence interval, 67
  considerations, 39, 55, 57, 58, 65, 69
  criterion, 97–100
  data evaluation, 39
  example
    log-normal distribution, 173
    normal distribution, 58–60
    Weibull distribution, 64, 165, 167
  Eyring model, 137
  *K*-factors, 97
  nomenclature, 42
  normal distribution, 70
  Weibull distribution, 131
Philosophy, *See also* Customer
  Deming's 14 points, 17
  do-it-smarter, 11–13
  management, 5, 15
  nominal dimension, striving for, 374
  variability, reduction of, 249
Physicists, 1, *See* engineers, scientists, and
    technicians
Plackett and Burman designs, 182
Playing games with the numbers, 104

attribute evaluations, 113
customer needs, 377
example
  automobile, 274
  certifying failure rate criterion, 357
  reducing cycle time, 30
  management philosophy, 15
  post-reliability test assessment, 155
  reliability testing, 357
  six sigma program, 334
  survey results, 330, 334
Poisson distribution, 74
  application, 69, 74, 85
  approximation for binomial, 86, 110
  *c* chart, 302
  confidence interval, 147, 155, 438–439
  criterion test, failure rate, 148–155
  example
    failure rate confidence interval, 147
    posttest statement, 154
    sequential test, 145
    time terminated test, 149, 151, 356
  factorial experiment, 201
  properties of, 378
  reduced sample size testing, 148, 149
  repairable system criterion testing, fixed
    duration, 132, 141–142, 148–155
  repairable system criterion testing,
    sequential, 144
  table, reference, 438–439
  test time, total, 146
  *u* chart, 303
Population, 37–38, 103, 481
Probability density function (PDF), 41, 64,
    481
  application, 119, 121, 232, 363, 368
  binomial distribution, 73, 379
  CDF, to, 58
  chi-square $(\chi)^2$ distribution, 80
  estimated, 383
  example, PDF, CDF, then a probability
    plot, 58
  exponential, 74, 380
  *F* distribution, 81
  log-normal distribution, 78
  normal distribution, 70, 378
  Poisson distribution, 74, 380
  probability plot summary, 64
  *t* distribution, 81
  Weibull distribution, 76, 380
Probability paper, 57, 385, 481
  log normal, 62, 463
  normal, 62, 462
  plot positions and interpretations, 60, 386

Weibull, 62, 385, 464
Probability Plotting, 3, 57–63, 65–67, 481
  application, 13, 98, 113, 125, 191, 299,
      309, 316
  best estimate, 99
  best fit line, 67, 164, 387
  comparing populations, 118, 126, 236
  concept, 57, 385
  confidence intervals, 67
  creation of, 64
  example
    comparing two populations, 118
    CUSUM, 309
    paired comparison, 120
    PDF, CDF, then a probability plot, 58
    percent of population statements, 98
    system stress to fail, 365
    system test, 356
  examples, list of, 62
  factorial experiment conclusions,
      confirmation of, 236
  factorial experiment effects, 62, 180, 191,
      206, 209, 213, 220, 227, 361–362
  factorial experiment residuals, 224
  factorial experiment trials, 127, 204, 232,
      355, 361–363, 365–367
  giving additional information, 45
  half-normal, 207, 209, 478
  histogram, in lieu of, 39
  knee in, 62, 99, 169
  lack of fit, 62–63, 98, 173, 389, 390
  log-normal, 62, 173, 463
  looking at data, 45, 462
  normal, 58, 62
  outlier, 62, 98, 119, 125
  paired comparison, 119
  plotting positions, 60, 386, 460–461
  sample size, 99
  table, plot positions, 460–461
  Weibull, 62, 163, 386, 464
Problems, *See* Chronic and Sporadic
    problems and Common and Special
    causes
  brainstorming, 24
  defining, 9, 13
  example, define right, 9, 356
  solving, 23
Process, 3, 482, *See also* Control charts,
    Chronic problems, Common causes,
    Special causes, Sporadic problems
  breakthrough sequence, 22
  Deming's 14 points, 20
  example
    process improvement, 26, 33

  reducing cycle time, 29
  flow chart, 27, 29, 31, 335–341, 482
  improvement, 15–20, 332, 338, 377
  monitoring, 290
  Poisson process, homogeneous, 69, 84, 85
  Poisson process, nonhomogeneous, 69,
      83, 85, 141, 155–160
  six sigma program, 334, 338
  stable, 20, 55, 297
  variability, 12, 245, 248
Process control chart, *See* Control chart
Process capability, 291
  acceptance of, 13, 249, 291
  application, 48, 243, 341, 342
  estimation of process variability, 205
  example, $C_p$ and $C_{pk}$, 311, 374
  indices ($C_p$ and $C_{pk}$), calculation of, 48,
      309
  process control, 291
  six sigma program, 312, 333, 335, 341, 342
Producers risk, *See* Beta (β) risk
Programmers, 1, 3, *See also* pass/fail
    functional testing


Quality, 3, 314
  breakthrough sequence, 22
  cause-and-effect diagram, 25
  changing from shear numbers, 20
  improvement, 19, 313, 332
  inspection, 18, 314
  leadership, 16
  manufacturing, 290–291
  six sigma, 332
  vital few, 22
Quality Function Deployment (QFD), 1, 319
    –382, 482
  alternative, simplified, 328
  considerations, 319
  example
    creating chart, 326
    with factorial experiment, 349
  six sigma program, 342
  Taguchi contributions, blending with, 355
Question, ask the right, 13, *See also* Do-it-
    smarter considerations
Quota, 15, 20, 26


*R* chart, *See* Control chart
$R^2$, 390, 396
Random, 89
  considerations, 12
  combining factorial trails, 211

Random (*Continued*)
  data, randomly generated, 44
  error, 47
  example
    automobile test, 36
    trap, 49
  factorial experiment trials, 178–180
  factorial test in lieu of sampling, 104, 113,
    198, 211, 232
  sampling, 37, 49
    continuous response in lieu of attribute,
      105, 113
    reliability test, 128–175
  sampling assumptions, 12, 54, 112, 139,
    143, 357
  sampling inferences, 91–127
  sampling needed, 10
  start of production sample, 143
  trial sequence, 179–180
  variable, 38, 378
Random effect model, 55, 176, 282, *See also*
  variance components
References, 14, 487
Regression, 202, 482
  all possible, *See* Mallows' $C_p$
  coefficients, model, 251
  computer output description, 393–396
  example, computer program, 400–416
  factorial experiment, 223, 227
  happenstance data, 229
  lack of fit, 390, 407
  least squares, 479
  levels, coded, 254, 474
  levels, natural, 254, 474
  Mallows' $C_p$, 220, 230, 480
  response surface methodology, 252, 260
  stepwise, 227
Reject Quality Level (RQL), 305, 482
Reliability testing, 1, 3, 69, 128–175, 482
  assumptions, 139, 142
  censored data, nonrepairable device, 58,
    474
  considerations, test duration, 173
  criterion test, 144–161, 357
  do-it-smarter considerations, 139, 160, 173
  early life failures, 142, 159, 164, 169, 173,
    316, 382
  example
    do-it-smarter considerations, 356
    experimentation trap, 53
  factorial experiment, 200
  growth model, 133
  hazard rate, 82–83
  intensity function, 69

nonrepairable device, 131, 162–175, *See*
    Log-normal distribution,
    Nonrepairable device reliability
    testing, Weibull distribution
  probability plotting, 62, 163, 173, 386, 463
  purpose of, 358
  repairable system, 83, 132, 141–161, *See
    also* Nonhomogeneous Poisson
    Process and Poisson distribution
  repairable system versus nonrepairable
    devices, 130
  sequential, 143–146
  strategy, 139, 356
  wear out failures, 142, 164, 173, 382
Residual analysis, 482, *See also* Factorial
  experiments
Resolution, 54, 223–226, 233–235
Responses, 3, 483, *See also* Attribute
  response, Continuous response, Logic
  pass/fail response, reliability testing,
  Do-it-smarter considerations
Response surface methodology, 1, 250–272,
  483, *See also* Mixture experiments
  algorithm designs, 250, 262, 268, 269, 271,
    472
  application, 181, 198, 202, 244, 355, 356
    process improvement, 33, 291
  Box–Behnken design, 255
  canonical form, 254, 474
  central composite design, 252–255
  computer output description, 395–396
  considerations, 270
  contour plot, 256, 270
  curvature, 190
  do-it-smarter considerations, 271
  example
    central composite design, 254
    computer program, 406–411
  implementation strategy, 271
  multicollinearity, 271, 480
  path of steepest accent, 272, 481
  six sigma program, 340, 342
  strategy, multi-experiment, 271
  variance inflation factor, 271, 486
Risk, 37, 43, *See also* Alpha, Beta,
  Consumer, Producer, Hypothesis testing
Robust, 483, *See also* Assumptions design,
  central limit theorem, 93
  comparison tests of means, 114
  confidence interval on mean, 45, 93
  confidence interval on standard deviation,
    45
  design, *See* Factorial Experiments
  Poisson distribution tests, 132–133, 142

Run-in, *See* Screen

*s* chart, *See* Control chart
Sample size, 483
  attribute, 105–107, 113, 200
  binomial, Poisson distribution
    approximation for, 147
  comparing two means, 115
  continuous response data, 92–93
  example
    attribute data, 107, 164
    continuous response data, 92
  factorial experiment, 179–180, 199, 200,
    397–398
  *K* factors, 98
  large, 9, 45
  percent of population, 99
  Poisson distribution, 146, 148
  question, 9
  reduction in, 148, 149, 170
  variability, less, 41
  Weibull distribution, 164, 170
Sampling, 3, *See also* Attribute response
    data, continuous response data,
    comparison, do-it-smarter
    considerations, random, reliability
    testing
  assumptions, 54
  chi-square ($\chi^2$) distribution, 80
  considerations, 12, 37–39, 54, 103
  continuous response, 91
    in lieu of attribute response, 105, 113
  distributions, 70
  do-it-smarter considerations, 358
  factorial alternative to random sampling,
    104, 113, 198, 211, 232
  *F* distribution, 81
  *t* distribution, 81
Scale parameter, *See* Weibull distribution
Scatter diagram, 336, 340, 483
*s* chart, *See* Control charts
Scientists, 1, *See* Engineers
Screen, manufacturing, 161, 169, 484, *See*
    Burn-in
  application, 160, 175
  example
    NHPP, 156
    Weibull distribution, 169
  repairable systems with changing failure
    rate, 155, 161
Screening experiment, 187, 195, 485
Search pattern strategy, 201, *See* Pass/fail
    functional testing

Sequential testing, 484
  binomial distribution, 112
  example, Poisson distribution, 145
  Poisson distribution, 144
Shape parameter, *See* Weibull Distribution
Shewhart control chart, 292, 305, 306, 315,
    484, *See also* Control charts
Single-sided, 484, *See also* hypothesis test
  attribute response evaluations, 111
  confidence interval, 45
  continuous response data, 72
  CUSUM chart, 305
  example
    comparing proportions, 123
    confidence interval on mean, 95
  normal distribution, 70
  Poisson distribution, 147
  probability plot, 110
  *t* distribution, 81
Six sigma program, 332–343, 484
  brainstorming, 338, 340
  example, $C_p$ and $C_{pk}$ calculations on an
    assembly, 312, 374
  process capability index, 309, 312
  product development steps, 338
  slogans, 20
  tools, 335–341
Slogans, 20
Software, *See* pass/fail functional testing
Special causes, 22, 484, *See also* Sporadic
    problems
  application, 290, 316
  Deming's 14 points, 17
  example, from *p* chart, 300
  six sigma program, 342
Specification, 89, 97, 484, *See also* Criterion
  considerations, 91, 99
  Deming's 14 points, 19
  example
    factorial, 363
    probability plot, 361
    reliability test with do-it-smarter
      considerations, 356
    tolerance analysis, 101
  factorial experiment input, 12
  loss function, 246, 247
  process capability, 310
  process creation, 374
  six sigma program, 333
  variability, 37
  variance components analysis, 243
Sporadic problem, 290, 484, *See also*
    Special causes
  application, 160

Sporadic problem (*Continued*)
  Deming's 14 points, 17
  Juran's corrective action, 22
  six sigma program, 342
Stability, process, *See* Control charts
Standard deviation (s, σ), 39, 41, 484, *See also* Variance
  applications, 100, 125–126
  binomial distribution, 379
  comparison tests, 114, 117
  confidence interval, 45, 96
  control chart, 292, 293
  CUSUM chart, 306, 309
  error, root mean square, 392, 394, 395, 404
  example, confidence interval, 97
  factorial experiment, response in, 248
  normal distribution, 378
  overall, 48
  Poisson distribution, 380
  pooling, 311
  population, 91
  probability plot, 118, 125–126
  sample, 41
  six sigma program, 333–334
Statistician, 1, 7
Statistical Process Control (SPC), 1, 89, 290 –293, *See also* Control chart
Supplier, *See* Vendor
  comparing, 2
  Deming's 14 points, 18
Surveys
  customer, 30, 328
  example, QFD, 326
  QFD, 320
Symbols, 468
System reliability testing, *See* Homogeneous Poisson process, Nonhomogeneous Poisson process, Poisson distribution, Reliability testing


Tables
  Analysis of Means (ANOM—Table I), 124, 431–436
  chi-square (χ²) distribution (Table G), 96, 122, 144, 145, 147, 428–429
  control chart factors (Table J), 293–294, 437
  *F* distribution (Table F), 117–118, 405, 411, 424–427
  factorial confounding between factors (Tables N1–N3), 185–245, 360, 362, 450–458
  factorial designs (Tables M1–M3), 182–

245, 253, 277, 282, 359, 365, 372, 398, 440–449
  Gamma function (Table H), 382, 430
  log-normal hazard paper (Table R2), 466
  log-normal probability paper (Table Q2), 463
  normal distribution (Tables A, B, and C), 92, 95, 106, 147, 418–420
  normal hazard paper (Table R1), 465
  normal probability paper (Table Q1), 98, 209, 462
  plot positions (Table P), 98, 165, 173, 209, 460–461
  Poisson distribution factors (Table K), 110, 111, 147, 149, 151, 163, 171, 356, 438–439
  *t* distribution (Tables D and E), 92, 96, 117, 121, 216, 405, 421–422
  test coverage, pass/fail functional (Table O), 277, 279, 459
  Weibull mean (Table L), 165, 440
  Weibull hazard paper (Table R3), 164, 467
  Weibull probability paper (Table Q3), 164, 464
Taguchi contributions, 3, 244–249, 485, *See also* Factorial experiments
  array, inner and outer, 248, 373, 479
  criterion considerations, 103
  do-it-smarter considerations, 289
  example, loss function, 247
  experiment designs, 244, 245, 349
  loss function, 243, 244, 245, 479
  parameter design, 355
  resolution III design with two-factor interactions, 195, 371
  signal-to-noise ratio, 248
  tolerance design, 355
  tolerancing, 103
  variability, reducing, 245, 248
*t* distribution, 81
  comparative tests, 114
  example, confidence intervals on mean, 95
  factorial analyses, 206, 208, 212, 221, 313, 402, 405
  mean, confidence interval on, 93
  table, 421–423
team
  advantage, 5
  Deming's 14 points, 19
  example
    process improvement, 26, 33
    reducing cycle time, 30
  factorial experiment factors, 178, 192, 346
  goal, 21

quality leadership, 16
Technicians, 1, *See also* Engineers
Test considerations
  assumptions
    customer usage, 133, 357
    listing, 371
  configurations, 274
  coverage, 273–277, 281, 289, 485
  definition, test, 485
  example
    reliability test with do-it-smarter
      considerations, 356
    pyramiding experiments, 344
  performance ratio, 112, 485
  strategy, 11, 344
  stress to failure, 365
  tolerance extremes, 355
  unified test strategy, 344
  traps, 49–54
Testing, *See* Attribute response data,
    Comparison, Continuous response data,
    Control chart, Factorial, Pass/fail
    functional testing, Reliability testing
Theory, in text, 8
Time-line chart, 340, 485
Time series, 54
Tolerance
  analysis, 100, 342, 486
  $C_p$ and $C_{pk}$, 309–312
  example, 100, 374
  philosophy in meeting, 248–249, 374
Training, 7, 19, *See* Education
Transformations
  count data, 237
  example, PDF, CDF, then a probability
    plot, 58
  factorial experiments, 223
  failure rate, 140
  lambda plots, 237
  logarithm, 80, 237, 248
  logit, 237, 479
  proportion data, 200, 237
  residual plots, 237
  table of, 237
Trend chart, 339, 485
Trivial many, 313, *See also* Pareto diagram
Two-sided, *See* Double-sided
Type I error, 45, 485
Type II error, 43, 485
Type III error, 23, 485

*u* chart, *See* Control charts
Uncensored data, probability plot positions,
    60, 386, 460–461
Uncertainty, 486, *See* delta
Use of text, 2

Variability, 37
  considerations, criterion, 97
  do-it-smarter considerations, 55
  example
    reduction of, 368
    tolerance analysis, 101
  illustration, 42
  loss function, 245
  reduction of, 12, 100, 232, 243, 244, 266
  sources, 48
  standard deviation, 39
  Taguchi contributions, 244–249
  tolerance analysis, 101
  total, 48, 202
Variance, 486, *See also* Standard deviation
  chi-square distribution, 80
  comparing two variances, 117
  example, comparing two, 118
  overall, 48
  pooled, 311
  stabilizing transformation, 237
  total, 48, 202
Variance components, 202
  analysis, 219, 238
  application, 49, 205, 243
  examples, 202, 203, 238, 241
    computer program, 406
  measurement sources, 47
Variance inflection factor, 271, 486
Variation, 19, 47, 127, *See also* Taguchi
    contributions
Vendor, 486, *See also* Certification,
    Criterion evaluation, Supplier
  control charts, 126–127
  criterion, 12
  customer relationships, 319
  do-it-smarter considerations, 126
  example, attribute response data, 107
  factorial experiments, 12, 127, 243
  qualification, 126–127
Verifying, 486, *See also* Certification
  failure criterion test alternative, 10
Vital few, 313, *See also* Pareto diagram
  break through sequence, 22

Wear-out, *See* Bath tub curve
Weibull distribution, two parameter 76, 486
  accelerated testing, 173

Weibull distribution (*Continued*)
  application, 69, 77, 85
  CDF, 381
  censored data, 58
  characteristic life, 77, 164, 165, 167, 170,
    381, 386, 474, *See also* scale
    parameter
  do-it-smarter considerations, 173
  example
    hazard plot, 64, 167
    probability plot, 165
    zero failure test, 171
  hazard plot, 64, 167, 172
  hazard rate, 82, 382
  nonlinear probability plot, 169
  nonrepairable device testing, 3, 69, 128,
    131, 162, *See also* nonrepairable
    device testing
  PDF, 57, 381
  plot positions, 60, 386
  probability paper, 62, 386
  probability plot, 60, 163, 172, 385, 386,
    460–461
    with convex shape, 169
  properties of, 380
  reduced sample size testing, 170
  scale parameter, 77, 131, 381, 483, *See*

    *also* Characteristic life
  screen, in manufacturing, 1, 161, 169, 484,
    *See also* Screen
  shape parameter, 77, 131, 164, 165, 167,
    170, 172, 381, 386, 484
  step stress, 139, 173
  table, mean, 440
  test with know shape parameter, 170
  transformation, 58
Weibull, three-parameter, 77
  application, 69, 77, 84, 85, 99, 169–170
  location parameter, 77, 381, 479
  PDF, 380
  properties of, 380
Work standards, 20


$\bar{x}$, *See* Mean
$\bar{x}$ chart, *See* Control chart
$X$ chart, *See* Control chart


Zero failure test option,
  attribute failure rate criterion, 110
  mean life criterion, 171
  system failure rate criterion, 149